ADHD and Developmental Disabilities

Contents

Preface

Attention Deficit Hyperactivity Disorder (ADHD) is a disorder of the brain. It is a developmental disability and its symptoms include extreme inattention, hyperactivity and impulsivity that impairs normal functioning. This book on ADHD and developmental disabilities discusses topics related to developmental disabilities, their treatment, pathophysiological processes and effective medical care for such diseases. ADHD usually manifests during childhood and treatments range from counseling to medication. This book includes some of the vital pieces of work being conducted across the world, on various topics related to ADHD and developmental disabilities. This book, with its detailed analyses and data, will prove immensely beneficial to professionals and students involved in this area at various levels.

After months of intensive research and writing, this book is the end result of all who devoted their time and efforts in the initiation and progress of this book. It will surely be a source of reference in enhancing the required knowledge of the new developments in the area. During the course of developing this book, certain measures such as accuracy, authenticity and research focused analytical studies were given preference in order to produce a comprehensive book in the area of study.

This book would not have been possible without the efforts of the authors and the publisher. I extend my sincere thanks to them. Secondly, I express my gratitude to my family and well-wishers. And most importantly, I thank my students for constantly expressing their willingness and curiosity in enhancing their knowledge in the field, which encourages me to take up further research projects for the advancement of the area.

Editor

1

Selective Impairment of Attentional Networks of Alerting in Wilson's Disease

Yongsheng Han[1,2], Fangfang Zhang[1], Yanghua Tian[1], Panpan Hu[1], Bo Li[2], Kai Wang[1]*

1 Department of Neurology, The First Affiliated Hospital of Anhui Medical University, Hefei, Anhui Province, PR China, **2** Institute of Neurology, Anhui University of Chinese Medicine, Hefei, Anhui Province, PR China

Abstract

Wilson's disease (WD) is typically affected by attention, which is one of the cognitive domains. The Attention Network Test (ANT) was developed to measure the functioning of the following three individual attentional networks: orienting, alerting, and executive control. The ANT has been used in a variety of neuropsychiatric conditions; however, it has not been used in WD. The aim of this study was to investigate the attentional function of WD patients, and 35 patients with early and moderate neurological WD, as well as 35 gender-, age-, and education-matched healthy controls performed the ANT. Remarkable differences between the patients and healthy controls were observed in the alerting network ($p = 0.007$) in contrast the differences in the orienting ($p = 0.729$) and executive control ($p = 0.888$) networks of visual attention. The mean reaction time in the ANT was significantly longer in the WD patients than in the controls ($p < 0.001$, 0.001). In the WD patients, there was an effect specifically on the alerting domain of the attention network, whereas the orienting and executive control domains were not affected.

Editor: Suliann Ben Hamed, Centre de Neuroscience Cognitive, France

Funding: These authors have no support or funding to report.

* Email: wangkai1964@126.com

Introduction

Wilson's disease (WD) is a rare autosomal recessive genetic disorder of copper metabolism that is characterized by hepatic and neurological symptoms. In 1912, Kinnier Wilson first described the disease as a syndrome that appears in between one in 30,000 and one in 100,000 individuals [1]. The consequences of this disorder are related to copper deposition in different tissues including the brain, liver, kidneys, and cornea [2]. Different parts of the brain are affected including the brainstem, cerebellum, thalamus, and subcortical white matter, whereas the most common damage frequently occurs in the basal ganglia [3,4,5]. The clinical expression is highly variable, with hepatic, neurological, or psychiatric symptoms predominating.

Approximately fifty percent of WD patients have psychiatric or neurological problems [6]. Cognitive changes have been reported since the first WD cases were described in 1912, although dystonia and dysarthria are the most common neurological signs. One of the most common impairments is memory change [7]; other cognitive changes have been reported in untreated cases, including dementia [8]. Neuropsychological evaluation evokes cognitive deficits in numerous domains, including focused attention, verbal learning, visuo-constructive ability, mental speed, verbal fluency, set-shifting ability, and visual memory, which are the most frequently damaged cognitive domains in WD patients [9]. Portala et al. [10] reported that symptomatic WD patients showed remarkably lower performance than normal controls on assessments of finger tapping, simple reaction time, short-term memory, word decoding speed, grammatical reasoning and maze perception.

Attention deficit is one of the most frequent symptoms of cognitive impairment in WD patients. In various studies, WD patients have been reported to have a deficit in one of the attentional systems. Seniow et al. observed marked attention impairment in a digit span test in WD patients [11]. Portala et al. found that 62% of WD patients present concentration difficulties and executive control problems in the allocation of attention [10,12]. Hegde et al. [4] reported that nearly one-half of WD patients experience impairment in sustained and focused attention. Lin et al. [13] reported on a child with WD with an attention deficit who had been misdiagnosed with attention deficit hyperactivity disorder (ADHD) for more than a year because he could not pay close attention and frequently left his seat in the classroom.

WD, Parkinson's disease (PD) and Huntington's disease (HD) are basal ganglia disorders. Zhou et al. [14] found that in using the attentional network test (ANT) to test the attention network, PD patients showed selective abnormality in the orienting network, and the alerting and executive control networks were not significantly different between the PD patients and the healthy controls. Couettea and his coworker reported attention deficit in HD patients, with a slowing of disengagement processes, which delayed the occurrence of exogenous processes such as inhibition of return (IOR) as well as endogenous strategies and re-orienting towards uncued locations where the testing target was expected to appear [15].

These studies show that PD and HD patients have impaired attention. Additionally, WD is a basal ganglia disorder, and we hypothesized that individuals with WD would have attention network function difficulties, with the basal ganglia playing a key role in impaired attention in WD patients. Differing from patients with other basal ganglia disorders, WD patients have obvious and visible MRI changes that provide a unique opportunity for exploration of attentional cognitive deficits in the substrate, leading to a better understanding of the role of the basal ganglia structures in higher cognitive functions [9]. The anatomy and connections of the basal ganglia indicate that these structures are crucial links between the parts of the brain which have classically been considered to be related to emotional functioning and that brain regions formerly considered to have largely motor functions. The basal ganglia play a very important role in the development and integration of psychomotor behaviors such as motor functioning, memory and attention [16].

On the basis of numerous neuroanatomical and cognition studies, Posner and Petersen divided the human attention system into three independent networks identified as alerting, orienting and executive control. Alerting is defined as the capability of completing and maintaining response readiness for an impending stimulus. Orienting is the selection of information from multiple sensory inputs. Executive control describes the ability to work out a conflict when faced with competing responses [17]. Each network is connected to specific anatomical areas and is dependent on specific neuromodulators [17]. The thalamic, frontal and parietal regions of the right hemisphere have links with the alerting system, and norepinephrine from the midbrain nucleus coeruleus regulates the alerting system. Sections of the superior parietal lobe, the temporoparietal junction and the frontal eye fields appear to be activated by the orienting system, which is modulated by acetylcholine. The midline frontal areas (the anterior cingulated cortex) and lateral prefrontal cortical regions are activated by the executive control network, which is modulated by dopamine [17,18].

The attentional network test (ANT) was developed to evaluate the efficiencies of the three attention networks in one experiment and was designed for normal subjects and various patient populations [17]. It has detected dissociations in the different networks in various populations [14,19,20,21,22]. No study has been published on the attention networks of WD patients. Attention is a vital prior condition for every "higher-order" cognitive process, such as working memory and executive function [23,24,25], ensuring that attention is very important. Whether there is a global attention deficit or a deficit in a specific attention network in WD patients is unknown. The primary goal of this study was to investigate whether specific changes in attentional networks could be found in WD patients versus healthy controls (HC) matched for age, gender, and educational level. We attempted to access the different attentional subcomponents and determine which were impaired or unaffected in the identical patient group. We hypothesized that WD patients would be more impaired than the HCs in attention tasks; however, this impairment depends on the attentional subcomponent involved in the task.

Materials and Methods

Ethics Statement

The study protocol was approved by the ethics committee of the Anhui Medical University. Each participant provided signed informed consent, and this research was in accordance with the Helsinki Declaration.

Subjects

We studied 35 WD patients and 35 HCs. The patients were recruited from the Institute of Neurology at Anhui University of Chinese Medicine, China. The WD diagnosis criteria [26] included the following: (1) presentation of extrapyramidal symptoms and signs, (2) corneal Kayser-Fleischer rings observed with a slit lamp, (3) serum ceruloplasmin <20 mg/dL or copper oxidase <0.21 mg/dL, and (4) a 24-h urinary copper concentration > 100 μg. Cranial magnetic resonance imaging (MRI) or computerized tomography (CT) scans were obtained for all the patients (thirty-four WD patients had MRI scans whereas one WD patient had a CT scan because sheet metal placement in his body prohibited an MRI scan). The following exclusion criteria included (1) patients with mental retardation (a score on the Wechsler Adult Intelligence Scale-Revised Chinese Version [WAIS-RC]-IQ <70 points), (2) patients with dysaudia and lalopathy, (3) patients with significant impairment of liver function (alanine aminotransferase >100 U or patients with liver cirrhosis), (4) patients with possible anxiety and depression (Hamilton Anxiety Scale [HAMA] and Hamilton Depression Scale [HAMD] >7 points), and (5) patients taking L-dopa or other drugs that affect cognitive function. No patients had visual acuity or field deficits. The patients were evaluated using the United Wilson's Disease Rating Scale (UWDRS) [27] to assess the entire spectrum of clinical symptoms. All the patients were receiving regular copper chelation therapy.

Thirty-five HCs matched for age, gender, education level, and intellectual level were recruited from a local volunteer group. All the subjects were right-handed, with normal speaking, writing, language expression, visual acuity, and comprehension skills. None of the HCs had a history of serious physical or mental illness. The clinical and demographic data of the WD patients and the HCs are shown in Table 1.

Neuropsychological background tests

The neuropsychological tests performed with all the subjects, comparing the HCs with the WD patients were as follows: (1) the WAIS-RC [28] was performed to measure intelligence; (2) the HAMA [29] and HAMD [30] were used to measure anxiety and depressive states; (3) a verbal fluency (animals/min) test [31,32] was applied to measure the frontal lobe functions; and (4) the digit span test [33], including forward and backward digits, investigated short-term memory and attention span.

Attention network test

The ANT was used as described by the authors of the test [17] to assess the attentional networks of the participants. A computerized 30-min task is designed to bond cued reaction time (RT) with a flanker task. The participants observed the stimuli shown on the computer screen and responded by pressing two response buttons. The stimuli comprised a row of five visual horizontal black lines that have arrowheads which point left or right, against a gray background. Whether the sides of two arrows are in the same, opposite or no direction determine the congruent, incongruent or neutral condition. The participants were required to decide the direction of a central arrow and press a left or a right key in accordance with the pointing direction. A series of spatial and alerting cues and flankers were introduced to test all three attentional networks, as described. The participants were guided to concentrate on a central cross-shaped fixation point presented for randomized 400 to 1600 ms, which was subsequently replaced for 100 ms by one of four warning cues that provide information about the impending target. The central arrow as a target could appear above or below the fixation point and was in the middle of

Table 1. Clinical and demographic data and Neuropsychological task performances of WD patients and HCs.

		WD (*N*=35)	HC (*N*=35)	*P*
Gender (M:F)		23/12	24/11	-
Age at investigation (years,mean±*SD*)		22.66 (3.50)	22.80 (3.42)	0.863
Years of school education (years,mean±*SD*)		11.26 (2.76)	11.60 (3.13)	0.629
Wechsler Adult Intelligence Scale-Revised Chinese version (WAIS-RC) (mean±*SD*)		99.34 (10.84)	101.53 (11.98)	0.388
Verbal fluency (mean±*SD*)		11.20 (2.15)	10.80 (1.48)	0.362
DT	Digits forwards (mean±*SD*)	7.77 (0.55)	7.94 (0.34)	0.119
	Digits backwards (mean±*SD*)	4.97 (1.15)	5.06 (1.18)	0.547
Hamilton Anxiety Scale (HAMA) (mean±*SD*)		2.86 (2.05)	2.14 (2.20)	0.164
Hamilton Depression Scale (HAMD) (mean±*SD*)		2.94 (2.09)	2.25 (2.20)	0.185
United Wilson's Disease Rating Scale (UWDRS) (mean±*SD*)		19.43 (9.86)	-	-
Duration of disease (years,mean±*SD*)		6.68 (4.94)	-	-

two flankers (arrows). Different equal-balanced-cues and flankers appeared in random order. The participants accomplished a 24-trial practice block and feedback was included after each trial. The subjects completed three experimental blocks of 96 trials with no feedback, with up to 2 min of rest between the blocks. The reaction times (RT) and accuracy were recorded. The four cue conditions were as follows: (1) no cue, the subjects were shown a cross for 100 ms that was the same as the first fixation; (2) a central cue, which was at the central fixation point; (3) a double cue, in which the cues were presented on the two possible target locations simultaneously (above and below the fixation point); and (4) a spatial cue, in which the cue was presented on the target location (above or below the central fixation point). The trials were presented randomly. Throughout the task, the participants were guided to concentrate on a centrally located fixation cross and to respond as rapidly and as accurately as possible (see Figure 1).

Calculation of attention network efficiencies

The differences in RTs originated from various experimental conditions to measure the alerting, orienting and executive control networks [17]. From the following raw reaction time data, the attention network efficiency values were calculated. The raw RTs with correct responses were omitted with a 100–1700 ms window to eliminate the effect from the outliers, and the RTs outside this window were not included. Subtracting the mean of the median RTs of the conditions with a double cue from the mean of the median RTs of the conditions with no cue could yield the alerting effect. Because neither of these conditions provides information on the spatial location of the target, subtraction provides the measure of alerting. The orienting effect was calculated by subtracting the mean of the median RTs of the conditions with a spatial cue from the mean of the median RTs of the conditions with a center cue. The subject was alerted in both conditions, however, only the spatial cue offered spatial information on where to orient. The conflict (executive) effect was calculated by subtracting the mean of the median RTs of the conditions with the congruent flankers from the mean of the median RTs in the conditions with the incongruent flankers.

Statistical analysis

SPSS 13.0 software was used in all the analyses. For the two-tailed tests, the level of significance was set at $p<0.05$. The group differences were evaluated by using nonparametric tests for 2-independent samples (Mann-Whitney U-test). The relationship between the patients' performance in the ANT and their clinical or neuropsychological ability was computed using Spearman's correlation.

Results

The neuropsychological background data

The means and standard deviations of the demographic and clinical characteristics of the WD patients and HCs showed no remarkable differences in gender, age and education; the WAIS-RC, HAMA, HAMD, DT, and VFT scores of the two groups are shown in Table 1. Thirty-four patients underwent MRI examinations, and the data showed instances of basal ganglia abnormality (18 of 34 had a high T2 signal and/or a lower T1 signal on MRI), mild cortical and/or subcortical atrophy (13 of 34), brainstem abnormality (10 out of 34) and thalamus abnormality (11 of 34); one patient had a CT scan that showed a mild subcortical atrophy (Figure 2).

The efficiencies of the three networks

Table 2 shows the mean raw RTs and accuracy for each cue condition of the ANT in the two groups. Table 3 and Figure 3 summarize the mean score and the standard error *(SE)* for each of the attention networks, the mean RT, and the global accuracy. There were longer ($Z=-4.305$, $p<0.001$) overall mean RTs in the WD patients than in the HCs; the accuracy rates were similar ($Z=-1.689$, $p=0.091$) in the two groups. Between the WD patients and the HCs, we found significant differences ($Z=-2.721$, $p=0.007$) in the baseline RT-adjusted alerting network scores. The differences between the groups in the orienting and executive network scores were insignificant ($Z=-0.347$, $p=0.729$; $Z=-0.141$, $p=0.888$).

The ratio could be applied to verify specific effects that are not affected by the overall reaction time because the response times (RTs) are longer in the WD patients. The median RT in each condition was divided by the participant's overall RT for every subject [20]. The ratio scores are shown in Table 2b. Based on these ratio scores, the WD patients were notably different in regard to the alerting network compared with the controls ($Z=-3.365$, $p=0.001$); there was no significant difference between the orienting and executive networks in the two groups ($Z=-1.204$, $p=0.229$; $Z=-1.380$, $p=0.168$).

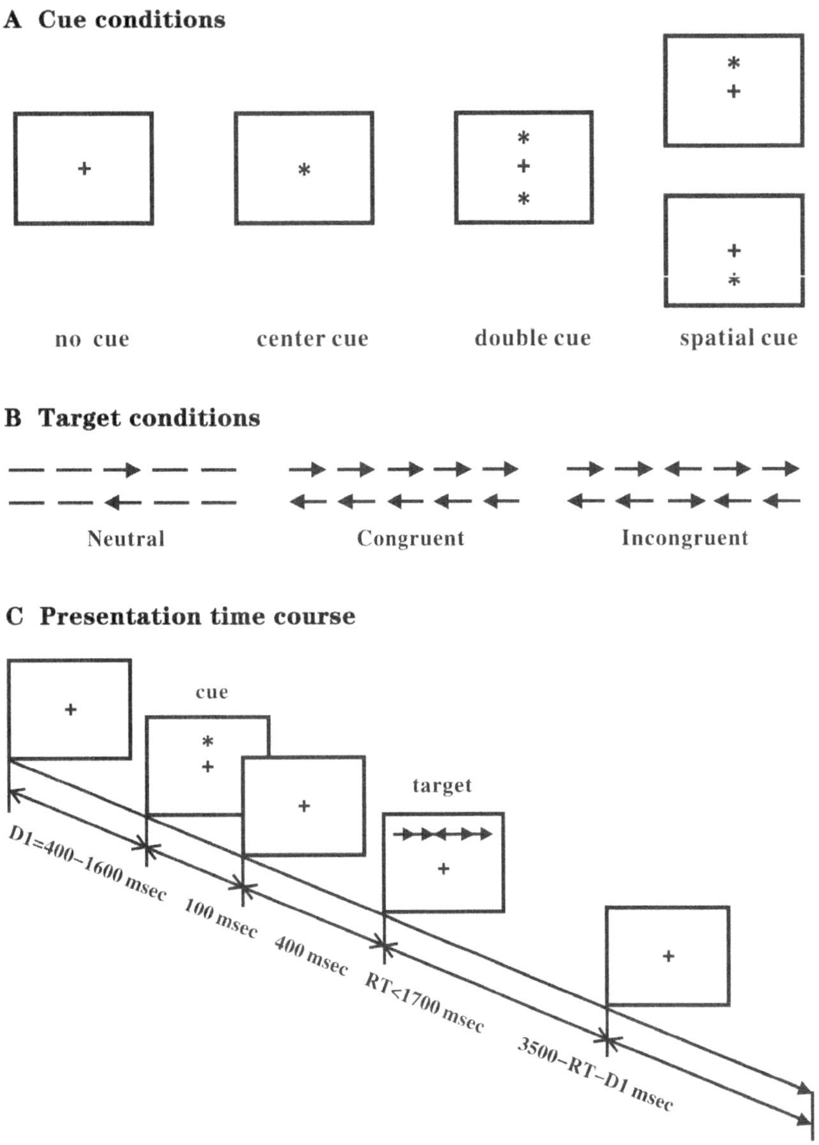

Figure 1. Experimental paradigm of the Attention Network Test. (A) The 4 cue conditions. (B) The 6 stimuli used in the present experiment. (C) An example of the procedure.

Correlations

The examination of the correlations between the networks indicates that the scores for the networks were not significantly related in the WD patients and HCs. We inspected the connection of the scores for the ANT with age and education level as well as the scores on the WAIS-RC, VFT, and UWDRS, and there were no significant interactions among these variables.

Discussion

The ANT is very sensitive to attention deficits in many neurological and psychiatric disorders such as PD, ADHD, multiple sclerosis (MS), Alzheimer's disease (AD), and schizophrenia [14,19,20,21,34,35]. The ANT has the advantage of comparing deficits in different attentional networks [17].

In this study, we first investigated attentional networks based on the ANT in WD patients. The most significant finding is a specific alteration of the alerting network in WD patients. This test is used as indicated by the significantly lower alerting effect in the ANT; no difference between the WD patients and HCs relating to the orienting and the executive control effects was shown. The findings of this study confirm our hypothesis. The deficits of the alerting network indicate that WD patients do not derive as much benefit as the HCs from temporal cue warnings. In accordance with the outcomes of the WAIS-RC, all of the WD patients were not cognitively impaired compared with the HCs, and the lower alerting effect demonstrated in patients suggests a smaller RT difference between the trials that with and without a warning cue. This finding might forecast the harm in using the warning cue to speed up response times or the capability of maintaining alertness with no cue. Even in the trials with no warning cue, the HCs had a more rapid mean RT than the in-trial WD patients with a warning cue (659 ms vs. 719 ms); it is hypothesized that the WD patients with slower overall RTs are lack the ability to completely use the additional helpful information of the warning cue to enhance their reaction times in the cued trials.

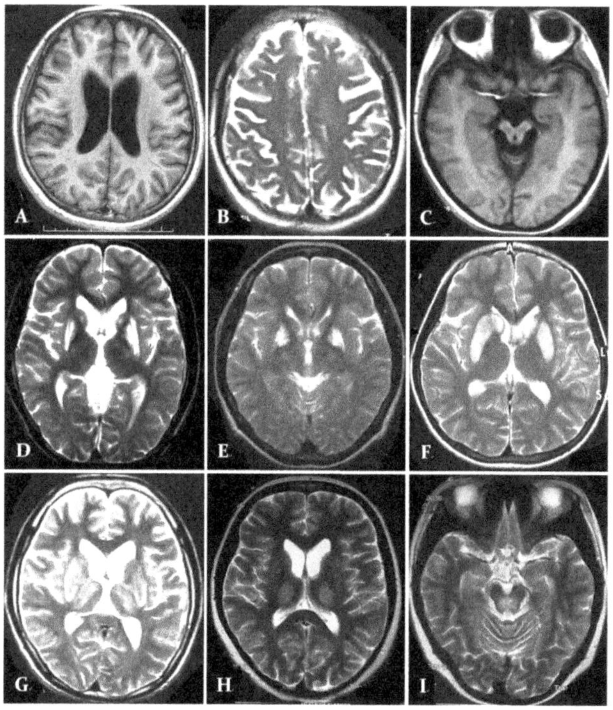

Figure 2. MRI with classically described changes in patients with Wilson's disease. A. Axial T1-W imaging a 18-year-old male patient shows diffuse subcortical atrophy. **B.** Axial T2-W imaging a 22-year-old male patient shows diffuse cortical atrophy. **C.** Axial T1-W imaging a 22-year-old male patient shows brainstem atrophy. **D.** Axial T2-W imaging a 24-year-old female patient shows bilateral putamen hyperintensity signal abnormalities. **E.** Axial T2-W imaging a 25-year-old male patient shows bilateral globus pallidus hyperintensity signal abnormalities. **F.** Axial T2-W imaging a 23-year-old male patient shows bilateral putamen and caudate nucleus hyperintensity signal abnormalities. **G.** Axial T2-W imaging a 20-year-old male patient shows bilateral basal ganglionic and thalamic hyperintensity in addition to diffuse atrophy . **H.** Axial T2-W imaging a 26-year-old female patient shows bilateral thalamic hyperintensity signal abnormalities . **I.** Axial T2-W imaging a 21-year-old male patient shows pons hyperintensity signal abnormalities.

The deficit found in WD in alerting attention is not distinct. A similar deficit was found in MS and ADHD, and it was reported in a study that MS and ADHD patients displayed a deficit in the alerting attention network and not in the orienting and executive attention networks [34,35,36]. Whether an identical underlying mechanism is involved requires further study.

Despite the existence of three independent attentional networks, some studies have found interactions in test performance, which has been found in HCs and patients [17,34,35]. In our study, we did not find any interaction between the alerting, orienting, and executive control networks in WD patients.

Depression, anxiety and tremor are common symptoms of WD, which could impede neuropsychological test performance [37,38]. In this study, UWDRS evaluation was conducted for WD patients, and they had a neurological UWDRS subscore of under 15. The statistical analysis was impaired by the low prevalence and lower degree of resting tremor and postural tremor in the upper limbs of the WD patients. Although WD movement disorder is not markedly obvious in WD patients, the RTs of the patients with WD are significantly longer than those of the HCs, which contributed to the WD patients having various degrees of upper limb movement awkwardness or tremor. The ratio score transformations are effective in uncovering the group effects in the processes, in a manner that is independent of global slowing. We calculated a ratio score transformation for each participant by dividing the mean RT and determined each condition by the participant's overall RT (Table 2b) for each of the three attentional networks [14]. In this study, the alerting ratio and the alerting RT of the WD patients were significantly lower than those of the HCs. The motor speed factor is not conducive to less efficient alerting attention in WD patients. Marina found that the most often diagnosed symptoms in WD patients are depression (36%) and anxiety (62%) [39]. In this study, the patients were not different from the controls in anxiety and depression, at least as measured by the HAMA and HAMD. Depression and anxiety do not account for our results. Our patients might be expected not to be especially anxious or depressed because our inclusion criteria asked for the total UWDRS scores to be below 30 in the WD patients and for the participants to have a low degree of physical disability, which might explain the low incidence of anxiety and depression in these patients.

The alerting network is a significant source of attention, and it maintains an adequate level of alertness. For optimal performance, it is crucial [40,41]. In an fMRI study that uses the ANT, the alerting contrast indicated a strong thalamic involvement as well as activation of the anterior and cortical site [18]. The alerting network manifested a specific decrease in the theta-, alpha-, and beta-band activity in the brain oscillations 200–450 ms after the warning signal [42]. In this study, cerebral MRI showed that approximately 11 of the 35 WD patients had abnormally high thalamus T2 signals and/or lower T1 signals, and 13 of 35 WD patients had cortical and/or subcortical atrophy. When analyzing the performance of the ANT in a study of healthy volunteers, only the alerting network was related to strong activation of the thalamus in the three attentional networks [18]. For decades, the thalamus has been reported to be related to arousal, attention and alertness [43]. In this study, approximately one-third of the patients had abnormal magnetic resonance signals in the thalamus; in most of the WD patients, the abnormal imaging involved the basal ganglia, brainstem signal changes and brain atrophy. Imaging studies examining brain areas have demonstrated that an activation of the thalamic, frontal, and parietal areas, particularly of the right hemisphere are involved in alerting control. In this study, few WD patients had abnormal images in the frontal and parietal areas, and it could be hypothesized that the link between the basal ganglia and cortex is involved in the efficiency of the alerting network. Middleton reported that several areas of the prefrontal cortex involved in higher order cognitive function are targets of output from the basal ganglia [44,45]. Excessive copper accumulates in the basal ganglia in WD patients. The function of the frontostriatal networks, which are involved in motor and cognitive function, are affected by these changes [46]. This area of investigation requires further study.

The attentional networks have been associated with various neuromodulators [47]. Pharmacological studies indicate that noradrenergic antagonists block the warning effect, whereas is does not influence orienting [48]. In such cases, there appears to be a double dissociation, with norepinephrine (NE) involved predominantly in the alerting network [48]. The decrease in the magnitude of the alerting effect results from the reduced levels of noradrenalin in the brain [48]. PET evidence of nigrostriatal dopaminergic dysfunction has been found in WD patients even after many years of penicillamine treatment. [49]. As shown for AD, the possible contribution of alerted NE levels to changes in the alerting effect in WD should be clarified.

Table 2. Mean reaction times and accuracy under each cue condition for WD patients and HCs.

Group	Flanker	Cue type			
		No cue	**Double cue**	**Center cue**	**Spatial cue**
Mean RTs (ms) and standard deviations					
WD	Congruent	720 (71)	692 (84)	705 (75)	668 (70)
	Incongruent	824 (67)	812 (77)	822 (71)	789 (76)
	neutral	656 (80)	625 (77)	629 (84)	610 (79)
Health Controls	Congruent	645 (97)	600 (95)	618 (95)	585 (102)
	Incongruent	752 (96)	732 (95)	742 (94)	702 (100)
	neutral	582 (93)	524 (90)	538 (93)	512 (92)
Accuracy (%) and standard deviations					
WD	Congruent	0.99 (0.02)	0.99 (0.02)	0.99 (0.03)	0.99 (0.02)
	Incongruent	0.96 (0.06)	0.95 (0.06)	0.97 (0.03)	0.96 (0.06)
	neutral	0.99 (0.02)	0.98 (0.04)	0.99 (0.02)	0.99 (0.03)
Health Controls	Congruent	0.99 (0.06)	0.99 (0.06)	0.99 (0.06)	0.99 (0.06)
	Incongruent	0.96 (0.09)	0.99 (0.08)	0.96 (0.08)	0.97 (0.09)
	neutral	0.99 (0.06)	0.96 (0.08)	0.99 (0.06)	0.99 (0.06)

Patients with WD are very vulnerable to the effects of attention, which might influence many other cognitive processes or motor functions; attention could be an important candidate for therapy. Recent studies have attempted to rehabilitate specific attentional networks. Strum et al. [50] found that a computerized rehabilitation program could improve specific attentional networks. Vigilance and alertness are the most elementary functions in the hierarchy, which is valuable for the normal operation of selective attention and divided attention. Allcock et al. reported that slowed RTs in computerized tasks are linked with increased fall frequency in PD patients [51]. Attention training might enhance walking and prevent falls in patients. Further study is required to determine whether attention rehabilitation programs could improve attention and motor function in WD patients.

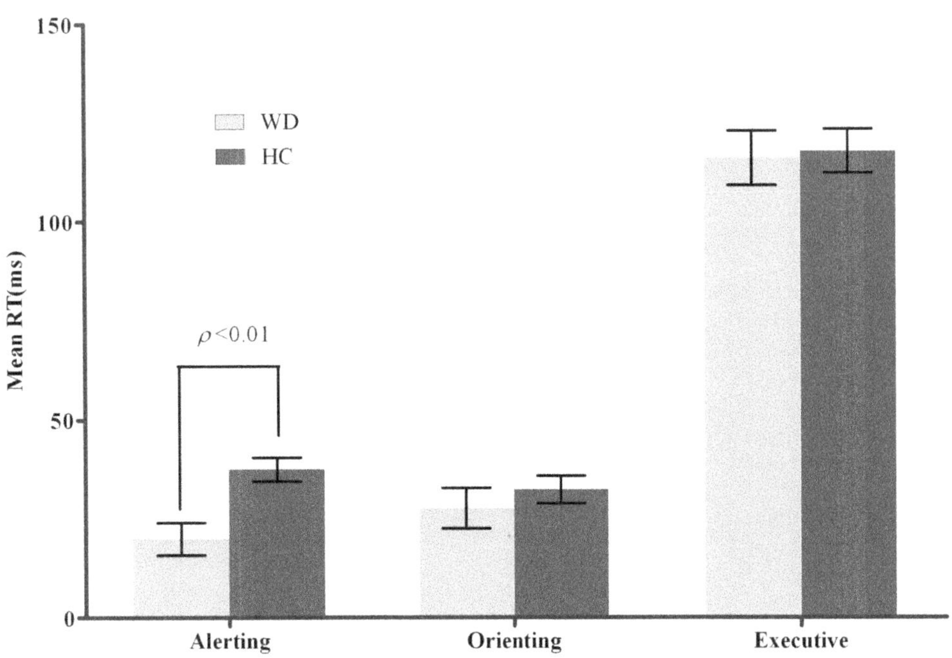

Figure 3 Mean RTs of the Alerting, Orienting and Executive network. Errors bars represent mean standard errors.

Figure 3. Mean RTs of the Alerting, Orienting and Executive network. Errors bars represent mean standard errors.

Table 3. Attention network scores (in RT and ratio score) and accuracy (%) of WD patients and HCs.

	WD (N=35) Mean±SE	HC (N=35)Mean±SE	Z	P
Alerting RT (ms)	20.00 (4.10)	37.54 (3.06)	−2.721	0.007
Ratio	0.029 (0.006)	0.061 (0.005)	−3.365	0.001
Orienting RT (ms)	27.66 (5.12)	32.34 (3.45)	−.347	0.729
Ratio	0.039 (0.007)	0.053 (0.006)	−1.204	0.229
Executive RT (ms)	116.20 (6.84)	117.99 (5.55)	−.141	0.888
Ratio	0.166 (0.010)	0.195 (0.014)	−1.380	0.168
Accuracy (%)	97.54 (0.41)	97.49 (1.05)	−1.689	0.091
Mean RT (ms)	709.14 (11.52)	625.80 (15.30)	−4.305	<0.001

Conclusions

Our study suggests that the ANT could be completed in WD patients and could facilitate the exploration of specific disease-related alterations in the alerting network. Future research is merited on the future activation of attentional networks in WD by simultaneous fMRI examination during the performance of ANT by a WD. Future studies should examine the interaction of attentional networks and the neuroendocrine system in WD.

Author Contributions

Conceived and designed the experiments: YH KW. Performed the experiments: YT FZ BL. Analyzed the data: YH PH. Contributed reagents/materials/analysis tools: YH FZ. Wrote the paper: YH.

References

1. Ala A, Walker AP, Ashkan K, Dooley JS, Schilsky ML (2007) Wilson's disease. Lancet 369:397–408.
2. Litwin T, Gromadzka G, Szpak GM, Jabłonka-Salach K, Bulska E, et al.(2013) Brain metal accumulation in Wilson's disease. J Neurol Sci 329:55–58.
3. Starosta-Rubinstein S, Young AB, Kluin K, Hill G, Aisen AM, et al. (1987) Clinical assessment of 31 patients with Wilson disease. Arch Neurol 44:365–370.
4. Hawkins RA, Maziotta JC, Phelps ME (1987) Wilson disease studied with FDG and positron emission tomography. Neurology 37:1707–1711.
5. Gajda J, Czlonkowska A, Kryst T (1994) Correlation of clinical manifestation and MRI findings in Wilson disease. J Neurol suppl 1:161.
6. Rathbun JK (1996) Neuropsychological aspects of Wilson's disease. Int J Neurosci 85:221–229.
7. Lang C (1989) Is Wilson's disease a dementing condition? J Clin Exp Neuropsychol 11:569–570.
8. Frotal NAF, Caramelli P, Barbosa ER (2009) Cognitive impairment in Wilson's disease. Dementia & Neuropsychologia 3(1):16–21.
9. Hegde S, Sinha S, Rao SL, Taly AB, Vasudev MK (2010) Cognitive profile and structural findings in Wilson's disease: A neuropsychological and MRI-based study. Neurol India 58:708–713.
10. Portala K, Levander S, Westermark, Ekselius L, von Knorring L (2001) Pattern of neuropsychological deficits in patients with treated Wilson's disease. Eur Arch Psychiatry Clin Neurosci 251:262–268.
11. Seniów J, Bak T, Gajda J, Poniatowska R, Czlonkowska A (2002) Cognitive functioning in neurologically symptomatic and asymptomatic forms of Wilson's disease. Mov Disord 17(5):1077–1083.
12. Portala K, Westermark K, von Knorring L, Ekselius L (2000) Psychopathology in treated Wilson's disease determined by means of CPRS expert and self-ratings. Acta Psychiatr Scand 101:104–109.
13. Lin JJ, Lin KL, Wang HS, Wong MC (2006) Psychological presentations without hepatic involvement in Wilson disease. Pediatr Neurol 35:284–286.
14. Zhou SS, Chen XW, Wang CQ, Yin CL, Hu PP, et al. (2012) Selective attention deficits in early and moderate stage Parkinson's disease. Neurosci Lett 509:50–55.
15. Couettea M, Bachoud-Levi AC, Brugieres P, Sieroff E, Bartolomeo P (2008) Orienting of spatial attention in Huntington's disease. Neuropsychologia 46:1391–1400.
16. Cristinzio C, Bononi M, Piacentini S,Albanese A,Bartolomeo P (2013) Attentional networks in Parkinson's disease. Behav Neurol 27 (4):1–6.
17. Fan J, McCandliss BD, Sommer T, Raz A, Posner MI (2002) Testing the efficiency and independence of attentional networks. J Cogn Neurosci 14:340–347.
18. Fan J, McCandliss BD, Fossella J, Flombaum JI, Posner MI (2005) The activation of attentional networks. Neuroimage, 26:471–479.
19. Lundervold AJ, Adolfsdottir S, Halleland H, Halmøy A, Plessen K, et al. (2011) Attention Network Test in adults with ADHD:the impact of affective fluctuations. Behav Brain Funct 7:2–8.
20. Wang K, Fan J, Dong Y, Wang CQ, Lee T, et al. (2005) Selective impairment of attentional networks of orienting and executive control in schizophrenia. Schizophr Res 78:235–241.
21. Fuentes LJ, Fernández PJ, Campoy G, Antequera MM, García-Sevilla J, et al. (2010) Attention network functioning in patients with dementia with Lewy bodies and Alzheimer's disease. Dement Geriatr Cogn Disord 29:139–145.
22. Leskin LP, White PM (2007) Attentional networks reveal executive function deficits in posttraumatic stress disorder. Neuropsychology 21:275–284.
23. Funahashi S (2001) Neuronal mechanisms of executive control by the prefrontal cortex. Neurosci Res 39:147–165.
24. Kubler A, Murphy K, Kaufman J, Stein EA, Garavan H (2003) Co-ordination within and between verbal and visuospatial working memory: Network modulation and anterior frontal recruitment. Neuroimage 20:1298–1308.
25. Posner MI, Petersen SE (1990) The attention system of the human brain. Annu Rev Neurosci 13:25–42.
26. Roberts EA, Schilsky ML (2008) Diagnosis and treatment of Wilson disease: An update. Hepatology, 47:2089–2111.
27. Leinweber B, Möller JC, Scherag A, Reuner U, Günther P, et al. (2008) Evaluation of the Unified Wilson's Disease Rating Scale(UWDRS) in German patients with treated Wilson's disease. Mov Disord 23:54–62.
28. Gong YX (1992) Wechsler Adult Intelligence Scale–Revised in China Version. Hunan Medical College, Changsha, Hunan/China.
29. Gjerris A, Bech P, Bøjholm S, Bolwig TG, Kramp P, et al. (1983) The Hamilton Anxiety Scale. Evaluation of homogeneity and inter-observer reliability in patients with depressive disorders. J Affect Disord 5:163–170.
30. Miller IW, Bishopb S, Normanc WH, Maddever H (1985) The Modified Hamilton Rating Scale for Depression: reliability and validity. Psychiatry Res 14:131–142.
31. Hanlly JR, Dewick HC, Davies ADM, Playeer J, Turnbull C (1990) Verbal fluency in Parkinson's disease. Neuropsychologia 28:737–741.
32. Henry JD, Crawford R (2004) Verbal fluency deficits in Parkinson's disease: a meta-analysis. J Int Neuropsychol Soc 10:608–622.
33. Blackburn HL, Benton AL (1957) Revised administration and scoring of the digit span test. J Consult Psychol 21:139–143.
34. Crivelli L, Farez MF, González CD, Fiol M, Amengual A,et al. (2012) Alerting network dysfunction in early multiple sclerosis. J Int Neuropsychol Soc 18 (4):757–763.
35. Urbanek C, Weinges-Evers N, Bellmann-Strobl J, Bock M, Dorr J, et al. (2010) Attention Network Test reveals alerting network dysfunction in multiple sclerosis. Mult Scler 16:93–99.
36. Booth JE, Carlson CL, Tucker DM (2007) Performance on a neurocognitive measure of alerting differentiates ADHD combined and inattentive subtypes: A preliminary report. Arch Clin Neuropsych 22:423–432.
37. Pacheco-Unguetti AP, Acosta A, Marqués E, Lupiáñez J (2011) Alterations of the attentional networks in patients with anxiety disorders. J Anx Disord 25:888–895.
38. Farrin L, Hull L, Unwin C (2003) Effects of depressed mood on objective and subjective measures of attention. J Neuropsych Clin Neurosci 15:98–104
39. Svetela M,Potrebic A, Pekmezovic T, Tomic A, Kresojevic N, et al. (2009) Neuropsychiatric aspects of treated Wilson's disease. Parkinsonism Relat Disord 15: 772–775.

40. Audet T, Mercier L, Collard S, Rochette A, Hébert R (2000)Attention deficits:is there a right hemisphere specialization for simple reaction time, sustained attention,and phasic alertness? Brain cogn 43:17–21
41. Posner MI, Petersen SE (1990)The attention system of the human brain. Annu Rev Neurosci 13:25–42.
42. Fan J, Byrne J, Worden MS, Guise KG, McCandliss BD, et al.(2007) The relation of brain oscillations to attentional networks. J Neurosci 27: 6197–6206.
43. Schiff ND (2008) Central thalamic contributions to arousal regulation and neurological disorders of consciousness. Ann N Y Acad Sci 1129:105–118.
44. Middleton FA, Strick PL (1994) Anatomical evidence for cerebellar and basal ganglia involvement in higher cognitive functions. Science 266:458–61.
45. Middleton FA, Strick PL (1995) Anatomical basis for basal ganglia involvement in working memory. Society for Neuroscience Abstracts 21:676.
46. Swainson R, Rogers RD, Sahakian BJ, Summers BA, Polkey CE, et al. (2000) Probabilistic learning and reversal deficits in patients with Parkinson's disease or frontal or temporal lobe lesions: Possible adverse effects of dopaminergic medication. Neuropsychologia 38 (5):596–612.
47. Green AE, Munafo MR, DeYoung CG, Fossella JA, Fan J, et al. (2008)Using genetic data in cognitive neuroscience: from growing pains to genuine insights. Nat Neurosci Rev 9:710–720.
48. Beane M, Marrocco RT (2004) Norepinephrine and acetylcholine mediation of the components of reflexive attention: implications for attention deficit disorders. Prog Neurobiol 74:167–181.
49. Snow BJ, Bhatt M, Martin WR, Li D, Calne DB (1991)The nigrostriatal dopaminergic pathway in Wilson's disease studied with positron emission tomography. J Neurol Neurosurg Psychiatry 54:12–17.
50. Strum W, Willmes K, Orgass B, Hartje W (1997) Do specific attention effects need specific training. Neuropsychol Rehab 7(2):81–103.
51. Allcock LM, Rowan EN, Steen IN, Wesnes K, Kenny RA, et al. (2009) Impaired attention predicts falling in Parkinson's disease. Parkinsonism Relat Disord 15 (2):110–115.

2

Individual Differences in Impulsivity Predict Head Motion during Magnetic Resonance Imaging

Xiang-zhen Kong[1,3¶], Zonglei Zhen[1,3¶], Xueting Li[1,3], Huan-hua Lu[1,3], Ruosi Wang[1], Ling Liu[1,3], Yong He[1,3], Yufeng Zang[4], Jia Liu[2,3]*

1 State Key Laboratory of Cognitive Neuroscience and Learning & IDG/McGovern Institute for Brain Research, Beijing Normal University, Beijing, China, **2** School of Psychology, Beijing Normal University, Beijing, China, **3** Center for Collaboration and Innovation in Brain and Learning Sciences, Beijing Normal University, Beijing, China, **4** Center for Cognition and Brain Disorders, Hangzhou Normal University, Hangzhou, China

Abstract

Magnetic resonance imaging (MRI) provides valuable data for understanding the human mind and brain disorders, but in-scanner head motion introduces systematic and spurious biases. For example, differences in MRI measures (e.g., network strength, white matter integrity) between patient and control groups may be due to the differences in their head motion. To determine whether head motion is an important variable in itself, or just simply a confounding variable, we explored individual differences in psychological traits that may predispose some people to move more than others during an MRI scan. In the first two studies, we demonstrated in both children (N = 245) and adults (N = 581) that head motion, estimated from resting-state functional MRI and diffusion tensor imaging, was reliably correlated with impulsivity scores. Further, the difference in head motion between children with attention deficit hyperactivity disorder (ADHD) and typically developing children was largely due to differences in impulsivity. Finally, in the third study, we confirmed the observation that the regression approach, which aims to deal with motion issues by regressing out motion in the group analysis, would underestimate the effect of interest. Taken together, the present findings provide empirical evidence that links in-scanner head motion to psychological traits.

Editor: Juan Zhou, Duke-NUS Graduate Medical School, Singapore

Funding: This work was supported by the National Natural Science Foundation of China (31230031, 91132703, 31221003 and 30800295) and the National Basic Research Program of China (2010CB833903). The funders had no role in study design, data collection and analysis, decision to publish, or preparation of the manuscript.

* Email: liujia@bnu.edu.cn

¶ These authors contributed equally to this work.

Introduction

Head motion during an MRI scan is undesirable, which not only displaces the brain in space, but also interferes with the MR signals [1,2,3,4,5]. Recent studies have further discovered that head motion introduces spurious biases [6,7,8,9,10] and poses difficulty in identifying signatures of neurological disorders, including attention deficit hyperactivity disorder (ADHD) and autism [8,11]. For example, in-scanner head motion decreases long-range functional connectivity [5,7]. Therefore, it is possible that the reduced functional connectivity between the medial prefrontal cortex (MPFC) and posterior cingulate cortex (PCC) observed in ADHD [12,13,14] may be largely due to more intensive head motion of patients with ADHD during scanning. Because head motion significantly confounds both MRI data acquisition and interpretation, it is necessary to characterize the nature of the motion: what makes people move their head during scanning, and why some people move more than others do?

One possible reason of head motion is that some individuals are unable to control their behaviors during scanning. Indeed, MRI data from patients with ADHD and autism contained more volumes with excessive head motion (e.g., > 2 mm) [15,16], implying that they move more intensively than healthy controls. Greater head motion is also found in neurological disorders such as multiple sclerosis [17]. Although some studies did not observe greater head motion in mental disorders such as schizophrenia (e.g., [18]), the failure may be due to low disease severity and small sample size [17]. In addition, the magnitude of head motion is reliable across multiple scans within an individual and varies significantly across individuals [8,9], suggesting that head motion might reflect a trait-like property of human participants. Importantly, a recent study shows that head motion during brain imaging reflects a neurobiological trait rather than simply a technical artifact, suggesting that head motion may be an indicator of a specific cognitive control capacity in the individual brain [19]. Taken together, we hypothesize that the psychological trait of impulsivity is a potential factor contributing to head motion during MRI scan, with impulsive individuals moving their head more intensively in an MRI scanner.

To test this hypothesis, we examined the relationship between head motion, measured during scanning, with the psychological trait of impulsivity measured outside the scanner. In Study 1, we examined whether individual differences in impulsivity assessed by Barratt impulsiveness scale (BIS) [20] significantly accounted for the variance in head motion. Thus, in Study 2, we investigated whether group differences in head motion between children with ADHD and typically developing children (TDC) reflected differences in impulsivity. All these results converged to demonstrate that head motion contains information regarding an individual's impulsivity and, thus, it provides a novel perspective in understanding motion effects in MRI data analyses and interpretation. Further, given that head motion was correlated with impulsivity, regressing out head motion in across-subject analyses as suggested by some studies [8,21] would result in the underestimation of the effect of interest. The final study confirmed this hypothesis by showing that simply regressing out head motion significantly reduced the association between the fMRI metric (i.e., amplitude of low frequency fluctuation, ALFF) and impulsivity.

Materials and Methods

2.1 Participants

Five hundred and eighty-one college students (mean age: 20.5 years; SD: 0.95; 327 females) from Beijing Normal University (BNU), Beijing, China, participated in Study 1. The dataset is part of the Brain Activity Atlas Project (BAAP, http://www.brainactivityatlas.org/). Participants reported no past or current psychiatric illness or history of neurological disorders. Both behavioral and MRI protocols were approved by the Institutional Review Board of Beijing Normal University. Written informed consent was obtained from all participants prior to the experiment. Fifteen outlier participants (2.6% of all participants) were excluded from further analyses; outliers were defined as being 2 SD below or above the group mean for head motion (see *Assessment of In-Scanner Head Motion*).

Participants for Study 2 and 3 included both ADHD and TDC from the ADHD-200 Consortium (http://fcon_1000.projects.nitrc.org/indi/adhd200/). Because the data were from multiple imaging centers, we only analyzed data collected from our imaging center to minimize variability across centers. This sub-dataset contained 245 children, 102 of whom were diagnosed with ADHD (mean age: 12.08 years, SD: 2.04; 12 females); the remaining 143 participants were TDC (mean age: 11.43 years, SD: 1.86; 59 females). Details on the inclusion criteria are available at the website of ADHD-200. Two children with ADHD (2% of the ADHD population) and 3 TDC (2% of the TDC population) showed excessive head motion (i.e., greater than 2 SD above the group mean of head motion for each group); therefore, were excluded from further analyses. Behavioral measures of hyperactivity/impulsivity were not available for 7 children with ADHD and 16 TDC; therefore, they were not included in further analyses either.

2.2 Assessment of Impulsivity

2.2.1 Barratt impulsiveness scale (BIS). In Study 1, impulsivity was assessed using the BIS [20], which was a 4-point Likert-type scale containing 30 items. In the BIS, higher values indicate greater levels of impulsivity. In addition to the total score as a comprehensive measure of impulsivity, BIS contains six components of impulsivity: attention (focusing on task at hand), cognitive instability (thought insertions and racing thoughts), motor (acting on the spur of the moment), perseverance (a consistent life style), self-control (planning and thinking carefully), and cognitive complexity (enjoying challenging mental tasks).

2.2.2 The ADHD Rating Scale (ADHD-RS) IV. In Study 2, the ADHD-RS IV was used to assess ADHD symptoms. This consists of a 4-point Likert-type scale containing 18 items, with each item corresponding to one of the 18 DSM-IV diagnostic criteria. Higher scores indicated greater ADHD-related behavior. ADHD-RS IV has 2 subscales: inattentive (difficulties in focusing on one thing) and hyperactivity/impulsivity (difficulties in behavioral inhibition). We focused on the hyperactivity/impulsivity subscale on the basis of our findings in Studies 1.

2.3 Assessment of In-Scanner Head Motion

2.3.1 Assessment of In-Scanner Head Motion from Diffusion Tensor Images. Diffusion tensor (DT) images were collected on a 3T scanner (Siemens Trio, with a Tim system) at the BNU Imaging Center for Brain Research, Beijing, China. Diffusion-weighted images were collected using a single-shot spin-echo echo-planar imaging (SE-EPI) sequence: repetition time (TR) = 7.2 s, echo time (TE) = 104 ms, flip angle = 90°, field of view (FOV) = 230 mm, matrix size = 128 × 128 mm, resolution = 1.8 × 1.8 × 2.5 mm^3, 49 slices, slice thickness = 2.5 mm. The diffusion weighting gradients were applied along 64 non-collinear directions using a b-value of 1000 s/mm^2, together with an acquisition without diffusion weighting (b = 0 s/mm^2). The total scan time was 7 min 48 s. Foam padding was used to restrict motion within the scanner.

DTI images were processed with FMRIB's Software Library (FSL, http://www.fmrib.ox.ac.uk/fsl). Volumes were realigned to the first volume with a rigid body transform correction with FMRIB's Linear Image Registration Tool (FLIRT), and rigid transformation matrices were obtained for each volume. To estimate in-scanner head motion, the root-mean-square (RMS) deviation, which summarizes 6 translations and rotations across 3 axes, was calculated from 2 transformations of 2 consecutive volumes [3]. That is, in-scanner head motion was measured as the summary measure of both translations and rotations of each brain volume relative to the preceding one as previous studies [8,9]. Finally, head motion was calculated by averaging the RMS deviations for all volumes.

2.3.2 Assessment of In-Scanner Head Motion from Resting-State functional MR Images. The resting-state fMRI data were from the ADHD-200 Consortium. Brain images were collected using a T2*-weighted gradient-echo EPI (GRE-EPI) sequence: TR = 2 s, TE = 30 ms, flip angle = 90°, FOV = 220 mm, matrix size = 64 × 64, 30 axial slices, slice thickness = 4.5 mm. Participants were instructed to keep their eyes closed and to relax during the scan. The total scan time lasted 8 min. Foam padding was used to restrict head motion within the scanner.

In-scanner head motion was calculated from the resting-state fMRI images using the same procedures described in Study 1.

2.4 Relationship between In-Scanner Head Motion and Impulsivity

2.4.1 Correlation Analysis. Pearson correlation analyses were used to examine the potential link between head motion and impulsivity scores in both adult and child datasets. In Study 1, the correlation between head motion and impulsivity total score was calculated. Given the multi-dimensional property of impulsivity [22,23,24], we further investigated which components of impulsivity [20] mainly contributed to the significant association. To account for multiple testing with these multiple components, we used the Bonferroni correction and considered significant only components for which $p < 0.05/6$. In addition, to ensure the findings robust to data non-normality and to avoid the influence of outliers, Spearman's rank-correlation coefficient was also calculated for each correlation analysis.

2.4.2 Mediation Analysis with Dataset from Children with or without ADHD. In this study, we used the mediation analysis [25,26] in order to test the mediation effect of impulsivity in the ADHD-TDC group difference in head motion. In other words, we aimed to test whether the difference between groups in the trait of impulsivity accounted for the difference in head motion between children with ADHD and children in the TDC group. In the mediation model, "a" represents the relation of an independent variable (i.e., X, or ADHD versus TDC) to a mediating variable (i.e., M, or impulsivity), "b" represents the relation of M to a dependent variable (i.e., Y, or head motion), "total" represents the relation of X to Y, and "direct" represents the relation of X to Y after being adjusted for M. The mediated effect may be calculated in two ways, as either "a*b" or "total – direct," both of which correspond to the reduction in the effect of X on Y when M was adjusted (for a review, see [26]). In this study, we conducted the mediation analysis with a tool provided by Wager et al. [27]. A bootstrapping procedure was applied to obtain an unbiased estimate of the indirect effect and a 99% confidence interval (CI). Specifically, the indirect effect was calculated by sampling with replacement where the sample size was equaled to the original one. This procedure was repeated 5000 times, which resulted in a distribution of the indirect effect. If 99% CI does not contain zero, the indirect effect is considered significant (i.e., $p < 0.01$). In the analysis, age and gender were treated as covariates.

2.5 Effects of head motion on neural correlates of impulsivity

2.5.1 Data preprocessing. Anatomical and resting-state functional data were preprocessed using both FSL (http://www.fmrib.ox.ac.uk/fsl) and AFNI (http://afni.nimh.nih.gov). The first 4 volumes were discarded for MRI signals to reach a steady state. Preprocessing steps of fMRI data included spatial Gaussian smoothing (FWHM = 6 mm), motion correction, intensity normalization, and removing linear trends. In addition, nuisance signals (i.e., six motion parameters, signals derived from cerebrospinal fluid and white matter masks after segmentation as well as global signals) were removed from the time courses using the general linear model.

2.5.2 Amplitudes of low frequencies fluctuation (ALFF). Recently, resting-state fMRI has emerged as a powerful approach for discovering neural signatures of both neurological and mental disorders (e.g., [28]). In the present study, we focused on the low frequency fluctuations (LFFs, 0.01-0.10 Hz) in the blood oxygen level-dependent (BOLD) signal at rest. Specifically, we employed an increasingly popular measure of LFFs, which is referred to as ALFF. ALFF reflects the strength of low frequency fluctuations of the brain under resting state. Among a variety of neural metrics in resting-state fMRI, ALFF becomes increasingly popular in identifying neural correlates of disorders such as ADHD [29] and autism [30]. In this study, ALFF values were calculated for each voxel based on a standard procedure [29]. Specifically, the time courses were first converted to the frequency domain using the fast Fourier transform. Then, the square root of power spectrum at each frequency was averaged across a frequency band of 0.01–0.10 Hz. Because low frequency fluctuations are most prominent in the gray matter, following analyses were conducted on the gray matter mask that included the voxels with a probability higher than 0.25 in the Harvard-Oxford brain template of the gray matter mask. It is worth noting that the ALFF was calculated with fMRI data that had been preprocessed with standard procedure, including head motion correction.

2.5.3 Statistical analysis. To examine possible effects of head motion on the neural correlates of impulsivity, we explored the association between the behavioral measure of impulsivity (i.e., Hyper/impulsivity scores) and the ALFF of the brain across ADHD children either with or without including head motion as a confounding factor in the general linear model. The statistical maps were corrected for multiple comparisons with clusters determined by $Z > 2.3$ voxel-wise thresholding and a family-wise error-corrected (FWE-corrected) cluster significance threshold of $p < 0.05$ [31].

Results

3.1 Head Motion and Impulsivity in Healthy Adults

Study 1 examined the potential link between in-scan head motion and impulsivity. Impulsivity was indexed for each participant by the total BIS score, with higher values indicating a greater level of impulsivity. In-scanner head motion was estimated as the average motion of each brain volume relative to the preceding one as previous studies [8,9] during DTI scan. The mean, SD, and reliability of each measure is mentioned in Table 1. Note that the reliability of in-scanner head motion was relatively high (i.e., 0.83), suggesting that it is unlikely random noise but may reflect a trait-like property of the participants (e.g., [9,32]). To test this instinct, next we examined the correlation between participants' in-scanner head motion and their scores in impulsivity.

We obtained a positive correlation between the magnitude of in-scanner head motion and self-reported impulsivity scores across participants ($r = 0.10$, $p = 0.02$; Spearman $rho = 0.10$, $p = 0.02$) (Fig. 1a). Further correlation analyses showed that among the 6 components of BIS impulsivity, only the self-control component contributed significantly to the association ($r = 0.14$, $p = 0.001$, Bonferroni corrected; Spearman $rho = 0.15$, $p < 0.0005$; Fig. 1b), whereas the rest of the components were not correlated with in-scanner head motion (cognitive complexity: $r = 0.02$, $p = 0.56$; attention: $r = 0.08$, $p = 0.07$; cognitive instability: $r = 0.07$, $p = 0.10$; motor: $r = 0.07$, $p = 0.12$; perseverance: $r = -0.001$, $p = 0.99$). Therefore, participants who tended to act without an appropriate amount of deliberation were more likely to have a larger amount of head motion during scanning, and such association was mainly due to difficulty with self-control. To test whether the motion-impulsivity correlation reported here was reliable, we randomly split the dataset into two halves ($N = 283$ for each sub-dataset). We observed the motion-impulsivity correlation in both sub-datasets (Sub-dataset 1: $r = 0.13$, $p = 0.027$; Spearman $rho = 0.17$, $p = 0.005$; Sub-dataset 2: $r = 0.14$, $p = 0.018$; Spearman $rho = 0.13$, $p = 0.030$), suggesting that the association is reliable.

3.2 Impulsivity as a Mediator of ADHD-TDC Group Difference in Head Motion

The dataset for Study 2 comes from the ADHD-200 Consortium, which consisted of resting-state fMRI data and clinical behavioral data collected from ADHD and TDC. Impulsivity was assessed by the hyperactivity/impulsivity subscale of the ADHD-RS IV, and their in-scanner head motion was estimated from the resting-state fMRI data with the same procedure used in Studies 1.

As expected, children with ADHD scored significantly higher in impulsivity than those in the TDC group ($t [215] = 12.9$, $p < 0.001$, two-tailed), and in-scanner head motion was significantly larger in children with ADHD than in children in the TDC group ($t [215] = 4.03$, $p < 0.001$, two-tailed) (Table 1). In addition, the

Table 1. Mean Scores (± SD) and Reliability Estimates for Each Task in the Study.

	Mean ± SD	Reliability
In-scanner Head Motion (mm, n = 566; from DTI data in adults)	0.28±0.05	0.83
BIS Impulsivity (n = 566)	62.16±8.45	0.73
Attention	10.36±2.03	0.38
Instability	6.75±1.57	0.51
Motor	12.90±3.01	0.66
Perseverance	7.56±1.55	0.24
Self-control	12.33±2.63	0.57
Complexity	12.27±2.19	0.38
	ADHD (n = 93)	**TDC (n = 124)**
In-scanner Head Motion (mm; from resting-state fMRI data in children)	0.11±0.04	0.09±0.03
Hyper/impulsivity	22.38±6.45	13.54±3.61

The reliability of In-scanner head motion was Spearman-Brown-corrected split-half reliability, and that of BIS Impulsivity was Cronbach's alpha for items in the questionnaire. Note that the reliabilities of the components of impulsivity (e.g., self-control) were medium, possibly because the number of items for each component was small (e.g., 6 items for self-control). ADHD: attention deficit hyperactivity disorder; TDC: typically-developing controls; BIS: Barratt impulsiveness scale.

correlation between head motion and impulsivity was observed in the children dataset ($r = 0.34$, $p < 0.001$). Similar patterns were observed in both ADHD children ($r = 0.26$, $p = 0.01$; Spearman rho $= 0.22$, $p = 0.03$) and TDC children ($r = 0.15$, $p = 0.10$; Spearman rho $= 0.19$, $p = 0.03$).

Furthermore, the mediation analysis [26] indicated that the difference between groups in head motion could be largely accounted for by the difference in impulsivity. In this model, the participant group (ADHD versus TDC) was the predictor, impulsivity was the mediator, and in-scanner head motion was the outcome. The mediation analysis showed that the difference in head motion between ADHD and TDC became insignificant (beta $= 0.09$, $p = 0.35$) after their association (beta $= 0.27$, $p < 0.001$) was adjusted by the mediator of impulsivity (Fig. 2). Bootstrap simulation ($n = 5000$) further confirmed that the indirect effect through impulsivity was significant ($p < 0.01$) with a 99% confidence interval of 0.0189 to 0.42. In other words, the difference between groups in the psychological trait of impulsivity accounted for the difference in head motion between children with ADHD and children in the TDC group.

3.3 Effects of Head Motion on Neural Correlates of Impulsivity

To deal with differences in head motion between participant groups, several groups have proposed to include head motion as a confounding variable in across-subject analyses [8,21]. However, given the above-mentioned link between head motion and impulsivity, the regression approach may reduce the power to detect neural correlates of impulsivity. To demonstrate this possibility, in the third study we examined how head motion affected the identification of impulsivity-related cortical regions in the ADHD children. To do this, we correlated the behavioral measure of impulsivity and the ALFF of the brain, the strength of low frequency neural fluctuations under a resting state [29]. Head

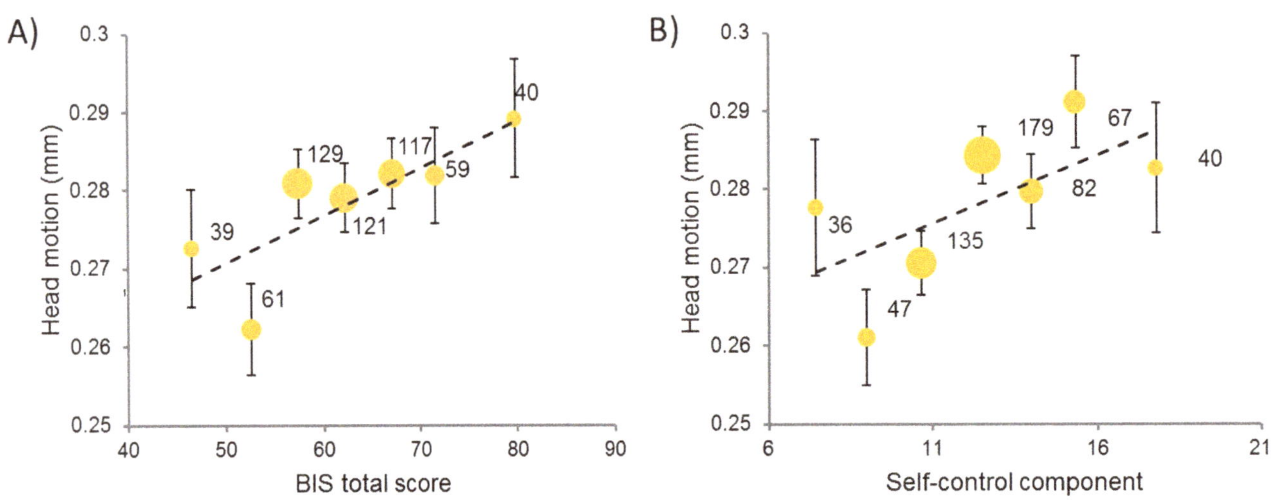

Figure 1. Binned scatter plots between in-scanner head motion and impulsivity indexed by (A) BIS total score, and (B) self-control component score. To avoid overlap for participants with similar scores, participants are binned into groups on the basis of impulsivity scores. The size of dots indicates the number of participants in the groups. Error bars indicate standard error of the mean (s.e.m).

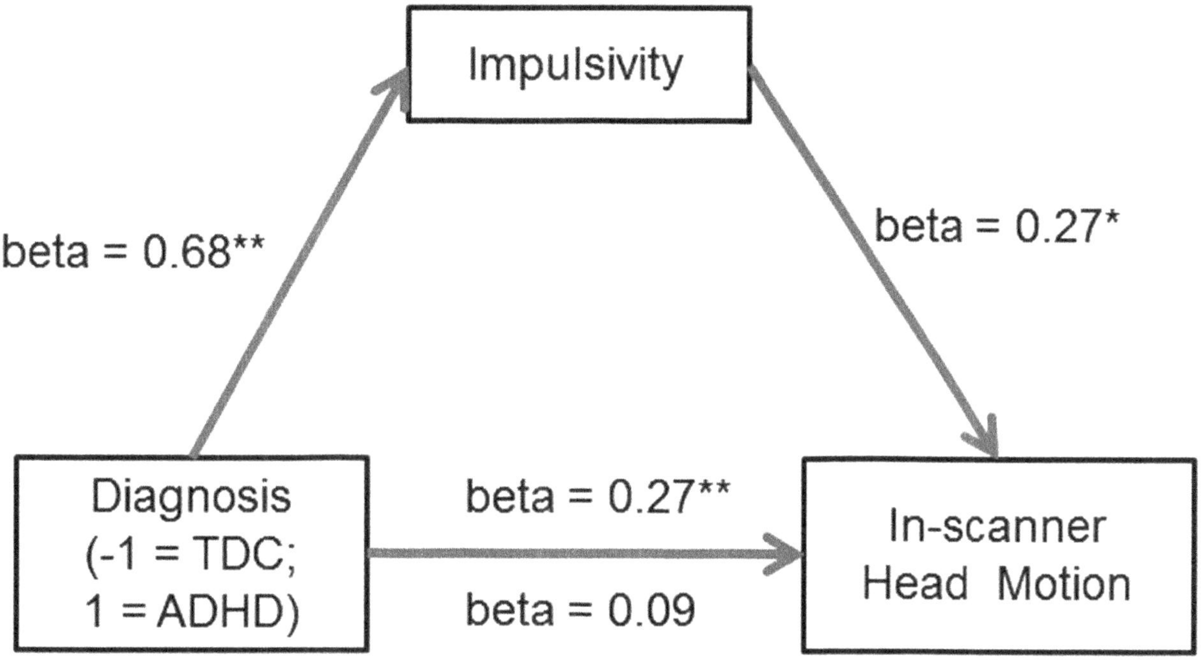

Figure 2. Impulsivity as a sufficient mediator of the difference in head motion between ADHD and TDC in the mediation analysis. Path coefficients are shown next to arrows indicating each link in the analysis. For the group difference in head motion, the value above the arrow indicates the zero-order correlation, and the value below the arrow represents the correlation after controlling the mediator of impulsivity. All values represent standardized betas. * indicates $p < 0.01$, ** indicates $p < 0.001$, two-tailed. ADHD: attention deficit hyperactivity disorder; TDC: typically developing children.

motion was either included as a confounding factor in the general linear model or not for the across-subject analysis.

When the variable of head motion was not regressed out, we found a significant association between the ALFF of the brain and impulsivity in the right orbital frontal cortex (MNI coordinates: 12, 62, −16; Z-value = 3.53, $p < 0.05$, FWE corrected) (Fig. 3, Top), which is a classic brain region related to impulsivity [33,34,35,36,37]. However, when head motion was considered as a confounding factor and then regressed out, the association was greatly weakened; indeed, no regions survived the multiple comparison correction (Fig. 3, Bottom).

Discussion

Many researchers have attempted using MRI to identify neural signatures for disorders in the brain to improve the ability to diagnose such disorders, but inevitable head motion during MRI scanning poses difficulties in both data acquisition and interpretation. In this study, we elucidated the nature of head motion by correlating head motion with psychological traits in large samples. In two studies, we found that the variance of head motion was partly accounted for by the individual differences in impulsivity. Importantly, the association was observed across participant groups (children and adults) and across imaging modalities (resting-state fMRI and DTI), suggesting that the association between head motion and impulsivity can be observed across data modalities and ages. In addition, the final study suggests that the regression approach, which aims to deal with the issue on head motion in across-subject analyses, likely underestimated the effect of interest.

A recent study [19] has found that distant connectivity primarily in the default mode network significantly correlates with individuals' head motion during brain imaging, suggesting that head motion is an indicator of a specific cognitive control capacity in the individual brain. Our study extended this finding by showing a reliable association between impulsivity and in-scanner head motion. Because the association was apparently more prominent in children with ADHD, the effect of head motion might be particularly important in patient-control studies. Indeed, we demonstrated that the group difference in head motion between ADHD and TDC children was fully mediated by their difference in impulsivity. Together with recent studies [17,19], our findings provide empirical evidence that the in-scanner head motion reflects trait-like properties of human participants, such as impulsivity, rather than just technical artifacts.

Note that the contribution of impulsivity to in-scanner head motion was small, possibly because of following reasons. First of all, in-scanner head does contain noise, which is evidenced by imperfect test-retest reliability of around 0.60 [9,19,38]. Therefore, together with the imperfect reliability of the measure on the impulsivity, the correlation coefficient of the motion-impulsivity is hardly larger than 0.60. Second, in this study the in-scanner head motion was measured at rest, and previous studies have shown that in the situation of low cognitive demands, the association between head motion and cognitive measures becomes weak [17]. Finally, the psychological trait of impulsivity is one of many factors that contribute to in-scanner head motion. Indeed, other psychological traits (e.g., conscientiousness, agreeableness, and anxiety), cognitive processes (e.g., high cognitive demands), and neurological/mental disorders (e.g., multiple sclerosis, schizophrenia) may also affect in-scanner head motion [17]. Having said this, the motion-impulsivity association cannot be simply ignored because of its small effect size. Instead, the association shall be taken into account especially in identifying neural signatures of some neurological/cognitive disorders because (1) the association is

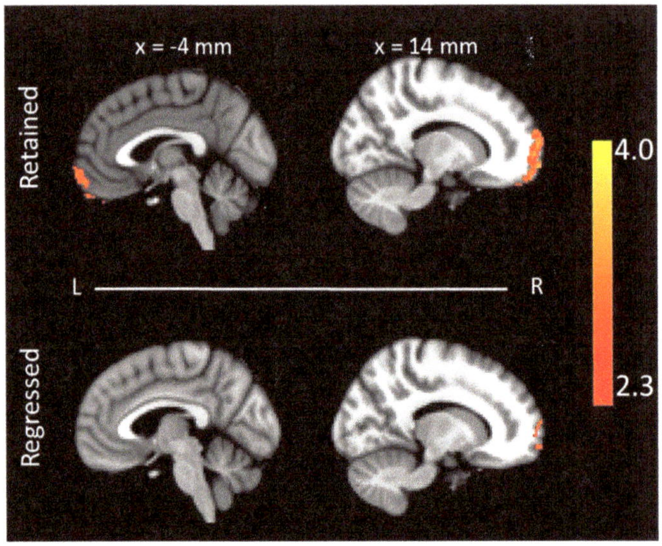

Figure 3. The neural correlates of impulsivity in the ADHD children. The ALFF value of the bilateral orbital frontal cortex and prefrontal cortex was positively correlated with the behavioral measure of impulsivity when the variable of head motion was either retained (top, $Z > 2.3$, $p < 0.05$, FWE corrected) or regressed out (bottom, $Z > 2.3$, uncorrected). The coordinate is in the MNI stereotactic space. ALFF: the amplitude of low-frequency fluctuation.

reliable across data modalities, subject populations, and ages, and (2) the association is likely more evident in population with impulsivity-related disorders (i.e., ADHD).

Recently, the neuroimaging field has become increasingly concerned about the confounding effect of in-scanner head motion on the interpretation of group differences in MRI measures, especially when the groups show differences in head motion. Accordingly, several groups have proposed to include head motion as a confounding variable in across-subject analyses to match head motion between groups [8,21]. However, the regression approach may reduce the ability to detect the effect of interest [8]. For instance, previous studies have shown that the correlation coefficient between age and the functional connectivity between the MPFC and PCC reduces almost by 50% when head motion is regressed [8,39]. One interpretation is that younger children move their head more intensively, which affects the quality of MRI data. Alternatively, head motion is associated with psychological or clinical traits (e.g., impulse control), cognitive processes [17], and even neurobiological substrates (e.g., functional connectivity [19]). Thus, regressing out head motion in the across-subject analysis likely underestimates the effect of interest. Consistent with the latter instinct, we found that the neural correlates of impulsivity indexed by ALFF greatly weakened when the regression approach was adopted. This result is in line with a recent finding that discarding data with severe motion artifacts, which is another approach proposed to deal with head motion, may introduce sampling bias [17].

On the other hand, it is unwise to conduct across-subject analyses without taking head motion into account, because head motion does interfere with the MR signals [1,2,3], and not modeling or removing head motion from MRI data surely produces spurious results [7,8]. However, to differentiate the variance of interest (i.e., motion-associated endophenotypes) from the variance of error (i.e., motion-induced artifacts) is difficult with current techniques. Therefore, we suggest several ways of dealing with the head motion issue. First, results shall be presented both with and without head motion being regressed out in group-level analyses. If any significant difference is observed, the authors shall discuss such difference not only in terms of random noises but also in terms of meaningful variables such as psychological traits or the severity of disorders. Specifically, cortical regions that are modulated by head motion may likely provide clues on the type of cognitive or psychological variables underlying such modulation. Besides, replication in an independent sample is helpful, because motion-induced artifacts are usually random and not specific to brain regions. Third, an ideal solution is to minimize head motion artifacts during data acquisition so that there is no need to model head motion in data analysis. Several approaches have been proposed, one of which is to develop algorithms prospectively co-registering all images, as articulated previously [9,17,40]. Because this approach can prevent motion-induced artifacts on MR signals at the time of acquisition, it is likely superior to traditional realignment-based corrections. Finally, with advances in MRI acquisition techniques such as multi-band sequences [41], motion-induced artifacts can be effectively limited by increasing sampling rate [38], for example.

In sum, our study found that the variable of head motion is not simply a random factor, but reflects valuable information regarding individuals' psychological traits. Specifically, we found that a portion of variance in head motion could be explained by impulsivity, especially in the population with higher level of impulsivity. Thus, our study invites a broad investigation of whether other psychological traits (e.g., conscientiousness and agreeableness) or psychiatric symptoms (e.g., anxiety and claustrophobia) might contribute to in-scanner head motion. Such a finding may ultimately elucidate the relationship among in-scanner behaviors, psychological traits, and neural signatures of neurological disorders.

Acknowledgments

We thank members of Liu Lab for help collecting data. All the data are available upon request.

Author Contributions

Conceived and designed the experiments: JL XZK. Performed the experiments: XTL HHL RSW LL XZK. Analyzed the data: XZK ZLZ. Contributed reagents/materials/analysis tools: XZK ZLZ YFZ. Contributed to the writing of the manuscript: XZK ZLZ YH YFZ JL.

References

1. Friston KJ, Williams S, Howard R, Frackowiak RS, Turner R (1996) Movement-related effects in fMRI time-series. Magn Reson Med 35: 346–355.
2. Bullmore ET, Brammer MJ, Rabe-Hesketh S, Curtis VA, Morris RG, et al. (1999) Methods for diagnosis and treatment of stimulus-correlated motion in generic brain activation studies using fMRI. Hum Brain Mapp7: 38–48.
3. Jenkinson M, Bannister P, Brady M, Smith S (2002) Improved optimization for the robust and accurate linear registration and motion correction of brain images. Neuroimage 17: 825–841.
4. Tijssen RH, Jansen JF, Backes WH (2009) Assessing and minimizing the effects of noise and motion in clinical DTI at 3 T.Hum Brain Mapp 30: 2641–2655.
5. Murphy K, Birn RM, Bandettini PA (2013) Resting-state FMRI confounds and cleanup. NeuroImage.
6. Ling J, Merideth F, Caprihan A, Pena A, Teshiba T, et al. (2012) Head injury or head motion? Assessment and quantification of motion artifacts in diffusion tensor imaging studies. Hum Brain Mapp33: 50–62.
7. Power JD, Barnes KA, Snyder AZ, Schlaggar BL, Petersen SE (2012) Spurious but systematic correlations in functional connectivity MRI networks arise from subject motion. Neuroimage 59: 2142–2154.
8. Satterthwaite TD, Wolf DH, Loughead J, Ruparel K, Elliott MA, et al. (2012) Impact of in-scanner head motion on multiple measures of functional connectivity: relevance for studies of neurodevelopment in youth. Neuroimage 60: 623–632.
9. Van Dijk KR, Sabuncu MR, Buckner RL (2012) The influence of head motion on intrinsic functional connectivity MRI. Neuroimage 59: 431–438.
10. Satterthwaite TD, Elliott MA, Gerraty RT, Ruparel K, Loughead J, et al. (2013) An improved framework for confound regression and filtering for control of motion artifact in the preprocessing of resting-state functional connectivity data. Neuroimage 64: 240–256.
11. Deen B, Pelphrey K (2012) Perspective: Brain scans need a rethink. Nature 491: S20.
12. Castellanos FX, Margulies DS, Kelly C, Uddin LQ, Ghaffari M, et al. (2008) Cingulate-precuneus interactions: a new locus of dysfunction in adult attention-deficit/hyperactivity disorder. Biol Psychiatry 63: 332–337.
13. Uddin LQ, Kelly AM, Biswal BB, Margulies DS, Shehzad Z, et al. (2008) Network homogeneity reveals decreased integrity of default-mode network in ADHD. J Neurosci Methods 169: 249–254.
14. Fair DA, Posner J, Nagel BJ, Bathula D, Dias TG, et al. (2010) Atypical default network connectivity in youth with attention-deficit/hyperactivity disorder. Biol Psychiatry 68: 1084–1091.
15. Durston S, Tottenham NT, Thomas KM, Davidson MC, Eigsti IM, et al. (2003) Differential patterns of striatal activation in young children with and without ADHD. Biol Psychiatry 53: 871–878.
16. Kaiser MD, Hudac CM, Shultz S, Lee SM, Cheung C, et al. (2010) Neural signatures of autism. Proc Natl Acad Sci U S A 107: 21223–21228.
17. Wylie GR, Genova H, Deluca J, Chiaravalloti N, Sumowski JF (2014) Functional magnetic resonance imaging movers and shakers: Does subject-movement cause sampling bias? Hum Brain Mapp35: 1–13.
18. Yoo SS, Choi BG, Juh R, Pae CU, Lee CU (2005) Head motion analysis during cognitive fMRI examination: application in patients with schizophrenia. Neurosci Res 53: 84–90.
19. Zeng LL, Wang D, Fox MD, Sabuncu M, Hu D, et al. (2014) Neurobiological basis of head motion in brain imaging. Proc Natl Acad Sci U S A.
20. Patton JH, Stanford MS, Barratt ES (1995) Factor structure of the Barratt impulsiveness scale. J Clin Psychol 51: 768–774.
21. Zuo XN, Di Martino A, Kelly C, Shehzad ZE, Gee DG, et al. (2010) The oscillating brain: complex and reliable. Neuroimage 49: 1432–1445.
22. Paulsen K, Johnson M (1980) Impulsivity: a multidimensional concept with developmental aspects. J Abnorm Child Psychol 8: 269–277.
23. Reynolds B, Penfold RB, Patak M (2008) Dimensions of impulsive behavior in adolescents: laboratory behavioral assessments. Exp Clin Psychopharmacol 16: 124–131.
24. Dvorak RD, Pearson MR, Kuvaas NJ (2013) The five-factor model of impulsivity-like traits and emotional lability in aggressive behavior. Aggress Behav 39: 222–228.
25. Preacher KJ, Hayes AF (2008) Asymptotic and resampling strategies for assessing and comparing indirect effects in multiple mediator models. Behav Res Methods 40: 879–891.
26. MacKinnon DP, Fairchild AJ, Fritz MS (2007) Mediation analysis. Annu Rev Psychol 58: 593–614.
27. Wager TD, Davidson ML, Hughes BL, Lindquist MA, Ochsner KN (2008) Prefrontal-subcortical pathways mediating successful emotion regulation. Neuron 59: 1037–1050.
28. Biswal BB, Mennes M, Zuo XN, Gohel S, Kelly C, et al. (2010) Toward discovery science of human brain function. Proc Natl Acad Sci U S A 107: 4734–4739.
29. Zang YF, He Y, Zhu CZ, Cao QJ, Sui MQ, et al. (2007) Altered baseline brain activity in children with ADHD revealed by resting-state functional MRI. Brain Dev 29: 83–91.
30. Supekar K, Uddin LQ, Khouzam A, Phillips J, Gaillard WD, et al. (2013) Brain hyperconnectivity in children with autism and its links to social deficits. Cell Rep 5: 738–747.
31. Worsley KJ (2001) Statistical analysis of activation images; Jezzard P, Matthews PM, Smith SM, editors. New York: Oxford University Press.
32. Yan CG, Cheung B, Kelly C, Colcombe S, Craddock RC, et al. (2013) A comprehensive assessment of regional variation in the impact of head micromovements on functional connectomics. Neuroimage.
33. Rolls ET (2004) The functions of the orbitofrontal cortex. Brain Cogn 55: 11–29.
34. Ridderinkhof KR, Ullsperger M, Crone EA, Nieuwenhuis S (2004) The role of the medial frontal cortex in cognitive control. Science 306: 443–447.
35. Lucantonio F, Stalnaker TA, Shaham Y, Niv Y, Schoenbaum G (2012) The impact of orbitofrontal dysfunction on cocaine addiction. Nat Neurosci 15: 358–366.
36. Cho SS, Pellecchia G, Aminian K, Ray N, Segura B, et al. (2013) Morphometric correlation of impulsivity in medial prefrontal cortex. Brain Topogr 26: 479–487.
37. Blair RJ (2004) The roles of orbital frontal cortex in the modulation of antisocial behavior. Brain Cogn 55: 198–208.
38. Kong XZ (2014) Association between in-scanner head motion with cerebral white matter microstructure: a multiband diffusion-weighted MRI study. PeerJ 2: e366.
39. Andrews-Hanna JR, Snyder AZ, Vincent JL, Lustig C, Head D, et al. (2007) Disruption of large-scale brain systems in advanced aging. Neuron 56: 924–935.
40. Yendiki A, Koldewyn K, Kakunoori S, Kanwisher N, Fischl B (2013) Spurious group differences due to head motion in a diffusion MRI study. Neuroimage.
41. Moeller S, Yacoub E, Olman CA, Auerbach E, Strupp J, et al. (2010) Multiband multislice GE-EPI at 7 tesla, with 16-fold acceleration using partial parallel imaging with application to high spatial and temporal whole-brain fMRI. Magn Reson Med 63: 1144–1153.

3

Differences in Visuo-Motor Control in Skilled vs. Novice Martial Arts Athletes during Sustained and Transient Attention Tasks: A Motor-Related Cortical Potential Study

Javier Sanchez-Lopez[1], Thalia Fernandez[1]*, Juan Silva-Pereyra[2], Juan A. Martinez Mesa[3], Francesco Di Russo[4,5]

1 Departamento de Neurobiología Conductual y Cognitiva del Instituto de Neurobiología, Universidad Nacional Autónoma de México, Juriquilla, Querétaro, México, **2** Proyecto en Neurociencias de la Facultad de Estudios Superiores Iztacala, Universidad Nacional Autónoma de México, Tlalnepantla, Estado de México, México, **3** Departamento de Psicología del Deporte, Instituto de Medicina del Deporte de Cuba, Cerro, Ciudad de La Habana, Cuba, **4** Dipartimento di Scienze Motorie Umane e della Salute, Università degli Studi di Roma "Foro Italico," Roma, Lazio, Italia, **5** Unità di Neuropsicologia, IRCCS Fondazione Santa Lucia, Roma, Lazio, Italia

Abstract

Cognitive and motor processes are essential for optimal athletic performance. Individuals trained in different skills and sports may have specialized cognitive abilities and motor strategies related to the characteristics of the activity and the effects of training and expertise. Most studies have investigated differences in motor-related cortical potential (MRCP) during self-paced tasks in athletes but not in stimulus-related tasks. The aim of the present study was to identify the differences in performance and MRCP between skilled and novice martial arts athletes during two different types of tasks: a sustained attention task and a transient attention task. Behavioral and electrophysiological data from twenty-two martial arts athletes were obtained while they performed a continuous performance task (CPT) to measure sustained attention and a cued continuous performance task (c-CPT) to measure transient attention. MRCP components were analyzed and compared between groups. Electrophysiological data in the CPT task indicated larger prefrontal positive activity and greater posterior negativity distribution prior to a motor response in the skilled athletes, while novices showed a significantly larger response-related P3 after a motor response in centro-parietal areas. A different effect occurred in the c-CPT task in which the novice athletes showed strong prefrontal positive activity before a motor response and a large response-related P3, while in skilled athletes, the prefrontal activity was absent. We propose that during the CPT, skilled athletes were able to allocate two different but related processes simultaneously according to CPT demand, which requires controlled attention and controlled motor responses. On the other hand, in the c-CPT, skilled athletes showed better cue facilitation, which permitted a major economy of resources and "automatic" or less controlled responses to relevant stimuli. In conclusion, the present data suggest that motor expertise enhances neural flexibility and allows better adaptation of cognitive control to the requested task.

Editor: Bart Rypma, University of Texas at Dallas, United States of America

Funding: This research was supported by the Programa de Apoyo a Proyectos de Investigación e Innovación Tecnológica (PAPIIT IN205212). The funder had no role in study design, data collection and analysis, decision to publish, or preparation of the manuscript.

* E-mail: thaliafh@yahoo.com.mx

Introduction

Sports performance depends on many different components, including cognitive and motor skills. Previous studies have reported the superior cognitive abilities of expert athletes, who are capable of quickly extracting important information and using this ability to identify the most relevant information [1,2,3,4,5]. In addition, experts can better modulate their cognitive and motor resources according to specific task demands [6].

A method that is commonly used to study how sports performance is enhanced is the analysis of the brain electrical activity. Previous studies have reported differences between expert athletes, less expert athletes and/or non-athletes studying EEG rhythms during eyes-closed resting state and concluding that these rhythms are enhanced in elite athletes compared to control subjects [7]. Additionally, this research group has investigated the task-related power decrease of EEG alpha activity as an index of cortical activation and they have observed that athletes' brains is characterized by a reduced cortical activation during a motor task [8,9], a sport judgments task [10] and the reactivity to eyes opening in the condition of resting state [11], in line with the "neural efficiency" hypothesis. Another analysis commonly used has been the event-related potentials (ERPs), which are regarded as direct correlates of information processing [12,13]. Most of the previous ERP studies on athletes have compared experts with beginners or non-athletes and have found differences between groups in the amplitude and latency of different ERP components.

These differences have been associated with expertise, sports discipline and level of task demand [14,15,16,17,18,19,20,21,22]. Additionally, movement-related cortical potential (MRCP) has been studied in this population. This activity has been associated with motor skill learning and performance. During a self-paced task, in the final seconds prior to voluntary movement production, there is an increase in electrical activity in the premotor and motor areas of the brain. One component of the MRCP, the Bereitschafts potential (BP), is a slowly rising negativity that occurs 1–2 s prior to movement onset. The BP is followed by a steeper gradient negativity, the negative slope (NS'), 400–500 ms prior to movement onset. These components are followed by the motor potential (MP), with the peak negativity occurring concomitantly with movement onset in contralateral central sites [23].

Several studies have investigated differences in the amplitude and onset time of the MRCP between expert and novice performers to aid our understanding of learning-related changes in brain functioning [24,25,26,27,28,29]. The main findings from these studies are that expert performers show smaller amplitude and later onset MRCPs prior to task performance than their novice counterparts. This fact has been observed in groups of expert clay target [24] and pistol shooters [30], elite and novice kendo martial art performers [25,26] and guitar players [27,28,29]. It has been concluded that experienced performers are able to plan and perform the task with reduced cortical activity compared to novices and that these differences can be attributed to long-term training by the expert group.

Compared to the aforementioned MRCP studies for self-paced movements, the MRCP in a stimulus-related task (externally triggered movements) has not been sufficiently studied in general and has never been studied as a function of expertise. Therefore, features of this brain electrical activity have not been defined as a function of expertise during stimulus-related tasks. In this sense, differences in MRCP between expert and novice athletes could be related not just to expertise but also to cognitive task demand, as found in ERP studies. Externally triggered MRCPs differ from self-paced MRCPs because external events affect motor preparation. Starting from stimulus onset, MRCP negativity is followed by a strong positivity in prefrontal and parietal areas, identified as the P3 complex in ERP studies. This activity depends on stimulus discrimination, response selection and execution. While parietal activity has been extensively studied because it corresponds to components of the ERP [31], prefrontal activity was discovered only recently and has been related to aging [31] and physical exercise [32]. The main components of this prefrontal activity are referred to as prefrontal negativity [33] [14] and prefrontal positivity (pP), depending on polarity, with pN preceding pP.

Many cognitive processes are required during athletic training and competition, including different types of attention, such as sustained attention, which maintains an athlete's focus throughout the competition, and transient attention, which allows perception of an opponent's cues, enabling a fast response. However, in the sport psychology literature, these processes have not been clearly defined. Previous ERP studies have shown that sustained and transient attention are processes clearly separated [34]. Moreover, skilled and novice athletes exhibit differences in both types of attention. Given that MRCP has been associated with motor skill learning and performance and also that externally triggered tasks involve an interaction between MRCP and cognitive processes, we hypothesized that two different processes would be found and that they would be reflected by differences in behavioral performance and MRCP between groups. Skilled athletes must show better capabilities in both sustained and transient attention tasks than novices. If skilled athletes are given a highly demanding task (i.e., physical or cognitive), they will use all of the necessary resources required by the task, whereas if an easier task is presented, they will be economical and will use less resources in responding to the task. Novice athletes have not developed all of the necessary resources to control their responses during a high-demand task. The goal of the present study was to identify behavioral and electrophysiological differences in MRCP between skilled and novice martial arts athletes during two different types of tasks: a sustained attention task and a transient attention task.

Experiment 1

To investigate the differences in MRCP between skilled and novice martial arts athletes on a sustained attention task, a continuous performance task (CPT) was used. In sustained attention tasks, participants are instructed in advance to attend to the same specific stimulus across all stimuli presented in the task. Every stimulus is a potential target that may require a response [34]. This task requires high levels of sustained attention. Given that combat requires long periods of sustained attention, this ability should be more developed in skilled martial arts athletes as a consequence of their training. Our hypothesis was that skilled athletes would show better performance and differences compared to novice athletes in both the negative and positive components of the MRCP related to high motor control.

Methods

Participants. Twenty-two martial arts athletes from three different combat disciplines (judo, taekwondo and kung-fu) were recruited. The participants were divided into two groups: a) 12 skilled athletes (mean age = 25.5 years, $SD = 10.6$) with more than five years of practice and the highest degree in their discipline and b) 10 novice athletes (mean age = 24.3 years, $SD = 9.7$) with less than one year of practice and the lowest degree in their discipline. All participants were healthy and had normal or corrected-to-normal vision. All subjects included in the study had scores in the normal range (>90) on the Wechsler Intelligence Scale and an attention deficit and hyperactivity disorder (ADHD) score greater than −1.80 in the task of variables of attention (TOVA), which indicates normal attention (see Table 1).

Ethics Statement. Participants were informed of their rights and provided written informed consent for participation in the study. Additionally, when participants enrolled in our study were minors, the written informed consent was obtained from their parents (mother or father) on behalf of them. This research was carried out ethically following the principles stated in the chapter five on ethics and medical research of the Declaration of Helsinki. Both this research and its informed consent were approved by the Ethics Committee of the Neurobiology Institute at the Universidad Nacional Autónoma de México.

Stimuli. Five different pointed arrows (2.95 cm width, 2.03 cm height; white on black background) were used. A sequence of arrows was presented in the center of a 17-inch VGA computer monitor at a viewing distance of 80 cm and visual angle of approximately $2.11 \times 1.45°$.

Continuous performance task. A sequence of 600 arrows divided into six blocks of 100 arrows was presented to each participant. The participants were instructed to respond to the target arrow (pointed right and downward) and not to respond when another arrow was shown. The target stimulus itself was presented in 20% of the trials and the non-target stimulus in 80%. The stimulus duration was 100 ms, and a variable interstimulus interval (1.2–1.5 s) was used.

Table 1. Group characteristics for chronological age, years of sport practice, ADHD score, Intelligence Quotient score and sport disciplines practiced.

Group	Age	Years of sport practice	ADHD score	IQ	Sport
Skilled $N=11$	25±11	9±6	1.7±1.9	105±7.7	Judo = 5
					TKD = 4
					Kung-fu = 3
Novice $N=10$	25±9	1±0	1.0±1.6	108±2.6	Judo = 3
					TKD = 2
					Kung-fu = 5
Skilled *vs.* Novice	NS	$p=.01$**	NS	NS	NS

NS = no significant differences between groups.
**$p \leq .01$.

Procedure. Participants were seated in a comfortable chair in a room with low light and instructed to respond by pressing a button with the right index finger as rapidly and accurately as possible when the target stimulus appeared during the task.

ERP recording. An electroencephalogram (EEG) was recorded with 32 Ag/Cl sintered surface electrodes mounted on an elastic cap (Electrocap) using NeuroScan SynAmps amplifiers (Compumedics NeuroScan) and Scan 4.5 software (Compumedics NeuroScan). The electrodes were referenced to linked earlobes. Electrooculograms were recorded from a supraorbital electrode and an electrode placed at the external canthus of the left eye. The EEG was digitized at a 500-Hz sampling rate and filtered using a band-pass filter set from 0.1 to 100 Hz. Electrode impedance was maintained below 5 kΩ.

Data analysis. Behavioral analysis was conducted using percentages of correct responses, which were transformed ARCSIN [SQRT(percentage/100)]. To analyze accuracy, a two-way ANOVA was performed with Group (skilled and novices) and Condition (target and non-target) as factors. A one-way ANOVA was also performed for reaction times.

The MRCP were computed offline using 2000-ms epochs from each subject in the target condition using motor response as the trigger. Each epoch consisted of 1500 ms preceding the motor response and 500 ms following the motor response. A baseline correction was performed using the initial 200 ms of the epoch. Epochs with voltage changes exceeding +100 μV were omitted from the final average. Vertical electro-oculogram artifacts were removed by applying an eye-movement correction algorithm [35]. Segments with artifacts and noisy electrical activity were rejected. The average number of EEG segments per condition and group was approximately equal (more than 60 trials).

Statistical analyses were performed on MRCP time windows selected by visual inspection according to previous literature [23]: The BP was divided into two components: early BP, measured as the mean amplitude between −800 and −400 ms, and the late BP, measured as the mean amplitude between −400 and −200 ms. The maximum negative amplitude was measured between −200 and −50 ms (N-115). To measure the positive activity around the response, the maximum positive amplitude between 0 and 100 ms (P50) was taken at electrodes from central, parietal and temporal areas. Additionally, the mean amplitude between −500 and −100 ms was considered in prefrontal areas where the pP positive activity was observed. The pN in the grand average was not clearly detected and was not analyzed.

For each component identified, an ANOVA statistical analysis was performed. Because the negative components were mainly observed in posterior areas prior to a motor response in skilled athletes and the same distribution was observed in a P50 component after motor response in novice athletes, only central, temporal and parietal electrodes were analyzed. Centro-Parietal (CP3, CP4, P3 and P4) and Temporo-Parietal (TP7–TP8 and T5–T6) electrodes were analyzed separately using Group (skilled and novice), Topography (central-parietal and parietal) and Laterality (left and right) as factors. To analyze electrodes on the centro-parietal midline (CPz and Pz), Group (skilled and novice) and Topography (centro-parietal and parietal) were used as factors. Finally, Group (skilled and novice) and Laterality (left, midline and right) were used as factors to analyze the prefrontal electrodes (Fp1, Fpz and Fp2). The Huynh-Feldt correction was applied to correct for the degrees of freedom. The minimum significant difference (MSD) criteria were used for post-hoc comparisons in the repeated-measures analyses. Only significant differences between groups and interactions that involved Group are reported.

Results

The behavioral results showed no significant differences between groups in the Group×Condition interaction for the rate of correct responses ($F(1,19)=.2$, $p=.7$). Similarly, there were no differences between groups in response times ($F(1,19)=.1$, $p=.7$) (Table 2).

Waveforms and topography maps are shown in Figures 1 and 2, respectively. The MRCPs initiated with a slow rising negativity (BP) approximately 1200 ms before the response with a radial distribution over the medial central areas in both groups. In novices, the BP also showed a bilateral positivity over temporal sites; in both groups, the BP reached the maximum negativity at approximately 115 ms before the response (N-115). In experts, a slow prefrontal positivity was also present concomitantly with the BP and was slightly larger over the hemisphere that was contralateral to the responding hand. These two activities terminated after the target stimulus onset, just before the response, and were substituted by a medial posterior parietal positivity corresponding to the stimulus-related P3 component, peaking approximately 50 ms after the response (P50). Statistical results are reported (Table 3).

Early BP (window from −800 to −400 ms). Electrodes on temporo-parietal sites showed significant differences between groups $F(1,20)=4.9$, $p=.03$, $\eta^2=.199$. Skilled athletes showed larger amplitudes in this negative component than novice athletes ($MD=1.3$ μV, $p=.03$). Centro-parietal and centro-parietal midline electrodes showed no significant differences between groups.

Table 2. Behavioral results for the CPT and c-CPT: percentages of target and non-target correct responses and response times for both the skilled and novice groups.

Task	Condition	Skilled	Novice
CPT	Target	$M = 97.84 \pm 2.14$	$M = 97.59 \pm 1.52$
	Non-target	$M = 99.46 \pm .43$	$M = 99.51 \pm .29$
	Response Time	$M = 420$ ms ± 51 ms	$M = 428$ ms ± 44 ms
c-CPT	Target	$M = 95.55 \pm 4.73$	$M = 95 \pm 4.48$
	Non-target	$M = 99.47 \pm .37$	$M = 99.69 \pm .29$
	Response Time	$M = 366$ ms ± 40 ms	$M = 357$ ms ± 51 ms

M = mean.

Late BP (window from −550 to −250 ms). Analysis of temporo-parietal electrodes in this time window showed significant differences between groups $F(1,20) = 4.8$, $p = .04$, $\eta^2 = .195$. A significant Group×Topography×Laterality interaction was found $F(1,20) = 5.4$, $p = .03$, *epsilon* = 1, where skilled athletes showed larger amplitudes than novices athletes, principally in the TP8 ($MD = 2.5$ µV, $p = .04$) and T6 ($MD = 2.7$ µV, $p = .005$) electrodes. No significant differences were observed on centro-parietal and centro-parietal midline electrodes.

pP (window from −500 to −100 ms). The results of the analysis on prefrontal electrodes showed significant differences between groups $F(1,20) = 5.0$, $p = .03$, $\eta^2 = .200$. Skilled athletes showed significantly larger Fp1 electrode amplitudes than did novices ($MD = 2.1$ µV, $p = .01$).

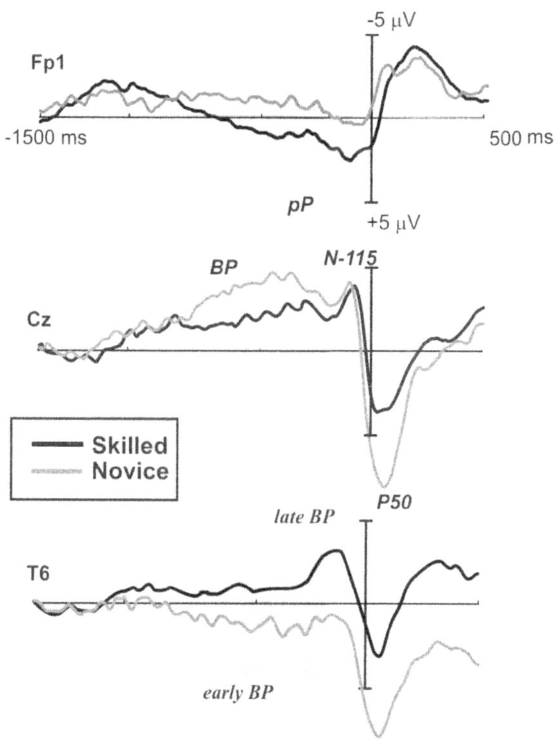

Figure 1. Grand average waveforms of MRCPs at the prefrontal, central and temporal electrodes for the CPT. Black lines indicate skilled athletes, and gray lines indicate novice athletes. Gray marks show windows where significant differences were found. Negativity is plotted up.

Maximum negative amplitude (~−115 ms). Analysis of temporo-parietal electrodes in this time window showed significant differences between groups $F(1,20) = 5.7$, $p = .02$, $\eta^2 = .223$. A significant Group×Topography×Laterality interaction was found $F(1,20) = 8.2$, $p = .009$, *epsilon* = 1, where skilled athletes showed larger amplitudes than novice athletes, principally in the TP7 ($MD = 4.2$ µV, $p = .02$), TP8 ($MD = 3.7$ µV, $p = .04$) and T6 ($MD = 4.2$ µV, $p = .01$) electrodes. No significant differences were observed on centro-parietal and centro-parietal midline electrodes.

P50. In this time window, differences in temporo-parietal electrodes between groups were found $F(1,20) = 4.9$, $p = .03$, $\eta^2 = .197$. The results showed larger amplitudes in novice athletes than in skilled athletes ($MD = 4.1$ µV, $p = .03$). No differences were found in centro-parietal and centro-parietal midline electrodes in this time window.

Discussion

We hypothesized that skilled and novice athletes would show differences in performance and MRCP components during a sustained attention task. Our analysis showed no significant differences in behavioral performance between the groups. However, some MRCP components did differ. The negativity of the BP did not differ between groups. However, in novices, the BP was larger on the medial central electrodes, and it showed a less radial distribution, yielding bilateral positivity in the temporal areas that was not present in skilled athletes. Furthermore, skilled athletes group showed a strong prefrontal positivity concomitant with the BP and disappearing with response onset. Activity around the time of the response was dominated by the parietal P50, which coincided with the P3 component. This activity was much larger in novices.

Previous MRCP studies [24,25,26,27,28,29,30] have found a reduction in the BP component in skilled participants and have attributed it to smaller and more economic motor preparation in the supplementary motor areas of skilled individuals. The present study did not confirm this notion statistically; however, the results showed a similar trend for BP negativity. More interestingly, novices, but not skilled athletes, showed a bilateral positive counterpart of the BP over bilateral temporal areas indicating that their BP activity is produced by sources in the bilateral SMA with different orientations that converge during the negativity in medial central areas and diverge during the positivity in temporal areas. Concordantly with the aforementioned studies, these differences may be associated with the activation of a smaller portion of the SMA in experts (presumably around the SMA sulcus) than in novices, which could have also activated the lateral wall of the SMA.

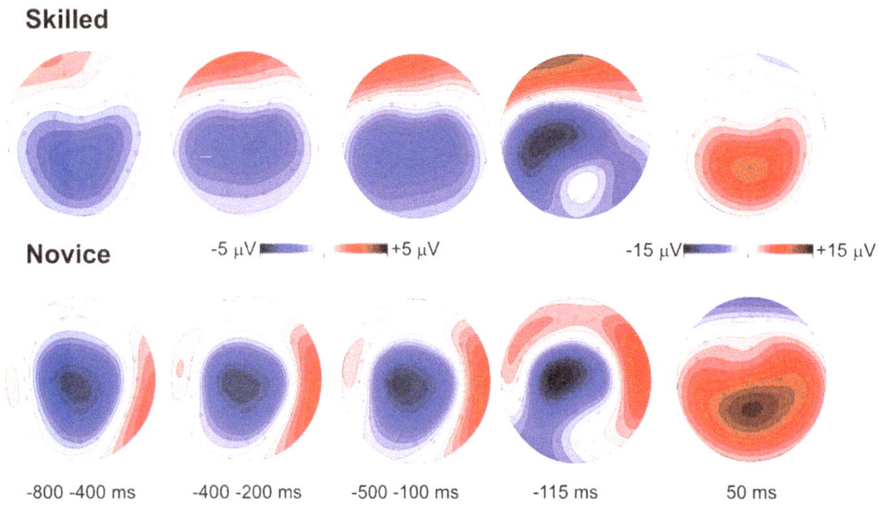

Figure 2. CPT amplitude maps for each time window analyzed where significant differences were found. Skilled athletes are shown above, and novice athletes are shown below.

The novel result here is the presence of a strong pP in skilled athletes compared to novice athletes. Differences between groups in prefrontal activity were found at Fp1, where skilled athletes showed larger amplitudes during a long period preceding motor response (from −600 to −150). Topography and laterality suggest that this prefrontal activity might be related to top-down supervision [36], which controls response selection during motor preparation. This prefrontal positivity has not been reported before using a CPT in athletes but was detected in recent MRCP studies using discriminative response tasks, such as go/no-go [31,32], fatiguing leg action [37] and bimanual coordination, where it has been associated with awareness of the upcoming response execution. Because the CPT requires sustained and controlled attention, we propose that the prefrontal positivity could be related to higher executive control of motor responses in skilled athletes. Considering both simultaneous pP and BP activity, it is likely that skilled athletes are able to allocate two different processes, i.e., motor response preparation and motor control preparation, simultaneously. The presence of greater anticipation in prefrontal areas in the skilled group is consistent with the idea that skilled martial arts competitors must be able to cognitively anticipate actions and strategies [1].

During a CPT, it is necessary to maintain attention for long time periods because the stimulus is a potential target that may require a response; thus, the subject must be able to sustain and control attention and motor response preparation. This assumption supports our results, which reveal that skilled athletes have better mechanisms to process both of these demands. In terms of real sport practice, it is known that fighters use strategies that include focusing their attention on their own performance and the performance of their opponent and maintaining their attention to plan the speed and power of their motor responses [38,39].

The positive peak found approximately 50 ms after a motor response coincided in timing and topography with the well-known stimulus-related P3 component associated with stimulus discrimination and motor response execution, but in this MRCP analysis, this peak should be considered a response-related P3. In this sense, considering that novice athletes showed greater amplitude in this component, we may assume that this group invests greater resources during this stage of the task. Skilled athletes, in contrast, invest more resources at earlier stages of a task to make the final result more efficient and accurate [1].

Table 3. Significant differences between groups in the amplitude of the MRCP components in the CPT.

Component	Topography	Electrodes	Mean Difference	$F_{(1,20)}$	p
Early BP	Temporo-parietal	$\text{All}_{(TP7,TP8,T5,T6)}$	1.3 μV(1)	4.9	.03
Late BP	Temporo-parietal	TP8	2.5 μV(1)	4.8	.04
		T6	2.7 μV(1)		
pP	Prefrontal	Fp1	2.1 μV(1)	5.0	.03
Maximum Negative Amplitude	Temporo-parietal	TP7	4.2 μV(1)	5.7	.02
		TP8	3.7 μV(1)		
		T6	4.2 μV(1)		
P50	Temporo-parietal	$\text{All}_{(TP7,TP8,T5,T6)}$	4.1 μV(2)	4.9	.03

(1)Amplitude was larger in skilled than novice athletes.
(2)Amplitude was larger in novice than skilled athletes.

Experiment 2

In the transient attention task, participants were instructed to respond only when the target stimulus was preceded by a signal stimulus. Many studies have shown that cued response preparation produces superior task performance compared to sustained response preparation [40,41]. c-CPT tasks involve transient attention and transient response preparation because advanced response preparation is only called for if the signal stimulus is presented [34]. Because the ability to respond automatically in combat when specific movements are detected in the opponent is necessary for high-level athletes, they are required to hone their capacity for quickly detecting a target in order to conserve resources. We hypothesized that skilled athletes would show better performance compared to novice athletes. We also expected to see differences between groups in both the negative and positive components in the MRCP due to less motor control and more automatic motor responses in skilled athletes.. The aim of this experiment was to assess MRCP differences between skilled and novice martial arts athletes during a transient attention task. A cued continuous performance task (c-CPT) was used.

Methods

Participants. The participants, characteristics and inclusion criteria were the same as for Experiment 1.

Stimuli. The same five different pointed arrows as in Experiment 1 were used. The instructions were changed to apply the same sequence to a transient attention task.

Cued continuous performance task. The participants were instructed to respond to the target arrow only if a specific arrow (warning stimulus) preceded it three stimuli before (go trial). Participants were presented with the following types of no-go trials: (i) target arrow not preceded by warning stimulus (false target); (ii) non-target arrow preceded by warning stimulus (false signal); and (iii) non-target arrow not preceded by warning stimulus (no cue trial). The warning-target sequence requiring the participant to make a motor response was presented in 10% of the trials. The warning stimulus itself was presented in 20% of the trials because it could precede the target or another stimulus. Thus, the occurrence of go and no-go trials was equiprobable.

Procedure. This experiment followed the same procedure and recording protocol as Experiment 1.

Data analysis. Statistical analyses was performed using MRCP time windows selected by visual inspection according to previous literature [23]: The early BP was measured as the mean amplitude between −900 and −600 ms, and the late BP was measured as the mean amplitude between −550 and −250 ms. To measure the positive activity around the response, the maximum amplitude between −50 and 50 ms (P10) was taken at electrodes from the central, parietal and temporal areas. Furthermore, the mean amplitude between −900 and −100 ms was also considered in prefrontal areas where the pP was observed. The pN in the grand average was not clearly detected.

For each value, an ANOVA statistical analysis was performed. Because a greater distribution of negativity was observed from the fronto-central to parietal areas in skilled athletes and the same effect was observed in the P10 component in novice athletes, fronto-central, central, temporal and parietal electrodes were analyzed. Central (FC3–FC4, C3–C4, CP3, CP4, P3 and P4) and Temporal (FT7–FT8, T3–T4, TP7–TP8 and T5–T6) electrodes were analyzed using Group (skilled and novice), Topography (frontal, central, centro-parietal and parietal) and Laterality (left and right) as factors. To analyze electrodes on the midline (FCz, Cz, CPz and Pz), Group (skilled and novice) and Topography (frontal, central, centro-parietal and parietal) were used as factors. Finally, Group (skilled and novice) and Laterality (left, midline and right) were used as factors to analyze the prefrontal electrodes (Fp1, Fpz and Fp2). The minimum significant difference (MSD) criteria were used for post-hoc comparisons in the repeated-measures analyses. Significant differences between groups were found and are reported. No significant interactions were found.

Results

As in Experiment 1, the behavioral results showed no significant differences between groups in the Group×Condition interaction for the rate of correct responses ($F(1,19)=.350$, $p=.561$). Similarly, there were no differences between groups in response times ($F(1,19)=.191$, $p=.668$) (See Table 2).

Waveforms and topography maps are shown in Figures 3 and 4, respectively. The MRCPs initiated with a slow rising negativity (BP) approximately 1500 ms before the response, with a radial distribution over the medial central areas in both groups. In this task, the BP slope was steeper than in the task used in Experiment 1. In both groups, the BP reached maximum negativity at approximately 400 ms before the response. Concomitantly with the BP, novices also showed a slow pP with a radial distribution. These two activities finished after the target stimulus onset, just before the response, and were substituted by a medial posterior parietal positivity corresponding to the stimulus-related P3 component, peaking approximately 10 ms after the response (P10). Statistical analysis of the electrophysiological data showed significant group differences, indicating that skilled athletes showed a larger BP than novices, whereas the pP and the P10 were smaller. Statistical results are reported below (Table 4)

Early BP (window from −900 to −600 ms). Electrodes on central sites showed significant differences between groups $F(1,20)=5.1$, $p=.03$, $\eta^2=.203$. Skilled athletes showed larger amplitudes in this negative component than novice athletes ($MD=2.2$ µV, $p=.03$). When electrodes on temporal sites were analyzed, significant group differences were found $F(1,20)=5.7$, $p=.02$, $\eta^2=.224$, with larger amplitudes in the skilled group compared to the novice group ($MD=1.7$ µV, $p=.02$). No significant differences were found when midline electrodes were analyzed.

Late BP (window from −550 to −250 ms). Analysis of central electrodes in this time window showed significant differences between groups $F(1,20)=6.1$, $p=.02$, $\eta^2=.234$. Skilled athletes showed larger amplitudes than novices athletes ($MD=3.2$ µV, $p=.02$). Similar results were found when temporal electrodes were analyzed $F(1,20)=7.6$, $p=.01$, $\eta^2=.276$, with skilled athletes consistently showing larger amplitudes than novices ($MD=2.6$ µV, $p=.01$). No differences were found in midline electrodes.

pP (window from −900 to −100 ms). The results of the analysis of prefrontal electrodes showed significant differences between groups $F(1,20)=4.1$, $p=.02$, $\eta^2=.239$. Novice athletes showed larger amplitudes in this positive component than skilled athletes ($MD=4.1$ µV, $p=.02$).

P10. In this time window, differences in temporal electrodes between groups were found $F(1,20)=5.5$, $p=.02$, $\eta^2=.216$. The results showed larger amplitudes in novice athletes than in skilled athletes ($MD=3.3$ µV, $p=.02$). No differences were found in central and midline electrodes in this time window.

Discussion

Our hypothesis about this transient attention task was that differences in performance and MRCP components would be found between groups. Analysis of performance showed no

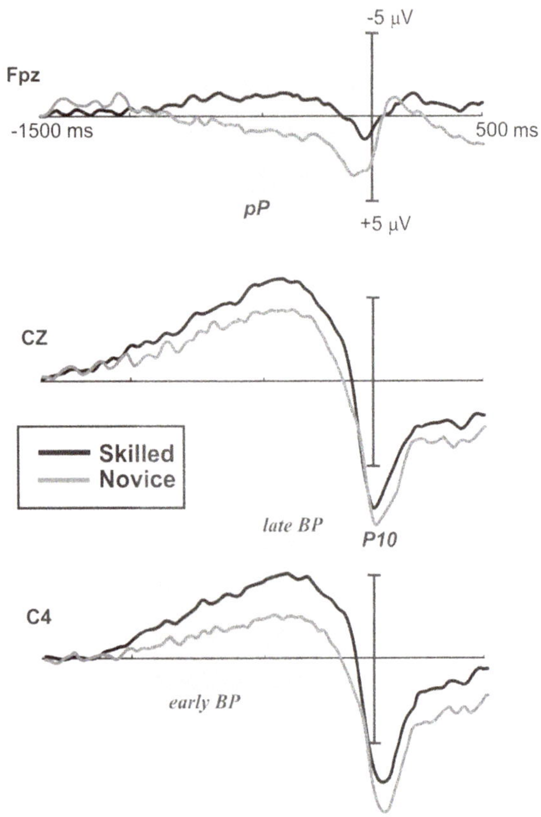

Figure 3. Grand average waveforms of MRCPs at the prefrontal and central electrodes for the c-CPT. Black lines indicate skilled athletes, and gray lines indicate novice athletes. Gray marks show windows where significant differences were found. Negativity is plotted up.

differences, but differences between groups were observed in the MRCP components. The skilled group showed larger BP amplitudes at central electrodes than novices. This result contradicted previous studies where self-paced tasks were used. Furthermore, larger positive amplitudes were observed preceding motor response at prefrontal electrodes in novice athletes compared to skilled athletes, which is contrary to the findings of the first experiment. Additionally, a larger positive amplitude (P10) was found in novice athletes after a motor response.

The cue CPT is a task where automatic mechanisms of attention are required, i.e., less controlled attention and motor responses. Skilled athletes showed larger and more distributed negative BP activity starting 900 ms before the motor response, which likely relates to higher motor preparation and greater anticipation. On the other hand, novice athletes showed less negativity, which most likely relates to less motor preparation and anticipation. Additionally, bilateral prefrontal positive activity was found in novice but not in skilled athletes, suggesting higher cognitive control during the task. In general, group differences could be based on greater motor preparation in skilled athletes and more controlled cognitive processing in novice athletes. With these results in mind, we propose that skilled athletes show more automatic mechanisms of anticipatory and mental preparation and respond with fewer attentional resources.

General Discussion

The aim of this study was to identify differences in motor-related cortical potential between skilled and novice martial arts athletes during sustained and transient attention tasks to study expertise effects. It has been proposed that sustained and transient tasks refer to two different types of cognitive processes [34]. Considering that sustained and transient attention are required during training and competition, we anticipated differences between groups due to the effects of expertise. There were no differences in behavioral performance in both tasks. One explanation could be that the stimuli were too easy to result in the expected differences. However, electrophysiological data can

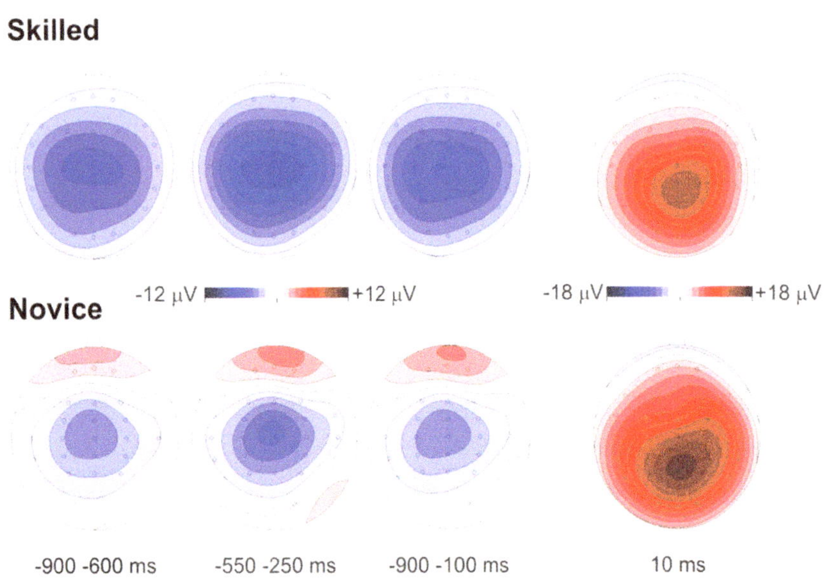

Figure 4. c-CPT amplitude maps for each time window analyzed where significant differences were found. Skilled athletes are shown above, and novice athletes are shown below.

Table 4. Significant differences between groups in the amplitude of the MRCP components in the c-CPT.

Component	Topography	Mean Difference	$F_{(1,20)}$	p
Early BP	Central	2.2 μV⁽¹⁾	5.1	.03
	Temporal	1.7 μV⁽¹⁾	5.7	.02
Late BP	Central	3.2 μV⁽¹⁾	3.2	.02
	Temporal	2.6 μV⁽¹⁾	2.6	.01
pP	Prefrontal	4.6 μV⁽²⁾	5.8	.02
P10	Temporal	3.3 μV⁽²⁾	5.5	.02

(1)Amplitude was larger in skilled than novice athletes.
(2)Amplitude was larger in novice than skilled athletes.

offer deeper analyses about the cognitive processes during task performance [42].

The MRCP results showed differences between groups, and these differences were distinct, depending on the type of task. Electrophysiological data in the CPT task indicated larger pP activity and greater posterior negativity distribution prior to a motor response in the skilled athletes, while novices showed significantly larger response-related P3 after a motor response in centro-parietal areas. We propose that skilled athletes are able to allocate two different but related processes simultaneously in the early stages of a task to control motor response preparation, which is consistent with CPT demand, where controlled attention and controlled motor responses are required. During the c-CPT task, novice athletes showed strong prefrontal positive activity before the motor response and a large response-related P3, whereas in skilled athletes, the prefrontal activity was absent. We propose that skilled athletes possess better cue facilitation, which permitted a major saving of resources and "automatic" or less controlled responses to relevant stimuli.

Two classes of attentional processing mechanisms have been proposed: automatic and controlled [43,44]. Automatic processes are fast, inflexible and consume little attentional capacity. Conversely, controlled processes are slow, attentionally demanding and controlled by the participant's intentions. In our study, skilled athletes showed brain electrical activity that suggests controlled sustained attention. In the transient attention task, skilled athletes were able to process information more automatically after cue stimulus than were novices. Overall, skilled athletes appeared to process information more quickly and to spend less of their available attentional resources on transient attention processing than novice athletes.

Conclusions

Our results indicated differences in visuo-motor processing between skilled and novice athletes during attentional tasks. Skilled athletes showed more controlled responses and greater anticipation in the early stages of the sustained attention task. Conversely, novice athletes showed more cognitive control and less motor preparation than skilled athletes during the transient attention task. Overall, there are differences in visuo-motor processing between groups, depending on the expertise level and requirements of the task. In general, the present data suggest that motor expertise enhances neural flexibility to allow better adaptation of cognitive control to a requested task.

Acknowledgments

The authors are grateful for the participant's cooperation in this study. The authors also acknowledge the technical assistance of Leonor Casanova, Lourdes Lara, Héctor Belmont and Marika Berchicci.

Author Contributions

Conceived and designed the experiments: JSL TF JSP JAMM. Performed the experiments: JSL. Analyzed the data: JSL TF JSP JAMM FDR. Wrote the paper: JSL TF JSP JAMM FDR. Contributed to final approval of the version to be published: JSL TF JSP JAMM FDR.

References

1. Anshel MH, Payne JM (2006) Application of Sport Psychology for Optimal Performance in Martial Arts. In: Dosil J, editor. The Sport Psychologist's Handbook A Guide for Sport-Specific Performance Enhancement Inglaterra: John Wiley & Sons pp. 353–374.
2. del-Monte L (2005) Relación entre la capacidad de concentración de la atención y el rendimiento en las judokas del Equipo Nacional de Cuba. ef deportes 87: 1–1.
3. Rushall BR (2006) Psychological Factors and Mental Skills in Wrestling. In: Dosil J, editor. The Sport Psychologist's Handbook A Guide for Sport-Specific Performance Enhancement. London: John Wiley & Sons
4. Blumenstaein B, Bar-Eli M, Tenenbaum G (2002) Brain and Body in Sport and Exercise. U.S.A: Wiley
5. Lavalle D, Kremer J, Moran AP, Williams M (2004) Sport Psychology. Contemporany Themes. London: Palgrave Macmillan.
6. Nougier V, Rossi B (1999) The development of expertise in the orientation of attention International Journal of Sport Psychology 30: 246–260.
7. Babiloni C, Marzano N, Iacoboni M, Infarinato F, Aschieri P, et al. (2010) Resting state cortical rhythms in athletes: a high-resolution EEG study. Brain Res Bull 81: 149–156.
8. Del Percio C, Babiloni C, Marzano N, Iacoboni M, Infarinato F, et al. (2009) "Neural efficiency" of athletes' brain for upright standing: a high-resolution EEG study. Brain Res Bull 79: 193–200.
9. Del Percio C, Infarinato F, Iacoboni M, Marzano N, Soricelli A, et al. (2010) Movement-related desynchronization of alpha rhythms is lower in athletes than non-athletes: a high-resolution EEG study. Clin Neurophysiol 121: 482–491.
10. Babiloni C, Marzano N, Infarinato F, Iacoboni M, Rizza G, et al. (2010) "Neural efficiency" of experts' brain during judgment of actions: a high-resolution EEG study in elite and amateur karate athletes. Behav Brain Res 207: 466–475.
11. Del Percio C, Infarinato F, Marzano N, Iacoboni M, Aschieri P, et al. (2011) Reactivity of alpha rhythms to eyes opening is lower in athletes than non-athletes: a high-resolution EEG study. Int J Psychophysiol 82: 240–247.
12. Picton TW, Bentin S, Berg P, Donchin E, Hillyard SA, et al. (2000) Guidelines for using human event-related potentials to study cognition: recording standards and publication criteria. Psychophysiology 37: 127–152.
13. Jennings JR, Coles MGH (1991) Handbook of cognitive psychophysiology: Central and autonomic nervous system approaches. Chichester, UK: Wiley.
14. Di Russo F, Taddei F, Apnile T, Spinelli D (2006) Neural correlates of fast stimulus discrimination and response selection in top-level fencers. Neurosci Lett 408: 113–118.

15. Fontani G, Lodi L (2002) Reactivity and event-related potentials in attentional tests: Effect of training. Perceptual and Motor Skills 94: 817–833.
16. Fontani G, Lodi L, Felici A, Migliorini S, Corradeschi F (2006) Attention in athletes of high and low experience engaged in different open skill sports. Perceptual and Motor Skills 102: 791–805.
17. Fontani G, Maffei D, Cameli S, Polidori F (1999) Reactivity and event-related potentials during attentional tests in athletes. Eur J Appl Physiol Occup Physiol 80: 308–317.
18. Hack J, Memmert D, Rupp A (2009) Attentional mechanisms in sports via brain-electrical event-related potentials. Res Q Exerc Sport 80: 727–738.
19. Hamon JF, Seri B (1989) Cortical reactivity during reaction time tests in sprinters. Neurophysiol Clin 19: 109–122.
20. Hung T-M, Spalding TW, Santa María DL, Hatfield BD (2004) Assessment of Reactive Motor Performance With Event-Related Brain Potentials: Attention Processes in Elite Table Tennis Players. Journal of Sport and Exercise Psychology 26.
21. Radlo SJ, Janelle CM, Barba DA, Frehlich SG (2001) Perceptual decision making for baseball pitch recognition: Using P300 latency and amplitude to index attentional processing. Research Quarterly for Exercise and Sport 72: 22–31.
22. Taddei F, Bultrini A, Spinelli D, Di Russo F (2012) Neural correlates of attentional and executive processing in middle-age fencers. Med Sci Sports Exerc 44: 1057–1066.
23. Shibasaki H, Hallett M (2006) What is the Bereitschaftspotential? Clinical Neurophysiology 117: 2341–2356.
24. Di Russo F, Pitzalis S, Aprile T, Spinelli D (2005) Effect of practice on brain activity: an investigation in top-level rifle shooters. Medicine & Science in Sports & Exercise 37: 1586–1593.
25. Hatta A, Nishihira Y, Higashiura T, Kim SR, Kaneda T (2009) Long-term motor practice induces practice-dependent modulation of movement-related cortical potentials (MRCP) preceding a self-paced non-dominant handgrip movement in kendo players. Neuroscience Letters 459: 105–108.
26. Kita Y, Mori A, Nara M (2001) Two types of movement-related cortical potentials preceding wrist extension in humans. Neuroreport 12: 2221–2225.
27. Wright DJ, Holmes P, Di Russo F, Loporto M, Smith D (2012) Reduced motor cortex activity during movement preparation following a period of motor skill practice. PLoS One 7: e51886.
28. Wright DJ, Holmes PS, Di Russo F, Loporto M, Smith D (2012) Differences in cortical activity related to motor planning between experienced guitarists and non-musicians during guitar playing. Human Movement Science 31: 567–577.
29. Wright DJ, Holmes PS, Smith D (2011) Using the movement-related cortical potential to study motor skill learning. Journal of Motor Behavior 43: 193–201.
30. Fattapposta F, Amabile G, Cordischi MV, Di Venanzio D, Foti A, et al. (1996) Long-term practice effects on a new skilled motor learning: an electrophysiological study. Electroencephalography and Clinical Neurophysiology 99: 495–507.
31. Berchicci M, Lucci G, Pesce C, Spinelli D, Di Russo F (2012) Prefrontal hyperactivity in older people during motor planning. Neuroimage 62: 1750–1760.
32. Berchicci M, Lucci G, Di Russo F (2013) Benefits of Physical Exercise on the Aging Brain: The Role of the Prefrontal Cortex. The Journals of Gerontology Series A: Biological Sciences and Medical Sciences.
33. Di Russo F, Taddei F, Apnile T, Spinelli D (2006) Neural correlates of fast stimulus discrimination and response selection in top-level fencers. Neuroscience Letters 408: 113–118.
34. Smid HG, de Witte MR, Homminga I, van den Bosch RJ (2006) Sustained and transient attention in the continuous performance task. J Clin Exp Neuropsychol 28: 859–883.
35. Gratton G, Coles MG, Donchin E (1983) A new method for off-line removal of ocular artifact. Electroencephalography and Clinical Neurophysiology 55: 468–484.
36. Norman W, Shallice T (1986) Attention to action. In: Davidson RJ, Schwartz GE, Shapiro D, editors. Consciousness and self regulation: Advances in research and theory. New York: Plenum. pp. 1–18.
37. Berchicci M, Menotti F, Macaluso A, Di Russo F (2013) The neurophysiology of central and peripheral fatigue during sub-maximal lower limb isometric contractions. Frontiers in Human Neuroscience 7: 135.
38. Abernethy B, Russell DG (1987) Expert-Novice Differences in an Applied Selective Attention Task Journal of Sport Psychology 9: 326–345.
39. Williams AM, Grant A (1999) Training perceptual skill in sport. International Journal of Sport Psychology 30: 194–220.
40. Brunia CH (1993) Waiting in readiness: gating in attention and motor preparation. Psychophysiology 30: 327–339.
41. Rosenbaum DA (1980) Human movement initiation: specification of arm, direction, and extent. J Exp Psychol Gen 109: 444–474.
42. Gazzaniga MN (1999) The new cognitive neurosciences. Cambridge: The MIT Press. 1276 p.
43. Shiffrin RM, Schneider W (1977) Controlled and automatic human information processing: II. Perceptual learning, automatic attending and a general theory. Psychological Review 84: 127–190.
44. Schneider W, Shiffrin RM (1977) Controlled and automatic human information processing: I. Detection, search, and attention. Psychological Review 84: 1–66.

4

PFOS Induces Behavioral Alterations, Including Spontaneous Hyperactivity That Is Corrected by Dexamfetamine in Zebrafish Larvae

Stefan Spulber[1]*, Pascal Kilian[1], Wan Norhamidah Wan Ibrahim[1,2], Natalia Onishchenko[1], Mazhar Ulhaq[3¤], Leif Norrgren[3], Sara Negri[4], Marcello Di Tuccio[4], Sandra Ceccatelli[1]

1 Dept of Neuroscience, Karolinska Institutet, Stockholm, Sweden, **2** Department of Biology, Faculty of Science, Universiti Putra Malaysia, Serdang, Selangor, Malaysia, **3** Department of Biomedicine and Veterinary Public Health, Swedish University of Agricultural Sciences, Uppsala, Sweden, **4** Environmental Research Center, Salvatore Maugeri Foundation – IRCCS, Pavia, Italy

Abstract

Perfluorooctane sulfonate (PFOS) is a widely spread environmental contaminant. It accumulates in the brain and has potential neurotoxic effects. The exposure to PFOS has been associated with higher impulsivity and increased ADHD prevalence. We investigated the effects of developmental exposure to PFOS in zebrafish larvae, focusing on the modulation of activity by the dopaminergic system. We exposed zebrafish embryos to 0.1 or 1 mg/L PFOS (0.186 or 1.858 μM, respectively) and assessed swimming activity at 6 dpf. We analyzed the structure of spontaneous activity, the hyperactivity and the habituation during a brief dark period (visual motor response), and the vibrational startle response. The findings in zebrafish larvae were compared with historical data from 3 months old male mice exposed to 0.3 or 3 mg/kg/day PFOS throughout gestation. Finally, we investigated the effects of dexamfetamine on the alterations in spontaneous activity and startle response in zebrafish larvae. We found that zebrafish larvae exposed to 0.1 mg/L PFOS habituate faster than controls during a dark pulse, while the larvae exposed to 1 mg/L PFOS display a disorganized pattern of spontaneous activity and persistent hyperactivity. Similarly, mice exposed to 0.3 mg/kg/day PFOS habituated faster than controls to a new environment, while mice exposed to 3 mg/kg/day PFOS displayed more intense and disorganized spontaneous activity. Dexamfetamine partly corrected the hyperactive phenotype in zebrafish larvae. In conclusion, developmental exposure to PFOS in zebrafish induces spontaneous hyperactivity mediated by a dopaminergic deficit, which can be partially reversed by dexamfetamine in zebrafish larvae.

Editor: Filippo Del Bene, Institut Curie, France

Funding: This work was funded by the Swedish Research Council (VR and Formas grants), Karolinska Institutet research grants, and by the Swedish Society for Medical Research (SSMF). The funders had no role in study design, data collection and analysis, decision to publish, or preparation of the manuscript.

Competing Interests: The authors have declared that no competing interests exist.

* E-mail: stefan.spulber@ki.se

¤ Current address: Department of Veterinary Basic Sciences, PMAS Arid Agriculture University, Rawalpindi, Pakistan

Introduction

Perfluorinated compounds (PFCs) are a family of chemical compounds that are very stable in the environment due to the carbon-fluorine bonds (reviewed in [1]). Perfluorooctane sulfonate (PFOS) is a member of the PFCs family that has been used in a wide range of industrial and commercial applications for the past 50 years and is the most commonly found in a large number of biomonitoring samples from the human general population and wildlife [2–4]. In the human population, the main route of exposure to PFOS is believed to be through consumption of contaminated food, such as fish, aquatic invertebrates, marine mammals, and other composite food, as well as contaminated drinking water [5–7]. The elimination half-life of PFOS (5.4 years in humans [8]) and its persistence in the environment raise concerns about the potential adverse impact on human health, particularly when the exposure occurs during early developmental stages (see [9]). PFOS has been detected in the umbilical cord and in maternal milk, and there is epidemiological evidence of dose-dependent increase in the risk of adverse birth outcomes [10–12]. Prenatal exposure to PFOS has not been found to be associated to neurodevelopmental deficits in children up to the age of 7 [8,13,14]. However, two cross-sectional studies report an association between blood levels of PFOS and impulsivity [15] and the prevalence of attention deficit hyperactive disorder (ADHD) [16] in children aged 9–11 and 12–15, respectively.

In rodents, developmental toxicity studies on the effects of PFOS have revealed reduction of fetal weight, reduced neonatal survival, defects in the peripheral nervous system, and behavioral alterations [17–20]. In addition, after maternal exposure, PFOS accumulates in the developing brain before the formation of the blood brain barrier (BBB) [21], and can also cross the BBB to a certain extent [22–24]. *In vitro* studies have shown that PFOS enhances the differentiation of cortical neural stem cells towards neuronal and oligodendroglial phenotypes [25], and that the neuronal differentiation induced in PC12 cells is shifted towards a cholinergic, rather than a dopaminergic phenotype [26].

Most developmental neurotoxicity data available on PFCs were generated using rodents as animal models. Zebrafish (*Danio rerio*) has emerged as an alternative animal model for pharmacological and toxicological studies due to the conserved neurotransmitter systems and molecular signaling pathways associated to behavioral responses (reviewed in [27,28]). The aim of this study was to investigate the effects of developmental exposure to PFOS on the activity pattern in zebrafish larvae, with special focus on the modulation of swimming activity by the dopaminergic system. To this end we exposed zebrafish embryos to PFOS at concentrations that do not increase the mortality or the incidence of embryonic malformations [29,30]. We analyzed the behavior at larval stage, with special focus on the pattern of spontaneous activity, as well as on the transient hyperactivity induced by a dark pulse (visual motor response, VMR) or by a vibrational stimulus (startle response). In light of the findings in zebrafish larvae, we further analyzed historical behavioral data from rodents [19] and found similar phenotypes in the spontaneous locomotion in mice exposed to PFOS during early developmental stages. Altogether, our data indicate that developmental exposure to PFOS results in behavioral alterations and a central dopamine signaling deficit which provide experimental evidence supporting the reported epidemiological association between exposure to PFOS and impulsivity [15,16].

Materials and Methods

Chemicals

PFOS (heptadecafluorooctanesulfonic acid potassium salt, CAS 2795-39-3, purity >98%) was purchased from Sigma-Aldrich, dissolved in DMSO (1 mg/mL), and stored at 4°C as stock solution for exposure in zebrafish embryos. For exposing pregnant mouse females, PFOS was dissolved in pure ethanol immediately before administration on palatable pieces of food (cookie bits that were readily consumed by the animals).

Animals: exposure and behavioural tests

All experimental procedures were performed in agreement with the Swedish animal protection legislation and European regulations, and were approved by the local Animal Ethics Committee (Stockholms Norra djurförsöksetiska nämnd).

Zebrafish. Wildtype AB zebrafish embryos were obtained from the zebrafish core facility at Karolinska Institutet. Breeding groups of adult fish (3 males and 2 females) were housed together overnight in 10 L spawning tanks containing environmental enrichment (commercially available aquaria decoration made of non-toxic plastic). Thirty minutes after turning the light on (9:00 a.m.), the fertilized eggs were collected and stored at 28.5°C until further processing. The eggs were washed twice with fresh E3 water (5 mM NaCl, 0.17 mM KCl, 0.33 mM $CaCl_2$, 0.33 mM $MgSO_4$; 0.05% methylene blue; pH 7.4) in order to remove all debris. This procedure was performed on a clean open lab bench, at room temperature, under constant illumination (approximately 500 lx). Stock PFOS was further diluted in DMSO to yield a final concentration of 0.1% DMSO in the rearing water. The zebrafish embryos were exposed to PFOS concentrations of either 0.1, or 1 mg/L (0.186 or 1.858 µM, respectively). The doses were selected based on our experience and earlier reports [30–32] to avoid a significant increase in the rate of embryonal malformations and lethality. Control embryos were exposed to 0.1% DMSO in E3 water. The exposure to PFOS was initiated about 2 hours post fertilization (hpf). The zebrafish larvae were then plated and maintained individually in 48-well plates (cylindrical wells, 10 mm inner diameter; VWR, Leuven, Belgium) in 750 µl E3 water at 28°C in a 10:14 h dark-light cycle (light on at 9 a.m.; 300 lx intensity, daylight-matching spectrum white light) until behavioral testing at 6 days post fertilization (dpf). The exposure followed a static, non-replacement regime (*i.e.* the rearing water was not refreshed or replaced throughout the experiment, according to OECD guidelines [33,34] and earlier reports [30,32,35]). All treatments were present in each plate, and the larvae were distributed such that an equal proportion from each group would be placed in wells at the periphery of the plate. The mortality, successful hatching, and the occurrence of embryonal malformations as assessed at the 24 (developmental failure/coagulation, light-induced coiling movements), 48 (developmental failure/coagulation, blood circulation, pericardial oedema, pigmentation), 72, and 120 hpf (hatching, eye development, swimming bladder inflation, morphological abnormalities such as scoliosis or bent spine), as well as after completing the behavioural experiments (6 dpf) using an inverted microscope (Nikon Ti-S) in brightfield configuration with a 4× objective. The larvae displaying morphological abnormalities at 6 dpf were excluded from analyses.

Determination of PFOS in zebrafish larvae by UPLC-MS/MS. The zebrafish larvae were killed by rapid cooling in ice-cold water immediately after the behavioural recording at 6 dpf. The larvae were then collected and stored in Eppendorf tubes with a minimal amount of rearing water to preserve the integrity of the organism until further processing. All larvae from an experiment were pooled per treatment to yield a sufficient amount of tissue (22±14 mg per treatment group from 6 independent experiments). The internal dosimetry was performed by liquid chromatography coupled with mass spectrometry using an Acquity UPLC system (Waters, Milford, MA, USA) coupled with a triple quadrupole Waters TQD mass spectrometer. The samples were homogenized with acetonitrile (100 µL x 10 mg) using an ultrasonic homogenizer (Omni-Ruptor 250, Omni International). An internal standard (Perfluorononanoic acid, PFNA) was added to 100 µL of supernatant and then the samples (2 µL) were diluted 1:40 with 2 mM ammonium acetate - methanol solution (50:50, v/v) before injection in UPLC. A calibration curve was prepared by spiking PFOS and PFNA standard to a pool of homogenized control larvae in the range from 100 to 1600 absolute ng of PFOS. Chromatographic separation was performed on an Acquity UPLC BEH C18 column (2.1×100 mm, 1.7 µm) maintained at 30°C, by gradient elution with a mixture containing variable proportions of 2 mM ammonium acetate buffer and methanol delivered at a flow rate of 0.5 mL/min. Under these conditions isomers of PFOS eluted at 1.6, 1.9, 2.1 and 2.5 minutes whereas PFNA eluted at 2.4 minutes. The total run time was 9 min. For the MS/MS detection, quantitative analysis was obtained in multiple reaction monitoring (MRM) in negative ion mode (ESI-). In particular for all the isomers of PFOS 499.0→79.8 m/z was used for quantification and 499.0 → 98.8 for confirmation; for PFNA 463.0→418.9 was selected. The limit of detection for PFOS (at a signal-to-noise ratio of 3) was 0.2 ng.

Behavioral tests and analyses in zebrafish larvae. We recorded the locomotor activity of 6 dpf zebrafish larvae at 50 frames per second (fps) under constant infrared illumination using integrated high throughput systems for videotracking and environmental control (ZebraBox™, ViewPoint, Lyon, France, and DanioVision, Noldus, Wageningen, The Netherlands). The larvae were detected by automated online image analysis using a dynamic subtraction algorithm with individual frame weight of 4%. All videotracking data was visually inspected for detection accuracy before inclusion in further analyses. The raw tracking data were exported and analyzed using routines custom developed in

Matlab™ R2012b environment (MathWorks Inc., Natick, MA, USA). To minimize the effect of missing samples (*e.g.* when the fish moved too fast over few frames, or too little to meet the automated detection criteria), the position of center of gravity was approximated using linear interpolation of x and y coordinates between the samples at the beginning and at the end of the missing samples sequence. For the analysis of bouts, we used a threshold of 0.2 mm/frame to filter out detection noise. A bout of activity was defined as the activity detected in a continuous sequence of frames during which the measured displacement of the center of gravity is above the threshold (see insert in Fig 1 A). Bouts separated by less than 40 ms (2 frames) were considered as a single bout. The following parameters were calculated for measuring the spontaneous activity bouts: frequency of occurrence, expressed in number of bouts per time unit (bouts/min); and average distance moved within the bout (mm).

Spontaneous activity. Before initiating the behavioural experiments, the temperature control system of the recording chamber (DanioVision™, Noldus) was allowed to run continuously until equilibrium was reached, and the temperature did not vary by more than 0.2°C over 5 min. The experimental workflow ensured that (1) the handling of the multi-well plate was limited to less than 30 s in total; (2) utmost care was taken to limit the vibrations transferred to the plate during handling; (3) the larvae did not experience major fluctuations in light intensity, particularly not towards sudden decrease (the light sources inside the recording chamber were on when the multi-well plate was placed inside, and the intensity of the lighting did not change except when testing the VMR). The larvae were allowed to acclimatize allowed to acclimatize for at least 15 min after transfer to the recording chamber. This procedure was found sufficient (pilot tests; not shown) for the spontaneous activity to be reliably recorded and analysed over reasonably long periods free from trends or trailing effects of changes in the environment. We estimated the average frequency of occurrence, and distance moved within spontaneous bouts over at least 3 min after the acclimatization period and prior to any further experimental challenge.

The visual motor response (VMR) is one of the earliest behavioral responses that can be recorded in freely moving zebrafish larvae (already at 4 dpf), and consists of a robust increase in swimming activity in response to a sudden decrease in the environmental light intensity [36–38]. Yet, at 4 dpf, the energy required for growth and swimming is provided by the protein-rich yolk, and although the larvae display a robust locomotor response to changes in light intensity, the spontaneous activity varies widely between individuals and does not support reliable estimations of baseline activity [39]. Therefore, the analysis of activity induced by dark pulses was performed at 6 dpf as follows: the larvae were placed in the DanioVision™ chamber and allowed to acclimatize for at least 15 min before starting the experiment (environmental temperature maintained at 28°C by means of a custom-built system for circulating temperature-controlled water; light intensity 3200–3500 lx). The baseline activity under constant illumination was recorded during the last 10 min of the acclimatization period. The larvae were then exposed to a dark pulse (10 min; light not detectable in the visible spectrum). The transition between light and dark was virtually instantaneous.

To characterize the hyperactivity induced by the dark pulse, we used two orthogonal parameters derived from the cumulative activity curve: the total locomotor activity and the index of curvature (IOC). IOC was calculated according to the formula below, as described by Fry et al. [40]: $IOC = \frac{(n-1)Rn - 2\sum_{i=1}^{n-1} Ri}{nRn}$, where R_i denotes the value of the i-th bin in the cumulative histogram. The IOC can assume values between $-(n-1)/n$ and $(n-1)/n$ (approaching -1 and 1, respectively, for very large n), where n is the number of observation bins (time intervals). If the activity is recorded predominantly in the beginning of the observation interval (*e.g.* if the animals habituate to the environment), IOC is negative, and the absolute value increases with the bias of distribution in activity measures. In contrast, an IOC value close to 0 indicates a uniform distribution of activity within the observation period. The rationale for calculating a parameter to describe the shape of the curve is that (1) the novelty-induced hyperactivity is a consistent finding in all animal models; (2) the locomotor activity necessarily decays with time as the animals habituate to the environment [41,42]; and (3) the shape of the habituation curve conveys ethologically relevant information, such as the rate of habituation or acquisition of reinforcement [40]. As compared to the measures of habituation described earlier [42,43], the IOC is a longitudinal measure of the activity and has the advantage of orthogonality in relation to global measures of activity.

The startle response consists of a brief increase in swimming activity (typically a single bout that is more intense than spontaneous bouts) shortly after the application of a stimulus (vibrational, acoustic, electric, or tactile), followed by a period of inactivity before resuming spontaneous activity [44] (Movie S1). The acoustic/vibrational startle response in particular develops in parallel with the auditory system and consistent behavioral responses can be recorded no sooner than 5 dpf in normal zebrafish larvae [45,46]. We have used a custom-built system consisting of a solenoid hitting the chassis of the recording chamber. The stimulus was triggered from the videotracking software (EthoVision XT 9, Noldus, Wageningen, The Netherlands) and was synchronized with the behavioral observation. The fish were allowed to habituate to the experimental environment for 4 minutes before delivering the first stimulus. The baseline activity was recorded during the last minute of the habituation period. A series of 10 equally spaced taps (1 min intervals) were delivered during each session. A startle response was validated only if we recorded a bout of activity within 0.5 s (25 frames) after triggering the stimulus. After validation, we analyzed the following parameters: average distance moved per time unit (1 s); latency to startle (measured as the delay between the application of the stimulus and the beginning of the first subsequent bout); distance moved within the bout; inactive period following the startle response (measured as the delay between the end of the startle response and the beginning of the first next bout) (see also Figure S1). We found no evidence of habituation (decreasing number of responsive larvae, or decreasing intensity of the startle response) in our system (data not shown), and estimated group means after averaging the values for each parameter across the validated startle responses for each larva.

Pharmacological challenges in zebrafish larvae. Apomorphine (Apotekt, Sweden), dexamfetamine (S(+)-amfetamine sulfate, Cat. No. A-127; RBI, Natick, MA, USA), quinpirole (Tocris Bioscience, Bristol, UK), and SKF-81297 (Tocris Bioscience, Bristol, UK) were dissolved in 0.1% DMSO E3water immediately before adding to the rearing water. The pharmacological compounds were delivered in 20 µL E3 medium/well 30 min prior to recording the swimming activity. The final concentrations in the rearing water were as follows: dexamfetamine – 1 and 10 µM; apomorphine – 2.5 and 5 µM; quinpirole – 10 and 20 µM; SKF-81297 – 25 and 50 µM. The doses and the timing of behavioural recording relative to the administration of the selected compounds were set based on previous reports (for dexamfetamine,

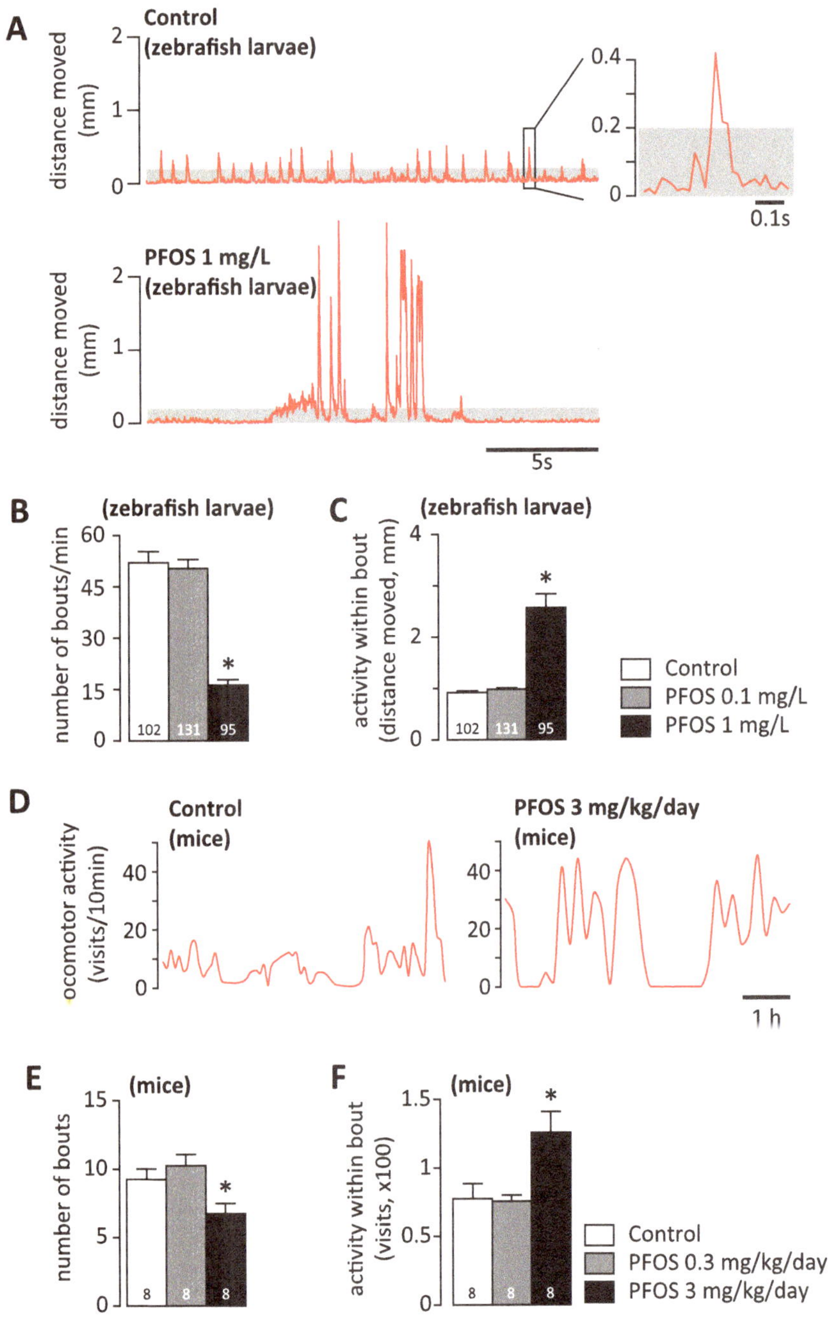

Figure 1. The structure of spontaneous locomotion in zebrafish larvae and mice during the active phase of the circadian cycle (light for zebrafish larvae, dark for mice). (A) Representative sequence of spontaneous activity (20 s) recorded at 6 dpf in one control and one larva exposed to 1 mg/L PFOS. In the control larva, the spontaneous activity consists of short, evenly spread bouts of swimming. In the larva exposed to 1 mg/L PFOS, the spontaneous activity consists of clusters of intense activity separated by extended periods of inactivity. Background noise (displacement below 0.2 mm/frame) shaded in gray; inset in top panel – magnification of a representative bout of spontaneous activity. (B) Quantification of frequency of spontaneous bouts of activity. Note the dramatic decrease in bout frequency induced by exposure to 1 mg/L PFOS. (C) Average distance moved during one spontaneous bout of activity. Zebrafish larvae exposed to 1 mg/L PFOS have a hyperactive phenotype characterized by a 2.5 fold higher distance swum during spontaneous bouts of activity. (D) Illustrative sequence of spontaneous locomotion during the active phase of the circadian cycle in one control and one mouse exposed to 3 mg/kg/dy PFOS during gestation. The spontaneous locomotor activity (visits) in the homecage is integrated over consecutive, non-overlapping 10 min bins and spline-interpolated for clarity. (E, F) Similar to the pattern found in zebrafish larvae, the mice exposed to 3 mg/kg PFOS display less frequent (E), but more intense (F) bouts of activity. B, C, E, F – one-way ANOVA followed by Dunnett's post-hoc test; * $p<0.05$ PFOS exposed vs. control. The number of independent observations is indicated at the bottom of each column in B, C, E and F.

apomorphine, and quinpirole see [47,48]) and dose-response curves tested in our lab (for SKF-81297). In particular the doses of dexamfetamine were selected so that the low dose would induce hyperactivity, and the high dose would suppress spontaneous activity in control larvae [48]. All plates were treated similarly in each experiment, *i.e.* all larvae in one plate received the same concentration of the compound, and the different concentrations were divided between plates originating from the same stock and spawning session. All experiments were repeated at least 3 times, and used fertilized eggs produced from different stocks. This design was carefully observed in order to minimize the bias of genetic background differences across stocks.

Historical behavioral data in mice. In light of the phenotypical alterations found in zebrafish, as well as to strengthen the relevance of zebrafish larvae as experimental model for developmental neurotoxicity, we further analyzed historical behavioral data from mice. The developmental exposure to PFOS in mice has been described earlier [19]. Briefly, pregnant C57Bl/6/Bkl dams (Scanbur BK, Sweden) received PFOS at a dose of 0.3 or 3 mg/kg/day throughout gestation (N = 6 per treatment). The locomotor activity was recorded in 8 male pups (5–6 weeks of age), randomly selected from all litters (maximum 2 pups from any litter were included). At weaning, the pups were implanted with sterile subcutaneous radio frequency identification (RFID) tags (ID-100A, Trovan Ltd., UK) under 4% isoflurane anesthesia. The transponders allowed unambiguous identification of animals throughout the experiment.

Monitoring and analysis of spontaneous locomotion in freely moving mice. The locomotor activity of freely moving mice was monitored using the TraffiCage™ system (NewBehavior, Zürich, Switzerland), as described elsewhere [19]. Briefly, the system consists of an array of radio frequency antennas to be placed under the cage with group-housed, freely moving mice. The antennas would read the RFID tags and provide an approximate location of each animal with a time resolution of 50 ms. The series of RFID detection were exported and analyzed using custom routines developed in Matlab™ R2012b. The time interval during which an animal is detected constantly by the same antenna is defined as "visit", and is described by time of first detection of a specific RFID and by its duration. When an animal is changing its location to a large enough extent to be detected by another antenna, a new visit is recorded. Visits that are longer than 10 min are considered inactive periods, consistent with resting/sleeping time (see also [19]). The number of visits was used as estimate of locomotor activity. The spontaneous locomotion is typically characterized by clusters of relatively short visits bounded by inactive periods, which we defined as "activity bouts". A bout of activity is therefore described by the moment of appearance (for classification of occurrence in relation to the phases of the circadian cycle), the intensity of activity it comprises (number of visits); and the duration (defined as the time interval between the end of an inactive period, and the beginning of the next inactive period). Given that the spontaneous activity analyzed during the dark phase is part of a virtually infinite sequence, the number of bouts is equal to the number of inactive periods. In order to match the zebrafish data on spontaneous activity, we analyzed only the dark phase of the circadian cycle (when mice are normally active). In addition, we analyzed the novelty-induced hyperactivity in mice. Thus, we monitored the locomotor activity for 2 h after transferring the animals to a new cage with fresh bedding (otherwise identical to the home cage). The handling and the sudden change in the environment typically induces an abrupt increase in exploration/locomotor activity, which subsides within 2–3 h in group-housed animals (see also [19]). We assessed the habituation to a new environment by estimating the total locomotor activity and the IOC.

Statistical analyses

All statistical analyses were performed using Statistica 10 software package (StatSoft Inc., Uppsala, Sweden). The data were analyzed by ANOVA (one-way, factorial, or repeated measures) as appropriate. Between-group differences were tested using post-hoc analysis: Dunnett's test for comparison against a single control group, as in one-way or repeated measures ANOVA design; and unequal N HSD test for comparisons against multiple controls as in simple factorial ("exposure" and "treatment" as factors) or between-group with replication factorial designs ("within-group" and "treatment" as factors). The ANOVA tables are shown in File S1. The threshold for statistical significance was set to 0.05 for all statistical analyses. All data are reported as average ± standard error of the mean.

Results

PFOS bioaccumulation in zebrafish larvae

The average concentration of PFOS measured in the zebrafish larvae was 21.6±5.4 ng/mg wet tissue and 213.5±62.7 ng/mg wet tissue in larvae exposed to 0.1 or 1 mg/L PFOS respectively. We did not find any effect of PFOS exposure on the viability, time of hatching, or incidence of developmental abnormalities (Table S1).

Alterations in the pattern of spontaneous activity

The spontaneous swimming activity in zebrafish is characterized by discrete bouts of activity separated by inactive intervals. This pattern, also described as "beat-and glide", is consistently displayed after the age of 4 dpf, and marks the developmental switch to increased spontaneous locomotion to support foraging [49–51]. However, although episodes of hyperactivity can be induced at 4 dpf (see [38]), the spontaneous activity is consistent over time and between individuals only at later stages, *i.e.* near the end of the yolk sac absorption and around the onset of the need for an external supply of energy [39,52,53]. The larvae exposed to 1 mg/L PFOS (Fig. 1 A) exhibit a dramatic disruption of the regular bout pattern, with a reduced frequency of activity bouts (Fig 1 B), but increased distance moved within a bout (Fig. 1 C). The shape and distribution of the activity bouts in larvae exposed to 0.1 mg/L PFOS was not different from controls (Fig. 1 B, C). Notably, the exposure to PFOS had a similar effect on the pattern of spontaneous locomotion in mice (Fig 1 D). We found a significant decrease in the number of spontaneous bouts of activity associated with an increase in the intensity of activity within the bout occurred only in the mice exposed to 3 mg/kg/day, but not in the 0.3 mg/kg/day PFOS-exposed mice (Fig. 1 E, F).

Alterations in the VMR (zebrafish larvae) and novelty-induced hyperactivity (mice)

The visual motor response (VMR) in zebrafish larvae describes the transient hyperactivity induced by a dark pulse during the light phase [36,38,52,54]. Controls and larvae exposed to 0.1 mg/L PFOS, displayed an increase in the frequency of activity bouts (Fig 2 A) in addition to increasing the activity within the bout (Figure S2). In contrast, the larvae exposed to 1 mg/L PFOS appear to respond only with an increase in the number of bouts that is invariable over time (Fig 2 A). The transition from light to dark is typically associated with a robust increase in swimming activity that gradually decays over time as the larvae habituate to the environment (Fig. 2 B; see also [38,54,55] and Movie S2). The total distance moved during a 10 min dark pulse was lower, and the rate of habituation was higher (larger negative IOC value) as compared to controls only in the larvae exposed to 0.1 mg/L PFOS (Fig. 2 C). In light of these findings, we re-analyzed the data we reported earlier [19], focusing on the novelty-induced hyperactivity in mice (Fig. 2 D), and found that mice exposed to

0.3 mg/kg/day PFOS display both less locomotor activity, and faster habituation (larger negative IOC value) as compared to controls and mice exposed to 3 mg/kg/day PFOS (Fig. 2 E).

The VMR experimental setting also allows for investigating the effects of the transitions between light and dark phases [54]. The transition from light to dark induces a peak of activity (about 10 s) before stabilizing to a plateau-like level, consistently higher than the activity before the transition. In contrast, the transition from dark to light is characterized by a brief increase in swimming activity followed by an abrupt suppression of spontaneous swimming activity to a level not only lower than the activity before transition, but also lower than spontaneous activity before the dark pulse (Fig. 2 F). In zebrafish larvae exposed to 1 mg/L PFOS we found a stronger behavioral response to changes in light intensity. Following the transition from light to dark, the change in locomotor activity had a biphasic pattern, with an abrupt increase in activity, followed by a transient decrease before reaching the plateau level. At the transition from dark to light, the PFOS-exposed larvae displayed sharp peak of activity followed by a longer period of relatively high activity before settling at a level lower than at the end of the dark period (Fig 2 F). Importantly, the transition from dark to light has the electrophysiological features of a startle response (*e.g.* activation of Mauthner cells [36]). Therefore, we approached the startle response to a vibrational

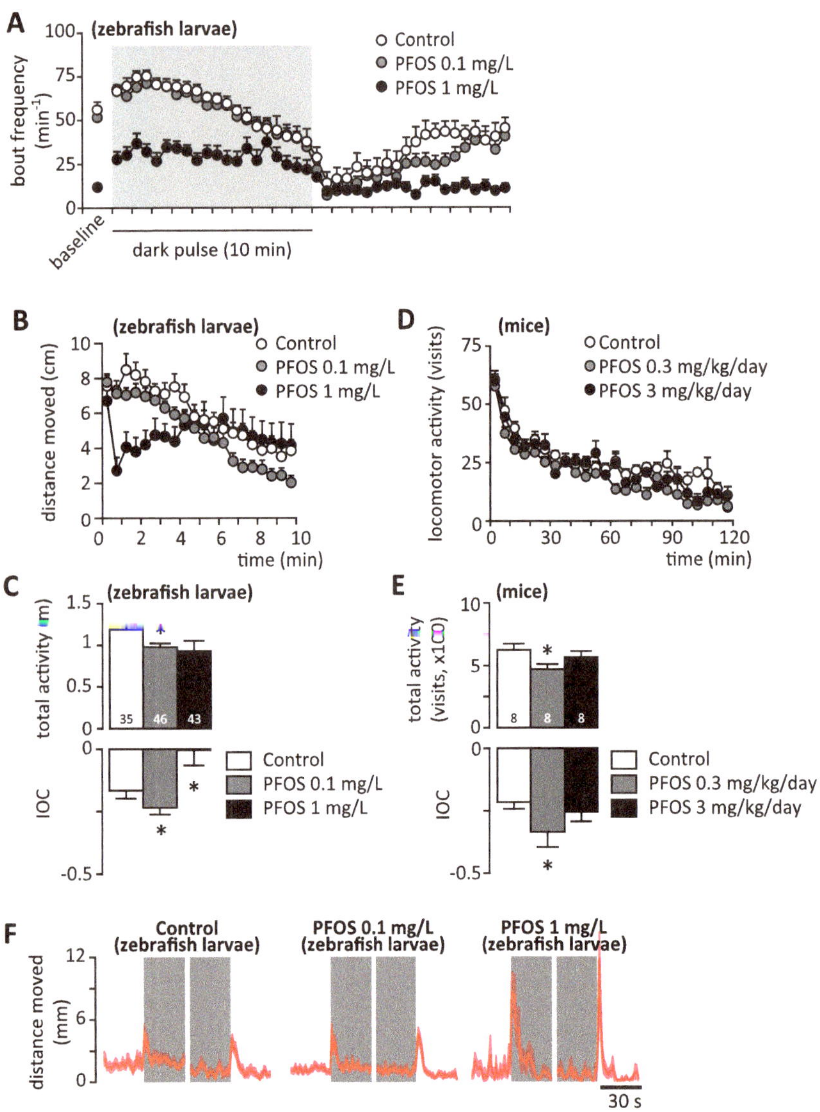

Figure 2. VMR in zebrafish larvae and novelty-induced hyperactivity in mice. (A) The dark pulse induces a similar pattern of fluctuations in the frequency of spontaneous bouts in larvae exposed to 0.1 mg/L PFOS as in controls. Larvae exposed to 1 mg/L PFOS respond with an increase in frequency that does not vary over time. In addition, the frequency of spontaneous bouts is restored directly to baseline level after the dark pulse. (B) Hyperactivity and habituation in zebrafish larvae during the dark pulse; 30 s timebins. (C) Quantification of total distance and IOC in zebrafish larvae. (D) Novelty-induced hyperactivity in mice. (E) Quantification of total distance moved and habituation rate (estimated by IOC) in mice. Note the similarity between the dose-response curves of the effect of exposure to PFOS on habituation in zebrafish and mice. (F) Swimming activity in zebrafish larvae at the transition between light and dark (gray shaded areas). The larvae exposed to 1 mg/L PFOS display hyperactive episodes of higher magnitude that last considerably longer than in controls. * $p<0.05$ PFOS exposed vs. control; ANOVA followed by Dunnett's post-hoc test. The number of independent observations is indicated at the bottom of each column in C and E. Graphs in A and B are based on the same number of observations reported in C; graphs in D are based on the same number of observations as in E.

stimulus in order to refine the investigation of the altered swimming activity induced by PFOS.

Alterations in the startle response

The spontaneous activity of 6 dpf larvae in baseline conditions is characterized by bouts occurring at a rate of around 50/min, which yields a sub-unit probability to record 1 bout of activity within each second. Therefore, we inferred that measuring the distance moved by individual larvae in 1 s long timebins would accurately isolate the startle bout from the background spontaneous activity in control larvae. We found that the startle response in control larvae typically consists of a single bout of activity (Fig. 3 A) with the amplitude about 2.5 times larger than in spontaneous bouts (Fig. 3 B, C); the latency to startle is about 200 ms (Fig. 3 D), and the spontaneous swimming activity is resumed after an inactive period of about 1 s (Fig. 3 E). The startle response in larvae exposed to 0.1 mg/L PFOS was similar to controls. In contrast, the startle response in larvae exposed to 1 mg/L PFOS is characterized by a longer latency to startle, and is followed by a cluster of bouts of amplitude similar to the spontaneous bouts which are separated by very short inactive periods (Fig. 3 A–E). In addition, the larvae exposed to 1 mg/L PFOS also exhibit an increase in activity 1 s before stimulation (Fig. 3 C). Therefore, the startle response in control larvae can be described as an amplitude-modulation of spontaneous swimming bouts, while in PFOS-exposed larvae the startle response appears as frequency modulation of the locomotor output.

To summarize, the developmental exposure to 1 mg/L PFOS induced changes in spontaneous swimming activity at baseline characterized by less frequent, but more intense bouts of activity as compared to controls. In addition, stimuli that normally induce only a brief hyperactive episode in control larvae, in PFOS exposed larvae induce abnormally prolonged hyperactive episodes consisting of series of bouts of constant amplitude. This results in a pattern of spontaneous activity that is fragmented and highly variable over time (Figure S3). A similar pattern has been described recently in a zebrafish model aimed at investigating the developmental effects of knocking down Latrophilin 3 (Lphn3.1), an ADHD susceptibility gene, which was characterized by less numerous and misplaced dopaminergic neurons [56]. The phenotype was rescued by acute administration of drugs used in the treatment of ADHD [56]. Therefore, in light of the epidemiological report on the association between ADHD and the exposure to perflourinated chemicals (including PFOS) [16], we investigated whether the calming effect of dexamfetamine could be reproduced in our model.

Effects of dexamfetamine and dopamine receptor agonists on spontaneous activity

We recorded the startle response in 6 dpf zebrafish larvae 30 min after spiking the rearing water with a catecholamine reuptake inhibitor, dexamfetamine (1 or 10 μM). The concentrations of dexamfetamine were selected based on the dose-response curves reported earlier [47,48], according to which 1 μM should stimulate, while 10 μM should suppress spontaneous activity in control zebrafish larvae. We found that 1 μM dexamfetamine induced hyperactivity in controls and in larvae exposed to 0.1 mg/L PFOS by increasing the frequency of spontaneous activity bouts, but did not alter the distance moved within a bout (Fig 4 A). At 10 μM, dexamfetamine reduced the number of bouts of spontaneous activity only in the larvae exposed to 0.1 mg/L PFOS. In contrast, dexamfetamine monotonically increased the frequency of bouts of spontaneous activity and reduced the activity within the bout in the larvae exposed to 1 mg/L PFOS.

To confirm the dopamine signaling deficiency, and investigate the effects of dopamine receptor agonists on specific phenotypes, we treated the zebrafish larvae with non-specific (apomorphine), and specific (quinpirole for D2, and SKF-81297 for D1) dopamine receptor agonists. In zebrafish larvae exposed to 1 mg/L PFOS we found that quinpirole increased the frequency of spontaneous swimming bouts, while SKF-81297 reduced the within-bout activity (Figure S4). As expected, apomorphine treatment had effects consistent with the activation of both D1 and D2 receptors in larvae exposed to 1 mg/L PFOS (Figure S4).

Effects of dexamfetamine and dopamine receptor agonists on the startle response

In controls, dexamfetamine increased the response rate (at 1 μM; Fig 4 B) and decreased the inactive period following the startle response (at both 1 and 10 μM; Fig 4 E), but did not alter the amplitude (Fig 4 C, D) or the latency (not shown) of the startle response. In larvae exposed to 0.1 mg/L PFOS, the only effect of dexamfetamine was a decrease in the inactive period (Fig 4 E. In larvae exposed to 1 mg/L PFOS, the increase in activity preceding the startle response was abolished by dexamfetamine (at both 1 and 10 μM; Fig. 4 C), and the duration of hyperactivity following the vibrational stimulus was reduced from 4.8 to 2.5 s (Fig 4. C, Figure S5). In addition, dexamfetamine monotonically increased the response rate (Fig 4 B), but had no effect on the latency (not shown) or the inactive period after the startle response (Fig 4 E) in larvae exposed to 1 mg/L PFOS.

The expected facilitating effect of dopamine receptor agonists on movement in the vibrational startle experiments manifested as a decrease in the latency to startle (induced by apomorphine), and in the inactive period (induced by apomorphine and quinpirole) in controls and larvae exposed to 0.1 mg/L PFOS (Figure S4). In larvae exposed to 1 mg/L PFOS, the dopamine receptor agonists had no effect on the parameters related to the startle response.

When we analyzed the amplitude of the activity bout induced by the vibrational stimulus in relation to the spontaneous activity bouts, we found that dexamfetamine treatment restored the amplitude modulation of the startle response in larvae exposed to 1 mg/L PFOS essentially by reducing the amplitude of spontaneous bouts (Fig 4 D).

Discussion

In this study we found that zebrafish larvae exposed to PFOS in the rearing water from 2 hpf display dose-dependent behavioural alterations: zebrafish larvae exposed to 0.1 mg/L PFOS habituate faster than controls during a dark pulse, while 1 mg/L PFOS induces a disorganized pattern of spontaneous activity and persistent hyperactivity. Similarly, mice exposed to 0.3 mg/kg/day PFOS habituated faster than controls to a new environment, while mice exposed to 3 mg/kg/day PFOS displayed more intense and disorganized spontaneous activity. To further investigate the hyperactivity induced by PFOS, we analysed the startle response to a vibrational stimulus and found that larvae exposed to 1 mg/L PFOS display sustained hyperactivity after stimulation. Both spontaneous and startle-induced hyperactivity were partly reversed by acute administration of dexamfetamine.

In this study we found that zebrafish larvae exposed to PFOS in the rearing water from 2 to 144 hpf accumulated the chemical in the body, in agreement with earlier reported pharmacokinetics data [30]. Given that PFOS readily permeates the chorion [30], and that short-term exposure to PFOS did not induce detectable alterations (Figure S6), it is reasonable to assume that the

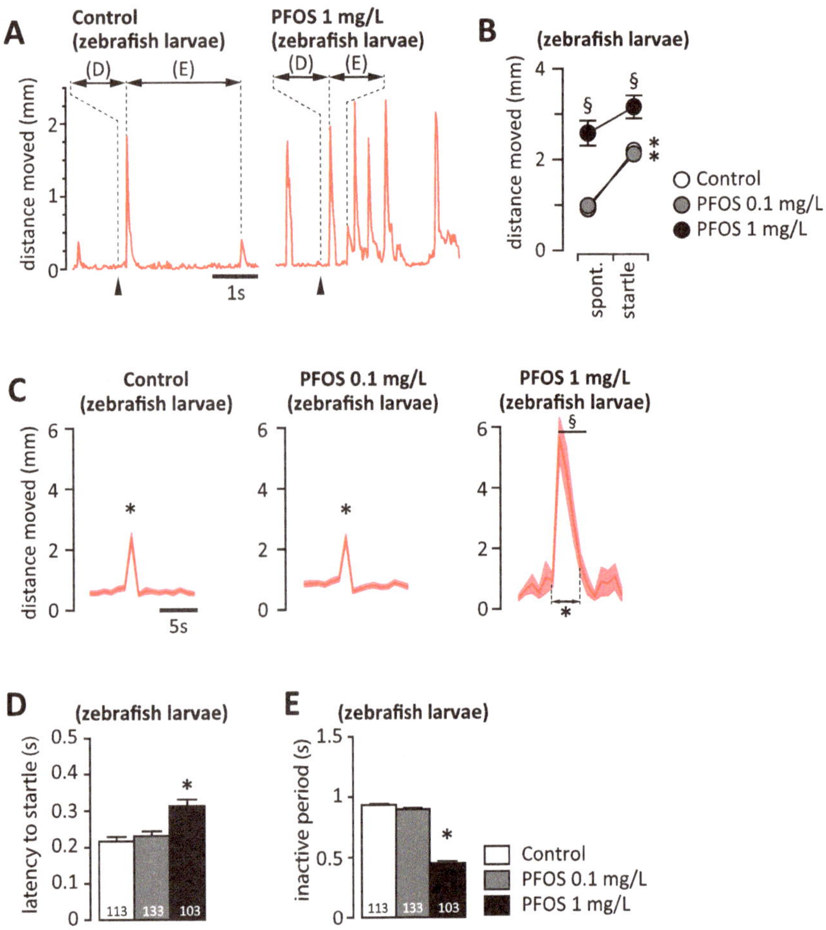

Figure 3. The effects of developmental exposure to PFOS on startle response in 6 dpf zebrafish larvae. (A) Typical vibrational startle response in a 6 dpf zebrafish larvae. Control larvae display a single bout of swimming activity after triggering the stimulus (arrowhead), followed by a prolonged silent period. Note that in control larvae, the swimming bout induced by the vibrational stimulus is considerably more robust than the spontaneous bouts (analysis shown in B), and is followed by a period of inactivity. In contrast, in larvae exposed to 1 mg/L PFOS, the vibrational stimulus is followed by a prolonged sequence of swimming bouts that have the amplitude similar to spontaneous bouts. The time interval between triggering the stimulus and the initiation of the bout is defined as latency to startle (analysis shown in D). The delay between the end of the startle bout and the following bout (analysis shown in E) can be defined as the latency to resume spontaneous swimming activity in control, but not in larvae exposed to 1 mg/L PFOS. (B) Comparison of the distance moved within spontaneous vs. stimulation-induced swimming bouts. Control larvae and larvae exposed to 0.1 mg/L PFOS consistently display a robust increase in the amplitude of activity bout in response to vibrational stimulation. In contrast, zebrafish larvae exposed to 1 mg/L PFOS swam significantly longer distances within spontaneous bout, but do not increase the distance moved in response to the vibrational stimulation. (C) Average distance moved integrated over 1s timebins. The increase in distance moved is accounted for by a single, more robust bout in controls (see A). In contrast, the amplitude of the startle response in larvae exposed to 1 mg/L PFOS is significantly larger than in controls, and it is presumably accounted for by more than 1 bout. In addition, the larvae exposed to 1 mg/L PFOS remain hyperactive for about 4 s after stimulation. The higher variability before in spontaneous activity before and after the startle response can be explained by irregularity in occurrence of spontaneous bouts. Note also that the larvae exposed to 1 mg/L PFOS display an increase in activity before the stimulation. (D, E) Analysis of the latency to startle (D) and inactive period (E). Zebrafish larvae exposed to 1 mg/L PFOS have longer latency to startle, and have shorter inactive period than controls or larvae exposed to 0.1 mg/L PFOS. B - repeated measures ANOVA followed by unequal N HSD post-hoc test; * $p<0.05$ startle vs. spontaneous; § $p<0.05$ PFOS exposed vs. controls. C –repeated measures ANOVA followed by unequal N HSD, or Dunnett's post-hoc test, respectively; § $p<0.05$ PFOS exposed vs. control; * $p<0.05$ vs. baseline. D, E - ANOVA followed by Dunnett's post-hoc test; * $p<0.05$ PFOS exposed vs. controls. The number of independent observations is indicated at the bottom of each column in D and E. The graphs in B and C are based on the same number of observation as reported in D and E.

behavioral effects are due to developmental damage, rather than to acute effects.

We found that the larvae exposed to 1 mg/L PFOS displayed disorganized spontaneous activity, characterized by less frequent, but more intense bouts. Similarly, mice prenatally exposed to 3 mg/kg/day PFOS displayed a decreased frequency associated with an increased intensity of spontaneous activity bouts. This pattern of alterations is suggestive of disturbances in the modulation of locomotion. To further investigate these alterations in zebrafish larvae, we induced sustained hyperactivity over a limited period by exposure to a dark pulse. The resulting fluctuations in distance moved was consistent with earlier reports and theoretical models [52,55,57]. The transition from light to dark induces an adaptive behavioral response that involves several regulatory circuits modulating spontaneous swimming [36]. In control larvae, the adaptation to dark consisted of a simultaneous modulation of bout frequency and activity within the bout. The monotonic decrease in swimming activity during the dark pulse is

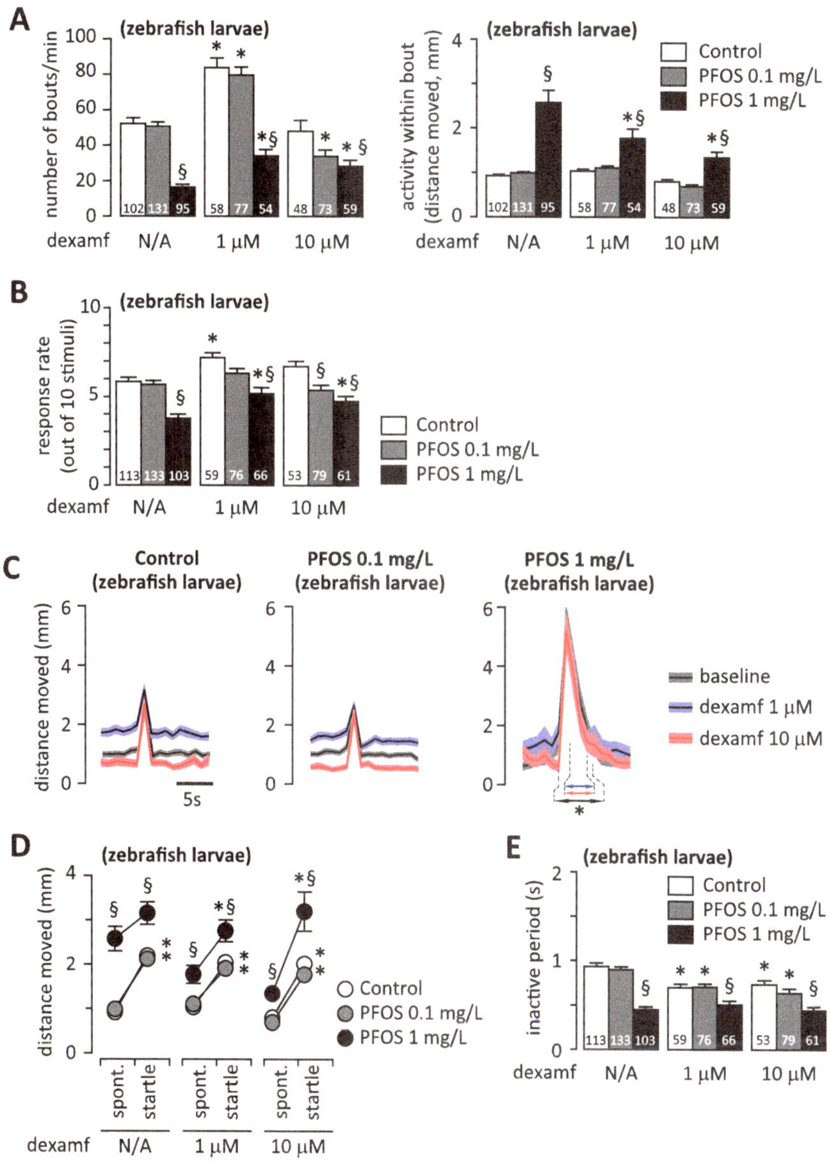

Figure 4. The effects of acute administration of dexamfetamine on spontaneous swimming and on startle response. (A) Dexamfetamine displays a bell-shaped dose-dependence of spontaneous bout frequency, but does not alter the distance swam per bout in controls and in larvae exposed to 0.1 mg/L PFOS. In contrast, dexamfetamine monotonically increases the frequency of spontaneous bouts of activity, and reduces the distance moved per bout in larvae exposed to 1 mg/L PFOS. (B) Average rate of response to vibrational stimulation. At baseline, the rate of response is significantly lower in the larvae exposed to 1 mg/L PFOS than in controls. Upon administration of dexamfetamine, the rate of response is increased only at 1 μM in controls, and at both doses in the larvae exposed to 1 mg/L PFOS. (C) Acute dexamfetamine administration alters the spontaneous activity before and after stimulation (presumably by altering the frequency of spontaneous bouts; see also A), but does not influence the amplitude of the startle response (accounted for by a single bout; see also D) in controls and larvae exposed to 0.1 mg/L PFOS. In larvae exposed to 1 mg/L PFOS, the amplitude of the startle response is not altered (presumably accounted for by more than one bout; see also D and E), but the duration of hyperactivity following the vibrational stimulation is shortened by both 1 and 10 μM dexamfetamine (see also Figure S5). (D) Dexamfetamine restores the amplitude-modulation of the activity bouts in larvae exposed to 1 mg/L PFOS by decreasing the distance moved for spontaneous bouts. (E) Dexamfetamine shortens the inactive period only in controls and in the larvae exposed to 0.1 mg/L PFOS. A, D - factorial ANOVA followed by unequal N HSD post-hoc test; § $p<0.05$ PFOS exposed vs. control; * $p<0.05$ vs. baseline. B- repeated measures ANOVA, followed by Dunnett's post hoc test with the first 3 samples as control (baseline); * $p<0.05$ vs. baseline. E - repeated measures ANOVA followed by unequal N HSD post-hoc test; * $p<0.05$ startle vs. spontaneous; § $p<0.05$ PFOS exposed vs. controls. The number of independent observations is indicated at the bottom of each column in A, B and E. Graphs in C and D are based on the same number of observation as reported in B and E.

indicative of habituation [55,58]. Interestingly, we found that the zebrafish larvae exposed to 0.1 mg/L PFOS did not display alterations in spontaneous activity, but habituated faster than controls. Similarly, mice exposed to PFOS at a dose that does not induce overt alterations in spontaneous locomotion were also found to habituate faster to a new environment. One can speculate that the defects in gating locomotion that result in a disorganized spontaneous activity pattern obscure the more subtle effect at motivational level. Alternatively, the different pattern of alterations in mice and zebrafish larvae may suggest that different mechanisms are responsible for the phenotype induced by developmental exposure to PFOS.

The larvae exposed to 1 mg/L PFOS displayed stereotypical adaptive changes in spontaneous activity with virtually no amplitude modulation of the activity bouts as compared to baseline, and very little variation in bout frequency during the dark pulse. The exaggerated response to the transition from light to dark was in agreement with the report by Huang et al [30]. In addition, we found that the larvae exposed to 1 mg/L PFOS displayed prolonged hyperactivity following the transition from dark to light. The behavioral modulation at the transition from dark to light shares kinematic and electrophysiological features with the startle response [36]. When we investigated the startle response to a vibrational stimulus, we found that the initial startle is followed by persistent hyperactivity in the larvae exposed to 1 mg/L PFOS. The rigidity in adaptation to changes in the environment is strongly suggestive of dopamine deficit, since it has been shown that dopamine signaling is required for behavioral variability [59,60].

The developmental exposure to 1 mg/L PFOS induced complex phenotypical alterations consisting of a hypokinetic component associated to hyperactivity. The hypokinetic phenotype is illustrated by the reduced frequency of spontaneous activity bouts, while the hyperactivity is illustrated by the increase in distance moved within spontaneous activity bouts and by the persistent hyperactivity following the startle response. In light of the dopamine deficiency hypothesis, we tested whether dopamine receptors agonists can correct the behavioral alterations. Indeed, we found that the hypokinetic component was partly reversed by acute administration of D2 agonists (apomorphine and quinpirole), which also facilitated the initiation of movement in control larvae. The hyperactive phenotype was corrected by the D1 agonists (apomorphine and SKF-81297), which in turn had no effect in controls at the doses applied in our study. Importantly, the effects of dexamfetamine were more extensive than the effects of the dopamine receptor agonists, and corrected the hyperactive phenotype in a monotonic dose dependent fashion. This suggests that the phenotype is caused by alterations in several diffuse neurotransmitter systems, such as noradrenaline and serotonin, in addition to the core defects in dopaminergic signaling. In zebrafish, the dopaminergic system is highly conserved [47,61,62], and plays an important role in regulating the swimming bouts in larvae [51]. A "hyperactive/impulsive motor phenotype" (consisting of clusters of very intense spontaneous activity) has been described recently in a zebrafish model established to investigate the effect of knocking down a homolog of Latrophilin 3 (Lphn3.1; one of the zebrafish orthologs of LPHN3, a susceptibility gene for ADHD [63]) during development [56]. The phenotype was reversed by acute administration of amfetamine-like psychostimulants commonly used for treating ADHD patients. In our study, the larvae exposed to 1 mg/L PFOS displayed clusters of intense spontaneous activity, as well as persistent hyperactivity following the startle response. In addition, the calming effect of dexamfetamine was replicated in larvae exposed to 1 mg/L PFOS, as illustrated by the dramatic correction of both spontaneous, and induced hyperactivity.

Several lines of evidence support the association of ADHD with alterations in dopamine signaling (reviewed in [64,65]). The core alteration behind the hyperactivity and impulsivity has been suggested to be a deficit in behavioral inhibition [66,67]. Impulsivity due to reduced behavioral inhibition has been shown to correlate with serum concentrations of PFOS in children independently from an actual diagnosis of ADHD [15]. In addition, the relative risk of being diagnosed with ADHD was found to increase with the level of PFOS in the peripheral blood [16]. An important limitation of the cross-sectional studies [15,16] is the unavailability of data on maternal exposure during pregnancy. Nevertheless, the age range in the study cohorts place the birth of the children in the early 1990's, a period corresponding to the peak in PFOS exposure in the general population [12,68]. Therefore, one can speculate that an early (developmental) exposure is very likely to have contributed to the outcomes analyzed in the cross-sectional studies. In the case of PFCs, an important source of exposure used to be the grease-resistant packaging [7] used for food with high fat content, such as fast-food products, chips and snacks, which in itself is documented to increase the risk of ADHD [69]. Here we show that in zebrafish exposure to PFOS during development induces hyperactivity and a dopaminergic signaling deficit that can be corrected by acute administration of dexamfetamine. Mice exposed to PFOS *in utero* exhibit similar alterations and dose-response curve. In conclusion, both experimental models show that exposure to PFOS during development induces core features of the phenotype observed in PFOS-exposed children.

Supporting Information

Figure S1 Analysis of relationships among the variables selected for analysis. (A) Loading plot for the first two factors extracted by means of PLS-DA (projection to latent structure – discriminant analysis) (see also [70]). The model included variables from both spontaneous activity (denoted by "r" in the beginning of the variable name) and startle response (denoted by "s" in the beginning of the variable name) in larvae that were not subject to pharmacological manipulations. Variables projecting symmetrically relative to the origin of the axes may be negatively correlated, while variables mapped very close together may be positively correlated. Note that the spontaneous activity within the bout (r_dist/bout) and the spontaneous bout frequency (r_bouts/min) mapped symmetrically relative to the origin of the axes, but the negative correlation was not confirmed. (B) It is obvious that the developmental exposure to PFOS 1 mg/L had significant influence on both variables, which rendered the multivariate approach uninformative. The most important information provided by the multivariate model above was that the variables we selected were orthogonal to a large-enough extent to justify their consideration as independent variables analysed separately in multifactorial models.

Figure S2 Analysis of hyperactivity induced by a dark pulse in 6 dpf zebrafish larvae (30 s timebins). The total distance moved within the bout does not differ between baseline and the dark period, but decreases during the dark period. The sudden increase at the transition between dark and light is due to the startle-like response (see text for details). The distance moved per bout drops after the transition from dark to light in controls and larvae exposed to 0.1 mg/L PFOS. In contrast, these fluctuations cannot be identified in larvae exposed to 1 mg/l PFOS, possibly because of the disorganized pattern of spontaneous activity (very high within-individual variations). Note, though, the dramatic variations at the transitions between light and dark phases in larvae exposed to 1 mg/L PFOS. The pattern of changes in the activity during the VMR testing is consistent with earlier reports and theoretical models [52,55,57]. In our experiment, the larvae had not been exposed to any dark period before recording the swimming activity. Therefore the spontaneous activity at baseline was constant and did not show significant long-term trends (not shown). In line with the analysis of the startle response, the amplitude modulation of the activity bouts is absent in the larvae exposed to 1 mg/l PFOS. Yet, the total distance swam during the 10 min dark pulse is not different from controls. Therefore, in agreement with earlier reports [39], several orthogonal parameters should be used for characterizing the swimming phenotype in zebrafish larvae. In addition, we argue that the characterization of alterations induced by exposure to potentially neurotoxic compounds in animal models must include the analysis of spontaneous activity alongside with induced behavioural responses.

Figure S3 Illustrative individual traces of spontaneous activity over 1 min (3 s timebins). Note the heavily fragmented pattern in the larvae exposed to 1 mg/l PFOS (right) as compared to controls (left). A similar pattern, described as "hyperactive/impulsive motor phenotype", was found in a zebrafish model investigating the role of Latrophilin 3 (Lphn3.1) in the etiology of ADHD [56].

Figure S4 Synoptic illustration of the effects of dopamine receptors agonists and D-amfetamine on activity bouts in 6 dpf zebrafish larvae. (A, B) Effects on spontaneous activity. Note that quinpirole (D2 receptor agonist) increases the frequency of bouts, but does not alter the activity within the bout, while SKF-81297 (D1 receptor agonist) reduces the activity within the bout, but does not change the frequency of spontaneous bouts. As expected, apomorphine (nonspecific dopamine receptor agonist) has an effect that shares features of both D1 and D2 receptor agonists. (C, D) Effects on the startle response. Note that the latency to startle in controls is affected only by apomorphine. Otherwise, dopamine receptors agonists have no effect at the doses we tested. In contrast, the inactive period is shortened by all compounds, except the D1 agonist SKF-81297. Neither the latency to startle, nor the inactive period are affected by any of the compounds in the larvae exposed to 1 mg/L PFOS. Factorial ANOVA followed by unequal N HSD post-hoc test; § $p<0.05$ PFOS exposed vs. control; * $p<0.05$ vs. baseline.

Figure S5 The effect of dexamfetamine on the startle-induced hyperactivity (SIH) in zebrafish larvae exposed to 1 mg/L PFOS. (A) SIH consists of a cluster of bouts of activity separated by short inactive periods (see also the main text for details). To estimate the duration of SIH, we measured the delay between the beginning of the startle response and the first occurrence of an inactive period longer than 0.7 s (i.e. 1 standard deviation longer than the average first inactive period following the startle response; see Fig 3E). The arrowhead indicates the moment when the stimulus was triggered. (B) Acute administration of dexamfetamine consistenly shortens the delay of occurrence of inactive periods longer than 0.7 s. One-way ANOVA followed by Dunnett's post-hoc test; * $p<0.05$ vs. baseline. The analysis described above is not applicable to controls or to larvae exposed to 0.1 mg/L PFOS because the inactive period following the startle response is not significantly different from the average delay between spontaneous bouts (see Fig 1B, 3E, 4A and 4E). In contrast, spontaneous bouts in zebrafish larvae exposed to 1 mg/L PFOS occur on average every 6 s at baseline, and every 1.5–2 s after dexamfetamine treatment (see Fig 4A). Neither apomorphine, nor specific dopamine receptor agonists had significant effects on SIH duration (not shown).

Figure S6 The effects of short-term exposure to PFOS 1 mg/L. Zebrafish larvae were exposed to 0.1 or 1 mg/L PFOS for 24 h before recording the VMR at 6 dpf. Control larvae received an equivalent amount of vehicle (DMSO). The final concentration of DMSO in the E3 water was 0.1%. (A) Distance moved in 30 s timebins before (baseline), during, and after a 10 min dark pulse. (B) Swimming activity at the transition between light and dark (gray shaded areas). The short-term exposure to PFOS had no significant effect on either distance moved, or reaction to sudden changes in light intensity.

Movie S1 Slow motion (0.05x) of a normal startle response recorded in 6 dpf zebrafish larvae. The light marks the moment of triggering the acoustic stimulus. Note that the fish initiates a brief sequence of swimming motions with a certain delay after the application of the stimulus and moves about 2 mm away from the initial position. Recorded at 100 fps; well diameter: 10 mm.

Movie S2 Visual motor response (VMR) in 6 dpf zebrafish larvae. The transition from light to dark (see marker at the bottom) induces a hyperactive reaction in the larvae. Note that the control larvae (top row) react almost instantaneously after turning the transition to dark, while the larvae exposed to 1 mg/L PFOS (bottom row) have a delayed, but exaggerated response. Recorded at 50 fps; well diameter: 10 mm.

Table S1 Embryonal mortality and malformation rates in zebrafish larvae exposed to 0.1 or 1 mg/L PFOS from 2 hpf until the timepoint for analysis.

File S1 ANOVA tables for the data shown in the main figures.

Acknowledgments

We thank Prof. Gilberto Fisone and Prof. Sven-Ove Ögren for their support in designing the pharmacological probing of the dopaminergic system; Prof. Abdel ElManira and Dr. Stefan Örn for the fruitful discussions on the zebrafish model.

Author Contributions

Conceived and designed the experiments: SS NO SC. Performed the experiments: SS PK WNWI NO MU SN MDT. Analyzed the data: SS SN. Contributed reagents/materials/analysis tools: LN SN SC. Wrote the paper: SS SC.

References

1. Fromme H, Tittlemier S, Völkel W, Wilhelm M, Twardella D (2009) Perfluorinated compounds—exposure assessment for the general population in Western countries. Int J Hyg Environ Health 212: 239–270.
2. Giesy JP, Kannan K (2001) Global Distribution of Perfluorooctane Sulfonate in Wildlife. Environ Sci Technol 35: 1339–1342.
3. Olsen GW, Huang H-Y, Helzlsouer KJ, Hansen KJ, Butenhoff JL, et al. (2005) Historical comparison of perfluorooctanesulfonate, perfluorooctanoate, and other fluorochemicals in human blood. Environ Health Perspect 113: 539–545.
4. Lau C, Anitole K, Hodes C, Lai D, Pfahles-Hutchens A, et al. (2007) Perfluoroalkyl acids: a review of monitoring and toxicological findings. Toxicol Sci 99: 366–394.

5. Quinete N, Wu Q, Zhang T, Yun SH, Moreira I, et al. (2009) Specific profiles of perfluorinated compounds in surface and drinking waters and accumulation in mussels, fish, and dolphins from southeastern Brazil. Chemosphere 77: 863–869.
6. Zhang T, Sun HW, Wu Q, Zhang XZ, Yun SH, et al. (2010) Perfluorochemicals in meat, eggs and indoor dust in China: assessment of sources and pathways of human exposure to perfluorochemicals. Environ Sci Technol 44: 3572–3579.
7. EFSA (2008) Opinion of the Scientific Panel on Contaminants in the Food chain on Perfluorooctane sulfonate (PFOS), perfluorooctanoic acid (PFOA) and their salts. EFSA J 653: 1–131.
8. Olsen GW, Burris JM, Ehresman DJ, Froehlich JW, Seacat AM, et al. (2007) Half-life of serum elimination of perfluorooctanesulfonate,perfluorohexanesulfonate, and perfluorooctanoate in retired fluorochemical production workers. Environ Health Perspect 115: 1298–1305.
9. Grandjean P, Landrigan PJ (2006) Developmental neurotoxicity of industrial chemicals. Lancet 368: 2167–2178.
10. Chen M-H, Ha E-H, Wen T-W, Su Y-N, Lien G-W, et al. (2012) Perfluorinated compounds in umbilical cord blood and adverse birth outcomes. PLoS One 7: e42474.
11. Apelberg BJ, Goldman LR, Calafat AM, Herbstman JB, Kuklenyik Z, et al. (2007) Determinants of Fetal Exposure to Polyfluoroalkyl Compounds in Baltimore, Maryland. Environ Sci Technol 41: 3891–3897.
12. Sundström M, Ehresman DJ, Bignert A, Butenhoff JL, Olsen GW, et al. (2011) A temporal trend study (1972-2008) of perfluorooctanesulfonate, perfluorohexanesulfonate, and perfluorooctanoate in pooled human milk samples from Stockholm, Sweden. Environ Int 37: 178–183.
13. Fei C, Olsen J (2011) Research | Children's Health Prenatal Exposure to Perfluorinated Chemicals and Behavioral or Coordination Problems at Age 7 Years: 573–578. doi:10.1289/ehp.1002026.
14. Fei C, McLaughlin JK, Lipworth L, Olsen J (2008) Prenatal exposure to perfluorooctanoate (PFOA) and perfluorooctanesulfonate (PFOS) and maternally reported developmental milestones in infancy. Environ Health Perspect 116: 1391–1395.
15. Gump BB, Wu Q, Dumas AK, Kannan K (2011) Perfluorochemical (PFC) exposure in children: associations with impaired response inhibition. Environ Sci Technol 45: 8151–8159.
16. Hoffman K, Webster TF, Weisskopf MG, Weinberg J, Vieira VM (2010) Exposure to polyfluoroalkyl chemicals and attention deficit/hyperactivity disorder in U.S. children 12-15 years of age. Environ Health Perspect 118: 1762–1767.
17. Johansson N, Fredriksson A, Eriksson P (2008) Neonatal exposure to perfluorooctane sulfonate (PFOS) and perfluorooctanoic acid (PFOA) causes neurobehavioural defects in adult mice. Neurotoxicology 29: 160–169.
18. Lau C, Butenhoff JL, Rogers JM (2004) The developmental toxicity of perfluoroalkyl acids and their derivatives. Toxicol Appl Pharmacol 198: 231–241.
19. Onishchenko N, Fischer C, Wan Ibrahim WN, Negri S, Spulber S, et al. (2011) Prenatal exposure to PFOS or PFOA alters motor function in mice in a sex-related manner. Neurotox Res 19: 452–461.
20. Zhang L, Li Y, Chen T, Xia W, Zhou Y, et al. (2011) Abnormal development of motor neurons in perfluorooctane sulphonate exposed zebrafish embryos. Ecotoxicology 20: 643–652.
21. Borg D, Bogdanska J, Sundström M, Nobel S, Håkansson H, et al. (2010) Tissue distribution of (35)S-labelled perfluorooctane sulfonate (PFOS) in C57Bl/6 mice following late gestational exposure. Reprod Toxicol 30: 558–565.
22. Chang S-C, Noker PE, Gorman GS, Gibson SJ, Hart J a, et al. (2012) Comparative pharmacokinetics of perfluorooctanesulfonate (PFOS) in rats, mice, and monkeys. Reprod Toxicol 33: 428–440.
23. Harada KH, Hashida S, Kaneko T, Takenaka K, Minata M, et al. (2007) Biliary excretion and cerebrospinal fluid partition of perfluorooctanoate and perfluorooctane sulfonate in humans. Environ Toxicol Pharmacol 24: 134–139.
24. Maestri L, Negri S, Ferrari M, Ghittori S, Fabris F, et al. (2006) Determination of perfluorooctanoic acid and perfluorooctanesulfonate in human tissues by liquid chromatography/single quadrupole mass spectrometry. Rapid Commun Mass Spectrom 20: 2728–2734.
25. Wan Ibrahim WN, Tofighi R, Onishchenko N, Rebellato P, Bose R, et al. (2013) Perfluorooctane sulfonate induces neuronal and oligodendrocytic differentiation in neural stem cells and alters the expression of PPARγ in vitro and in vivo. Toxicol Appl Pharmacol 269: 51–60.
26. Slotkin TA, MacKillop EA, Melnick RL, Thayer KA, Seidler FJ (2008) Developmental neurotoxicity of perfluorinated chemicals modeled in vitro. Environ Health Perspect 116: 716–722.
27. Maximino C, Herculano AM (2010) A review of monoaminergic neuropsychopharmacology in zebrafish. Zebrafish 7: 359–378.
28. Panula P, Sallinen V, Sundvik M, Kolehmainen J, Torkko V, et al. (2006) Modulatory neurotransmitter systems and behavior: towards zebrafish models of neurodegenerative diseases. Zebrafish 3: 235–247.
29. Shi X, Du Y, Lam PKS, Wu RSS, Zhou B (2008) Developmental toxicity and alteration of gene expression in zebrafish embryos exposed to PFOS. Toxicol Appl Pharmacol 230: 23–32.
30. Huang H, Huang C, Wang L, Ye X, Bai C, et al. (2010) Toxicity, uptake kinetics and behavior assessment in zebrafish embryos following exposure to perfluorooctanesulphonicacid (PFOS). Aquat Toxicol 98: 139–147.
31. Ulhaq M, Carlsson G, Örn S, Norrgren L (2013) Comparison of developmental toxicity of seven perfluoroalkyl acids to zebrafish embryos. Environ Toxicol Pharmacol 36: 423–426.
32. Hagenaars A, Vergauwen L, De Coen W, Knapen D (2011) Structure–activity relationship assessment of four perfluorinated chemicals using a prolonged zebrafish early life stage test. Chemosphere 82: 764–772.
33. OECD (2013) Test No. 236: Fish Embryo Acute Toxicity (FET) Test. OECD Guidelines for the Testing of Chemicals, Section 2. OECD Publishing. pp. 1–22. doi:10.1787/9789264203709-en.
34. OECD (2013) Test No. 210: Fish, Early-life Stage Toxicity Test. OECD Guidelines for the Testing of Chemicals, Section 2. OECD Publishing. pp. 1–24. doi:10.1787/9789264203709-en.
35. Ali S, Champagne DL, Richardson MK (2012) Behavioral profiling of zebrafish embryos exposed to a panel of 60 water-soluble compounds. Behav Brain Res 228: 272–283.
36. Burgess H, Granato M (2007) Modulation of locomotor activity in larval zebrafish during light adaptation. J Exp Biol 210: 2526–2539.
37. Colwill RM, Creton R (2011) Imaging escape and avoidance behavior in zebrafish larvae. Rev Neurosci 22: 63–73.
38. Emran F, Rihel J, Dowling JE (2008) A behavioral assay to measure responsiveness of zebrafish to changes in light intensities. J Vis Exp: 1–6.
39. Ingebretson JJ, Masino MA (2013) Quantification of locomotor activity in larval zebrafish: considerations for the design of high-throughput behavioral studies. Front Neural Circuits 7: 109.
40. Fry W, Kelleher RT, Cook L (1960) A mathematical index of performance on fixed-interval schedules of reinforcement. J Exp Anal Behav 3: 193–199.
41. Wong K, Elegante M, Bartels B, Elkhayat S, Tien D, et al. (2010) Analyzing habituation responses to novelty in zebrafish (Danio rerio). Behav Brain Res 208: 450–457.
42. Roberts AC, Bill BR, Glanzman DL (2013) Learning and memory in zebrafish larvae. Front Neural Circuits 7: 126.
43. Stewart AM, Cachat J, Green J, Gaikwad S, Kyzar E, et al. (2013) Constructing the habituome for phenotype-driven zebrafish research. Behav Brain Res 236: 110–117.
44. Burgess HA, Granato M (2007) Sensorimotor gating in larval zebrafish. J Neurosci 27: 4984–4994.
45. Tanimoto M, Ota Y, Horikawa K, Oda Y (2009) Auditory input to CNS is acquired coincidentally with development of inner ear after formation of functional afferent pathway in zebrafish. J Neurosci 29: 2762–2767.
46. Zeddies DG, Fay RR (2005) Development of the acoustically evoked behavioral response in zebrafish to pure tones. J Exp Biol 208: 1363–1372.
47. Irons TD, Kelly PE, Hunter DL, Macphail RC, Padilla S (2013) Acute administration of dopaminergic drugs has differential effects on locomotion in larval zebrafish. Pharmacol Biochem Behav 103: 792–813.
48. Irons TD, MacPhail RC, Hunter DL, Padilla S (2010) Acute neuroactive drug exposures alter locomotor activity in larval zebrafish. Neurotoxicol Teratol 32: 84–90.
49. Masino MA, Fetcho JR (2005) Fictive swimming motor patterns in wild type and mutant larval zebrafish. J Neurophysiol 93: 3177–3188.
50. Wiggin TD, Anderson TM, Eian J, Peck JH, Masino MA (2012) Episodic swimming in the larval zebrafish is generated by a spatially distributed spinal network with modular functional organization. J Neurophysiol 108: 925–934.
51. Lambert AM, Bonkowsky JL, Masino M a (2012) The conserved dopaminergic diencephalospinal tract mediates vertebrate locomotor development in zebrafish larvae. J Neurosci 32: 13488–13500.
52. Padilla S, Hunter DL, Padnos B, Frady S, MacPhail RC (2011) Assessing locomotor activity in larval zebrafish: Influence of extrinsic and intrinsic variables. Neurotoxicol Teratol 33: 624–630.
53. Liu Y-C, Bailey I, Hale ME (2012) Alternative startle motor patterns and behaviors in the larval zebrafish (Danio rerio). J Comp Physiol A Neuroethol Sens Neural Behav Physiol 198: 11–24.
54. Ellis LD, Seibert J, Soanes KH (2012) Distinct models of induced hyperactivity in zebrafish larvae. Brain Res 1449: 46–59.
55. MacPhail RC, Brooks J, Hunter DL, Padnos B, Irons TD, et al. (2009) Locomotion in larval zebrafish: Influence of time of day, lighting and ethanol. Neurotoxicology 30: 52–58.
56. Lange M, Norton W, Coolen M, Chaminade M, Merker S, et al. (2012) The ADHD-susceptibility gene lphn3.1 modulates dopaminergic neuron formation and locomotor activity during zebrafish development. Mol Psychiatry 17: 946–954.
57. Staddon JER, MacPhail RC, Padilla S (2010) The dynamics of successive induction in larval zebrafish. J Exp Anal Behav 94: 261–266.
58. Best JD, Berghmans S, Hunt JJFG, Clarke SC, Fleming A, et al. (2008) Non-associative learning in larval zebrafish. Neuropsychopharmacology 33: 1206–1215.
59. Costa RM, Lin S-C, Sotnikova TD, Cyr M, Gainetdinov RR, et al. (2006) Rapid alterations in corticostriatal ensemble coordination during acute dopamine-dependent motor dysfunction. Neuron 52: 359–369.
60. Costa RM (2011) A selectionist account of de novo action learning. Curr Opin Neurobiol 21: 579–586.
61. Sallinen V, Torkko V, Sundvik M, Reenilä I, Khrustalyov D, et al. (2009) MPTP and MPP+ target specific aminergic cell populations in larval zebrafish. J Neurochem 108: 719–731.

62. Anichtchik O V, Kaslin J, Peitsaro N, Scheininà M, Panula P (2004) Neurochemical and behavioural changes in zebrafish Danio rerio after systemic administration of 6-hydroxydopamine: 443–453. doi:10.1046/j.1471-4159.2003.02190.x.
63. Arcos-Burgos M, Jain M, Acosta MT, Shively S, Stanescu H, et al. (2010) A common variant of the latrophilin 3 gene, LPHN3, confers susceptibility to ADHD and predicts effectiveness of stimulant medication. Mol Psychiatry 15: 1053–1066.
64. Genro JP, Kieling C, Rohde L a, Hutz MH (2010) Attention-deficit/hyperactivity disorder and the dopaminergic hypotheses. Expert Rev Neurother 10: 587–601.
65. Del Campo N, Chamberlain SR, Sahakian BJ, Robbins TW (2011) The roles of dopamine and noradrenaline in the pathophysiology and treatment of attention-deficit/hyperactivity disorder. Biol Psychiatry 69: e145–57.
66. Barkley RA (1997) Behavioral inhibition, sustained attention, and executive functions: constructing a unifying theory of ADHD. Psychol Bull 121: 65–94.
67. Bari A, Robbins TW (2013) Inhibition and impulsivity: Behavioral and neural basis of response control. Prog Neurobiol 108: 44-79.
68. Haug LS, Thomsen C, Becher G (2009) Time trends and the influence of age and gender on serum concentrations of perfluorinated compounds in archived human samples. Environ Sci Technol 43: 2131–2136.
69. Howard AL, Robinson M, Smith GJ, Ambrosini GL, Piek JP, et al. (2011) ADHD is associated with a "Western" dietary pattern in adolescents. J Atten Disord 15: 403–411.
70. Spulber S, Bartfai T, Winblad B, Schultzberg M (2011) Morphological and behavioral changes induced by transgenic overexpression of interleukin-1ra in the brain. J Neurosci Res 89: 142–152.

5

Brain Morphology in Children with Epilepsy and ADHD

Ricardo Saute[1], Kevin Dabbs[2], Jana E. Jones[2], Daren C. Jackson[2], Michael Seidenberg[3], Bruce P. Hermann[2]*

1 Faculty of Medicine, Pontificia Universidade Catolica do Rio Grande do Sul (PUCRS), Porto Alegre, Brazil, **2** Department of Neurology, University of Wisconsin School of Medicine and Public Health, Madison, Wisconsin, United States of America, **3** Department of Psychology, Rosalind Franklin University of Science and Medicine, North Chicago, Illinois, United States of America

Abstract

Background: Attention deficit hyperactivity disorder (ADHD) is a common comorbidity of childhood epilepsy, but the neuroanatomical correlates of ADHD in epilepsy have yet to be comprehensively characterized.

Methods: Children with new and recent-onset epilepsy with (n = 18) and without (n = 36) ADHD, and healthy controls (n = 46) underwent high resolution MRI. Measures of cortical morphology (thickness, area, volume, curvature) and subcortical and cerebellar volumes were compared between the groups using the program FreeSurfer 5.1.

Results: Compared to the control group, children with epilepsy and ADHD exhibited diffuse bilateral thinning in the frontal, parietal and temporal lobes, with volume reductions in the brainstem and subcortical structures (bilateral caudate, left thalamus, right hippocampus). There were very few group differences across measures of cortical volume, area or curvature.

Conclusions: Children with epilepsy and comorbid ADHD exhibited a pattern of bilateral and widespread decreased cortical thickness as well as decreased volume of subcortical structures and brainstem. These anatomic abnormalities were evident early in the course of epilepsy suggesting the presence of antecedent neurodevelopmental changes, the course of which remains to be determined.

Editor: Yoko Hoshi, Tokyo Metropolitan Institute of Medical Science, Japan

Funding: This work was supported by the National Institute of Neurological Disorders and Stroke (NINDS) 2RO1-44351 and the Clinical and Translational Science Award (CTSA) program, previously through the National Center for Research Resources (NCRR) grant 1UL1RR025011, and now by the National Center for Advancing Translational Sciences (NCATS), grant 9U54TR000021. The funders had no role in study design, data collection and analysis, decision to publish, or preparation of the manuscript.

Competing Interests: The authors have declared that no competing interests exist.

* E-mail: hermann@neurology.wisc.edu

Introduction

Attention deficit hyperactivity disorder (ADHD) is a common neuropsychiatric disorder in children and adolescents. The prevalence rate varies across individual studies, but is similar among pooled results regardless of the diagnostic procedure used and the countries or regions of the populations examined, ranging from 5.9 to 7.1% [1]. ADHD has substantial implications for quality of life in childhood as it is strongly associated with factors such as school performance, emotional adjustment, and peer relationships [2]. If persistent into adulthood, particularly if untreated, ADHD can be associated with lower socioeconomic status, work difficulties with frequent job changes, and other life problems [2].

Children with epilepsy have an increased prevalence of mental health disorders that include ADHD, mood and anxiety disorders, autistic spectrum disorder and conduct problems. These issues have been demonstrated repeatedly in epidemiological and clinical studies which have reported rates 4–5 times higher than the general population and 2.5 times higher than in individuals with other non-neurological chronic conditions [3–6]. ADHD in particular has been identified as a common comorbidity by several groups with rates varying from 21 to 31.5%—approximately 5 times higher than the general population [5–10].

Despite the elevated rate of ADHD in youth with epilepsy and its potential relevance for children's well-being [10], only a few neuroimaging investigations of this comorbidity have been published. It is not well established yet whether the mechanisms and neurobiological substrates of this disorder in children with epilepsy are similar to those in children without epilepsy. To our knowledge, the only examination of brain structure and ADHD in children with epilepsy was a prior analysis by our group [7] which examined total cortical lobar volumes as well as volumes of the cerebellum and brainstem. However, these analyses did not include examination of more contemporary metrics of cortical anatomy including thickness, area and curvature, nor a broader survey of subcortical structures, all of which are now possible with newer image processing systems which may yield new insights regarding the alterations in brain morphology associated with ADHD in children with epilepsy.

In the present study, we conducted a broad and comprehensive characterization of the neuroanatomical correlates of ADHD in childhood epilepsy. We included children with epilepsy with and without ADHD, as well as healthy controls, for the purpose of determining features specifically associated with ADHD that are not associated with epilepsy more generally. Additionally, in order to avoid confounding factors such as chronic seizure activity or long term anti-epileptic drug (AED) effects, as well as the cumulative social and psychological consequences of the disorder, we restricted our examination to children with new- and recent-onset epilepsy.

Methods

Participants

A total of 100 research participants comprised three groups of children: new and recent-onset epilepsy with ADHD (Epilepsy ADHD+, n = 18) and without ADHD (Epilepsy ADHD-, n = 36), and typically-developing first-degree cousin controls (n = 46). All participants were aged 8–18 years and attended regular schools. Children with epilepsy were recruited from the pediatric neurology clinics at three Midwestern medical centers (University of Wisconsin-Madison, Marshfield Clinic, Dean Clinic) and met the following inclusion criteria: (i) newly diagnosed epilepsy within the past 12 months; (ii) no other developmental disabilities (e.g. autism); (iii) no other neurological disorder, and (iv) normal clinical MRI. Children with epilepsy underwent routine MRI as part of their diagnostic workup and all scans were interpreted as unremarkable by the clinical neuroradiologists. This point was later confirmed by the research pediatric neurologist when reviewing the cases for study participation. Inclusion in the Epilepsy ADHD+ group required a diagnosis of ADHD according to DSM-IV [12] criteria (see *Assessment of ADHD* below). Exclusion criteria for controls were: (i) any initial precipitating event (e.g. simple or complex febrile seizures); (ii) any seizure or seizure-like episode; (iii) diagnosed neurological disease; (iv) loss of consciousness greater than 5 min; or (v) other family history of a first-degree relative with epilepsy or febrile convulsions; (vi) ADHD. Further demographic and clinical features of the three groups are provided in Table 1. Table 1 shows that there were 25 children/adolescents with localization-related epilepsies (LRE) and 29 with idiopathic generalized epilepsies (IGE). Of the total epilepsy group, 7 were on no medications, 46 were on monotherapy and 1 was on polytherapy. There were no differences between the ADHD+/− groups and demographic features (age, gender) or epilepsy characteristics (age of onset, duration of epilepsy, number of medications, epilepsy syndrome). IQ was lower in the Epilepsy ADHD+ group compared to the Epilepsy ADHD- and Controls groups, but nevertheless fell in the average range.

First-degree cousins were used as controls rather than siblings or other potential controls groups because: (i) first-degree cousins are more genetically distant from the participants with epilepsy and thus less pre-disposed than siblings to shared genetic factors that may contribute to anomalies in brain structure and cognition; (ii) a greater number of first-degree cousins were available than siblings in the target age range and (iii) the family link was anticipated to facilitate participant recruitment and especially retention over time (which is our intent) compared to more general control populations (e.g. unrelated school mates).

This project represents an extension of our previous report [7] but includes several distinguishing features. The sample is partially but not completely overlapping as some T1 only scans were unacceptable for current analysis compared to the prior investigation that used T1, T2 and proton density (PD) weighted images—thus more recent participants with acceptable T1 scans were included. The neuroimaging analyses are completely distinct and comprehensive in scope as will be described below. Finally, the epilepsy control group (ADHD-) is quite different. In order to have an "uncomplicated" epilepsy group, we selected children not only without ADHD, but without reported academic problems as well (e.g., special learning services, tutors, grade retention). Since academic problems are often comorbid with ADHD, and they exist in a significant proportion of children with epilepsy without ADHD, it was felt to be important to eliminate these children from the epilepsy control group (ADHD-).

Assessment of ADHD

To determine ADHD status the Kiddie–Schedule for Affective Disorders and Schizophrenia–Present and Lifetime Version (K-SADS-PL) was used [13]. This is a semi-structured diagnostic interview designed to assess current and previous episodes of psychopathology in children and adolescents using DSM-IV criteria [12]. The KSADS-PL has been utilized in several studies of children with epilepsy to identify rates of psychiatric comorbidity including ADHD [14,15]. The K-SADS-PL was administered by interviewing both the parent and the child separately. In the current study, two interviewers were specially trained to administer the clinical interview, and interviews were randomly selected for review to ensure diagnostic consistency. Fifteen

Table 1. Demographic and clinical characteristics of participants (means and standard deviations).

Variable	Control (n = 46)	Epilepsy ADHD- (n = 36)	Epilepsy ADHD+(n = 18)[a]
Age (y)	13.08 (3.26)	13.47 (3.41)	12.11 (3.15)
Sex (% female)	27 (58%)	20 (56%)	7 (39%)
FSIQ	110.20 (11.21)	109.81 (11.81)	93.44 (9.23)*
Seizure onset age (y)	—	12.56 (3.37)	11.02 (3.26)
Epilepsy duration (m)	—	8.58 (3.72)	8.33 (3.05)
AED's (0/1/2+)	—	6/30/0	1/16/1
Syndrome (IGE/LRE)	—	21 (58%)/15 (42%)	8 (44%)/10 (56%)
ADHD medication (1+)	—	—	7

[a]ADHD subtypes: Inattentive (n = 9); Hyperactive-Impulsive (n = 3); Combined (n = 3); NOS (n = 3).
FSIQ: Full-scale intelligent quotient.
AED: Anti-epileptic drug.
IGE: Idiopathic generalized epilepsy.
LRE: Localization-related epilepsy.
*$p<0.05$ compared to Control and Epilepsy ADHD- groups.

percent of participants were randomly selected for independent review to ensure reliability of diagnoses and reduce rater drift. Interviewers were not blinded to seizure history as this often arose spontaneously during the interview. There was no association between ADHD+/− and epilepsy syndrome (IGE vs. LRE) ($p = 0.34$), age of onset ($p = 0.12$), duration of epilepsy ($p = 0.80$), or AED number $p = 0.13$).

MRI acquisition

Images were obtained on a 1.5T GE Signa MRI scanner (GE Healthcare, Waukesha, WI, U.S.A.). Sequences acquired for each participant were T1-weighted, three-dimensional (3D) spoiled gradients recall (SPGR) using the following parameters: TE = 5 ms, TR = 24 ms, flip angle = 40 degrees, NEX = 1, slice thickness = 1.5 mm, slices = 124, plane = coronal, field of view (FOV) = 200 mm, matrix = 256×256. All MR images were inspected before image processing. Image quality was rated on a five-point scale (0 = poor 4 = excellent) and we required a minimum quality rating of 3 or better for the scan to be included in this analysis. Further details regarding MRI processing are provided in the supporting information file Methods S1.

Human Subjects

This study was reviewed and approved by the Institutional Review Boards of all participating institutions (University of Wisconsin-Madison, Marshfield Clinic, Dean Clinic). On the day of study participation families and children gave informed consent and assent, respectively. All procedures were consistent with the Declaration of Helsinki [11]. The investigators obtained informed written consent from the next of kin, caretakers, or guardians on behalf of the minors/children participants involved in the study. Those study participants age 18 completed written informed consent.

Analyses

Analyses focused on differences between the Epilepsy ADHD+, Epilepsy ADHD- and control groups in regard to cortical thickness, area, volume and curvature, as well as volumes of subcortical and brain stem structures. For cortical measurements, a surface-based group analysis using Freesurfer's statistical tool Qdec was performed. The participants' surface data were smoothed using 10, 15 or 20 mm FWHM kernels to optimize significant regions. A general linear model was then applied at each vertex to test for group differences in cortical thickness, area, volume and curvature. Age and gender were modeled as covariates for all measures while intracranial volume (ICV) was added as a covariate for measures of cortical area, volume and curvature. To correct for multiple comparisons, a Monte-Carlo simulation was implemented with an initial cluster-forming threshold set to $p<0.05$. Clusters were then tested against an empirical null distribution of maximum cluster size built using synthesized Z-distributed data across 10,000 permutations, producing cluster-wise p-values (CWP) fully corrected for multiple comparisons. A False Discovery Rate (FDR) of $p<0.05$ was also independently applied to correct for multiple comparisons. Finally, we examined subcortical structure volumes previously reported to be abnormal in epilepsy and/or ADHD using multivariate analysis of covariance (MANCOVA), with age, gender and ICV as covariates.

Results

Cortical thickness (vertex analysis)

Figure 1 and Table 2 depict the results of the Monte Carlo simulation comparing Epilepsy ADHD+ to healthy controls. All surviving significant (CWP<0.05) clusters represent areas of decreased cortical thickness in the Epilepsy ADHD+ group versus healthy controls. Affected regions in the left hemisphere include: 1) caudal and rostral middle frontal areas, superior aspect of the frontal lobe, pre and postcentral gyri, superior and inferior aspects of the parietal lobe, supramarginal gyrus, cuneus, lateral aspect of the occipital lobe; and posterior areas of inferior, middle and superior aspects of the temporal lobe and banks of the superior temporal sulcus; 2) paracentral lobule, precuneus, posterior and caudal anterior aspects of the cingulate cortex, and superior medial aspect of the frontal lobe; and 3) pars triangularis, pars opercularis, lateral extremity of the pre and postcentral gyri, insula, and transverse temporal gyrus. Affected areas in the right hemisphere include: 1) inferior aspects of the parietal lobe, lateral aspects of the occipital lobe, fusiform gyrus, and posterior areas of inferior, middle and superior aspects of the temporal lobe and banks of the superior temporal sulcus; 2) pars opercularis, pars triangularis, rostral and caudal middle frontal areas, pre and postcentral gyri, and supramarginal gyrus; and 3) superior aspect of the frontal lobe, caudal middle frontal area, paracentral gyrus, and rostral anterior, caudal anterior and posterior aspects of the cingulate cortex.

Figure 2 depicts the results of the Monte Carlo simulation comparing Epilepsy ADHD+ to Epilepsy ADHD- children. The Epilepsy ADHD+ group exhibits significant cortical thinning in several left hemisphere regions including: 1) inferior and superior aspects of the parietal lobe, post and precentral gyrus, supramarginal gyrus, lateral aspect of the occipital lobe, and inferior and middle aspects of the temporal lobe; 2) precentral gyrus, pars opercularis, and caudal middle, rostral middle and superior aspects of the frontal lobe; and 3) posterior cingulate cortex, precuneus, paracentral lobule, and superior medial aspect of the frontal lobe. The Epilepsy ADHD+ group also exhibits a cluster of decreased thickness in the right cerebral cortex, including: 5) pars opercularis, pars triangularis, rostral and caudal middle frontal areas, pre and postcentral gyri, supramarginal gyrus, superior aspect of the frontal lobe, and paracentral lobule. There were no cortical thickness differences between the Epilepsy ADHD- and controls after correction for multiple comparisons.

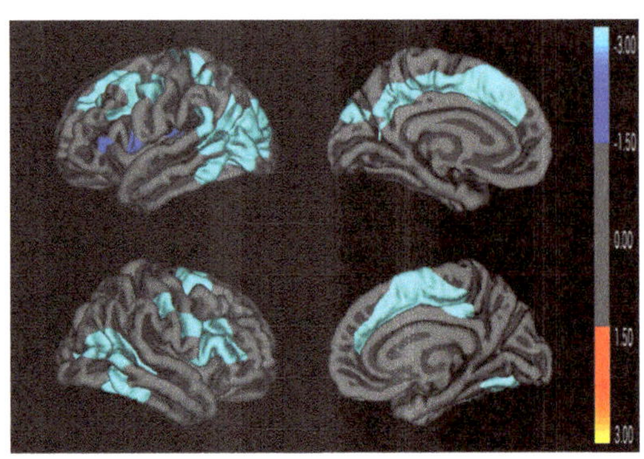

Figure 1. Cortical thickness comparison between epilepsy ADHD+ and control groups. Monte Carlo cluster-wise simulation: Blue colors indicate significant clusters where the Epilepsy ADHD+ group is thinner than the control group.

Table 2. Regions of significant differences in vertex analyses of cortical thickness (CT) and cortical area (CA).

Comparison Groups	Region of Interest	Cluster size (mm^2)	P corrected	Tal. Coord. (x y z)
CT: Epi ADHD+ vs. Control	L superior parietal	18015.46	0.0001	−23.4 −76.1 18.4
	L paracentral	4909.15	0.0001	−18.0 −31.7 37.8
	L insula	2336.06	0.0188	−31.0 −24.0 13.5
	R inferior parietal	5444.41	0.0001	37.9 −56.8 17.5
	R pars opercularis	5207.25	0.0001	41.4 7.9 18.6
	R superior frontal	5277.92	0.0001	7.6 −2.5 53.3
CT: Epi ADHD+ vs. Epi ADHD-	L inferior parietal	8318.56	0.0001	−38.0 −48.8 33.5
	L caudal middle frontal	3843.39	0.0001	−40.2 14.9 44.7
	L posterior cingulate	1972.37	0.0436	−13.1 −33.5 38.3
	R pars opercularis	6338.68	0.0001	44.0 21.1 16.4
CA: Epi ADHD- vs. Control	L middle temporal	1320.29	0.0457	−59.0 −36.3 −11.1

Cortical surface area, volume and curvature (vertex analysis)

Figure 3 reveals a significant cluster of greater surface area in Epilepsy ADHD- compared to healthy control groups in the left middle and inferior temporal regions. There were no differences in area in comparisons involving the Epilepsy ADHD+ group. Analyses of cortical volume did not yield any significant difference among groups after correction for multiple comparisons. Cortical volume is the product of two independent components, cortical thickness and surface area. In the case where one is increasing and the other is decreasing the volume change can be zero.

Cortical surface curvature assesses differences in small areas (peak of gyri and sulci), making FDR a more appropriate correction. The curvature index is zero for a locally flat surface and the magnitude increases as the surface becomes more spiked. Sulci and gyri are distinguished by positive and negative curvatures, respectively. Minor dissimilarities surviving FDR are found in two group comparisons (supporting information file Figure S1). Epilepsy ADHD+ participants demonstrate a small region of increased curvature in the lateral orbitofrontal cortex and an area of decreased curvature in the fusiform gyrus, compared to epilepsy ADHD- participants. Epilepsy ADHD- participants exhibit increased curvature compared to controls in three regions: 1) the inferior portion of the parietal lobe, 2) posterior cingulate cortex, and 3) precuneus; as well as a small area of decreased curvature at the isthmus of the cingulate cortex.

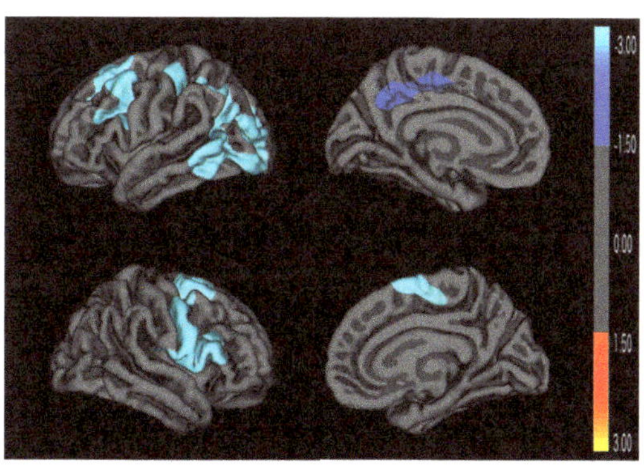

Figure 2. Cortical thickness comparison between Epilepsy ADHD+ and Epilepsy ADHD- groups. Monte Carlo cluster-wise simulation: Blue colors indicate significant clusters where the Epilepsy ADHD+ group is thinner than the Epilepsy ADHD- group.

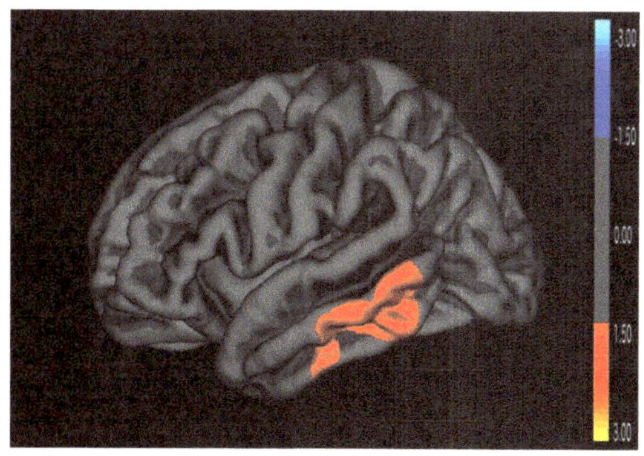

Figure 3. Cortical area comparison between Epilepsy ADHD- and control groups. Monte Carlo cluster-wise simulation: Red colors indicate significant clusters where the Epilepsy ADHD- group is larger in area than the control group.

Subcortical volumes

A summary of the volumetric analyses of subcortical structures and cerebellum is provided in Table 3. Three patterns of results can be appreciated. First, an arguably strong ADHD association was characterized by greater abnormality (reduced volume) in the Epilepsy ADHD+ participants compared to *both* the Epilepsy ADHD- and the control groups, who did not differ from one another. The right caudate showed this degree of specificity. Second, a more common pattern of association was characterized by greater abnormality in the ADHD+ compared to *either* the ADHD- *or* the control group, with the ADHD- and control groups again not differing from one another. Regions of interest demonstrating this pattern included total subcortical grey matter, brainstem, left caudate, left thalamus, and right hippocampus. Third, there was a general relationship of epilepsy characterized by both epilepsy groups (ADHD+ and ADHD-) differing significantly from the controls, with the epilepsy groups not differing from each other. Regions of interest showing this pattern included volumes of the right thalamus, and total cerebellum (due to left cerebellum).

Table 3. Subcortical volume comparisons between groups.

Association	Region of Interest	Control	Epilepsy ADHD-	Epilepy ADHD+
ADHD	R caudate	4052	4063	3770*#
	Total subcortical GM	203171	199105	195759*
	Brainstem	20818	20587	19767*
	L caudate	4024	4015	3800*
	L thalamus	7744	7622	7487*
	R hippocampus	4404	4434	4191#
Epilepsy	R thalamus	8082	7846*	7631*
	Cerebellum	149152	144560*	143296*
	L cerebellum	74389	71890*	71411*

*$p<0.05$ compared to control group.
#$p<0.05$ compared to Epilepsy ADHD- group.

Discussion

In this study a comprehensive set of analyses were performed to characterize alterations in cortical morphology, subcortical structures, and cerebellum that may be associated with ADHD in children with epilepsy. By incorporating children with epilepsy with and without ADHD, we were able to identify anatomical abnormalities associated with epilepsy more generally versus abnormalities associated more specifically with ADHD. Three core findings emerged from this investigation: 1) ADHD in children with epilepsy is associated with a distributed pattern of anatomic abnormality involving the cortex and subcortical structures, the cortical morphological abnormalities characterized overwhelmingly by reduced cortical thickness in bilateral areas of the frontal, parietal, and temporal lobes, with minor or no group differences in metrics of cortical surface area, volume or curvature; 2) Children with epilepsy and ADHD exhibited significantly smaller subcortical volumes of the caudate, thalamus, hippocampus, and brainstem; 3) A more general association with epilepsy, unrelated to the presence or absence of ADHD, was seen in reduced volumes of the cerebellum and thalamus. These findings will be reviewed below.

First, the main finding is a diffusely distributed pattern of neuroanatomical abnormality in children with epilepsy and ADHD compared to children with epilepsy but without ADHD and typically-developing controls. These results involve broad and widespread cortical and subcortical areas suggesting associations between altered brain networks in ADHD that participate in executive function, attention, and sensorimotor systems [16]. The Epilepsy ADHD+ group exhibited significant cortical thinning in areas related to the dorsal attention network including the left intraparietal sulcus, left superior areas of the parietal lobe, superior frontal and precentral gyrus; as well as in ventral attention network areas such as the supramarginal gyrus and the temporoparietal junction in the left and the inferior frontal gyrus in the right hemisphere [17], supporting more general developmental ADHD findings. Cortical thinning is also the notable characteristic of ADHD in the general population [18–28].

We found minimal differences in cortical area or volume when examining the Epilepsy ADHD+ group. Nevertheless, two studies have reported decreased cortical area in children with ADHD compared to controls [29,30]. Curvature analysis revealed very modest differences between children with epilepsy with versus without ADHD, these findings restricted to two small regions and not emerging in the comparison between Epilepsy ADHD+ and controls, indicating that this may be an incidental finding of uncertain clinical significance. Shaw et al. also found no differences in their gyrification index (a measure comparable to curvature) between ADHD and controls [30].

Second, at the subcortical level, children with epilepsy and ADHD differed significantly from the Epilepsy ADHD- and control groups in the volume of the right basal ganglia, as well as from either the Epilepsy ADHD- or the control group, with the latter two groups comparable to each other across volumes of the left caudate, left thalamus, right hippocampus, and brainstem, with additional reduced volume of total subcortical grey matter. Several of these results are consistent with meta-analyses and reviews of ADHD in the general population [31–35]. These studies were based primarily on structural MRI differences using voxel-based morphometry between children with ADHD and healthy controls, with the most constant findings involving smaller right caudate [31,34,35], right putamen and right globus pallidus [31,33,35] in children with ADHD. Left caudate [31] volume has also been shown to be decreased, although with less consistency across studies. Additionally, abnormalities in shape analyses – which we did not examine in the present investigation – have been reported in the basal ganglia, hippocampus and amygdala in children with ADHD [32]. These meta-analyses have not identified changes in thalamus, probably because of the relatively small number of investigations targeting this structure and the lack of segregation of specific thalamic nuclei [36]. However, two recent publications provide new insights regarding the potential role of thalamus morphometry in ADHD. Ivanov and colleagues demonstrated significantly smaller regional volumes bilaterally in the pulvinar nuclei in children with ADHD compared to healthy controls despite their finding of no significant difference in total thalamus volume. Moreover, those individuals treated with stimulant medication exhibited pulvinar measurements more similar to controls than those under no treatment [37]. Further, Xia and colleagues reported reduced volume in the right and left thalamus in youth with ADHD in comparison to healthy controls, although this finding was not significant in the left hemisphere when controlling for age and gender. Examining subdivisions within the thalamus, significant volume differences were found in the ventral anterior, medial dorsal, and pulvinar nuclei in the left but not right thalamus [38]. These results, together with our finding of diminished left thalamic volume in ADHD, are consistent with anatomic evidence implicating the thalamus in cortical-striatal-thalamic-cortical loops that are significant substrates for higher cognitive functions, including attention [39].

Brainstem volume, likewise, is understudied in the ADHD literature, but our result is physiologically reasonable, given that the brainstem hosts the reticular activating system and is the production site for neurotransmitters with a key role in ADHD [40,41]; and there is reported probable involvement of this structure in attention manifestations of various neuropsychiatric disorders [42]. Cerebellar atrophy has long been considered a consequence of epilepsy chronicity/severity or the effects of specific medications, namely phenytoin [43], but here we find cerebellar atrophy in children with new onset (and not chronic) epilepsy and no children had been prescribed or taken phenytoin. This result was driven largely by volumetric reduction in the left cerebellum. The volume of the left thalamus follows the same pattern, indicating an association with epilepsy as well. In contrast to our results, one of the most robust regions of decreased volume in a ROI based meta-analysis of general ADHD was the cerebellum, in particular the posterior inferior vermis [34], but here no such effect was found. Cerebellar volume reduction is a recurrent finding in the epilepsy literature, even though it seems to be more prominent in chronic cases [44–48]. Accordingly, thalamic volume is shown to be decreased bilaterally in investigations of both focal and generalized epilepsy syndromes [26,49–51].

In the epilepsy ADHD literature several clinical seizure features, including seizure frequency [52], clinical control of seizures [52], number of antiepileptic drugs [7], and duration of epilepsy [7,9], are reported as unassociated with the frequency of ADHD diagnosis or reported symptoms. ADHD studies in epilepsy samples usually detect more inattentive subtype than in developmental ADHD [7,9,53,54]. Finally, ADHD symptoms in children with epilepsy have been reported to improve with stimulant medication in in the same way they do in the general population [54–57].

In summary, this study indicates that ADHD, a common comorbidity in pediatric epilepsy, is associated with thinning of cortical regions and diminution of subcortical structures related to attention, executive function and sensorimotor networks.

There are differences in the neuroimaging results of this investigation compared to our previous report [7] which might be due to number of factors. First and foremost, the epilepsy control group (ADHD-) is substantially different and more rigorously defined. To derive a clearly "uncomplicated" epilepsy group, we selected children not only without ADHD but also without reported academic problems as well, that is, children who had been provided with a variety of academic services or academic adjustments for achievement problems. These included special school-based learning services, tutors, grade retention, formal individual education plans, and other provisions. Since academic problems are often comorbid with ADHD, and they exist in a significant proportion of children with epilepsy without ADHD, we felt it appropriate to exclude these children from the epilepsy control group (i.e., ADHD-). Second, our previous study utilized an entirely different image processing system (Brains2) which combined T1, T2 and PD images for tissue segmentation supplemented by VBM to measure gray matter volume, while the current study examines gray matter surface based features (thickness, area, volume and curvature). Although these two measurements of gray matter volume in general are correlated, differences can exist as each imaging technique indexes different biological signals [58]. Volume based VBM observes the proportion of gray matter voxels, based on signal intensity threshold, compared to voxels representing other tissue type such as white matter and cerebrospinal fluid (CSF) [59]. As such, gray matter volume measured in VBM can be sensitive to changes in gray matter and CSF volumes as well as differences in cortical surface curvature, which cannot be distinguished from each other. Gray matter thickness measures the distance between white-gray matter boundary to cortical surface, which is less affected by adjacent CSF volume and cortical curvature and primarily reflects packing density and arrangement of neuronal cells [60]. In summary, distinctions in cohort characteristics between the current and our previous study likely influenced the neuroimaging findings with additional contribution from differences in morphometric analysis techniques. Note that neuroimaging findings in the current study are in line with the general ADHD literature, which have consistently shown cortical thinning with a similar anatomical distribution.

Limitations, Strengths, and Future Directions

Our study has both limitations and strengths. Regarding limitations, first noted is that the number of children with epilepsy and ADHD is modest. Second, we were not able to include an ADHD group without epilepsy as too few controls met criteria for ADHD, thereby precluding a true 2×2 analysis. Third, because of the modest sample size, it was not possible to perform analyses examining ADHD as a function of the known subtypes including inattentive, hyperactive, and combined—a very important task for the future. Fourth, the mechanisms that underlie the ADHD comorbidity in epilepsy remain an open question. This investigation does not inform that point. One avenue we are currently investigating is whether family history/family aggregation of ADHD is a pertinent consideration. Despite these limitations, the strengths of the paper include that fact that ADHD is an important complication of childhood epilepsy, the diagnosis of which was defined rigorously based on DSM-IV diagnosis from the K-SADS-PL rather than a parent report questionnaire which thereby improved diagnostic reliability. We included measures of cortical morphology that went beyond cortical thickness, measures that have been understudied in epilepsy in general and epilepsy and ADHD in particular. Because of that, we felt that there was utility in examining these measures comprehensively and indeed it appears that alterations in cortical thickness are a primary correlate of ADHD in epilepsy. Moving forward, we are tracking these children prospectively (2 years and 5-6 years later) and plan to focus on their longitudinal trajectories in the future.

Conclusions

ADHD is a common co-occurring condition in childhood epilepsy. This comorbidity of epilepsy has anatomical correlates that are detectable early in the course of the epilepsy suggesting that the altered neuroanatomy is not due to epilepsy chronicity or treatment. The etiology of this anatomical signature and its prospective course remain to be characterized, as does the life course of children with epilepsy with ADHD compared to children with epilepsy without ADHD.

Supporting Information

Figure S1 Cortical curvature comparisons. A) FDR corrected significant differences in curvature. Blue colors indicate regions in which the Epilepsy ADHD+ group has decreased curvature relative to the Epilepsy ADHD- group (fusiform region). Red colors indicate regions in which the Epilepsy ADHD+ group has increased curvature relative to the Epilepsy ADHD- group (lateral orbitofrontal prefrontal region). B) FDR corrected significant differences in curvature in the right hemisphere. Blue colors indicate regions in which the Epilepsy ADHD - group has decreased curvature compared to the control group. Red colors indicate regions in which the Epilepsy ADHD - group has increased curvature compared to the control group.

Methods S1 MRI processing details.

Acknowledgments

We thank Raj Sheth MD and Monica Koehn MD for study participation and subject recruitment. Also greatly appreciated are Dace Almane, Melissa Hanson, Kate Young, and Bjorn Hanson for overall study coordination, participant recruitment, cognitive assessment, and data management. We also thank Alan McMillian, PhD, Beth Meyerand, PhD, and Jack Lin MD for consultation regarding image analysis.

Author Contributions

Conceived and designed the experiments: BH JJ MS RS. Performed the experiments: BH JJ. Analyzed the data: RS KD DJ. Wrote the paper: BH RS KD.

References

1. Willcutt EG (2012) The prevalence of DSM-IV attention-deficit/hyperactivity disorder: a meta-analytic review. Neurotherapeutics 9: 490–499.
2. Spencer TJ, Biederman J, Mick E (2007) Attention-deficit/hyperactivity disorder: diagnosis, lifespan, comorbidities, and neurobiology. Ambul Pediatr 7: 73–81.
3. Rutter M, Graham P, Yule W (1970) A neuropsychiatric study in childhood. London: S.I.M.P./William Heineman Medical Books.
4. Davies S, Heyman I, Goodman R (2003) A population survey of mental health problems in children with epilepsy. Dev Med Child Neurol 45: 292–295.
5. Berg AT, Caplan R, Hesdorffer DC (2011) Psychiatric and neurodevelopmental disorders in childhood-onset epilepsy. Epilepsy Behav 20: 550–555.
6. Russ SA, Larson K, Halfon N (2012) A national profile of childhood epilepsy and seizure disorder. Pediatrics 129: 256–264.
7. Hermann B, Jones J, Dabbs K, Allen CA, Sheth R, et al. (2007) The frequency, complications and aetiology of ADHD in new onset paediatric epilepsy. Brain 130: 3135–3148.
8. Dunn DW, Austin JK, Harezlak J, Ambrosius WT (2003) ADHD and epilepsy in childhood. Dev Med Child Neurol 45: 50–54.
9. Sherman EM, Slick DJ, Connolly MB, Eyrl KL (2007) ADHD, neurological correlates and health-related quality of life in severe pediatric epilepsy. Epilepsia 48: 1083–1091.
10. Cohen R, Senecky Y, Shuper A, Inbar D, Chodick G, et al. (2012) Prevalence of Epilepsy and Attention-Deficit Hyperactivity (ADHD) Disorder: A Population-Based Study. J Child Neurol.
11. World Medical Association Declaration of Helsinki (1991) The Journal of Law, Medicine & Ethics 19: 264–265.
12. American Psychiatric Association (2000) American Psychiatric Association: Diagnostic and Statistical Manual of Mental Disorders, Fourth Edition, Text Revision.
13. Kaufman J, Birmaher B, Brent D, Rao U (1997) Schedule for Affective Disorders and Schizophrenia for School-Age Children-Present and Lifetime version (K-SADS-PL): Initial reliability and validity data. Journal of the American Academy of Child & Adolescent Psychiatry 36: 980–988.
14. Ott D, Siddarth P, Gurbani S, Koh S, Tournay A, et al. (2003) Behavioral disorders in pediatric epilepsy: unmet psychiatric need. Epilepsia 44: 591–597.
15. Caplan R, Siddarth P, Gurbani S, Hanson R, Sankar R, et al. (2005) Depression and anxiety disorders in pediatric epilepsy. Epilepsia 46: 720–730.
16. Cortese S, Kelly C, Chabernaud C, Proal E, Di Martino A, et al. (2012) Toward systems neuroscience of ADHD: a meta-analysis of 55 fMRI studies. Am J Psychiatry 169: 1038–1055.
17. Luo L, Rodriguez E, Jerbi K, Lachaux JP, Martinerie J, et al. (2010) Ten years of Nature Reviews Neuroscience: insights from the highly cited. Nat Rev Neurosci 11: 718–726.
18. Bohland JW, Saperstein S, Pereira F, Rapin J, Grady L (2012) Network, anatomical, and non-imaging measures for the prediction of ADHD diagnosis in individual subjects. Front Syst Neurosci 6: 78.
19. Hoekzema E, Carmona S, Ramos-Quiroga JA, Richarte Fernandez V, Picado M, et al. (2012) Laminar thickness alterations in the fronto-parietal cortical mantle of patients with attention-deficit/hyperactivity disorder. PLoS One 7: e48286.
20. Narr KL, Woods RP, Lin J, Kim J, Phillips OR, et al. (2009) Widespread cortical thinning is a robust anatomical marker for attention-deficit/hyperactivity disorder. J Am Acad Child Adolesc Psychiatry 48: 1014–1022.
21. Proal E, Reiss PT, Klein RG, Mannuzza S, Gotimer K, et al. (2011) Brain gray matter deficits at 33-year follow-up in adults with attention-deficit/hyperactivity disorder established in childhood. Arch Gen Psychiatry 68: 1122–1134.
22. Almeida LG, Ricardo-Garcell J, Prado H, Barajas L, Fernandez-Bouzas A, et al. (2010) Reduced right frontal cortical thickness in children, adolescents and adults with ADHD and its correlation to clinical variables: a cross-sectional study. J Psychiatr Res 44: 1214–1223.
23. Shaw P, Lerch J, Greenstein D, Sharp W, Clasen L, et al. (2006) Longitudinal mapping of cortical thickness and clinical outcome in children and adolescents with attention-deficit/hyperactivity disorder. Arch Gen Psychiatry 63: 540–549.
24. Shaw P, Eckstrand K, Sharp W, Blumenthal J, Lerch JP, et al. (2007) Attention-deficit/hyperactivity disorder is characterized by a delay in cortical maturation. Proc Natl Acad Sci U S A 104: 19649–19654.
25. Makris N, Biederman J, Valera EM, Bush G, Kaiser J, et al. (2007) Cortical thinning of the attention and executive function networks in adults with attention-deficit/hyperactivity disorder. Cereb Cortex 17: 1364–1375.
26. Alhusaini S, Doherty CP, Scanlon C, Ronan L, Maguire S, et al. (2012) A cross-sectional MRI study of brain regional atrophy and clinical characteristics of temporal lobe epilepsy with hippocampal sclerosis. Epilepsy Res 99: 156–166.
27. Qiu MG, Ye Z, Li QY, Liu GJ, Xie B, et al. (2011) Changes of brain structure and function in ADHD children. Brain Topogr 24: 243–252.
28. Duerden EG, Tannock R, Dockstader C (2012) Altered cortical morphology in sensorimotor processing regions in adolescents and adults with attention-deficit/hyperactivity disorder. Brain Res 1445: 82–91.
29. Wolosin SM, Richardson ME, Hennessey JG, Denckla MB, Mostofsky SH (2009) Abnormal cerebral cortex structure in children with ADHD. Hum Brain Mapp 30: 175–184.
30. Shaw P, Malek M, Watson B, Sharp W, Evans A, et al. (2012) Development of cortical surface area and gyrification in attention-deficit/hyperactivity disorder. Biol Psychiatry 72: 191–197.
31. Frodl T, Skokauskas N (2012) Meta-analysis of structural MRI studies in children and adults with attention deficit hyperactivity disorder indicates treatment effects. Acta Psychiatr Scand 125: 114–126.
32. Shaw P, Rabin C (2009) New insights into attention-deficit/hyperactivity disorder using structural neuroimaging. Curr Psychiatry Rep 11: 393–398.
33. Ellison-Wright I, Ellison-Wright Z, Bullmore E (2008) Structural brain change in Attention Deficit Hyperactivity Disorder identified by meta-analysis. BMC Psychiatry 8: 51.
34. Valera EM, Faraone SV, Murray KE, Seidman LJ (2007) Meta-analysis of structural imaging findings in attention-deficit/hyperactivity disorder. Biol Psychiatry 61: 1361–1369.
35. Nakao T, Radua J, Rubia K, Mataix-Cols D (2011) Gray matter volume abnormalities in ADHD: voxel-based meta-analysis exploring the effects of age and stimulant medication. Am J Psychiatry 168: 1154–1163.
36. Shaw P (2010) The shape of things to come in attention deficit hyperactivity disorder. Am J Psychiatry 167: 363–365.
37. I, Bansal R, Hao X, Zhu H, Kellendonk C, et al. (2010) Morphological abnormalities of the thalamus in youths with attention deficit hyperactivity disorder. Am J Psychiatry 167: 397–408.
38. Xia S, Li X, Kimball AE, Kelly MS, Lesser I, et al. (2012) Thalamic shape and connectivity abnormalities in children with attention-deficit/hyperactivity disorder. Psychiatry Res 204: 161–167.
39. Mega MS, Cummings JL (1994) Frontal-subcortical circuits and neuropsychiatric disorders. J Neuropsychiatry Clin Neurosci 6: 358–370.
40. Aston-Jones G, Cohen JD (2005) Adaptive gain and the role of the locus coeruleus-norepinephrine system in optimal performance. J Comp Neurol 493: 99–110.
41. Aston-Jones G, Rajkowski J, Cohen J (1999) Role of locus coeruleus in attention and behavioral flexibility. Biol Psychiatry 46: 1309–1320.
42. Mirsky AF, Duncan CC (2001) A nosology of disorders of attention. Ann N Y Acad Sci 931: 17–32.
43. Hermann BP, Bayless K, Hansen R, Parrish J, Seidenberg M (2005) Cerebellar atrophy in temporal lobe epilepsy. Epilepsy Behav 7: 279–287.
44. Sandok EK, O'Brien TJ, Jack CR, So EL (2000) Significance of cerebellar atrophy in intractable temporal lobe epilepsy: a quantitative MRI study. Epilepsia 41: 1315–1320.
45. Liu RS, Lemieux L, Bell GS, Sisodiya SM, Bartlett PA, et al. (2002) The structural consequences of newly diagnosed seizures. Ann Neurol 52: 573–580.
46. Hagemann G, Lemieux L, Free SL, Krakow K, Everitt AD, et al. (2002) Cerebellar volumes in newly diagnosed and chronic epilepsy. J Neurol 249: 1651–1658.
47. Oyegbile TO, Bayless K, Dabbs K, Jones J, Rutecki P, et al. (2011) The nature and extent of cerebellar atrophy in chronic temporal lobe epilepsy. Epilepsia 52: 698–706.

48. Dabbs K, Becker T, Jones J, Rutecki P, Seidenberg M, et al. (2012) Brain structure and aging in chronic temporal lobe epilepsy. Epilepsia 53: 1033–1043.
49. Pail M, Brazdil M, Marecek R, Mikl M (2010) An optimized voxel-based morphometric study of gray matter changes in patients with left-sided and right-sided mesial temporal lobe epilepsy and hippocampal sclerosis (MTLE/HS). Epilepsia 51: 511–518.
50. Saini J, Sinha S, Bagepally BS, Ramchandraiah CT, Thennarasu K, et al. (2013) Subcortical structural abnormalities in juvenile myoclonic epilepsy (JME): MR volumetry and vertex based analysis. Seizure 22: 230–235.
51. Kim JH, Kim JB, Seo WK, Suh SI, Koh SB (2013) Volumetric and shape analysis of thalamus in idiopathic generalized epilepsy. J Neurol.
52. Sherman EM, Brooks BL, Akdag S, Connolly MB, Wiebe S (2010) Parents report more ADHD symptoms than do teachers in children with epilepsy. Epilepsy Behav 19: 428–435.
53. Dunn DW, Austin JK, Perkins SM (2009) Prevalence of psychopathology in childhood epilepsy: categorical and dimensional measures. Dev Med Child Neurol 51: 364–372.
54. Koneski JA, Casella EB, Agertt F, Ferreira MG (2011) Efficacy and safety of methylphenidate in treating ADHD symptoms in children and adolescents with uncontrolled seizures: a Brazilian sample study and literature review. Epilepsy Behav 21: 228–232.
55. Yoo HK, Park S, Wang HR, Lee JS, Kim K, et al. (2009) Effect of methylphenidate on the quality of life in children with epilepsy and attention deficit hyperactivity disorder: and open-label study using an osmotic-controlled release oral delivery system. Epileptic Disord 11: 301–308.
56. Kattimani S, Mahadevan S (2011) Treating children with attention-deficit/hyperactivity disorder and comorbid epilepsy. Annals of Indian Academy of Neurology 14: 9–11.
57. Santos K, Palmini A, Radziuk AL, Rotert R, Bastos F, et al. (2013) The impact of methylphenidate on seizure frequency and severity in children with attention-deficit-hyperactivity disorder and difficult-to-treat epilepsies. Dev Med Child Neurol 55: 654–660.
58. Narr KL, Bilder RM, Toga AW, Woods RP, Rex DE, et al. (2005) Mapping cortical thickness and gray matter concentration in first episode schizophrenia. Cereb Cortex 15: 708–719.
59. Bullmore ET, Suckling J, Overmeyer S, Rabe-Hesketh S, Taylor E, et al. (1999) Global, voxel, and cluster tests, by theory and permutation, for a difference between two groups of structural MR images of the brain. IEEE Trans Med Imaging 18: 32–42.
60. Selemon LD, Rajkowska G, Goldman-Rakic PS (1998) Elevated neuronal density in prefrontal area 46 in brains from schizophrenic patients: application of a three-dimensional, stereologic counting method. J Comp Neurol 392: 402–412.

6

Prepuberal Stimulation of 5-HT7-R by LP-211 in a Rat Model of Hyper-Activity and Attention-Deficit: Permanent Effects on Attention, Brain Amino Acids and Synaptic Markers in the Fronto-Striatal Interface

Lucia A. Ruocco[1¶], Concetta Treno[1], Ugo A. Gironi Carnevale[1], Claudio Arra[2], Gianpiero Boatto[3¶], Maria Nieddu[3], Cristina Pagano[4], Placido Illiano[4], Fabiana Barbato[4], Angela Tino[4¶], Ezio Carboni[5], Giovanni Laviola[6], Enza Lacivita[7], Marcello Leopoldo[7], Walter Adriani[6], Adolfo G. Sadile[1]*

1 Department of Experimental Medicine, School of Medicine, II University of Naples, Napoli, Italy, **2** Animal facility, National Cancer Institute, Napoli, Italy, **3** Department of Chemistry and Pharmacy, University of Sassari, Sassari, Italy, **4** Istituto di Cibernetica "Eduardo Caianiello" - CNR, Pozzuoli, Napoli, Italy, **5** Department of Biomedical Sciences, University of Cagliari, Cagliari, Italy, **6** Section of Behavioural Neuroscience, Department of Cell Biology and Neurosciences, Istituto Superiore di Sanità, Roma, Italy, **7** Department of Medicinal Chemistry, University of Bari, Bari, Italy

Abstract

The cross-talk at the prefronto-striatal interface involves excitatory amino acids, different receptors, transducers and modulators. We investigated long-term effects of a prepuberal, subchronic 5-HT7-R agonist (LP-211) on adult behaviour, amino acids and synaptic markers in a model for Attention-Deficit/Hyperactivity Disorder (ADHD). Naples High Excitability rats (NHE) and their Random Bred controls (NRB) were daily treated with LP-211 in the 5th and 6th postnatal week. One month after treatment, these rats were tested for indices of activity, non selective (NSA), selective spatial attention (SSA) and emotionality. The quantity of L-Glutamate (L-Glu), L-Aspartate (L-Asp) and L-Leucine (L-Leu), dopamine transporter (DAT), NMDAR1 subunit and CAMKIIα, were assessed in prefrontal cortex (PFC), dorsal (DS) and ventral striatum (VS), for their role in synaptic transmission, neural plasticity and information processing. Prepuberal LP-211 (at lower dose) reduced horizontal activity and (at higher dose) increased SSA, only for NHE but not in NRB rats. Prepuberal LP-211 increased, in NHE rats, L-Glu in the PFC and L-Asp in the VS (at 0.250 mg/kg dose), whereas (at 0.125 mg/kg dose) it decreased L-Glu and L-Asp in the DS. The L-Glu was decreased, at 0.125 mg/kg, only in the VS of NRB rats. The DAT levels were decreased with the 0.125 mg/kg dose (in the PFC), and increased with the 0.250 mg/kg dose (in the VS), significantly for NHE rats. The basal NMDAR1 level was higher in the PFC of NHE than NRB rats; LP-211 treatment (at 0.125 mg/kg dose) decreased NMDAR1 in the VS of NRB rats. This study represents a starting point about the impact of developmental 5-HT7-R activation on neuro-physiology of attentive processes, executive functions and their neural substrates.

Editor: Judith Homberg, Radboud University, Netherlands

Funding: Young Investigator "ADHD-sythe" Project 2009–2012 and ERA-net PrioMedChild "NeuroGenMRI" Project 2011–2015 from the Italian Ministry of Health (local unit to LAR, Principal Investigator WA). The funders had no role in study design, data collection and analysis, decision to publish, or preparation of the manuscript.

Competing Interests: The authors have declared that no competing interests exist.

* E-mail: agsadile@alice.it

¶ LAR, GB and AT are equal first authors on this work.

Introduction

The interface between the prefrontal cortex (PFC) and the striata represents the neural substrate for the parallel processing of cognitive and non-cognitive information [1,2]. Therefore, this neural site has been the target of neurophysiological and imaging studies in relation to neuropsychiatric problems [3,4]. The neurogenetic approach in model systems has been used so far to study complex behaviour [5,6] and its neural substrates. This approach will likely lead to a better understanding of neuropsychiatric problems such as Attention-Deficit Hyperactivity Disorder (ADHD), Autism, Schizophrenia and Depression.

In the mammalian brain, the communication between the PFC and the dorsal/ventral striatum involves the amino acid L-Glutamate (L-Glu) acting through different ionotropic [7] and metabotropic receptors, transduction mechanisms and various modulators [8,9]. The latter include dopamine (DA), norepinephrine (NE), serotonin (5-HT), and histamine. A series of clinical, pharmacological, biochemical and molecular biology studies have supported the "dopamine hypothesis" in the last fifty years [10,11], which has yielded a wealth of information giving rise to a major knowledge in the field of neurosciences. For instance, in the case of ADHD, DA-ergic psychostimulant drugs like methylphenidate (MPH) and the amphetamines have been largely used. Notwithstanding, the amino acid transmission between the PFC and the striata is modulated by 5-HT that is released by axon terminals of raphe nuclei and may operate through seven receptor families. Among these, the 5-HT7 receptor subtype is the target of LP-211, a newly synthesised selective agonist [12,13]. It is likely to hypothesise that this receptor could serve a new therapeutic target for ADHD and other neuropsychiatric problems sharing attention deficit.

Therefore, in this manuscript we attempt to investigate long-term effects of a prepuberal, subchronic treatment, by LP-211, on adult behaviour, amino acid transmitters and synaptic markers, using a well documented rat model for ADHD [14]. Animal models for studying ADHD can be of genetic and non-genetic type [15]. The Naples High Excitability (NHE) rat is a classically validated genetic model, which reproduces the mesocortical variant of ADHD [6,14,16,17]. In particular, their profile is characterised by a dysfunctioning mesocortical DA branch with an attention deficit, hyperactivity and altered executive functions. Therefore, adolescent male rats of the Sprague-Dawley-derived NHE line, and their Naples Random-Bred (NRB) [6,16] controls, received daily exposure to LP-211 (0.0, 0.125, 0.250 or 0.500 mg/kg), from post-natal day 30–31 to 43–44.

By using a multidisciplinary approach, here we show that prepuberal LP-211 yields long lasting changes on adult behaviour, improving spatial attention in a dose dependent manner, associated with modified expression of pre- and post-synaptic markers.

The results of the present experiments may represent an important starting point to explore how selective 5-HT7 receptor stimulation can impact upon the neurophysiology of attentive processes, executive functions and their neural substrates. This may, in turn, lead to a better understanding of developmental neuropsychiatric disorders that share activity, attention and executive function problems.

Results

Body weight

To evaluate possible LP-211 developmental-treatment influences on body growth, the body weight was measured in all groups analyzed. There were no differences across groups in NHE and NRB rats. In fact, separate two-way factorial ANOVAs on NHE and NRB rats, with treatment x time (as covariate), showed no main effect for treatment but only for age (time, $F = 4111.3$ and 832.94; $df = 1/26$ and $2/45$; $p<0.0001$ for both) with no interaction.

Long-term behavioural effects of adolescent LP-211 in rats

Behavioural tests were carried out on young adult rats (pnd 70–75 days) so that long-term effects of prepuberal subchronic LP-211 treatment could be determined. The behavioural tests consisted of short exposure of the rats to spatial novelties paradigms, i.e. Làt and Olton mazes. The main variables were total activity, non selective and selective spatial attention (NSA, SSA), and emotionality index in Broadhurst's terms [18]. Exposure to spatial novelties within a Làt maze (Figure 1A–C) yielded no significant treatment effect for NHE and NRB rats, in separate univariate ANOVAs for indices of activity, i.e. both horizontal activity (HA, panel A) and vertical activity (VA, panel B) as well as rearing duration (RD, panel C). Exposure to spatial novelties within a Olton's eight-arm radial maze shows that LP-211 treatment reduced exploratory HA activity only in the NHE rats (Figure 2A) (one-way ANOVA: effect for treatment ($F = 3.56$; $df = 3/20$; $p< 0.033$) and for time ($F = 4.886$; $df = 5/110$; $p<0.000$) with no treatment per time interaction). The post-hoc LSD test confirmed that the reduction of HA produced by LP-211 was due to the 0.125 mg/kg dose ($p<0.0064$). On the other hand, the vertical activity in both NHE and NRB rats, VA and RD, were not influenced by prepuberal LP-211 treatment (one-way ANOVAs: no significant treatment effect on VA and RD) as was observed in the Làt maze (Figure 2B–C).

For the selective spatial attention (SSA), the two markers of non-reinforced SSA are depicted in Figure 3 panels A and B, respectively. The position of the First repetitive arm Entry (FE) significantly improved only in NHE rats, as demonstrated by one-way ANOVA ($F = 3.908$; $df = 3/20$; $p<0.024$). Post-hoc LSD test showed that the higher score was due to the 0.250 mg/kg dose of LP-211 ($p<0.0087$). In contrast, the other parameter, i.e. the total Number of alley Visits needed To Criterion (NVTC), was not different among groups, as demonstrated by one-way ANOVA. The defecation score, used as an emotionality index in Broadhurst terms, was not different across treatment groups and behavioural tasks (Làt and Olton mazes), as demonstrated by separate Kruskal–Wallis tests within the NHE and NRB rats.

Long-term effects of LP-211 on biochemical parameters in adult rats

It is very well known the role of excitatory amino acids in the synaptic dialogue between the pre-frontal cortex (PFC) and the dorsal/ventral striatum (DS/VS) [19,20]. L-Glu and L-Asp can play a role in synaptic transmission, neural plasticity and information processing [21]. After the completion of behavioural tests, the various groups of rats were analyzed for the *ex-vivo* levels of the amino acids L-Glu, L-Asp and L-Leucine in the PFC, DS and VS by LC/MS/MS. The choice of L-Asp was based on its hypothesised role in neurotransmission as suggested by D'Aniello et al. [22] and for its proposed involvement in the formation of N-Methyl D-aspartate (NMDA). In fact, L-Asp can be converted into the stereoisomer D-aspartate by the racemase enzyme, then be inserted as such into NMDA by the N-Methyl transferase and act as an agonist at NMDA receptors [22,23].

Excitatory amino acids L-Glu and L-Asp were expressed as a ratio over L-Leu that does not participate into neurotransmission. Moreover, they were measured in the soluble fraction that corresponds to the one sampled by the microdyalisis method [24]. Data pertaining to the forebrain sites are shown (Figure 4A: NHE and Figure 4B: NRB).

Prefrontal Cortex. Separate one-way ANOVAs on NHE and NRB rats showed an increased ratio of L-Glu/L-Leu ($F = 6.14$; $df = 2/15$, $p<0.011$) for LP-211 at 0.250 mg/kg dose in the NHE line (Figure 4A). Conversely, no significant changes were observed for any of the doses in NRB rats (Figure 4B). Furthermore, the level of L-Asp/L-Leu did not vary in the PFC of NHE or NRB rats for any of the doses (Figure 4A–B).

Dorsal Striatum. In the DS, separate one-way ANOVAs on NHE and NRB rats revealed a decreased L-Glu/L-Leu ratio only for the 0.125 mg/kg dose ($F = 7.23$; $df = 2/15$, $p<0006$) in the NHE line. In contrast, no significant difference was observed in the levels of L-Glu/L-Leu in the NRB line. Furthermore, the L-Asp/L-Leu ratio was also reduced at the 0.125 mg/kg dose ($F = 11.50$; $df = 2/15$, $p<0.001$) in the NHE rats. No significant changes were observed across amino acids and LP-211 doses in the NRB rats (Figure 4B).

Ventral Striatum (or nucleus accumbens). Finally, the levels of L-Glu/L-Leu in the VS of NHE rats showed no significant differences. Separate one-way ANOVAs on NHE and NRB rats demonstrated a reduced L-Glu/L-Leu ratio in the VS for the 0.125 mg/kg dose ($F = 6.43$; $df = 2/15$; $p<0.010$), only in

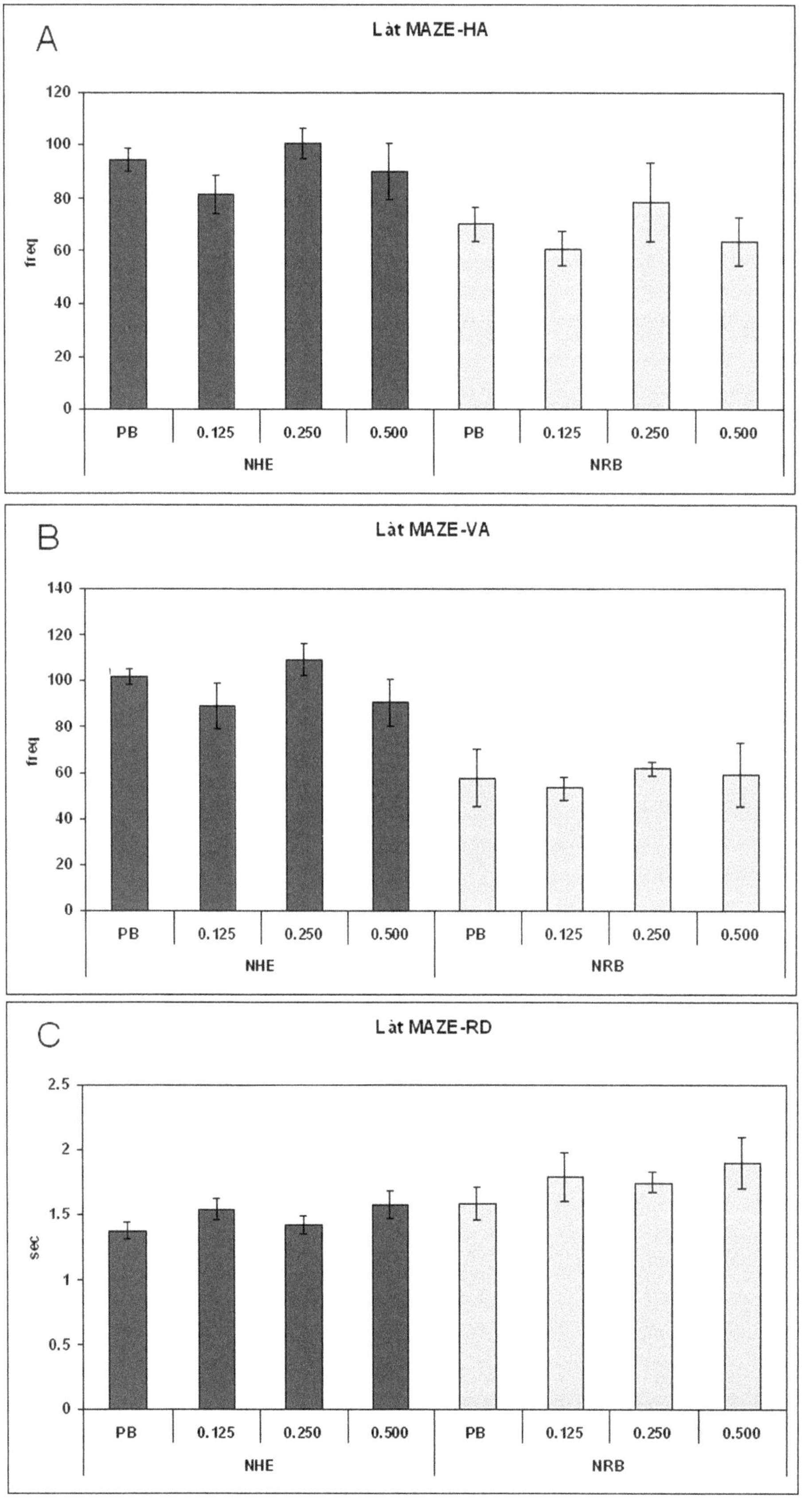

Figure 1. Long term behavioural effects of prepuberal subchronic LP-211 treatment on activity and non selective attention in the Làt maze for adult NHE and NRB rats. The frequency of corner crossings (A), the frequency of rearings (B), and their duration (C) after vehicle or treatment with 0.125, 0.250 or 0.500 mg/kg LP-211 are reported as mean ± SEM, (N = 6/group). For statistical analysis see the Results section.

NRB rats (Figure 4B). Moreover, there was an increased L-Asp/L-Leu ratio ($F = 7.887$, $df = 2/14$, $p<0.005$) for the 0.250 mg/kg dose in the NHE line (Figure 4A). The increased L-Glu in the PFC and L-Asp in the VS, produced by the 0.250 mg/kg dose within the NHE line, were the most relevant findings from the point of view of fronto-striatal cross talk.

Long-term effects of LP-211 on neuronal substrate in adult rats

Long term changes in neural substrates were detected using, as molecular probes, the synaptic transmission markers dopamine transporter (DAT), NMDAR1 subunit and calcium-calmodulin-dependent kinase type II alfa (CaMKIIα). DAT has been chosen as presynaptic marker [25,26], NMDAR1 as postsynaptic marker [27], whereas CaMKIIα served as an intracellular coincidence detector device [28]. Data pertaining to specific brain areas are shown in Figures 5, 6, 7, 8, and 9.

Ex-vivo levels of DAT protein. In the PFC, the one-way ANOVA on the DAT level of NHE rats, treated with vehicle, 0.125 mg/kg or 0.250 mg/kg LP-211, showed a significant reduction at 0.125 mg/kg dose ($F = 14.02$; $df = 1/9$; $p<0.006$) (Figure 5A). This reduction was about 20% of the vehicle control. The dose of 0.250 mg/kg had no significant effect. Conversely, no significant difference was found in the PFC of NRB rats (Figure 5B). In the DS, separate one-way ANOVAs showed no significant effects due to treatment on DAT level of NHE and NRB rats (Figure 5A–B). In the VS, the one-way ANOVA on DAT level of NHE rats, treated with vehicle or LP-211, showed a significant treatment effect only at the 0.250 mg/kg dose (Figure 5A). In fact, there was an increase in DAT protein level ($F = 14.39$; $df = 1/10$; $p<0.004$) that accounted for 100%. In contrast, no significant differences were observed again in NRB rats (Figure 5B). Finally, within the Mesencephalon (ME), the separate one-way ANOVAs, on DAT level for NHE and NRB rats, showed no significant effect due to prepuberal treatment with vehicle or LP-211 (Figure 5A–B).

Ex vivo levels NMDAR1 protein. The goal of these experiments was to verify whether the higher density of the NMDAR1 subunit, found in the PFC of NHE rats, could be modified by stress-associated vehicle injections and/or LP-211 treatment at adolescence. NMDAR1 protein level in the PFC of NHE and NRB rats, under basal conditions, are shown in Figure 6A. Separate one-way ANOVAs showed a higher NMDAR1 level in NHE rats ($F = 10.10$; $df = 1/7$; $p<0.019$). This increase was about 75% compared to the NRB controls. A higher level of NMDAR1 was also found within the VS (Figure 6B) of NHE rats, but one-way ANOVA showed no significant difference versus controls.

NMDAR1 protein levels in the brain areas (PFC; DS; VS) of NHE rats, treated with vehicle, 0.125 mg/kg or 0.250 mg/kg LP-211, are shown in Figure 7A. The separate one-way ANOVAs revealed no significant differences for NMDAR1 levels in the PFC, the DS and the VS of NHE rats, and this for all LP-211 treatment dosages. No significant changes were identified from the analysis of the PFC and DS data from NRB rats (Figure 7B). In the VS of NRB rats, treated with LP-211 at 0.125 mg/kg dose, the protein level was about 45% of that found in the vehicle-treated controls ($F = 18.65$; $df = 1/8$; $p<0.003$). A very similar but not significant reduction was observed for the 0.250 mg/kg dose.

Ex-vivo levels of CaMKIIα protein. The spatio-temporal coincidence detector CaMKIIα [28] was chosen for its integrator function in the intracellular traffic signalling, in relation to complex behaviours. Therefore, LP-211 treatment could modify this molecular device. CaMKIIα protein levels were analysed by western blot in the forebrain of NHE and compared to NRB rats, to determine the long-term effect of the adolescent treatment with vehicle, 0.125 mg/kg or 0.250 mg/kg LP-211 (Figure 8). Separate one-way ANOVAs on NHE and NRB rats showed, under basal conditions, a lower level of CaMKIIα in the PFC ($F = 6.19$; $df = 1/7$; $p<0.042$) of NHE compared to NRB rats (Figure 8A). This reduction accounted for 29.6% of the NRB level assumed as 100%. By contrast, an increased protein level was observed in the DS ($F = 6.13$; $df = 1/11$; $p<0.033$; Figure 8B). No significant differences were observed in the VS (Figure 8C). Long lasting effects of LP-211 prepuberal treatment were not observed in NHE and NRB rats (Figure 9A and B, respectively).

Discussion

The rationale for these studies was to investigate whether and to what extent a prepuberal subchronic stimulation of serotonin 7 subtype receptors (5-HT7-R), by the selective LP-211 agonist, would produce long term effect on adult behaviour, amino acid transmitters and synaptic markers. This was carried out using a validated animal model of hyperactivity and attention deficit, the NHE line, and compared to the NRB control rats.

A prepuberal subchronic design was chosen based on the assumption that i) the prepuberal period is "critical" for the organisation of neural networks in the developing forebrain, and that these sites are sensitive to genotype x environment interactions [29]; ii) that repeated administration of a 5-HT7-targeting agonist would trigger a cascade of events leading eventually to enhanced neural plasticity [30–32].

By using a multi-disciplinary approach, we show that adolescent exposure to LP-211 yields long lasting changes on adult behaviour, improving spatial attention in a dose dependent manner, associated with modified pre/post synaptic markers.

Long term behavioural effects persisting into adulthood

Prepuberal subchronic treatment apparently modified neural circuits underlying locomotor activity, NSA and SSA, as monitored in adulthood by exposure to two spatial novelty paradigms (i.e. Làt and Olton mazes). Under basal conditions, the NHE rats showed a higher frequency of leanings than NRB rats [14]. In NHE rats, 0.125 mg/kg LP-211 during adolescence reduced adult horizontal activity. The sub-chronic prepuberal treatment with the intermediate 0.250 mg/kg LP-211 dose produced significantly improved SSA that persisted into adulthood, even though it had no long-term effect on the frequency of rearings and leanings. The performance of these animals in the Olton's maze was almost perfect, indicating enhanced attention to spatial information and suggesting improved hippocampal function. The LP-211 treatment of adolescent rats has been recently demonstrated [33] to rearrange forebrain networks, with a central role of hippocampal connections, a finding which in turn confirms the emerging importance of 5-HT7 receptors for learning and memory processes. Thus, results are consistent with previous reports in rats [13,34].

In particular, the stimulation of 5-HT(7) receptors could alternatively have been induced by a mixed 5-HT(1A/7) agonist with the help of a 5-HT(1A) selective antagonist [35–37]. This classic approach has been presently overcome by the availability of a direct 5-HT(7) agonist. It has been suggested that 5-HT(7) stimulation impairs short-term memory while improving long-term memory, and that acquisition requires silencing of 5-HT(7) while consolidation requires its activation [13,34,38]. For instance, 5-HT(7) antagonists are able to reverse a working memory deficit [39]. No effect has been reported under our experimental

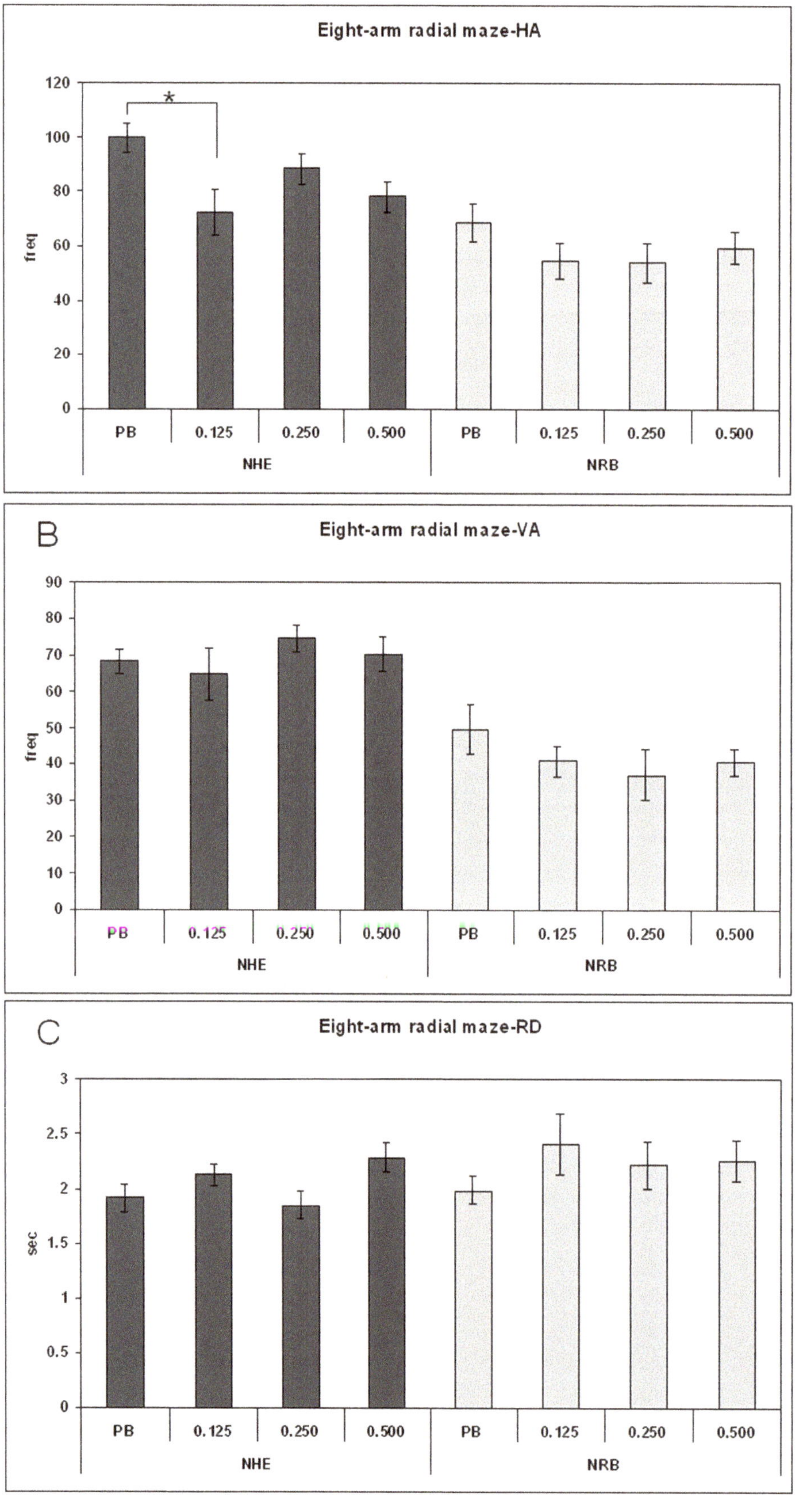

Figure 2. Long term behavioural effects of prepuberal subchronic LP-211 treatment on activity and non selective attention in the Olton maze for adult NHE and NRB rats. The horizontal activity (A), the frequency of rearings (B) and their duration (C) after vehicle or treatment with 0.125, 0.250 or 0.500 mg/kg LP-211 are reported as mean ± SEM, (N = 6/group). For statistical analysis see the Results section (* $p<0.01$).

conditions (of prepuberal subchronic LP-211 exposure) on anxiety level, as monitored by elevated Zero-maze in the NHE rat line [40]. Therefore, we hypothesize that the beneficial effect of LP-211 on SSA might be due to enhanced attentive processes/mechanisms rather than to reduced emotionality. The absence of an effect by LP-211 on behavioural variables in the Làt maze, and the reduced horizontal activity in the Olton's maze, might be tentatively explained by the differential effect of 5-HT(7) stimulation on egocentric versus allocentric spatial mapping [38]. Indeed, spatial mapping in these two paradigms reveals a different neural mechanism: egocentric in the Làt maze and allocentric in the Olton's maze [41]. Thus, we have identified a second significant effect on spatial orientation, in addition to that induced previously by intranasal dopamine (INDA) treatment with the 0.150 mg/kg dose [42].

Long term effects on amino acids and synaptic markers into adulthood

Excitatory amino acids. The ratio of Glutamate and Aspartate over Leucine, an amino acid not involved in neuro-

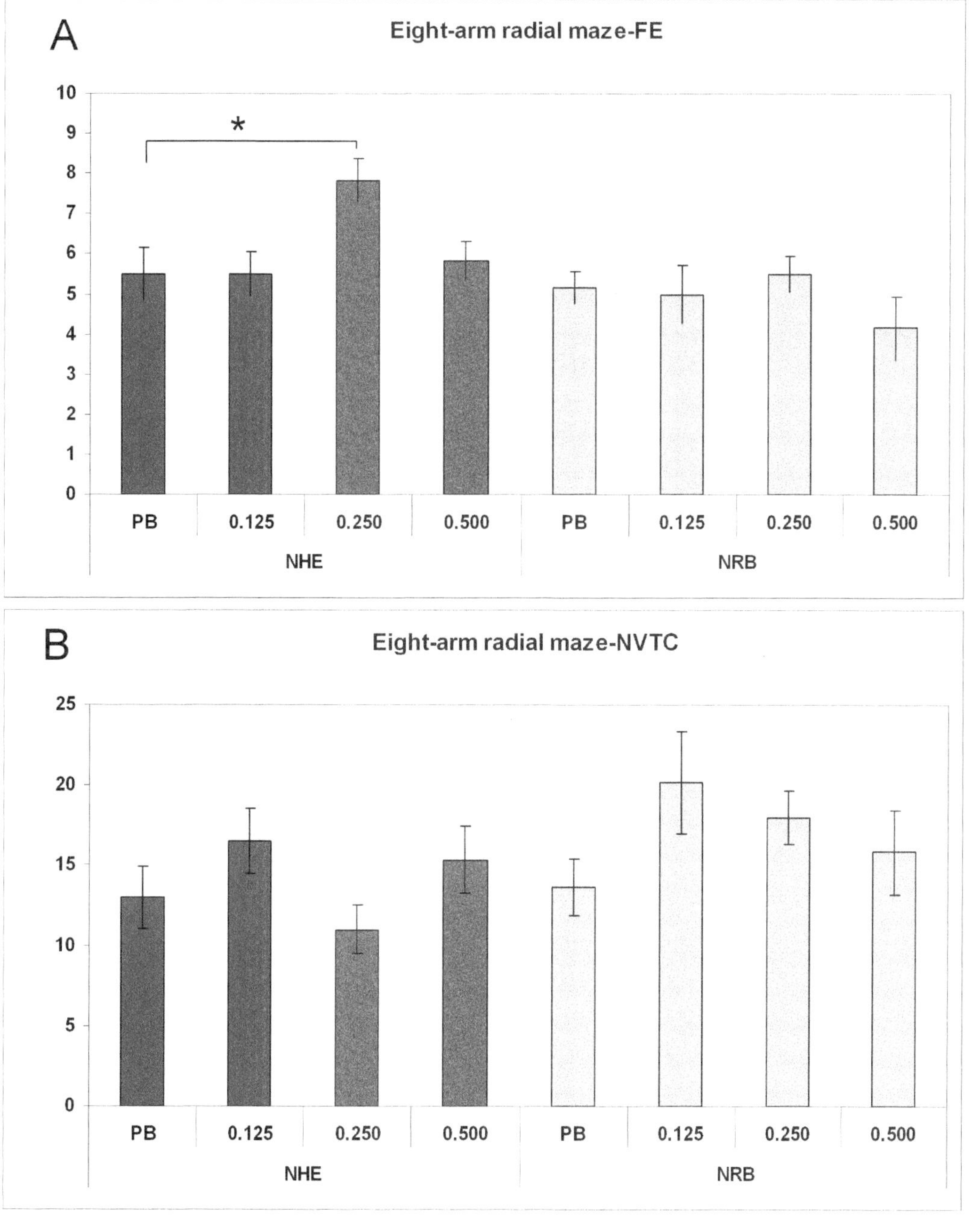

Figure 3. Long term behavioural effects of prepuberal subchronic LP-211 treatment in the Olton maze. Spatial selective attention: the position of first repetitive arm visit (FE; panel A) and number of arm visits before all arms are visited (NVTC; panel B) are reported for the NRB and NHE rats. An efficient rat will explore the eight arms only one time, thus the best score should be 9 for first error, and 8 for number of arm visits to criterion. Data after vehicle or treatment with 0.125, 0.250 or 0.500 mg/kg LP-211 are presented as mean ± SEM, (N = 6/group). For statistical analysis see the Results section (* $p<0.01$).

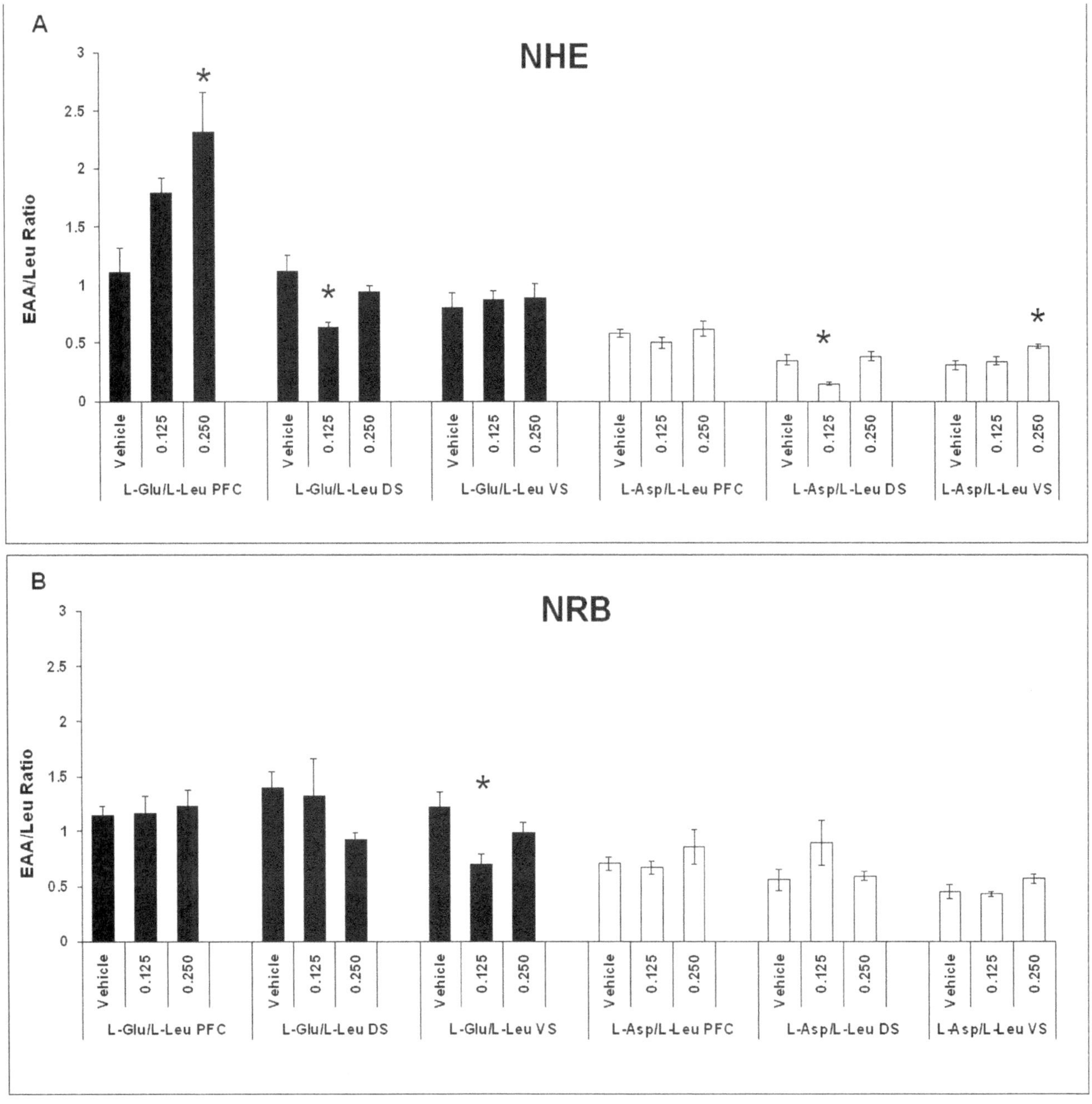

Figure 4. Level of Glu/Leu (black) and Asp/Leu (white) expressed as ratio in PFC, DS and VS of NHE (panel A) and NRB (panel B) rats. Data after vehicle or treatment with 0.125 or 0.250 mg/kg LP-211 are presented as mean ± SEM, (N = 6/group). For statistical analysis see the Results section (* $p < 0.02$).

transmission, pertained only to the soluble forms and was comparable to that measured in micro-dialysis [24]. This was presently an attempt to study, within *ex vivo* tissues, the compartmentalisation of excitatory amino acids in the mammalian brain. The soluble form includes amino acids that can be washed out with cold saline together with part of the neuro-glial component. Amino acids are distributed in three main heterogeneous pools, for which a homeostasis has been proposed by Kalivas [43]. These include a very large metabolic pool (10 milliMoles) of neuro-glial origin, a smaller vesicular pool and an even smaller extra synaptic pool [44]. In addition, they are not independent as L-Glu, first stored in the glial pool, is transferred to the neuron as glutamine, then is deaminated back to L-Glu and finally packed into vescicles to be secreted into the synaptic cleft. Therefore, and even though the metabolic compartment overwhelms the others by its size (10 mM), the higher level of L-Glu should be proportionally distributed among the three pools. On the other hand, L-Asp was measured, as mentioned in the Introduction, because of its hypothesised role in the formation of NMDA molecules, which are agonists at the NMDA receptor sites. Therefore, L-Asp data should be considered in conjunction with NMDAR1 binding sites (see below). We predict that the beneficial effect of adolescent LP-211 is due to altered amino acid transmission. This, in turn, may prevent glutamate neurotoxicity

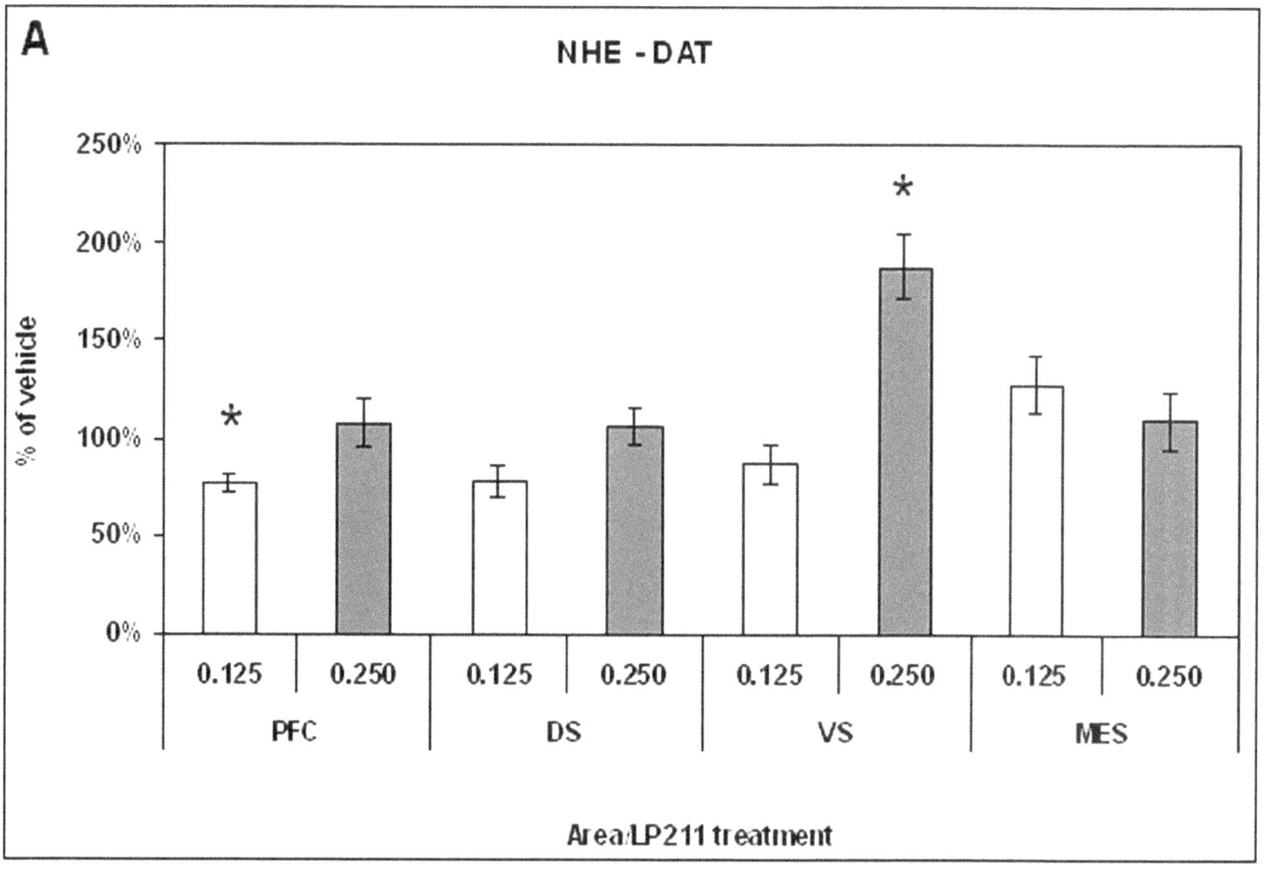
A
NHE - DAT
250%
200%
150%
100%
50%
0%
% of vehicle
*
*
0.125
0.250
PFC
DS
VS
MES
Area/LP211 treatment

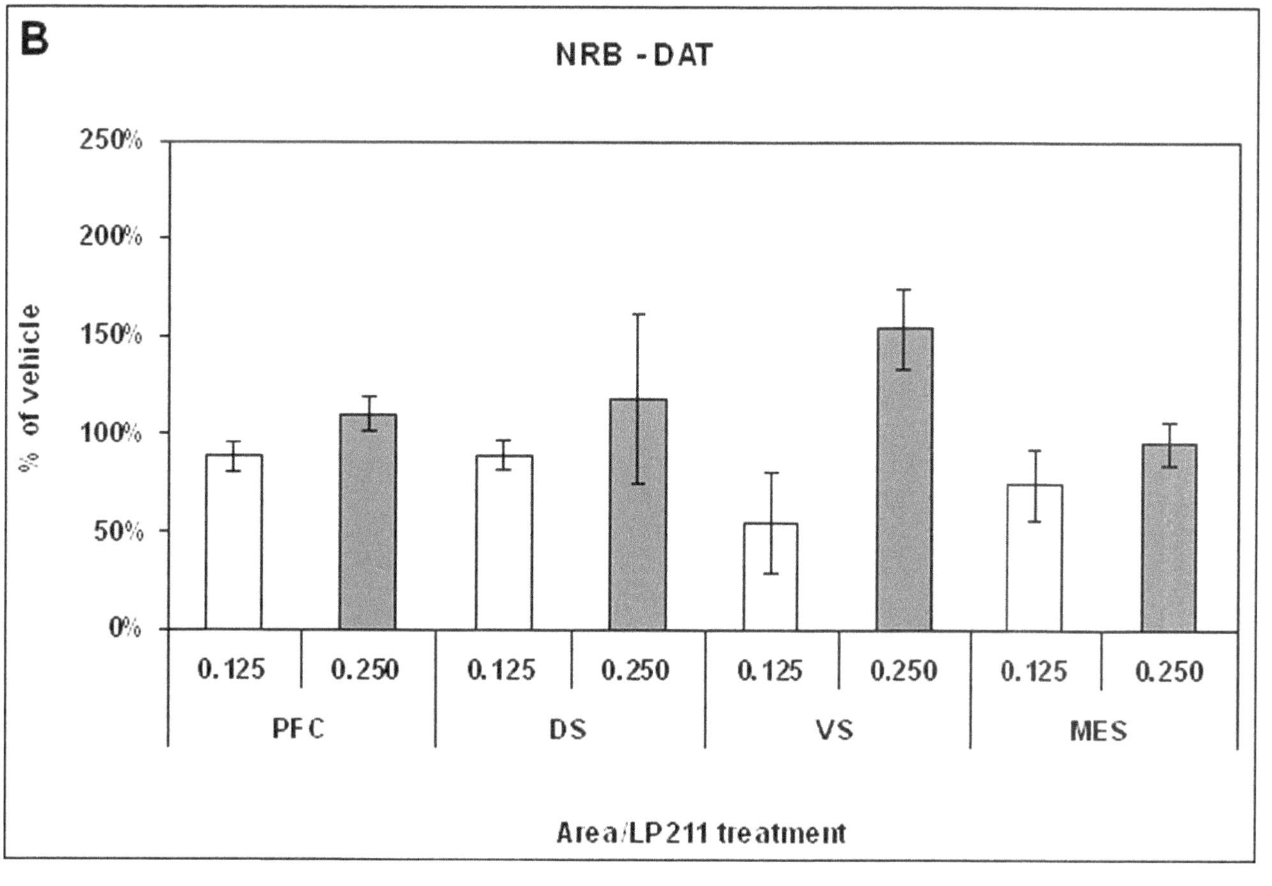
B
NRB - DAT
250%
200%
150%
100%
50%
0%
% of vehicle
0.125
0.250
PFC
DS
VS
MES
Area/LP211 treatment

Figure 5. Level of DAT protein measured by western blot in the PFC, DS, VS and ME of NHE (panel A) and NRB (panel B) rats after adolescent treatment with 0.125 or 0.250 mg/kg LP-211. Data are given as % of vehicle response ± standard error. For statistical analysis see the Results section (* $p<0.05$).

- that imaging studies have shown to be the basis for right fronto-striatal atrophy in ADHD [45,46]. Adolescent exposure to LP-211 yielded indeed two major consequences: i) it decreased L-Glu and L-Asp in the DS after treatment with the 0.125 mg/kg dose and ii) it increased L-Glu in PFC and L-Asp in the VS after treatment with the 0.250 mg/kg dose, both in the NHE rats. L-Glu also decreased, after prepuberal subchronic treatment with 0.125 mg/kg LP-211, only in the VS of control NRB rats. Thus, prepuberal exposure to serotonergic stimulation permanently modifies neural areas and forebrain circuits underlying activity, motivation and attention, but not emotionality. By focussing on the prefronto-striatal interface, the most relevant change was produced by adolescent exposure to 0.250 mg/kg LP-211, with persistent amino acid changes found in both PFC and VS of an animal model for hyperactivity and attention deficit.

Synaptic markers. The presynaptic DAT, the post-synaptic NMDAR1 and CaMKIIα markers, studied under basal conditions, showed that NMDAR1 levels within the PFC of NHE rats were higher, in comparison with NRB rats; by contrast, no differences were found within the DS. Moreover, NHE rats showed a significant reduction in the amount of CaMKIIα within the PFC, while previous findings [47,14] have shown that DAT level within the PFC is higher for NHE. Conversely, an increased level of CaMKIIα was detected in the DS while the VS did not show any difference between NHE and NRB rats. Finally, the

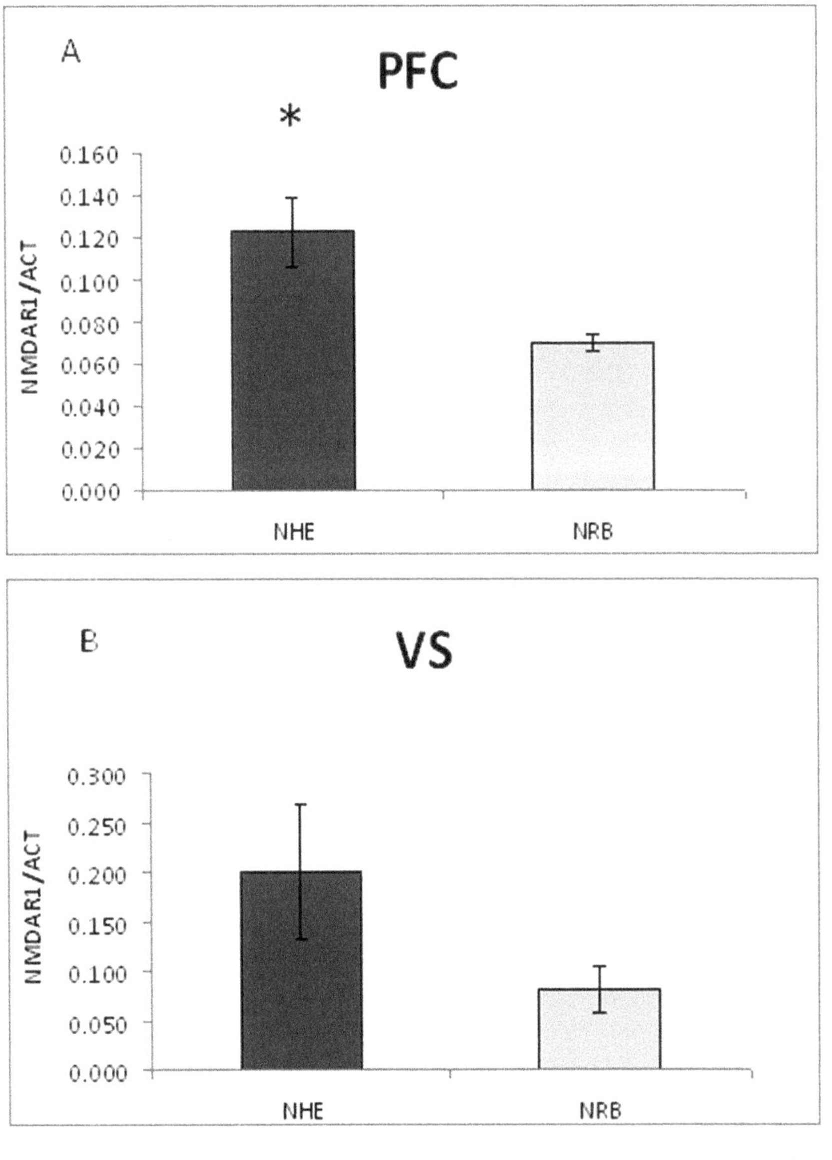

Figure 6. Level of NMDAR1 protein measured in the PFC (panel A) and VS (panel B) of NHE and NRB rats under basal conditions. Data are presented as mean ± standard error. For statistical analysis see the Results section (* $p<0.05$).

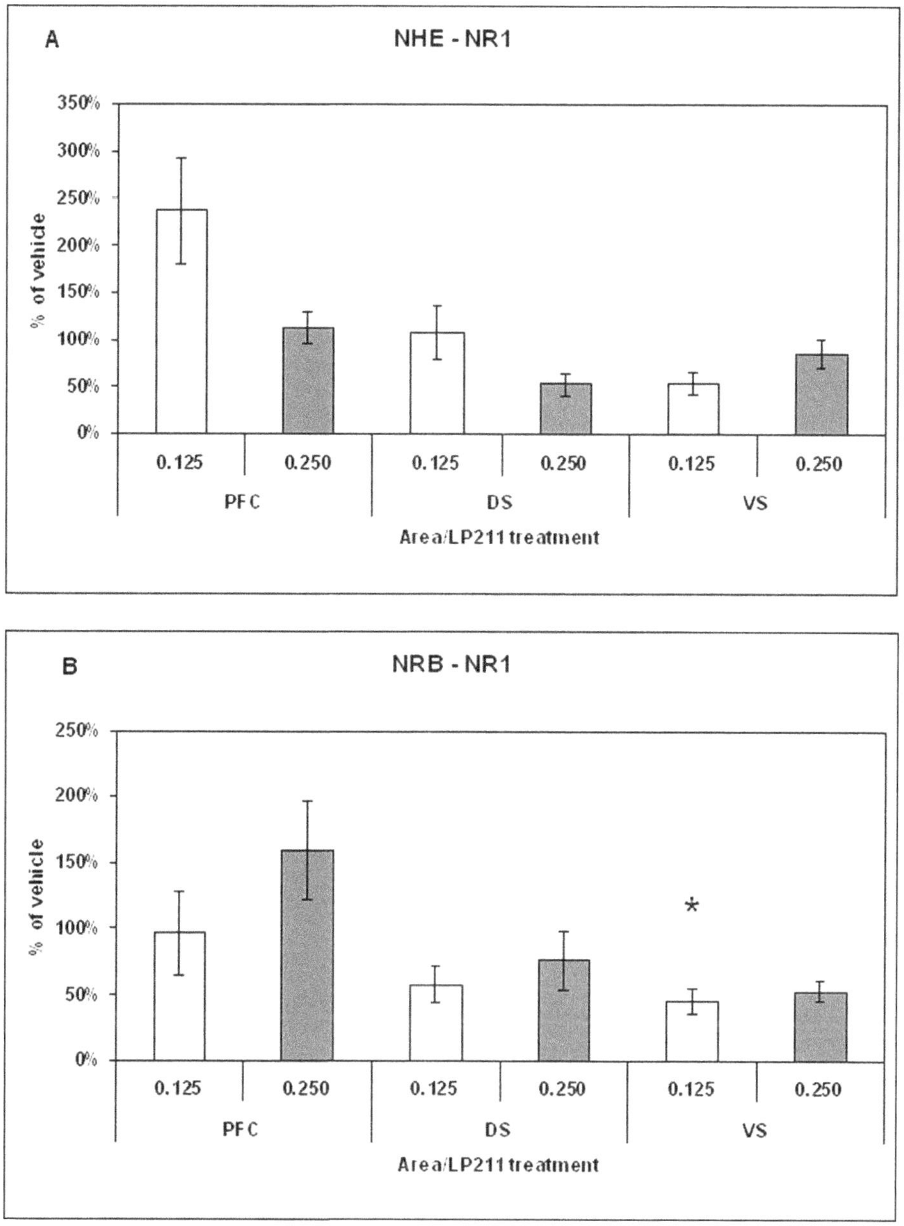

Figure 7. Level of NMDAR1 protein measured by western blot in the forebrain sites of NHE (panel A) and NRB (panel B) rats after adolescent treatment with 0.125 or 0.250 mg/kg LP-211. Data are presented as % of vehicle response ± standard error. For statistical analysis see the Results section (* $p<0.05$).

level of CaMKIIα in the mesencephalon - though very low [48] - was found to be higher in NHE rats.

Treatment with LP-211 during adolescence gave the following findings that persisted into adulthood: 1) DAT level in the PFC was decreased at the 0.125 mg/kg dose and conversely increased in the VS at the 0.250 mg/kg, but only in NHE rats. The adolescent prepuberal treatment produced no differences in all areas of NRB control subjects; 2) NMDAR1 was decreased in the VS of NRB rats when previously faced with the prepuberal subchronic exposure to a 0.125 mg/kg dose; 3) prepuberal subchronic LP-211 exposure exerted no long-term effect on CaMKIIα levels in either line and in all areas. It is noteworthy that CaMKIIα level has been reported to be lower in the forebrain of animal models for ADHD, such as SHR and NHE rats [49–51].

Altogether, the most relevant change was produced by the 0.250 mg/kg dose of LP-211: adolescent exposure to this dose generated, as a sequel into adulthood, an improved spatial orientation as well as persistently elevated L-Asp and DAT levels in the VS and L-Glu levels in the PFC. The simplest interpretation of these results is that the cross-talk between the PFC and VS might have been improved.

Prefronto-striatal interface in model systems

The "dialogue" between the PFC and both the DS and VS, occurring through glutamate and aspartate, is modulated mainly by DA, NA, 5-HT and histamine. Our experimental evidence suggests that only two signaling modulators (DA and 5-HT) are effective in inducing long-term changes within neural networks,

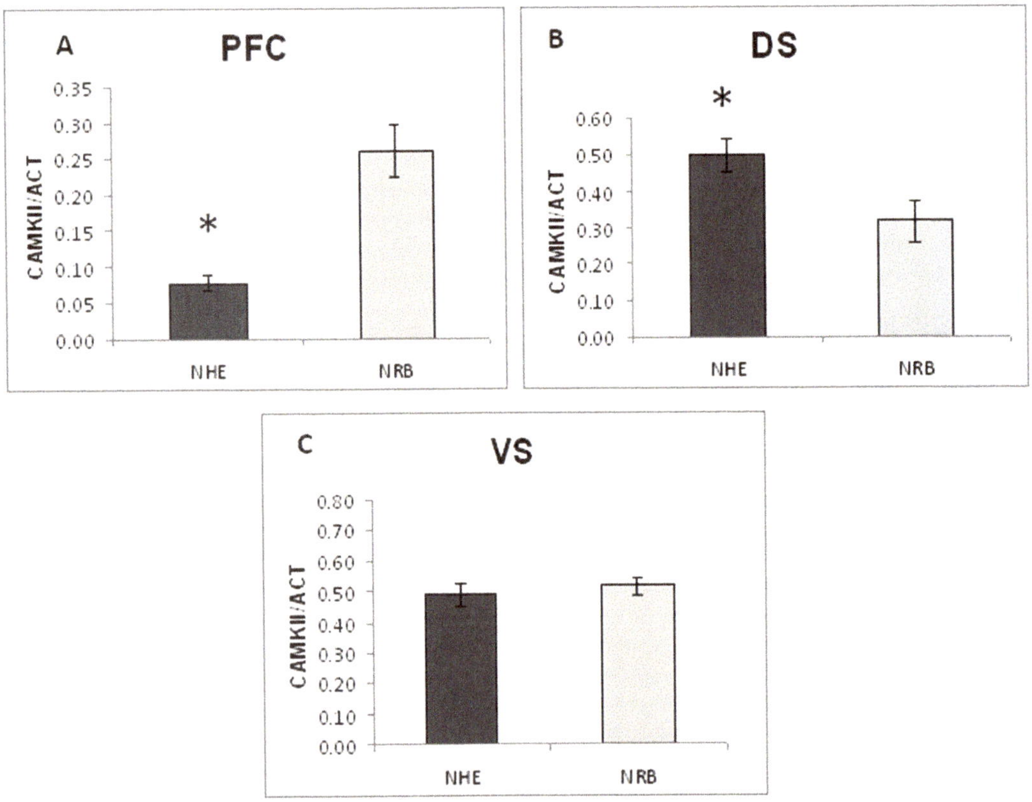

Figure 8. Level of CaMKIIα protein measured in the PFC (panel A), DS (panel B) and VS (panel C) of NHE and NRB rats under basal conditions. Data are presented as mean ± standard error. For statistical analysis see the Results section (* $p<0.05$).

which are known to underlie attentive and motivational processes. In fact, prepuberal subchronic treatments with MPH and ATX, which block the reuptake of DA/NE and NE, respectively, did not similarly alter the SSA in adult rats, in spite of significant effects on DA, NA, 5-HT and metabolites at the prefronto-striatal interface in NHE rats [52]. By contrast, we found previously that an INDA-based prepuberal subchronic treatment is effective at a low dose (0.075 mg/kg) [53].

This profile of effects is likely to be explained because DA has the following functions: i) at mesencephalic level, DA can interact with DA-D2 autoreceptors, associated with hyper-polarising potassium conductances, thereby reducing the firing rate of DA neurons [54] and ii) at 0.150 mg/kg dose, DA can induce the synthesis of neurotrophic factors of the BDNF type [55]. On the other hand, the MPH-induced DA increase, caused by MPH itself and ATX, clearly suggests that the DA signal is much more effective in the absence of other modulator signals.

The fact that the developmental stimulation of 5-HT7 receptors (by the selective agonist LP-211) is just as effective as DA-related drugs in modifying the long-term SSA in NHE rats requires further experimental investigations. One clue is given by the fact that 5-HT7 is found to be functionally linked to forebrain limbic networks, which comprise the amygdala, VS, orbital PFC, and thalami [33]. Moreover, a recent report [56] demonstrated that serotonin acts on inhibitory interneurons in the PFC through Gs proteins. The PFC-mediated inhibitory control over subcortical structures might well be mediated by 5-HT7 receptor via its basal level of activation and possibly through neuroplastic processes [57].

Therefore, we can assume that the positive effect of adolescent exposure to 0.250 mg/kg LP-211 on SSA, in association with enhanced levels of amino acids and DAT in the PFC and VS, is possibly due to the stimulation of serotonergic more effective transducers independent of CaMKIIα. Alternatively, this positive effect might be explained by more complex circuits, leading - eventually - to the re-modeling of cognitive maps: in this context, recent findings [33] point to enhanced transmission between limbic networks including the hippocampus, that might explain the improved SSA (essential to build spatial maps). Furthermore, the same approach has confirmed the hypothesis that the mesocortical DA branch is, in the NHE rat model, at a higher functional state [14,16,17]. In addition, the subchronic treatments using other selective agonists of the 5-HT7 receptors, during the prepuberal period, may induce medium/long term effects on selective spatial attention, underpinned by synaptic markers such as DAT, NMDAR1 but not CaMKIIα.

Finally, the concentration of CaMKIIα [28], which is a coincidence spatio-temporal detector device, was reduced in the PFC of NHE rats under basal conditions and increased in the DS as compared to NRB. Interestingly, the reduced CaMKIIα levels in the PFC were associated with a reduced spatial orientation of the NHE rats in the Olton's maze. On the other hand, adolescent exposure to LP-211 did not change the level of CaMKIIα in the forebrain, but significantly improved the SSA. In fact, as mentioned in the Introduction, CaMKIIα is a molecular device that integrates neural signals at higher complexity levels, as demonstrated by Yovell and Abrams [58]. They studied the phosphorylation of the Aplysia membrane proteins by this kinase in the presence of serotonin. The CaMKIIα protein is localised

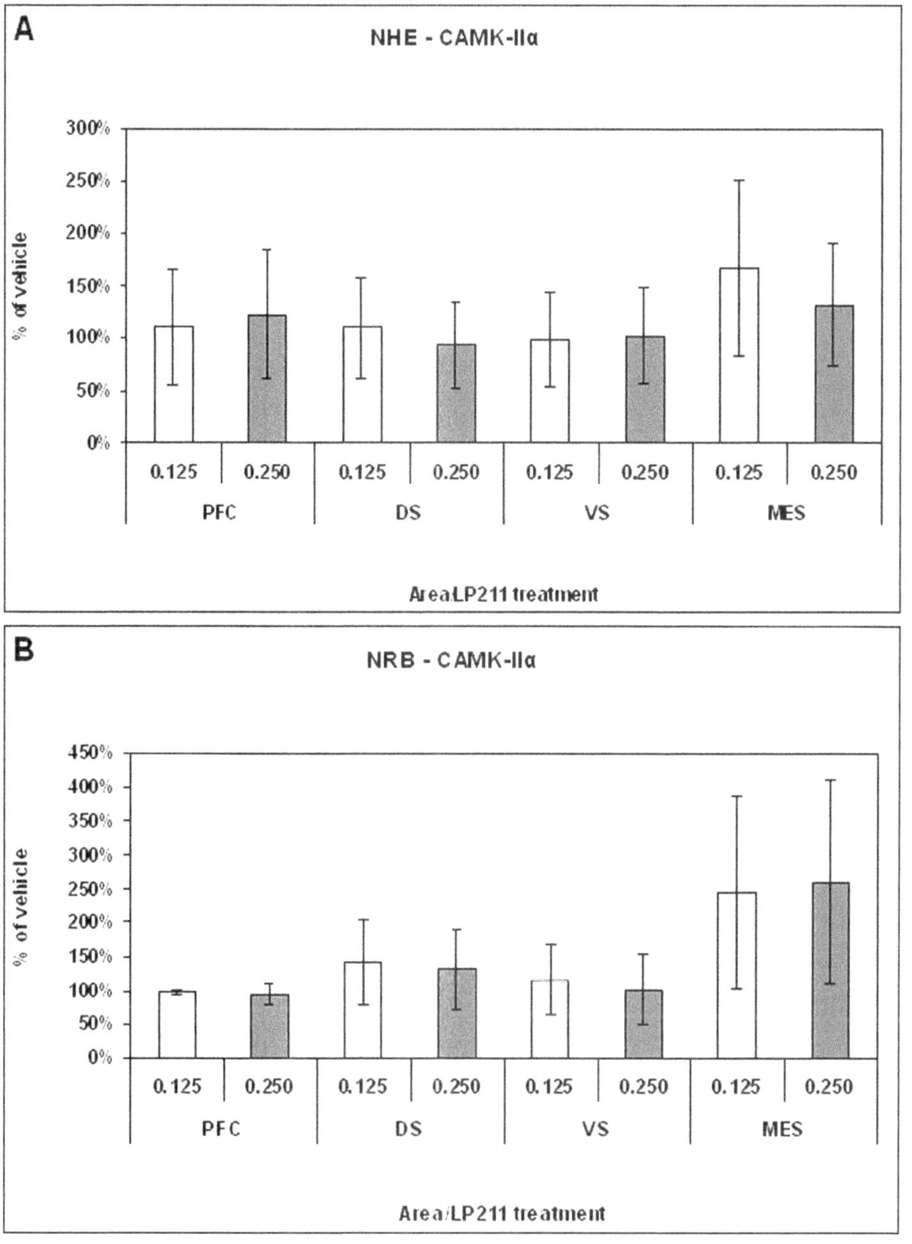

Figure 9. Level of CaMKIIα protein measured by western blot in NHE (panel A) and NRB (panel B) rats after adolescent treatment with 0.125 or 0.250 mg/kg LP-211. Data are presented as % of vehicle response ± standard error.

mainly at post-synaptic level, but it is also present at pre-synaptic levels. The addition of calcium and serotonin within 8 sec significantly increased the phosphorylation of the Aplysia membrane proteins by the kinase, thereby demonstrating a classical Pavlovian conditioning in a test tube [58,59].

Interestingly, recent findings from our laboratory do point to a disintegrated interface in the PFC of NHE rats, as monitored by immuno-chemical markers [60]. This, in turn, might explain a functional "vulnus" in the default mode network that includes the medial PFC, anterior cingolate, as well as lateral-parietal and temporal cortices, as proposed in [61–65].

Materials and Methods

Animals

Prepuberal male rats of the Sprague–Dawley-derived NHE line (n = 24) and of the NRB control line (n = 24), from our animal colony, were used throughout the experiments. Rats were housed in groups of two inside Makrolon cages (425 mm×266 mm×150 mm, floor area 820 cm^2; Techniplast, Italy) under standard conditions. An artificial 12:12 reverse light–dark (LD) cycle was obtained by turning on the lights from 7 pm to 7 am. All other parameters fulfilled the requirements of the Guide for the Care and Use of Laboratory Animals, implemented by the Italian Legislative Decree 116/1992 that covers all scientific procedures involving the use of live animals. The European

Directive 2010/63 on the protection of animals used in scientific experiments, revisioning the Directive 86/609, is currently being enacted into Italian legislation, and will be applicable to future research protocols. All present experiments were covered by an authorisation from Ministero della Salute, for which ethical advice was issued from Istituto Superiore di Sanità (authorization to AGS, n. prot. 422/2009 dated 08-04-09, duration 36 months). The 3Rs principles were taken into account in order to seek for alternatives to animal use, to reduce the number of animals used and to refine the protocols for limitation of animal suffering.

Prepuberal treatment

At weaning on postnatal day (pnd) 28, rats were randomly assigned to treatment and control groups (n = 6/group), which received i.p. vehicle or LP-211 (0.0, 0.125, 0.250 or 0.500 mg/kg). LP-211 was dissolved in phosphate buffer (vehicle) with 1% and 2% DMSO for the lower doses and the highest one, respectively. Treatments were given daily during the dark phase between 10:00 am and 11:00 am, for 14 days from pnd 30–31 to 43–44, as already published [40]. Thirty days after last drug or vehicle injection, all the rats were tested in the Làt maze and, 24 hrs later, in the eight-arm radial maze (Olton's maze).

Drugs

A new selective 5-HT7 receptor agonist, namely N-(4-cyanophenylmethyl)-4-(2-diphenyl)-1-piperazinehexanamide (LP-211), was synthesized and provided by EL and ML [12]; drug dosage was chosen according to previous experience [40] by GL and WA. DMSO was obtained from Sigma-Aldrich (Milano, Italy).

Làt-maze

Apparatus. The Làt-maze consisted of a 60 cm×60 cm× 40 cm box made of special poly-vinyl-chloride (PVC) material (KÖMACEL^R), closed by a cover of the same material. A smaller transparent-plastic 30 cm×30 cm×40 cm box was inserted in the middle, thus providing a 60 cm long, 15 cm wide and 40 cm high square-shaped exploratory corridor. See [66] for details. The box was illuminated by a white, cold 4 W lamp placed 60 cm above the floor in the centre of the cover, providing 0.1–0.2 μW/cm^2. A set of two such boxes was located in a sound attenuated experimental room.

Procedure. At the beginning of the dark phase of an inverted light/dark L/D cycle (between 9 am and 4 pm), the rats were individually exposed to the Làt-maze and allowed to explore the corridor for 10 min. In order to minimise the interference with the arousal state, pairs of rats from the same home cage were tested at the same time. The animals' behaviours were monitored by a high resolution CCD camera and stored on a DVD recorder to be analyzed off-line. The number of corner crossings (HA), frequency (VA) and duration (RD) of rearings on hind-limbs, or leanings against the walls with one or both forepaws, were measured in 1-min blocks. The reliability index was quite high ($r = 0.914$; $df = 198$; $p<0.001$). At the end of the test, the fecal boluses were counted and the floor was wiped with a wet sponge.

Eight-arm radial maze (Olton's maze)

Apparatus. The apparatus consisted of eight arms (8 cm×60 cm) extending from an octagonal centre platform (18.5 cm diameter). The distance from the platform centre to the end of each arm was 69.25 cm. The apparatus was constructed of grey PVC with a smooth surface, and side walls (14 cm high, transparent Plexiglas). The maze was placed on the floor of a dimly lit room, surrounded by a circular higher wall without visual cues. Rat behaviour was monitored by a high resolution CCD camera and stored on DVD to be analysed off-line.

Procedure. In the Olton's maze, each rat was placed on the centre platform into a cardboard cylinder to avoid immediate escape into an arm. The trial began with the removal of the cylinder and the rat was allowed to explore. The main parameters considered in the Olton's maze were horizontal activity (HA: number of alley visits); frequency (VA) and duration (RD) of rearings on the hind-limbs. The number of arms visited before the first repetition occurred (first entry, FE), and number of arms visited before completion of visits to all eight arms (number of visits to criterion, NVTC), were also recorded. The latter two indices are markers of non-reinforced SSA.

Dissection of brain areas

The animals were sacrificed by a guillotine at pnd 77. The brain was removed and put on a surface of ice-cold saline. After removal of the olfactory tubercles, the first coronal cut was made at 4.20 AP from Bregma, using the stereotaxic coordinates of *The Rat Brain Atlas* as reference [67]. By this method, a tiny tissue included both PFC and cingulate cortex area 1. The entire upper portion of the striatum (i.e. DS), which included the caudate-putamen (CPu) and globus pallidus (CG), was removed by a sagittal pinch extending between 2.20 and −3.8 AP, up to 7 mm DV in depth. Then, ventral striatum (i.e. VS) was removed by sagittal pinch between 2.70 to 0.48 AP, 1 mm from the midline and about 1 mm in depth, thus including the nucleus accumbens.

Amino acids

Extraction procedure. Vehicle, LP-211 0.125 and 0.250 mg/kg groups were analysed. The 0.500 mg/kg group was excluded because it did not show any significant effect in the behavioural analysis. Brain samples were homogenised in 1 ml ice-cold saline in an Eppendorf and centrifuged at 7,500 g at 4°C for 20 min. The supernatant was filtered and used for LC/MS/MS analysis of the free amino acids L-Glu, L-Asp and L-Leu.

Liquid chromatography/tandem mass spectrometry. The detection was performed using a Varian 310-MS triple quadrupole mass spectrometer (Varian, Palo Alto, CA, USA). All the analytes were detected in the positive ionisation mode and with selected reaction monitoring (SRM) mode (Table 1). The settings of the ESI source were as follows: spray voltage, 5000 V; capillary temperature 300°C; sheath gas pressure (spraying), 20 arbitrary units; auxiliary gas pressure (desolvating), 10 arbitrary units; and ion sweep gas pressure (curtain), 5 arbitrary units. The collision cell (Q2) pressure was 2.2 mTorr of argon. The collision energies were optimised for maximum detection of each product ion (Table 1). Chromatographic separation was achieved with a ProStar^{TM} 300 HPLC system (Varian, Palo Alto, CA, USA) on a Varian Polaris® C_{18}column (5 μm, 2.1 mm×100 mm) at a flow rate of 0.3 mL/min. The mobile phase consisted of aqueous 0.1% formic acid (A) and acetonitrile (B). Samples were eluted with a linear gradient from 10 to 90% B in 5 min. At 5:01 min, solvent B was decreased from 90% to 10% and remained constant for 5 min. The total run time was 10 min.

CaMKIIα, DAT, and NMDAR1

Protein extracts. Membrane and cytosolic protein fractions were prepared as described in [68] with minor modification. Tissues were homogenized in a glass/Teflon potter in cold 0.32 M sucrose buffer pH 7.4 containing 1 mM HEPES, 0.1 mM EGTA and 0.1 mM phenylmethylsulfonyl fluoride, in the presence of

Table 1. LC/MS/MS parameters.

Analyte	RT (min)	SRM transitions *(m/z)*	CE (eV)
Aspartate	1.36	134.0→134.0	4.0
		134.0→116.0	4.0
Glutamate	1.38	148.0→148.0	4.0
		148.0→130.0	7.5
Leucine	1.42	132.2→132.2	4.0
		132.2→86.0	10.0

commercial cocktails of protease (Roche, Monza, Italy) and phosphatase (Sigma-Aldrich) inhibitors. The homogenate was centrifuged at 1,000 g for 10 min resulting in a pellet (P1) that corresponded to the nuclear fraction. The supernatant (S1) was then centrifuged at 13,000 g for 15 min to obtain a clarified fraction of cytosolic proteins (S2) and a pellet (P2) corresponding to the crude membrane fraction. The latter was homogenised in a glass/Teflon potter in 1% Triton X-100 buffer containing 50 mM Tris-HCl pH 7,4–300 mM NaCl, 5 mM EDTA and 0,02% Sodium Azide. The total protein content was measured according to the Bradford Protein Assay procedure (Bio-Rad, Milan, Italy), using bovine serum albumin as the calibration standard.

Gel electrophoresis and immunoblotting. Sodium dodecyl sulfate-polyacrylamide gel electro-phoresis (SDS-PAGE) and transfer of proteins to nitrocellulose membranes were performed according to conventional methods with minor modifications. The proteins were solubilised in loading buffer at 54°C for 45 min, and then separated on 10% polyacrylamide gels and transferred onto PVDF membranes (GE Healthcare) in transfer buffer (25 mM Tris, 192 mM glycine, pH 8.3, 20% methanol). The membranes were incubated with blocking buffer, 5%ECL blocking agent (GE Healthcare) in PBST (0.1 M phosphate buffered saline, pH 7.4, 0.1% Tween-20), for 1 h at room temperature. The blots were incubated overnight at 4°C with one of the following primary antibodies: NMDAR1 (1:300 anti-NMDAR1; Chemicon-Millipore AB9864); CaMKIIα (1:2000 Anti-CaM Kinase IIα, Clone 6G9; Upstate-Millipore #05-532); DAT (1:500 anti-Dopamine Transporter; Millipore AB2231); internal standard: Actin (1:500 anti-Actin; Sigma A2066); or Actin (1:3000 anti–Actin, Clone C4; Chemicon-Millipore MAB1501).

After three 10 min washes in PBST, the blots were incubated for 1 h at room temperature with horseradish peroxidase-conjugated secondary antibody (anti-rabbit or anti-mouse ECL anti-rabbit IgG, HRP-linked Whole Ab; GE Healthcare NA934, NA931). After washing, immuno-complexes were visualised by chemiluminescence using the ECL western blotting kit (GE Healthcare) according to the manufacturer's instructions. All protein bands were within linear range of the standard curves, and were normalised to actin levels on the same membrane. Quantity One software (BioRad Laboratories, Hercules, CA, USA) was used for standardisation and quantisation of protein bands obtained by western blot analysis.

Statistics

The fulfilment of the requirements for parametric analysis (normality, variance, etc.) was assessed by specific tests (Kolmogorov–Smirnov and Levene, Box test of equality of covariance matrices) and appropriate transformations were used when necessary. Behavioural variables in the Làt and Olton's radial maze were submitted to a one-way factorial analysis of variance (ANOVA) for treatment followed by post-hoc test LSD for single comparison.

Defecation scores were submitted to a non-parametric test by Kruskal–Wallis. The rejection level was set at $p>0.05$ after correction of the alpha-level by the Hölm's procedure [69]. All statistical analyses on behavioural and neurochemical data were performed by SPSS software. All data are stored on a hard disk of a PC in our laboratory and a back-up copy in also saved in a mobile HD unit. They will be kept at least for the next ten years and can be made available on request.

Acknowledgments

L.A. Ruocco, A. Tino, and G.P. Boatto share equal first-authorship, as they lead the three cooperating groups. W. Adriani was PI of the Young Investigator "ADHD-sythe" (including the Second University of Naples, LAR as responsible of local unit) Project and the ERA-net "NeuroGen-MRI".

Author Contributions

Conceived and designed the experiments: LAR AGS WA AT GB. Performed the experiments: LAR CT MN AT CP PI FB. Analyzed the data: LAR UAGC AT MN CP PI FB. Contributed reagents/materials/analysis tools: LAR GB AT AGS EL ML CA. Wrote the paper: LAR AGS AT GB WA EC GL.

References

1. Sesack SR, Grace AA (2010) Cortico-Basal Ganglia reward network: microcircuitry. Neuropsychopharmacology 35: 27–47. 10.1038/npp.2009.93 [doi].
2. Arnsten AF, Wang MJ, Paspalas CD (2012) Neuromodulation of thought: flexibilities and vulnerabilities in prefrontal cortical network synapses. Neuron 76: 223–239. 10.1016/j.neuron.2012.08.038 [doi].
3. Hirano S, Yamada M (2013) Network analyses in neuroimaging studies. Brain Nerve 65: 659–667. 1416101517 [pii].
4. Arnsten AF (2009) Toward a new understanding of attention-deficit hyperactivity disorder pathophysiology: an important role for prefrontal cortex dysfunction. CNS Drugs 23 Suppl 1: 33–41. 10.2165/00023210-200923000-00005 [doi].
5. Sadile AG (1993) What can genetic models tell us about behavioral plasticity? Rev Neurosci 4: 287–303.
6. Gironi Carnevale UA, Vitullo E, Varriale B, Ruocco LA, Sadile AG (2007) A classical Mendelian cross-breeding study of the Naples high and low excitability rat lines. Behav Brain Res 183: 130–140.
7. Mayer ML (2011) Emerging models of glutamate receptor ion channel structure and function. Structure 19: 1370–1380. 10.1016/j.str.2011.08.009 [doi].
8. Niciu MJ, Kelmendi B, Sanacora G (2012) Overview of glutamatergic neurotransmission in the nervous system. Pharmacol Biochem Behav 100: 656–664. 10.1016/j.pbb.2011.08.008 [doi].

9. Marmiroli P, Cavaletti G (2012) The glutamatergic neurotransmission in the central nervous system. Curr Med Chem 19: 1269–1276. CMC-EPUB-20120217-001 [pii].
10. Bauer M, Praschak-Rieder N, Kasper S, Willeit M (2012) Is dopamine neurotransmission altered in prodromal schizophrenia? A review of evidence. Curr Pharm Des 18: 1568–1579. CPD-EPUB-20120118-011 [pii].
11. Genro JP, Kieling C, Rohde LA, Hutz MH (2010) Attention-deficit/hyperactivity disorder and the dopaminergic hypotheses. Expert Rev Neurother 10: 587–601. 10.1586/ern.10.17 [doi].
12. Hedlund PB, Leopoldo M, Caccia S, Sarkisyan G, Fracasso C, et al. (2010) LP-211 is a brain penetrant selective agonist for the serotonin 5-HT(7) receptor. Neurosci Lett 481: 12–16. 10.1016/j.neulet.2010.06.036 [doi].
13. Leopoldo M, Lacivita E, Berardi F, Perrone R, Hedlund PB (2011) Serotonin 5-HT7 receptor agents: Structure-activity relationships and potential therapeutic applications in central nervous system disorders. Pharmacol Ther 129: 120–148. 10.1016/j.pharmthera.2010.08.013 [doi].
14. Ruocco LA, Sadile AG, Gironi Carnevale UA (2009) Modeling the Mesocortical Variant of ADHD: the Naples High Excitability rats. In: Gordon S.M, Mitchell A.M., editors. Attention Deficit Hyperactivity Disorder. New York: Nova Science. pp. 85–106.
15. Davids E, Zhang K, Tarazi FI, Baldessarini RJ (2003) Animal models of attention-deficit hyperactivity disorder. Brain Res Rev 42: 1–21.
16. Viggiano D, Vallone D, Welzl H, Sadile AG (2002) The Naples high-and low excitability rats: selective breeding, behavioral profile, morphometry and molecular biology of the mesocortical dopamine system. Behav Genet 32: 315–333.
17. Viggiano D, Vallone D, Ruocco LA, Sadile AG (2003) Behavioural, pharmacological, morpho-functional molecular studies reveal a hyper-functioning mesocortical dopamine system in an animal model of ADHD. Neurosci Biobehav Rev 27: 683–689.
18. Broadhurst PL (1960) Experiments in psychogenetics: application of biometrical genetics to the inheritance of behavior. In: Eysenck HJ, editor. Experiments in personality. Vol. I. Psychogenetics and Psycho-pharmacology. London: Routledge, Regan Paul. pp. 1–102.
19. Girault JA (2012) Integrating neurotransmission in striatal medium spiny neurons. Adv Exp Med Biol 970: 407–429. 10.1007/978-3-7091-0932-8_18 [doi].
20. Ruocco LA, Di Pizzo A, Gironi Carnevale UA, Murolo M, Sadile AG, et al. (2009) Excitatory amino acids in the forebrain of the naples high-excitability rats: neurochemical and behavioural effects of subchronic D-aspartate and its diethyl ester prodrug. Behav Brain Res 198: 37–44.
21. Errico F, Rossi S, Napolitano F, Catuogno V, Topo E, et al. (2008) D-aspartate prevents corticostriatal long-term depression and attenuates schizophrenia-like symptoms induced by amphetamine and MK-801. J Neurosci 28: 10404–10414. 10.1523/JNEUROSCI.1618-08.2008 [doi].
22. D'Aniello A (2007) D-Aspartic acid: an endogenous amino acid with an important neuro-endocrine role. Brain Res Rev 53: 215–234.
23. Ruocco LA, Gironi Carnevale UA, Sica A, Arra C, Topo E, et al. (2009) Elevated forebrain excitatory L-glutamate, L-aspartate and D-aspartate in Naples high-excitability rats. Behav Brain Res 198: 24–28. 10.1016/j.bbr.2008.11.029 [doi].
24. Di Chiara G, Tanda G, Carboni E (1996) Estimation of in-vivo neurotransmitter release by brain microdialysis: the issue of validity. Behav Pharmacol 7: 640–657.
25. Adriani W, Koot S, Columba-Cabezas S, Romano E, Travaglini D, et al. (2012) Immunization with DAT fragments is associated with long-term striatal impairment, hyperactivity and reduced cognitive flexibility in mice. Behav Brain Funct 8: 54. 10.1186/1744-9081-8-54 [doi].
26. Adriani W, Zoratto F, Laviola G (2012) Brain processes in discounting: consequences of adolescent methylphenidate exposure. Curr Top Behav Neurosci 9: 113–143. 10.1007/7854_2011_156 [doi].
27. Paoletti P, Bellone C, Zhou Q (2013) NMDA receptor subunit diversity: impact on receptor properties, synaptic plasticity and disease. Nat Rev Neurosci 14: 383–400. 10.1038/nrn3504 [doi].
28. Huang CS, Shi SH, Ule J, Ruggiu M, Barker LA, Darnell RB, Jan YN, Jan LY (2005) Common molecular pathways mediate long-term potentiation of synaptic excitation and slow synaptic inhibition. Cell 123: 105–118. 10.1016/j.cell.2005.07.033 [doi].
29. Dobbing J (1968) Vulnerable periods in developing brain. In: Davidson AN, Dobbing J, editors. Applied neurochemistry. Philadelphia: Davis. pp. 287–316.
30. Andersen SL, Dumont NL, Teicher MH (1997) Developmental differences in dopamine synthesis inhibition by (+/−)-7-OH-DPAT. Naunyn Schmiedebergs Arch Pharmacol 356: 173–181.
31. Teicher MH, Krenzel E, Thompson AP, Andersen SL (2003) Dopamine receptor pruning during the peripubertal period is not attenuated by NMDA receptor antagonism in rat. Neurosci Lett 339: 169–171. S0304394002014751 [pii].
32. Teicher MH, Andersen SL, Hostetter JC (1995) Evidence for dopamine receptor pruning between adolescence and adulthood in striatum but not nucleus accumbens. Dev Brain Res 89: 167–172. 016538069500109Q [pii].
33. Canese R, Zoratto F, Altabella L, Porcari P, Mercurio L, de Pasquale F, et al. (2013) Persistent modification of forebrain networks and metabolism in rats following adolescent exposure to a 5-HT7 agonist. Psychopharmacology, in press.
34. Perez-Garcia G, Meneses A (2009) Memory time-course: mRNA 5-HT1A and 5-HT7 receptors. Behav Brain Res 202: 102–113. 10.1016/j.bbr.2009.03.027 [doi].
35. Eriksson TM, Golkar A, Ekstrom JC, Svenningsson P, Ogren SO (2008) 5-HT7 receptor stimulation by 8-OH-DPAT counteracts the impairing effect of 5-HT(1A) receptor stimulation on contextual learning in mice. Eur J Pharmacol 596: 107–110. 10.1016/j.ejphar.2008.08.026 [doi].
36. Manuel-Apolinar L, Meneses A (2004) 8-OH-DPAT facilitated memory consolidation and increased hippocampal and cortical cAMP production. Behav Brain Res 148: 179–184. S0166432803001864 [pii].
37. Perez-Garcia G, Gonzalez-Espinosa C, Meneses A (2006) An mRNA expression analysis of stimulation and blockade of 5-HT7 receptors during memory consolidation. Behav Brain Res 169: 83–92. 10.1016/j.bbr.2005.12.013 [doi].
38. Sarkisyan G, Hedlund PB (2009) The 5-HT7 receptor is involved in allocentric spatial memory information processing. Behav Brain Res 202: 26–31. 10.1016/j.bbr.2009.03.011 [doi].
39. Bonaventure P, Aluisio L, Shoblock J, Boggs JD, Fraser IC, et al. (2011) Pharmacological blockade of 5-HT(7) receptor reverses working memory deficits in rats by normalizing cortical glutamate neurotransmission. PLoS One 6: e20210. 10.1371/journal.pone.0020210 [doi].
40. Ruocco LA, Romano E, Treno C, Lacivita E, Arra C, et al. (2013) Emotional and risk seeking behavior after prepuberal subchronic or adult acute stimulation of 5-HT7-Rs in Naples High Excitability rats. Synapse, Nov 25. [Epub ahead of print] 10.1002/syn.21724 [doi].
41. Berke JD, Breck JT, Eichenbaum H (2009) Striatal versus hippocampal representations during win-stay maze performance. J Neurophysiol 101: 1575–1587. 10.1152/jn.91106.2008 [doi].
42. Ruocco LA, de Souza Silva MA, Topic B, Mattern C, Huston JP, Sadile AG (2009) Intranasal Application of Dopamine Reduces Activity and Improves Attention in Naples High Excitability Rats that Feature the Mesocortical Variant of ADHD. Eur Neuropsycopharmacol 19: 693–701.
43. Kalivas PW (2009) The glutamate homeostasis hypothesis of addiction. Nat Rev Neurosci 10: 561–572. 10.1038/nrn2515 [doi].
44. Waagepetersen HS, Sonnewald U, Schousboe A (2007) Glutamine, glutamate and GABA: metabolic aspects. In: Abel Lajtha, editor. Handbook of Neurochemistry and Molecular Neurobiology. Amino Acid and Peptides in the Nervous System. New York: Springer. pp. 1–22.
45. Filipek PA, Semrud-Clikeman M, Steingard RJ, Renshaw PF, Kennedy DN, Blederman J (1997) Volumetric MRI analysis comparing attention-deficit hyperactivity disorder and normal controls. Neurology 48: 589–601.
46. Kelly AM, Margulies DS, Castellanos FX (2007) Recent advances in structural and functional brain imaging studies of attention-deficit/hyperactivity disorder. Curr Psychiatry Rep 9: 401–407.
47. Viggiano D, Ruocco LA, Sadile AG (2003) Dopamine phenotype and behaviour in animal models: in relation to attention deficit hyperactivity disorder. Neurosci Biobehav Rev 27: 623–637.
48. Ochiishi T, Yamauchi T, Terashima T (1998) Regional differences between the immunohistochemical distribution of Ca2+/calmodulin-dependent protein kinase II alpha and beta isoforms in the brainstem of the rat. Brain Res 790: 129–140. S0006-8993(98)00058-4 [pii].
49. Marco EM, Adriani W, Ruocco LA, Canese R, Sadile AG, Laviola G (2011) Neurobehavioral adaptations to methylphenidate: The issue of early adolescent exposure. [Special issue] Neurosci Biobehav Rev 35: 1722–1739. 10.1016/j.neubiorev.2011.02.011 [doi].
50. Papa M, Sagvolden T, Sergeant JA, Sadile AG (1996) Reduced CaMKII-positive neurones in the accumbal shell of an animal model of Attention-Deficit Hyperactivity Disorder. Neuroreport 7: 3017–3020.
51. Papa M, Sellitti S, Sadile AG (2000) Remodeling of neural Networks in the anterior forebrain of an animal model of hyperactivity and attention deficit as monitored by molecular imaging probes. Neurosci Biobehav Rev 24: 149–156.
52. Ruocco LA, Gironi Carnevale UA, Treno C, Sadile AG, Melisi D, et al. (2010) Prepuberal subchronic methylphenidate and atomoxetine induce different long-term effects on adult behaviour and forebrain dopamine, norepinephrine and serotonin in Naples High-Excitability rats. Behav Brain Res 210: 99–106. 10.1016/j.bbr.2010.02.020 [doi].
53. Illiano P, Pagano C, Tino A, Boatto G, Nieddu M, et al. (2011) Prepuberal subchronic intranasal DA differentially affects dopamine transporter and modifies L-Glutamate, L-Aspartate and L-Leucine content in the fronto-striatal interface of Naples High-Excitability rats. Soc Neurosci Abstr.
54. Grace AA, Bunnney BS, Moore H, Todd CL (1997) Dopamine-cell depolarization block as a model for the therapeutic actions of anti-psychotic drugs. Trends Neurosci 20: 31–37.
55. Fumagalli F, Cattaneo A, Caffino L, Ibba M, Racagni G, et al. (2010) Subchronic exposure to atomoxetine up-regulates BDNF expression and signalling in the brain of adolescent spontaneously hypertensive rats: comparison with methyl-phenidate. Pharmacol Res 62: 523–529. 10.1016/j.phrs.2010.07.009 [doi].
56. Masana M, Santana N, Artigas F, Bortolozzi A (2012) Dopamine neurotransmission and atypical antipsychotics in prefrontal cortex: a critical review. Curr Top Med Chem 12: 2357–2374. CTMC-EPUB-20121221-8 [pii].
57. Speranza L, Chambery A, Di Domenico M, Crispino M, Severino V, et al. (2013) The serotonin receptor 7 promotes neurite outgrowth via ERK and Cdk5 signaling pathways. Neuropharmacol 67: 155–167. 10.1016/j.neuropharm.2012.10.026 [doi].

58. Yovell Y, Kandel ER, Dudai Y, Abrams TW (1987) Biochemical correlates of short-term sensitization in Aplysia: temporal analysis of adenylate cyclase stimulation in a perfused-membrane preparation. Proc Natl Acad Sci U S A 84: 9285–9289.
59. Yovell Y, Abrams TW (1992) Temporal asymmetry in activation of Aplysia adenilate cyclase by calcium and transmitters may explain temporal requirement of conditioning. Proc Natl Acad Sci U S A 89: 6526–6554.
60. Ruocco LA, Vallone D, Treno C, Tino A, Sadile AG (2011) Higher density of NMDAR1 subunit in medial prefrontal cortex of the Naples High-Excitability Rats. Molecular mechanisms in Neuroscience, Accademia Nazionale dei Lincei, Roma, Italy.
61. Esposito F, Aragri A, Pesaresi I, Cirillo S, Tedeschi G, et al. (2008) Independent component model of the default-mode brain function: combining individual-level and population-level analyses in resting-state fMRI. Magn Reson Imaging 26: 905–913. 10.1016/j.mri.2008.01.045 [doi].
62. Esposito F, Aragri A, Latorre V, Popolizio T, Scarabino T, et al. (2009) Does the default-mode functional connectivity of the brain correlate with working-memory performances? Arch Ital Biol 147: 11–20.
63. Gusnard DA, Raichle ME (2001) Searching for a baseline: functional imaging and the resting human brain. Nat Rev Neurosci 2: 685–694. 10.1038/35094500 [doi].
64. Greicius MD, Krasnow B, Reiss AL, Menon V (2003) Functional connectivity in the resting brain: a network analysis of the default mode hypothesis. Proc Natl Acad Sci U S A 100: 253–258. 10.1073/pnas.0135058100 [doi].
65. Raichle ME, Snyder AZ (2007) A default mode of brain function: a brief history of an evolving idea. Neuroimage 37: 1083–1090. 10.1016/j.neuroimage.2007.02.041 [doi].
66. Sadile AG, Gironi Carnevale UA, Vitullo E, Cioffi LA, Welzl H, Bättig K (1988) Maze learning of the Naples High- and Low-Excitability rat lines. Adv Biosci 70: 177–180.
67. Paxinos G, Watson C (2007) The Rat Brain in Stereotaxic Coordinates. London: Academic Press.
68. Fumagalli F, Frasca A, Racagni G, Riva MA (2008) Dynamic regulation of glutamatergic postsynaptic activity in rat prefrontal cortex by repeated administration of antipsychotic drugs. Mol Pharmacol 73: 1484–1490. 10.1124/mol.107.043786 [doi].
69. Hölm S (1979) A simple sequentially rejective multiple test procedure. Scand J Stat 6: 65–70.

Robust Resilience and Substantial Interest: A Survey of Pharmacological Cognitive Enhancement among University Students in the UK and Ireland

Ilina Singh[1]*, Imre Bard[2], Jonathan Jackson[2]

1 Department of Social Science, Health & Medicine, Kings College London, London, United Kingdom, 2 Department of Methodology, London School of Economics & Political Science, London, United Kingdom

Abstract

Use of 'smart drugs' among UK students is described in frequent media reports as a rapidly increasing phenomenon. This article reports findings from the first large-scale survey of pharmacological cognitive enhancement (PCE) among students in the UK and Ireland. Conducted from February to September 2012, a survey of a convenience sample of 877 students measured PCE prevalence, attitudes, sources, purposes and ethics. Descriptive and logistic regression statistical methods were used to analyse the data. Lifetime prevalence of PCE using modafinil, methylphenidate or Adderall was under 10%, while past regular and current PCE users of these substances made up between 0.3%–4% of the survey population. A substantial majority of students was unaware of and/or uninterested in PCE; however about one third of students were interested in PCE. PCE users were more likely to be male, British and older students; predictors of PCE use included awareness of other students using PCEs, ADHD symptomatology, ethical concerns, and alcohol and cannabis use. The survey addresses the need for better evidence about PCE prevalence and practices among university students in the UK. We recommend PCE-related strategies for universities based on the survey findings.

Editor: Harriet de Wit, University of Chicago, United States of America

Funding: The survey was funded by the LSE Sticerd Foundation and LSE Personal Research Fund. The funders had no role in study design, data collection and analysis, decision to publish or preparation of the manuscript.

Competing Interests: The authors have declared that no competing interests exist.

* Email: ilina.singh@kcl.ac.uk

Introduction

Prevalence of pharmacological cognitive enhancement

The past five years have seen increasing debate about cognitive enhancement, emerging initially in the United States and then more recently in the United Kingdom and Europe. A general definition of cognitive enhancement is provided in Hildt & Franke [1]:

> Cognitive enhancement is the use of drugs, biotechnological strategies or other means by healthy individuals aiming at the improvement of cognitive functions such as vigilance, concentration or memory without any medical need. [1:2].

The use of prescription drugs for non-medical purposes has driven some of the controversy over cognitive enhancement. The academic literature on pharmacological cognitive enhancement (PCE) has focused primarily on three pharmacological substances: methylphenidate (e.g. Ritalin) and its related compounds; mixed amphetamine salts, traded in the United States under the name Adderall; and modafinil (Provigil). Methylphenidate and mixed amphetamine salts are psychostimulants, and are the most common forms of pharmacological treatment for Attention Deficit/Hyperactivity Disorder (ADHD). Modafinil is used as a treatment for narcolepsy.

PCE has invoked increasing media scrutiny in many countries around the world [2–4], with special emphasis placed on the non-medical use of prescription drugs by university students. Several national ethics advisory bodies have addressed PCE (5), including the US President's Council on Bioethics, the UK Parliament, and the Italian National Bioethics Commission [6–8].

A salient topic in the debate is non-medical use of prescription drugs as 'smart drugs' or 'study aids' among university students. PCE prevalence data is available primarily from research among US university students, in which estimates of non-prescription stimulant drug use range from 5%–35% [9–10], with members of fraternities and sororities often showing the highest rates [11].

Documentation of PCE prevalence in Europe has been both less systematic and less comprehensive than in the US. Looking across a range of different studies, PCE prevalence estimates in different EU Member States range from 0.8% to 16%, depending on country, university and type of drug used [12–19]. Moreover, variation in study sample and methods, and research design quality, complicates comparative understanding of PCE prevalence across the EU [20].

Research on PCE prevalence in the UK is particularly sparse. The only published study to date is an investigation of prescription drug abuse that includes PCE as one form of drug misuse. From a sample of 1614 students and 489 university staff at a university in Wales [19], a total of 37 students (0.02%) reported having used stimulant drugs without a prescription; of these respondents, three reported having used prescription stimulants in order to study.

The other source of systematic evidence available on PCE prevalence in the UK derives from a population survey conducted by the Wellcome Trust (http://www.wellcome.ac.uk/About-us/Publications/Reports/Public-engagement/WTX058859.htm). The Wellcome Monitor, which included seven questions on cognitive enhancement, found low PCE prevalence in the general population. Approximately 2% of adult respondents and 1% of young people aged 14–18 admitted to PCE using Ritalin or Adderall. No respondents had used modafinil for PCE. One third of both adults and young people held that regular or occasional use of pharmacological cognition enhancement was acceptable.

In the absence of research evidence, journalism is the most widely cited source of information about UK PCE prevalence. In 2009 the student newspaper at Cambridge University, *The Varsity*, surveyed 1000 students and found a 10% PCE prevalence rate. The survey queried students about "taking medication without prescription to help them work" [21]. Information about the survey is limited to a short article in the student paper.

Limitations of PCE survey evidence

While large-scale surveys of PCE can in principle provide us with a high level understanding of PCE prevalence, published PCE surveys tend to have several limitations. Prevalence data are often misrepresented because drug use practices and purposes are not elicited as part of the survey. Drug use practices are important because lifetime prevalence can easily be misrepresented as frequent and on-going use when an individual has in fact used the drug only once or twice. In turn, this can lead to overestimates of current PCE prevalence, and can help to foster a false picture of PCE as a widespread and ongoing practice [20]. Drug use purposes are also important to distinguish in a PCE survey. As Partridge [22] has argued, reported misuse of prescription stimulants is often assumed to mean that misuse is aimed specifically at cognition enhancement, when the true purpose may instead be recreational.

Surveys have rarely investigated the ethical dimensions of PCE. Evidence from qualitative studies in the US suggests that PCE users tend to conceive of PCE as being both safe and morally unproblematic [23–25]. A small interview study among German university students found that ethical considerations were a relatively low priority in PCE decision-making. Medical and legal dimensions played a more important role than ethical considerations in students' reasoning about the use of caffeine as a 'smart drug' as compared to PCE [26]. Two studies with Cambridge University students found that participants condemned PCE when there were long-term negative effects on health and when PCE was seen to confer an unfair advantage in exam situations [27].

Rationale for the current study

Despite the lack of evidence for PCE prevalence in the UK, there is an increasing level of concern and activity around PCE, encouraged in the media and extending to public debate and Parliamentary and Home Office activity [28]. Within these debates, prevalence estimates for PCE in the UK are derived from poor quality sources, as outlined above. Characteristics of UK PCE users and practices, as well as PCE sources, are the subject of widespread speculation [3]. Attitudes toward PCE in the UK also lack systematic investigation.

The aim of the current study was to conduct a national survey of PCE among UK and Irish university students in order to gain better understanding of PCE in a population hypothesized to be active PCE users.

Methods

A survey of a convenience sample of students enrolled in universities in the UK and Ireland was conducted from February to September 2012. Participants were recruited using on-line methods, including social media sites and national university student mailing lists.

The survey was developed on the basis of a review of the available empirical studies of PCE, as well as a series of focus groups involving 70 university students. Before launching, the survey was piloted with 13 university students and questions were revised on the basis of their feedback. The final survey included measures of knowledge of smart drugs, drug use patterns (prevalence, last-year and last-month prevalence, drug use motivations and frequency), eventual prescription use of cognition enhancers (which also included questions about non-prescribed ways of use as well as diversion), questions on ethics, and two psychological instruments: the 6-item World Health Organisation (WHO) version of the Adult ADHD Self-report Scale (http://www.hcp.med.harvard.edu/ncs/asrs.php) and the Rosenberg Self-Esteem Scale (https://personality-testing.info/tests/RSE.php).

The survey was conducted using Surveygizmo (www.surveygizmo.com) under a domain (www.thesmartdrugstudy.com) purchased and set up for the purposes of the project.

Respondents were presented with the following definition:

> Smart drugs, also known as cognitive enhancers, are prescription and non-prescription substances that people use to improve their cognitive functioning and performance.

From a list containing 27 substances (in randomized order) respondents were asked to mark those they considered to be 'smart drugs' based on the above definition; they also had the option to enter additional drugs into a textbox if they considered an important substance to be missing from the list. For the purposes of this study we considered the following drugs to be cognition enhancers: methylphenidate, modafinil, Adderall, donepezil, piracetam, and atomoxetine.

When assessing drug use prevalence we distinguished among 6 different categories of use for each of the 27 drugs listed on the survey:

1) I have never heard of it
2) I never tried it and was never interested
3) I never tried it but considered doing so
4) I tried it a few times in the past
5) I used it regularly in the past
6) I use it nowadays

To differentiate substance use groups, we created four distinct and mutually exclusive categories of user groups for the most commonly identified PCEs (modafinil, methylphenidate and Adderall).

1) Respondents who indicated that they had never heard of, or that they were not interested in methylphenidate, modafinil and Adderall
2) Respondents who indicated their interest in at least one of three substances but had never tried any of the them
3) Respondents who had used methylphenidate, modafinil, or Adderall but not for the purpose of enhancing cognitive performance (non-PCE-type use)

Table 1. Participant characteristics ($n = 877$).

	%	*n*
Gender		
Male	46%	403
Female	53%	467
Not recorded	1%	7
Degree		
Undergraduate	75%	660
Postgraduate	22%	192
Other	3%	25

4) Respondents who had used at least one smart drug for the purpose of enhancing cognitive performance (PCE users).

To obtain a detailed understanding of drug use purposes, respondents were asked to indicate all the relevant motivations for using each substance, by choosing from a list containing 18 options or entering their individual answer into an open-ended textbox.

We asked those respondents who indicated an interest in modafinil, methylphenidate or Adderall, but who had not actually used these substances, to provide reasons why they had not used the drugs in question. Respondents described their reasons in a text-entry box on the survey. Answers were coded by two independent coders into 14 previously agreed categories (see www.thesmartdrugstudy.com for further information). When respondents gave several reasons why interest had not converted to use, each reason was individually coded and categorised. When responses were coded into different categories by the two coders, then the final result is the rounded-up average of the two coders' results.

Respondents were asked whether PCE use by students in an academic setting is ethically problematic. Three more specific questions were also asked: whether PCE use by students is like doping in sports, whether PCE use by students constitutes cheating, and if students feel pressure to use PCEs at university. A Likert-type scale was used to query respondents on ethical issues. Responses on each question were analysed for the four PCE user-types described earlier.

Statistical analysis was conducted using Stata 11, generating standard cross-tabulations, frequency tables and mean comparisons.

We also fitted a series of multinomial logistic regression models to examine the predictors of drug usage for modafinil, methylphenidate, Adderall and caffeine, in which we differentiated among the four user groups identified above. We used ordinal logistic (or proportional odds) modelling to estimate the factors associated with moving up or down the four user group categories for each drug. The potential predictors were: gender, age (17–20, 21–24, 25–29 and 30+), ethnicity (White British, other White, and non-White), alcohol use, cannabis use, awareness of other people at university using smart drugs, ADHD score, self-esteem score, and beliefs about the ethics of using smart drugs to improve academic performance.

The statistical technique groups adjacent values of the ordinal response into two groups, "high" (i.e. higher-numbered) and "low", divided at each level j = 1;:::;C-1 in turn. For drug use and awareness, there are three such groupings:

Table 2. What is a smart drug? ($n = 877$).

Substance	% of respondents identifying it as a smart drug	Substance	% of respondents identifying it as a smart drug
1. caffeine pills	42.1%	15. LSD	6.2%
2. methylphenidate	41.5%	16. MDMA	5.7%
3. energy drinks	33.9%	17. DMT	4.3%
4. vitamin supplements	29.2%	18. magic mushrooms	4.3%
5. modafinil	25.9%	19. sleeping pills	4.2%
6. Adderall	25.3%	20. Relevin	3.9%
7. speed	22.4%	21. crystal meth	3.8%
8. piracetam	13.1%	22. mephedrone	3.3%
9. ephedrine	9.2%	23. alcohol	2.6%
10. marijuana	9.3%	24. pain killers	2.6%
11. donepezil	8.9%	25. ketamine	2.5%
12. tobacco	8.3%	26. tranquilizers	22.2%
13. cocaine	7.8%	27. heroin	1.5%
14. atomoxetine	6.8%		

Table 3. Smart Drug Prevalence (n = 877).*

		methylphenidate *n* (%)	modafinil *n* (%)	Adderall *n* (%)	caffeine pills *n* (%)
Unaware		154 (17.6%)	514 (58.6%)	434 (49.5%)	13 (1.5%)
Uninterested		507 (57.8%)	213 (24.3%)	304 (34.7%)	302 (34.4%)
Considered		164 (18.7%)	80 (9.1%)	110 (12.5%)	129 (14.7%)
Past occasional	**PCE use**	22 (2.5%)	18 (2.1%)	12 (1.4%)	109 (12.4%)
	Other use	15 (0.7%)	10 (1.1%)	7 (0.8%)	141 (16.1%)
Past regular	**PCE use**	6 (1%)	6 (0.7%)	3 (0.3%)	49 (5.6%)
	Other use	2 (0.2%)	2 (0.2%)	2 (0.2%)	43 (4.9%)
Current	**PCE use**	7 (0.8%)	30 (3.4%)	3 (0.3%)	55 (6.3%)
	Other use	0 (0%)	4 (0.5%)	2 (0.2%)	36 (4.1%)

*Table 3 contains synthesized information from two questions. Prevalence – based on the six options listed – and purposes, focusing on PCE. Respondents could choose from 17 other purposes besides PCE; a subset of the data on other purposes is reported in Table 4. 'PCE use' was defined as a respondent who indicated PCE alone or in any combination; 'other use' was defined as a respondent who did not indicate PCE, but did indicate any other purpose.

- used [high] vs. (considered, uninterested, unaware) [low]
- (used, considered) [high] vs. (uninterested, unaware) [low]
- (used, considered, uninterested) [high] vs. (unaware) [low]

The regression coefficient of an explanatory variable X is then interpreted as the log odds ratio (and its exponential as the odds ratio) associated with a one-unit increase in X, for the choice of the high rather than low value in these dichotomies, with the same odds ratio applied to each way of grouping the response levels. Blocks of variables were added one at a time resulting in six models (Model I includes demographic variables, Model II adds alcohol use and cannabis use, Model III adds awareness of other people at university using smart drugs, and so on) to assess the effect of incrementally adjusting for other factors.

The proportional odds assumption was tested using the Brant test [29]. The test indicated no problems for all variables but the 'beliefs about the ethics of using smart drugs to improve academic performance' variable, added in Model VI for each of the drugs. Because the other predictors in the fitted ordered logistic models conformed to the proportional odds assumption, and because the findings from the multinomial logistic regression models indicated the same pattern of relationships, (controlling for ethical beliefs), we proceed with discussion of results from this analysis. We also interpret the results from the fitted multinomial logistic regressions when it comes to beliefs about the ethics of using smart drugs to improve academic performance in light of the Brant test.

Results

The final sample size was 877. Two respondents who completed the survey were excluded because they reported taking a fake drug called 'Relevin' [30]. We also dropped 14 respondents from the sample who said they had used cognitive enhancers for a medical indication and had a legitimate prescription.

Table 1 outlines the demographic profile of the sample. 75% of students in the sample reported being undergraduates. Participation was almost equally split between males and females. The mean age of participants was 22.7 years old. Participants were drawn from 104 universities in the UK and Ireland; a majority of respondents (79%) reported enrolment at a Russell Group university. The Russell Group is an association of the leading research universities in the United Kingdom. Our sample includes students from 23 of the 24 Russell Group member institutions. Universities most frequently represented in the survey were: Bristol University ($n = 161$), Manchester University ($n = 96$), Cardiff University ($n = 88$), London School of Economics ($n = 86$), Cambridge University ($n = 77$), Oxford University ($n = 34$) and University College London ($n = 32$).

Smart drugs

The five substances most frequently identified as 'smart drugs' were caffeine pills, methylphenidate, energy drinks, vitamin supplements, and modafinil (See Table 2 below for complete list). A small proportion of the sample (2%) was able to identify all 6 substances our study considered to be cognition enhancers, while 44% of respondents identified none as a smart drug.

PCE prevalence

We measured lifetime prevalence for the three prescription drugs most commonly used for PCE (methylphenidate, modafinil and Adderall). We also conducted a comparative analysis with

Table 4. Drug use purposes for modafinil, methylphenidate, Adderall and caffeine pills, as reported by users of these substances.

Substance Users	Enhance Cognition *n* (%)	Offset sleep deprivation *n* (%)	Enhance mood *n* (%)	Curiosity *n* (%)
modafinil, $n = 70$	54 (77.1%)	43 (61.4%)	12 (17.1%)	15 (21.4%)
methylphenidate, $n = 52$	35 (67.3%)	14 (26.9%)	10 (19.2%)	19 (36.5%)
Adderall, $n = 28$	18 (64.3%)	8 (28.6%)	6 (21.4%)	13 (46.4%)
caffeine pills, $n = 432$	213 (49.3%)	265 (61.3%)	46 (10.6%)	35 (8.1%)

Note that respondents could select more than one purpose for each drug.

Table 5. ***n* = 877.** User group categories on the basis of familiarity with methylphenidate, modafinil and Adderall.

User groups		n (%)
Unaware/not interested	Unaware of all PCEs	123 (14.0%)
	Uninterested in all PCEs	127 (14.5%)
	Unaware of some of the PCEs and uninterested in the other PCEs	336 (38.3%)
Considered using at least one PCE		179 (20.4%)
Non-CE type user (at least one drug)		30 (3.4%)
PCE-type user (at least one drug)		82 (9.4%)

caffeine, which a majority of students identified as a cognitive enhancer. Table 3 presents the breakdown for these four substances.

Lifetime prevalence for methylphenidate was 5.9%. The drug was unknown to almost 18% of our sample; 19% had considered trying it and 58% reported that they had never had interest in trying it. About 4% of users had taken methylphenidate for PCE, while about 1% had taken it for non-PCE use.

Modafinil was simultaneously the most unknown and the most frequently used cognition enhancer. Lifetime prevalence for modafinil was 8%. Lifetime prevalence for PCE use was 6.2%, which suggests that modafinil was used primarily for PCE purposes by this sample of students. Almost 59% of students had never heard of modafinil, while about 24% said they were never interested in trying it. Nine percent of students had considered trying modafinil.

Lifetime prevalence for Adderall was 3.2% overall and 2% for PCE use. Around 50% of respondents were unaware of Adderall; over a third were uninterested in it; and about 13% had considered using the drug.

In the case of the psychostimulants (methylphenidate and Adderall) there was a marked difference between the number of respondents who had tried the drug in the past and those who were current users. Respondents were five times more likely to be past users of methylphenidate than current users. Similarly, respondents were four times more likely to be past users of Adderall than current users. Modafinil use patterns differed from methylphenidate and Adderall use patterns; there was a slightly higher number of current users than past users of modafinil.

In comparison with the prescription medications, the lifetime prevalence for caffeine pills was 49.4%, with 24.3% lifetime prevalence for cognitive enhancement. A very small proportion of respondents were unfamiliar with caffeine pills (1.5%), while over 10% identified as current users, with current users choosing caffeine pills for cognitive enhancement than for other purposes.

Drug use motivations

Table 4 shows four of the most commonly indicated drug use motivations for modafinil, methylphenidate, Adderall and caffeine pills, by users of these substances (note that respondents could indicate more than one reason).

All four substances were used, to varying degrees, to 'enhance cognition', 'offset sleep deprivation', and to 'enhance mood'. Not included in Table 4 are the substances that were most commonly used to 'enhance cognition' and to 'offset sleep deprivation' by students in the sample as a whole (n = 877). These substances were energy drinks and caffeine tablets: 30% of the total sample had used energy drinks to enhance cognition; 45% had used energy drinks to offset sleep deprivation; 24% had used caffeine tablets to enhance cognition; 30% had used caffeine tablets to offset sleep deprivation.

User groups characteristics

Considering methylphenidate, Adderall and modafinil together, two thirds of the sample was not interested in these drugs for any purpose. This category was broken down into three further groups. Fourteen percent of respondents said that they had never heard of any of the three smart drugs. Another 14.5% of students responded that they were never interested in any of the three drugs. The remaining 38% of respondents in this category were unaware of some, and uninterested in the other, substances.

Around 20% of students had considered using at least one of the three drugs, and 9.4% of the sample had used one of these drugs to improve cognitive performance at least once. About 3% of respondents had used one of these three drugs for purposes other than cognitive enhancement. Table 5 details this breakdown of the results.

Table 6. ADHD ASRS Score by user group, *n* = 877.

User groups		Mean	Std. Err.	95% confidence interval	
Unaware/not interested	Unaware of all PCEs	2.4	0.1	2.2	2.7
	Uninterested in all PCEs	2.4	0.1	2.1	2.7
	Unaware of some of the PCEs and uninterested in the other PCEs	2.6	0.1	2.4	2.7
Considered using at least one PCE		3.1	0.1	2.9	3.3
Non-CE type user (at least one drug)		3.1	0.3	2.4	3.7
PCE-type user (at least one drug)		2.7	0.2	2.3	3.1

Table 7. Reasons for not using by those who have considered a PCE.

	Considered modafinil but not tried yet ($n=78$)	Considered methylphenidate but not tried yet ($n=161$)	Considered Adderall but not tried yet ($n=105$)
	n (%)	*n* (%)	*n* (%)
Lack of availability	28 (35.9%)	83 (51.6%)	56 (53.3%)
Concerns about side-effects	13 (16.7%)	25 (15.5%)	14 (13.3%)
Illegality	9 (11.5%)	14 (8.7%)	11 (10.5 s%)

Note that only the three most common reasons are shown.

Self-reported ADHD-symptoms

In this sample, none of the four drug user groups received a score consistent with clinically significant symptomatology of adult ADHD (see Table 6).

Conversion from interest in PCEs to use of PCEs

Table 7 details the three most common reported reasons given by respondents for why their interest in modafinil, methylphenidate and Adderall for PCE purposes did not convert to substance use. Lack of availability was the most common reason why interested students had not yet tried one of these three drugs, particularly in the case of the stimulant drugs. About half of students interested in PCE using stimulants cited lack of availability as the reason interest had not converted to use.

Not shown in the table is the finding that lack of availability was given as the sole reason why interest did not convert to use in a majority of cases (in 61/83 [74%] cases for methylphenidate, in 18/28 [64%] cases for modafinil, and in 40/56 [71%] cases for Adderall). The next most frequently cited reasons for non-conversion of interest to use were concerns about side effects, and concerns about the illegality of use.

Successful access to the stimulants (methylphenidate and Adderall), and modafinil was achieved via diverse routes. Adderall and methylphenidate were obtained primarily from friends. Modafinil was sourced primarily from an on-line distributor, such as an on-line pharmacy. Table 8 provides an overview of findings on the sources of PCEs.

Ethics

The results of the broad ethics question are summarised in Table 9. Views on the ethics of PCE in academia were related to respondents' experience of and attitudes toward PCEs. Among those who were unaware of, or uninterested in, modafinil, Adderall and methylphenidate, 13% were neutral and a majority (69.2%) agreed or strongly agreed that PCE in academic contexts is ethically problematic. Respondents who had considered PCE, or who had used PCEs, found PCE in academia to be less problematic. Among respondents who had considered PCE, 20% were neutral about the ethics of PCE use in academia, and almost 45% agreed or strongly agreed that PCE use in academia was problematic. Among PCE users, about 16% were neutral and almost 21% agreed or strongly agreed that PCE use in academia is problematic. In comparison to other user groups, the aware but disinterested group tended to have stronger positive and stronger negative opinions about the ethics of PCE use in academic settings. A very small minority (6.4%) of respondents in this group strongly disagreed that PCE in academia is ethically problematic while just under half of respondents (45.7%) strongly agreed with the statement.

Responses to the comparisons between PCE and doping in sports, and PCE and cheating were similarly dependent on user group, with those who had considered PCE and those who were PCE users less likely than the unaware/uninterested respondents to validate the comparisons. The comparison with cheating drew the strongest opinions from PCE users, 72% strongly disagreed with the comparison and no PCE users strongly agreed. Those who had considered PCE tended to disagree or strongly disagree that PCE was like cheating (29% and 32% respectively), or like doping in sports (21% and 22% respectively). About one fifth of those unaware/uninterested in PCE were neutral on both these comparisons. About one third of unaware/uninterested respondents disagreed to some extent with the comparison between PCE and cheating. However, 63% of these respondents endorsed the comparison between PCE and doping (27% agreed and 36% strongly agreed), and just under half of these respondents endorsed the comparison between PCE and cheating (24% agreed and 27% strongly agreed).

Across all user groups, a majority of respondents disagreed or strongly disagreed with the statement: "I would feel pressured to

Table 8. Source of PCEs reported by users of these substances.

Source of drug	Modafinil *n* (%)	Methylphenidate *n* (%)	Adderall *n* (%)
Family	0 (0%)	2 (4.1%)	1 (3.6%)
Friends	15 (21.4%)	37 (75.5%)	25 (89.3%)
Drug dealer	0 (0%)	2 (4.1%)	1 (3.6%)
Online	45 (64.3%)	1 (2.0%)	1 (3.6%)
Ambiguous entry	8 (11.4%)	7 (14.3%)	0 (0%)
Total	**69 (100%)**	**49 (100%)**	**28 (100%)**

Table 9. PCE in academia is ethically problematic ($n = 877$).

	Unaware/uninterested in some PCEs *n* (%)	Completely unaware *n* (%)	Uninterested *n* (%)	Considered *n* (%)	Non-PCE-use *n* (%)	PCE-use *n* (%)
Strongly disagree	26 (7.8%)	16 (13.0%)	8 (6.4%)	32 (17.9%)	8 (26.7%)	32 (39.0%)
Disagree	34 (10.2%)	10 (8.1%)	5 (4.0%)	32 (17.9%)	6 (20%)	20 (24.4%)
Neutral	43 (12.8%)	16 (13.0%)	16 (12.6%)	35 (20.0%)	3 (10%)	13 (15.6.%)
Agree	108 (32.2%)	37 (30.1%)	40 (31.5%)	46 (25.7%)	7 (23.3%)	15 (18.3%)
Strongly agree	124 (37.0%)	44 (35.8%)	58 (45.7%)	34 (19.0%)	6 (20%)	2 (2.4%)
Total	335 (100%)	123 (100%)	127 (100%)	179 (100%)	30 (100%)	82 (100%)

use PCEs if I knew other people used them." The frequency of disagreement diminished as PCE became more of a reality, such that about 80% of the unaware/uninterested group disagreed or strongly disagreed with the statement; 53% of the group that had considered PCE use disagreed or strongly disagreed; and 52% of PCE users disagreed or strongly disagreed. Across groups, the highest proportion of respondents in agreement with the statement was found in the PCE user group; 22% of PCE users agreed with the statement; and 11% of PCE users agreed strongly with the statement. Those who were PCE users or who had considered PCE were more than twice as likely as other groups to agree that they might feel pressure to use PCEs.

Predictors of PCE use

Tables 10–13 present the findings from a series of ordinal logistic regression models fitted for each of the modafinil, methylphenidate, Adderall and caffeine user groups.

Focusing on Model VI in each of the four tables (Tables 10–13), females and people in the youngest age group (ages 17–20) were less likely to use modafinil, methylphenidate and Adderall (but not caffeine) compared to males and the other age groups (conditioning on alcohol and cannabis use, awareness, beliefs about the ethics of using smart drugs to improve academic performance, and so on). White British students were more likely to use caffeine than non-White and non-British White students, and non-British White students were less likely than British White (and non-White) students to use modafinil. Alcohol and cannabis use were both positively associated with methylphenidate and with caffeine use, but this partial association did not hold for modafinil and Adderall.

ADHD symptoms were not generally related to smart drug use, although ADHD symptoms were a weak and positive predictor of methylphenidate use. Awareness of other people at university using smart drugs was strongly and positively associated with use of modafinil and methylphenidate and moderately associated with use of Adderall and caffeine.

Finally, we interpret the findings from multinomial logistic regressions for each of modafinil, methylphenidate and Adderall. The belief that it is unethical to use smart drugs to improve academic performance increased the predicted odds of moving from unaware to uninterested, but the same belief decreased the predicted odds of moving from uninterested to having considered taking the drug, and of moving from having considered taking the drug to actually having taken it.

Discussion

This article has reported the findings from the smart drug survey (www.thesmartdrugstudy.com), which is the first comprehensive national survey on cognitive enhancement among students enrolled at UK and Irish universities. The survey investigated cognitive enhancement in four areas: prevalence, practices, motivations, and ethics.

We defined a 'smart drug' for participants in order to address the problem of ambiguity around the concept. In order to avoid conflation with prescription drug users, we excluded students with prescriptions for methylphenidate, modafinil and Adderall in the survey. We employed a dimensional approach to understanding PCE prevalence to distinguish the level of *current* and *ongoing* use of PCEs in the university setting from *past* and *occasional* use. A dimensional investigation of PCE use therefore minimizes the risk of over-estimating PCE as a current problem in university settings. Such an approach is also a better means of evaluating the extent to which PCE poses a risk of drug dependence, because it differentiates occasional drug practices from sustained PCE.

Despite anecdotal reports of high rates of PCE in UK universities, a majority of students surveyed in this study were unaware of and/or uninterested in PCEs. Collectively, students in these user groups made up 67% of the study sample.

PCE users were likely to be British male students nearing the end of an undergraduate degree course or at postgraduate level. Current users, and regular past users of methylphenidate and Adderall made up less than 1% of the study sample, respectively. Under 6% of students had used methylphenidate or Adderall as a cognitive enhancer at least once. Modafinil was the most commonly used PCE; just over 8% of the study sample had used modafinil at least once. Modafinil was the only drug for which the proportion of past users and current users was almost equal (4.1% and 3.9% of the study population, respectively). Methylphenidate, the most widely known PCE among surveyed students, was also the substance that students were least interested in trying as a cognitive enhancer (relative to modafinil, Adderall and caffeine).

While students have concerns about the ethics of PCE in the university, there is little indication of strong principled disagreement with PCE. In general, the level of concern about the ethics of PCE use varied with students' interest in and use of PCEs, with those who had considered PCE and used PCE reporting lower levels of ethical concern than those who were uninterested and/or unaware. Nevertheless, our findings suggest that moral considerations may be positively associated with a sustained lack of interest among students in accessing and in using PCEs.

Concerns about peer pressure or coercion to use PCEs were very low among all students. Interestingly, concern about coercion grew with interest in and with personal use of PCE; we also found that awareness of PCE use in the peer group strongly predicted personal use. Taken together, these findings suggest that direct and indirect peer pressure may be mechanisms by which PCE spreads within groups in the university context. Such group dynamics warrant further investigation, particularly as they may help to

Table 10. Ordinal logistic regression predicting knowledge and use of modafinil. +

Predictors	Model ^^					
	I	II	III	IV	V	VI
Female (reference category: male)	0.434***	0.435***	0.420***	0.414***	0.409***	0.450***
	(−6.20)	(−5.99)	(−6.17)	(−6.25)	(−6.26)	(−5.41)
age 21–24 (reference category: age 17–20)	2.001***	2.017***	1.951***	1.919***	1.911***	1.982***
	−4.56	−4.61	−4.35	−4.23	−4.20	−4.41
age 25–29 (reference category: age 17–20)	1.680*	1.682*	1.743*	1.718*	1.712*	1.670*
	−2.35	−2.34	−2.49	−2.42	−2.41	−2.29
age 30+ (reference category: age 17–20)	2.584**	2.491**	2.758***	2.748***	2.751***	2.703***
	−3.20	−3.05	−3.38	−3.36	−3.36	−3.30
Ethnicity: not-white (reference category: British white)	1.163	1.086	1.064	1.072	1.070	1.058
	−0.79	−0.41	−0.31	−0.35	−0.34	−0.28
Ethnicity: white but not British (reference category: British white)	0.597**	0.588**	0.566**	0.565**	0.566**	0.558**
	(−2.66)	(−2.73)	(−2.89)	(−2.90)	(−2.89)	(−2.96)
Alcohol use (ranges from 1/never tried to 4/use weekly or more)		0.912	0.930	0.935	0.937	0.938
		(−1.30)	(−1.01)	(−0.93)	(−0.90)	(−0.89)
Cannabis use (ranges from 1/never tried to 4/use weekly or more)		1.033	0.982	0.997	0.997	0.948
		−0.43	(−0.24)	(−0.04)	(−0.04)	(−0.68)
Awareness of other people at University using smart drugs (dichotomous: no and yes)			2.048***	2.049***	2.054***	1.997***
			−5.10	−5.10	−5.11	−4.89
ADHD score (ranges from 0 to 6)				0.939	0.930	0.927
				(−1.51)	(−1.62)	(−1.70)
Self-esteem score (ranges from 0 to 30)					0.993	0.993
					(−0.58)	(−0.54)
Beliefs about the ethnics of using smart drugs to improve academic performance (ranges from 1 to 5, where 1 means 'strongly disagree' and 5 means 'strongly agree' that it is 'ethically problematic')						0.867**
						(−2.62)
Sample size (*N*)	887	887	886	886	886	886

+ Outcome variable has four mutually exclusive categories: unaware, uninterested, have considered, and have used (including currently use) each drug.
^^ Parameter estimates are odd-ratios, i.e. exponentiated coefficients. Standard errors in parentheses.
*** $p<.001$,
** $p<.01$,
* $p<.05$.

explain why PCE use in certain UK universities is anecdotally reported to be high, while PCE use across UK universities appears to be low [11].

In line with patterns of recreational drug use, curiosity motivated occasional PCE for those substances that were less available to students, perhaps because the stimulant drugs were more likely to be sourced opportunistically from friends and family. Alcohol and cannabis use were associated with methylphenidate use as a cognitive enhancer, giving some further weight to concerns about the intersection of PCE with recreational drug use. At the same time, methylphenidate PCE use was also weakly associated with ADHD symptomatology, suggesting that, in a subset of students, PCE may approach self-medication [31]. Cannabis is another substance associated with self-medication of ADHD [32]. The relationship between use of stimulants for PCE, ADHD symptomatology, and cannabis use is complex and requires focused investigation.

Our findings lend themselves to at least two plausible interpretations. One interpretation is that the data indicate substantial resilience to PCE among UK and Irish university students. Resilience here is defined as: low lifetime prevalence of PCE and very low levels of consistent use of PCEs, in a setting in which there is awareness of and interest in PCEs. Resilience has not been well documented or described in the literature on cognitive enhancement to date. On the basis of this study, resilience cannot be attributed wholly to a lack of interest in cognitive enhancement. Caffeine, delivered in tablets and energy drinks, was reported to be a common and consistently used cognitive enhancer. Further studies should differentiate attitudes to cognitive enhancement and attitudes toward *pharmacological*

Table 11. Ordinal logistic regression predicting knowledge and use of methylphenidate. +

Predictors	Model ^^					
	I	II	III	IV	V	VI
Female (reference category: male)	0.445***	0.568***	0.562***	0.579***	0.559***	0.635**
	(−5.99)	(−4.05)	(−4.10)	(−3.88)	(−4.09)	(−3.07)
age 21–24 (reference category: age 17–20)	1.513**	1.493**	1.410*	1.467*	1.451*	1.511**
	−2.80	−2.70	−2.29	−2.54	−2.47	−2.72
age 25–29 (reference category: age 17–20)	2.069***	1.920**	1.984**	2.030**	2.012**	1.990**
	−3.41	−3.02	−3.16	−3.27	−3.23	−3.18
age 30+ (reference category: age 17–20)	2.400**	2.542**	3.026***	3.033***	3.048***	2.960***
	−2.97	−3.13	−3.69	−3.71	−3.72	−3.65
Ethnicity: not-white (reference category: British white)	0.664*	0.841	0.817	0.812	0.810	0.802
	(−2.10)	(−0.85)	(−0.98)	(−1.01)	(−1.02)	(−1.07)
Ethnicity: white but not British (reference category: British white)	0.723	0.767	0.716	0.718	0.728	0.720
	(−1.76)	(−1.43)	(−1.79)	(−1.78)	(−1.70)	(−1.76)
Alcohol use (ranges from 1/never tried to 4/use weekly or more)		1.156*	1.202*	1.198*	1.205*	1.210**
		−2.01	−2.55	−2.49	−2.57	−2.61
Cannabis use (ranges from 1/never tried to 4/use weekly or more)		1.638***	1.545***	1.506***	1.511***	1.426***
		−6.60	−5.73	−5.36	−5.39	−4.51
Awareness of other people at University using smart drugs (dichotomous: no and yes)			2.485***	2.513***	2.533***	2.433***
			−6.46	−6.53	−6.57	−6.26
ADHD score (ranges from 0 to 6)				1.151***	1.121**	1.119*
				−3.39	−2.58	−2.53
Self-esteem score (ranges from 0 to 30)					0.978	0.979
					(−1.72)	(−1.68)
Beliefs about the ethics of using smart drugs to improve academic performance (ranges from 1 to 5, where 1 means 'strongly disagree' and 5 means 'strongly agree' that it is 'ethically problematic')						0.839**
						(−3.26)
Sample size (*N*)	887	887	886	886	886	886

+ Outcome variable has four mutually exclusive categories: unaware, uninterested, have considered, and have used (including currently use) each drug.
^^ Parameter estimates are odd-ratios, i.e. exponentiated coefficients. Standard errors in parentheses.
*** $p<.001$,
** $p<.01$,
* $p<.05$.

cognitive enhancement. Low uptake of PCE among UK and Irish university students may reflect concerns about drugs as the means of cognitive enhancement, rather than reflecting the desirability of cognitive enhancement as an end [33].

Another interpretation of the survey findings focuses on the relatively high proportion of students who showed an interest in PCE. Students who had considered using PCEs (20.4%) and students who had used a PCE at least once (9.4%) collectively made up one-third of the study sample. A key question here is why student interest in, and initial experimentation with PCE does not convert at higher rates to current ongoing use of PCEs. One clear answer from this survey is lack of availability of PCEs.

Upon closer examination, the data suggest a nuanced relationship between availability and PCE use. Availability is likely a key factor in different *patterns* of PCE use. These patterns of use are also moderated by awareness of PCEs. We note that despite the relatively greater availability of modafinil in the UK, it is still the most unknown PCE relative to methylphenidate and Adderall, with nearly 60% of students reporting that they had never heard of it. Although students reported more difficulty accessing the prescription stimulants, more students were past users of methylphenidate (44 students) than past users of modafinil (36 students). However, *current* modafinil users exceeded current methylphenidate users by a ratio of approximately 3:1.

The ease of internet access to modafinil is probably a factor in the ongoing use of this drug, resulting in a relatively higher proportion of current modafinil users despite the substantial lack of awareness about and interest in the drug. Similarly, the lack of availability of methylphenidate and Adderall in the UK is a probable factor in the relatively lower rates of ongoing use of these substances for cognitive enhancement, despite higher levels of awareness of and interest in these drugs.

Table 12. Ordinal logistic regression predicting knowledge and use of Adderall. +

Predictors	Model ^^					
	I	II	III	IV	V	VI
Female (reference category: male)	0.520***	0.582***	0.581***	0.591***	0.568***	0.450***
	(−5.05)	(−4.04)	(−4.04)	(−3.90)	(−4.14)	(−5.41)
age 21–24 (reference category: age 17–20)	1.295	1.298	1.274	1.293	1.285	1.982***
	−1.80	−1.81	−1.68	−1.77	−1.73	−4.41
age 25–29 (reference category: age 17–20)	1.267	1.216	1.243	1.256	1.250	1.670*
	−1.15	−0.95	−1.05	−1.10	−1.08	−2.29
age 30+ (reference category: age 17–20)	0.740	0.715	0.771	0.771	0.778	2.703***
	(−0.98)	(−1.08)	(−0.83)	(−0.83)	(−0.80)	−3.300
Ethnicity: not-white (reference category: British white)	1.155	1.155	1.136	1.132	1.127	1.058
	−0.78	−0.75	−0.66	−0.64	−0.62	−0.28
Ethnicity: white but not British (reference category: British white)	1.185	1.192	1.157	1.164	1.174	0.558**
	−0.96	−0.99	−0.82	−0.85	−0.90	(−2.96)
Alcohol use (ranges from 1/never tried to 4/use weekly or more)		0.927	0.943	0.940	0.945	0.938
		(−1.10)	(−0.85)	(−0.88)	(−0.82)	(−0.89)
Cannabis use (ranges from 1/never tried to 4/use weekly or more)		1.283***	1.237**	1.223**	1.228**	0.948
		−3.47	−2.94	−2.76	−2.81	(−0.68)
Awareness of other people at University using smart drugs (dichotomous: no and yes)			1.627***	1.634***	1.645***	1.997***
			−3.68	−3.71	−3.75	−4.89
ADHD score (ranges from 0 to 6)				1.069	1.039	0.927
				−1.65	−0.88	(−1.70)
Self-esteem score (ranges from 0 to 30)					0.976	0.993
					(−1.94)	(−0.54)
Beliefs about the ethics of using smart drugs to improve academic performance (ranges from 1 to 5, where 1 means 'strongly disagree' and 5 means 'strongly agree' that it is 'ethically problematic')						0.867**
						(−2.62)
Sample size (*N*)	887	887	886	886	886	886

+ Outcome variable has four mutually exclusive categories: unaware, uninterested, have considered, and have used (including currently use) each drug.
^^ Parameter estimates are odd-ratios, i.e. exponentiated coefficients. Standard errors in parentheses.
*** $p<.001$,
** $p<.01$,
* $p<.05$.

Finally, we note that these PCE use patterns might look very different if students found PCE to make a remarkable difference in their academic performance and achievement. We would expect to find a higher rate of consistent PCE use under such circumstances; more demand for, and wider availability of PCEs in universities; and a higher likelihood of conversion from interest to use. From the current use pattern data, we infer that students who use PCEs are not finding them to make a remarkable difference to their academic progress.

Limitations

As noted above, this survey was not based on a random sample. Results of convenience sample surveys may be biased, due to participant self-selection and other factors. We used an on-line survey tool rather than traditional survey approaches, which were considered too costly and unfeasible due to access and administration barriers. On-line surveys can have advantages compared to paper-based surveys [34], including ease of access and guaranteed anonymity.

We were unable to conduct extensive reliability and validity tests of individual survey questions, beyond the efforts outlined in the methods section. Methodological inconsistency is a major barrier to comparisons of PCE studies across and within countries. We hope that transparent publication of our methods and findings on the survey website will enable further testing of the questions as well as more consistency among future surveys of PCE.

Conclusion

In May, 2014 the BBC reported that the UK Advisory Council on the Misuse of Drugs would carry out a review of 'smart drug

Table 13. Ordinal logistic regression predicting knowledge and usage of caffeine. +

Predictors	Model ^^					
	I	II	III	IV	V	VI
Female (reference category: male)	0.731*	0.944	0.929	0.935	0.904	1.059
	(−2.41)	(−0.42)	(−0.53)	(−0.48)	(−0.72)	−0.39
age 21–24 (reference category: age 17–20)	1.131	1.109	1.069	1.075	1.063	1.110
	−0.86	−0.70	−0.45	−0.48	−0.41	−0.70
age 25–29 (reference category: age 17–20)	1.354	1.242	1.244	1.247	1.237	1.209
	−1.41	−0.99	−1.00	−1.01	−0.97	−0.85
age 30+ (reference category: age 17–20)	0.729	0.801	0.852	0.854	0.849	0.810
	(−1.05)	(−0.72)	(−0.52)	(−0.51)	(−0.53)	(−0.67)
Ethnicity: not-white (reference category: British white)	0.417***	0.549**	0.540**	0.539**	0.538**	0.519**
	(−4.67)	(−3.00)	(−3.08)	(−3.09)	(−3.10)	(−3.26)
Ethnicity: white but not British (reference category: British white)	0.514***	0.549***	0.536***	0.537***	0.540***	0.523***
	(−3.79)	(−3.34)	(−3.45)	(−3.44)	(−3.40)	(−3.56)
Alcohol use (ranges from 1/never tried to 4/use weekly or more)		1.265**	1.290***	1.288***	1.296***	1.302***
		−3.27	−3.51	−3.50	−3.57	−3.61
Cannabis use (ranges from 1/never tried to 4/use weekly or more)		1.659***	1.606***	1.595***	1.603***	1.492***
		−6.33	−5.87	−5.75	−5.79	−4.79
Awareness of other people at University using smart drugs (dichotomous: no and yes)			1.557**	1.556**	1.574***	1.492**
			−3.27	−3.26	−3.34	−2.92
ADHD score (ranges from 0 to 6)				1.030	1.003	1.000
				−0.71	−0.07	0.00
Self-esteem score (ranges from 0 to 30)					0.978	0.979
					(−1.70)	(−1.67)
Beliefs about the ethics of using smart drugs to improve academic performance (ranges from 1 to 5, where 1 means 'strongly disagree' and 5 means 'strongly agree' that it is 'ethically problematic')						0.809***
						(−3.86)
Sample size (*N*)	887	887	886	886	886	886

+ Outcome variable has four mutually exclusive categories: unaware, uninterested, have considered, and have used (including currently use) each drug.
^^ Parameter estimates are odd-ratios, i.e. exponentiated coefficients. Standard errors in parentheses.
*** $p<.001$,
** $p<.01$,
* $p<.05$.

use' (www.news.live.**bbc**.co.uk/newsbeat/27207469). Our research represents the most comprehensive survey of PCE to date among UK and Irish university students. We found a mixed picture of high 'resilience' combined with relatively high interest in PCE. Lifetime prevalence of PCE using modafinil, methylphenidate or Adderall was 9.4%; past regular and current PCE users of these substances made up between 0.3%–4% of the survey population. PCE users were more likely to be male, older and British; and they were very likely to be aware of other PCE users. ADHD symptomatology was weakly correlated with use of methylphenidate for PCE. Principled ethical disagreement with PCE was low; those students who thought PCE was unethical were less likely to develop an interest in, or desire to access PCE. Use of stimulants and modafinil for non-PCE purposes was low; however, alcohol and cannabis use predicted PCE.

The present study suggests two simultaneous paths for universities to take in relation to PCE: monitoring and education. UK and Irish universities should discuss reasons and strategies to monitor PCE availability and circulation. On the basis of this study, we feel it would be unreasonable for universities to institute drastic monitoring measures, because students show themselves to be sufficiently resilient to PCE without direct intervention. Moreover, university student life is ideally characterised by increasing autonomy and responsibility; these values should not be undermined through PCE surveillance activities.

Universities should take account of the level of interest in cognitive enhancement and educate students to make responsible decisions about PCEs. We recognise that 'responsible' decision-making in relation to misuse of prescription drugs, could be taken to mean that in all cases students should not misuse such drugs for PCE. However, we favour a pragmatic approach in which 'responsible decision-making' is characterised by raising awareness of the ethics, risks and benefits of pharmacological means of cognitive enhancement, relative to other means. As part of this endeavour, universities should focus on deflating the media hype around PCE and correcting the wrong impression that sustained use of 'smart drugs' is highly prevalent among UK students.

Acknowledgments

We are grateful to members of the Independent Scientific Committee on Drugs (ISCD) for support with this study and for helpful comments on the manuscript.

Author Contributions

Conceived and designed the experiments: IS IB. Performed the experiments: IS IB. Analyzed the data: IB JJ IS. Wrote the paper: IS IB JJ.

References

1. Hildt E (2013) Cognitive enhancement - A critical look at the current debate. In E Hildt, AG Franke, eds. Cognitive enhancement: An interdisciplinary perspective. London: Springer 1–14.
2. AAP (2013) Stress of study leads some to try 'academic doping', The Australian, 20 August. http://www.theaustralian.com.au/higher-education/stress-of-study-leads-some-to-try-academic-doping/story-e6frgcjx-1226699737256. Accessed 23 February 2014.
3. Paton G (2013) Universities warned of 'explosion' in use of smart drugs, The Telegraph 28 September http://www.telegraph.co.uk/education/university education/10340244/Universities-warned-of-explosion-in-use-of-smart-drugs.html. Accessed 20 February, 2014.
4. Sky News (2013) 'Smart Drug' Modafinil Risks Student Health, 28 September. http://news.sky.com/story/1147488/smart-drug-modafinil-risks-student-health Accessed 20 February, 2014.
5. Pustovrh T, Mali F (2013) Exploring some challenges of the pharmaceutical cognitive enhancement discourse: Users and policy recommendations. Neuroethics: 1–22.
6. Presidents Council on Bioethics (2003) Beyond therapy: Biotechnology and the pursuit of happiness. New York: Harper Collins.
7. Parliamentary Office of Science and Technology (POST) (2007) Better brains. No. 285. Parliamentary Office copyright www.parliament.uk/parliamentary_offices/post.cfm Accessed 10 February, 2014.
8. Comitato Nazionale per la Bioetica (13 March, 2013) Neuroscience and pharmacological cognitive enhancement: Bioethical aspects http://www.governo.it/bioetica/eng/opinions.html Accessed 23 February, 2014.
9. Smith ME, Farah MJ (2011) Are prescription stimulants "smart pills"? The epidemiology and cognitive neuroscience of prescription stimulant use by normal healthy individuals. Psychological Bulletin 137(5): 717.
10. Wilens TE, Adler LA, Adams J, Sgambati S, Rotrosen J, et al. (2008) Misuse and diversion of stimulants prescribed for ADHD: a systematic review of the literature. J Am Acad Child Adolesc Psychiatry 47(1): 21–31. doi: 10.1097/chi.0b013e31815a56f1
11. DeSantis A, Noar SM, Webb E (2010) Speeding through the frat house: A qualitative exploration of nonmedical ADHD stimulant use in fraternities. Journal of Drug Education 40(2): 157–171
12. Franke AG, Bonertz C, Christmann M, Huss M, Fellgiebel A, et al. (2011) Non-medical use of prescription stimulants and illicit use of stimulants for cognitive enhancement in pupils and students in Germany. Pharmacopsychiatry 44(02): 60–66.
13. Eickenhorst P, Vitzthum K, Klapp BF, Groneberg D, Mache S (2012) Neuroenhancement among German university students: Motives, expectations, and relationship with psychoactive lifestyle drugs. Journal of Psychoactive Drugs, 44(5): 418–427.
14. Singh I, Filipe AM, Bard I, Bergey M, Baker L (2013) Globalization and cognitive enhancement: emerging social and ethical challenges for ADHD clinicians. Curr Psychiatry Rep 15(9): 385–9.
15. Maier LJ, Liechti ME, Herzig F, Schaub MP (2013) To dope or not to dope: Neuroenhancement with prescription drugs and drugs of abuse among Swiss university students. PLoS ONE 8(11): e77967. doi: 10.1371/journal.pone.0077967
16. Ott R, Biller-Andorno N (2014) Neuroenhancement among Swiss students - A comparison of users and non-users. Pharmacopsychiatry 47(1): 22–8.
17. Castaldi S, Gelatti U, Orizio G, Hartung U, Moreno-Londono AM, et al. (2012) Use of cognitive enhancement medication among northern Italian university students. Journal of Addiction Medicine 6(2): 112–117.
18. Humle T, Friislund M (2010) 'Study drugs' vinder frem på universiteter. Information. http://www.information.dk/236139. Accessed 2014 February 23.
19. Holloway K, Bennett T (2012) Prescription drug misuse among university staff and students: A survey of motives, nature and extent. Drugs: education, prevention and policy. 19(2): 137–144.
20. Ragan I, Bard I, Singh I (2012) What should we do about student use of cognitive enhancers? An analysis of current evidence. Neuropharmacology 64: 588–95.
21. Lennard N (2009) One in ten takes drugs to study. Varsity Student Newspaper. March 6 http://www.varsity.co.uk/news/1307. Accessed 2014 February 20.
22. Partridge B (2013) A bubble of enthusiasm: How prevalent is the use of prescription stimulants for cognitive enhancement? In E . Hildt, AG . Frank (eds) Cognitive enhancement: An interdisciplinary perspective. Springer Netherlands: 39–47.
23. DeSantis AD, Webb E, Noar S (2008) Illicit use of prescription ADHD medications among college students: a multi-methodological approach. Journal of American College Health 57(3): 315–323.
24. Workman TA, Eells G (2010) Assessing the Risks and Issues: Prescription Drug Abuse on Campus http://www.stetson.edu/law/conferences/highered/archive/media/higher-ed-archives-2010/assessing-the-risks-and-issues.pdf. Accessed 2014 February 23.
25. DeSantis AD, Hane AC (2010) "Adderall is definitely not a drug": Justifications for the illegal use of ADHD stimulants. Substance Use & Misuse 45(1–2): 31–46.
26. Franke AG, Lieb K, Hildt E (2012) What users think about the differences between caffeine and illicit/prescription stimulants for cognitive enhancement. PLOS One. DOI: 10.1371/journal.pone.0040047
27. Scheske C, Schnall S (2012) The ethics of "smart drugs": Moral judgments about healthy people's use of cognitive-enhancing drugs. Basic and Applied Social Psychology 34(6): 508–515.
28. Hansard HC (2013) Deb 4, cc1072W–1073W.
29. Brant R (1990) Assessing proportionality in the proportional odds model for ordinal logistic regression. Biometrics, 46: 1171–1178.
30. EMCDDA (2002) Handbook for surveys on drug use among the general population. http://www.emcdda.europa.eu/html.cfm/index58052EN.html. Accessed 2014 Jan 26.
31. Peterkin AL, Crone CC, Sheridan MJ, Wise TN (2010) Cognitive performance enhancement: Misuse of self-treatment. J Atten Disord. doi: 10.1177/1089054710365980
32. Ly C, Gehricke JG (2013) Marijuana use is associated with inattention in men and sleep quality in women with Attention-Deficit/Hyperactivity Disorder: A preliminary study. Psychiatry Research 2010: 1310–1312.
33. Bergström LS, Lynöe N (2008) Enhancing concentration, mood and memory in healthy individuals: an empirical study of attitudes among general practitioners and the general population. Scandinavian Journal of Public Health 36(5): 532–537.
34. Reips UD (2002) Standards for Internet-based experimenting. Experimental Psychology 49 (4): 243–56.

8

Epidemiology of Treated Attention-Deficit/Hyperactivity Disorder (ADHD) across the Lifespan in Taiwan: A Nationwide Population-Based Longitudinal Study

Charles Lung-Cheng Huang[1,2], Chin-Chen Chu[3,4], Tain-Junn Cheng[5,6,7], Shih-Feng Weng[8,9]*

1 Department of Psychiatry, Chi Mei Medical Center, Tainan, Taiwan, **2** School of Medicine, Kaohsiung Medical University, Kaohsiung, Taiwan, **3** Department of Anesthesiology, Chi Mei Medical Center, Tainan, Taiwan, **4** Department of Recreation and Health-Care Management, Chia-Nan University of Pharmacy and Science, Tainan, Taiwan, **5** Department of Neurology and Occupational Medicine, Chi Mei Medical Center, Tainan, Taiwan, **6** Department of Occupational Safety, College of Environment, Chia Nan University of Pharmacy and Science, Tainan, Taiwan, **7** Department of Occupational and Environmental Medicine, National Cheng Kung University Hospital, Tainan, Taiwan, **8** Department of Medical Research, Chi Mei Medical Center, Tainan, Taiwan, **9** Department of Hospital and Health Care Administration, Chia Nan University of Pharmacy and Science, Tainan, Taiwan

Abstract

Objectives: We used insurance claims of a nationally representative population-based cohort to assess the longitudinal treated prevalence and incidence of attention-deficit/hyperactivity disorder (ADHD) in children, adolescents and adults.

Methods: Participants were identified from among National Health Insurance enrollees in Taiwan from 1999 to 2005. We identified study subjects who had at least one service claim during these years with a principal diagnosis of ADHD. A total of 6,173 patients were recorded in the treated ADHD cohort during the 6-year study.

Results: There was a significant increase in the treated prevalence rate of ADHD during the study period, from 64.65 per 100,000 in 2000 to 145.40 per 100,000 in 2005 ($p = .001$). An increase in the treated incidence rate of ADHD, from 44.67 per 100,000 in 2000 to 81.20 per 100,000 in 2005, was also observed ($p = .013$). However, the treated prevalence of ADHD was still lower than that of the community data in Taiwan. The peak treated prevalence of ADHD was at age 7–12 years for both males and females, and the peak treated incidence of ADHD was at age 0–6 for females and age 7–12 for males. Overall, the treated incidence and prevalence rates dropped abruptly after age 13–18 (both $p < .001$) for males and females ($p < .001$ for both). Male vs. female ratios of treated prevalence and incidence were both above 1 before age 25–30 years, but below 1 thereafter.

Conclusion: Although an increasing number of people with ADHD sought treatment during 1999–2005 in Taiwan, the treated prevalence of ADHD was still lower than that of the community data. The treated incidence and prevalence of ADHD fell dramatically after age 13–18. However, more women than men sought treatment in adulthood. There may be under-diagnosis and under-treatment of ADHD, especially among females and adults.

Editor: Philip Allen, University of Akron, United States of America

Funding: This research was supported by the Chi-Mei Medical Center, Tainan, Taiwan (CMFHR10131). The funders had no role in study design, data collection and analysis, decision to publish, or preparation of the manuscript.

Competing Interests: The authors have declared that no competing interests exist.

* E-mail: also99@gmail.com

Introduction

Attention-deficit/hyperactivity disorder (ADHD) is characterized by behavioral symptoms of inattention, hyperactivity, and impulsivity across the life cycle and is associated with considerable morbidity and disability [1,2]. Although it has long been recognized that ADHD is one of the most prevalent psychiatric disorders among children [3], the fact that this disorder often persists into adulthood and has a devastating impact has only recently become the focus of attention [4,5,6]. ADHD affects approximately 3% to 12% of school-aged children and adolescents [7,8,9,10,11], with a higher prevalence among males [7,9,10]. The symptoms may decline with age [12,13,14]. Nevertheless, the available data suggest that ADHD has a persistence rate of 15% to 78% into adulthood [4,13,15], depending on how one defines persistence. Epidemiology data on adult ADHD are limited, but several attempts have been made to gather this data and yielded prevalence estimates in the range of 1–6% [11,14,16,17].

ADHD impacts several domains of the lives of those who suffer from its symptoms, their family, and society [5,18,19]. Patients with untreated ADHD are associated with poorer long-term self-esteem and social functioning outcomes than non-ADHD controls [20,21]. Treatment for ADHD is associated with reduced core symptoms and improvement in outcomes [4,20,21]. However, it has been suggested that ADHD is underdiagnosed and undertreated [22,23], especially in girls [24] as well as in adults [25,26,27]. In spite of the public health implications due to the high prevalence and considerable morbidity and disability in

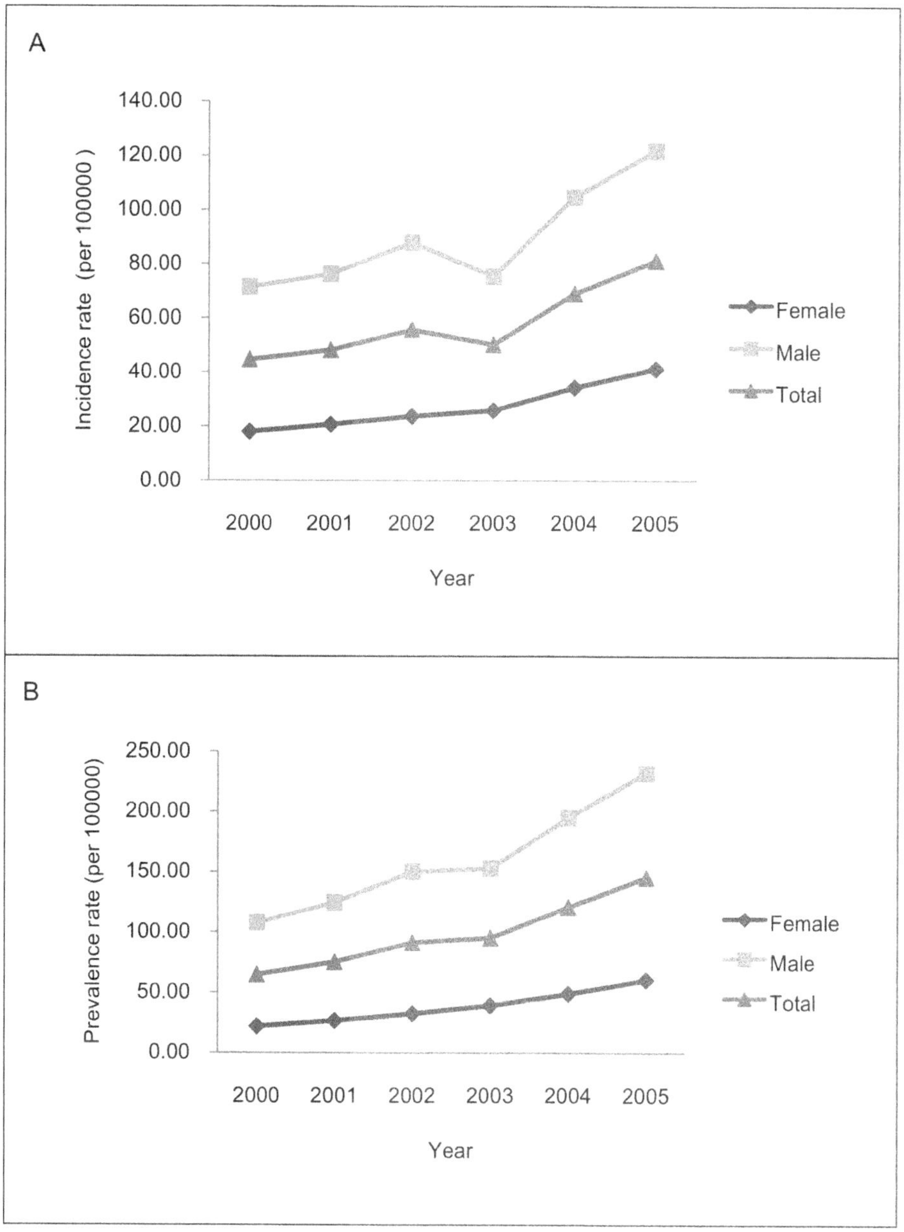

Figure 1. Overall 6-year healthcare-seeking incidence and prevalence of ADHD by years. (A) The trend analyses of year tested by linear regression were women (beta = 4.55; P = 0.002), men (beta = 9.29; P = 0.023), and total (beta = 6.85; P = 0.013). (B) The trend analyses of year tested by linear regression were women (beta = 7.61; P<0.001), men (beta = 23.85; P = 0.001), and total (beta = 15.56; P = 0.001).

childhood and adulthood as a result of ADHD, only a few data exist on the treatment patterns of ADHD in routine clinical practice [25,26,28], and knowledge regarding the adult group remains sparse [25,26]. Take Taiwan for example, where only one previous study known to us has estimated the epidemiology of treated ADHD in children aged 1–8 years [29]. This study reported a cumulative incidence up to age 8 of 2.69% for ADHD in 2004. There is evidence that factors such as genetic disposition, neurochemical abnormalities, neuropsychological deregulation, and environmental factors persist across the lifespan or change age-dependently [6,30]. Nevertheless, basic information on how the treated prevalence and incidence of ADHD varies by age and gender remains poorly described. Another gap in the current ADHD literature is that, although there have been both cross-sectional [26,31] and longitudinal epidemiological estimates [28,29] of treated ADHD, few studies [25] have explored the longitudinal trends of ADHD prevalence and incidence across the lifespan, using nationwide datasets. To our knowledge, only one study has examined the prevalence and incidence trends of pharmacologically treated ADHD in children, adolescents, and adults [25]. The authors found that a trend of increasing prescribing prevalence of ADHD drug treatment was observed within each age category from 2003 to 2008 in UK. Prevalence of prescribing to adult patients increased; however the numbers treated are much lower than published estimates of the prevalence of ADHD. The databank used in that study consisted of information provided by general practitioners in the UK, however. In an attempt to fill this gap, we designed a study to evaluate the annual incidence and prevalence of pharmacologically-treated ADHD (may include other nonpharmacological and multimodal management for adjuvant therapy) in healthcare-seeking children, adolescents, and adults among a nationally representative general population in Taiwan for the period 1999 to 2005. The inclusion of 6 years of data with a wide age range allowed us to investigate longitudinal trends of treated ADHD prevalence and incidence across the lifespan.

Methods

Sample

In this study, the medical claims data were retrieved from the Taiwan's National Health Insurance Research Database (NHIRD). The confidentiality of individuals was protected using encrypted personal identification to avoid the possibility of the ethical violations related to the data. Exemption was obtained from the institutional review board of Chi Mei Medical Center. The study sample was taken from the database of medical claims, including outpatient (ambulatory) care, hospital inpatient care, dental services, and prescription drugs provided by the National Health Research Institutes (NHRI) in Taiwan for use in related healthcare service studies. The Longitudinal Health Insurance Database 2005 is a sub-dataset of the NHIRD that contains all claims data (from 1996 to 2011) of one million beneficiaries who were randomly selected in 2005. The data consists of outpatient (ambulatory) care and inpatient care records and the registration files of the Taiwan NHIRD; as many as 93.1% of the residents of Taiwan in 1999 and 99.2% in 2009 were enrolled in the national health insurance system. There were no statistically significant differences in age and sex between the sample group and all enrollees.

The Definition of ADHD

Using the International Classification of Disease, 9th Revision, Clinical Modification (ICD-9-CM) diagnostic criteria [2], study subjects were identified as those who had at least one service claim (either outpatient or inpatient care) with a principal diagnosis of ADHD (ICD-9-CM: 314.XX) between 1999 and 2005.

In Taiwan, most of ADHD patients are diagnosed and treated by psychiatrists. They are diagnosed through clinical interview, scale assessment, and neuropsychological test (e.g. attention ability) in either outpatient or inpatient care. The physicians register the diagnosis code of the patient to the national health insurance system according to the ICD-9-CM diagnostic criteria. The treatment is pharmacotherapy mostly, but may also include nonpharmacological and multimodal management for adjuvant therapy, such as psychoeducation, counseling, behavioral intervention, and family therapy.

The Treated Prevalence of ADHD

Study subjects described above were defined as the prevalent cases from 1999 to 2005. The treated prevalence of ADHD from 1999 to 2005 was also calculated. The treated prevalence of ADHD was calculated with the number of total study subjects at the beginning of each year as the denominator and the number of prevalent cases of ADHD in each year as the numerator.

The Treated Incidence (Newly Diagnosed) of ADHD

The study subjects who were defined as having ADHD during the year and had not been defined as having ADHD during the previous years were defined as incident cases. The treated incidence of ADHD for each year was calculated from 1999 to 2005. The denominator was the person-years that were contrib-

Table 1. Incidence rate and prevalence rate of ADHD in Taiwan, 1999~2005.

	N (Incidence rate per 100,000 per year)			N (prevalence rate per 100,000 per year)			M/F ratio of incidence	M/F ratio of prevalence
	Female	Male	Total	Female	Male	Total		
1999				101 (22.16)	420 (93.83)	521 (57.67)		4.23
2000	82(17.97)	325(71.46)	407 (44.67)	99 (21.70)	490 (107.74)	589 (64.65)	3.98	4.97
2001	97 (20.73)	351 (76.23)	448 (48.26)	124 (26.50)	573 (124.44)	697 (75.08)	3.68	4.70
2002	111 (23.69)	410 (87.82)	521 (55.70)	152 (32.45)	701 (150.14)	853 (91.19)	3.71	4.63
2003	125 (25.86)	353 (75.36)	478 (50.22)	189 (39.10)	716 (152.85)	905 (95.08)	2.91	3.91
2004	166 (34.27)	494 (104.80)	660 (69.06)	236 (48.72)	918 (194.76)	1154 (120.75)	3.06	4.00
2005	208 (41.25)	604 (121.82)	812 (81.20)	304 (60.30)	1150 (231.94)	1454 (145.40)	2.95	3.85
Total	789	2537	3326	1205	4968	6173		

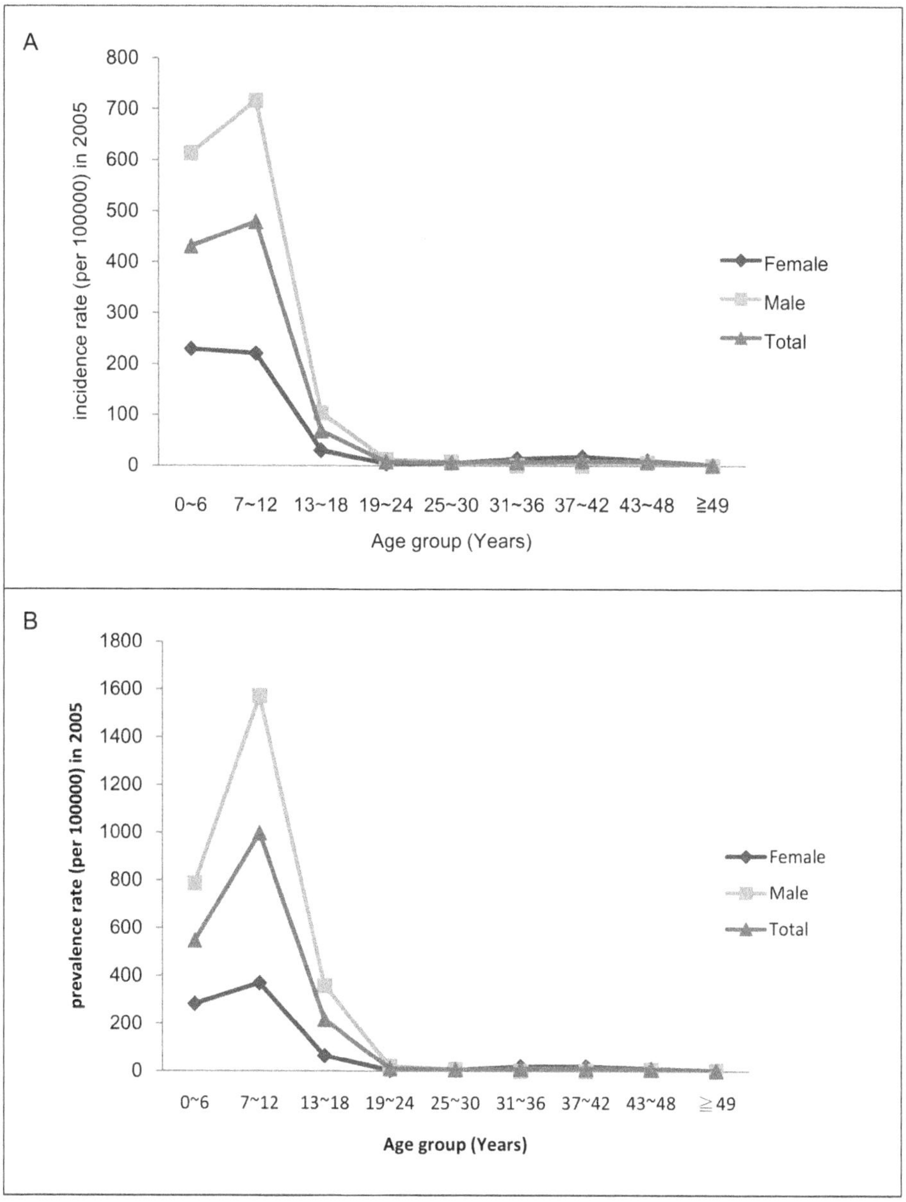

Figure 2. Healthcare-seeking incidence and prevalence of ADHD by age stratification in 2005. (A) Chow test (breakpoint age 13~18) in women (F = 168.64; P<0.001), men (F = 146.24; P<0.001), and total (F = 167.34; P<0.001). (B) Chow test (breakpoint age13~18) in women (F = 85.19; P<0.001), men (F = 43.48; P<0.001), and total (F = 48.49; P<0.001).

uted by the study subjects. The study subjects who were alive at the end of the year contributed one person-year to the denominator. The study subjects who died during the year contributed one-half person-year to the denominator. The numerator was the number of incident cases.

Measurements and Statistical Analysis

We obtained the information on age and sex directly from the Bureau of National Health Insurance (BNHI)'s insured file. Age was categorized into one of 8 groups comprising every 6 years from 0 to 48 years (e.g., 0–6, 7–12, etc.), and older than 49 years. The trend analyses of years were tested by linear regression using overall 6-year treated incidence and prevalence of ADHD. The Chow test [32], a particular test for structural change to determine whether the coefficients in a regression model are the same in separate sub-samples, was used to specify the breakpoint (e.g., age 13–18 years) in terms of the position of the observation.

The SAS statistical package SAS System for Windows, version 9.3.1 (SAS Institute Inc, Cary, North Carolina, USA) was used to perform the analyses in this study.

Results

A total of 6,173 patients were enrolled in the treated (healthcare-seeking) ADHD cohort during the 6-year study.

There was a significant increase in the prevalence rate of treated ADHD using linear regression for trend analyses of years, from 64.65 per 100,000 in 2000 to 145.40 per 100,000 in 2005 (beta = 15.56, $p = .001$). Increasing trends were found for both males (beta = 23.85, $p = .001$) and females (beta = 7.61, $p < .001$).

Table 2. Age- and sex-specific incidence (newly diagnosed) of ADHD by age stratification in 2005.

	N (incidence rate (per 100,000))			N (prevalence rate (per 100,000))			M/F ratio of incidence	M/F ratio of prevalence
	Female	Male	Total	Female	Male	Total		
0~6	82 (229.48)	241 (613.47)	323 (430.56)	101 (282.65)	309 (786.56)	410 (546.54)	2.67	2.78
7~12	86 (220.45)	305 (716.85)	391 (479.41)	144 (369.13)	669 (1572.38)	813 (996.84)	3.25	4.26
13~18	12 (29.88)	45 (103.67)	57 (68.21)	26 (64.74)	155 (357.10)	181 (216.60)	3.47	5.52
19~24	2 (4.00)	5 (12.33)	7 (7.73)	2 (4.00)	8 (19.72)	10 (11.04)	3.08	4.93
25~30	3 (5.31)	4 (7.74)	7 (6.47)	3 (5.31)	4 (7.74)	7 (6.47)	1.46	1.46
31~36	7 (13.74)	0 (0.00)	7 (7.03)	10 (19.63)	0 (0.00)	10 (10.05)	0.00	0.00
37~42	9 (17.91)	0 (0.00)	9 (8.95)	10 (19.90)	0 (0.00)	10 (9.94)	0.00	0.00
43~48	5 (10.45)	3 (6.24)	8 (8.34)	5 (10.45)	3 (6.24)	8 (8.34)	0.60	0.60
≥49	2 (1.50)	1 (0.76)	3 (1.13)	3 (2.24)	2 (1.52)	5 (1.89)	0.51	0.68

M/F ratio = male-to-female ratio.

There was a trend toward an increase in the incidence rate of treated ADHD, from 44.67 per 100,000 in 2000 to 81.20 per 100,000 in 2005 (beta = 6.85, $p = .013$), although there was a decrease in 2003. The treated prevalence and incidence rates of ADHD were both higher in males than in females for every calendar year. However, decreasing trends were noticed for the male-to-female ratio of treated incidence and prevalence during 2000–2005, ranging from 3.98 to 2.95 and 4.97 to 3.85, respectively (Table 1, Figure 1).

In 2005, the treated prevalence of ADHD was 231.94 per 100,000 for males and 60.30 per 100,000 for females, and the treated incidence was 121.82 per 100,000 for males and 41.25 per 100,000 for females. The peak treated prevalence of ADHD was in the 7–12 years age group for both males and females, and the peak treated incidence was at age 0–6 years for females and 7–12 years for males. Overall, the treated incidence rate dropped abruptly after age 13–18 years ($F = 168.64$, $p < .001$) for both males and females (both $p < .001$) using Chow test. The treated prevalence rate also dropped abruptly after age 16–18 years ($F = 48.49$, $p < .001$), for both males and females (both $p < .001$) (Table 2, Figure 2).

The overall male-to-female ratios of the treated prevalence and incidence of ADHD were 3.85 and 2.95, respectively. Male-to-female ratios of treated prevalence ranged from 1.46 to 5.52 before age 25–30 years, but fell below 1 thereafter. Male-to-female ratios of treated incidence ranged from 1.46 to 3.47 before age 25–30 years, but fell below 1 thereafter (Figure 3).

Discussion

Our study is among the few that have examined healthcare-seeking ADHD patients across their lifespan, with a long observation period and a large sample of a general population, using data from Taiwan's NHIRD. We designed a study to evaluate the annual incidence and prevalence of pharmacologically-treated ADHD in healthcare-seeking children, adolescents, and adults among a nationally representative general population in Taiwan for the period 1999 to 2005.

Trends of Treated Prevalence and Incidence of ADHD

Overall, prevalence of treated ADHD increased during 2000–2005 from 64.65 per 100,000 to 145.40 per 100,000 patients. An increase in the treated incidence rate of ADHD was also observed, from 44.67 per 100,000 to 81.20 per 100,000. These findings are in line with figures reported in the literature, which show an increase in the prevalence of ADHD treatment during the past decade in the UK [25], the Netherlands [28], and the USA [33,34]. Only one previous study known to us has estimated the epidemiology for treated ADHD in Taiwan [29]. The authors reported on the treated incidence in children aged 1–8 years from 1996–2004, and also found an elevated incidence rate for treated ADHD in later birth cohorts.

The results of this study suggest an increase in the prevalence and incidence of treated ADHD in Taiwan throughout the study period; however, the highest treated prevalence figure reported (15.7 per 1000 male patients aged 7–12 years) is below those reported in Germany (50 per 1000) [26], the Netherlands (21 per 1000) [28], and the USA (29 per 1000) [34], although is in line with the data from the UK (15.4 per 1000) [25]. It is worth noting that this number remains lower than the global prevalence of ADHD in community children and adolescents in Taiwan, which was estimated to be 9.9% and 3.3–7.5%, respectively [9,10].

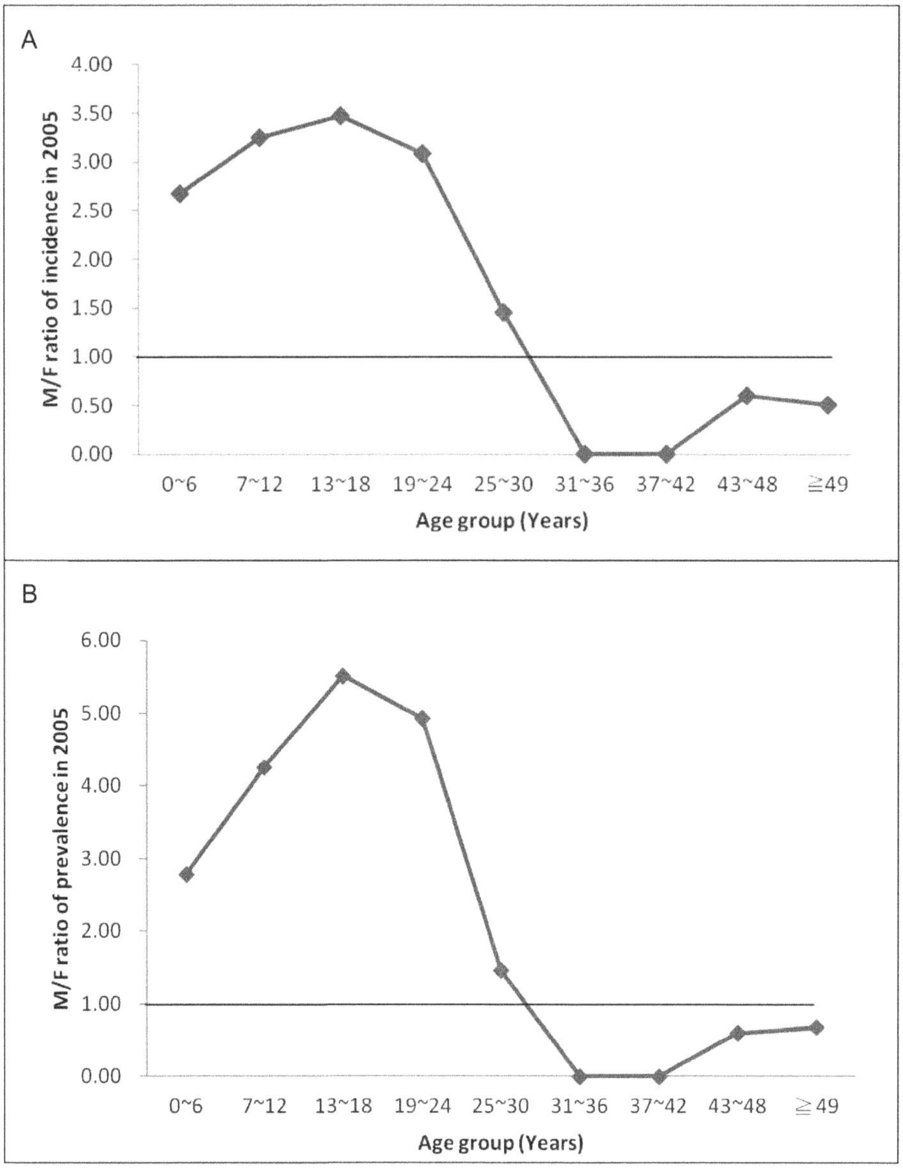

Figure 3. Male-to-female ratio of incidence and prevalence of ADHD by age stratification in 2005. M/F ratio = male-to-female ratio.

Under-diagnosis and Under-treatment of Adult ADHD

Our data showed that the peak treated prevalence of ADHD was at age 7–12 years for both males and females. These findings are in line with figures reported in Western countries, including Germany [26], the UK [25], and the USA [34]. It was surprising that the treated incidence and prevalence rates for both males and females dropped abruptly after age 13–18 years. A recent study by McCarthy et al. used The Health Improvement Network (THIN) database to examine the epidemiology of pharmacological treatment in children, adolescents and adults between 2003 and 2008 in UK primary care [25]. They also demonstrated a dramatic fall in treated incidence and prevalence rates after age 13–17 years. Furthermore, the highest treated prevalence rate among adults in our study was 0.20 per 1000 male patients aged 19–24 years, which was much lower than the estimated figure for ADHD in the general population.

There may be several explanations for the under-treatment of ADHD patients in their adulthood. In Taiwan, Ritalin (methylphenidate) is the only stimulant that has been included in the benefit package of the National Health Insurance program for use in the treatment of ADHD in adults [35]. Concerta (prolonged-release methylphenidate) and Strattera (atomoxetine HCl) are only indicated as continuation treatment for adults who started their treatment with this medication in childhood or adolescence. The strict regulation may hamper the treatment of adult ADHD patients. Lack of awareness of this disorder among the general population and even clinical practitioners may be another important reason for the under-treatment of adults. A retrospective claims database analysis covering the insured population of Nordbaden in Germany also revealed that ADHD was rarely detected in the adult population [26]. In addition, most patients were not seen by a mental health specialist, and physician involvement was highly concentrated.

Gender Effect on Treated Prevalence and Incidence of Healthcare-seeking ADHD

The present study has demonstrated that although the prevalence and incidence rates of treated ADHD were both higher in male patients for every calendar year, decreasing trends were noted for the male-to-female ratio throughout the study period, for both treated incidence and prevalence. These findings are in line with figures reported in the literature, which showed prevalence and incidence rates of drug prescribing were both consistently higher among boys than girls, although the greatest increases over time were observed in female patients [28,33]. McCarthy et al. also found that while the proportions of prescribing prevalence for males were higher in the various age categories over time, the rates of increase in treated prevalence were greater in females than males, for patients aged 6–12 years, 13–17 years, and 25–45 years [25].

The general impression that male ADHD are much more likely to be clinically diagnosed and treated is mostly based on studies among children and adolescents [28,33], rather than adult population. We found it interesting that the male to female ratios of treated prevalence and incidence were both above 1 before age 25 to 30 years, but below 1 thereafter. To our knowledge, a reverse male to female ratio of treated prevalence and incidence after adulthood has rarely been reported. Of the studies examining gender effects on the epidemiology of healthcare-seeking ADHD across the lifespan, one did not find a reverse ratio [26], and another found a reverse incidence ratio only among patients older than 45 years [25]. Since there was no evidence of a higher prevalence among females in the general population in the literature, there is a possibility that the higher treated incidence and prevalence among healthcare-seeking women in their adulthood may be associated with previously under-recognized ADHD. This finding echoes the argument of a previous study that ADHD may be under-identified in girls [24].

Limitations and Strengths

This study has some limitations, however. The ADHD diagnoses used in the study were from administrative claims data reported by physicians, which may not be as precise as diagnoses made by structured interview with specific diagnostic criteria. Still another limitation of this study is that the sample size of adult patients was relatively small. Despite these considerations, the present study has important implications for practice and research. Our study is one of the few to explore longitudinal trends in the treated prevalence and incidence of healthcare-seeking ADHD patients across the lifespan, using nationwide datasets. The use of a nationwide population-based database such as this has advantages, such as (1) the large sample size; (2) preventing selection bias in recruiting study subjects; (3) avoiding the recall bias of patients when filling out questionnaires; (4) it may be more representative of the real world, i.e., allowing us to understand what is actually happening under the general conditions of clinical practice. This study has added to the existing body of knowledge on age and gender effects on the epidemiology of treated ADHD in clinical settings, in particular to the ADHD healthcare-seeking figures in adulthood.

Conclusions

Epidemiologic data from Taiwan's NHIRD in current study showed that although increasing numbers of people with ADHD had sought treatment during 1999–2005 in Taiwan, the treated prevalence of ADHD was still lower than in community data. The unique findings of this study were that there may be an under-diagnosis and under-treatment of ADHD, especially among females and adults. Nevertheless, more women than men sought treatment in their adulthood. This study has added to the existing body of knowledge on age and gender effects on the epidemiology of treated ADHD in clinical settings, in particular to the ADHD healthcare-seeking figures in adulthood. Furthermore epidemiologic studies can clarify whether the patterns of ADHD diagnosis and treatment in community and clinical settings is appropriate. Population-based epidemiologic studies may shed important new light on how we understand ADHD, as well as its natural history, treatment, and consequences.

Acknowledgments

Our study was based in part on data from the National Health Insurance Research Database provided by the Bureau of National Health Insurance, Department of Health, and managed by the National Health Research Institutes in Taiwan. We would also like to acknowledge Mr. James Ascencio for his assistance during the study period.

Author Contributions

Conceived and designed the experiments: CLCH CCC. Analyzed the data: SFW. Contributed reagents/materials/analysis tools: TJC. Wrote the paper: CLCH.

References

1. American Psychiatric Association (2000) Diagnostic and Statistical Manual of Mental Disorders-Text Revision. (DSM-IV-TR). Washington: APA.
2. World Health Organization (1992) International Classification of Diseases, 9th Revision, Clinical Modification. (ICD-9-CM). Ann Arbor: Commission on Professional and Hospital Activities, WHO.
3. Bird HR, Canino G, Rubio-Stipec M, Gould MS, Ribera J, et al. (1988) Estimates of the prevalence of childhood maladjustment in a community survey in Puerto Rico. The use of combined measures. Arch Gen Psychiatry 45: 1120–1126.
4. Wender PH, Wolf LE, Wasserstein J (2001) Adults with ADHD. An overview. Ann N Y Acad Sci 931: 1–16.
5. Spencer TJ, Biederman J, Mick E (2007) Attention-deficit/hyperactivity disorder: diagnosis, lifespan, comorbidities, and neurobiology. J Pediatr Psychol 32: 631–642.
6. Schmidt S, Petermann F (2009) Developmental psychopathology: Attention Deficit Hyperactivity Disorder (ADHD). BMC Psychiatry 9: 58.
7. Scahill L, Schwab-Stone M (2000) Epidemiology of ADHD in school-age children. Child Adolesc Psychiatr Clin N Am 9: 541–555, vii.
8. Wolraich ML, Hannah JN, Pinnock TY, Baumgaertel A, Brown J (1996) Comparison of diagnostic criteria for attention-deficit hyperactivity disorder in a county-wide sample. J Am Acad Child Adolesc Psychiatry 35: 319–324.
9. Gau SS, Chong MY, Chen TH, Cheng AT (2005) A 3-year panel study of mental disorders among adolescents in Taiwan. Am J Psychiatry 162: 1344–1350.
10. Wang YC, Chong MY, Chou WJ, Yang JL (1993) Prevalence of attention deficit hyperactivity disorder in primary school children in Taiwan. J Formos Med Assoc 92: 133–138.
11. Polanczyk G, Rohde LA (2007) Epidemiology of attention-deficit/hyperactivity disorder across the lifespan. Curr Opin Psychiatry 20: 386–392.
12. Biederman J, Mick E, Faraone SV (2000) Age-dependent decline of symptoms of attention deficit hyperactivity disorder: impact of remission definition and symptom type. Am J Psychiatry 157: 816–818.
13. Faraone SV, Biederman J, Mick E (2006) The age-dependent decline of attention deficit hyperactivity disorder: a meta-analysis of follow-up studies. Psychol Med 36: 159–165.
14. Simon V, Czobor P, Balint S, Meszaros A, Bitter I (2009) Prevalence and correlates of adult attention-deficit hyperactivity disorder: meta-analysis. Br J Psychiatry 194: 204–211.
15. Biederman J, Petty CR, Clarke A, Lomedico A, Faraone SV (2011) Predictors of persistent ADHD: an 11-year follow-up study. J Psychiatr Res 45: 150–155.
16. Fayyad J, De Graaf R, Kessler R, Alonso J, Angermeyer M, et al. (2007) Cross-national prevalence and correlates of adult attention-deficit hyperactivity disorder. Br J Psychiatry 190: 402–409.

17. Kessler RC, Adler L, Barkley R, Biederman J, Conners CK, et al. (2006) The prevalence and correlates of adult ADHD in the United States: results from the National Comorbidity Survey Replication. Am J Psychiatry 163: 716–723.
18. Klassen AF, Miller A, Fine S (2004) Health-related quality of life in children and adolescents who have a diagnosis of attention-deficit/hyperactivity disorder. Pediatrics 114: e541–547.
19. Swensen AR, Birnbaum HG, Secnik K, Marynchenko M, Greenberg P, et al. (2003) Attention-deficit/hyperactivity disorder: increased costs for patients and their families. J Am Acad Child Adolesc Psychiatry 42: 1415–1423.
20. Harpin V, Mazzone L, Raynaud JP, Kahle J, Hodgkins P (2013) Long-Term Outcomes of ADHD: A Systematic Review of Self-Esteem and Social Function. J Atten Disord.
21. Shaw M, Hodgkins P, Caci H, Young S, Kahle J, et al. (2012) A systematic review and analysis of long-term outcomes in attention deficit hyperactivity disorder: effects of treatment and non-treatment. BMC Med 10: 99.
22. Sayal K, Ford T, Goodman R (2010) Trends in recognition of and service use for attention-deficit hyperactivity disorder in Britain, 1999–2004. Psychiatr Serv 61: 803–810.
23. Cuffe SP, Moore CG, McKeown R (2009) ADHD and health services utilization in the national health interview survey. J Atten Disord 12: 330–340.
24. Biederman J (1998) Attention-deficit/hyperactivity disorder: a life-span perspective. J Clin Psychiatry 59 Suppl 7: 4–16.
25. McCarthy S, Wilton L, Murray ML, Hodgkins P, Asherson P, et al. (2012) The epidemiology of pharmacologically treated attention deficit hyperactivity disorder (ADHD) in children, adolescents and adults in UK primary care. BMC Pediatr 12: 78.
26. Schlander M, Schwarz O, Trott GE, Viapiano M, Bonauer N (2007) Who cares for patients with attention-deficit/hyperactivity disorder (ADHD)? Insights from Nordbaden (Germany) on administrative prevalence and physician involvement in health care provision. Eur Child Adolesc Psychiatry 16: 430–438.
27. Wender PH (1998) Attention-deficit hyperactivity disorder in adults. Psychiatr Clin North Am 21: 761–774, v.
28. Hodgkins P, Sasane R, Meijer WM (2011) Pharmacologic treatment of attention-deficit/hyperactivity disorder in children: incidence, prevalence, and treatment patterns in the Netherlands. Clin Ther 33: 188–203.
29. Chen CY, Liu CY, Su WC, Huang SL, Lin KM (2007) Factors associated with the diagnosis of neurodevelopmental disorders: a population-based longitudinal study. Pediatrics 119: e435–443.
30. Rowland AS, Lesesne CA, Abramowitz AJ (2002) The epidemiology of attention-deficit/hyperactivity disorder (ADHD): a public health view. Ment Retard Dev Disabil Res Rev 8: 162–170.
31. Perwien A, Hall J, Swensen A, Swindle R (2004) Stimulant treatment patterns and compliance in children and adults with newly treated attention-deficit/hyperactivity disorder. J Manag Care Pharm 10: 122–129.
32. Chow GC (1960) Tests of Equality Between Sets of Coefficients in Two Linear Regressions. Econometrica 28: 591–605.
33. Cox ER, Halloran DR, Homan SM, Welliver S, Mager DE (2008) Trends in the prevalence of chronic medication use in children: 2002–2005. Pediatrics 122: e1053–1061.
34. Zuvekas SH, Vitiello B, Norquist GS (2006) Recent trends in stimulant medication use among U.S. children. Am J Psychiatry 163: 579–585.
35. National Health Insurance Administration (2013) Drug coverage items and payment standard. Taipei: Ministry of Health and Welfare, editor.

9

Dissociable Patterns in the Control of Emotional Interference in Adults with Attention-Deficit/ Hyperactivity Disorder (ADHD) and in Adults with Alcohol Dependence

Ivo Marx[1]*, John Krause[1,2], Christoph Berger[1,3], Frank Häßler[3]

1 Department of Psychiatry and Psychotherapy, University Medicine Rostock, Rostock, Germany, 2 Department of Forensic Psychiatry, University Medicine Rostock, Rostock, Germany, 3 Department of Child and Adolescent Psychiatry, Psychotherapy and Neurology, University Medicine Rostock, Rostock, Germany

Abstract

Objectives: To effectively manage current task demands, attention must be focused on task-relevant information while task-irrelevant information is rejected. However, in everyday life, people must cope with emotions, which may interfere with actual task demands and may challenge functional attention allocation. Control of interfering emotions has been associated with the proper functioning of the dorsolateral prefrontal cortex (DLPFC). As DLPFC dysfunction is evident in subjects with ADHD and in subjects with alcohol dependence, the current study sought to examine the bottom-up effect of emotional distraction on task performance in both disorders.

Methods: Male adults with ADHD (n = 22), male adults with alcohol dependence (n = 16), and healthy controls (n = 30) performed an emotional working memory task (n-back task). In the background of the task, we presented neutral and negative stimuli that varied in emotional saliency.

Results: In both clinical groups, a working memory deficit was evident. Moreover, both clinical groups displayed deficient emotional interference control. The n-back performance of the controls was not affected by the emotional distractors, whereas that of subjects with ADHD deteriorated in the presence of low salient distractors, and that of alcoholics did not deteriorate until high salient distractors were presented. Subsequent to task performance, subjects with ADHD accurately recognized more distractors than did alcoholics and controls. In alcoholics, picture recognition accuracy was negatively associated with n-back performance, suggesting a functional association between the ability to suppress emotional distractors and successful task performance. In subjects with ADHD, performance accuracy was negatively associated with ADHD inattentive symptoms, suggesting that inattention contributes to the performance deficit.

Conclusions: Subjects with ADHD and alcoholics both display an emotional interference control deficit, which is especially pronounced in subjects with ADHD. Beyond dysfunctional attention allocation processes, a more general attention deficit seems to contribute to the more pronounced performance deficit pattern in ADHD.

Editor: Linda Chao, University of California, San Francisco, United States of America

Funding: The authors have no support or funding to report.

Competing Interests: The authors have declared that no competing interests exist.

* Email: ivo.marx@med.uni-rostock.de

Introduction

Attention-Deficit/Hyperactivity Disorder (ADHD) is a childhood-onset syndrome consisting of inattentive, hyperactive, and impulsive characteristics [1]. Approximately 65% of children and adolescents with ADHD show partial remission by the age of 25, whereas 15% continue to meet full DSM-IV criteria [2]. Given a prevalence rate of 2.9% to 4.4%, ADHD is one of the most common psychiatric disorders in adulthood [3,4]. Compared to children with ADHD, affected adults show fewer hyperactive symptoms, but their inattentive and impulsive symptoms persist [5]. These symptoms cause complications in areas such as work, social life, and relationships [6,7]. Subjects with ADHD are often susceptible to alcoholism [8–10]. It has been shown that the risk of developing an alcohol use disorder is increased by a factor of 1.7 in children with ADHD [11]. Furthermore, adult alcoholics with ADHD have been found to begin to exceed the critical level of alcohol use earlier [8] and show a pattern of longer-lasting abuse [12] compared with non-ADHD alcoholics.

Deficits in emotion regulation (ER) have been reported in children and adolescents [13–17] as well as in adults with ADHD (for a review, see [18]). ER deficits seem to be prominent especially in the combined subtype [13–14], which suggests an association with hyperactive-impulsive symptoms and therefore with deficient inhibitory control of inadequate emotional expression. Studies that have focused on the expressive aspect of emotional dysregulation in children with ADHD have found an increased expression of negative affect in potentially frustrating situations [14,15,17]. Importantly, emotional dysregulation has been negatively associated with social status and peer preference [14,15], which underlines the relevance of these deficits for everyday life. Likewise, deficits in ER have been reported in alcohol-dependent subjects [19,20] and have been linked with alcohol dependency severity [21,22]. Because the severity of alcohol dependency has been related to inhibition deficits [23], a connection between deficient inhibitory capacities and impaired ER is suggested. Thus, ER deficits may be caused by deficient inhibitory control over emotional responses in both ADHD and alcohol dependence.

Barkley [24] suggests that deficits in emotional self-regulation in subjects with ADHD arise from increased emotional impulsivity (i.e., a lowered threshold and increased speed of responding to emotional cues), which itself is the result of a lack of effortful executive control. Executive control thus does not reflect a unitary construct but rather represents an accumulation of cognitive functions that subserve adaptive, goal-directed behavior. For example, executive functions encompass the allocation of attention toward task-relevant information, the inhibition of task-irrelevant information, planning, and behavior monitoring (for reviews, see [25,26]). In Barkley's model [24], self-regulation, or executive control, is conceptualized as a sequential construct that incorporates the inhibition of emotion-induced inappropriate behavior, self-calming, attention refocusing, and organized goal orienting. Likewise, Nigg and Casey [27] argue that ER deficits in ADHD are the result of a dysregulation of the frontolimbic circuitry that incorporates the amygdala, ventral striatum, and prefrontal top-down modulatory areas. Expanding the network of emotion processing according to the current state of research in healthy subjects, the regions most commonly involved in the generation of emotions involve the amygdala, the ventral striatum, the ventromedial prefrontal cortex, and the insula. However, executive control is exerted mainly by the dorsolateral prefrontal cortex (DLPFC), the anterior cingulate cortex, the ventrolateral prefrontal cortex, and the dorsomedial prefrontal cortex (for a review, see [28]).

Despite the fact that subjects with ADHD and subjects with alcohol dependence seem to suffer from top-down ER deficits, little is known about their prerequisites, the bottom-up effects of dysfunctional emotion processing. In this sense, deficient attentional control of interfering emotional stimuli or a lowered threshold for emotional cues [24] might cause emotional over-reagibility, which, in turn, might be a prerequisite for subsequent deficits in effortful behavioral control. Attentional control is thus defined as the ability to orient attention to task-relevant information while inhibiting task-irrelevant information [29–31], a function that has been shown to rely on the DLPFC [32].

One way to examine the attentional control of interfering emotional stimuli in experimental contexts is by using paradigms of emotional interference control. In these paradigms, cognitive tasks are imposed that require a continuous orienting of attention to task-relevant information. While the subjects work on the task, emotionally salient but task-irrelevant distractors are imposed, and an experimenter examines how these distractors interfere with attentional control (i.e., the degree to which performance deteriorates in the distractor's presence when compared with its absence) [33]. Assuming a limited number of attentional resources in the individual, task-irrelevant but emotionally salient distractors interfere with the primary task and cause a "fight for resources". In this way, the bottom-up effect of emotional distraction and a lack of cognitive control cause an over-allocation of resources to the emotional distractors and an under-allocation of resources to the primary task, which results in impaired task performance. According to this "neuro-competitive" model introduced by Iordan, Dolcos, and Dolcos [34], increased susceptibility to emotional interference is believed to be grounded in an imbalance of activity between the dorsal executive control system (incorporating the DLPFC and the lateral parietal cortex) and the ventral emotion processing system (incorporating the amygdala, the ventrolateral prefrontal cortex, and the medial prefrontal cortex), whereby a hypofunction of the executive control system causes impaired executive control over emotional responses. This model is supported by recent meta-analytic findings [35] that have identified the neuronal structures that are responsible for emotion processing (amygdala, superior temporal gyrus, insula, medial anterior cingulate cortex), cognitive control (supplementary motor area, superior parietal lobule, DLPFC), and the integration of emotion processing and cognitive control processes (subgenual anterior cingulate cortex, precuneus). Furthermore, the authors found the DLPFC and the inferior parietal lobule to be specifically involved in the processing of task-irrelevant emotional distractors, which underlines their unique role in attention allocation processes.

In the current study, we implemented a working memory ("n-back") task that requires attentional control as exerted by the DLPFC [36]. At the same time, we induced emotional interference by presenting pictures of varying emotional salience while participants performed the working memory task. Given its key role in emotional interference control by attention allocation processes [35], DLPFC functionality should be affected by emotional content; that is, emotionally salient but task-irrelevant stimuli should withdraw attention from the working memory task and should result in poorer task performance in terms of prolonged response times and decreased performance accuracy.

Testing this hypothesis in adults with ADHD, Marx et al. [37] recently found that those with the disorder displayed enhanced distractibility by emotionally salient stimuli in terms of lower performance accuracy when compared with non-affected controls. Specifically, the performance of subjects with ADHD deteriorated in the presence of emotionally low salience distractors, but that of the controls did not deteriorate until emotionally high salience distractors were presented. However, to our knowledge, no comparable research examining emotional interference control in alcoholics exists. Because working memory (WM) deficits have been demonstrated in individuals with ADHD [38,39] and in individuals with alcoholism [40], suggesting DLPFC dysfunction, and because both disorders show ER deficits, it remains unclear whether the disorders share a common dysfunction in the emotion processing system or whether deficient emotional interference control is specific to ADHD. WM deficits have been shown to be comparably stable in the course of ADHD [40,41], but these deficits seem to vary as a function of abstinence duration in alcohol-dependent individuals, with medium-sized effects emerging for short-term (up to one month) and intermediate-term (up to one year) abstinence and small effect sizes emerging for long-term abstinence (more than one year) [40]. Thus, WM deficits seem "trait-like" in adults with persisting ADHD and "state-like" in adults with alcohol dependency depending on the duration of abstinence, such that subjects with ADHD might be more susceptible to emotional interferences.

The current study aims to compare adults with ADHD (without comorbid alcohol dependence) and adults with alcohol dependence (without comorbid ADHD) relative to healthy control subjects in their ability to cope with emotional interferences while performing an emotional working memory ("n-back") task. First, we expect all groups to display performance deterioration as a function of task difficulty and the degree of distractor salience.

Second, we expect individuals with ADHD and alcoholic individuals to display WM deficits in comparison to controls. Third, because the two disorders have emotion processing deficits in common, we expect both groups of patients to be more distractible by task-irrelevant emotional stimuli, as indicated by larger performance deterioration under emotionally arousing conditions in comparison to controls. Fourth, because DLPFC dysfunction seems to be more stable over time in ADHD, the emotional interference effect should be more accentuated in the ADHD group compared with the alcoholism group. Fifth, because enhanced emotional distractibility implies a larger amount of attention allocation to emotional distractors, we expect that the ADHD group and alcoholic individuals will memorize the emotional stimuli better than the control group will, with alcoholic subjects outperforming those with ADHD.

Methods

Participants

As there is no prior knowledge of gender differences in emotional interference control in subjects with ADHD and in subjects with alcohol dependence, we decided to only include males to control for potential confounding variables associated with gender. The inclusion of males only was driven by sampling considerations. The gender ratio is balanced in adults with ADHD [42], while it is increased by a factor of two to three in alcoholics in favor of males [43–45]. Moreover, comorbid disorders hardly differ between alcohol-dependent males and females [44], whereas gender-related differences are present in subjects with ADHD [46,47]. This is another potentially confounding variable that we aimed to control for.

The study sample consisted of 68 male participants (22 subjects with ADHD, 16 subjects with alcohol dependence, and 30 healthy controls) who were 18 to 45 years old. The participants in the ADHD condition were recruited from the ADHD outpatient service of the Department of Psychiatry and Psychotherapy at the University Medicine Rostock. University hospital employees and students who were recruited via announcements served as controls. All participants with ADHD and 21 controls represent the male subsample of subjects who took part in the previously published study by Marx et al. [37]. Inpatients engaging in detoxification at the Department of Psychiatry and Psychotherapy and inpatients from a local specialist hospital for addictive disorders (Friedrich-Petersen-Klinik) formed the group of subjects with alcohol dependence.

The diagnostic procedure for all of the participants included extensive psychiatric examination using the Structured Clinical Interview for DSM-IV Axis I and II Disorders (SCID) [48] and the Personality Styles and Disorders Inventory (PSSI) [49]. Adult ADHD was assessed using German versions of the Barkley Interview [50], the Wender-Reimherr Interview [51], and the following questionnaires: a short version of the Wender Utah Rating Scale (WURS-k) [52], which was used to quantify ADHD symptoms in childhood; the Conners' Adult ADHD Rating Scales (CAARS-S:L) [53]; a short self-rating questionnaire based on the DSM-IV criteria (ADHS-SB) [51], which was used to assess current ADHD symptoms; and the Barratt Impulsiveness Scale (BIS-10) [54]. The ADHD diagnosis was assigned by a senior clinical psychiatrist and included the following criteria: a WURS-k sum score ≥30 points [55]; an age- and gender-adjusted total ADHD symptom subscale score of ≥1.5 SD above the mean on the CAARS-S:L; substantial impairment in more than one setting; and clinically relevant psychological strain. Alcohol dependence was diagnosed by means of the SCID, and additional information was gathered concerning the year of first alcohol consumption, the amount of alcohol consumed prior to treatment, the number of detoxifications, and the number of other alcohol-related treatments. In addition, the Alcohol Withdrawal Scale (AWS) [56] was used to assess whether alcohol withdrawal symptoms were currently observable in the participants. Participants who scored above 0 were excluded from the study. The intellectual capacity of all subjects was assessed with a short version of the Wechsler Adult Intelligence Scale-Revised (HAWIE-R) [57]. The alcohol-dependent and control subjects underwent the same diagnostic procedure as the subjects with ADHD.

The exclusion criteria for all of the participants included an IQ lower than 80, a neurological or endocrine disorder known to affect brain function, previous head injury, current depressive disorder, lifetime schizophrenia spectrum disorder, and borderline personality disorder. Furthermore, severe cognitive dysfunction (amnestic syndrome, dementia), current intoxication, symptoms of alcohol withdrawal, and severe impairment of liver functioning as measured by the Gamma GT served as exclusion criteria in the alcohol dependency group. Additionally, addiction in the ADHD group and in the control group as well as ADHD in the alcohol dependency group and in the control group served as exclusion criteria.

In the ADHD group, 16 subjects were combined subtype, five were primarily inattentive, and one subject was primarily hyperactive/impulsive. Half of the subjects were drug naïve; the others had taken methylphenidate previously but were free of any medication for a minimum of 72 h prior to testing. Within the ADHD group, one subject suffered from adjustment disorder, and seven subjects had a personality disorder (other than BPD). In the alcohol dependence group, one subject suffered from a panic disorder, one suffered from a THC addiction, two suffered from polytoxicomania, and three had a personality disorder (other than BPD). The three experimental groups did not differ from each other with regard to age, but subjects with alcohol dependence had lower IQ values compared with the ADHD and control subjects. It should be noted that the relatively high IQ values could be due to the use of the short version of the WAIS, which depends on relatively old German norms. Rather than examining a group of only well-educated subjects, educational and occupational levels were mixed in the experimental groups. The subjects with ADHD displayed increased ADHD symptom severity compared with the alcohol-dependent subjects, and the alcohol-dependent subjects displayed increased ADHD symptom severity compared with the controls. The basic demographic and clinical sample characteristics are shown in Table 1.

Experimental Tasks and Measures

Initially, a classical n-back task was applied. In this task, participants are presented with stimuli and are asked to indicate whether the currently presented stimulus is the same as the one presented n steps earlier in the sequence. The task consisted of eight 1-back and eight 2-back blocks, which were presented randomly. Each block consisted of 14 letters (4 targets, 10 distractors), and the subjects were asked to indicate targets by pressing the left mouse button ("yes") and distractors by pressing the right mouse button ("no"). The respective n-back condition was indicated by the number "1" or "2", which appeared at the beginning of each block. The entire task was preceded by two practice trials for each n-back condition.

Subsequently, the participants performed the emotional variant of the task [37]: they worked on the n-back task while simultaneously being presented with emotional background picture stimuli. The subjects were explicitly instructed to ignore

Table 1. Basic Demographic and Clinical Characteristics.

	ADHD		ALC		CON		F(2,65)	Post-Hoc
	M	SD	M	SD	M	SD		
Age	28.23	6.09	32.60	6.43	29.51	7.79	1.88	
IQ	128.14	17.44	113.44	16.92	126.79	13.55	4.83**	ALC<CON, ADHD
CAARS-S:L							F(2,62)	
Inattention	90.05	22.84	55.35	29.59	32.80	29.15	25.06***	CON <ALC <ADHD
Hyperactivity/Impulsivity	76.95	31.77	43.11	32.74	18.23	26.57	22.74***	CON<ALC<ADHD
ADHD Total	88.66	23.74	52.91	30.42	20.33	23.96	41.73***	CON<ALC<ADHD
Drinking units per day before admission			31.56	19.00				
Years since ≥ 3 DSM criteria fulfilled			8.88	5.37				
Number of detoxifications			1.69	2.60				
Number of other alcohol-related treatments			0.81	1.05				

ADHD = Subjects with ADHD, ALC = Alcoholics, CON = Controls. M = Mean, SD = Standard Deviation. *p<.05, **p<.01, *** p<.001.

the emotionally laden pictures and to process the task as quickly and as accurately as possible. The task consisted of nine 1-back and nine 2-back blocks, where each n-back condition consisted of 3 blocks with 14 neutral, low emotionally salient, or high emotionally salient pictures. Each block contained 14 randomly presented stimuli (4 targets, 10 distractors), and both the pictures within the blocks and the blocks themselves were presented in random order. Each picture was presented for a duration of 3,000 ms. After 1,250 ms had elapsed, the n-back letter was presented in the middle of the screen for a duration of 500 ms. In total, 252 affective pictures were presented, with ratings ranging from "1" (negative valence; low arousal) to "9" (positive valence; high arousal): 84 neutral (valence: M = 5.25, SD = 0.25; arousal: M = 2.39, SD = 0.84), 84 low salience negative (valence: M = 2.67, SD = 0.49; arousal: M = 5.14, SD = 0.49), and 84 high salience negative pictures (valence: M = 2.15, SD = 0.49; arousal: M = 6.39, SD = 0.45). All of the negative and 32 of the neutral pictures were taken from the International Affective Picture System [58], and 52 of the neutral stimuli were collected and evaluated in the department's own research laboratory. The stimuli will be provided upon request to the corresponding author.

After completing the emotional n-back task, all of the subjects performed a surprise recognition memory task in which all 256 pictures that had been used in the first task and 54 new pictures (18 per salience category) were presented in randomized order. The participants were asked to indicate on a four-point scale whether the picture had been presented before (1 = no, certain 2 = no, uncertain, 3 = yes, uncertain, 4 = yes, certain).

Dependent Variables

For both versions of the n-back task, the median of the reaction time for correctly identified targets (RT) and the individual discrimination indices for performance accuracy (d′) were used as dependent variables, with the d′ calculated based on the signal detection theory as follows: d′ = z (hits/number of targets) – z (false alarms/number of distractors). The resulting value range was -4.66≤x≤+4.66, with more negative values indicating poorer performance. For the recognition task, the ratings were binarized (known and unknown) prior to computation of the d′.

Covariates of Interest

The Questionnaire of Current Motivation (QCM) [59] is an 18-item questionnaire that was designed to assess the current motivational aspects of task completion, including the dimensions of task interest, perceived challenge, mastery confidence, and incompetence fear, according to the cognitive-motivational process model [60]. Subjects are asked to evaluate the items on a seven-point Likert rating scale (from 1 = disagree to 7 = agree), with higher scores reflecting higher task-related motivation. Differences in education history (subjects with ADHD more often attend special schools, repeat grades, receive special educational services and are less likely to graduate from school) [61,62], self-esteem, and control beliefs (subjects with ADHD have a more external locus of control and suffer from lower self-esteem) [63–65] may differentially affect task-related motivation in experimental groups; therefore, the QCM was considered a possible covariate of interest in the present study to rule out systematic motivational group differences that might have existed prior to the experimental manipulation of reward options in the present study and that might independently impact the dependent variables. The prognostic value of the QCM was demonstrated by showing that mastery confidence and incompetence fear predicted learning performance in a complex, computer-simulated system [60]. Moreover, the task properties (self-regulated vs. question guided) and characteristics of the subject ("slow learners" vs. "fast learners") were demonstrated to mediate the association of task interest and challenge with learning success [59]. In this study, we adopted the following QCM items: (1) "I enjoy doing this kind of task," (2) "The task seems very interesting to me," (3) "I'm very curious about how well I will perform the task," and (4) "I'm a little bit scared that I could make a fool of myself". The subjects answered these four items subsequent to the practice trial. The individual mean score, with item four inverted, served as an indicator of the potential motivational group differences in task engagement.

Procedure

The examination took place at the research laboratory of the Department of Psychiatry and Psychotherapy, University Medicine Rostock. After the study purposes were explained to the subjects non-specifically, the subjects were seated in the quiet and dimmed experiment room and worked on the experimental tasks. Both of the n-back tasks were projected onto a white screen using a Sanyo 285 LCD Z2 projector. The subjects' distance to the screen was approximately 138 inches, and the screen had a width of 51 inches. The visual angle was 21 degrees. The experimental paradigm was presented using presentation software (Neurobehavioral Systems Inc., Berkeley, CA, USA), which was installed on a desktop PC (Compaq HP dc 5700; CPU: Pentium 4, 3 GHz; 1 GB RAM). The total duration of the test was approximately 60 minutes.

The study was conducted in accordance with the latest version of the Declaration of Helsinki. The ethics committee of the Faculty of Medicine of the University of Rostock approved this study (registration number: A 2012–0020). The subjects were provided with information about the task to be performed and the study procedure, and written informed consent was obtained from all of the participants. All of the subjects were able to consent (i.e., they were able to understand, reproduce, and draw a rational conclusion based on the information provided in the written subject information). Subjects who did not have the capacity or ability to consent were excluded according to the exclusion criteria.

Statistical Analyses

The data were analyzed using SPSS version 17 (SPSS Inc., Chicago, IL, USA). Tests of the group differences in socio-demographic and clinical data and task-related motivation were performed using univariate analyses of variance (ANOVAs). The group differences in the dependent variables (RT, d′) were analyzed using repeated-measures ANCOVAs with the diagnostic group (subjects with ADHD; alcohol-dependent subjects; controls) as the between-subjects factor, the n-back level (1-back; 2-back) and emotional salience (neutral; low emotionally salient; high emotionally salient) as the within-subject factors, and IQ as the covariate. In cases of significant main or interaction effects, post-hoc group comparisons were conducted. Multiple comparisons were corrected using the Bonferroni procedure. Prior to the analyses, the raw data were z-transformed to examine extreme outliers ($z>3.0$). Two extreme outliers were detected and were replaced by the respective group means. The significance level for all of the tests was $p \leq 0.05$. The partial eta-squared (η_p^2) is reported as a measure of the effect size.

Results

Because psychostimulants have been demonstrated to improve working memory performance [66] by improving prefrontal cortex activity [67,68], we compared the drug-naïve ADHD subjects with those who had discontinued their medication in relation to the dependent variables in the classical n-back task prior to all subsequent analyses. No subgroup differences were observed for RT or d′ (all $ps>0.05$). Importantly, the ADHD subgroups did not differ from each other with regard to age, $t(20) = -0.07$, $p = .95$, *ns*, intellectual capacity, $t(20) = -0.20$, $p = .84$, *ns*, or task-related motivation, $t(20) = 1.00$, $p = .33$, *ns* and were thus analyzed as a group.

Task-Related Motivation

The experimental groups did not differ from each other in terms of their initial task-related motivation, $F(2,65) = 1.97$, $p = .15$, *ns*. The three experimental groups displayed an intermediate motivational level (subjects with ADHD: $M = 4.32$, $SD = 1.17$; alcoholics: $M = 4.45$, $SD = 1.35$; controls: $M = 4.94$, $SD = 1.11$).

Classical N-back Task

No group differences for RT emerged (all $ps>0.05$), but a between-subjects effect of working memory load was found for d′, $F(2,63) = 12.17$, $p<.001$, $\eta_p^2 = .28$, and post-hoc comparisons indicated that subjects with ADHD and alcohol-dependent subjects were both impaired relative to controls (CON vs. ADHD: $p<.001$; CON vs. ALC: $p = .007$; ADHD vs. ALC: $p = 1.00$) (see Figure 1). No further significant effects emerged (all $ps>0.05$). The mean reaction times and accuracy scores for the classical n-back task are presented in Table 2.

Emotional N-back Task

Working memory load affected d′, $F(1.61) = 5.97$, $p = .02$, $\eta_p^2 = .09$, with all subjects responding less accurately in the 2-back condition compared with the 1-back condition. Likewise, the emotional salience of the background picture stimuli affected d′, $F(2,122) = 3.26$, $p = .04$, $\eta_p^2 = .05$, in all subjects. The post-hoc analyses revealed that performance accuracy decreased gradually when the salience of the background pictures increased (neutral vs. low salience pictures: $p = .04$; neutral vs. high salience pictures: $p< .001$; low salience vs. high salience pictures: $p = .04$). Group differences emerged both for RT, $F(2,60) = 3.25$, $p = .05$, $\eta_p^2 = .10$, and for d′, $F(2,61) = 5.84$, $p = .005$, $\eta_p^2 = .16$. Alcohol-dependent subjects displayed prolonged RTs relative to controls (CON vs. ADHD: $p = .85$, *ns*; CON vs. ALC: $p = .04$; ADHD vs. ALC: $p = .47$, *ns*), and subjects with ADHD displayed decreased d′ compared with controls (CON vs. ADHD: $p = .004$; CON vs. ALC: $p = 1.00$, *ns*; ADHD vs. ALC: $p = .16$, *ns*) (see Figure 1). Furthermore, an emotion x group interaction effect emerged both for RT, $F(4,120) = 3.75$, $p = .007$, $\eta_p^2 = .11$, and for d′, $F(4,122) = 3.56$, $p = .009$, $\eta_p^2 = .10$. RTs differed between the groups when high salience pictures were presented, $F(2,65) = 3.21$, $p = .05$, $\eta_p^2 = .10$, but the subsequently conducted post-hoc tests yielded insignificant results (all $ps>.05$). When emotional distractor salience increased, performance accuracy deteriorated in subjects with ADHD, $F(2,38) = 11.08$, $p<.001$, $\eta_p^2 = .37$, and in alcohol-dependent subjects, $F(2,30) = 6.05$, $p = .006$, $\eta_p^2 = .29$, but not in controls, $F(2,58) = 2.79$, $p = .07$, *ns*. The performance of subjects with ADHD deteriorated in the presence of low salience pictures (neutral vs. low salience pictures: $p = .009$; neutral vs. high salience pictures: $p<.001$; low salience vs. high salience pictures: $p = 1.00$, *ns*), whereas that of alcohol-dependent subjects did not deteriorate until high salience pictures were presented (neutral vs. low salience pictures: $p = .84$, *ns*; neutral vs. high salience pictures: $p = .001$; low salience vs. high salience pictures: $p = .20$, *ns*) (see Figure 2). No further effects were significant (all $ps>0.05$). The

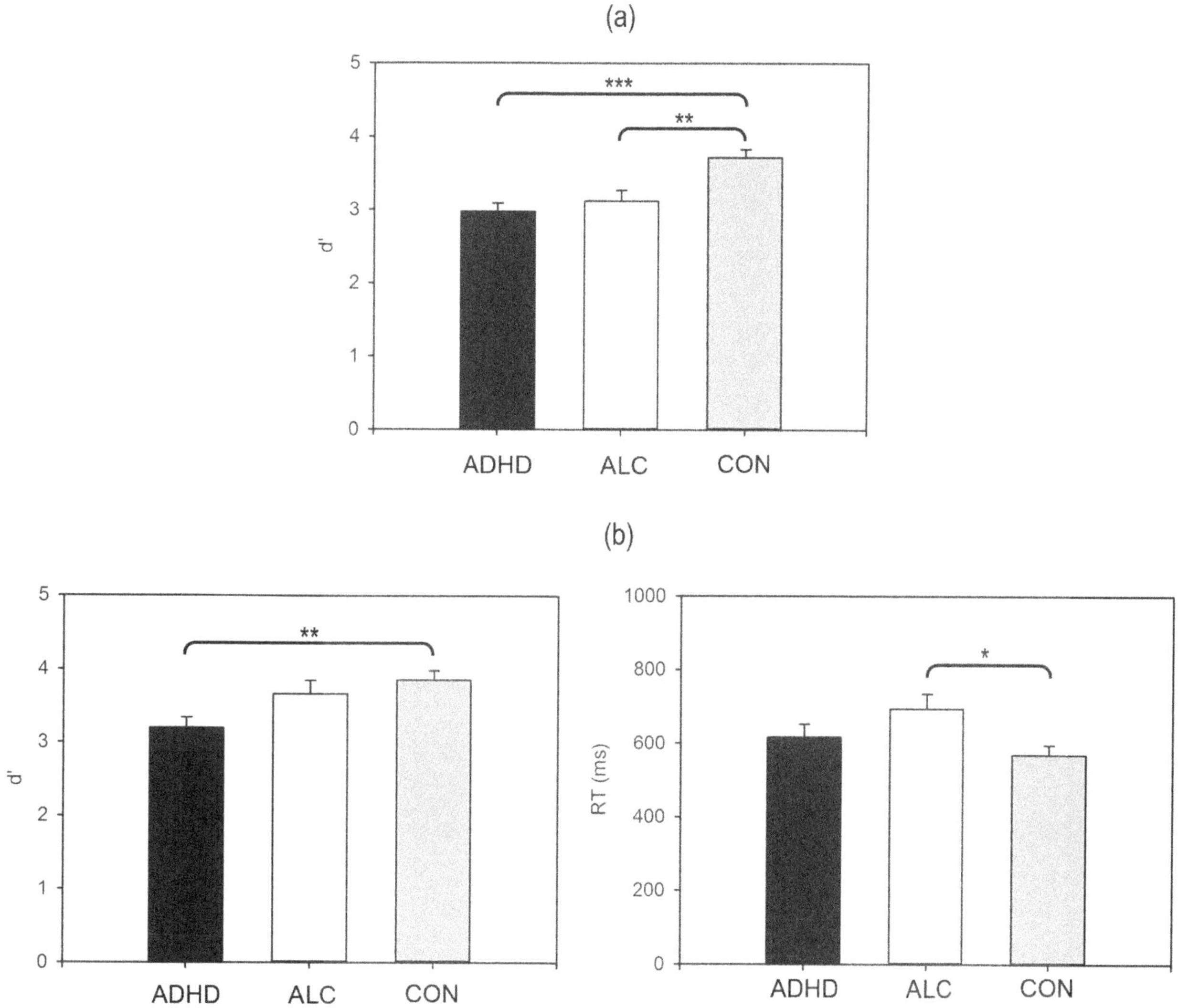

Figure 1. Between-Subjects Effect for the Classical N-back Task (a); Between-Subjects Effects for the Emotional N-back Task (b). ADHD = ADHD group, ALC = alcoholics, CON = control group. d' = discriminability score, RT = reaction time in milliseconds. *p<.05, **p<.01, ***p< .001.

mean reaction times and accuracy scores for the emotional n-back task can be derived from Table 3.

Surprise Recognition Memory Task

The three experimental groups differed significantly in their picture recognition performance, $F(2,56) = 8.73$, $p < .001$, $\eta_p^2 = .24$, with subjects with ADHD outperforming both alcohol-dependent subjects and controls (CON vs. ADHD: $p = .003$; CON vs. ALC: $p = 1.00$, *ns*; ADHD vs. ALC: $p = .002$) (see Figure 3). No further effects were significant (all $ps > 0.05$). The accuracy scores for the surprise recognition memory task are provided in Table 4. All between-subjects effects and between-within interaction effects are displayed in Figure 1.

Association between N-Back Task Performance and Picture Recognition Accuracy

Overall performance accuracy as measured by the average d' across all experimental conditions was negatively associated with subsequent picture recognition in alcohol-dependent subjects ($r = -0.53$, $p = .05$) but not in subjects with ADHD ($r = -0.15$, $p = .55$, *ns*) or controls ($r = 0.04$, $p = .85$, *ns*).

Association between N-Back Task Performance and Inattentive and Hyperactive/Impulsive Symptoms

The correlation analyses between the CAARS-S:L DSM-IV inattention and hyperactivity/impulsivity subscale sum scores and overall performance accuracy revealed that in subjects with ADHD ($r = -0.50$, $p = .03$) and in controls ($r = -0.37$, $p = .05$), but not in alcohol-dependent subjects ($r = 0.09$, $p = .75$, *ns*), d' was negatively correlated with inattention, whereas no significant correlations emerged for hyperactivity/impulsivity (all $ps > 0.05$).

Discussion

The current study sought to examine the pattern of emotional interference control in adult males with ADHD and in adult males with alcohol dependence. Given the role of the DLPFC in coping with emotional distractors and based on the knowledge of common but differentially pronounced DLPFC dysfunction in

Table 2. Descriptive Statistics for the Classical N-back Task Performance.

	ADHD		ALC		CON		Group	N-back	N-back x Group
	M	SD	M	SD	M	SD	F(2,63)	F(1,63)	F(2,63)
Reaction Time (ms)							1.70	0.81	0.88
1-back	591.83	140.22	637.59	202.54	558.05	153.82			
2-back	729.51	237.42	762.55	215.01	639.87	216.98			
							F(2,63)	F(1,63)	F(2,63)
Performance Accuracy (d')							12.17***	3.38(*)	0.57
1-back	3.26	0.44	3.09	0.88	3.92	0.54			
2-back	2.81	0.87	2.81	0.95	3.62	0.82			

ADHD = Subjects with ADHD, ALC = Alcoholics, CON = Controls. Group = between-subjects effect of experimental group membership, N-back = within-subjects effect of task difficulty, N-back x Group = within-between-subjects interaction effect. M = Mean, SD = Standard Deviation. (*)p<.10, *p<.05, **p<.01, *** p<.001.

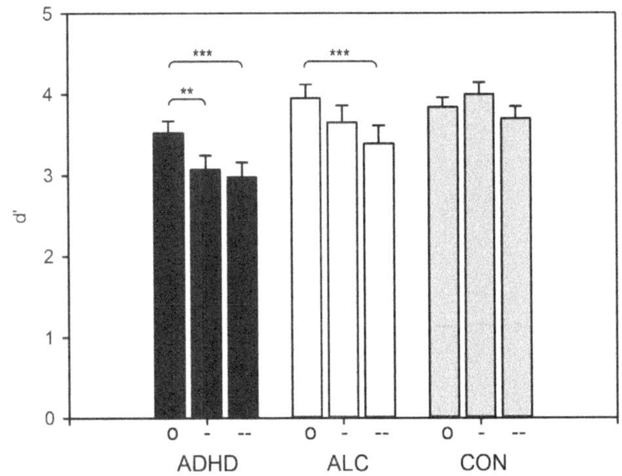

Figure 2. Experimental Group x Distractor Salience Level Interaction Effect for the Emotional N-back Task. ADHD = ADHD group, ALC = alcoholics, CON = control group. o = neutral distractors, - = low emotionally salient distractors, - - = high emotionally salient distractors. d' = discriminability score. *p<.05, **p<.01, ***p<.001.

subjects with ADHD and in subjects with alcohol dependence, we expected both clinical groups to display WM deficits and emotional interference control deficits when compared with controls, with the emotional interference control deficit being more accentuated in those with ADHD.

As expected, WM deficits were observed in both clinical groups, with a dissociation of the quality of this deficit emerging in the emotional version compared with the classical version of the task. Whereas both clinical groups displayed decreased performance accuracy compared with the controls in the classical task, subjects with ADHD displayed decreased performance accuracy but alcohol-dependent subjects displayed increased response times in the emotional version of the task. This effect might be interpreted as indicating that alcohol-dependent subjects, by taking more time to make their decisions, were able to ensure performance quality that paralleled that of the control group, suggesting a less pronounced WM deficit in alcohol-dependent subjects.

Moreover, a deficit in coping with emotional interferences was found in both clinical groups. Whereas the controls displayed stable performance accuracy across all salience levels (i.e., they were not at all susceptible to the emotional content of the implemented pictorial distractors), the performance of subjects with ADHD deteriorated in the presence of low salience pictures, whereas that of alcohol-dependent subjects did not deteriorate until high salience pictures were presented. Thus, the emotional interference control deficit was more pronounced in subjects with ADHD. This interpretation is underlined by three facts: (1) Subjects with ADHD accurately recognized more distractor pictures from the emotional n-back task subsequent to task performance, indicating larger attention allocation to the emotional distractors or, in other words, impaired interference control relative to alcoholics and controls. (2) Picture recognition accuracy was negatively associated with WM performance in the alcoholic group but not in the ADHD and control groups, suggesting an association between the ability to suppress emotional distractors and success in n-back task performance solely in alcohol-dependent subjects. This association might be lacking in the controls because they fully concentrated on the primary task, as suggested by their lack of susceptibility to the emotional distractors, whereas subjects with ADHD might overallocate their

Table 3. Descriptive Statistics for the Emotional N-back Task Performance.

	ADHD		ALC		CON		Group	N-back	N-back x Group	Emotion	Emotion x Group
	M	SD	M	SD	M	SD	F(2,60)	F(1,60)	F(2,60)	F(2,120)	F(4,120)
Reaction Time (ms)							3.25*	0.43	0.44	0.55	3.75**
1-back											
neu	568.97	133.42	633.38	158.32	535.26	153.06					
low	549.50	149.97	674.90	158.63	534.39	147.44					
high	632.89	168.32	692.43	134.38	581.55	159.67					
2-back											
neu	676.51	214.79	725.01	167.03	585.75	190.45					
low	580.01	157.57	672.03	188.44	584.76	171.96					
high	711.76	236.21	719.69	150.51	599.79	185.79					
							F(2,61)	F(1,61)	F(2,61)	F(2,122)	F(4,122)
Performance Accuracy (d')							5.84**	5.97*	2.87$^{(*)}$	3.26*	3.56**
1-back											
neu	3.84	0.57	3.92	0.75	4.06	0.66					
low	3.37	1.01	3.60	0.76	4.10	0.53					
high	3.36	0.98	3.29	1.04	3.83	0.84					
2-back											
neu	3.34	1.34	3.62	0.99	3.72	0.69					
low	2.85	1.51	3.53	0.72	3.94	0.74					
high	2.76	1.30	3.08	0.85	3.68	0.89					

ADHD = Subjects with ADHD, ALC = Alcoholics, CON = Controls. Group = between-subjects effect of experimental group membership, N-back = within-subjects effect of task difficulty, N-back x Group = within-between-subjects interaction effect, Emotion = within-subjects effect of the emotional salience of the background picture stimuli, Emotion x Group = within-between-subjects interaction effect. M = Mean, SD = Standard Deviation. neu = neutral pictures, low = low emotional salience, high = high emotional salience. $^{(*)}p<.10$, $^{*}p<.05$, $^{**}p<.01$, $^{***}p<.001$.

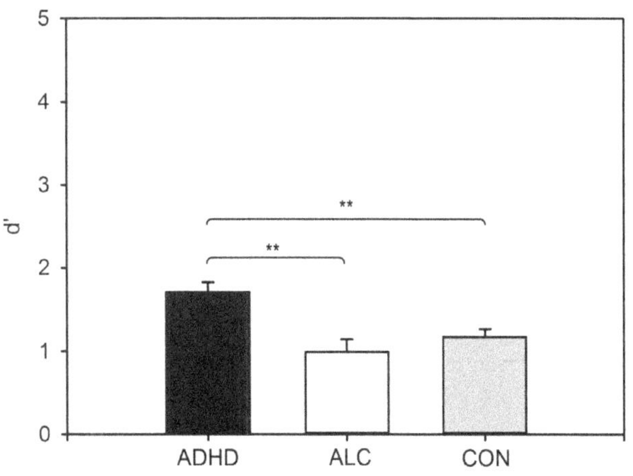

Figure 3. Between-Subjects Effect for the Surprise Memory Recognition Task. ADHD = ADHD group, ALC = alcoholics, CON = control group. d' = discriminability score. *p<.05, **p<.01, ***p<.001.

attention to distractors, as suggested by their breakdown in performance accuracy with increasing distractor salience. (3) Consequently, in subjects with ADHD and in the controls but not in alcohol-dependent subjects, performance accuracy was negatively associated with ADHD inattentive symptoms, suggesting that inattention seems to contribute to the emotional interference control deficit in ADHD but not in alcohol dependence.

With regard to task validity, all subjects displayed decreased performance accuracy in the 2-back condition compared with the 1-back condition as well as gradually decreasing performance accuracy with increasing distractor salience in the emotional version of the task. Thus, although the manipulation of working memory load and distractor salience was successful in the emotional version of the task, the effect of WM load was not found in the classical version. Despite sensitivity to WM deficits in the clinical groups, the less complex task may have been too easy to provoke significant differences between the conditions, and the effect of WM load may have become more apparent in the more complex task that included additional visual stimulation.

Longitudinal studies are needed to examine the stability of the emotional interference deficit in subjects with ADHD and in alcohol-dependent subjects. Because DLPFC integrity seems permanently impaired in subjects with ADHD [40,41] but seems to vary more strongly as a function of abstinence duration in alcohol-dependent subjects [40], longitudinal studies would allow for the examination of recovery effects, which should be more prominent in the alcoholic group. Furthermore, longitudinal studies would allow for the examination of emotional interference control deficits resulting from prolonged alcoholism when working memory deficits become more severe.

In our study, we included males exclusively, but it would be interesting to include females in future studies. To the best of our knowledge, no research has addressed gender differences in emotional interference control in subjects with ADHD and in alcoholics, but a recently conducted study in healthy subjects using an emotional variant of the Stroop Task found no gender differences at the electrophysiological level [69]. However, there is some evidence for gender differences in the classical variant of the Stroop Task, which assesses cognitive interference control. This evidence demonstrates that females outperform males both in healthy subjects [70] and in subjects with ADHD [71]. However,

Table 4. Descriptive Statistics for the Surprise Recognition Memory Task.

	ADHD		ALC		CON		Group	N-back	N-back x Group	Emotion	Emotion x Group
	M	SD	M	SD	M	SD	F(2,56)	F(1,56)	F(2,56)	F(2,112)	F(4,112)
Performance Accuracy (d')							8.73***	0.06	2.80(*)	1.05	0.93
1-back											
neu	1.69	0.69	0.98	0.52	1.14	0.60					
low	2.09	0.84	1.05	0.73	1.57	0.48					
high	2.11	0.81	1.31	0.69	1.61	0.69					
2-back											
neu	1.16	0.69	0.68	0.59	0.62	0.56					
low	1.65	0.84	0.84	0.79	1.02	0.52					
high	1.61	0.65	1.00	0.81	1.07	0.51					

ADHD = Subjects with ADHD, ALC = Alcoholics, CON = Controls. Group = between-subjects effect of experimental group membership, N-back = within-subjects effect of task difficulty, N-back x Group = within-between-subjects interaction effect, Emotion = within-subjects effect of emotional salience of the background picture stimuli, Emotion x Group = within-between-subjects interaction effect. M = Mean, SD = Standard Deviation. neu = neutral pictures, low = low emotional salience, high = high emotional salience. (*)p<.10, *p<.05, **p<.01, *** p<.001.

the results still seem inconclusive for subjects with ADHD because other studies have found no gender differences [72,73]. Functional imaging studies on emotion processing in healthy subjects suggest that females respond more strongly to negative emotional stimuli [74,75], but males more strongly recruit regulatory areas [76]. The latter finding is also evident in self-ratings of emotional control, in which males report suppressing their emotions to a larger degree than do women [77]. Furthermore, it has been found that differences in brain structure between females and males are associated with differences in ER and emotion expression [78]. More precisely, females were found to have larger right orbitofrontal and ventromedial prefrontal cortex volumes, and a larger ventromedial prefrontal cortex volume is associated with using emotion suppression strategies less often and with a more intense emotion expression. Thus, future studies are required to analyze whether the stronger emotional responsiveness and less frequent use of emotion regulation strategies in females might facilitate an increased susceptibility to emotional interferences or whether their possibly superior interference control might compensate for this.

Beyond emotional interference control, future research should address the impact of gender differences on the development of comorbid affective disorders in subjects with ADHD and in alcoholics. For example, Biederman et al. [79,80] found that girls with ADHD develop higher rates of major depressive disorder and anxiety disorders in their young adult years than do boys with ADHD, and Retz-Junginger, Rösler, Müller, and Retz [81] found that adult females with ADHD, who displayed elevated levels of emotional dysregulation when compared with males, were overrepresented among the clients of their outpatient services. In this sense, females with ADHD seem to be at particular risk for the development of affective disorders when compared with males with ADHD, which may be due to gender differences in emotion processing.

Limitations

Some methodological limitations of our study need to be considered. First, we included only male subjects. Thus, our results cannot be generalized to female subjects. Second, although the exclusion of comorbid psychiatric disorders that may have affected test performance resulted in a higher specificity of our findings, the impact of these comorbidities on emotional interference control will have to be examined in future studies. The importance of both gender and comorbidity aspects is suggested, for example, by recent findings demonstrating that females with ADHD, when compared with males, display higher rates of comorbid mood disorders [47] and borderline personality disorder [46]; both of these disorders have emotional interference control deficits [82–88]. These findings suggest larger impairment in coping with emotional interferences in females than in males with ADHD. However, males and females with ADHD have been found to display differential brain activation patterns while performing the n-back task, with males, but not females, being impaired relative to controls [89]. These findings suggest that females with ADHD might be better able to block out emotional distractors [90], which might parallel the impact of higher relevant comorbidity. Third, it should be noted that in the present study, the probability to detect group differences was reduced due to limited statistical power. This limitation might be especially true for the classical n-back task and the surprise recognition memory task, for which trend effects have been found.

Conclusions

The results of the present study suggest that subjects with ADHD and alcohol-dependent subjects share dysfunctions in a frontal-parietal-cerebellar network subserving working memory [91,92], as measured by their impaired n-back task performance relative to controls. Additionally, we were able to demonstrate that both clinical groups display an emotional interference control deficit, and this deficit is even more pronounced in subjects with ADHD. Whereas the performance of subjects with ADHD deteriorated in the presence of low emotionally salient distractors, the performance of alcohol-dependent subjects did not deteriorate until highly salient distractors were presented. Based on our data, we speculate that in subjects with ADHD, differences in attention allocation processes (as indicated by higher distractor recognition rates and a lack of negative correlation between task performance and subsequent distractor identification) and a more general attention deficit (as indicated by a positive correlation between n-back task performance and clinical ratings of ADHD inattentive symptoms) contribute to the more pronounced deficit pattern. However, this hypothesis should be tested in future studies.

Considering the high comorbidity between ADHD and alcohol dependence, it remains unclear whether the emotional interference control deficit is more pronounced in subjects with both conditions. This is a question that should be addressed in future studies. Moreover, further research should consider how deficient emotional interference control is associated with behavioral markers of emotional dysregulation and adult comorbid psychopathology. In the case of emotion regulation, for example, it has been shown that children with more severe emotion dysregulation differ from those with milder impairment in terms of higher rates of unipolar and bipolar mood disorders, oppositional defiant disorders, and conduct disorders [93]. Because emotion regulation is preceded by the modulation of interfering emotionally laden stimuli in emotion processing and because emotional interference control seems to be deficient especially in subjects with ADHD, the regulatory deficit might mediate the link between impaired emotional interference control and adult psychopathology in subjects with the disorder.

Acknowledgments

The authors would like to thank the patients and employees from Friedrich-Petersen-Klinik for their participation and support. We also thank Mrs. Wencke Lubojanski for her highly committed clinical support.

Author Contributions

Conceived and designed the experiments: IM CB FH. Performed the experiments: JK. Analyzed the data: IM CB JK. Contributed reagents/materials/analysis tools: IM CB. Wrote the paper: IM JK. Performed clinical diagnostics: JK IM. Recruited the subjects: JK IM. Interpreted the data: IM JK FH. Revised the manuscript for important intellectual content: FH. Final approval: IM JK CB FH.

References

1. American Psychiatric Association (2000) Diagnostic and statistical manual of mental disorders (4th ed., text rev.). Washington, DC: Author.
2. Faraone SV, Biederman J, Mick E (2006) The age-dependent decline of attention deficit hyperactivity disorder: a meta-analysis of follow-up studies. Psychol Med 36: 159–165.
3. Faraone SV, Biederman J (2005) What is the prevalence of adult ADHD? Results of a population screening of 966 adults. J Attent Disord 2: 384–391.
4. Kessler RC, Adler L, Barkley R, Biederman J, Conners CK, et al. (2006) The prevalence and correlates of adult ADHD in the United States: results from the National Comorbidity Survey Replication. Am J Psychiatry 163: 716–723.

5. Biederman J, Mick E, Faraone SV (2000) Age-dependent decline of symptoms of attention deficit hyperactivity disorder: impact of remission definition and symptom type. Am J Psychiatry 157: 816–818.
6. Biederman J, Petty CR, Woodworth KY, Lomedico A, Hyder LL, et al. (2012) Adult outcome of attention-deficit/hyperactivity disorder: a controlled 16-year follow-up study. J Clin Psychiatry 73: 941–950.
7. Rösler M, Casas M, Konofal E, Buitelaar J (2010) Attention deficit hyperactivity disorder in adults. World J Biol Psychiatry 11: 684–698.
8. Ohlmeier MD, Peters K, Te Wildt B, Zedler M, Ziegenbein M, et al. (2008) Comorbidity of alcohol and substance dependence with attention-deficit/hyperactivity disorder (ADHD). Alcohol Alcohol 43: 300–304.
9. Shekim WO, Asarnow RF, Hess E, Zaucha K, Wheeler N (1990) A clinical and demographic profile of a sample of adults with attention deficit hyperactivity disorder, residual state. Compr Psychiat 31: 416–425.
10. Smith BH, Molina BSG, Pelham WE (2002) The clinically meaningful link between alcohol use and attention deficit hyperactivity disorder. Alcohol Res Health 26: 122–129.
11. Lee SS, Humphreys KL, Flory K, Liu R, Glass K (2011) Prospective association of childhood attention-deficit/hyperactivity disorder (ADHD) and substance use and abuse/dependence: a meta-analytic review. Clin Psychol Rev 31: 328–341.
12. Wilens TE (2004) Impact of ADHD and its treatment on substance abuse in adults. J Clin Psychiatry 65: 38–45.
13. Anastopoulos AD, Smith TF, Garrett ME, Morrissey-Kane E, Schatz NK, et al. (2011) Self-regulation of emotion, functional impairment, and comorbidity among children with ADHD. J Atten Disord 15: 583–592.
14. Maedgen JW, Carlson CL (2000) Social functioning and emotional regulation in the attention deficit hyperactivity disorder subtypes. J Clin Child Psychol 29: 30–42.
15. Melnick SM, Hinshaw SP (2000) Emotion regulation and parenting in AD/HD and comparison boys: linkages with social behaviors and peer preference. J Abnorm Child Psychol 28: 73–86.
16. Sjöwall D, Roth L, Lindqvist S, Thorell LB (2013) Multiple deficits in ADHD: executive dysfunction, delay aversion, reaction time variability, and emotional deficits. J Child Psychol Psychiatry 54: 619–627.
17. Walcott CM, Landau S (2004) The relation between disinhibition and emotion regulation in boys with attention deficit hyperactivity disorder. J Clin Child Adolesc Psychol 33: 772–782.
18. Retz W, Stieglitz RD, Corbisiero S, Retz-Junginger P, Rösler M (2012) Emotional dysregulation in adult ADHD: What is the empirical evidence? Expert Rev Neurother 12: 1241–1251.
19. Fox HC, Hong KA, Sinha R (2008) Difficulties in emotion regulation and impulse control in recently abstinent alcoholics compared with social drinkers. Addic Behav 33: 388–394.
20. Thorberg FA, Lyvers M (2006) Negative Mood Regulation (NMR) expectancies, mood, and affect intensity among clients in substance disorder treatment facilities. Addict Behav 31: 811–820.
21. Fairholme CP, Nosen EL, Nillni YI, Schumacher JA, Tull MT, et al. (2013) Sleep disturbance and emotion dysregulation as transdiagnostic processes in a comorbid sample. Behav Res Ther 51: 540–546.
22. Kuvaas NJ, Dvorak RD, Pearson MR, Lamis DA, Sargent EM (2013) Self-regulation and alcohol use involvement: a latent class analysis. Addict Behav 39: 146–152.
23. Sjoerds Z, van den Brink W, Beekman AT, Penninx BW, Veltman DJ (2013) Response inhibition in alcohol-dependent patients and patients with depression/anxiety: a functional magnetic resonance imaging study. Psychol Med 9: 1–13.
24. Barkley RA (2010) Deficient emotional self-regulation: a core component of attention-deficit/hyperactivity disorder. Journal of ADHD & Related Disorders, 1, 5–37.
25. Funahashi S (2001) Neuronal mechanisms of executive control by the prefrontal cortex. Neurosci Res 39: 147–165.
26. Hofmann W, Schmeichel BJ, Baddeley AD (2012) Executive functions and self-regulation. Trend Cogn Sci 16: 174–180.
27. Nigg JT, Casey BJ (2005) An integrative theory of attention-deficit/hyperactivity disorder based on the cognitive and affective neurosciences. Development and Psychopathology, 17, 785–806.
28. Ochsner KN, Silvers JA, Buhle JT (2012) Functional imaging studies of emotion regulation: a synthetic review and evolving model of the cognitive control of emotion. Ann NY Acad Sci 1251: E1–E24.
29. Casey BJ, Durston S, Fossella JA (2001) Evidence for a mechanistic model of cognitive control. Clin Neurosci Res 1: 267–282.
30. Miller EK, Cohen JD (2002) An integrative theory of prefrontal cortex activation. Ann Rev Neurosci 24: 167–202.
31. Norman DA, Shallice T (1986) Attention to action: Willed and automatic control of behavior. In R. J. Davidson, C. E. Schwartz & D. Shapiro (Eds.), Consciousness and self-regulation: Advances in research and theory (Vol. 4, pp. 1–18). New York: Plenum Press.
32. Abe M, Hanakawa T (2009) Functional coupling underlying motor and cognitive functions of the dorsal premotor cortex. Behav Brain Res 198: 13–23.
33. Casey BJ, Thomas KM, Welsh TF, Livnat R, Eccard CH (2000). Cognitive and behavioral probes of developmental landmarks for use in functional neuroimaging. In M. Ernst & J. M. Rumsey (Eds.), Functional Neuroimaging in Child Psychiatry (pp. 155–168). New York: Cambridge University Press.
34. Iordan AD, Dolcos S, Dolcos F (2013) Neural signatures of the response to emotional distraction: a review of evidence from brain imaging investigations. Front Hum Neurosci 7: 200.
35. Cromheeke S, Mueller SC (2013) Probing emotional influences on cognitive control: an ALE meta-analysis of cognition emotion interactions. Brain Struct Funct (accepted).
36. Rottschy C, Langner R, Dogan I, Reetz K, Laird AR, et al. (2012) Modelling neural correlates of working memory: a coordinate-based meta-analysis. Neuroimage 60: 830–846.
37. Marx I, Domes G, Havenstein C, Berger C, Schulze L, et al. (2011) Enhanced emotional interference on working memory performance in adults with ADHD. World J Biol Psychiatry 12 (S1): 70–75.
38. Boonstra AM, Oosterlaan J, Sergeant JA, Buitelaar JK (2005) Executive functioning in adult ADHD: a meta-analytic review. Psychol Med 35: 1097–1108.
39. Schoechlin C, Engel RR (2005) Neuropsychological performance in adult attention-deficit hyperactivity disorder: meta-analysis of empirical data. Arch Clin Neuropsych 20: 727–744.
40. Stavro K, Pelletier J, Potvin S (2012) Widespread and sustained cognitive deficits in alcoholism: a meta-analysis. Addict Biol 18: 203–213.
41. Halperin JM, Trampush JW, Miller CJ, Marks DJ, Newcorn JH (2008) Neuropsychological outcome in adolescents/young adults with childhood ADHD: profiles of persisters, remitters and controls. J Child Psychol Psychiatry 49: 958–966.
42. Simon V, Czobor P, Bálint S, Mészáros A, Bitter I (2009) Prevalence and correlates of adult attention-deficit hyperactivity disorder: meta-analysis. Br J Psychiatry 194: 204–211.
43. Compton WM, Thomas YF, Stinson FS, Grant BF (2007) Prevalence, correlates, disability, and comorbidity of DSM-IV drug abuse and dependence in the United States: results from the national epidemiologic survey on alcohol and related conditions. Arch Gen Psychiatry 64: 566–576.
44. Goldstein RB, Dawson DA, Chou SP, Grant BF (2012) Sex differences in prevalence and comorbidity of alcohol and drug use disorders: results from wave 2 of the National Epidemiologic Survey on Alcohol and Related Conditions. J Stud Alcohol Drugs, 73, 938–950.
45. Haberstick BC, Young SE, Zeiger JS, Lessem JM, Hewitt JK, et al. (2013) Prevalence and correlates of alcohol and cannabis use disorders in the United States: results form the national longitudinal study of adolescent health. Drug Alcohol Depend 136: 158–161.
46. Cumyn L, French L, Hechtman L (2009) Comorbidity in adults with attention-deficit hyperactivity disorder. Can J Psychiatry 54: 673–683.
47. Groß-Lesch S, Dempfle A, Reichert S, Jans T, Geissler J, et al. (2013) Sex- and subtype-related differences in the comorbidity of adult ADHD. J Atten Disord
48. Wittchen H, Zaudig M, Fydrich T (1997) Strukturiertes Klinisches Interview für DSM-IV (SKID). Göttingen: Hogrefe.
49. Kuhl J, Kazén M (1997) Persönlichkeits- Stil- und Störungs-Inventar (PSSI): Handanweisung. Göttingen: Hogrefe.
50. Barkley RA (1998) Attention-deficit hyperactivity disorder: a handbook for diagnosis and treatment, 2nd edn. New York: Guilford Press.
51. Rösler M, Retz-Junginger P, Retz W, Stieglitz R-D (2008) HASE –Homburger ADHS-Skalen für Erwachsene. Göttingen: Hogrefe.
52. Retz-Juninger P, Retz W, Blocher D, Weijers HG, Trott GE, et al. (2002). Wender Utah rating scale. The short-version for the assessment of the attention-deficit hyperactivity disorder in adults. Nervenarzt 73: 830–838.
53. Conners C, Erhardt D, Sparrow E (1998) The Conners Adult ADHD Rating Scale-Long Version (CAARS-S:L). Toronto: Multi-Health Systems.
54. Barratt ES (1985) Impulsiveness subtraits: Arousal and information processing. In: Spence JT, Izard CE, editors.Motivation, emotion and personality. Amsterdam: North Holland/Elsevier Science.
55. Retz-Junginger P, Retz W, Blocher D, Stieglitz RD, Georg T, et al. (2003) Reliability and validity of the Wender-Utah-Rating-Scale short form. Retrospective assessment of symptoms for attention deficit/hyperactivity disorder. Nervenarzt 74: 987–993.
56. Wetterling T, Kanitz R-D, Besters B, Fischer D, Zerfass B, et al. (1997) A new rating scale for the assessment of the alcohol-withdrawal syndrome (AWS Scale). Alcohol Alcohol 32: 753–760.
57. Tewes U (1994) Hamburg-Wechsler-Intelligenztest für Erwachsene – Revision 1991 (HAWIE-R). Bern: Huber.
58. Lang PJ, Bradley MM, Cutberth BN (2008) International affective picture system (IAPS): Affective ratings of pictures and instruction manual. Technical Report A-8. Gainesville, FL: University of Florida.
59. Rheinberg F, Vollmeyer R, Burns BD (2001) QCM: a questionnaire to assess current motivation in learning situations. Diagnostica 47: 57–66.
60. Vollmeyer R, Rheinberg F (1998) Motivationale Einflüsse auf Erwerb und Anwendung von Wissen in einem computersimulierten System. Zeitschrift für Pädagogische Psychologie 12: 11–23.
61. Murphy KR, Barkley RA, Bush T (2002) Young adults with attention deficit hyperactivity disorder: subtype differences in comorbidity, educational, and clinical history. J Nerv Ment Dis 190: 147–157.
62. Taanila AM, Hurtig TM, Miettunen J, Ebeling HE, Mailanen IK (2009) Association between ADHD symptoms and adolescents' psychosocial wellbeing: a study of the Northern Finland birth cohort 1986. Int J Circumpolar Health 68: 133–142.

63. Carlson CL, Mann M, Alexander DK (2000) Effects of reward and response cost on the performance and motivation of children with AD/HD. Cognit Ther Res 24: 87–98.
64. Niederhofer H (2008) Attributions for school success and failure by adolescent students with and without attention deficit hyperactivity disorder. Psychol Rep 102: 616–620.
65. Rucklidge J, Brown D, Crawford S, Kaplan B (2007) Attributional styles and psychosocial functioning of adults with ADHD. J Atten Disord 10: 288–298.
66. Strand MT, Hawk LW, Bubnik M, Shiels K, Pelham WE (2012) Improving working memory in children with attention-deficit/hyperactivity disorder: the separate and combined effects of incentives and stimulant medication. J Abnorm Child Psychol 40: 1193–1207.
67. Cubillo A, Smith AB, Barrett N, Giampietro V, Brammer M, et al. (2013) Drug-specific laterality effects on frontal lobe activation of atomoxetine and methylphenidate in attention deficit hyperactivity disorder boys during working memory. Psychol Med 44: 633–646.
68. Wong CG, Stevens MC (2012) The effects of stimulant medication on working memory functional connectivity in attention-deficit/hyperactivity disorder. Biol Psychiatry 71: 458–466.
69. Putman P, Arias-Garcia E, Pantazi I, van Schie C (2012) Emotional Stroop interference for threatening words is related to reduced EEG delta-beta coupling and low attentional control. Int J Psychophysiol 84: 194–200.
70. Van der Elst W, Van Boxtel MP, Van Breukelen GJ, Jolles J (2006) The Stroop color-word test: influence of age, sex, and education; and normative data for a large sample across the adult age range. Assessment 13: 62–79.
71. Bálint S, Czobor P, Comlósi S, Mészáros Á, Simon V, et al. (2009) Attention deficit hyperactivity disorder (ADHD): gender- and age-related differences in neurocognition. Psychol Med 39: 1337–1345.
72. Rucklidge JJ, Tannock R (2002) Neuropsychological profiles of adolescents with ADHD: effects of reading difficulties and gender. J Child Psychol Psychiatry 43: 988–1003.
73. Van Mourik R, Oosterlaan J, Sergeant JA (2005) The Stroop revisited: a meta-analysis of interference control in AD/HD. J Child Psychol Psychiatry 46: 150–165.
74. Domes G, Schulze L, Böttger M, Grossmann A, Hauenstein K, et al. (2010) The neural correlates of sex differences in emotional reactivity and emotion regulation. Hum Brain Mapp 31: 758–769.
75. Stevens JS, Hamann S (2012) Sex differences in brain activation to emotional stimuli: a meta-analysis of neuroimaging studies. Neuropsychologia 50: 1578–1593.
76. Mak AK, Hu ZG, Zhang JX, Xiao Z, Lee TM (2009) Sex-related differences in neural activity during emotion regulation. Neuropsychologia 47: 2900–2908.
77. Melka SE, Lancaster SL, Bryant AR, Rodriguez BF (2011) Confirmatory factor and measurement invariance analyses of the emotion regulation questionnaire. J Clin Psychol 67: 1283–1293.
78. Welborn BL, Papademetris X, Reis DL, Rajeevan N, Bloise SM, et al. (2009) Variation in orbitofrontal cortex volume: relation to sex, emotion regulation and affect. Soc Cogn Affect Neurosci 4: 328–339.
79. Biederman J, Monuteaux M, Mick E, Spencer T, Wilens T, et al. (2006) Young adult outcome of attention deficit hyperactivity disorder: a controlled 10-year follow-up study. Psychol Med 36: 167–179.
80. Biederman J, Petty CR, Monuteaux MC, Fried R, Byrne D, http://www.ncbi.nlm.nih.gov/pubmed?term=Mirto%20T%5BAuthor%5D&cauthor=true&cauthor_uid=20080984 et al. (2010) Adult psychiatric outcomes of girls with attention deficit hyperactivity disorder: 11-year follow-up in a longitudinal case-control study. Am J Psychiatry 167: 409–417.
81. Retz-Junginger P, Rösler M, Müller R, Retz W (2012) Impact of gender on the utilization of outpatient health service for adult ADHD. Psychiatr Prax 39: 345–348.
82. Dichter GS, Felder JN, Smoski MJ (2009) Affective context interferes with cognitive control in unipolar depression: an fMRI investigation. J Affect Disord 114: 131–142.
83. Domes G, Winter B, Schnell K, Vohs K, Fast K, et al. (2006) The influence of emotions on inhibitory functioning in borderline personality disorder. Psychol Med 36: 1163–1172.
84. Joormann J, Nee DE, Berman MG, Jonides J, Gotlib IH (2010) Interference resolution in major depression. Cogn Affect Behav Neurosci 10: 21–33.
85. Mensebach C, Wingenfeld K, Driessen M, Rullkoetter N, Schlosser N, et al. (2009). Emotion-induced memory dysfunction in borderline personality disorder. Cogn Neuropsychiatry 14: 524–541.
86. Rey G, Desseilles M, Favre S, Dayer A, Piguet C, et al. (2014) Modulation of brain response to emotional conflict as a function of current mood in bipolar disorder: preliminary findings from a follow-up state-based fMRI study. Psychiatr Res 223: 84–93.
87. Segrave RA, Thomson RH, Cooper NR, Croft RJ, Sheppard DM, et al. (2012) Emotive interference during cognitive processing in major depression: an investigation of lower alpha 1 activity. J Affect Disord 141: 185–193.
88. Wang KS, Labar M, Smoski MZ, Rosenthal F, Dolcos TR, et al. (2008) Prefrontal mechanisms for executive control over emotional distraction are altered in major depression. Psychol Res 163: 143–155.
89. Valera EM, Brown A, Biederman J, Faraone SV, Makris N, et al. (2010) Sex differences in the functional neuroanatomy of working memory in adults with ADHD. Am J Psychiatry 167: 86–94.
90. Burgess GC, Depue BE, Ruzic L, Willcutt EG, Du YP, et al. (2010) Attentional control activation relates to working memory in attention-deficit/hyperactivity disorder. Biol Psychiatry 67: 632–640.
91. Hautzel H, Mottaghy FM, Specht K, Müller HW, Krause BJ (2009) Evidence of a modality-dependent role of the cerebellum in working memory? An fMRI study comparing verbal and abstract n-back tasks. Neuroimage 47: 2073–2082.
92. Schmidt H, Jogia J, Fast K, Christodoulou T, Haldane M, et al. (2009) No gender differences in brain activation during the N-back task: An fMRI study in healthy individuals. Hum Brain Mapp 11: 3609–3615.
93. Biederman J, Petty CR, Day H, Goldin RL, Spencer T, et al. (2012) Severity of the aggression/anxiety-depression/attention child behavior checklist profile discriminates between different levels of deficits in emotional regulation in youth with attention-deficit hyperactivity disorder. J Dev Behav Pediatr 33: 236–243.

10

Organizing Heterogeneous Samples Using Community Detection of GIMME-Derived Resting State Functional Networks

Kathleen M. Gates[1]*, Peter C. M. Molenaar[2], Swathi P. Iyer[3], Joel T. Nigg[3,4], Damien A. Fair[3,4,5]

1 Department of Psychology, University of North Carolina, Chapel Hill, North Carolina, United States of America, 2 Department of Human Development and Family Studies, The Pennsylvania State University, State College, Pennsylvania, United States of America, 3 Department of Behavioral Neuroscience, Oregon Health & Sciences University, Portland, Oregon, United States of America, 4 Department of Psychiatry, Oregon Health & Sciences University, Portland, Oregon, United States of America, 5 Advanced Imaging Research Center, Oregon Health & Sciences University, Portland, Oregon, United States of America

Abstract

Clinical investigations of many neuropsychiatric disorders rely on the assumption that diagnostic categories and typical control samples each have within-group homogeneity. However, research using human neuroimaging has revealed that much heterogeneity exists across individuals in both clinical and control samples. This reality necessitates that researchers identify and organize the potentially varied patterns of brain physiology. We introduce an analytical approach for arriving at subgroups of individuals based entirely on their brain physiology. The method begins with Group Iterative Multiple Model Estimation (GIMME) to assess individual directed functional connectivity maps. GIMME is one of the only methods to date that can recover both the direction and presence of directed functional connectivity maps in heterogeneous data, making it an ideal place to start since it addresses the problem of heterogeneity. Individuals are then grouped based on similarities in their connectivity patterns using a modularity approach for community detection. Monte Carlo simulations demonstrate that using GIMME in combination with the modularity algorithm works exceptionally well - on average over 97% of simulated individuals are placed in the accurate subgroup with no prior information on functional architecture or group identity. Having demonstrated reliability, we examine resting-state data of fronto-parietal regions drawn from a sample (N = 80) of typically developing and attention-deficit/hyperactivity disorder (ADHD) -diagnosed children. Here, we find 5 subgroups. Two subgroups were predominantly comprised of ADHD, suggesting that more than one biological marker exists that can be used to identify children with ADHD based from their brain physiology. Empirical evidence presented here supports notions that heterogeneity exists in brain physiology within ADHD and control samples. This type of information gained from the approach presented here can assist in better characterizing patients in terms of outcomes, optimal treatment strategies, potential gene-environment interactions, and the use of biological phenomenon to assist with mental health.

Editor: Juan Zhou, Duke-NUS Graduate Medical School, Singapore

Funding: This work was supported in part by NIH (http://grants.nih.gov/grants/oer.htm) grants R01 MH86654 (JTN), K99/R00 MH091238 (DAF), R01 MH096773 (DAF), and R21 EB015573 (KMG), the Oregon Clinical and Translational Research Institute (http://www.ohsu.edu/xd/research/centers-institutes/octri/) (DAF), the Medical Research Foundation (http://www.ohsu.edu/xd/about/foundation/about/medical-research-foundation/) (DAF), and and NSF grant 1157220 (http://www.nsf.gov/funding/) (PCMM). The funders had no role in study design, data collection and analysis, decision to publish, or preparation of the manuscript.

Competing Interests: The authors have declared that no competing interests exist.

* E-mail: kmgates@unc.edu

Introduction

For many clinical disciplines disease status is initially identified from symptoms and verified via biological measures. For example, insomnia may be brought to a doctor's attention based on patient self-report, but the symptom can be attributed to diverse causes including lifestyle changes, hyperthyroidism, or Cushing's disease. Only through biological testing can the cause be identified and an appropriate treatment plan created. In contrast, the diagnosis and categorization of mental health disorders, such as attention-deficit/hyperactivity disorder (ADHD), typically relies solely on observable symptom clusters [1]. It is possible, if not likely [2,3], that as with insomnia multiple mechanisms may lead to similar symptom clusters for a given mental disorder as defined by the Diagnostic and Statistical Manual of Mental Disorders (currently, DSM-5) or International Classification of Diseases (ICD). Clusters of symptoms that culminate to a diagnosis may relate to different neurobiological etiologies despite being under the same broad diagnostic category [4].

While it is largely agreed that the above possibility exists, studies examining the etiology of any given disorder typically ignore the potential heterogeneity that exists within current symptom-based classifications. In accordance with the current standard, analyses are conducted as though both the diagnostic group *and* the comparison control group represent two homogeneous populations. This approach makes two assumptions: (1) that the neurobiology for predefined diagnostic groups is distinct from those in another predefined group; and (2) that individuals are homogeneous within these predefined groups. A critical review of literature reveals that these assumptions are rarely met [5–7].

Moreover, assuming within-group homogeneity will likely cause misleading results at the aggregate level [8–10] in addition to missing important features for subpopulations within a given category.

This reality does not imply that current diagnostic categorization is completely arbitrary or not informative. However, it does present a significant barrier in the development of genetic and biological markers to assist in accurate diagnoses for a given disorder. Although small literatures have made attempts to parse fMRI data across individuals using various statistical methods (e.g., [11]), none have been sufficiently accepted to fall into wide use. Furthermore, efforts to subdivide based solely on biological features are still extremely rare (with notable exception using heart rate data [12]). The development of treatments, preventative, and intervention strategies for a given individual also suffer from this confound. Motivated by these issues, we present an approach for arriving at the potentially varied neurobiological etiologies related to a given mental health disorder, and show its utility in characterizing ADHD.

Specifically, we organize individuals into subgroups based on their brain connectivity maps. Brain connectivity maps have been used to identify systematic differences between subgroups and conditions in both clinical and non-clinical populations (e.g., [5,13]). On these dynamic features of the individual, we conduct community detection to arrive at subgroups of individuals based entirely on their functional brain architecture. This approach will enable new insights into the number of biologically-based subgroups within any diagnostic category, including typically developing populations, by looking at the functional connectivity of regions.

We sought an approach that would be widely applicable, accessible, and useful. Since we wished to move away from classification of surface symptoms and towards classification based on neurobiological features of the brain, we required an algorithm for arriving at data-driven classification using no *a priori* information regarding category status or symptoms but rather uses features of brain functioning that are in line with current theories and approaches for understanding brain processes. Accordingly, several points of consideration helped guide the search for an optimal approach. For one, the method must be useful on data that comes from non-invasive techniques for understanding brain physiology. Additionally, since not all individuals with mental disorders are capable of doing difficult paradigms and experimental designs differ greatly across sites, the method should not require examining responses to experimental manipulation. Two, given that brain processes can best be thought of as coordinated activity of disparate regions across time [14,15], we necessitated an approach for arriving at precise brain connectivity maps that quantifies relations among brain regions across time for each individual. This requires a state-of-the-art statistical method tailored to the data that detects signal from noise. Three, the algorithm must organize the individual-level models into subgroups based on brain connectivity estimates without prior classification information.

Our method (see Figure 1) satisfies these requirements by combining: (1) functional MRI (fMRI) collected while participants are not engaged in a specific task (i.e. resting-state functional connectivity MRI – rs-fcMRI; [16]); (2) unified structural equation modeling (uSEM) [17,18] conducted with Group Iterative Multiple Model Estimation (GIMME) [10] to ensure accurate individual level measurements of functional connectivity among brain regions; and (3) a widely used community detection algorithm [19], modularity, to arrive at data-driven subgroups of individuals based on brain processes rather than clusters of signs and symptoms. A benefit of rs-fcMRI is that it is developmentally and contextually more variable than brain structural measures, making it a highly attractive place to start towards the goal of identifying subgroups of individuals based on similar brain processes. Furthermore, it can be administered at across any age range, species, or cognitive ability. Prior rs-fcMRI analyses have revealed that there is ongoing information processing between spatially disparate regions of the brain even during rest, and differences in these observed processes relate to cognitive performance as well as psychiatric disorders. Connectivity maps conducted on rs-fcMRI data thus carry vast potential to advance understanding of normative and suboptimal brain processes. Taken together, our approach is a robust and easily applied method that utilizes functional connectivity networks to arrive at brain-based subgroups with no prior classification information.

Methods

GIMME

A necessary requirement for any project aiming to make inferences from directed functional connectivity maps is that they be reliable. Recent work demonstrated that most methods fail in their ability to recover both the presence and direction (i.e., which ROI statistically predicts the other ROI as opposed to bidirectional correlation between the two) of brain connections for individuals [20]. We utilize one of the only approaches to date that has been shown to reliably recover these parameters in heterogeneous and homogeneous samples of individuals: Group Iterative Multiple Model Estimation (GIMME; http://www.nitrc.org/projects/gimme/) [10]. GIMME first looks across individuals to detect signal from noise to arrive at a map that contains lagged and contemporaneous directed connections that exist for the majority ("group map"). In a second step GIMME identifies individual-level connections using the group-derived parameter patterns as a starting point. This has been shown to vastly improve reliability and precision of individual-level connections [10]. GIMME estimates the weight of these connections from within a unified Structural Equation Model (uSEM) [17] framework. Unified SEM contains both lagged and contemporaneous directed relations among regions, making it ideal for biological systems that likely contain these effects as detailed in [18].

Subgrouping with community detection

For the final step, we utilize Newman's commonly used modularity algorithm [19] found in the Brain Connectivity Toolbox (http://www.brain-connectivity-toolbox.net) to arrive at data-driven subgroup classifications of individuals using solely the results from the directed functional connectivity analysis. Prior work in fMRI using this modularity algorithm required that the researcher set an arbitrary threshold, or cutoff point, for what constitutes similarity between any two given individuals. Researchers would then arrive at thresholds by looking for consistency in community detection results at multiple thresholds (e.g., [2,21,22]). Rather than rely on subjective cut-offs we utilized an entirely data-driven approach to thresholding guided by the same principals.

Modularity uses an input matrix which indicates the relatedness among N nodes, which in this case is $n = 1 \ldots N$ individuals. To obtain this matrix, a first step in the present approach is to vectorize each individual's contemporaneous connection weights as estimated by GIMME. Recent work suggests that contemporaneous relationships best capture neuronal relations from BOLD data [20]. Including the lagged relations via uSEM ensures unbiased estimates of these contemporaneous relations [18]. Given

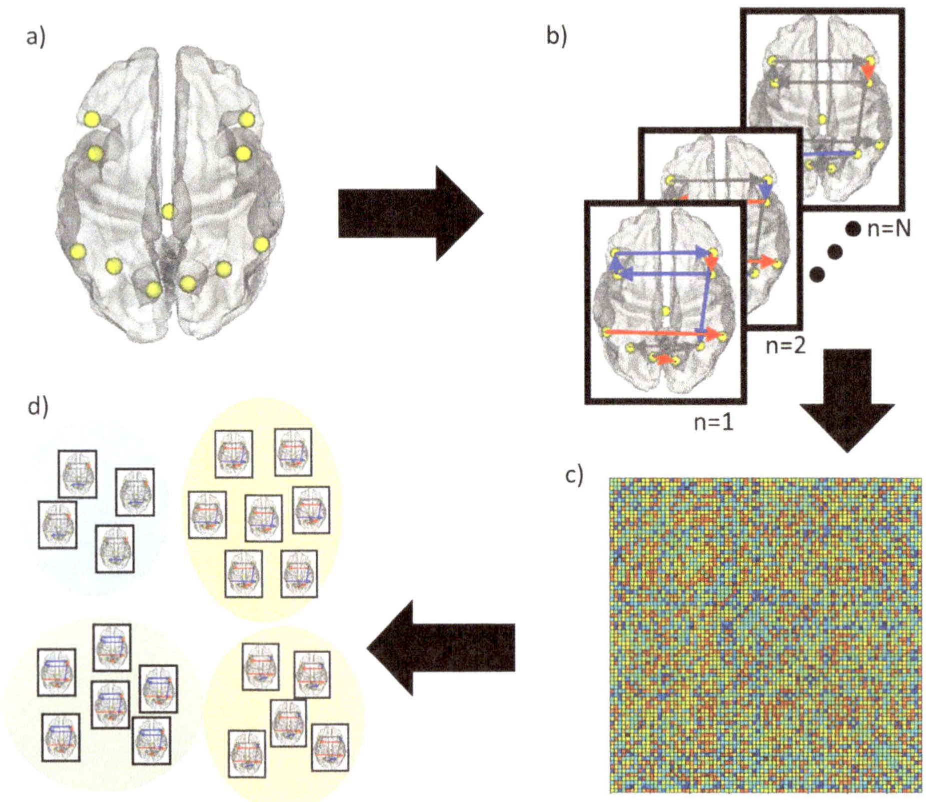

Figure 1. Schema of analytic process. Analysis were conducted using the following steps: a) obtain timeseries of functional MRI observations from regions of interest; b) arrive at directed functional connectivity maps for each individual using GIMME; c) correlate each individual's vector of connection weights with every other individual's vector for a similarity matrix; d) apply Newman's modularity maximization algorithm to similarity matrix to arrive at subgroups of individuals based on similar brain connectivity patterns.

the high degree of heterogeneity seen in the individual-level connections, including the individual-level paths may result in groups too small to offer any value over individual-level analysis. Thus we aim to subgroup individuals based on the similarities they share in their values in the sample-level paths. While only the sample-level connections are included to arrive at a correlation coefficient for each pair of individuals, it is necessary to estimate the individual-level connections when identifying the final models because these connections will ensure precise estimates of the connections we wish to use [23]. An added benefit is that sample-level connections will have normally distributed estimates across individuals, making it appropriate for the correlation analysis to follow.

The strength of linear dependence for the beta vector of each individual "i" with the beta vector of each other individual "j" is computed to produce a correlation matrix X. Following common practice in fMRI the weighted N by N matrix X is then binarized to create an A matrix where A_{ij} indicates if individual "i" is similar to individual "j" according to a given threshold r:

$$A_{ij}\begin{cases} 1 & \text{if } X_{ij} \geq r \\ 0 & \text{if } X_{ij} < r \end{cases} \tag{1}$$

which can then be used in Newman's modularity maximization algorithm; full equations for the method are explained in [19].

Deciding on the value for r, the threshold for which individuals are considered similar constitutes a pivotal decision in the algorithm. Researchers commonly select thresholds (or solutions) that provide the highest modularity index. Two criteria drive our threshold selection algorithm. One, the classification must be reliable across multiple runs. The modularity index can demonstrate considerable variability across iterations because it is sensitive to starting conditions that change randomly across runs. Researchers do not always consider this specific problem. Two, each individual must be reachable (i.e. have a connected path from one individual to another) by most other individuals at the given threshold [15]. Here, reachability is defined as the average number of individuals that each person can reach.

The modularity algorithm [19] is conducted at each threshold 100 times. To investigate the first criteria, the stability of Q across these 100 community detection attempts is examined. Figure 2 illustrates the instability seen in the Q value. This instability corresponds to different subgroup denotations, such that choosing a subgroup assignment for one run might differ from a second run at the same threshold. As depicted in Figure 2 and the top panel of Figure 3, the Q index becomes unstable at certain thresholds. This is a due to the program being sensitive to starting conditions, which change randomly across each run. An optimal r threshold would provide community solutions that are stable across each run, indicating that the solution is robust to different starting points.

Our next criterion is the reachability index. For each threshold we see that the reachability drops prior to the Q index reaching maximum instability (Figure 3, middle panel). This supports our decision to choose a threshold that occurs prior to the drop off in

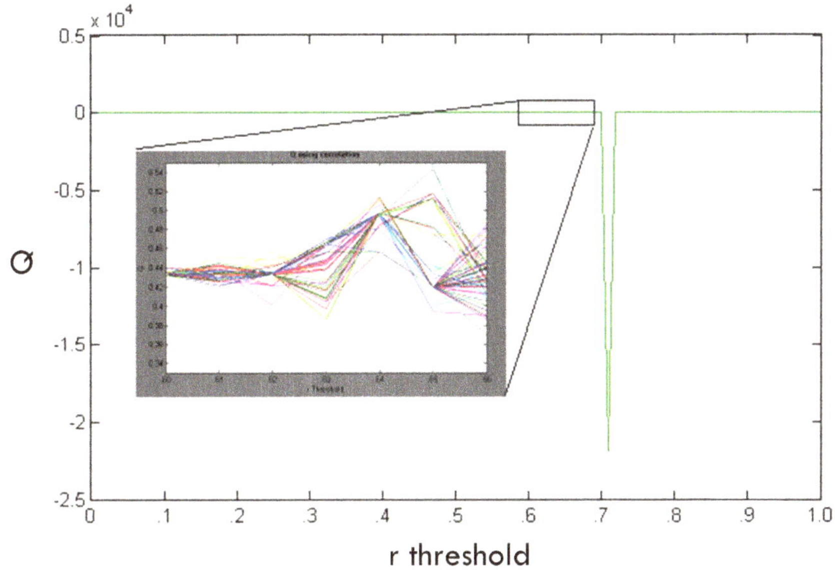

Figure 2. Instability in Q index. This is taken across 100 iterations at each threshold from 0.0 to 1.0 at .01 increments.

reachability as this relates to community quality. The middle panel of Figure 3 depicts the process for finding the drop in reachability. A line is generated from the first to last point of the average reachability across *r* thresholds. Next, we find the greatest distance from this line to the reachability values using perpendicular angles to determine the point at which reachability drops.

The bottom panel of Figure 3 shows the Q estimates for each threshold (conducted 100 times) up until the point where reachability drops. Please note that even at low values some thresholds are unstable, as indicated by fluctuations in the Q, whereas others reliably obtain the same Q across 100 attempts. Simulated and empirical data reveal that when Q is stable for this specific binary modularity algorithm, the subgroups are also stable

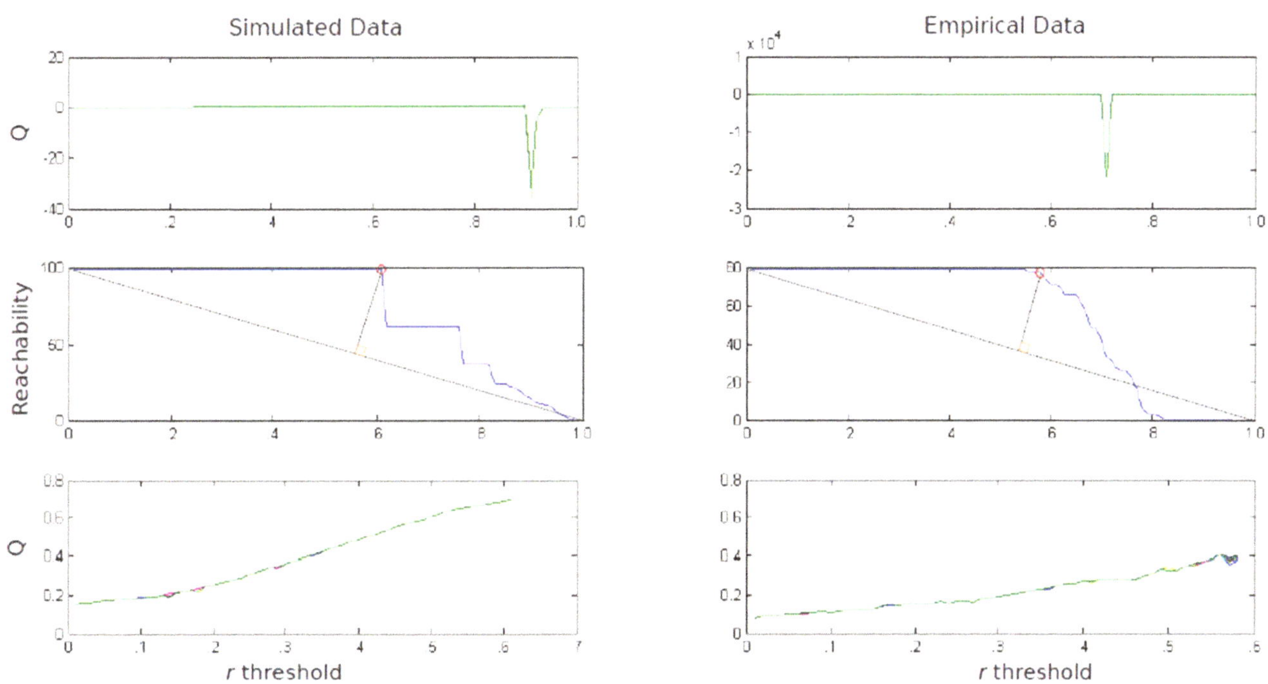

Figure 3. Q index and reachability across thresholds. Q values across all thresholds (top panel); average number of individuals each individual can reach at each threshold (i.e., reachability) and visual depiction (grey, dotted lines) of approach for defining the point at which reachability begins to decrease (middle panel); Q values (bottom panel) up until drop in reachability (denoted with a red circle in the middle panel). The optimal r thresholds with maximum stability, Q index value, and reachability criteria were .60 and .56 for the simulated data example presented here (1 of 100 runs) and empirical data, respectively.

(see Results below). The standard deviation of Q across 100 estimates is used to quantify stability. We select the threshold for which the Q index has maximum stability; in the event of a tie, the highest *r* with the highest Q is selected. The correlation threshold *r* is set and the above A matrix is created accordingly and used in the binary modularity algorithm [19].

Verifying the robustness of community detection solution

We followed the analytic plan outlined by Kerrer and colleagues [24] for testing the robustness of community structures in our simulated and empirical data. We quantified the difference between each run using the variation of information (VI) criterion developed by Meilă [25]. We use the VI index here to look at the robustness of community structures across varying levels of perturbations. This helps identify if the community structure is dependent on a small proportion of the data points and thus easily attributed to chance. First, we arrived at a final solution for each of the simulated and empirical data examples as outlined above. Here, "network" refers to the binary matrix of similarity at the chosen *r* threshold. Second, we randomly perturb the networks in a manner that retains the degree, or the number of edges, for each individual (i.e., vertex) by removing edges in the original network and placing it between two other individuals in the same network [24]. We conducted perturbations across probability levels which ranged from none (0) to completely random (1) at .025 increments. Each network (i.e., the 100 simulated data sets and the empirical data results) were randomly perturbed at each probability level 100 times. Third, we conducted community detection algorithm with data-driven thresholding for each of the perturbed networks to arrive at community structures. Finally, we took the community structures from the perturbed networks and measured the variation of information between these community assignments and the original one.

Comparing connectivity maps between subgroups

Variation in the connection weights of specific connections between two given ROIs has long been a focal point of fMRI research [17]. Having arrived at data-driven subgroups, group-level weights are compared between the subgroups to see how each subgroup differs from the average of the other subgroups. ANOVA with false discover rate (FDR) correction, at alpha of 0.05, was used to look at differences in beta weights for group-level connections [26]. As a comparison to the typical method for examining ADHD brain connectivity patterns, we also compare the connection weights between the control and ADHD groups using the diagnostic categorization.

Data

Simulated data

Simulated time series of fMRI data for 10 brain regions for 100 individuals were used to demonstrate feasibility and reliability of our approach following the approach outlined in [10]. For the present simulation, each individual has a time series of length 200 scans (at 2 TRs). All ROIs for all individuals have autoregressive effects of weight 0.60. In addition to these and as depicted in Figure 4a, 9 contemporaneous paths exist for all individuals comprising this sample. These paths are generated to have a weight (technically "beta") of 0.50 unless specified otherwise. For each subgroup, 3 of the 9 group-level beta estimates differ from .5 by ±.2 (refer to Figures 4b–e for specifics). Additionally, in each subgroup there exists one unique connection that randomly occurs across individuals comprising that subgroup using a binomial distribution with a probability of 0.5. This last level of heterogeneity adds in some individual-level variation within the group. The degree of similarity to expect as well as the variability in connection weights has been informed by previous research that used individual-level connectivity maps to examine a priori defined subgroups (e.g., [5])

Empirical data set

We demonstrate the utility of this approach in a sample of 80 children (29 females and 51 male) aged 7–12 years old, of which 40% met DSM-IV and DSM-5 diagnostic criteria for Attention-Deficit/Hyperactivity Disorder (ADHD) by a multi-method, multi-informant, best-estimate procedure that we have described in detail elsewhere [27,28] and summarized below. Written informed consent was obtained from parents and written informed assent from all child participants in accordance with the guidelines of the Oregon Health and Sciences University (OHSU) Research Integrity Office (IRB). The OHSU IRB approved this study.

Psychiatric diagnoses were based on multi-method, multi-informant research evaluations by our team with 1) *Kiddie Schedule for Affective Disorders and Schizophrenia* - KSADS-I [29,30] administered to a parent, 2) parent and teacher (short form) *Conners' Rating Scale-3rd Edition* [31] and Strengths and Difficulties Questionnaire (SDQ), (3) IQ and academic screening, (4) behavioral observations by a clinical interviewer, and then 5) a best-estimate clinical review by a board certified child psychiatrist and licensed clinical neuropsychologist. They independently assigned all appropriate diagnoses, with adequate agreement (kappa>.75 for all disorders with base rate >5% in a larger sample of several hundred children they have reviewed) and kappa >.80 for ADHD. They conferenced any disagreements and readily reached agreement or else the case was excluded. Estimates of intelligence were evaluated with a three-subtest short form (Block Design, Vocabulary, and Information) of the *Wechsler Intelligence Scale for Children, Fourth Edition* (WISC-IV) [32]. Demographic details including diagnostic status and IQ is provided in the Table 1.

Children were excluded if they did not meet DSM-IV criteria for ADHD or criteria for typically developing control. Children were also excluded for an IQ<75, or if a history of neurological illness, chronic medical problems, sensorimotor handicap, autistic disorder, mental retardation, or significant head trauma (with loss of consciousness) was identified by parent report. Children were also excluded if they had evidence of psychotic disorder or bipolar disorder on the structured parent psychiatric interview or were in a current major depressive episode. Children prescribed short-acting stimulant medications were scanned after a minimum washout of five half-lives (i.e., 24–48 hours depending on the preparation); all other psychoactive medications were a rule-out. Typically developing control children (TDC) were excluded for presence of conduct disorder, major depressive disorder, or history of psychotic disorder, as well as for presence of ADHD. All children were right handed.

Data Acquisition and Processing

Participants were scanned using a 3.0 Tesla Siemens Magnetom Tim Trio scanner (Siemens, Erlangen, Germany) with a twelve-channel head-coil at the OHSU Advanced Imaging Research Center. One high-resolution T1-weighted MPRAGE sequence lasting 9 minutes and 14 seconds (TR = 2300 ms, TE = 3.58 ms, orientation = sagittal, 256×256 matrix, resolution = 1^3 mm) was collected. Blood-oxygen level dependent (BOLD)-weighted functional imaging data were collected in an oblique plane (parallel to the ACPC) using T2*-weighted echo-planar imaging

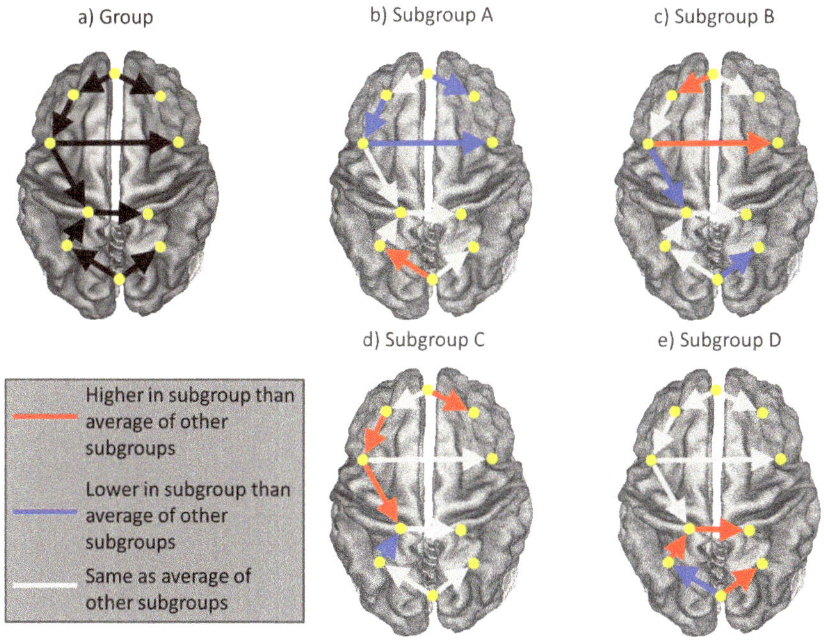

Figure 4. Patterns of effects used to simulate data and results.

(TR = 2500 ms, TE = 30 ms, flip angle = 90°, FOV = 240 mm, 36 slices covering the whole brain, slice thickness = 3.8 mm, in-plane resolution = 3.8×3.8 mm). Steady state magnetization was assumed after 5 frames (~10 s). Three runs of 3.5 minutes each were obtained. During rest periods subjects were instructed to stay still, and fixate on a standard fixation-cross in the center of the display.

All functional images were preprocessed in the same manner to reduce artifacts. These steps included: (i) removal of a central spike caused by MR signal offset, (ii) correction of odd vs. even slice intensity differences attributable to interleaved acquisition without gaps, (iii) correction for head movement within and across runs, and (iv) within-run intensity normalization to a whole brain mode value of 1,000. Atlas transformation of the functional data was computed for each individual via the MPRAGE scan. Each run then was resampled in atlas space [33] on an isotropic 3 mm grid, combining movement correction and atlas transformation in one interpolation [34]. All subsequent operations were performed on the atlas-transformed volumetric time series.

Functional connectivity preprocessing followed prior methods [35–37]. These steps included: (i) a temporal band-pass filter (0.009 Hz<f<0.08 Hz) and spatial smoothing (6 mm full width at half maximum), (ii) regression of the whole brain signal averaged over the whole brain, (iii) regression of ventricular signal averaged from ventricular region of interest (ROI), and (iv) regression of white matter signal averaged from white matter ROI. Regression of first order derivative terms for the whole brain, ventricular, and white matter signals were also included in the correlation preprocessing. These preprocessing steps are thought to reduce spurious variance unlikely to reflect neuronal activity [38].

Table 1. Demographics of empirical sample.

	ADHD	TDC	Statistic
Mean Age in Years	9.68 (1.52)	9.13 (1.20)	t = 1.83, df = 78, p = .07
% Male	78%	46%	χ^2 = 4.77, df = 1, p = .03
IQ	110.81 (15.11)	116.92 (13.75)	t = 1.76, df = 70, p = .08

Standard deviation in parentheses. Eight values for IQ are missing (5 ADHD, 3 TDC).

Subjects underwent several rigorous steps to correct for head motion during scanning. At the first level of correction (i.e., traditional motion correction), motion was measured relative to a reference frame (in this case, the middle frame of a BOLD run) and quantified using an analysis of head position based on rigid body translation and rotation. This procedure results in the rigid body transform defined by six motion parameters (3 translation, 3 rotation) typically generated by most functional MRI software tools. These 6 parameters were used as regressors in preprocessing to remove potential motion related artifact. In addition, in an effort to remove participants with egregious motion, we began our analysis by filtering those subjects with high movement runs based on root mean square (RMS). The data derived from the 6 motion parameters needed to realign head movement on a frame-by-frame basis were calculated as RMS values for translation and rotation in the x, y, and z planes in millimeters. Total RMS values were calculated on a run-by-run basis for each participant. Participant's BOLD runs with movement exceeding 1.5 mm RMS were removed. Last, frame-to-frame displacement (FD) was calculated for every time point. FD was calculated as a scalar quantity using a formula that sums the values for framewise displacement in the six rigid body parameters ($FDi = |\Delta dix| + |\Delta diy| + |\Delta diz| + |\Delta \alpha i| + |\Delta \beta i| + |\Delta \gamma i|$, where $\Delta dix = d(i-1)x - dix$, and similarly for the other five rigid body parameters) [21]. At each time point, if the FD was greater than 0.2 mm, the frame was excluded from the subject's time series by a placeholder row of missing values so the temporal ordering of scans was retained for uSEM analysis.

We selected 11 regions of interest based on prior work by Dosenbach and colleagues [22,39,40]. These regions termed the fronto-parietal network (see Figure 5a) were selected based on their implied role in adaptive task level control that surfaces in resting state studies [40,41] and atypical nature in studies of ADHD [42,43]. Table 2 lists the 11 ROIs and coordinates. Time series were computed for each of the cortical regions by averaging the signal intensity across all voxels within a 10 mm sphere for each time point.

Results

Simulated data

For the simulated data, GIMME was able to recover all of the connections which existed at the group level for each of the 100 sets of data (see Figure 4a). After considering individual-level connections (which varied systematically across subgroups), on average 99.73% (std. = 0.09%, range = 95–100% across the 100 data sets) of the connections across all individuals were recovered accurately (i.e., both the presence and direction were correct). The community detection algorithm described above then identified the subgroups excellently: 97.23% (std. = 1.87%, range = 92–100%) of the individuals within each data set were placed in subgroups with those who shared their simulated brain map pattern. ANOVA results consistently revealed significant differences in connection weights across the subgroups that corresponded with the patterns used to create the data that was consistent across the 100 simulated data sets (Figure 4b–e). This, taken together with the reliable recovery of subgroup classification, verifies that the present approach appropriately groups individuals who are indeed similar.

As an added check, we tested the modularity approach on randomly generated graphs to ensure robustness of our solution as described in the methods [24]. The subgroups were consistently recovered in the simulated data and were robust to minor perturbations. Figure 6a displays the results from a representative simulated data set (number 11 of 100). The simulated data results adhere to the ideal pattern described by Karrer and colleagues. The community assignments remain similar for the simulated individuals until a perturbation level of about .5 (i.e., random assignment of 50% of the edges), at which point 20% of the vertices are assigned different communities than the original and we see this variation of information increasing steadily past this point. The randomly generated graphs, by contrast, experience a sharp increase in variation of information at the slightest perturbation. Indeed, over 40% of the vertices have different community assignments after perturbing about two percent of the edges.

Table 2. Coordinate locations of regions in Talaraich space.

Region	X	Y	Z
L dlPFC	−43	22	34
R dlPFC	43	22	34
L FC	−41	3	36
R FC	41	3	36
midcingulate	0	−29	30
L IPL	−51	−51	36
R IPL	51	−47	42
L IPS	−31	−59	42
R IPS	30	−61	39
L precuneus	−9	−72	37
R precuneus	10	−69	39

"dlPFC" = dorsolateral prefrontal cortex; "FC" = frontal cortex; "IPS" = intraperietal sulcus; "IPL" = inferior parietal lobule; "R" preceding these ROI names and abbreviations denotes right and "L" denotes left.

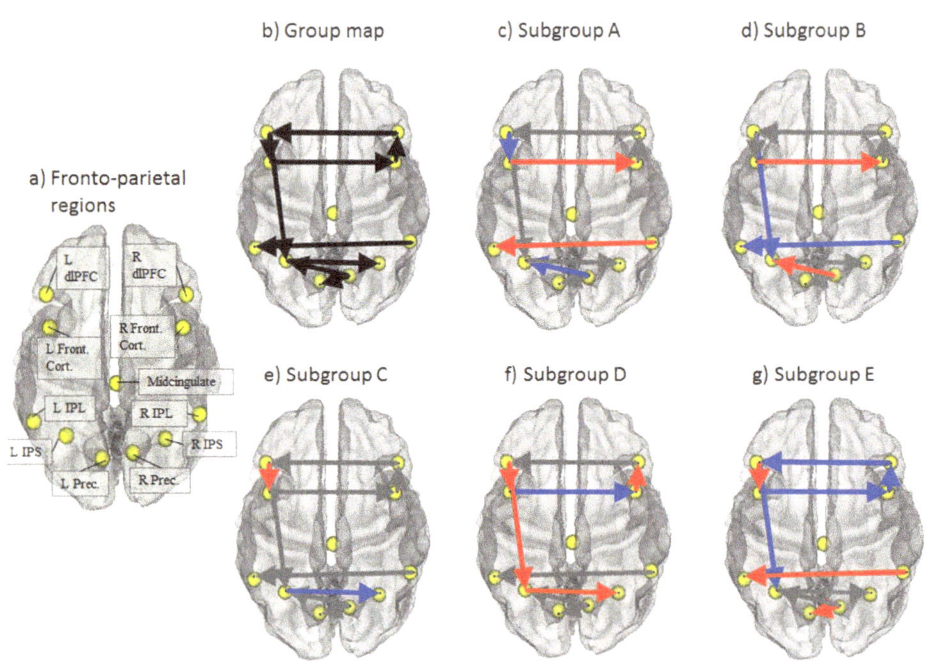

Figure 5. Regions and results from empirical sample. Red lines indicate the subgroup had higher connection values than the average of the other subgroups; blue lines indicate the subgroup had lower connection values than the average of the other subgroups; gray paths indicate the connection values were similar to the average of other subgroups. Abbreviations: "dlPFC" = dorsolateral prefrontal cortex; "FC" = frontal cortex; "IPS" = intraperietal sulcus; "IPL" = inferior parietal lobule; "R" preceding these ROI names and abbreviations denotes right and "L" denotes left.

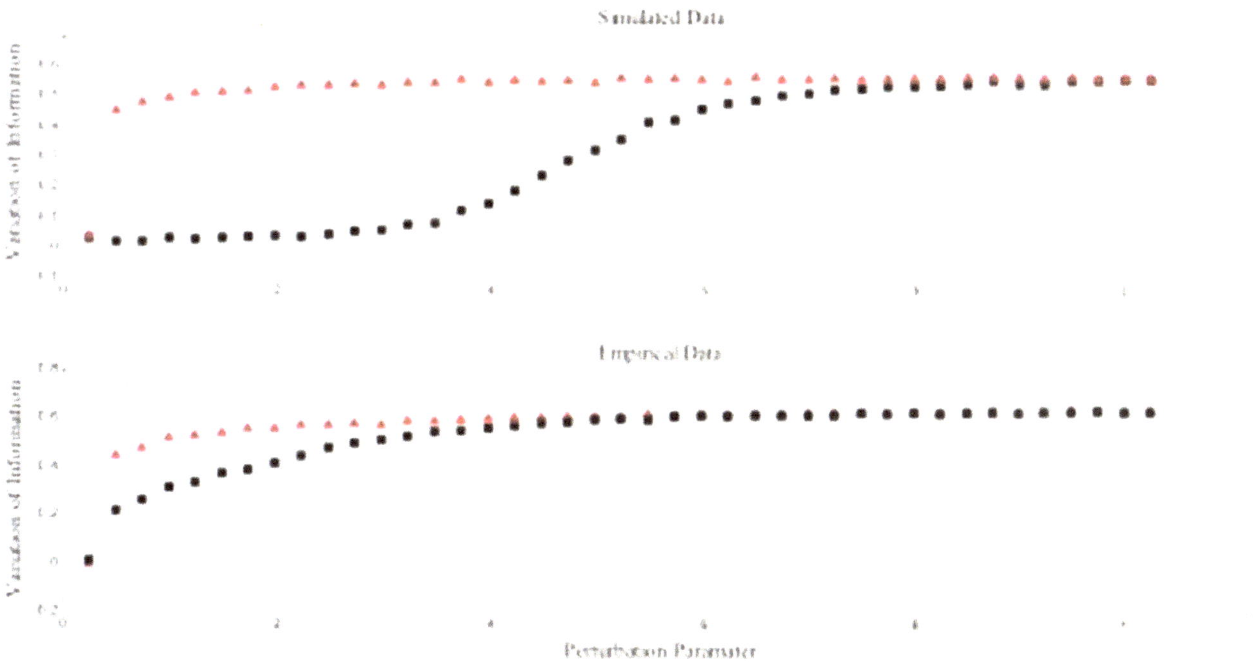

Figure 6. Variation of information (VI) in simulated and empirical data across varying degrees of perturbation. Red triangles indicate VI values obtained from random perturbations; black squares correspond to VI values obtained on the original matrices.

Empirical data

The connectivity map depicted in Figure 5b provides the connectivity pattern of the fronto-parietal region set common for the majority of individuals in the whole sample (i.e. connections found to be significant for the majority, or the "group map"). In addition, a number of connections surfaced at the individual level (not pictured). Every individual had at least one connection in addition to those found at the group-level, and every potential connection between regions was found for at least one person. Hence there appears to be some connections that exist for the majority of individuals while there also exists a large degree of heterogeneity in the structure of connections as evidenced by the extra connections uncovered at the individual level. This finding highlights the need to use a method such as GIMME which is geared towards detecting signal from noise to reliably arrive at the presence of individual-level connections which in turn improve upon the precision of connection weight estimates.

We first compared path weights by considering the ADHD and Typically Developing samples to be two homogenous groups, akin to how current research projects are typically conducted. That is, we placed and analyzed the individuals into groups based on their diagnostic status. Here, our search is limited to differences between these two diagnostically defined groups. Tests for significant differences between ADHD and TDC on the path weights revealed no significant differences. Hence it appears the within-group heterogeneity washed out effects of interest that we were able to isolate by enabling for heterogeneity within the diagnostic categories.

We then applied the community detection algorithm to group individuals based on their brain patterns of connectivity as opposed to their diagnostic status. The community detection approach arrived at 5 subgroups of individuals. Regarding the robustness of the solution as quantified using VI, the curves for the empirical and random data remain distinct and thus the network of individuals can be said to show community structure (see Figure 6b; [24]). Since there are a higher proportion of males than females diagnosed with ADHD, we first investigated if males and females were evenly distributed across the subgroups. The proportions of males and females in each of the subgroups were not different than what one would expect by chance ($\chi^2 = 3.65$, df = 4, $p = .456$). ADHD and TDC participants, however, were placed in different subgroups at levels greater than chance ($\chi^2 = 12.32$, df = 4; $p = .015$; Figure 7). Of note, 38% of the controls are in subgroup A (see Table 3 for results). Subgroups B and D contain a high percentage of the ADHD children, who make up a large part of these subgroups. The smaller subgroups C and E are disproportionately control, but contain relatively small percentages of the control sample. Taken together, subgroups A, C, and E are subgroups with low likelihood for ADHD and as such have an organization of brain physiology that we term "protective." That is, individuals with brain connectivity maps similar to those found in these groups will likely not have ADHD. Subgroups B and D appear to have brain organizations that place them at higher likelihood for having ADHD. These findings demonstrate that heterogeneity exists within both control and ADHD populations, and that the potential differences between the two

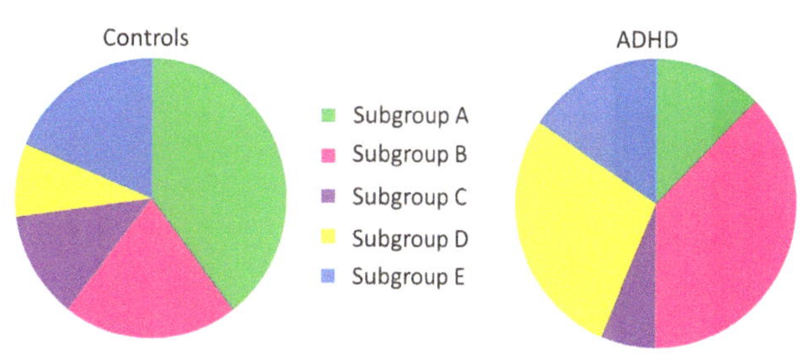

Figure 7. Subgroup make-up: Controls and ADHD.

Table 3. Group affiliation by ADHD diagnostic category.

	Subgroup				
	A	B	C	D	E
Control (N = 48)	18	10	7	4	9
% of Control	38%	21%	15%	8%	19%
% within Subgroup	82%	45%	77%	31%	64%
ADHD (N = 32)	4	12	2	9	5
% of ADHD	13%	38%	6%	28%	16%
% within Subgroup	18%	55%	22%	69%	36%

categories are washed out when assuming within-group homogeneity.

Numerous differences in the connection weights existed across the groups (Figures 5c–g). For instance, subgroup A (protective) was the only subgroup to have stronger interhemispheric connections than the average of the other subgroups in both the anterior and posterior regions. In subgroup B (risk), by comparison, the statistical prediction of the left inferior parietal lobule (L IPL) from the right inferior parietal lobule (R IPL) was weaker, but like subgroup A had strong directed influence of the left frontal cortex (L FC) on the R FC. Importantly, subgroup B had lower directed connectivity strength from the left dorsolateral prefrontal cortex (L dlPFC) to the left intraparietal sulcus (L IPS), which is consistent with previous research on deficits in attention [44]. However for this connection, subgroup D (also a risk group for ADHD) evidenced a stronger directed connection, suggesting that more than one pathway for attention deficits exists. Indeed, subgroup D (risk) appears to have decreased connectivity from the L FC to the R FC when compared to the average of the other groups, indicating a potential biological marker for ADHD in addition to the L dlPFC and L IPS deficit found in subgroup B and previous research. Subgroup E (protective) had decreased connectivity on a number of connections predominantly associated with the frontal regions. Taken together, there appears to be different physiological markers within the ADHD diagnostic category as well as different profiles within the control sample.

Discussion

The current analysis presents a beginning effort at establishing empirically driven, brain-based subtypes in mental disorders. We combined and extended state-of-the-art methods to arrive at a dynamic community detection approach for characterizing differences in brain physiology, tested it using Monte Carlo simulations, and validated the approach with empirical data. Our approach differs from current implementations in at least two meaningful ways. For one, similarities among individuals are assessed using the entire pattern of connections as opposed to alternative methods that simply take one aspect, such as one connection weight or statistical parametric maps. In this way our approach is directly in line with the current understanding of brain functioning as best understood as the connectivity between disparate regions as opposed to isolated areas. Two, no assumptions are made regarding the classification of individuals. Traditional methods, such as machine learning or discriminant analysis, require *a priori* distinction of subgroups based on the construct of interest (e.g., gender, age, clinical category, performance). Humans are multidimensional and can be categorized on various axes [2,45]. For this reason, a complementary way to look at group differences is presented here. The present approach organizes individuals based on their functional brain physiology, from which researchers can then examine how a given group relates to demographic, clinical, and performance characteristics.

The feasibility of using GIMME and community detection to arrive at data-driven subgroups of individuals based on brain physiology was demonstrated via our simulations. As seen previously [10], GIMME reliably recovered the presence and true direction of connections at the group and individual levels and is one of the few approaches that can do so [46]. Next, a widely used algorithm for arriving at subgroups, the modularity approach [19], was used for subgroup classification. This procedure was modified to arrive at the optimal solution in an entirely data-driven fashion. Subgroup designations were accurately made using the GIMME individual-level connectivity map estimates.

The empirical data example offered concrete evidence for theories that have hitherto been untested. That is, within diagnostic categories there exists heterogeneity in brain physiologies. In particular, researchers have made strong assertions that clinical diagnoses may result from multiple etiologies [3,4]. This possibility has been noted in ADHD as well as Autism Spectrum Disorder [3,47]. Most evidence for this phenomenon has been from neuropsychological data and behavior or symptom report (e.g., [2]), with recent evidence suggesting heterogeneity in the biological components as well [48]. In this sample, ADHD appears to have at least two main biological manifestations related to the fronto-parietal regions that differentiated individuals within this diagnostic category. In line with previous research [44], one of the ADHD-dominant subgroups did have weaker dorsolateral prefrontal cortex connection with the inferior parietal sulcus. However, the other ADHD-dominant subgroup had increased connectivity between these two regions but had decreased connectivity between the right and left frontal cortex. Hence grouping all ADHD individuals together may not capture all of the informative characteristics of the disorder and in this sample, washed out meaningful differences.

Although the majority of ADHD-diagnosed children fell into two subgroups, about a third were spread across the three subgroups comprised of predominantly typically developing control. This further supports the notion that many mechanisms exist by which children may meet criteria for ADHD [2]. If these results were taken at face value, we might propose for example that the current diagnostic criteria capture a group with a developmental brain trajectory that A) is at risk, and B) is sensitive to our functional MR measurements. We also would propose that another group with ADHD has either typical brain development or a pathology that likes outside of the brain systems examined here or for which our MR measurements are not sensitive to. Nonetheless, the work supports the potential of a biologically based nosology in the future.

A final important finding was that children identified as typically developing controls were found in every subgroup. Indeed, some individuals had biological markers that are similar to those in a clinical category yet did not meet the level for a clinical diagnosis. Investigating contextual indices that may protect those at biological risk for developing a disorder provides another utility for data-driven subgroup classifications. Thus it is interesting to consider that the brain findings here may reflect liability for ADHD in a biologically at risk subgroup, rather than ADHD per se—the controls in these groups may represent individuals at risk for ADHD who had sufficient protective factors in their development (or their genome) to avoid exhibiting the syndrome.

It will be interesting to follow these groups over time to evaluate whether this type of hypothesis holds true over time.

Importantly, the fact that typically developing controls may be heterogeneous in functional brain architecture, or brain "profiles", is not a new concept either. A long line of research in the social sciences has urged researchers to examine processes at the individual level rather than aggregate as is typically done in cross-sectional studies [45,49–51]. Support for this notion is found in fMRI data, where individual differences in brain patterns relating to indices such as performance [17,52] and gender [13] have been found in normative samples. The approach presented here provides a bridge between group-level aggregation and individual-level analysis. *A priori* grouping based solely on diagnostic category would miss the heterogeneity that exists within a diagnostic category, whereas conducting individual-level analysis would result in unique maps from which no meaningful inferences could be made.

Amidst the heterogeneity within diagnostic categories, subgroups emerged that were predominantly clinical or control, supporting some degree of biological validity to the existing nosology. Although both ADHD and control individuals surfaced in each of the five brain-based groups, the composition of each subgroup contained a disproportionate number of the diagnostic categories. Hence, our method can be used to identify disease-associated brain physiologies much like the current approach of comparing predefined a diagnostic group to a control group. Varied interhemispheric and posterior-anterior functional connections differentiate predominantly ADHD-comprised subgroups from predominantly control subgroups in our study. Data in the ADHD literature examining functional differences in the diagnostic subtypes (i.e. Combined type, and Inattentive type) lend support for this particular finding [2]. Most important, the approach presented here can help researchers better understand between-group differences alongside within-group heterogeneity.

The present work builds from prior subgrouping algorithms that have demonstrated success. However, community detection does not come without shortcomings. One, the popularity of community detection algorithms in fMRI research has grown substantially in a short time. Along with this growth there has been an influx of algorithms that seek to improve upon the traditionally used ones (e.g., [53]). The proliferation of community detection programs has occurred quickly enough such that they have yet to be formally compared and evaluated to identify which ones are best for which situations (e.g., number of individuals in each "true" group, number of subgroups in a sample, unequal group sizes, small sample sizes) and what scientific questions. The Newman algorithm [19], as applied here, is widely used, but is likely not optimal for all situations. Importantly, many community detection approaches in the fMRI literature have been tested on relatively large adjacency matrices and, while useful, may not be optimal for smaller matrices where the nodes are participants.

Two, a few options exist regarding the generation of the similarity matrices (i.e., the adjacency matrix that indicates how similar each individual's connectivity weights are to each other individual) that were ultimately used with the community detection algorithm. For instance, the connectivity mapping results may vary based on preprocessing decisions, such as global signal regression (GSR). We used GSR because it offers a number of benefits such as improving the correspondence between resting-state correlations and anatomy [54] and motion correction at the time series level [55,56]. There is the possibility that GSR altered connectivity patterns [57,58], which in turn may change the degree of similarity of individuals and thus the resulting community designations. Hence future work can investigate the impact of these decisions on resulting subgroup designations.

Other options exist regarding the features of the connectivity maps used to generate the similarity matrix. We also could have created the similarity matrix using the estimates for lagged paths in addition to or instead of the contemporaneous path estimates. Since contemporaneous paths seem to hold information regarding neuronal relationships, we chose to use these. Lagged effects, and by extension, coherence in the frequency domain, could also be informative in creating groups. Future work is also needed to investigate approaches for arriving at the similarity matrix in a manner that utilizes the individual-level paths in addition to the sample-level ones. We utilize sample-level paths since they are normally distributed across individuals and thus appropriate for obtaining correlation values denoting similarity in values for use with the community detection algorithm. Additionally, the high degree of heterogeneity with regards to the individual-level paths necessitated that we omit these when creating the similarity matrices since including individual-level results via a distance measure (as opposed to correlation) resulted in groups that were too small to offer any value over individual-level analysis. As the solution to this problem is not straightforward, more work needs to be done to identify methods that arrive at similarity matrices that are appropriate for data that is not normally distributed.

Data of a substantial sample size are often capable of being split into a multitude of valid subgroup arrangements. What determines a given demarcation rests predominantly on the features (in our case connections) chosen to show similarities or differences between individuals and the algorithm chosen to demarcate the sample. What is most important in this line of work is to identify the subgroups that are most meaningful with regard to clinical translation. Thus, the work presented here will need to be validated further by examining how the subgroups predict outcomes and/or respond to treatment differently (as seen in [2]), and how different contextual factors interact with the brain physiology to predict diagnostic classification that can guide prevention efforts. The method presented here is a step towards this goal. Having demonstrated the feasibility and utility of dynamic community detection, more work is needed across multiple domains of inquiry to exploit the extent to which understanding heterogeneity in brain physiology can be helpful in guiding treatment, prevention, and intervention efforts.

Author Contributions

Conceived and designed the experiments: DAF JTN. Performed the experiments: DAF JTN. Analyzed the data: KMG SPI. Contributed reagents/materials/analysis tools: KMG. Wrote the paper: DAF KMG. Conceived analytic plan: DAF KMG PCMM.

References

1. Kapur S, Phillips AG, Insel TR (2012) Why has it taken so long for biological psychiatry to develop clinical tests and what to do about it? Mol Psychiatry 17: 1174–1179.
2. Fair DA, Bathula D, Nikolas MA, Nigg JT (2012) Distinct neuropsychological subgroups in typically developing youth inform heterogeneity in children with ADHD. Proc Natl Acad Sci U S A 109: 6769–6774.
3. Volkmar FR, Lord C, Bailey A, Schultz RT, Klin A (2004) Autism and pervasive mental disorders. Journal of Child Psychology and Psychiatry 45: 135:170.
4. Gottesman II, Gould TD (2003) The endophenotype concept in psychiatry: Etymology and strategic intentions. . American Journal of Psychiatry 160: 636–645.

5. Hillary FG, Medaglia JD, Gates K, Molenaar PC, Slocomb J, et al. (2011) Examining working memory task acquisition in a disrupted neural network. Brain 134: 1555–1570.
6. Miller MB, Van Horn JD (2007) Individual variability in brain activations associated with episodic retrieval: a role for large-scale databases. Int J Psychophysiol 63: 205–213.
7. Miller MB, Van Horn JD, Wolford GL, Handy TC, Valsangkar-Smyth M, et al. (2002) Extensive Individual Differences in Brain Activations Associated with Episodic Retrieval are Reliable Over Time. Journal of Cognitive Neuroscience 14: 1200–1214.
8. Ramsey JD, Hanson SJ, Hanson C, Halchenko YO, Poldrack RA, et al. (2010) Six problems for causal inference from fMRI. Neuroimage 49: 1545–1558.
9. Seghier ML, Lazeyras F, Pegna AJ, Annoni JM, Khateb A (2008) Group analysis and the subject factor in functional magnetic resonance imaging: analysis of fifty right-handed healthy subjects in a semantic language task. Hum Brain Mapp 29: 461–477.
10. Gates KM, Molenaar PC (2012) Group search algorithm recovers effective connectivity maps for individuals in homogeneous and heterogeneous samples. Neuroimage 63: 310–319.
11. Kherif F, Poline J-B, Mériaux S, Benali H, Flandin G, et al. (2003) Group analysis in functional neuroimaging: selecting subjects using similarity measures. NeuroImage 20: 2197–2208.
12. Friedman B, Santucci A (2003) Idiodynamic profiles of cardiovascular activity: A P-technique approach. Integrative Physiological & Behavioral Science 38: 295–315.
13. Beltz AM, Gates KM, Engels AS, Molenaar PC, Pulido C, et al. (2013) Changes in alcohol-related brain networks across the first year of college: a prospective pilot study using fMRI effective connectivity mapping. Addict Behav 38: 2052–2059.
14. Sporns O, Chialvo DR, Kaiser M, Hilgetag CC (2004) Organization, development and function of complex brain networks. Trends Cogn Sci 8: 418–425.
15. Tononi G, Sporns O, Edelman GM (1994) A measure for brain complexity: relating functional segregation and integration in the nervous system. Proceedings of the National Academy of Sciences 91: 5033–5037.
16. Biswal BB, Yetkin FZ, Haughton VM, Hyde JS (1995) Functional connectivity in the motor cortex of resting human brain using echo-planar MRI. . Magnetic resonance in medicine 34: 537–541.
17. Kim J, Zhu W, Chang L, Bentler PM, Ernst T (2007) Unified structural equation modeling approach for the analysis of multisubject, multivariate functional MRI data. Hum Brain Mapp 28: 85–93.
18. Gates KM, Molenaar PC, Hillary FG, Ram N, Rovine MJ (2010) Automatic search for fMRI connectivity mapping: an alternative to Granger causality testing using formal equivalences among SEM path modeling, VAR, and unified SEM. Neuroimage 50: 1118–1125.
19. Newman ME (2006) Modularity and community structure in networks. Proc Natl Acad Sci U S A 103: 8577–8582.
20. Smith SM, Miller KL, Salimi-Khorshidi G, Webster M, Beckmann CF, et al. (2011) Network modelling methods for FMRI. Neuroimage 54: 875–891.
21. Power JD, Fair DA, Schlaggar BL, Petersen SE (2010) The development of human functional brain networks. Neuron 67: 735–748.
22. Fair DA, Cohen AL, Power JD, Dosenbach NUF, Church JA, et al. (2009) Functional Brain Networks Develop from a "Local to Distributed" Organization. PLoS Comput Biol 5: e1000381.
23. Kutner MH, Nachtsheim C, Neter J (2004) Applied linear regression models: McGraw-Hill/Irwin.
24. Karrer B, Levina E, Newman MEJ (2008) Robustness of community structure in networks. Physical Review E 77.
25. Meilă M (2007) Comparing clusterings—an information based distance. Journal of Multivariate Analysis 98: 873–895.
26. Storey JD (2002) A direct approach to false discovery rates. Journal of the Royal Statistical Society: Series B (Statistical Methodology) 64: 479–498.
27. Musser ED, Galloway-Long HS, Frick PJ, Nigg JT (2013) Emotion Regulation and Heterogeneity in Attention-Deficit/Hyperactivity Disorder. Journal of the American Academy of Child & Adolescent Psychiatry 52: 163–171. e162.
28. Nikolas MA, Nigg JT (2013) Neuropsychological performance and attention-deficit hyperactivity disorder subtypes and symptom dimensions. Neuropsychology 27: 107.
29. Kaufman J, Birmaher B, Brent D, Rao U, Flynn C, et al. (1997) Schedule for Affective Disorders and Schizophrenia for School-Age Children-Present and Lifetime Version (K-SADS-PL): initial reliability and validity data. J Am Acad Child Adolesc Psychiatry 36: 980–988.
30. Puig-Antich J, Ryan N (1986) The schedule for affective disorders and schizophrenia for school-age children. Pittsburg: Western Psychiatric Institute and Clinic.
31. Conners CK (2008) Conners 3rd Edition Manual; Rayes M, Hartawidjojo V, editors. Toronto: Multi-Health Systems Inc.
32. Wechsler D (2003) Wechsler Intelligence Scale for Children Technical and Interpretive Manual. San Antonio, TX: The Psychological Corporation.
33. Talairach J, Tournoux P (1988) Co-Planar Stereotaxic Atlas of the Human Brain. Rayport M, translator. New York: Thieme Medical Publishers, Inc.
34. Lancaster JL, Glass TG, Lankipalli BR, Downs H, Mayberg H, et al. (1995) A Modality-Independent Approach to Spatial Normalization of Tomographic Images of the Human Brain. Hum Brain Mapp 3: 209–223.
35. Fair DA, Schlaggar BL, Cohen AL, Miezin FM, Dosenbach NU, et al. (2007) A method for using blocked and event-related fMRI data to study "resting state" functional connectivity. Neuroimage 35: 396–405.
36. Fox MD, Snyder AZ, Vincent JL, Corbetta M, Van Essen DC, et al. (2005) The human brain is intrinsically organized into dynamic, anticorrelated functional networks. Proc Natl Acad Sci U S A 102: 9673–9678.
37. Fair DA, Cohen AL, Dosenbach NU, Church JA, Miezin FM, et al. (2008) The maturing architecture of the brain's default network. Proc Natl Acad Sci U S A 105: 4028–4032.
38. Fox MD, Raichle ME (2007) Spontaneous fluctuations in brain activity observed with functional magnetic resonance imaging. Nat Rev Neurosci 8: 700–711.
39. Dosenbach NU, Visscher KM, Palmer ED, Miezin FM, Wenger KK, et al. (2006) A core system for the implementation of task sets. Neuron 50: 799–812.
40. Dosenbach NU, Fair DA, Miezin FM, Cohen AL, Wenger KK, et al. (2007) Distinct brain networks for adaptive and stable task control in humans. Proc Natl Acad Sci U S A 104: 11073–11078.
41. Dosenbach NU, Fair DA, Cohen AL, Schlaggar BL, Petersen SE (2008) A dual-networks architecture of top-down control. Trends Cogn Sci 12: 99–105.
42. Silk T, Vance A, Rinehart N, Egan G, O'boyle M, et al. (2005) Fronto-parietal activation in attention-deficit hyperactivity disorder, combined type: functional magnetic resonance imaging study. The British Journal of Psychiatry 187: 282–283.
43. Silk T, Vance A, Rinehart N, Bradshaw J, Cunnington R (2008) Dysfunction in the Fronto-Parietal Network in Attention Deficit Hyperactivity Disorder (ADHD): An fMRI Study. Brain Imaging and Behavior 2: 123–131.
44. Liston C, McEwen BS, Casey BJ (2009) Psychosocial stress reversibly disrupts prefrontal processing and attentional control. Proceedings of the National Academy of Sciences of the United States of America 106: 912–917.
45. Molenaar PC (2004) A manifesto on psychology as idiographic science: Bringing the person back into scientific psychology, this time forever. Measurement 2: 201–218.
46. Mumford JA, Ramsey JD (2014) Bayesian networks for fMRI: A primer. Neuroimage 86: 573–582.
47. Betancur C (2011) Etiological heterogeneity in autism spectrum disorders: more than 100 genetic and genomic disorders and still counting. Brain Res 1380: 42–77.
48. Fair D, Nigg JT, Iyer S, Bathula D, Mills KL, et al. (2013) Distinct Neural Signatures Detected for ADHD Subtypes After Controlling for Micro-Movements in Resting State Functional Connectivity MRI Data. Frontiers in Systems Neuroscience 6.
49. Molenaar PC (2008) On the implications of the classical ergodic theorems: analysis of developmental processes has to focus on intra-individual variation. Dev Psychobiol 50: 60–69.
50. Lamiell JT (1981) Toward an idiothetic psychology of personality. American Psychologist 36: 276–289.
51. Nesselroade JR, Baltes PB (1979) Longitudinal research in the study of behavior and development: Academic Pr.
52. Nichols TT, Gates KM, Molenaar PCM, Wilson SJ (In Press) Greater BOLD activity but more efficient connectivity is associated with better cognitive performance within a sample of nicotine-deprived smokers. . Addict Biol.
53. Blondel VD, Guillaume J-L, Lambiotte R, Lefebvre E (2008) Fast unfolding of communities in large networks. Journal of Statistical Mechanics: Theory and Experiment 2008: P10008.
54. Fox MD, Zhang D, Snyder AZ, Raichle ME (2009) The global signal and observed anticorrelated resting state brain networks. Journal of neurophysiology 101: 3270–3283.
55. Satterthwaite TD, Wolf DH, Ruparel K, Erus G, Elliott MA, et al. (2013) Heterogeneous impact of motion on fundamental patterns of developmental changes in functional connectivity during youth. Neuroimage 83: 45–57.
56. Yan CG, Cheung B, Kelly C, Colcombe S, Craddock RC, et al. (2013) A comprehensive assessment of regional variation in the impact of head micromovements on functional connectomics. Neuroimage 76: 183–201.
57. Gotts SJ, Saad ZS, Jo HJ, Wallace GL, Cox RW, et al. (2013) The perils of global signal regression for group comparisons: a case study of Autism Spectrum Disorders. Frontiers in human neuroscience 7.
58. Saad ZS, Gotts SJ, Murphy K, Chen G, Jo HJ, et al. (2012) Trouble at rest: how correlation patterns and group differences become distorted after global signal regression. Brain connectivity 2: 25–32.

11

Tracing Developmental Trajectories of Oppositional Defiant Behaviors in Preschool Children

Lourdes Ezpeleta[1]*, Roser Granero[1], Núria de la Osa[1], José Blas Navarro[2], Eva Penelo[2], Josep M. Domènech[1]

1 Unitat d'Epidemiologia i de Diagnòstic en Psicopatologia del Desenvolupament, Departament de Psicologia Clínica i de la Salut, Universitat Autònoma de Barcelona, Barcelona, Spain, 2 Departament de Psicobiologia i Metodologia de les Ciències de la Salut, Universitat Autònoma de Barcelona, Barcelona, Spain

Abstract

Objective: Previous studies on developmental trajectories have used ad hoc definitions of oppositional defiant behaviors (ODB), which makes it difficult to compare results. This article defines developmental trajectories of ODB from ages 3–5 based on five different standard measurements derived from three separate instruments.

Method: A sample of 622 three-year-old preschoolers, followed up at ages 4, 5, and 6, was assessed with the five measures of oppositionality answered by parents and teachers. Growth-Mixture-Modeling (GMM) estimated separate developmental trajectories for each ODB measure for ages 3 to 5.

Results: The number of classes-trajectories obtained in each GMM depended on the ODB measure, but two clear patterns emerged: four trajectories (persistent low, decreasers, increasers/high increasers, persistent moderate/persistent high) or three trajectories (persistent low, decreasers, increasers/high increasers). Persistent high trajectories accounted for 4.4%–9.5% of the children. The trajectories emerging from the different ODB measures at ages 3 to 5 discriminated disruptive disorders, comorbidity, use of services, and impairment at age 6, and globally showed a similar pattern, summarizing longitudinal information on oppositionality in preschool children in a similar way.

Conclusions: Trajectories resulting from standard scales of the questionnaires have predictive validity for identifying relevant clinical outcomes, but are measure-specific. The results contribute to knowledge about the development of ODB in preschool children.

Editor: Karen Lidzba, University Children's Hospital Tuebingen, Germany

Funding: Funding was from Spanish Ministry of Economy and Competitiveness grant PSI2012-32695. The funders had no role in study design, data collection and analysis, decision to publish, or preparation of the manuscript.

Competing Interests: The authors have declared that no competing interests exist.

* Email: lourdes.ezpeleta@uab.cat

Introduction

The recognition that some disorders have their roots in the preschool period and that these problems are stable and continue into later life [1] has recently led to substantial growth in the study of psychopathology among pre-schoolers. Oppositional defiant disorder (ODD) is among the most prevalent disorders in this age range [2,3]. The varied concurrent and successive comorbidity shown by ODD [4], along with its associated problems in terms of daily functioning in different contexts [5], highlight the importance of efforts to understand and prevent this disorder.

The study of developmental trajectories enables us to understand the evolution of disorders, with regard to their level and to their growth or decline over time [6]. Such study helps researchers identify the causes and consequences of the behaviors traced. In this sense, the identification of trajectories constitutes a highly valuable strategy for our knowledge of psychopathologies, their associated factors and the predictive associations between them. The results of these types of studies are also useful for identifying groups of children with different needs over the course of their development, and for designing proper therapeutic and preventive interventions. The preschool age is when interventions may be most effective [7], and it is therefore important to study this developmental period closely.

Data for ODD developmental trajectories from early preschool ages are scarce. Miner and Clarke-Stewart [8] studied the normative trajectories of externalizing behaviors in a sample of the general population from ages 2 to 9, which was assessed five times with a short externalizing behavior scale from the Child Behavior Checklist (CBCL) [9,10], filled out by mothers and teachers. There was a decline in externalizing behavior from 2 to 9 years old, which was most pronounced from 2 to 7 and then became more gradual. It is also of note that mothers rated children higher than teachers did. Peticlerc et al. [11] used three items of the CBCL/1½-5 that were indicative of disregard for rules (defiant, not guilty, insensitive to punishment), an important dimension of oppositional defiant and conduct disorder, and found four trajectories in a sample of 1,942 children aged 29 months to 74 months: very low (9.1%), low (56.9%), moderate (29.7%), and chronic (4.3%). The trajectories were stable and reflected different degrees of severity. Males, maternal antisocial behavior, and postpartum depression in a parent were most likely to be associated with a chronic trajectory. In a sample of boys from low-income families, tracked from 1.5 to 10 years of age, Shaw et al. [12] found four trajectories of conduct problems, defined through five items of the CBCL (cruelty to animals, disobedience, fights, physical attacks, temper tantrums), as answered by the mothers: low (10.1%), moderate desisters (33.2%), medium decline (49.9%) and chronic (6.7%). Children in the chronic group scored high in fearlessness, and their mothers were younger, more depressed and more child-rejecting. All of these studies were based on the modification of existing measures and produced different definitions, which impedes comparisons.

Previous work on developmental trajectories has contributed to an understanding of the externalizing disorders, but it also has some shortcomings. First, some of these studies have been overly focused on boys and on samples from low socioeconomic levels, which limits the generalizability of results. Trajectories have also mostly been derived based on just one informant (the mothers) and one instrument, and the use of varying and idiosyncratic definitions also makes it difficult to compare results across studies. Furthermore, there are concerns that diagnostic instruments and screening/scale scores do not tap the same phenomena, since screens are only modestly associated with diagnosis. Therefore, it is worthwhile finding out whether the same trajectories emerge when ODD symptoms based on a diagnostic interview are assessed, as opposed to scale scores. In the emerging field of preschool psychopathology there is a need for cross-instrument data on developmental trajectories, as traced using different assessment tools, not only for consolidating the field, but also with a view to providing appropriate estimations of the evolution of disorders in this segment of the population. In this way it may be possible to improve service provision. The aim of this study is to contribute data on the characteristics of developmental trajectories of oppositional defiant behaviors (ODB) obtained with three of the most widely-used instruments for the assessment of this disorder (DSM-IV diagnostic interview, CBCL and Strengths and Difficulties Questionnaire -SDQ) in a sample of Spanish three-year-olds in their first year of preschool education. There were two specific objectives: 1) to trace the developmental trajectories of ODB from ages 3 to 5, based on different instruments and using the scales that clinicians and researchers most typically employ; and 2) to ascertain the discriminative ability of these trajectories for different outcomes at age 6 in order to evaluate the usefulness of each instrument for this purpose. The results of this study may help clinicians and researchers interested in the evolution of ODB at these ages to choose the most appropriate instrument according to their goals, which might in turn improve identification of the needs of affected children.

Method

Participants

The data analyzed in this work come from a longitudinal study on psychopathological risk factors from age 3 described in [3] (Figure S1 online). The sample design involved a two-phase sampling. In the first phase a random group of 2,283 families obtained from the census of 3-year-old preschoolers in Barcelona (Spain) were contacted and invited to participate. In total, 1,341 families (58.7%) agreed to take part (33.6% of high socioeconomic status, 43.1% middle and 23.3% low; 50.9% were boys). To ensure the participation of children with possible behavioral problems, the first phase sampling applied the parent-rated SDQ^{3-4} conduct problems scale [13] plus four ODD DSM-IV-TR symptoms, which were used as screening for ODB problems. Two groups were potentially considered: screen positive (all children with SDQ^{3-4} scores ≥4, Percentile 90, or with a positive response for any of the 8 DSM-IV ODD symptoms) and screen negative (a random group comprising 28% of children who did not reach the positive threshold). The number of refusals in this stage of the sampling was $n = 135$ (10.6%), and these children did not differ in sex ($p = .815$) or type of school ($p = .850$) from those who did agree to participate (the only difference was in SES, with higher participation ratio for high socioeconomic levels, 86.2% *vs.* 73.6%; $p = .007$).

The second sampling phase involved the n = 622 children (417 from the positive screen group −49.4% boys− and 205 from the negative screen −51.2% boys), who were selected for the follow-up. The first complete assessment of this sample was at age 3. Demographic characteristics are shown in Table 1 (and Table S1 online). At age 4,603 children remained in the follow-up (303 boys), at age 5 there were 570 (288 boys), and at age 6 there were 511 (256 boys). No differences in sex ($\chi^2 = 1.39$, df = 1, $p = .29$), SES ($\chi^2 = 5.27$, df = 2, $p = .08$) or type of school ($\chi^2 = 0.51$, df = 1, $p = .53$) were found on comparing completers and drop-outs.

Measures

The *Diagnostic Interview of Children and Adolescents for Parents of Preschool Children* (DICA-PPC [14]) is a semi-structured interview for parents of children aged 3 to 7 that follows the DSM-IV-TR criteria [15]. The schedule is interviewer-based, as it is the interviewer who decides about the presence/absence of the symptoms, considering the answers provided by the parents and the definitions of the symptoms in the manual. The characteristics of the symptoms, the methods of identifying those characteristics and how to code the symptoms were taught during the training. An intensive training period lasting one week included an overview of the developmental psychology and psychopathology of preschool children, as well as interviewing skills. Subsequently, a longer training period was made up of 4 phases: 1) Study of the interview schedule; 2) Practice interviews and role-playing in simulated interviews; 3) Listening to and coding of audio-recorded real interviews; and 4) Observation and coding of live interviews. The criterion for being ready for the field was to obtain a mean agreement with an expert kappa ≥0.80 for all the questions in at least five interviews. The team of interviewers consisted of two Ph.D. clinical psychologists, three psychologists with masters degrees and five psychology students.

Inter-interviewer agreement was examined in a pilot study with 13 interviews involving children from public pediatric primary care, whose families accepted to participate. Mean age of the children was 5.54 years (SD = 0.97). For each interview the kappa coefficient [16] between the interviewer and each of the observers (raters) was calculated for all the interview questions and for the diagnoses. The interviews were recorded and then rated by a team of five interviewers, resulting in 65 observations. All the interviewers took the role of "interviewer" and "raters". Kappa coefficients of the rating of all the interview questions ranged from.64 to.94 (mean kappa.78, 95% CI:.73 to.83) indicating good to excellent agreement between interviewers. The agreement was significant and very good for disruptive behavior disorders ($\kappa = .91$).

Presence/absence of the eight ODD symptoms was used to derive trajectories. The diagnoses analyzed as outcomes were disruptive behavior disorders (ADHD, ODD and CD), depressive disorders (major depression, dysthymia and minor depression) and anxiety disorders (separation and generalized anxiety, specific and social phobia), in addition to the number of CD-aggressive symptoms (bullying, fighting, weapon use, cruelty to people, cruelty to animals, stealing with confrontation, and forced sex) and

Table 1. Demographic Characteristics of the Sample ($N = 622$).

Age (mean; *SD*)		3.8	(0.33)
Sex (*N*;%)	Male	311	(50.0)
Race/ethnicity (*N*;%)	Non-Hispanic white	557	(89.5)
	Hispanic-American	46	(7.4)
	Other	19	(3.1)
Family socioeconomic status (*N*;%)	High	205	(33.0)
	Mean-high	280	(45.0)
	Low	137	(22.0)

CD-non-aggressive symptoms (fire-raising, vandalism, breaking and entering, lying, and stealing without confrontation). Comorbidity was defined as the presence of more than one disorder among those assessed in the diagnostic interview. Use of services was registered after assessment of the symptoms of each disorder. The interviewer recorded whether a professional had been consulted about the symptoms and whether the child received any treatment for the symptoms (psychological, pharmacological or other).

The *Child Behavior Checklist* (CBCL/1½-5 [17]) measures behavioral and emotional problems according to parents' perception. The aggressive behavior empirical scale (18 items; *not true, somewhat true, very true*) and the DSM-scale of oppositional defiant problems (5 items) were used to derive the oppositional defiant behaviors. Cronbach's alpha of the scales in the sample was, respectively, .84 and .74.

The *Strengths and Difficulties Questionnaire* (SDQ [13]) is a brief screening questionnaire for the mental health of children. The conduct problems scale (5 items; *not true, somewhat true, certainly true*) was completed by parents and teachers. Cronbach's alpha in the sample was, respectively, .59 and .73.

The *Children's Global Assessment Scale* (CGAS [18]) is a global measure of functional impairment rated by the interviewer based on information from the diagnostic interview. Scale scores range from 1 (maximum impairment) to 100 (normal functioning). Scores above 70 indicate normal adaptation.

All the measures were administered yearly. Table S4 online shows the items in each scale of the instruments used for the trajectories, as well as the item scores and the scale's theoretical range.

Procedure

The project was approved by the ethics review committee of the authors' institution (Comissió d'Etica en l'Experimentació Animal I Humana). Informed written consent was obtained from parents of the children participating in the study, as approved by the ethics committee, in which the confidentiality of data was guaranteed. In Spain, preschool education is financed from public funds, and 3-year-olds are in preschool education. Families were recruited at the schools and also gave written consent. All families of children from P3 (3-year-olds) in the participating schools were invited to answer the SDQ[3-4]. Families who agreed and met the screening criteria were contacted by telephone and interviewed at the school for each assessment. The interviewer team, which included two clinical psychologists with Ph.D., two psychologists with masters degrees and psychology students, was specifically trained, and all interviewers were blind to screening group (see [14]). All interviews were audio-recorded and supervised. After the interview, the interviewer completed the CGAS, and the teacher's SDQ was given out for completion before the end of the academic year. The data were collected once a year between November 2009 and July 2013, with an average interval between the first and second assessment of 11.01 months (SD = 1.15) and 12.45 months (SD = 1.19) between the second and third assessment. Average interval between parent-family assessment and teacher's report in the follow-ups was 1.41 months (SD = 1.79).

Statistical Analysis

The trajectories were obtained through Growth-Mixture-Modeling (GMM) in MPlus7 using the sampling weight procedure within the Variable command to account for the multi-sampling design (each child was weighted by the inverse proportion to the probability of selection in the second phase of the sampling), defining the Robust Maximum Likelihood (MLR) estimator in the Analysis command (a full-information method [19,20]) and using Lo-Mendell-Rubin [21] as a measure to determine the number of classes. Five individual GMMs estimated separate developmental trajectories for each ODB measure (DSM-IV-ODD symptoms, CBCL-behavior scale, CBCL-DSM-ODB scale, SDQ-Parents conduct scale and SDQ-Teachers conduct scale) registered for the children's ages: 3-4-5 years old. Selection of the number of trajectories for each of the five measures considered was based on [22]: a) the lowest Bayesian information criterion (BIC) for the model (compared with other solutions); b) entropy (measure of the model's discriminative capacity for classifying children, that is, its ability to identify individuals following the different trajectories) above .80; c) high on-diagonal average values (around .80) in the matrix containing the probabilities of membership (that is, high average latent class probabilities for most likely latent class membership by latent class); d) no less than 4% of participants in a class/trajectory (to allow statistical comparisons); and e) the best clinical interpretability.

The discriminant capacity of trajectories on psychopathology and functioning at age 6 was estimated with the SPSS20-Complex Samples (CS) module. A design was drawn up according to the multi-stage sampling, assigning to each child a weight equal to the inverse proportion of the probability of selection in the second phase of the sampling. Logistic regression models (CSLOGISTIC procedure) were obtained for binary outcomes and General Linear Models (CSGLM procedure) were applied to quantitative criteria, both defining Robust estimation. These analyses were adjusted for the presence of comorbidities other than those included in the models at baseline (age 3 years) to obtain the specific discriminant capacity of the trajectories. Predictive capacity for the trajectories was estimated through the change in R^2 (ΔR^2), comparing the second step-block including the trajectories with the previous step-block including only the covariate "other comorbidity".

Results

Table S2, online, shows the goodness-of-fit for the GMM analyses. Different candidate models were considered for each measure with a number of trajectories/groups ranging from one to four (more groups were not considered due to the lack of convergence and/or very small classes). The final models selected yielded the lowest BIC indices (except for the parent-rated SDQ-conduct and CBCL/1½-5 DSM-ODB, but the three-group models were retained as the final solutions because fit criteria were not obtained for solutions with larger numbers of classes-trajectories), good entropy, high on-diagonal values in the matrix with the average latent class probabilities, and adequate sample size and clinical interpretability. Figure 1 shows the final model selected for each measure. No statistical differences between trajectories were found for sex or SES.

Trajectories derived from DSM-IV-ODD symptoms reported by parents

The results of the GMM identified four trajectories of ODD symptoms. Trajectory 1 ($N = 373$, 60.0%) represented those children with a persistently low number of ODD symptoms from ages 3 to 5 ($\bar{x} = 0.32$, 0.42 and 0.39); trajectory 2 ($N = 131$, 21.1%) represented decreasers in ODD symptoms, starting at age 3 with a high mean number of symptoms (3.1) and with a low mean by age 5 (0.65); trajectory 3 ($N = 80$, 12.9%) represented increasers, that is, children starting with 1.33 mean symptoms at age 3, and showing an increase in mean number of symptoms to 3.32 at age 5; and trajectory 4 ($N = 38$, 6.1%) represented those with a persistently high number of symptoms ($\bar{x} = 4.52$, 4.45 and 4.37); this group had a mean number of symptoms above the DSM-IV diagnostic threshold across the three assessments.

Trajectories derived from parents' CBCL/1½-5 empirical and DSM scales

For the CBCL-aggressive behavior scale, four trajectories were identified. Four children were excluded from the GMM due to missing-values in the three follow-ups for this ODB measure. Trajectory 1 ($N = 394$, 63.8%) represented persistently low mean scores on the scale from ages 3 to 5 ($\bar{x} = 6.73$, 4.92 and 3.11); trajectory 2 ($N = 38$, 6.1%) represented decreasers in aggressive behavior scores who started with a high mean score (17.2) at age 3 and had lower means by ages 4 (11.2) and 5 (5.13); trajectory 3 ($N = 159$, 25.7%) represented persistently moderate scores (mean scores 9.95, 10.2 and 10.5 at ages 3, 4, and 5, respectively); and trajectory 4 ($N = 27$, 4.4%) represented the high increasers ($\bar{x} = 15.3$, 17.7, 20.1), that is, children who remained at high scores above cut-off in the three assessments, and even showed increases in these scores.

For the CBCL DSM-ODB scale, three trajectories were identified. Five children were excluded from the GMM due to missing values in the three follow-ups for this ODB measure. Trajectory 1 ($N = 481$, 78.0%) represented persistently low scores on the DSM-ODB scale from ages 3 to 5 ($\bar{x} = 2.47$, 2.00, 1.54); trajectory 2 ($N = 78$, 12.6%) represented decreasers with mean scores of 6.19, 4.19 and 2.19 at ages 3, 4 and 5, respectively; and trajectory 3 ($N = 58$, 9.4%) represented high increasers, that is, children with a high mean number of symptoms at age 3 (5.34), and who showed an increase in mean score at ages 4 (6.02) and 5 (6.71), also remaining above cut-off at all three assessment points.

Trajectories derived from the parent- and teacher-reported SDQ conduct scale

For the conduct scale of the SDQ completed by parents, three trajectories emerged. Trajectory 1 ($N = 490$, 78.8%) represented persistently low scores on the conduct scale from ages 3 to 5 ($\bar{x} = 2.18$, 1.53, 0.89); trajectory 2 ($N = 56$, 9.0%) represented decreasers in conduct scale scores with means of 5.52, 3.60 and 1.67 for ages 3, 4 and 5, respectively; and trajectory 3 ($N = 76$, 12.2%) represented increasers, that is, children starting with a mean score of 3.09 at age 3, and whose mean score had increased by ages 4 (3.56) and 5 (4.04).

For the SDQ conduct scale answered by teachers, four trajectories were identified. Two children were excluded from the GMM due to missing values in the three follow-ups for this ODB measure. Trajectory 1 ($N = 399$, 64.4%) represented persistently low scores between ages 3 and 5 on the conduct scale ($\bar{x} = 0.96$, 0.69, 0.42); trajectory 2 ($N = 94$, 15.2%) represented decreasers in conduct scale scores with means from 4.77, 3.05 and 1.32 for ages 3, 4 and 5, respectively; trajectory 3 ($N = 68$, 11.0%) represented increasers, that is, children starting with a mean score for symptoms at age 3 of 1.10 and whose mean score had increased by ages 4 (2.24) and 5 (3.39); and trajectory 4 ($N = 59$, 9.5%) represented persistently high scores, these children maintaining a high mean score above cut-off at ages 3, 4, and 5 (5.22, 5.19, and 5.16, respectively).

Agreement between trajectories

The kappa (κ) and the global agreement (relative observed concordance between classes) was estimated for similar trajectories yielded by the different instruments: one concordance matrix was calculated for the 4-class trajectories solutions (DSM-IV-ODD, CBCL-aggressive and SDQ-conduct-parents) and another for the 3-class trajectories solutions (CBCL-DSM-ODB and SDQ-conduct-teachers). Agreement indexes were low: DSM-IV-ODD and CBCL-aggressive $\kappa = .32$ (65.9% global agreement), DSM-IV and SDQ parents $\kappa = .24$ (67.6% agreement), CBCL-aggressive and SDQ parents $\kappa = .31$ (72.1% agreement), and CBCL-DSM-ODB and SDQ teacher $\kappa = .10$ (61.4% agreement).

Discriminant capacity of the trajectories

The shape and number of trajectories yielded by the parents' CBCL DSM-ODB were similar to those of the parents' SDQ-conduct; the parents' DSM-IV trajectories were similar to those of the teachers' SDQ-conduct; and the trajectory of the parents' CBCL-aggressive was the most distinctive. Table 2 summarizes the ability of this set of trajectories to discriminate DSM-IV diagnoses, comorbidity, use of services, functional impairment and the number of CD symptoms at age 6 (detailed information in Table S3, online). These results are adjusted for the presence of comorbidities other than those included in the model at baseline (i.e., for the prediction of ADHD at 6 years, ADHD, ODD, conduct disorder, depression and anxiety at 3 years were controlled for), to obtain the adjusted predictive capacity for the trajectories in relation to outcomes (ΔR^2 values tabulated correspond to the change in predictive capacity between the first step entering the covariate "other comorbidities" and the second step adding the trajectories). All instruments yielded statistically significant predictions for disruptive disorders (ADHD and ODD) (except the DSM-IV, which did not significantly discriminate ADHD), depression, comorbidity, use of services and impairment. DSM-IV trajectories showed very good discriminative power (significant ΔR^2 coefficients above 20%) for ODD and depression, and good predictive capacity (significant ΔR^2 coefficients above

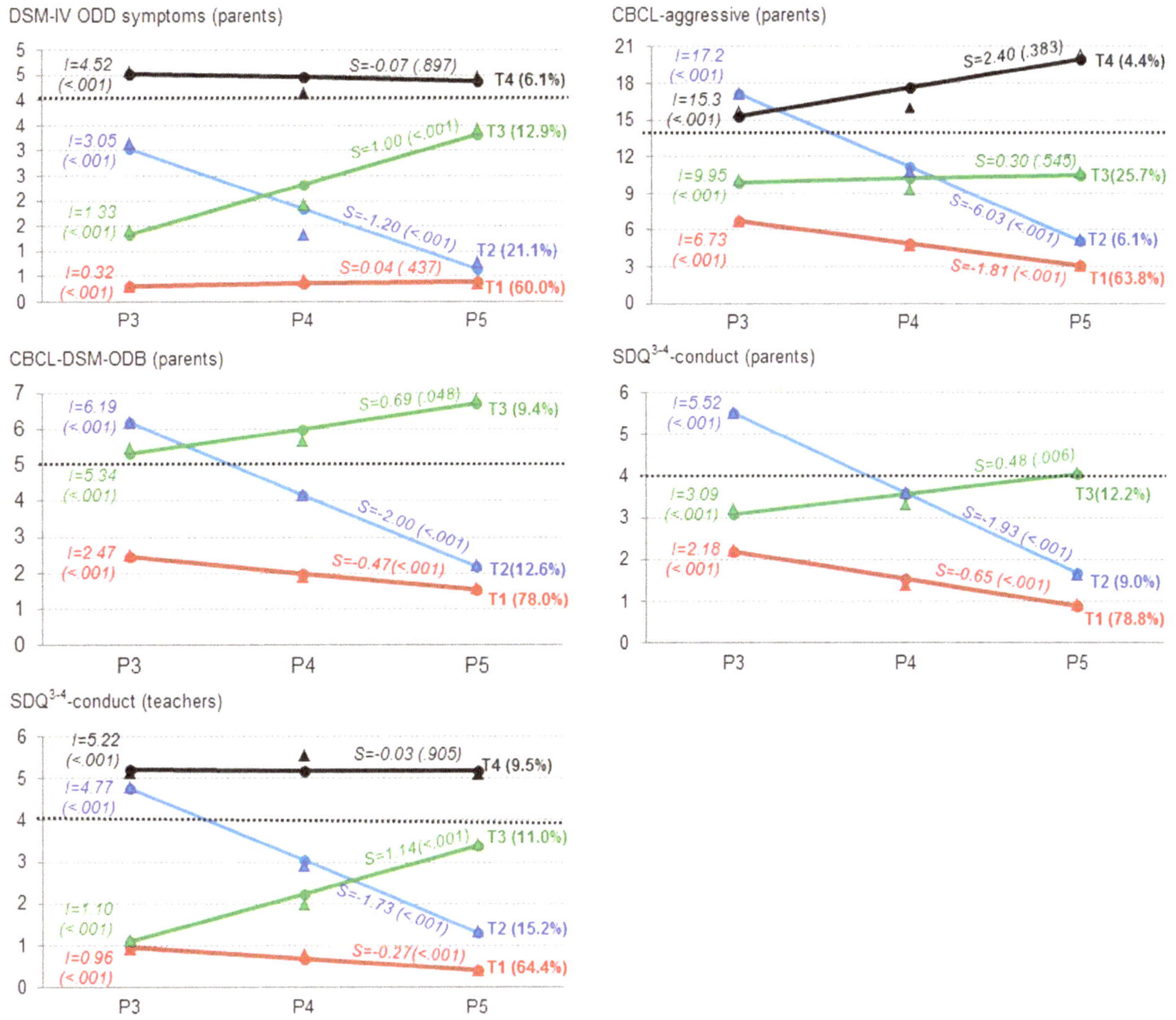

Figure 1. Developmental trajectories for ODB in the different instruments, children's age on X-axis and raw score on Y-axis (broken line represents the cut-off of diagnosis for DSM-IV definition and percentile 90 at baseline in the sample for dimensional measures; triangle represents observed empirical values). I=intercept, S=slope (in brackets, p-value).

Figure 1. Developmental trajectories for ODB in the different instruments, children's age on X-axis and raw score on Y-axis (broken line represents the cut-off of diagnosis for DSM-IV definition and percentile 90 at baseline in the sample for dimensional measures; triangle represents observed empirical values). *S = slope (in brackets, p-value).*

10%) for the group of disruptive disorders, impairment and comorbidity. CBCL-aggressive was the best measure for predicting the disruptive disorders group, ADHD, comorbidity and use of services. CBCL DSM-ODB and the parent SDQ showed good predictive capacity for disruptive disorders (particularly ODD) and depression. The teacher SDQ showed good predictive power for disruptive disorders (and particularly ADHD), and very good predictive power for depression. No significant predictor emerged for anxiety disorders at age 6. The only significant predictor of the number of CD aggressive symptoms at age 6 was teacher SDQ trajectories, but the effect size of this prediction was small. For the number of CD non-aggressive symptoms the significant predictors were CBCL- DSM-ODB and SDQ, but the effect sizes of ΔR^2 values were low.

Discussion

This study identified several developmental trajectories of oppositional-disorder-related behavior from ages 3 to 5 for the different definitions of the instruments used. The trajectories identified showed good ability to discriminate disruptive disorders, depression, comorbidity, use of services and impairment at age 6. Goodness-of-fit, clinical interpretability and convergence supported the validity of the empirical trajectories.

The number of trajectories ranged between 3 (for CBCL-DSM-ODB and parents' SDQ) and 4 (for the DSM-IV, CBCL-

Table 2. Discriminative Ability of the Trajectories (columns) for outcomes (rows): Diagnoses, Comorbidity, Use of Services and Functional Impairment at Age 6 (ΔR^2).

	DSM-IV ODD	CBCL- Aggressive	CBCL- ODB	SDQ Parent	SDQ Teacher
[1]Disruptive disorders	**.152**	**.223**	**.162**	**.136**	**.144**
[1]ADHD	.028	**.136**	**.044**	**.050**	**.129**
[1]ODD	**.247**	**.198**	**.182**	**.131**	**.074**
[1]Depression	**.272**	**.134**	**.101**	**.123**	**.207**
[1,3]Anxiety disorders	.002	.015	.010	.004	.012
[1]Comorbidity	**.096**	**.175**	**.056**	**.035**	**.065**
[1]Use of services	**.048**	**.099**	**.022**	**.034**	**.040**
[2]Impairment (CGAS: total)	**.152**	**.136**	**.058**	**.043**	**.033**
[2]# CD aggressive symptoms	.014	.016	.037	.019	**.038**
[2]# CD non-aggressive symptoms	.013	.025	**.020**	**.026**	**.021**

[1]Logistic Regression for binary outcomes and [2]General Linear Model for quantitative.
[3]Includes separation-generalized anxiety, specific-social phobia.
Results adjusted for other comorbidities at baseline (age 3).
ΔR^2: change in R^2 when entering the trajectories in comparison with the previous step including only the covariate "other comorbidity".
Bold: significant ΔR^2 ($p < .05$).

aggressive and teachers' SDQ). The trajectories yielded by each instrument accounted for different children, as shown by the low agreement indexes. This finding suggests that the composition of trajectories is specific to each definition, and that the instruments are not measuring exactly the same construct, thus highlighting the advisability of using various instruments answered by different reporters in the assessment of children with oppositional defiant disorders. We did not find differences between trajectories for sex or SES, which is in line with the results of recent studies in preschoolers that found no association of SES with diagnosis [2] and no sex differences for trajectories [23], pointing out that sex differences emerge later in development.

A persistently low trajectory was always found, accounting for the majority of non-symptomatic children at age 3 who maintained this level until age 5 (range from 60% to 78%). Using standard definitions from a range of instruments, the parents and teachers in our study discriminated the oppositional behaviors as non-normative in the preschool age range.

For all instruments it was possible to identify a decreasers trajectory. In 6.1% to 21% of the children that start out with marked negativistic behavior, the developmental trajectory in these behaviors is a decreasing one. An increaser trajectory was identified for the DSM-IV and SDQ-conduct (parents and teachers). This trajectory accounts for 11% to 12.9% of cases. Finally, for the DSM-IV, CBCL-aggressive and SDQ-teachers, a stable high trajectory was found. The proportion of children in the high trajectory varied across the different instruments used, from 4.4% (CBCL-aggressive behavior) to 9.5% (SDQ-conduct teacher) (the parents' SDQ-conduct did not yield a chronic trajectory). Previous studies have shown the stability of disruptive behavior over long periods of time [24] and highlighted the usefulness of the study of developmental trajectories for focusing intervention and prevention initiatives. High and mean-level trajectories permit the identification of groups of children that should be the target of preventive efforts. Given the concurrent and successive comorbidity associated with ODD, preventive intervention oriented toward ODD may be successful for reducing not only disruptive disorders, but also the chain of disorders associated with ODD [25].

Although not for all the instruments, we were able to trace trajectories according to two informants: parents and teachers in the case of the SDQ conduct scale. Keiley et al. [26] reported that the trajectories of scores on the externalizing scale (Achenbach's instruments) from ages 5 to 12 were lower in the case of mothers and higher for teachers. Similarly, in our study, considering the SDQ answered by both parents and teachers, parents tended to report a decrease in conduct problems from ages 3 to 5, while teachers identified a group of children who maintained high scores in conduct problems for all three assessments. The discrepancies observed between parents and teachers might be attributable, in part, to differences in the context or situation in which the child's behavior is observed [27]. In accordance with Keiley et al. [26], we also observed that the development of conduct problems differs according to reporter or context. Recently, ODD has been conceptualized as a source-specific phenomenon: different groups of children, with different characteristics, are identified depending on the informant and on how the information is combined [28]. However, the characteristics of the informant (psychological problems, stress, socioeconomic status, perspective on the behavior, etc.), family status, and the characteristics of the child (problem type, non-clinical population) can also contribute to the discrepancies [29]. Therefore, for the study of the developmental trajectories of ODB it would seem advisable to have available information from several reporters. We also noted that trajectories were "measure-specific", which has implications for research and clinical practice: the results depend on the instrument used.

Also of interest in the field of ODD is the good capacity of the ODB trajectories – with all instruments – to predict depression (10% to 27% of the variability of depression was explained by the trajectories). Several studies have associated ODD with emotional symptoms at different ages. For instance, Copeland et al. [30] showed that ODD in adolescence increased the risk of depression in early adult life. Also, Stringaris and Goodman [31] point out that ODD and depression share irritability symptoms, which may account for their predictive association. The present findings indicate that the pattern of prediction may be observable early in life, which entails strong potential for prevention.

Another important finding from this study concerns the relevance of knowing which trajectory a child belongs to, as a useful predictor of outcomes at age 6. To give two examples, pertaining to any of the DSM-IV trajectories discriminated the presence of ODD at a level of 24.7% capacity, and the CBCL-aggressive trajectories explained 22.3% of the group of disruptive disorders at age 6. Depending on the purpose, clinicians and researchers may want to choose one of the instruments, taking into account the specifically-defined trajectories traced. For example, if the objective is to predict comorbidity at age 6, as related to oppositional behaviors, the most predictive definition is that derived from CBCL-aggressive; if the outcome studied is ODD, or impairment, then the solution derived with the DSM-IV-ODD may be the best option.

In summary, our study contributes to knowledge of the field through the identification of several developmental trajectories of oppositional behaviors according to different definitions. It is important to note that the trajectories identified via different instruments tended to concur, and using different definitions, the trajectories summarized longitudinal information on oppositionality in a closer way. However, some discrepancies in the evolution of the ODD problem were observed (not all the trajectories were similar), and this may be inherent to the differences between individual definitions. All definitions could be useful for the study of oppositional behaviors, and all had predictive validity for different outcomes at age 6. However, some limitations should be considered in interpreting these results. First, with the aim of permitting statistical comparison, this study only considered as final GMM with no less than 4% of participants in a class-trajectory, and this may be affecting the results, since this criterion reduces the more finely graded differences between different courses within the ODD spectrum. More research is needed to further test the validity of the resulting trajectories. The questionnaire scales include some items that represent symptoms of CD, but these were a minority in the set, and our objective was to provide clinicians and researchers with the trajectories yielded by the complete scales of the instruments and scores that they routinely use. Also, families with low socioeconomic status participated less than families from other levels, and this could have led to bias. Our results, then, do indeed contribute to the body of knowledge about the development of ODD in preschool children, and suggest future lines of enquiry for research on stability and protective and risk factors for early oppositional-defiant behaviors.

Supporting Information

Figure S1 Study design. SDQ: Strengths and Difficulties Questionnaire; ODD: Oppositional Defiant Symptoms; P3: first year of preschool education (age 3); P4: second year of preschool education (age 4); P5: third year of preschool education (age 5); 1E: first year of elementary school (age 6)

Table S1 Demographic Characteristics of the Sample ($N = 622$).

Table S2 Fitting Indices for Growth-Mixture-Modeling.

Table S3 Comparison between Trajectories on Outcomes at Age 6.

Table S4 Item content of the scales used for the trajectories in each instrument.

Author Contributions

Conceived and designed the experiments: LE. Performed the experiments: LE NdlO. Analyzed the data: RG JBN EP JMD. Wrote the paper: LE RG.

References

1. Reef J, van Meurs I, Verhulst FC, van der Ende J (2010) Children's problems predict adults' DSM-IV disorders across 24 years. Journal of the American Academy of Child and Adolescent Psychiatry 49: 1117–1124.
2. Bufferd SJ, Dougherty LR, Carlson GA, Klein DN (2011) Parent-reported mental health in preschoolers: findings using a diagnostic interview. Comprehensive Psychiatry 52 359–369.
3. Ezpeleta L, Osa Ndl, Doménech JM (2014) Prevalence of DSM-IV disorders, comorbidity and impairment in 3-year-old Spanish preschoolers. Social Psychiatry and Psychiatric Epidemiology 49: 145–155.
4. Maughan B, Rowe R, Messer J, Goodman R, Meltzer H (2004) Conduct Disorder and Oppositional Defiant Disorder in a national sample: developmental epidemiology. Journal of Child Psychology and Psychiatry 45: 609–621.
5. Ezpeleta L, Keeler G, Erkanli A, Costello EJ, Angold A (2001) Epidemiology of psychiatric incapacity in children and adolescents. Journal of Child Psychology and Psychiatry 42: 901–914.
6. Nagin D, Tremblay RE (1999) Trajectories of boys' physical aggression, opposition, and hyperactivity on the path to physically violent and nonviolent juvenile delinquency. Child Development 70: 1181–1196.
7. Luby JL, Belden AC, Spitznagel E (2006) Risk factors for preschool depression: the mediating role of early stressful life events Journal of Child Psychology and Psychiatry 47: 1292–1298.
8. Miner JL, Clarke-Stewart KA (2008) Trajectories of externalizing behavior from age 2 to age 9: Relations with gender, temperament, ethnicity, parenting, and rater. Developmental Psychology 44: 771–786.
9. Achenbach TM (1991) Manual for the Child Behavior Checklist/4–18 and 1991 profile. Burlington, VT: University of Vermont Department of Psychiatry.
10. Achenbach TM (1992) Manual for the Child Behavior Checklist/2–3 and 1992 profile. Burlington, VT: University of Vermont Department of Psychiatry.
11. Petitclerc A, Boivin M, Dionne G, Zoccolillo M, Tremblay RE (2009) Disregard for rules: the early development and predictors of a specific dimension of disruptive behavior disorders. Journal of Child Psychology and Psychiatry 50: 1477–1484.
12. Shaw DS, Lacourse E, Nagin DS (2005) Developmental trajectories of conduct problems and hyperactivity from ages 2 to 10. Journal of Child Psychology and Psychiatry 46: 931–942.
13. Goodman R (2001) Psychometric properties of the Strenghts and Difficulties Questionnaire. Journal of the American Academy of Child and Adolescent Psychiatry 40: 1337–1345.
14. Ezpeleta L, Osa Ndl, Granero R, Doménech JM, Reich W (2011) The Diagnostic Interview for Children and Adolescents for Parents of Preschool Children. Psychiatry Research 190: 137–144.
15. American Psychiatric Association (2000) DSM-IV Diagnostic and statistical manual of mental disorders. Washington, DC: American Psychiatric Press.
16. Cohen J (1960) A coefficient of agreement for nominal scales. Educational and Psychological Measurement 20: 37–46.
17. Achenbach TM, Rescorla LA (2000) Manual for the ASEBA preschool-age forms & Profiles. Burlington, VT: University of Vermont, Research Center for Children, Youth & Families.
18. Shaffer D, Gould MS, Brasic J, Ambrosini P, Fisher P, et al. (1983) A Children's Global Assessment Scale (CGAS). Archives of General Psychiatry 40: 1228–1231.
19. Enders CK, Bandalos DL (2001) The relative performance of full information maximum likelihood estimation for missing data in structural equation models. Structural Equation Modeling 8: 430–457.
20. Graham JW (2009) Missing data analysis: Making it work in the real world. Annual Review of Psychology 60: 549–576.
21. Lo Y, Mendell N, Rubin D (2001) Testing the number of components in a normal mixture. Biometrika 88: 767–778.
22. Nylund KL, Asparouhov T, Muthén BO (2007) Deciding on the number of classes in latent class analysis and growth misture modeling: a monte carlo simulation study. Structural Equation Modeling 14: 535–569.
23. Tremblay RE (2010) Developmental origins of disruptive behaviour problems: the 'original sin' hypothesis, epigenetics and their consequences for prevention. Journal of Child Psychology and Psychiatry 51: 341–367.
24. Reef J, Diamantopoulou S, van Meurs I, Verhulst FC, van der Ende J (2011) Developmental trajectories of child to adolescent externalizing behavior and adult DSM-IV disorder: results of a 24-year longitudinal study. Social Psychiatry and Psychiatric Epidemiology 46: 1233–1241.
25. Rowe R, Costello EJ, Angold A, Copeland WE, Maughan B (2010) Developmental pathways in oppositional defiant disorder and conduct disorder. Journal of Abnormal Psychology 119: 726–738.

26. Keiley MK, Bates JE, Dodge KA, Pettit GS (2000) A cross-domain growth analysis: Externalizing and internalizing behaviors during 8 years of childhood. Journal of Abnormal Child Psychology 28: 161–179.
27. Dirks MA, De Los Reyes A, Briggs-Gowan M, Cella D, Wakschlag LS (2012) Embracing not erasing contextual variability in children's behavior - theory and utility in the selection and use of methods and informants in developmental psychopathology. Journal of Child Psychology and Psychiatry 53: 558–574.
28. Drabick DAG, Gadow KD, Loney J (2007) Source-specific oppositional defiant disorder: Comorbidity and risk factors in referred elementary schoolboys. Journal of the American Academy of Child and Adolescent Psychiatry 46: 92–101.
29. De los Reyes A, Kazdin AE (2005) Informant discrepancies in the assessment of childhood psychopathology: a critical review, theoretical framework, and recommendations for further study. Psychological Bulletin 131: 483–509.
30. Copeland WE, Shanahan L, Costello EJ, Angold A (2009) Childhood and Adolescent Psychiatric Disorders as Predictors of Young Adult Disorders. Archives of General Psychiatry 66: 764–772.
31. Stringaris A, Goodman R (2009) Longitudinal outcome of youth oppositionality: irritable, headstrong, and hurtful behaviors have distinctive predictions. Journal of the American Academy of Child Adolescent Psychiatry 48: 404–412.

Associations between Acetaminophen Use during Pregnancy and ADHD Symptoms Measured at Ages 7 and 11 Years

John M. D. Thompson[1], Karen E. Waldie[2]*, Clare R. Wall[3], Rinky Murphy[4], Edwin A. Mitchell[1] and the ABC study group[¶]

1 Department of Paediatrics, The University of Auckland, Auckland, New Zealand, 2 School of Psychology, The University of Auckland, Auckland, New Zealand, 3 Discipline of Nutrition, The University of Auckland, Auckland, New Zealand, 4 Department of Medicine, The University of Auckland, Auckland New Zealand

Abstract

Objective: Our aim was to replicate and extend the recently found association between acetaminophen use during pregnancy and ADHD symptoms in school-age children.

Methods: Participants were members of the Auckland Birthweight Collaborative Study, a longitudinal study of 871 infants of European descent sampled disproportionately for small for gestational age. Drug use during pregnancy (acetaminophen, aspirin, antacids, and antibiotics) were analysed in relation to behavioural difficulties and ADHD symptoms measured by parent report at age 7 and both parent- and child-report at 11 years of age. The analyses included multiple covariates including birthweight, socioeconomic status and antenatal maternal perceived stress.

Results: Acetaminophen was used by 49.8% of the study mothers during pregnancy. We found significantly higher total difficulty scores (Strengths and Difficulty Questionnaire parent report at age 7 and child report at age 11) if acetaminophen was used during pregnancy, but there were no significant differences associated with any of the other drugs. Children of mothers who used acetaminophen during pregnancy were also at increased risk of ADHD at 7 and 11 years of age (Conners' Parent Rating Scale-Revised).

Conclusions: These findings strengthen the contention that acetaminophen exposure in pregnancy increases the risk of ADHD-like behaviours. Our study also supports earlier claims that findings are specific to acetaminophen.

Editor: Kenji Hashimoto, Chiba University Center for Forensic Mental Health, Japan

Funding: The initial study was funded by the Health Research Council of New Zealand. The 12 month postal questionnaire was funded by Hawkes Bay Medical Research Foundation. The 3.5 year follow-up study was funded by Child Health Research Foundation, Becroft Foundation and Auckland Medical Research Foundation. The 7 year follow-up study was funded by Child Health Research Foundation. The 11 year follow-up was funded by Child Health Research Foundation and the National Heart Foundation. E. A. Mitchell and J. M. D. Thompson are supported by Cure Kids. The 3½, 7 and 11 year follow-ups were conducted in the Children's Research Centre which is supported in part by the Starship Foundation and the Auckland District Health Board. The funders had no role in study design, data collection and analysis, decision to publish, or preparation of the manuscript.

Competing Interests: The authors have declared that no competing interests exist.

* Email: k.waldie@auckland.ac.nz

¶ Members of the ABC study group can be found in the acknowledgments.

Introduction

JAMA Pediatrics recently published a potentially alarming finding: Acetaminophen taken during pregnancy increased the risk of attention-deficit/hyperactivity disorder (ADHD) symptoms in their 7 year old offspring [1]. The use of acetaminophen in pregnancy led to an increased likelihood of offspring taking prescribed ADHD medications (e.g., methylphenidate) and an increased likelihood of hyperkinetic disorder (a severe form of ADHD). ADHD is the most common neurodevelopmental disorder, affecting over 5–10% of the school age population, and is characterised by inattention, hyperactivity and impulsivity [2]. Despite having an early onset, ADHD is most commonly diagnosed and treated between the ages 7 and 12 years [3] and is reported to persist through to adolescence and beyond in about 80% of cases [4].

The finding that even low doses of acetaminophen (indicated by the number of weeks of drug exposure) can affect behaviour 7 years later is alarming because acetaminophen (paracetamol) is the most commonly used antenatal drug [5]. If supported, understanding the biological mechanism underlying the acetaminophen-behaviour link would likely take precedent in tandem with efforts to inform the general public of the newly identified risks of this commonly used over-the-counter drug. The finding is also noteworthy because of the many strengths of the above study. Firstly, the sample consisted of a large cohort of mothers (64 322 individuals enrolled in the Danish National Birth Cohort) and multiple child outcomes were included (Strengths and Difficulties Questionnaire [SDQ], medication use for ADHD, and hospital records for hyperkinetic disorder. Secondly, the longitudinal research was sampled prospectively, meaning that the results were unlikely affected by recall bias. Finally, the analyses controlled for a wide range of factors that might influence both medication-taking in pregnant mothers (e.g., reported fever, inflammatory problems) and ADHD symptoms in offspring (e.g., birthweight, antenatal smoking and alcohol use).

In an Editorial in the same issue of *JAMA Pediatrics,* Cooper et al. [6] underscore the importance of the acetaminophen findings but also highlight some of the study weakness. They rightly stress that the correlational design of the study (among other factors) does not permit us to infer causation. As such, the authors urge caution when interpreting the study results until the findings are replicated and extended. One such recommendation by the authors to extend the study was to examine other drugs taken during pregnancy to determine if the drug-ADHD association was specific to acetaminophen.

Towards this end, the aim of the present study was to determine the association between drugs commonly taken during pregnancy, including acetaminophen, and ADHD in child members of the prospective Auckland Birthweight Collaborative (ABC) longitudinal study. Aspirin, antacids, and antibiotics were the other drugs, besides acetaminophen, that were analysed in relation to SDQ total difficulties (and sub-scales) at 7 and 11 years of age. We also measured ADHD symptoms with more specificity than the SDQ by using the Conners' Behavioural Rating Scale: Revised (CRS:R) parent report at ages 7 and 11 years. Our analyses included multiple covariates, including those controlled for in the Danish study. We also included other factors previously shown to be related to SDQ in our study, including antenatal maternal perceived stress. Children of mothers who report antenatal stress have been shown to have a range of poorer neurodevelopmental outcomes, including ADHD [7,8].

Methods

Participants

The Auckland Birthweight Collaborative (ABC) Study has been described in detail elsewhere [9]. In brief, the study originally selected children at birth, between October 1995 and November 1997. Children were selected over the entire time period from the Auckland District Health Board, and from October 1995 to August 1997 in the Waitemata District Health Board. All small for gestational age (SGA) infants ($<=10^{th}$ percentile for gestation and sex) and a random selection of appropriate for gestational age infants (AGA) were selected during the study, such that the number in each group were approximately equal. Infants were excluded from the study if they were not resident and born in the designated study regions, were preterm, were from multiple births or had congenital abnormalities likely to affect subsequent growth or development.

The study consisted of 1714 children at birth of which 871 had mothers who were self-identified as being of European ethnicity. The study has followed the children at 1 year (via a postal questionnaire), and with face to face assessments at 3.5, 7 and 11 years of age. Only European children were followed up after 3.5 due to the poor response rate for other ethnic groups at the previous time point. At all follow-ups mothers of respondents have been found to be more likely than non-respondents to have a tertiary education ($p=0.05$), to be married ($p<0.0001$), to have high socio-economic status ($p<0.0001$), not to have smoked during their pregnancy ($p<0.0001$) and to be older ($p=0.0001$). Respondents and non-respondents did not differ in other obstetric and social variables, including the gestational age, birthweight and gender of their infant, parity, type of delivery, maternal social support or maternal stress levels.

At birth, demographics and information about maternal health, perceived stress, drug use, and other lifestyle factors during pregnancy was collected by maternal interview and obstetric records. When children were aged approximately 12 months information about feeding practices, home environment, physical development of the child and maternal parenting stress and social support was collected via postal questionnaire. Children aged 3.5 years were assessed on measures of cognitive and physical development. Mothers were interviewed regarding the child's health, diet and development during the early years of life and demographic information was collected regarding the child's family environment, including socio-economic status [10]. When children were aged 7 years, information was again collected from maternal interview about children's physical activity, diet, behaviour and health. Mothers and children were assessed when the child was aged 11 years. Maternal interview collected demographic information, information about physical activity, diet and health of the child and maternal measures of stress and social support. Children completed questionnaires regarding bullying, self esteem, depression, headaches, behaviour and emotional difficulties.

The study received ethical approval at each phase from the Northern regional ethics committee. Signed consent for the study was given by the parents of the children and assent also given by the child.

Measures

Drug Use

Data on paracetemol use was obtained by interviewer-administered questionnaires with the mother soon after the birth of her child. Specifically, ascertainment of drug use was obtained by the following question "Did you have any of these medicines or treatments during your pregnancy". Amongst this list were: a) anti-inflammatories; b) aspirin based pain killers e.g. Aspro, Disprin) other pain killers e.g. Panadol (acetaminophen); d) antacids.

Strengths and Difficulties Questionnaire

Symptoms of ADHD were measured at ages 7 and 11 years using the parent format of the Strengths and Difficulties Questionnaire (SDQ) and also using the child format at age 11 [11].

Compared with other child behaviour rating scales the SDQ is considered to be a brief measure of child behaviour which inquires about 25 positive and negative emotional and behavioural attributes. Each child is given a score for 5 subscales each consisting of 5 items. The subscales relate to difficulties in conduct, emotion, hyperactivity-inattention, peer group relationships and pro-social behaviour. Each item is scored on a 3 point Likert scale of 0 = '*not true*', 1 = '*somewhat true*' and 2 = '*certainly true*'. The total scores for each subscale are calculated by summing scores on items relevant to a particular problem. The SDQ has a test-retest stability of 0.62 after 4 to 6 months and the internal consistencies of the subscales range from 0.62 to 0.75 [12].

The Total Difficulties score is calculated by summing all four deficit focused subscales (Emotional symptoms; Hyperactivity; Conduct problems; Peer problems). Scores range from 0 to 40. A total of 587 children age 7 years and 614 age 11 years had available data on all five SDQ scales.

Conners' Behavioural Rating Scale: Revised - Long Format (CRS:R-L)

The CRS:R-L is a measure of child and adolescent behaviour which is available for children age 6 to 17 years [13]. The CRS: R-L parent questionnaire, used here, consists of 80 items and each item is scored on a four point Likert scale. Responses indicate the extent to which each symptom applies to the target child. Symptoms are scored 0 = '*not at all true*' 1 = '*just a little true*', 2 = '*pretty much true*' and 3 = '*very much true*'. Three of the CRS:R-L subscales relate to the DSM-IV diagnostic criteria for (1) ADHD Inattentive type, (2) ADHD Hyperactive-Impulsive type, and (3) ADHD Combined type. Three subscales referred to as Conners Global Indices (CGI) are also provided (Restless-Impulsive subscale, Emotional Liability, Total subscale reflecting general problematic behaviour). The Conners' ADHD Index is used to identify a probable diagnosis of ADHD. Total raw scores for each of the CRS: R-L subscales are summed and converted to T-scores, which are standardised by a child's age and sex [14].

The CRS-R is one of the most popular of the DSM-IV based rating scales used in research and clinical settings. The parent versions of the CRS:R-L was used here to measure child behaviour, particularly symptoms of ADHD. A total of 575 children aged 7 years had scorable data for the CRS:R-L parent version and 617 children aged 11 years had scorable data.

Statistical analysis

We analysed SDQ and Conners scores continuously in univariable analysis using t-tests and logistic regression and for multivariable analysis using generalised linear models to control for potential confounders to assess the differences between those with each medication use during pregnancy and those without. Distributions of both the SDQ and Conners were skewed so we also undertook analyses using log transformed data to confirm the results found using the untransformed data.

Multivariable models were controlled for variables that we have previously reported to be related to ADHD symptoms in children and variables considered to be potential confounders in the relationship between medication use and ADHD symptoms.

All statistical analyses were carried out for this paper was generated using SAS/STAT software, Version 9.3 of the SAS System for Windows (SAS Institute Inc., Cary, NC, USA). and were tested with a significance level set at $p<0.05$.

Results

We investigated the relationships of the use of acetaminophen (49.8%), anti-inflammatories (1.3%), aspirin (5.3%), antacids (17.4%), and antibiotics (23.5%) in relation to the strengths and difficulties questionnaire at 7 years of age (parent) and 11 years of age (parent and child).

Presented in Table 1 are the descriptive statistics for the SDQ Total Difficulties scores at 7 and 11 years of age by medication taken during pregnancy. We found significantly higher total scores on all 3 SDQ formats if acetaminophen was used during pregnancy, but there were no significant differences associated with any of the other drugs. Additionally to provide a direct comparison with the original analyses we analysed the relationship with the categorical cutoff for defining borderline/abnormal scores. Our power is reduced for this analysis though we found stronger odds ratios at the univariable level than the original study SDQ at 7 (OR = 2.1 95% CI = (0.0, 5.0)), but smaller odds ratios with parent SDQ at 11 (OR = 1.2 95% CI = (0.6, 2.5)) and child SDQ at 11 (OR = 1.0 95% CI = (0.6, 1.6)).

Table 1. Means (standard deviations) and differences with 95% confidence intervals (CI) of Strengths and Difficulties Questionnaire (SDQ) Total Difficulties scores at 7 and 11 years of age by medication taken during pregnancy.

	Prevalence	Parent SDQ Total at 7			Parent SDQ Total 11			Child SDQ Total at 11		
		Yes μ (s.d)	No μ (s.d)	Difference 95% CI	Yes μ (s.d)	No μ (s.d)	Difference 95% CI	Yes μ (s.d)	No μ (s.d)	Difference 95% CI
Parecetamol	49.8%	8.0 (5.0)	6.7 (4.6)	**1.2 (0.4, 2.0)**	7.6 (5.2)	6.7 (5.0)	**0.8 (0.0, 1.6)**	10.3 (5.0)	9.3 (5.0)	**0.9 (0.1, 1.7)**
Anti-inflamatories	1.3%	6.2 (3.5)	7.5 (4.9)	−1.3 (−3.5, 0.9)	7.5 (6.8)	7.2 (5.1)	0.3 (−2.7, 3.2)	10.7 (5.3)	9.9 (5.0)	0.8 (−2.1, 3.7)
Aspirin	5.3%	7.9 (5.5)	7.4 (4.8)	0.5 (−1.5, 2.4)	7.8 (6.4)	7.2 (5.1)	0.6 (−1.8, 3.0)	10.2 (5.7)	9.9 (5.0)	0.3 (−1.8, 2.4)
Antacids	17.4%	7.3 (5.0)	7.5 (4.8)	−0.1 (−1.0, 0.7)	7.3 (5.4)	7.2 (5.1)	0.1 (−0.8, 1.0)	9.6 (4.8)	10.0 (5.1)	−0.4 (−1.3,0.5)
Antibiotics	23.5%	7.8 (4.8)	7.3 (4.9)	0.5 (−0.4, 1.4)	7.8 (5.3)	7.0 (5.0)	0.8 (−0.1, 1.7)	10.2 (5.0)	9.8 (5.0)	0.4 (−0.5, 1.3)

We further analysed the relationship of acetaminophen on the sub-scales of the SDQ, in univariable and multivariable analyses (controlling for all potential confounders, see Table 2). Notably the acetaminophen use group had higher scores at each age for all difficulty sub-scales and lower scores for the pro-social scales. We found a consistent effect with the total difficulties scale, though the parental scale at 11 did not quite reach statistical significance at the 5% level. Similarly consistent negative effects were seen for the emotional sub-scale with similar effects for the parental SDQ at 7 and 11. Lower scores were also seen for the conduct subscale on the parental SDQ at 7 and the child SDQ at 11.

Additionally the effects of acetaminophen on the Conners scales showed similar results at 7 years of age (see Table 3). This showed consistently higher (poorer) scores for all but the DSM IV inattentive score and DSM IV inattentive symptoms at 7 years of age. Likewise there were higher scores with all scales for the acetaminophen group for the 11 year old data. However, only the DSM IV- hyperactive impulsive scores at 11 showed a statistically significant difference at the univariable level.

Discussion

In this New Zealand birth cohort study with prospective follow up we found that the children of mothers who used acetaminophen during pregnancy were at increased risk of having symptoms of ADHD as defined by screening questionnaires (the SDQ and Connors Rating System) at 7 and 11 years of age. These findings strengthen the contention that acetaminophen exposure in pregnancy increases the risk of ADHD-like behaviours, as published by Liew et al [1]. Our study also supports the earlier report that the findings are specific to acetaminophen, as there were no associations found with other commonly used drugs in pregnancy (aspirin, antacids and antibiotics).

More specifically, there was a significant effect of acetaminophen use on parent scored SDQ total difficulties at age 7 after controlling for potential confounders. Particularly problematic at age 7 were emotional and conduct problems. Child- but not parent-reported total difficulties at age 11 remained significant in multivariable analyses. Child-reported problems with conduct and hyperactivity/inattention were particularly salient. The hyperactivity-inattention subscale consists of the following items: *'restless, overactive, cannot stay still for long', 'constantly fidgeting or squirming', 'easily distracted, concentration wanders', 'can stop and think things out before acting' and 'sees tasks through to the end, good attention span'.*

There was also a significant effect of acetaminophen use on parent scored CRS:R-L ADHD symptoms at age 7 after controlling for the potential confounders. These were specific to subscales relating to the DSM-IV diagnostic criteria for ADHD Hyperactive-Impulsive type. Other subscales showing a significant multivariable effect included the CGI Restless-Impulsive subscale (indicates symptoms of restlessness, impulsivity and inattentiveness) and the CGI Emotional Liability subscale (identifies individuals who are prone to emotional responses and behaviours than would be expected to be typical, such as outbursts of crying or anger). Interestingly, for the CRS:R-L the association between acetaminophen use during pregnancy and parent-reported ADHD symptoms was not consistent at 11 years. It is not clear why the finding did not remain significant.

It is also not clear why the SDQ child reported ADHD symptoms remained significant at age 11 but not parent-reported problems. Self-reported problem behaviour has been shown to be a more valid indicator of mental and physical health than parent-reported problems [15–17]. It is also well known that ADHD has a complex etiology. It could be that other, more positive and enriching, environmental exposures begin to dilute the neurological outcome of acetaminophen over time. Acetaminophen was hypothesized to act as a hormone disrupter and thus alter fetal brain development [1]. Unfortunately we do not yet have data relating to ADHD symptoms measured after puberty. We also did not have information on dosage of acetaminophen use or trimester of use. Early life acetaminophen exposure may be significant determinants ADHD only at higher doses of the pain killer. In addition, other environmental factors not measured may also act through epigenetics to modify disease risk and neurological outcomes. More research is needed to provide a more precise assessment of risk and consequences of acetaminophen use during pregnancy.

Other limitations should be considered while interpreting our results. Firstly, the follow-up rate of 59 to 70% of the original population is clearly a potential source of bias. Nonetheless, this is unlikely to cause any systematic bias because the percentage of

Table 2. Univariable and Multivariable differences of continuous Strengths and Difficulties Questionnaire (SDQ) scores between the offspring of mothers who took acetaminophen in pregnancy and those that did not at 7 and 11 years of age (95% confidence intervals in parentheses).

	Parent SDQ at 7		**Parent SDQ at 11**		**Child SDQ at 11**	
	Univariable	**Multivariable***	**Univariable**	**Multivariable***	**Univariable**	**Multivariable***
Total difficulties	**1.2 (0.2, 1.4)**	**1.1 (0.2, 2.0)**	**0.8 (0.0, 1.6)**	0.8 (−0.1, 1.8)	**0.9 (0.1, 1.7)**	**1.1 (0.2, 2.0)**
Emotion	**0.4 (0.1, 0.7)**	**0.4 (0.0, 0.7)**	**0.5 (0.2, 0.8)**	**0.5 (0.1, 0.9)**	**0.3 (0.0, 0.6)**	0.2 (−0.2, 0.6)
Conduct	**0.3 (0.0, 0.5)**	**0.2 (0.0, 0.5)**	0.0 (−0.2, 0.3)	0.0 (−0.3, 0.3)	0.1 (−0.2, 0.3)	**0.3 (0.0, 0.6)**
Hyperactivity	0.3 (−0.1, 0.7)	0.4 (−0.1, 0.8)	0.1 (−0.2, 0.5)	0.1 (−0.3, 0.6)	**0.4 (0.0, 0.7)**	**0.4 (0.0, 0.8)**
Peer Esteem	**0.3 (0.0, 0.5)**	0.1 (−0.2, 0.4)	0.1 (−0.1, 0.4)	0.2 (−0.1, 0.5)	0.2 (−0.1, 0.4)	0.2 (−0.1, 0.5)
Prosocial	−0.1 (−0.4, 0.2)	−0.1 (−0.5, 0.2)	−0.1 (−0.4, 0.2)	−0.1 (−0.4, 0.3)	0.0 (−0.2, 0.3)	0.0 (−0.3, 0.3)

*Controlled for SGA status, sex, age mother left school, maternal smoking during pregnancy, paternal smoking during pregnancy, marital status at birth, parity, socio-economic status, maternal pre-pregnancy BMI, maternal stress in the last month of pregnancy, alcohol consumption in the first trimester, living with the child's biological father at 3.5 and child activity levels at 3.5, high fever during pregnancy, visiting GP for psychological conditions including depression and anxiety, taking medication during pregnancy for psychological conditions.

Table 3. Univariable and Multivariable differences of continuous parental Conners' scores between the offspring of mothers who took acetaminophen in pregnancy and those that did not at 7 and 11 years of age (95% confidence intervals in parentheses).

	Parent Conners at 7		Parent Conners at 11	
	Univariable	**Multivariable***	**Univariable**	**Multlvariable***
Conners ADHD index	**1.6 (0.3, 2.9)**	1.5 (−0.1, 3.0)	0.8 (−0.5, 2.1)	0.5 (−1.1, 2.1)
CGI restless-impulsive	**2.1 (0.7, 3.6)**	**2.1 (0.4, 3.7)**	0.3 (−1.1, 1.6)	−0.1 (−1.7, 1.6)
CGI emotional lability	**2.6 (1.1, 4.1)**	**3.0 (1.3, 4.7)**	1.2 (−0.3, 2.6)	0.6 (−1.1, 2.4)
CGI total	**2.5 (1.1, 3.9)**	**2.6 (1.0, 4.2)**	0.6 (−0.7, 1.9)	0.1 (−1.5, 1.8)
DSM IV inattentive	1.1 (−0.2, 2.4)	0.7 (−0.8, 2.2)	0.6 (−0.8, 2.0)	0.2 (−1.5, 1.9)
DSM IV- hyperactive impulsive	**2.0 (0.5, 3.5)**	**2.0 (0.3, 3.6)**	**1.2 (0.0, 2.5)**	1.3 (−0.2, 2.7)
DSM-IV total	**1.6 (0.3, 3.0)**	1.5 (−0.1, 3.0)	1.0 (−0.3, 2.3)	0.8 (−0.7, 2.3)
DSM inattentive symptoms	0.0 (−0.1, 0.2)	0.0 (−0.2, 0.1)	0.0 (−0.1, 0.2)	0.0 (−0.2, 0.2)
DSM hyperactive-impulsive symptoms	**0.2 (0.0, 0.4)**	**0.2 (0.0, 0.4)**	**0.1 (0.0, 0.2)**	0.1 (−0.1, 0.2)

*Controlled for SGA status, sex, age mother left school, maternal smoking during pregnancy, paternal smoking during pregnancy, marital status at birth, parity, socio-economic status, maternal pre-pregnancy BMI, maternal stress in the last month of pregnancy, alcohol consumption in the first trimester, living with the child's biological father at 3.5 and child activity levels at 3.5, high fever during pregnancy, visiting GP for physchological conditions includingdepression and anxiety, taking medication during pregnancy for psychological conditions.

SGA and AGA children remained steady at all phases of the study- at 41and 59% respectively. Secondly, because data was only obtained from European mothers and offspring, generalization of the results should be limited to children of European ethnicity. Thirdly, selection bias may be a problem if one or both of the parents also had ADHD. Unfortunately we have no information on the ADHD status of the parents.

A strength of this study is that the longitudinal design of the research was sampled prospectively and the analyses controlled for a wide range of factors that might influence medication-taking in pregnant mothers (e.g., reported fever, inflammatory problems) and ADHD symptoms in offspring (e.g., birthweight, antenatal smoking and alcohol use). Interestingly controlling for all these factors had little effect on the size of the effect. In addition to the Danish study, we were also able to support the outcomes of the SDQ with more specificity by using the CRS-R parent report at both 7 and 11years. We were also were able to control for the effect of antenatal perceived stress.

There is a balance of weighing up the risk associated with taking acetaminophen during pregnancy and that of not taking it in the presence of potentially serious conditions such as maternal fever. In this study the reported prevalence of maternal fever in pregnancy was less than 5%, compared to approximately 50% who took acetaminophen during pregnancy.

Acknowledgments

The ABC study group also includes Mrs Elizabeth Robinson, Dr David Becroft and Professor Chris Wild. We acknowledge the assistance of Gail Gillies, Barbara Rotherham, and Helen Nagels for contacting or assessing the participants. We sincerely thank the parents and children for participating in this study.

Author Contributions

Conceived and designed the experiments: JMDT KEW CW RM EAM. Performed the experiments: JMDT KEW CW RM EAM. Analyzed the data: JMDT. Contributed reagents/materials/analysis tools: JMDT. Wrote the paper: JMDT KEW CW RM EAM. The ABC study group: ER DB CW. Collected data: GG BR HN.

References

1. Liew Z, Riutz B, Rebordosa C, Lee PC, Olsed J (2014) Acetaminophen use during pregnancy, behavioural problems, and hyperkinetic disorders. JAMA Pediat. Doi:10.1001/jamapediatrics.2013.4914.
2. Linnet KM, Wisborg K, Agerbo E, Secher N-J, Thomsen PH, et al. (2006) Gestational age, birth weight, and the risk of hyperkinetic disorder. Arch Dis Child 91: 655–660.
3. Bhutta AT, Cleves MA, Casey PH, Cradock MM, Anand K (2002) Cognitive and behavioral outcomes of school-aged children who were born preterm - A meta-analysis. JAMA 288: 728–737.
4. Mannuza S, Klein RG, Moulton JL, Kessler RC, Aguilar-Gaxiola S, et al. (2003) Persistence of attention-deficit hyperactivity disorder into adulthood: What have we learned from the prospective follow-up studies? J Atten Disord 7: 93–100.
5. Werler MM, Mitchell AA, Hernandez-Diaz S, Honein MA (2005) Use of over-the-counter medications during pregnancy. Am J Obstet Gynecol 193: 771–777.
6. Cooper M, Langley K, Thapar A (2014) Antenatal acetaminophen use and attention-deficit/hyperactivity disorder: An interesting observed association but too early to infer causality. JAMA Pediat. Doi:10.1001/jamapediatrics. 2013.4914.
7. Van den Bergh B, Marcoen A (2004) High antenatal maternal anxiety is relatied to ADHD symptoms, externalizing problems and anxiety in 8- and 9-year-olds. Child Development 75: 1085–1097.
8. Rodriguez A, Bohlia G (2005) Are maternal smoking and stress during pregnancy related to ADHD symptoms in children? J Child Psych Psychiatr 46: 246–254.
9. Thompson JM, Clark PM, Robinson E, Becroft DM, Pattison NS, et al. (2001) Risk Factors for Small-For-Gestational-Age Babies: The Auckland Birthweight Collaborative Study. J Pediatr Child Health 37: 369–375.
10. Elley WB, Irving JC (1985) The Elley-Irving socioeconomic index 1981 census revision. NZ J Ed Studies 20: 115–128.
11. Goodman R (1999) The extended version of the Strengths and Difficulties Questionnaire as a guide to child psychiatric caseness and consequent burden. J Child Psych Psychiatr Allied Disciplines 40: 791–799.
12. Goodman R (2001) Psychometric Properties of the Strengths and Difficulties Questionnaire. J American Child Adolesc Psychiatr 40: 1337–1345.
13. Conners CK (2001) Development of the CRS-R. In Conners CK, Ed. *Conners' Rating Scales-Revised* (pages 83–98). North Tonawanda, NY: Multi-Health Systems.

14. Conners CK, Sitarenios G, Parker JD, Epstein JN (1998) The revised Conners' Parent Rating Scale (CPRS-R): factor structure, reliability, and criterion validity. J Abnorm Child Psychol 26: 257–268.
15. McDougall J, Bedell G, Wright V (2013) The youth report version of the Child and Adolescent Scale of Participation (CASP): Assessment of psychometric properties and comparison with parent report. Child: Care, Health & Development 39: 512–522.
16. Shoval G, Mansbach-Kleinfeld I, Farbstein I, Kanaaneh R, Lubin G, et al. (2013) Self versus maternal reports of emotional and behavioral difficulties in suicidal and non-suicidal adolescents: an Israeli nationwide survey. European Psychiatr: J Assoc European Psychiatrists 28: 235–239.
17. Achenbac T, McConaughy S, Howell C (1987) Child and adolescent behavioural and emotional problems: implications of cross-informant correlations for situational specificity. Psychol Bull 101: 2.

13

Auditory and Visual Sustained Attention in Children with Speech Sound Disorder

Cristina F. B. Murphy*, Luciana O. Pagan-Neves, Haydée F. Wertzner, Eliane Schochat

Department of Physical Therapy, Speech-Language Pathology and Occupational Therapy, School of Medicine, University of São Paulo, São Paulo, Brazil

Abstract

Although research has demonstrated that children with specific language impairment (SLI) and reading disorder (RD) exhibit sustained attention deficits, no study has investigated sustained attention in children with speech sound disorder (SSD). Given the overlap of symptoms, such as phonological memory deficits, between these different language disorders (i.e., SLI, SSD and RD) and the relationships between working memory, attention and language processing, it is worthwhile to investigate whether deficits in sustained attention also occur in children with SSD. A total of 55 children (18 diagnosed with SSD (8.11±1.231) and 37 typically developing children (8.76±1.461)) were invited to participate in this study. Auditory and visual sustained-attention tasks were applied. Children with SSD performed worse on these tasks; they committed a greater number of auditory false alarms and exhibited a significant decline in performance over the course of the auditory detection task. The extent to which performance is related to auditory perceptual difficulties and probable working memory deficits is discussed. Further studies are needed to better understand the specific nature of these deficits and their clinical implications.

Editor: Kevin Paterson, University of Leicester, United Kingdom

Funding: This work was supported by Fundação de Amparo à Pesquisa do Estado de São Paulo (2009/50453-6). The funders had no role in study design, data collection and analysis, decision to publish, or preparation of the manuscript.

Competing Interests: The authors have declared that no competing interests exist.

* E-mail: crist78@yahoo.com

Introduction

Speech sound disorder is the most frequently occurring pediatric communication disorder [1]. The main characteristics of speech sound disorder involve difficulties in acquiring the phonological representation of speech sound systems and a limited capacity to accurately produce the sounds of the native speakers language [2,3]. Recent studies have also demonstrated the presence of deficits in speech perception and in phonological tasks that assess phoneme awareness and phonological memory [4–6]. Poor phonological representations of speech sound systems are often attributed to deficits that involve phonological memory [5,7,8]. For example, Kenney et al [5] investigated the performance of adults with persistent developmental speech disorders on tests of verbal and non-verbal short term memory. The results of this study revealed that the speech disorders group performed significantly worse in nonverbal rhythm, tonal memory and verbal short-term memory.

It is also well-established that children with SSD are also at increased risks for specific language impairment [9], later reading disability (RD) and developmental dyslexia [10–12]. For example, in a longitudinal study, Peterson et al [12] investigated the relationship between childhood SSD and literacy development. These authors noted that children with histories of SSD are more likely to develop reading disorders. Broomfield and Dodd [9] also found strong bidirectional comorbidity between SSD and LI based on referrals to pediatric speech and language therapy services. Recent genetic studies have also shown that RD, SSD and ADHD share the same genetic locus at 6p22 [13–15]. This relationship could lead to related phenotypic characteristics and an overlap of cognitive symptoms among these three disorders [16].

Given this expected cognitive overlap and the high comorbidity of attention deficit hyperactivity disorder (ADHD) and language disorders [17], recent research has investigated whether attention deficits are also overlapping symptoms of SLI and RD [18–23]. Finneran et al [18] investigated the performance of 4- to 6-year-old children with SLI on a visual sustained attention task. When compared to typically developing children (TD), the children with SLI were significantly less accurate but not significantly slower than the TD children on the test of visual sustained attention. In a study conducted by Spaulding et al [19], children with SLI also exhibited poorer performance than did typically developing children on an auditory sustained attention task, which supports the idea that children with SLI exhibit attention difficulties. Spaulding et al [19] found no differences between the groups in visual sustained attention tasks. Ebert and Kohnert [20] performed a meta-analysis and concluded that deficits in sustained attention seem to be part of the language impairment profile, particularly in tasks that use auditory-linguistic stimuli. Several studies have also confirmed the existence of attention deficits in children with dyslexia [21–23]. For example, Facoetti and Molteni [22] showed that children with dyslexia have difficulties in focusing attention on text and simultaneously inhibiting distractor stimuli.

No study has investigated sustained attention in children with SSD; however, given the presence of sustained attention deficits in children with SLI and RD and the well-established relationship between SLI, SSD and RD, it is worthwhile to examine whether this deficit also occurs in children with SSD. According to Gomes et al [24], all components of attention have a role in language acquisition; for example, to accurately identify and interpret incoming linguistic information, sustained attention is required to maintain focus on the speech input, to attend to relevant information and to ignore irrelevant information [18]. Moreover, because attention is closely related to phonological working memory, it is plausible that attention plays a role in language processing.

The current research aims to examine the performance of children with SSD on auditory and visual sustained attention tests. As in most of the studies of children with SLI and RD [18,20], this study assessed attention using continuous performance test protocols. These protocols assess performance with tasks that require the participant to remain prepared to respond to an infrequent target (e.g., digits, letters or symbols) over an extended period of time and measure both the maintenance of attention and inhibitory control. The outcome measures are the number of targets detected (HITS), the number of false alarms meaning incorrect responses to nontarget stimuli (FAs) and the response times (RTs). In terms of sensory modalities, Spaulding et al [19] found that the attention deficits of children with SLI are restricted to auditory stimuli. This finding was confirmed by Ebert and Kohnert [20] in a meta-analysis. In contrast, Finneran et al [18] found deficits for visual stimuli. Due to this controversy, we assessed both sensory modalities in the present study to provide more details about the performance of children with SSD in attention tests.

Methods

Ethics statement

This study was conducted at the Department of Physical Therapy, Speech-Language Pathology and Occupational Therapy in the School of Medicine at the University of Sao Paulo and was approved by the Research Ethics Committee of the Analysis of Research Projects of the Hospital das Clínicas, Medicine School, University of São Paulo, under protocol number 575/09. A written consent form with detailed information about the aim and the protocols of the study was also approved by this ethics committee. All parents provided written informed consent on behalf of their children prior to participation in the study.

Participants

A total of 55 children were invited to participate in this study: 18 diagnosed with SSD (SSD group) and 37 typically developing children (TD group). The children in the SSD group were recruited through the Laboratory of Investigation in Phonology within the departments of Physical Therapy, Speech-Language Pathology and Audiology and Occupational Therapy of the School of Medicine at the University of São Paulo and diagnosed using the Phonology [25] and Vocabulary Test [26] from the Infantile Language Test-ABFW [27]. The phonology test consists in a picture naming task (with 34 words corresponding to 90 consonants) and a task with imitation of single words (with 39 words corresponding to 107 consonants). The Percentage of Consonants Correct- Revised (PCC-R) [28] index was calculated separately for both tasks [29–31]. None of these children were undergoing rehabilitation. The children in the TD group were recruited from the general community. The inclusion criteria for this group were the absence of speech sound errors on the Phonology Test from the ABFW, normal hearing and no previous speech-language interventions. The children in both groups were monolingual Brazilian-Portuguese learners.

The inclusion criteria common to both groups were as follows: aged between 7 and 12 years; IQ > 80 (based on the WISC-IV); and no familial or personal history of diagnosed or suspected auditory, otological or neurological disorder or injuries. Additionally, the participants were required to demonstrate normal tympanometric and acoustic reflexes and symmetrical auditory sensitivity within normal limits (≤ 15 dB HL for octave frequencies from 250 to 8000 Hz and ≤ 5 dB HL at any interaural frequency difference). After recruitment, both groups were required to pass a screening battery that consisted of the following: a medical history interview, an audiological evaluation, non-verbal auditory perceptual measures (i.e., the Frequency Pattern Test [32] and Gap in Noise Test [33]), language tests (the ABFW Test – Picture Naming and Repetition of Words), a short-term memory test (the Digit Span Test) and a non-verbal IQ test (the RAVEN Test of Coloured Progressive Matrices with Brazilian norms [34] and a conversion table for IQ values [35]). The language test (i.e., the ABFW Test) was also administered to the TD group to confirm the absence of speech sound disorders.

Procedures and measures

After the groups were established, a series of tests was applied to investigate the attention skills of both groups.

In the present research, two attention tests were developed using E-Prime Professional Software. The protocols of these tests were loosely modeled on previously published tests [36,37], and the length of the task and the protocol parameters were also based on previously published protocols [38–40].

In the visual test, digits between 1 and 7 were presented on a screen, and the participants were instructed to press a button as quickly as possible every time a 1 or a 5 appeared. The auditory task was identical to the visual version except that the participants heard the digit spoken over a set of calibrated headphones. The auditory stimuli consisted of recordings of digits between 1 and 7 being read in a quiet recording studio by a female adult whose native language was Brazilian Portuguese (phonetic transcription of the stimuli: [’uw, ’doʲs, ’tejs, ’kʷatrʊ, ’sijk, ’seʲs, ’sɛtʃi]). The duration of the recorded digits was fixed at approximately 500 msec regardless of the number of syllables in the numeral. The stimuli were presented binaurally at a comfortable listening level that corresponded to a sound pressure level of 70 dB (A). The duration of each test was approximately 6 minutes, and each test consisted of 210 trials that were divided into 3 blocks of 70. The division of the tests into 3 blocks enabled us to investigate the vigilance decline effect, which measures the decline in performance over the course of the experiment. For each trial, the digit appeared during the first 500 msec of the trial and was followed by an inter-stimulus interval of 1000 msec (Figure 1). Three performance measures were compared across blocks: HITs, FAs and RTs (i.e., response times).

Participants were tested individually in a quiet, well-lit laboratory on campus. The order of the visual and auditory tests was counterbalanced across participants. Before each test, each participant was given the appropriate instructions and asked to perform approximately 15 practice trials.

Statistical analyses

The data were analyzed using SPSS version 18.0 (SPSS, Chicago, IL). Repeated-measures ANOVAs were performed to analyze intra- and inter-group (TD and SSD) differences. Mauchly's sphericity test was used to test the assumption that the data were spherical, and post hoc analyses (Bonferroni) were performed to identify the mean performance measures that differed significantly. The Kolmogorov-Smirnov test was used to

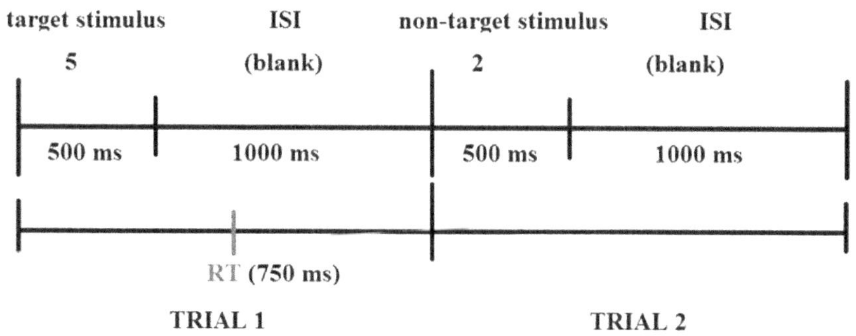

Figure 1. Example of two trials of the visual test: the first with a target stimulus (5) and the response time (RT) of 750 ms; the second with a non-target stimulus (2). ISI: inter-stimulus interval.

assess the normality of the data from each group, and the data were normalized using a logarithmic transformation. Pearson's correlations were calculated to determine the relationship between performance on the attention and memory tests. According to Dancey & Reidy [41], $r = 0.10$ to 0.30 demonstrates a weak correlation, $r = 0.40$ to 0.60 demonstrates a moderate correlation, and $r = 0.70$ to 1.0 demonstrates a strong correlation.

Results

Screening battery performance

The results of the initial test battery and the inclusion criteria (i.e., the IQ test and the audiological evaluation) led to the exclusion of 2 children from the SSD group and 4 children from TDT group. Table 1 displays the characteristics of both groups including mean age, gender, language, IQ, short-term memory and audiological performance. Comparisons between groups were performed using analyses of variance (ANOVAs).

Analyses of variance (ANOVAs) revealed significant between-group differences in the language tests (repetition [$F(3,35) = 18.795$, $p<0.001$, $\eta2 = 0.617$] and naming [$F(3,35) = 20.764$, $p<0.001$, $\eta2 = 0.640$]), in the Digit Span test [$F(1,53) = 40.02$, $p<0.001$, $\eta2 = 0.43$] and in both of the auditory perceptual tasks [Frequency Pattern ($p<0.001$) and GIN ($p<0.001$)]. No differences were found in age [$F(1,53) = 2.50$, $p<0,12$] or IQ ($p = 0.115$).

Attention tests

Table 2 displays the performance of both groups on the visual and auditory attention tests in terms of HITs, FAs and RTs.

Analyses of variance (ANOVAs) revealed a significant between-group difference in one of the auditory attention test measures; i.e., the auditory false alarm measure [$F(1,53) = 5.93$, $p = 0.02$, $\eta2 = 0.10$].

Figure 2 displays the results from all auditory and visual attention tests for both groups. Differences across the three blocks in all measures (i.e., HIT, FA and RT) were analyzed.

There were no significant declines in performance in terms of HIT rate in either the visual [$F(2,72) = 1.03$, $p = 0.36$] or auditory modalities [$F(2,72) = 2.66$, $p = 0.08$] in the TD group. In the SSD group, there was no significant decline in the visual modality [$F(2,34) = 0.44$, $p = 0.64$]; however, in contrast to the results of the TD group, the SSD group exhibited a significant decline in HIT rate in the auditory modality [$F(2,34) = 6.55$, $p<0.01$]. Post-hoc analyses using Bonferroni's adjustment for multiple comparisons

Table 1. Performance characteristics of the SSD and TD groups on the screening battery.

Variables	SSD (n = 18)	TD (n = 37)	p
Gender (n)			
Girls (%)	33,3	44	
Boys (%)	66,6	56	
Age (M ± DP)	8.11±1.2	8.76±1.4	0.012
Language tasks (M ± DP)			
Picture naming (%)	80.34±12.17	100±0.0	**<0.001**
Repetition of words (%)	80.27±12.33	100±0.0	**<0.001**
Short-term memory			
Digit Span	3.83±0.61	5.43±1.14	**<0.001**
Auditory tests			
Audiological evaluation	No alteration	No alteration	
Frequency Pattern Test	41.1±16.93	73.1±22.29	**<0.001**
Gap in Noise Test	7.13±2.35	4.5±0.7	**<0.001**
IQ score (Raven test)	106.47±8.1	111.41±16.4	0.265

Table 2. Means and Standard Deviations of the Performance Measures for All Experimental Conditions for both groups.

Measures	*Group*	*Mean*	*SD*	*F*	*p-value*	η^2
Visual HIT	TD	55,92	7,7	0,2	0,62	
	SSD	56,44	2,5			
Visual False Alarme	TD	2,38	3,2	2,3	0,13	
	SSD	4,17	5,458			
Visual RT	TD	645,72	98,2	3,0	0,09#	
	SSD	692,67	85,7			
Auditory HIT	TD	46,03	10,3	0,2	0,62	
	SSD	44,67	7,5			
Auditory False Alarm	TD	5,30	4,0	5,93	0,02*	0,10
	SSD	9,00	7,1			
Auditory RT	TD	1104,93	73,9	3,33	0,07#	
	SSD	1065,13	79,7			

revealed that the differences between blocks 1 and 2 ($p = 0.02$) and between blocks 1 and 3 ($p<0.01$) were significant.

The false alarm rates were similar for both modalities and both groups; there were no significant differences in performance across blocks in either group (TD group–visual [$F(2,72) = 1.37$, $p = 0.26$] and auditory [$F(2,72) = 2.63$, $p = 0.08$]; SSD group–visual [$F(2,34) = 0.40$, $p = 0.67$] and auditory [$F(1,45, 24.83) = 0.23$, $p = 0.72$]. However, although neither group exhibited declines in performance across blocks, the SSD group performed significantly worse than did the TD group in terms of auditory false alarms (FA block 1 [$F(1,53) = 5.93$, $p = 4.85$, $\eta2 = 0.08$] and FA block 3 [$F(1,53) = 4.04$, $p = 0.05$, $\eta2 = 0.07$]).

Response time increased significantly for both groups in both modalities; TD group–visual [$F (2.72) = 7.98$, $p<0.01$, $\eta2 = 0.18$] and auditory [$F (2,72) = 8.93$, $p<0.01$, $\eta2 = 0.$[illegible]]; SSD group–visual [$F (2,34) = 15.47$, $p<0.01$, $\eta2 = 0.48$] and auditory [$F (2,34) = 5.52$, $p<0.01$, $\eta2 = 0.25$.] Post-hoc analyses using Bonferroni's adjustment for multiple comparisons revealed that, in the TD group, blocks 1 and 3 were different in the visual modality ($p< 0.001$) and that there was a trend toward significance between blocks 1 and 2 in the auditory modality ($p = 0.06$). In the SSD group, blocks 1 and 3 in the visual modality were different ($p< 0.01$), and blocks 2 and 3 in the auditory modality were different ($p<0.01$). Although both groups exhibited significant declines in performance in this specific measure, there was no group effect, which indicates that the changes in performance across the blocks of the tests were similar across groups (visual RT [$F(1,53) = 3.57$, $p>0.05$, $r = 0.06$] and auditory RT [$F(1,53) = 2.33$, $p>0.05$, $r = 0.04$]). Indeed, the only significant difference in RT occurred in the last block of the auditory modality [$F (1,53) = 5.13$, $p = 0.03$, $\eta2 = 0.09$].

Given the worse performance of the SSD group in terms of auditory false alarms, we also included the Figure 3, with the distribution of the participants by the number of auditory false alarms. In all blocks, the comparison between both trend lines demonstrate the superior performance of the most participants of the TD group, compared with the SSD group.

Correlations

Tables 3 show the correlations between the auditory, language, memory and attention performance measurements.

For the TD group, there was a moderate, negative correlation between auditory FA and age, visual RT and FPT, Auditory HIT and GIN. There was also a moderate, positive correlation between Auditory HIT and FPT, visual RT and GIN. For the SSD group, there was a moderate, positive correlation between visual RT and GIN.

Discussion

The purpose of the present study was to assess auditory and visual sustained attention in children with SSD. First, it is important to discuss the performance characteristics of the SSD and TD groups on the screening battery. As expected, the SSD group exhibited poorer performances on both language tests (i.e., the picture naming and repetition of words tests). Moreover, the SSD group also exhibited poorer performances on the short-term memory test and both of the auditory perceptual tests (i.e., the Frequency Pattern Test and the GIN Test). In terms of memory abilities, our results corroborate those of a previous study in that both studies found that SSD children exhibited poorer short-term memory performance as measured with the digit span task [13]. The authors of this previous study suggested that children with SSD and children with language or reading impairments have difficulties in developing memory traces of speech input that are sustained for a sufficient duration to abstract acoustic features for phonological encoding. Regarding auditory perceptual performance, no study has applied the tests used in the present research to investigate the auditory perceptual skills of children with SSD; however, several researchers have found the same nonverbal auditory perception difficulties in children with specific language delays and dyslexia [42,43]. In summary, the performance of both groups in the language and memory tests confirms the significantly worse language skills of the SSD group compared to the TD group.

Based on the 3 measures analyzed, the SSD exhibited poorer sustained attention for auditory but not visual stimuli as indicated by a significant decline in HITs as the test progressed. The SSD group also demonstrated a greater number of false alarms in both the visual and auditory modality when compared to the TD comparison group.

As both between-group differences occurred in the auditory modality, we hypothesize that these results are related to the poorer performances of the SSD group in both auditory

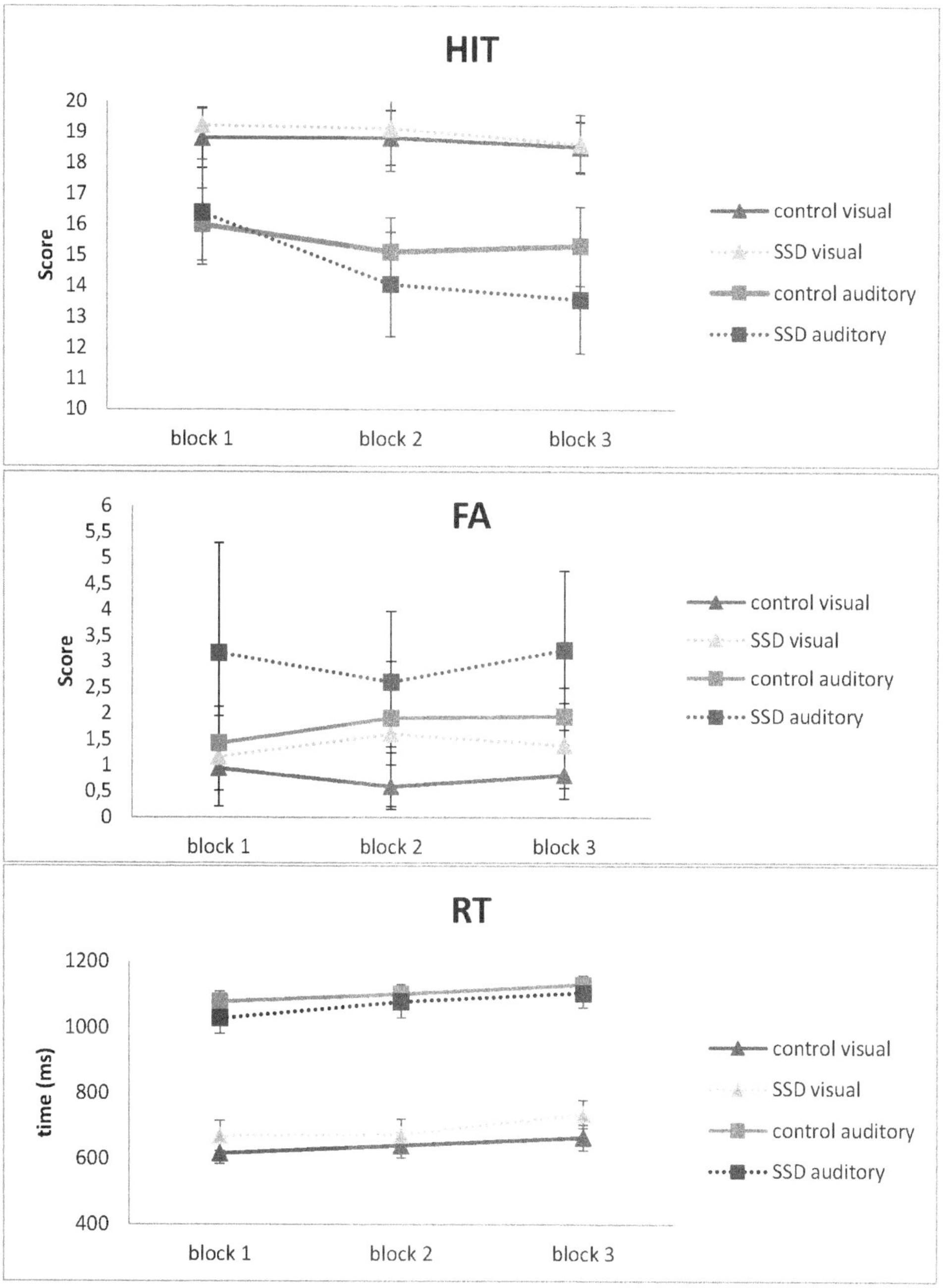

Figure 2. Performance along blocks for both groups. FA (false alarm); RT (response time).

perceptual measures. Thus, the nonverbal auditory perceptual impairments of the children with SSD might lead to difficulties in properly discriminating auditory stimuli. Consequently, these children may adopt a strategy of anticipating the stimuli, which would produce numerous false alarms. Moreover, the significant decline in auditory HIT performance over the course of the test suggests that the task was more difficult for these children in the auditory modality and thus caused fatigue. These results corroborate the findings of Spaulding et al [19] that demonstrated that children with SLI perform poorly on auditory sustained attention tasks compared to typically developing children. Furthermore, as in the present study, Spaulding et al found no differences in visual sustained attention tasks. Finneran et al [18] also noted that, because children with SLI have impairments in auditory processing skills (which may negatively affect task performance), auditory attention tests should not be used. Therefore, similar to the studies that have been conducted on SLI groups [18,19], in the present research, the poorer performance of the SSD group might reflect auditory processing impairments and not sustained attention impairments per se. Despite that, no significant correlation was found between auditory false alarms and both auditory tasks in the current research. Given that the present auditory tasks (FP and GIN) are specifically related to the auditory temporal processing, further studies should investigate others aspects of auditory processing.

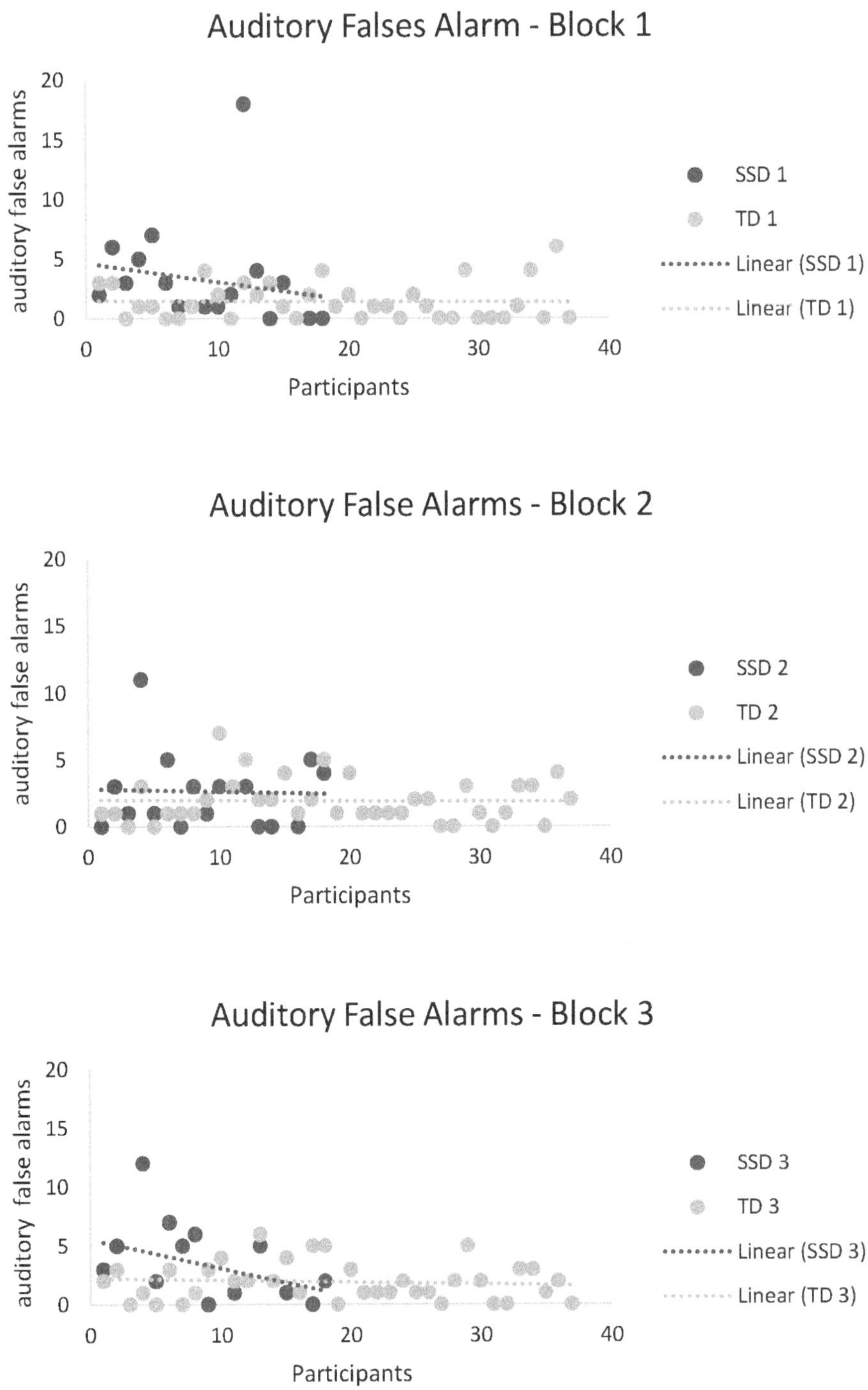

Figure 3. Distribution of the participants by the number of auditory false alarms.

Another hypothesis regarding the poorer performance of the SSD group is related to impulsivity skills. According to Riccio et al [44], false responses are an indication of impulsivity; therefore, the current results might suggest that the impulse control skills of the SSD group were less mature. No study has investigated this specific behavior in children with SSD, but it is well-documented that younger children exhibit more impulsive behavior than do older children. Furthermore, Diamond [45] argued that the poor performance of young children could be attributed to a combination of insufficient working memory and immature inhibitory functioning skills that are associated with the prefrontal region. In a recent review, Bari and Robbins [46] also noted that several fMRI and PET studies have associated deficits in go/no-go tasks with the medial portion of the prefrontal cortex; this region is

Table 3. Correlation between performance measures of TD and SSD group.

	Age		Digit Span		FPT		GIN		Naming		Repetition		Visual HIT		Visual FA		Visual RT		Auditory HIT		Auditory FA	
	TD	**SSD**	**TD**	**SSD**	**TD**	**SSD**	**TD**	**SSD**	**TD**	**SSD**	**TD**	**SSD**	**TD**	**SSD**	**TD**	**SSD**	**TD**	**SSD**	**TD**	**SSD**	**TD**	**SSD**
Digit Span	0.19	0.10							—		—											
FPT	**0.49***	−0.11	**0.43***	−0.40					—		—											
GIN	**−0.38***	**−0.49***	0.036	−0.14	**−0.42***	0.03			—		—											
Naming	—	0.04	—	0.07	—	0.28	—	0.07	—		—											
Repetition	—	0.12	—	0.13	—	0.24	—	0.13	—	**0.96***	—											
Visual HIT	0.06	0.27	0.16	−0.18	0.08	−0.10	0.16	−0.13	—	−0.00	—	−0.00										
Visual FA	−0.15	0.03	−0.21	−0.06	−0.21	0.03	0.16	0.28	—	−0.02	—	0.06	−0.23	−0.12								
Visual RT	−0.27	−0.43	−0.30	−0.05	**−0.49***	−0.12	**0.46***	**0.46***	—	−0.05	—	−0.03	0.08	−0.08	**0.40***	−0.18						
Auditory HIT	0.23	**0.47***	**0.32***	0.18	**0.46***	0.07	**−0.55***	−0.18	—	0.33	—	0.34	**0.59***	**0.43***	−0.03	−0.16	**−0.39***	−0.42				
Auditory FA	**−0.43***	−0.01	−0.28	0.23	−0.30	−0.29	**0.37***	0.02	—	−0.27	—	−0.27	0.05	−0.24	**0.54***	**0.50***	**0.41***	−0.20	−0.25	−0.26		
Auditory RT	−0.06	−0.24	−0.14	−0.01	−0.22	0.15	0.18	0.34	—	0.12	—	0.17	0.26	0.27	0.14	**−0.53***	**0.72***	0.16	−0.21	0.34	0.08	−0.69

also associated with working memory skills [47]. While attempting to construct a model to understand the behavior of ADHD children, Barkley [48] noted that poor behavioral inhibition (like that observed in ADHD) might lead to secondary deficits in working memory and associated functions. Working memory load also seems to be associated with declines in performance, such as the decline in auditory HIT performance observed in the present research. According to Davies and Parasuraman [49], such decrements in vigilance represent deteriorations in accuracy or detection speed over time. These declines occur primarily when stimulus events are presented rapidly in successive discrimination tasks as in the current research. According to Parasuraman [50], in such situations, decrements in sensitivity over time are linked to working memory requirements and the depletion of attentional resources throughout the period of vigilance. The current study did not investigate working memory performance in children with SSD; therefore, further studies are needed to better understand whether these possible immature behaviors and decrements in vigilance decrement are associated with working memory impairments in children with SSD.

The current study had some limitations. The sample size of the study group was relatively small, which may reduce the generalizability of the results of this study. Furthermore, both attention tasks measured sustained attention abilities. Therefore, further studies should consider larger samples and investigate other aspects of attention, such as selective attention.

In conclusion, the children with SSD performed worse on the auditory attention test; these children produced more false alarms and exhibited a significant decline in HIT performance over the course of the auditory test. The extent to which performance is related to difficulties in auditory perceptual abilities and probable working memory deficits is unclear. Further studies are necessary to better understand the nature of this poor performance and its clinical consequences in terms of rehabilitation.

Conclusion

Children with SSD disorders exhibited poorer performance on the auditory attention test than did the TD group; the children with SSD produced a greater number of false alarms, and their auditory HIT performance declined significantly over the course of the test. Further studies are needed to better understand the specific nature of these deficits and their clinical implications.

Author Contributions

Conceived and designed the experiments: CBM ES. Performed the experiments: CBM LOPN. Analyzed the data: CBM HFW. Wrote the paper: CBM LOPN HFW ES.

References

1. Bishop DVM (2010) Which neurodevelopmental disorders get researched and why? PLoS One 5(11): e 15112.
2. Fey ME (2008) Phonological and treatment articulation and phonology: inextricable constructs in speech pathology. Lang Speech Hear Ser Sch 23:225–32.
3. Tkach JA, Chen X, Freebairn LA, Schmithorst VJ, Holland SK, et al. (2011) Neural correlates of phonological processing in speech sound disorder: a functional magnetic resonance imaging study. Brain Lang 119(1):42–9.
4. Bird J, Bishop D (1992). Perception and awareness of phonemes in phonologically impaired children. European J Dis Comm 27: 289–311.
5. Kenney MK, Barac-Cikoja D, Finnegan K, Jeffries N, Ludlow CL (2006) Speech perception and short-term memory deficits in persistent developmental speech disorder. Brain Lang 96:178–90.
6. Leitao S., & Fletcher J (2004) Literacy outcomes for students with speech impairment: Long-term follow-up. Int J Lang Commun Disord, 39: 245–256.
7. Bird J, Bishop D (1992) Perception and awareness of phonemes in phonologically impaired children. Eur J Disord Commun 27:289–311.
8. Raitano NA, Pennington BF, Tunick RA, Boada R, Shriberg LD (2004) Pre-literacy skills of subgroups of childrenwith speech sound disorders. J Child Psychol Psychiatry 45:821–35.
9. Broomfield J, Dodd B (2004) Children with speech and language disability: caseload characteristics. Int. J. Lang. Comm. Dis. 39(3):303–24.
10. Bird J, Bishop DVM, Freeman NH (1995) Phonological awareness and literacy development in children with expressive phonological impairments. J Speech Lang Hear Res 38: 446–462.
11. Larrivee LS, Catts HW (1999) Early reading achievement in children with expressive phonological disorders. Am J Speech-Lang Pat 8:118–128.
12. Peterson RL, Pennington BF, Shriberg LD, Boada R (2009) What influences literacy outcome in children with speech sound disorder? J Speech Lang Hear Res. 52(5):1175–88.
13. Fisher SE, DeFries JC (2002) Developmental dyslexia: Genetic dissection of a complex cognitive trait. Nat Rev Neurosci 3: 767–780.
14. Smith SD, Pennington BF, Boada R, Shriberg LD (2005) Linkage of speech sound disorder to reading disability loci. J Child Psychol Psyc 46: 1057–1066.
15. Willcutt EG, Pennington BF, Smith SD, Cardon LR, Gayan J, et al. (2002) Quantitative trait locus for reading disability on chromosome 6p is pleiotropic for attention-deficit/ hyperactivity disorder. Am J Med Genet 114: 260–268.
16. McGrath LM, Hutaff-Lee C, Scott A, Boada R, Shriberg LD, et al. (2008) Children with comorbid speech sound disorder and specific language impairment are at increased risk for attention-deficit/hyperactivity disorder. J Abnorm Child Psychol 36(2):151–63.
17. Pennington BF, Bishop DV (2009) Relations among speech, language, and reading disorders. Annu Rev Psychol 60:283–306.
18. Finneran DA, Francis AL, Leonard LB (2009) Sustained attention in children with specific language impairment (SLI). J Speech Lang Hear Res. 52(4):915–29.
19. Spaulding TJ, Plante E, & Vance R (2008) Sustained selective attention skills of preschool children with specific language impairment: Evidence for separate attentional capacities. J Speech Lang Hear Res 51: 16–34.
20. Ebert KD, Kohnert K (2011) Sustained attention in children with primary language impairment: a meta-analysis. J Speech Lang Hear Res. 54(5):1372–84.
21. Marzocchi GM, Ornaghi S, Barboglio S (2009) What are the causes of the attention deficits observed in children with dyslexia? Child Neuropsychol 15(6):567–81.
22. Facoetti A, Molteni M (2000). Is attentional focusing an inhibitory process at distractor location? Cognitive Brain Research 10, 185–188.
23. Facoetti A, Zorzi M, Cestnick R, Lorusso ML, Molteni M, et al. (2006). The relationship between visuo-spatial attention and non-word reading in developmental dyslexia. Cogn Neuropsychol 23: 841–855.
24. Gomes H, Molholm S, Christodoulou C, Ritter W, & Cowan N (2000). The development of auditory attention in children. Front Biosci 5: 108–120.
25. Wertzner HF (2004) Fonologia. In: Andrade CRF, Befi-Lopes DM, Fernandes FDM, Wertzner HF ABFW - Teste de Linguagem Infantil nas Áreas de Fonologia, Vocabulário, Fluência e Pragmática. São Paulo: Pró-Fono.5–40.
26. Befi-Lopes DM Vocabulário (2004) In:Andrade CRF, Befi-Lopes DM, Fernandes FDM, Wertzner HF ABFW - Teste de Linguagem Infantil nas Áreas de Fonologia, Vocabulário, Fluência e Pragmática. São Paulo: Pró-Fono. pp.33–49.
27. Andrade CRF, Befi-Lopes DM, Fernandes FDM, Wertzner HF (2004) ABFW - Teste de Linguagem Infantil nas Áreas de Fonologia, Vocabulário, Fluência e Pragmática. São Paulo: Pró-Fono.
28. Shriberg LD, Austin D, Lewis BA, Mcsweeny JL, Wilson DL (1997) The percentage of consoants correct (PCC) metric: Extensions and reability data. J. Speech Lang Hear Res 40: 708–722.
29. Wertzner HF, Amaro L, Galea DES. (2007) Phonological performance measured by speech severity indices compared with correlated factors. Sao Paulo Med J 125(6):309–14.
30. Wertzner HF, Claudino GL, Galea DES, Patah LK, Castro MM. (2012) Phonological measures in children with phonological disorders. Rev Soc Bras Fonoaudiol 17(2):189–95.
31. Wertzner HF, Pereira K, Silva TZ, Pagan-Neves LO. (2013) The use of severity measures and speech inconsistency in children with speech sound disorders. Audiology Communication Research 18(3):213–9.
32. Musiek FE. (1994) Frequency (pitch) and duration patterns tests. J. Am. Acad. Audiol 5 (4): 265–268.
33. Musiek FE, Shinn JB, Jirsa R, Bamiou DE, Baran JA, et al. (2005) GIN (gaps in noise) test performance in subjects with confirmed central auditory nervous system involvement. Ear Hear 26(6):608–18.
34. Angelini AL, Alves ICA, Custódio EM, Duarte WF, Duarte JLM (1999) Manual das matrizes progressivas de Raven. São Paulo: Centro Editor de Testes e Pesquisas em Psicologia.
35. Strauss E, Sherman E, Spreen O (2006) A Compendium of Neuropsychological Tests. 3rd ed. New York: Oxford.
36. Gordon M (1983) The Gordon diagnostic system. Boulder CO: Gordon Systems.
37. Mahone EM, Pillion JP, Hoffman J, Hiemenz JR, Denckla MB (2005) Construct validity of the auditory continuous performance test for preschoolers. Dev Neuropsychol 27(1):11–33.

38. Guy J, Rogers M., Cornish K (2012) Age-related changes in visual and auditory sustained attention in preschool-aged children. Child Neuropsychol 19(6):601–14.
39. Seli P, Cheyne JA, Barton KR, Smilek D (2012) Consistency of sustained attention across modalities: Comparing visual and auditory versions of the SART. Can J Exp Psychol 66(1): 44–50.
40. Aylward GP, Brager P, Harper DC (2002) Relations between visual and auditory continuous performance tests in a clinical population: a descriptive study. Dev Neuropsychol 21(3): 285–303.
41. Dancey C, Reidy J (2006) Estatística sem matemática para psicologia: usando SPSS para Windows. Porto Alegre: Artmed.
42. Tallal P, Piercy M (1973) Developmental aphasia: impaired rate of non-verbal processing as a function of sensory modality. Neuropsychol. 11: 389–98.
43. Tallal P (1980) Auditory temporal perception, phonics and reading disabilities in children. Brain Lang. 9:182–98.
44. Riccio CA, Cohen MJ, Hynd GW, Keith RW (1996) Validity of the Auditory Continuous Performance Test in differentiating central processing auditory disorders with and without ADHD. J Learn Disabil 29(5):561–6.
45. Diamond A (1990) Developmental time course in human infants and infant monkeys, and the neural bases of inhibitory control in reaching. In: A Diamond, editor. The development and neural bases of higher cognitive functions. New York: New York Academy of Sciences. pp. 637–676.
46. Bari A, Robbins TW (2013) Inhibition and impulsivity: Behavioral and neural basis of response control. Prog Neurobiol 108:44–79.
47. Petit L, Courtney SM, Ungerleider LG, Haxby JV (1998) Sustained activity in the medial wall during working memory delays. The Journal of Neuroscience: the Official Journal of the Society for Neuroscience 18: 9429–9437.
48. Barkley RA (1997) Behavioral inhibition, sustained attention, and executive functions: constructing a unifying theory of ADHD. Psychol Bull 121: 65–94.
49. Davies DR, Parasuraman R (1982) The psychology of vigilance London: Academic Press.
50. Parasuraman R (1979) Memory load and event rate control sensitivity decrements in sustained attention. Science 205: 924–927.

14

Facial Mimicry in 6–7 Year Old Children with Disruptive Behavior Disorder and ADHD

Peter Deschamps[1]*, Nicolette Munsters[2], Leon Kenemans[2], Dennis Schutter[2], Walter Matthys[1,3]

1 Department of Psychiatry, Brain Center Rudolf Magnus, University Medical Center Utrecht, Utrecht, The Netherlands, 2 Department of Experimental Psychology, Helmholtz Research Institute, Utrecht University, Utrecht, The Netherlands, 3 Department of Child and Adolescent Studies, Utrecht University, Utrecht, The Netherlands

Abstract

Background: Impairments in facial mimicry are considered a proxy for deficits in affective empathy and have been demonstrated in 10 year old children and in adolescents with disruptive behavior disorder (DBD). However, it is not known whether these impairments are already present at an earlier age. Emotional deficits have also been shown in children with attention-deficit/hyperactivity disorder (ADHD).

Aims: To examine facial mimicry in younger, 6–7 year old children with DBD and with ADHD.

Methods: Electromyographic (EMG) activity in response to emotional facial expressions was recorded in 47 children with DBD, 18 children with ADHD and 35 healthy developing children.

Results: All groups displayed significant facial mimicry to the emotional expressions of other children. No group differences between children with DBD, children with ADHD and healthy developing children were found. In addition, no differences in facial mimicry were found between the clinical group (i.e., all children with a diagnosis) and the typically developing group in an analysis with ADHD symptoms as a covariate, and no differences were found between the clinical children and the typically developing children with DBD symptoms as a covariate.

Conclusion: Facial mimicry in children with DBD and ADHD throughout the first primary school years was unimpaired, in line with studies on empathy using other paradigms.

Editor: Nicholas P. Holmes, University of Reading, United Kingdom

Funding: Dennis J.L.G Schutter was supported by an Innovational Research Grant (VIDI 452-07-012) from the Netherlands Organization for Scientific Research (NWO). The funders had no role in study design, data collection and analysis, decision to publish, or preparation of the manuscript.

Competing Interests: The authors have declared that no competing interests exist.

* E-mail: p.k.h.deschamps@umcutrecht.nl

Introduction

Empathy is the ability to share and understand the emotions of other people with whom we interact and plays an important role in the development of prosocial behavior and inhibition of antisocial and aggressive behavior [1,2]. It is assumed that empathy is initiated by the observation of another's emotional state, followed by a cascade of phenomena [3] that have been studied on an emotional (sharing another's emotional state), cognitive (understanding another's emotional state) and behavioral level (e.g., targeted helping) [4]. Although the precise mechanism, how mimicry is related to the development of individual differences in empathy, remains unclear [3], adequate responses to the emotional states of others also involve the activation of corresponding facial, vocal or postural expressions, called mimicry. Previous facial mimicry studies in school-aged children (mean age 10 years) and adolescents (mean age 13 years) with disruptive behavior disorder (DBD) suggest deficits in response to negative but not positive emotions [5–7].

Several important issues concerning facial mimicry responses in children with DBD need further exploration. First, it remains unclear how early in development abnormalities in responses to emotional expressions start to emerge. The empathic ability of aggressive children may become increasingly impaired as social demands in peer interactions rapidly increase. Hence, deficits in facial mimicry might already be present in children with DBD at the start of school age (6–7 years old). On the other hand, studies using paradigms other than facial electromyography (facial EMG) (e.g., behavioral observation) suggest that aggressive preschoolers do not differ from their healthy developing peers in their response to the emotions of others [8,9]. The primary goal of the present study was to determine whether 6 to 7 year old children with DBD already show facial mimicry impairment. Second, despite high co-morbidity of attention-deficit/hyperactivity disorder (ADHD) and DBD and high co-occurrence of ADHD symptoms in children with DBD and DBD symptoms in children with ADHD, little attention has been paid to the influence of ADHD on emotion perception and processing in children with DBD [10,11]. Several studies in children with ADHD have shown that emotion processing might also be impaired, to some extent, in boys with ADHD [12–17]. Interestingly, it has been argued that deficits in responding to the emotions of others in children with ADHD are at least partially accounted for by the co-existence of DBD [15] and that in boys with DBD, deficits might at least partially be related to ADHD [18].

The present study aimed to address these issues by examining facial mimicry responses to emotional facial expressions in a sample of 6–7 year old children with DBD, in children with ADHD, and in healthy developing children. Two lines of approach were followed. First, three groups were compared, i.e., children with DBD, children with ADHD, and typically developing children. Second, while comparing the clinical group (i.e., all children with a diagnosis) to the typically developing group, first the effect of DBD on facial mimicry was examined with ADHD symptoms as a covariate, and second the effect of ADHD was examined with DBD symptoms as a covariate.

Methods

Participants

A sample of 100 children ranging from six to seven years old with a previous clinical diagnosis of DBD (i.e., either oppositional defiant disorder (ODD) or conduct disorder (CD)) and/or ADHD was recruited at the Outpatient Clinic of the Department of Child and Adolescent Psychiatry, University Medical Center Utrecht. Children were excluded from participating if a clinical diagnosis of ADHD or DBD was not confirmed (n = 3) in the Diagnostic Interview Schedule for Children (DISC module E) [19] or when they had an estimated IQ below 70 (n = 8) based on the vocabulary and block design subsets of the Wechsler Intelligence Scale for Children III-Dutch version [20,21]. Eighteen children were excluded as they had taken methylphenidate (n = 18) on the day of testing, despite instructions to cease medication prior to assessment. Furthermore, in six children from the clinical groups no EMG data were collected, either caused by technical difficulties, lack of cooperation or anxiety in the children. The final patient group for analyses comprised 65 children.

The healthy developing control group consisted of 37 children from regular elementary schools in the vicinity of Utrecht who did not meet criteria for a clinical diagnosis of ADHD or DBD on the DISC and had an estimated IQ within the normal range. No EMG data were collected in three children from the control group due to technical difficulties or anxiety. The Medical Ethics Committee of the University Medical Centre Utrecht approved the study protocol and parents gave written informed consent prior to participation.

Measurements

The DISC module E interview [19] was used to distinguish patient groups. For our first categorical approach, we pooled children with DBD with ADHD (n = 41) and children with DBD without comorbid ADHD (n = 6) in one DBD group. The other patient group consisted of children with ADHD without a comorbid DBD diagnosis (n = 18). Because of the small sample size of the DBD-only group, an analysis comparing this group to other groups was not appropriate. The group of children with DBD (n = 47) included both children with ODD (n = 41) and those with CD (n = 6). For our second approach, a total patient group was analyzed including 65 children with a diagnosis of DBD (n = 6), ADHD (n = 18) or DBD with comorbid ADHD (n = 41).

The Child Behavior Checklist 6–18 (CBCL) and Teacher Report Form (TRF) [22] were collected and used to quantify attention problems and rule-breaking/aggressive behavior.

Table 1 shows the characteristics of the sample used for final data analyses, divided in the DBD group with and without comorbid ADHD, ADHD only group and healthy control group. Analyses presented in Table 1 show that children in the DBD group were on average 4 months younger than the TD children. Furthermore children in the DBD and ADHD groups contained fewer girls, and these children had lower estimated IQ and lower socio-economic status (SES) than children in the control group. Children in the DBD group did not differ from children in the ADHD group in sex, estimated IQ or SES, but were significantly younger. As expected, the three groups significantly differed on attention problems and rule-breaking/aggressive behavior.

Facial EMG data collection

Film clips with dynamic emotional facial expressions, created at our laboratory, were used in the present study [23]. In these film clips, each with a total duration of 6400 ms, five different children (two boys and three girls) expressed anger, sadness, fear and happiness as illustrated in Figure 1. Clips started with a 1600 ms static of a neutral expression which served as baseline, followed by a 1600 ms morph into a dynamic emotional expression and ended with a 3200 ms static of the full-blown emotion. Each film clip was preceded by an inter-stimulus interval (a black screen), followed by a central fixation cross with a duration of 1000 ms. In total 32 movie clips were presented, once in a semi-random sequence in a first block (16 clips, 4 children × 4 emotions), and once in a semi-random sequence in a second block (16 clips, 4 children × 4 emotions). The size of the pictures was 21.5 cm height by 16 cm width. They were viewed from a distance of 95 cm. Furthermore, during the task, there were four trials in which a cartoon character was presented during an emotional film clip. Children were instructed to push a response button when the character appeared on screen in order to maintain the child's attention to the faces.

Table 1. Descriptives.

Characteristics	TD	ADHD	DBD	*F* (df = 96)	Contrasts
	(*n* = 34)	(*n* = 18)	(*n* = 47)		
	M (SD)	*M (SD)*	*M (SD)*		
Age	7.1 (0.5)	7.1 (0.7)	6.7 (0.5)	6.90*	TD, ADHD > DBD
Sex: male/female	17/17	8/10	11/36	6.65*	TD ≠ ADHD, DBD
estimated IQ	110 (20)	103 (17)	100 (19)	3.20*	TD > ADHD, DBD
SES	7.0 (2.1)	5.1 (1.9)	5.6 (1.5)	8.27*	TD > ADHD, DBD
CBCL T score					
-Attention	52.7 (4.0)	67.0 (8.4)	66.8 (7.9)	47.07*	TD < ADHD, DBD
-Rule-breaking	53.0 (4.3)	58.0 (6.8)	61.9 (6.4)	22.73*	TD < ADHD < DBD
-Aggression	53.5 (5.6)	63.4 (8.9)	70.8 (7.8)	55.34*	TD < ADHD < DBD
TRF T score					
-Attention	52.0 (3.1)	59.9 (9.7)	61.6 (7.5)	19.71*	TD< ADHD, DBD
-Rule-breaking	50.9 (2.6)	54.9 (5.4)	58.8 (7.7)	16.66*	TD < ADHD < DBD
-Aggression	52.2 (3.7)	60.8 (5.6)	64.5 (10.8)	22.03*	TD< ADHD, DBD

Note: * $p<0.05$.

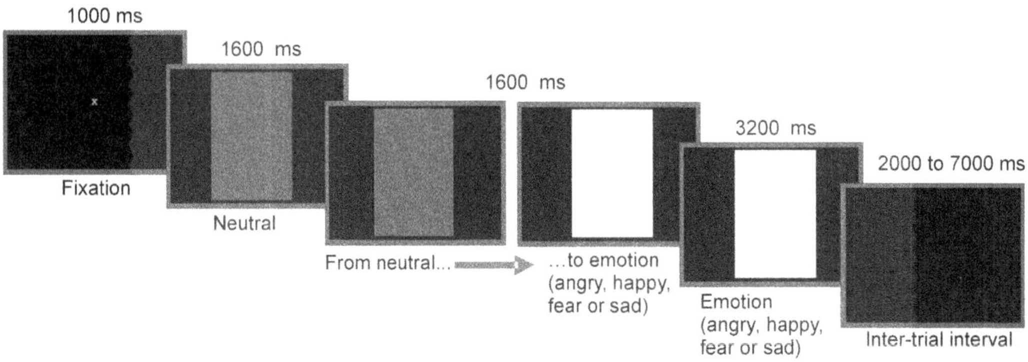

Figure 1. Example trial of the passive viewing task. Each trial started with a central fixation cross, followed by a film clip. The clips started with a neutral expression (in the figure represented by a gray rectangle), followed by a morph into a dynamic emotional expression and ended with a still of the full-blown emotion (in the figure represented by a white rectangle). Each trial ended with an inter-stimulus interval.

The data collected during these trials and during the four familiarization trials were excluded from further analyses.

EMG activity was recorded from bipolar montages from the corrugator supercilii (corrugator), zygomaticus major (zygomaticus), frontalis medialis (frontalis) and depressor anguli oris (depressor), according to the guidelines given by Fridlund and Cacioppo [24]. Ag-AgCl electrodes with a diameter of 4 mm, filled with conductive electrode gel (Signa gel, Parker Laboratories, Inc., Fairfield, New Jersey, U.S.A.), were placed on the left side of the face to obtain maximal reactions [25]. Raw EMG recordings were made with the ActiveTwo system (BioSemi, Amsterdam, The Netherlands) relative to the common mode sense (CMS). The ground consisted of the active CMS and passive driven right leg (DRL) electrode placed on the forehead that form a feedback loop driving the subject's average potential as close as possible to the analog-to-digital converter (i.e., the amplifier "zero") reference voltage in the A/D-box. The EMG signal was sampled at 2048 Hz.

Procedure

EMG data were collected while the child was seated in a chair in front of a computer screen in a dimly lit room at their own school. To ensure participants were at ease, they first had a small talk with the experimenter and completed the two WISC-III subtests. Children were instructed to watch the film clips carefully and to push a button when a popular cartoon character appeared. They were told they would receive a small present as a reward upon finishing the task. Between the two blocks of the passive viewing task, the experimenter ensured that the child was both comfortable and motivated. Additionally, during the task an experimenter encouraged the children to pay attention and recorded the time segments when the child was not looking at the computer screen to provide a measure of visual inattention. Total duration of the facial EMG task was approximately 12 minutes.

Data reduction and analysis

EMG signals were filtered offline (high-pass 20 Hz, 48dB/octave) and full wave rectified using Brain Vision Analyzer Software (Brain Products GmbH, Munich). Trials marked by the experimenter during the task indicating that the child was not looking at the computer screen, were excluded from further analysis. The average number of trials removed per participant was 1.82 (SD 0.41) out of 32 trials in the typically developing group, 3.68 (SD 0.60) in the DBD with/without ADHD group and 4.95 (SD 1.16) in the ADHD only group.

Raw EMG data were segmented into 100 ms epochs. All values were expressed as a percentage of individual baseline activity, defined as the mean activity during 1600 ms neutral facial expression preceding onset of the morph. Averaged activity during the interval starting 500 ms after the beginning of the morphed dynamic expression and ending 500 ms after the beginning of the static expression at the end of the morphed clip was used for further analyses (total time 1600 ms). Mean EMG responses across this 1600 ms period, expressed as a percentage change from baseline activity, were calculated for each emotion-muscle combination (averages of all stimuli for that emotion-muscle combination in the two blocks). Data points that exceeded 3 SD above or below the grand mean change score of the emotion condition were marked as outliers and excluded from further analysis [26]. Mean EMG responses as expressed in percentage change from baseline activity were calculated for each emotion-muscle combination (averages of all responses for that emotion-muscle combination in the two blocks).

Based on previous research of our group [23], facial EMG composite scores were calculated on basis of the absolute mimicry response to all four emotional presentations. Since mimicry to happy facial expressions consists of both smiling activity (i.e., increase in zygomaticus muscle) and relaxation of frowning activity (i.e., decrease in corrugator muscle), to calculate the total mimicry response to happy facial expressions (HAPPY), we used the following formula: [happy mimicry = (% change in zygomaticus activation during happy stimulus presentation compared to neutral face baseline - % change in corrugator activation during happy stimulus presentation compared to neutral face baseline)/2]. Thus, we calculated the overall mean of the positive change in zygomaticus and the negative change in corrugator activity in response to happy facial expressions compared to neutral face baseline. Likewise, angry facial mimicry consists of an increase in frowning and a decrease in smiling activity, the total angry score (ANGRY) consisted of the overall mean of the positive change in corrugator and the negative change in zygomaticus activity in response to angry facial expressions (formula: [angry mimicry = (% change in corrugator activation during stimulus presentation compared to baseline- % change in zygomaticus presentation during stimulus presentation compared to baseline)/2)]. The total fear score (FEAR) consisted of the positive change of frontalis activity in response to fearful facial expressions, and the total sad score (SAD) consisted of the positive change in frontalis, corrugator and depressor activity in response to sad facial expressions (formula: [sad mimicry = (% change in frontalis + % change in corrugator + % change in depressor compared to neutral face baseline)/3]).

Statistical analyses were performed using PASW Statistics 18.0 (IBM Company, Chicago, Illinois). Initially, we validated the composite scores within the healthy control group, as this group was not identical to the group used in our previous study [23]. Using one-sample t-tests, we checked whether the separate muscles of the composite scores changed significantly during presentation of the emotional film clips, compared to the activity during the neutral face baseline.

First, a multivariate analysis of variance (MANOVA) was conducted to examine whether facial mimicry differed in children with DBD, children with ADHD only, and healthy controls. Dependent variables were the facial mimicry response composite scores to sad, fearful, angry and happy facial expressions (SAD, FEAR, ANGRY and HAPPY MIMICRY). MIMICRY was entered as a within subjects factor with two levels (baseline and activation during stimulus presentation). GROUP was entered as between subjects variable with three levels (DBD with or without ADHD, ADHD and healthy controls).

Second, multivariate analyses of variance (MANOVA) were conducted to compare the facial mimicry response scores (SAD, FEAR, ANGRY and HAPPY MIMICRY) in the overall patient group with the typically developing children (GROUP) with the parent and teacher reported attention and aggression symptom scores entered as covariates.

In all tests, the alpha level of significance was set at $p<0.05$ (two-tailed).

Results

The independent sample t-tests within the healthy control group showed that all four composite scores consisted of the hypothesized muscle activation patterns (all p-values <0.05). In particular, in line with predictions, the presentation of angry facial expressions showed a significant increase in corrugator activity compared to the pre-stimulus neutral face baseline ($t(33) = 3.03$, $p = 0.005$) and a significant decrease in zygomaticus activity ($t(33) = -2.31$, $p = 0.027$). Following presentation of happy facial expressions, children showed an expected significant decrease in corrugator activity ($t(33) = -3.98$, $p<0.001$) and a significant increase in zygomaticus activity ($t(33) = 3.41$, $p = 0.002$). Presentation of fearful facial expressions led to an increase in frontalis activity compared to baseline ($t(33) = 4.64$, $p<0.001$). Sad facial expressions induced a significant increase in corrugator ($t(33) = 4.57$, $p<0.001$), frontalis ($t(33) = 4.45$, $p<0.001$) and depressor ($t(33) = 2.21$, $p = 0.034$) activity compared to baseline.

A significant main effect of MIMICRY was found, demonstrating that overall, the presented stimuli resulted in facial mimicry ($F(4,93) = 21.49$, $p<0.001$).

Univariate analyses showed a significant effect of MIMICRY in response to SAD ($F(1,96) = 33.90$, $p<0.001$), FEAR ($F(1,96) = 27.89$, $p<0.001$), ANGRY ($F(1,96) = 46.45$, $p<0.001$) and HAPPY ($F(1,96) = 32.00$, $p<0.001$) facial expressions.

We did not find a significant multivariate main effect of GROUP ($F(8,188) = 0.80$, $p = 0.60$), indicating no differences in facial mimicry between clinical groups and healthy developing children (see Figure 2).

An additional MANOVA comparing the activation of the individual muscles (i.e., zygomaticus and corrugator in response to happy and angry expressions, frontalis in response to fear and corrugator, frontalis and depressor in response to sad) between the three groups showed no multivariate effect of group ($F(16,180) = 0.740$, $p = 0.75$) meaning that the absence of a group effect in the main analysis was not due to the use of composite scores.

Next, a second additional analysis was conducted within the boys to assure the imbalance of sex in our groups could not explain the lack of a group difference. This analyses yielded similar results as the main analysis and showed no main effect of group ($F(8,116) = 0.92$, $p>0.50$).

Finally, four analyses were conducted to examine the effect of GROUP (all patients versus typically developing children) on facial mimicry with attention and aggression symptom scores as covariates respectively, reported by either parents (CBCL attention and CBCL aggression t scores) or teachers (TRF attention and TRF aggression t scores). No significant multivariate effect of GROUP was found in any of the MANOVAs with these individual factors entered as covariate (all $p>0.15$). Of note, no significant correlations were found between facial mimicry and the CBCL Attention t score ($F(4,93) = 0.87$, $p = 0.48$), CBCL Aggression t score ($F(4,93) = 1.40$, $p = 0.24$), TRF Attention t score ($F(4,91) = 0.62$, $p = 0.65$), TRF Aggression t score ($F(4,91) = 1.11$, $p = 0.36$).

Discussion

In the present study no evidence was found for impaired facial mimicry in 6–7 year old children with ADHD as compared to healthy controls. Also, no differences were found in facial mimicry between children with DBD and healthy controls. However, since the group of children with DBD without ADHD in our study sample was not sufficiently large, we had to pool the children with DBD with and without comorbid ADHD. Nevertheless, no differences in facial mimicry were found between the clinical group (i.e., all children with a diagnosis) and the typically developing group in an analysis with ADHD symptoms as a covariate, and no differences were found between the clinical children and the typically developing children with DBD symptoms as a covariate.

Results of an absence of facial mimicry deficits in our sample of 6–7 year olds with DBD are in keeping with studies using other paradigms (e.g., behavioral observation) that suggest that aggressive school-aged children and adolescents [2,27] but not younger children and preschoolers [8,9] respond less to the emotions of others compared to their healthy developing peers. Since in 10 year old children and adolescents with DBD diminished facial EMG responses have been demonstrated [5–7], one may speculate that EMG responses to emotional facial expressions are still intact in 6–7 year old children and that decreases in mimicry responses start after the beginning of school age.

However, there are other possible explanations why we did not find a group difference. Children in our study were younger than those in previous studies that showed facial mimicry deficits in DBD [5–7]. Since throughout development into late childhood and adolescence, symptoms of DBD are known to persist in certain, and decline in other children [28,29], our sample might have included children with less severe psychopathology. The symptom scores on the CBCL filled in by parents and the TRF in the present study indeed were lower as compared to those in previous studies [5–7]. Also, children in our study were recruited from an outpatient population, whereas in previous studies children were recruited from inpatient and day-treatment settings [5,6] or special schools for adolescents with severe behavioral problems [7]. Importantly, the present study sample contained only a few children with CD and the others were diagnosed with

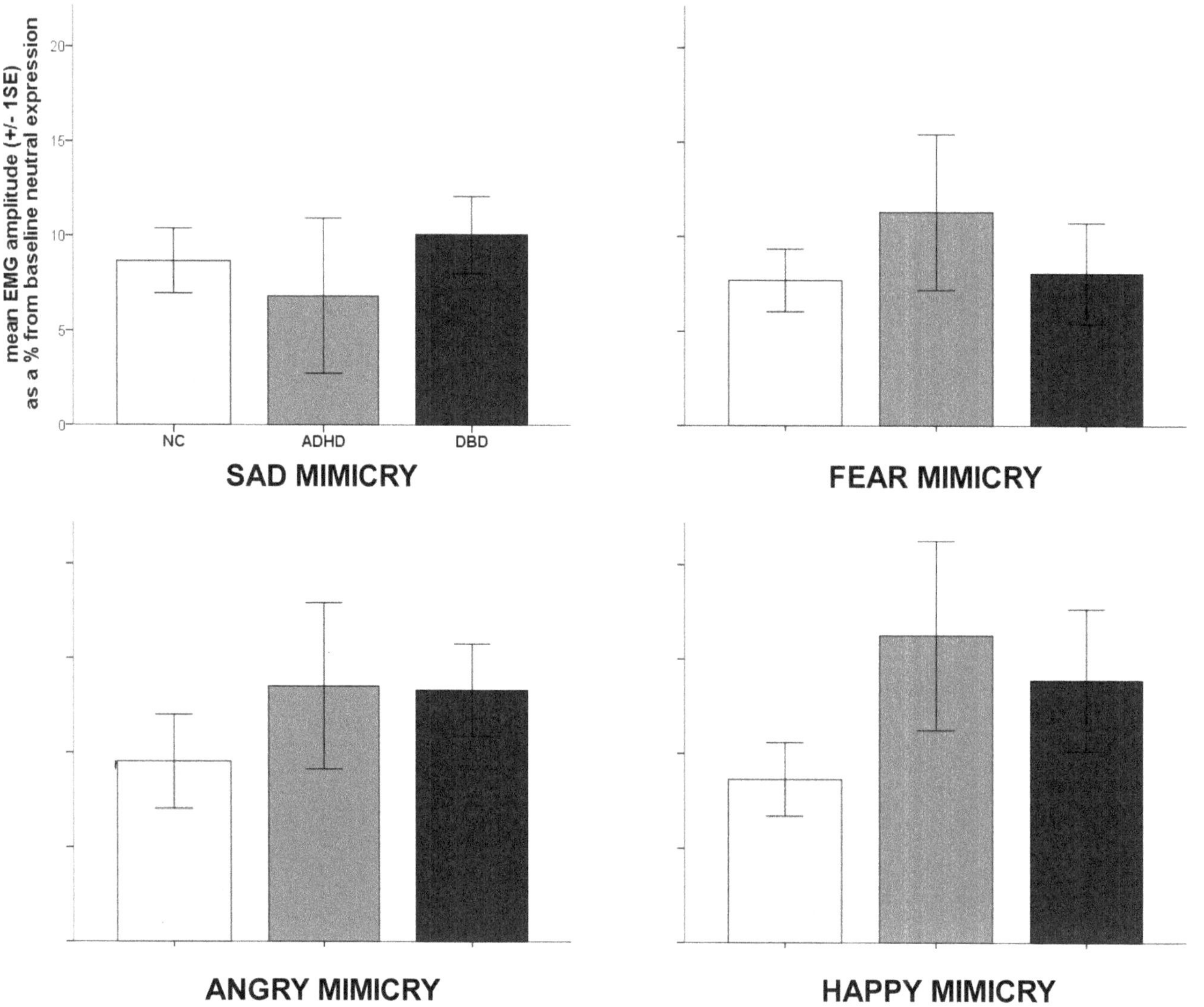

Figure 2. Facial mimicry response to emotional facial expressions in DBD, ADHD and healthy controls. No significant differences were shown between groups in mean EMG amplitude as a percentage from baseline neutral expression for SAD, FEAR, ANGRY and HAPPY MIMICRY presented for healthy controls, children with attention-deficit/hyperactivity disorder (ADHD) and children with disruptive behavior disorder (DBD). Error bars represent +/− 1 standard error.

ODD, whereas in other studies twenty percent [5,6] to almost half of the DBD sample consisted of CD children [7]. Recently, it has been suggested that the neurobiology of ODD may be different from CD [30,31] as ODD differs from CD in symptomatology, comorbidity and development [32–35]. Overall, this points towards less severe and different psychopathology in our young outpatient group as a possible explanation for the lack of a group difference.

Facial mimicry in children with ADHD thus far had not been studied, but previous studies using other paradigms had suggested deficits in emotion processing in children with ADHD. Several studies in children with attention problems and ADHD have shown that their facial emotion recognition skills [12–14] and empathic responsiveness to emotions [15–17] tend to be less well developed compared to healthy children. However, we could not show deficits in facial mimicry in ADHD compared to typically developing children.

With regard to the role of sex differences, our study sample differed from previous studies on facial mimicry in children with DBD as those studies did not examine girls. Little is known about the influence of sex on the development of facial mimicry, but studies in adults have suggested females might show more facial mimicry, although only in response to happy facial expressions [36,37]. To further examine whether the sex ratio in our study influenced the main findings, we conducted an additional analysis within the group of boys in our study. This analysis showed that, as in the overall sample, boys with DBD or ADHD showed no deficits in facial mimicry. Hence it is unlikely that the presence of girls in our sample influenced our main finding. However, it should be noted that due to the small sample sizes in the subgroup analyses, these analyses were likely to be statistically underpowered to detect this effect.

Finally, there are several methodological differences in our study compared to previous work to consider. First, only one other study examined facial EMG responses to child stimuli [6]. While stimuli of adults are useful to study emotional responsiveness in adult-child interactions, they might provide only limited information on social interactions between children. Next, the procedure and analysis in the present study was developed to maximize attention paid to the stimuli. Namely, children were encouraged to pay attention, motivated with the promise of a reward, an instruction was inserted in the paradigm to catch a cartoon character, and trials marked with visual inattention were excluded from further analysis. This could have reduced the influence of attention problems on deficits in facial mimicry. Two other studies found evidence for a positive moderating influence of increased attention on emotion processing in adults with low empathy and antisocial behavior using a fear-potentiated startle paradigm [38] and in children using a fear recognition task [39]. Both studies suggest that deficits in emotion processing can be at least temporarily corrected by instructing subjects to focus on the eyes of other people and guiding their attention towards relevant parts of the presented stimuli. Until future studies assess facial mimicry simultaneously with objective procedures, like eye-tracking, to verify actual attendance to the stimuli, it remains difficult to unravel whether previous findings of impaired mimicry are partly driven by a lack of attention. Further study is needed to explore whether young children with DBD and/or ADHD are only capable to adequately make use of their mimicry system under optimal conditions, i.e., conditions that need not be ecologically valid. It might well be that in children with ADHD a continuous lack of proper attention to relevant parts of emotional facial stimuli in daily live has a negative effect on the development of emotion processing and recognition.

Since in 10 year old children and adolescents with DBD diminished facial EMG responses have been demonstrated [5–7], one may speculate that EMG responses to emotional facial expressions are still intact in 6–7 year old children and decreases in mimicry responses start after the beginning of school age. Longitudinal studies using facial EMG and other physiological assessment methods are needed to shed light on the development of responsiveness to visual and other sensory modalities of emotional stimuli of other children. Further study should identify whether, at what age, and in which subgroups (e.g. those with CD versus those with ODD) children with DBD become impaired in their responding to emotions, and which factors affect altered emotional responsiveness. In conclusion, this study demonstrates that 6–7 year old children with DBD and ADHD exhibit normal facial mimicry to emotional facial expressions.

Acknowledgments

The authors would like to thank Arne Popma and Koen van Lith for their kind assistance in the data collection.

Author Contributions

Conceived and designed the experiments: PD LK DS WM. Performed the experiments: PD NM. Analyzed the data: PD NM LK DS WM. Contributed reagents/materials/analysis tools: PD DS LK WM. Wrote the paper: PD NM LK DS WM.

References

1. Eisenberg N, Miller PA (1987) The relation of empathy to prosocial and related behaviors. Psychol Bull 101: 91–119.
2. Miller PA, Eisenberg N (1988) The relation of empathy to aggressive and externalizing/antisocial behavior. Psychol Bull 103: 324–344.
3. Hofelich AJ, Preston SD (2012) The meaning in empathy: distinguishing conceptual encoding from facial mimicry, trait empathy, and attention to emotion. Cognition and Emotion 26: 119–128.
4. de Waal FB (2008) Putting the altruism back into altruism: the evolution of empathy. Annual Reviews Psychology 59: 279–300.
5. de Wied M, van Boxtel A, Zaalberg R, Goudena PP, Matthys W (2006) Facial EMG responses to dynamic emotional facial expressions in boys with disruptive behavior disorders. Journal of Psychiatric research 40: 112–121.
6. de Wied M, van Boxtel AV, Posthumus JA, Goudena PP, Matthys W (2009) Facial EMG and heart rate responses to emotion-inducing film clips in boys with disruptive behavior disorders. Psychophysiology 46: 996–1004.
7. de Wied M, van Boxtel A, Matthys W (2012) Verbal, Facial and Autonomic Responses to Empathy-Eliciting Film Clips by Disruptive Male Adolescents with High Versus Low Callous-Unemotional Traits. J Abnorm Child Psychol 4: 211–223.
8. Gill KL, Calkins SD (2003) Do aggressive/destructive toddlers lack concern for others? Behavioral and physiological indicators of empathic responding in 2-year-old children. Developmental Psychopathology 15: 55–71.
9. Feshbach ND, Roe K (1968) Empathy in six- and seven-year-olds. Child Dev 39: 133–145.
10. Sterba S, Egger HL, Angold A (2007) Diagnostic specificity and nonspecificity in the dimensions of preschool psychopathology. Journal of child psychology and psychiatry, and allied disciplines 48: 1005–1013.
11. Martel MM, Gremillion M, Roberts B, Eye von A, Nigg JT (2010) The structure of childhood disruptive behaviors. Psychological Assessment 22: 816–826.
12. Williams LM, Hermens DF, Palmer D, Kohn M, Clarke S, et al. (2008) Misinterpreting emotional expressions in attention-deficit/hyperactivity disorder: evidence for a neural marker and stimulant effects. Biol Psychiatry 63: 917–926.
13. Pelc K, Kornreich C, Foisy ML, Dan B (2006) Recognition of emotional facial expressions in attention-deficit hyperactivity disorder. Pediatr Neurol 35: 93–97.
14. Sinzig J, Morsch D, Lehmkuhl G (2008) Do hyperactivity, impulsivity and inattention have an impact on the ability of facial affect recognition in children with autism and ADHD? European Child and Adolescent Psychiatry 17: 63–72.
15. Marton I, Wiener J, Rogers M, Moore C, Tannock R (2009) Empathy and social perspective taking in children with Attention-Deficit/Hyperactivity Disorder. J Abnorm Child Psychol 37: 107–118.
16. Dyck MJ, Ferguson K, Shochet IM (2001) Do autism spectrum disorders differ from each other and from non-spectrum disorders on emotion recognition tests? Eur Child Adolesc Psychiatry 10: 105–116.
17. Braaten EB, Rosen LA (2000) Self-regulation of affect in attention deficit-hyperactivity disorder (ADHD) and non-ADHD boys: differences in empathic responding. J Consult Clin Psychol 68: 313–321.
18. Yuill N, Lyon J (2007) Selective difficulty in recognising facial expressions of emotion in boys with ADHD. General performance impairments or specific problems in social cognition? Eur Child Adolesc Psychiatry 16: 398–404.
19. Shaffer D, Fisher P, Lucas CP, Dulcan MK, Schwab-Stone ME (2000) NIMH Diagnostic Interview Schedule for Children Version IV (NIMH DISC-IV): description, differences from previous versions, and reliability of some common diagnoses. Journal of the American Academy of Child and Adolescent Psychiatry 39: 28–38.
20. Sattler JM (1992) Assessment of Children (3rd edition). San Diego, CA: Jerome M Sattler Publisher.
21. Kort W, Schittekatte M, Dekker PH, Verhaeghe P, Compaan EL, et al. (2005) Wechsler Intelligence Scale for Children-third edition, Dutch version. Psychological Corporation, London.
22. Achenbach TM, Rescorla LA (2001) Manual for the ASEBA School-Age Forms & Profiles. Burlington, VT: University of Vermont, Research Center for Children, Youth, & Families.
23. Deschamps PK, Schutte I, Kenemans JL, Matthys W, Schutter DJ (2012) Electromyographic responses to emotional facial expressions in 6–7year olds: A feasibility study. Int J Psychophysiol 85:195–9.
24. Fridlund AJ, Cacioppo JT (1986) Guidelines for human electromyographic research. Psychophysiology 23: 567–589.
25. Dimberg U, Petterson M (2000) Facial reactions to happy and angry facial expressions: evidence for right hemisphere dominance. Psychophysiology 37: 693–696.
26. Larsen JT, Norris JI (2009) A facial electromyographic investigation of affective contrast. Psychophysiology 46: 831–842.
27. Eisenberg N, Eggum ND, Di Giunta L (2010) Empathy-related Responding: Associations with Prosocial Behavior, Aggression, and Intergroup Relations. Social Issues and Policy Review 4: 143–180.
28. Frick PJ, Loney BR (1999) Outcomes of children and adolescents with oppitional defiant disorder and conduct disorder. In HC Quay & A Hogan (Eds), Handbook of disruptive behavior disorders New York: Plenum: 507–524.
29. Lahey BB, Loeber R, Hart EL, Frick PJ, Applegate B, et al. (1995) Four-year longitudinal study of conduct disorder in boys: patterns and predictors of persistence. J Abnorm Psychol 104: 83–93.
30. Matthys W, Vanderschuren LJMJ, Schutter DJLG, Lochman JE (2012) Impaired neurocognitive functions affect social learning processes in oppositional defiant disorder and conduct disorder: implications for interventions. Clin Child Fam Psychol Rev 15: 234–246.

31. Matthys W, Vanderschuren LJMJ, Schutter DJLG (2013) The neurobiology of oppositional defiant disorder and conduct disorder: altered functioning in three mental domains. Dev Psychopathol 25: 193–207.
32. Rowe R, Costello EJ, Angold A, Copeland WE, Maughan B (2010) Developmental pathways in oppositional defiant disorder and conduct disorder. J Abnorm Psychol 119: 726–738.
33. Nock MK, Kazdin AE, Hiripi E, Kessler RC (2007) Lifetime prevalence, correlates, and persistence of oppositional defiant disorder: results from the National Comorbidity Survey Replication. Journal of child psychology and psychiatry, and allied disciplines 48: 703–713.
34. Stringaris A, Goodman R (2009) Longitudinal outcome of youth oppositionality: irritable, headstrong, and hurtful behaviors have distinctive predictions. J Am Acad Child Adolesc Psychiatry 48: 404–412.
35. Stringaris A, Goodman R (2009) Three dimensions of oppositionality in youth. J Child Psychol Psychiatry 50: 216–223.
36. Dimberg U, Lundquist LO (1990) Gender differences in facial reactions to facial expressions. Biol Psychol 30: 151–159.
37. Sonnby-Borgström M, Jonsson P, Svensson O (2008) Gender differences in facial imitation and verbally reported emotional contagion from spontaneous to emotionally regulated processing levels. Scand J Psychol 49: 111–122.
38. Newman JP, Curtin JJ, Bertsch JD, Baskin-Sommers AR (2010) Attention moderates the fearlessness of psychopathic offenders. Biol Psychiatry 67: 66–70.
39. Dadds MR, Perry Y, Hawes DJ, Merz S, Riddell AC, et al. (2006) Attention to the eyes and fear-recognition deficits in child psychopathy. British Journal of Psychiatry 189: 280–281.

15

Prenatal Origins of Temperament: Fetal Growth, Brain Structure, and Inhibitory Control in Adolescence

Wolff Schlotz[1,2,3]*, Keith M. Godfrey[2,4], David I. Phillips[2]

1 Institute of Psychology, University of Regensburg, Regensburg, Germany, 2 MRC Lifecourse Epidemiology Unit, Southampton, United Kingdom, 3 Faculty of Social and Human Sciences, University of Southampton, Southampton, United Kingdom, 4 NIHR Southampton Biomedical Research Centre, University of Southampton and University Hospital Southampton NHS Foundation Trust, Southampton, United Kingdom

Abstract

Objective: Individual differences in the temperamental dimension of effortful control are constitutionally based and have been associated with an adverse prenatal developmental environment, with structural brain alterations presenting a potential mechanism. We investigated this hypothesis for anatomically defined brain regions implicated in cognitive and inhibitory motor control.

Methods: Twenty-seven 15–16 year old participants with low, medium, or high fetal growth were selected from a longitudinal birth cohort to maximize variation and represent the full normal spectrum of fetal growth. Outcome measures were parent ratings of attention and inhibitory control, thickness and surface area of the orbitofrontal cortex (lateral (LOFC) and medial (MOFC)) and right inferior frontal gyrus (rIFG), and volumetric measures of the striatum and amygdala.

Results: Lower birth weight was associated with lower inhibitory control, smaller surface area of LOFC, MOFC and rIFG, lower caudate volume, and thicker MOFC. A mediation model found a significant indirect effect of birth weight on inhibitory control via caudate volume.

Conclusions: Our findings support a neuroanatomical mechanism underlying potential long-term consequences of an adverse fetal developmental environment for behavioral inhibitory control in adolescence and have implications for understanding putative prenatal developmental origins of externalizing behavioral problems and self-control.

Editor: Cornelis B. Lambalk, VU University Medical Center, Netherlands

Funding: This work was supported by grants from the Medical Research Council and Wessex Medical Research. Subjects were drawn from a cohort study originally funded by Wellbeing of Women. WS was supported by German Research Foundation (Deutsche Forschungsgemeinschaft) fellowship grant DFG SCHl 1708/1-1. KMG is supported by the National Institute for Health Research through the NIHR Southampton Biomedical Research Centre. The funders had no role in study design, data collection and analysis, decision to publish, or preparation of the manuscript.

Competing Interests: The authors have declared that no competing interests exist.

* E-mail: wolff.schlotz@ur.de

Introduction

Effortful control (EC) is a temperamental dimension that describes individual differences in self-regulation, or the ability to exert behavioral control, including attentional focusing and inhibitory control [1]. Children and adolescents high in EC are able to inhibit a dominant response or activate a subdominant response, to maintain a sustained focus of attention, and to plan behavior. Individual differences in EC are likely to affect individual adjustment, success, health and well-being later in life. For example, low EC has been shown to be a risk factor for both internalizing and externalizing problems [2,3,4,5,6], might have evocative effects on mother's teaching strategies [7], and influence academic development [8]. Recently, a related but broader construct of self-control in childhood, including lack of control, persistence and attention as well as impulsivity, has been shown to predict adult physical health, substance dependence, personal finances and criminal offending [9]. Because of such broad and substantial potential consequences, investigating the origins of individual differences in EC is of high relevance.

Differences in EC are thought to be constitutionally based, which implies a biological basis. It has been suggested that genetic factors as well as maturation and experience are the primary factors affecting individual differences in EC [1]. Besides these factors, individual differences in behavior and mental health have been associated with an adverse prenatal developmental environment [10,11]. Birth weight across the full normal range is an indicator of prenatal adversity and has been associated with EC and executive functions in children [12,13,14]. In addition, a number of studies demonstrated associations of birth weight with symptoms of attention-deficit/hyperactivity disorder (ADHD) [12,15,16,17,18,19,20]. Because EC and ADHD symptoms are conceptually and empirically related [3,21], we have suggested that EC might mediate the association between prenatal adversity and ADHD symptoms [12].

However, the mechanisms underlying the association between birth weight and EC are unknown. A number of studies recently demonstrated associations between birth weight and global and regional brain morphology across the full normal range of birth weight in broad age samples including children, adolescents and adults [22,23,24]. Structural changes in brain development might be associated with individual differences in temperamental traits such as EC later in life [12,25]. In this study, we explore if specific alterations in brain structure might present a mechanism for putative fetal origins of EC in adolescence.

It has been suggested that EC is based on the executive attention network, which is involved in resolving conflict between other brain networks and is thought to underlie cognitive and emotional self-regulation [26]. Functional neuroimaging of activation during tasks that require cognitive control or response inhibition suggested that the executive attention network consists of the anterior cingulate cortex (ACC) and prefrontal, particularly orbitofrontal, cortical areas [26,27]. Consistently, effortful control has been shown to be associated with left orbitofrontal cortex (OFC) volume in adolescents [25], and structural deficits in ADHD have repeatedly been observed in OFC and anterior cingulate areas [28].

However, as mentioned above, EC is a heterogeneous construct including lower order facets, particularly attention and inhibitory control. Akin to this heterogeneity it has been suggested that executive attention functions, reflected in anterior cingulate activation, should be distinguished from executive motor control [29], or, similarly, cognitive control from control over overt behavior, e.g. motor inhibition and impulse control [30]. Inhibitory motor control has been shown to implicate prefrontal cortical areas and fronto-striatal circuits, with the right inferior frontal gyrus (rIFG) and striatum, particularly caudate, thought to be important areas for effective response inhibition [31,32,33,34,35]. Support for the relevance of a fronto-striatal pathway in inhibitory motor control comes from observations of activation in the lateral and medial frontal cortex, putamen and caudate during response inhibition tasks [36,37,38,39,40,41]; deficits in volumes of prefrontal cortical and basal ganglia structures in ADHD patients [28,32,42,43]; and correlations of frontal gray matter and caudate volume with physician and parent ratings of ADHD symptoms [44]. In addition, higher ratings on nonplanning, motor and cognitive impulsivity were associated with higher bilateral caudate activity during an inhibitory control task [39] and lower OFC volume [45,46,47]. In support of the notion that prenatal factors might affect the development of this pathway, a recent study has demonstrated shape contraction and smaller volume of the caudate bilaterally in boys with relatively low birth weight born at a short gestational age [48], and birth weight was shown to be correlated with caudate volume in another study [22].

In addition, a number of studies suggested a neural basis for impulse control based on a circuit including ventromedial prefrontal cortex (VMPFC), anterior cingulate cortex (ACC) and amygdala [39,49]. As impulsivity is a construct closely related to (low) inhibitory control, this circuit might also be implicated in long-term effects of prenatal adversity on inhibitory control, and recent data has reported a link between prenatal maternal depression and lower fractional anisotropy and axial diffusivity in the right amygdala of infants at birth (but no association with amygdala volume) [50], as well as associations between maternal cortisol levels in early gestation and child left amygdala volume at 7 years of age [51].

Based on these findings we hypothesized that an adverse prenatal developmental environment might lead to deficits in attention and inhibitory control in adolescence, and that such associations would be based on effects of prenatal adversity on brain development resulting in specific structural changes. The aim of our study was to investigate in a longitudinal birth cohort (1) whether birth weight across the normal spectrum (an indicator of fetal adversity) is associated with attention and inhibitory control in adolescence, and (2) if structural characteristics of OFC, rIFG, ACC, striatum and amygdala statistically mediate such associations.

Materials and Methods

Study design and participants

This is a follow-up study of children of mothers recruited for a longitudinal birth cohort study at 17 or less weeks of gestation at the Princess Anne Maternity Hospital in Southampton, UK [52]. A subgroup of 139 singleton children was recruited for a study when they were 7–9 years old [53,54]. For the follow-up study reported here, families of this subsample were contacted again when the children were approximately 14–15 years old. The local NHS National Research Ethics Service Committee Oxfordshire REC B approved the study and both parent and children gave written informed consent. Participants received a reimbursement of £140 to cover travel costs and their time invested.

Data on birth weight and gestational age were used to generate groups of participants to be recruited for the MRI study with the aim of having the full normal spectrum of fetal growth represented by the sample. In a first step, five participants born before the 37th week of gestation were excluded to prevent any confounding effect of preterm birth. The remaining 134 participants were then allocated to five groups based on sex-specific fetal growth (FG; birth weight adjusted for gestational age) by regressing birth weight on gestational age and using quintiles of the residuals for group allocation separately for males and females. This resulted in equally sized groups of low FG (n = 27), low-medium FG (n = 27), medium FG (n = 27), medium-high FG (n = 27) and high FG (n = 26). To represent the full normal spectrum of FG and increase power of the hypothesis tests only those 80 participants in the low, medium and high FG groups were included in the study. Of those, addresses of 27 were not traceable; the remaining participants were contacted by telephone and screened for exclusion criteria. Twenty-four participants were excluded because they wore dental braces (n = 6), did not want to participate (n = 12), reported symptoms of claustrophobia (n = 2), had metal implants (n = 2) or suffered from epilepsy (n = 1), and one participant was surplus to requirements. Thus, 29 adolescents were recruited into the MRI study. After MRI scanning, one participant was excluded due to poor image quality, and one participant had a very small total brain volume at 2.5 SD below the sample mean and therefore was excluded from all brain analyses. Thus, the resulting total sample size was $n = 27$ ($n_{lowFG} = 8$; $n_{mediumFG} = 12$; $n_{highFG} = 7$). The 27 participants included in the study did not differ from the 53 excluded in terms of age, sex, birth weight, and gestational age (all *p*s>.24).

Measurements

Data collected at birth. At birth, the infant's weight was measured using digital scales; the infant's gestational age at birth was calculated from the date of the last menstrual period, confirmed by ultrasound [52].

Temperamental factors. Inhibitory control and attention were measured by parent reports on two subscales of the Early Adolescent Temperament Questionnaire – Revised (EATQ-R) [55]. The scale Attention measures the capacity to focus and shift attention when desired (6 items; Cronbach's alpha = .81). Item examples are "Finds it easy to really concentrate on a problem" and "When interrupted or distracted, forgets what s/he was about to say" (reverse scored). The scale Inhibitory Control measures the capacity to plan and to suppress inappropriate responses (5 items; Cronbach's alpha = .58). Item examples are "Has a hard time waiting his/her turn to speak when excited" (reverse scored), and "Is usually able to stick with his/her plans and goals". The scores on the two scales in this sample correlated significantly ($r = .50$, $p = .006$).

MR imaging

Imaging data were acquired at the Oxford Centre for Clinical Magnetic Resonance Research, John Radcliffe Hospital, Oxford, UK, on a 3.0 Tesla TIM Trio scanner (Siemens, Erlangen, Germany). T1-weighted structural images for the structural analysis were acquired using a 3D magnetization prepared rapid gradient echo (MPRAGE) sequence. The voxel resolution was $1 \times 1 \times 1$ mm^3 with an acquisition matrix of $174 \times 192 \times 192$ and the following parameters: TR = 2040 ms; TE = 4.7 ms; inversion time (TI) = 900 ms; flip angle = 8°. Acquisition duration for this sequence was 5 min and 56 s. The sequence was acquired twice during the same session for each adolescent.

Image analysis

Cortical reconstruction and volumetric segmentation was performed with the FreeSurfer v5.1.0 imaging analysis suite (https://surfer.nmr.mgh.harvard.edu). This process included motion correction and averaging of the two T1-weighted images acquired for each subject, removal of non-brain tissue, and segmentation of white matter and subcortical grey matter volumetric structures [56]. Cortical thickness and surface area were obtained by reconstructing the grey/white matter boundary and the pial surface of the cortex [56]. Cortical thickness was calculated as the closest distance from the grey/white matter boundary to the pial surface at each surface location. Average cerebral cortical thickness and area for regions of interest (ROIs) were based on automated parcellation of the cortex into units based on gyral and sulcal structure using the Desikan-Killiany atlas [57]. Total brain volume was calculated by the volume of all brain labels [56].

Anatomical cortical ROIs were defined as the medial orbitofrontal cortex (MOFC), lateral orbitofrontal cortex (LOFC), ACC (comprising rostral and caudal anterior cingulate) and rIFG (comprising pars opercularis, pars triangularis and pars orbitalis). Exact anatomical boundaries and reliability of the parcellation are described elsewhere [57]. Average cortical thickness (CT) and surface area (SA) of these ROIs were used for hypothesis testing. Volumetric subcortical segmentation was based on validated automated procedures [56]; subcortical ROIs comprised the striatal areas of caudate, putamen and pallidum, and the amygdala. Figure 1 shows the ROIs for this study. Apart from rIGF, we used the total (left + right) CT, SA or volume of the structures, as we had no *a priori* hypotheses on hemisphere specificity. In addition, results of an exploratory whole-brain analysis are shown in the supporting information (for results of surface area analysis see Figure S1 in File S1; for results of cortical thickness analysis see Figures S2 and S3, both in File S1).

Statistical analysis

The main analysis focused on a potential mediating effect of structural brain characteristics for associations between fetal adversity and behavioral measures of attention and inhibitory control. Indicators of average CT, SA and volume were exported from FreeSurfer into Stata v12.1 (StataCorp, College Station, Texas). We used birth weight as a continuous predictor of brain structure and behaviour in hierarchical least squares multiple linear regression models. Potential mediation effects were tested by estimating path models including indirect effects using Mplus v6.11 (Muthén & Muthén, Los Angeles, California). Tests were conducted in the following order. First, associations between birth weight and behavioral measures (attention, behavioral inhibition) were tested. Second, associations between fetal adversity and brain structure in adolescence were tested by regressing structural brain characteristics of the ROIs defined above on birth weight. Third, behavioral measures were regressed on those structural brain indicators that showed significant associations with birth weight in the step before. All three association tests should reveal statistically significant associations for a mediating effect to be plausible. Therefore, mediation models were tested only for those behavioral measures and brain structures that fulfilled these criteria. To control for potential sex differences in birth weight and brain structure, all analyses were adjusted for sex. Brain analyses were additionally adjusted for intracranial volume (ICV) by including ICV as a covariate into the regression. To explore potential prenatal and postnatal confounding variables, we also included maternal smoking and drinking alcohol during pregnancy, parity and social class as covariates in additional models. All hypotheses were tested using a significance level of $p < .05$.

Results

Table 1 shows characteristics of the study participants. Gender proportions were similar in the three groups (Fisher's exact test, $p = .90$), and mean age did not significantly differ between the groups ($F = 0.22$, $p = .80$). As intended by design, groups had a similar mean gestational age ($F = 0.32$, $p = .73$), whereas mean birth weight differed between groups (Low v Medium FG: $t = 2.67$, $p = .016$; Low v High FG: $t = 5.37$, $p < .001$; Medium v High FG: $t = 4.79$, $p < .001$). Thus, the total sample represents fetal growth adjusted for gestational age across the full normal spectrum of birth weight.

Birth weight and behavior

Birth weight significantly predicted inhibitory control ($\beta = 0.41$, $p = .043$, $\Delta R^2 = .15$), but not attention ($\beta = 0.06$, $p = .76$). Thus, consistent with our hypothesis, adolescents born at higher birth weight showed more behavior indicative of higher inhibitory control as reported by their parents, with birth weight explaining 15% of the variance in inhibitory control. In contrast, attention was not significantly related to fetal growth. Adjusting the models for maternal smoking, drinking alcohol, parity and social class did not change the results (supporting information, Table S1 in File S1).

Birth weight and brain structure

Birth weight was positively associated with total brain volume ($\beta = 0.33$, $p = .001$, $\Delta R^2 = .10$), total gray matter ($\beta = 0.26$, $p = .023$, $\Delta R^2 = .06$) and white matter volume ($\beta = 0.34$, $p = .022$, $\Delta R^2 = .10$).

Table 2 shows the results of regressions of cortical ROIs on birth weight. Whereas adolescents born at a higher birth weight showed larger SA in rIFG and both medial and lateral OFC, no significant associations were observed for ACC. Birth weight was also significantly negatively related to thickness of the medial OFC, explaining between 10 and 22% of variance in cortex morphology. Figure 2 illustrates the statistically significant associations found.

Results of regression analysis testing associations of birth weight with volumes of subcortical ROIs are shown in Table 3. Caudate volume showed a significant positive association, with birth weight explaining 21% of the variance in caudate volume. This effect is illustrated Figure 2. In contrast, volumes of the other investigated subcortical structures were not significantly related to birth weight.

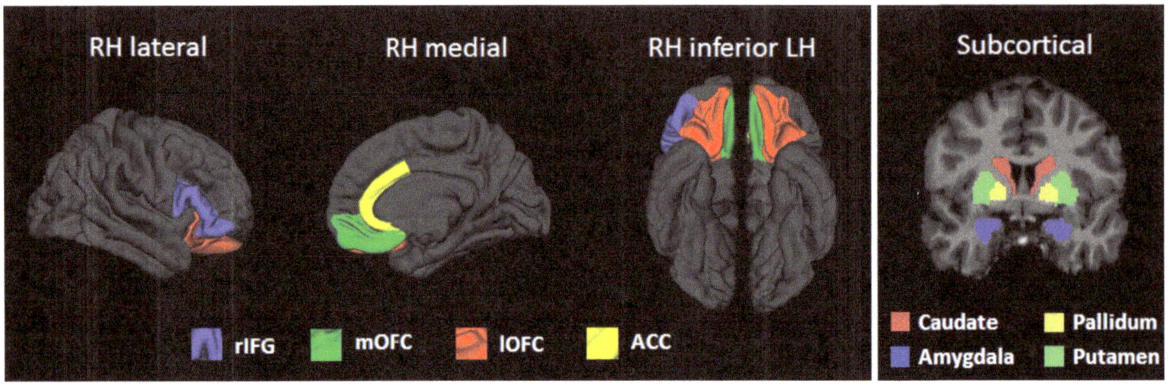

Figure 1. Cortical and subcortical anatomical target regions of interest (ROIs) for this study. LH: Left hemisphere; RH: Right hemisphere; rIFG: Right inferior frontal gyrus; LOFC: lateral orbitofrontal cortex; MOFC: medial orbitofrontal cortex; ACC: Anterior cingulate cortex.

Adjusting the models for maternal smoking, drinking alcohol, parity and social class did not change the results (supplemental material, Table S1 in File S1).

Inhibitory control, birth weight and brain structure

Results so far suggest SA of rIFG, LOFC and MOFC, CT of MOFC, and caudate volume as potential mediators of the relationship between birth weight and inhibitory control. To establish a potential mediational path, we next tested for associations between these structural indices and inhibitory control scores. Regression models showed no significant relationship for any of the cortical structures, all explaining almost no variance in inhibitory control (rIFG SA: $\beta = 0.06$, $p = .82$, $\Delta R^2 = .00$; LOFC SA: $\beta = 0.09$, $p = .71$, $\Delta R^2 = .01$; MOFC SA: $\beta = 0.05$, $p = .85$, $\Delta R^2 = .00$; MOFC CT: $\beta = -0.03$, $p = .89$, $\Delta R^2 = .00$). In contrast, caudate volume was significantly and positively associated with inhibitory control, explaining 20% of variance ($\beta = 0.53$, $p = .015$, $\Delta R^2 = .20$), thus qualifying as a potential mediator of the relationship between birth weight and inhibitory control.

A formal mediation test using path analysis tested the indirect effect of birth weight on inhibitory control via caudate volume (Figure 3). Confirming results presented above, paths from birth weight to caudate and from caudate to inhibitory control were highly significant, and the initially significant association between birth weight and inhibitory control became non-significant when caudate volume was entered in the model. The model confirmed that the indirect pathway effect from birth weight to inhibitory control via caudate volume was significant (indirect $\beta = 0.29$; $p = .025$).

Discussion

The results of our study suggest that an adverse fetal developmental environment, indicated by fetal growth across the full normal spectrum, may affect inhibitory control in adolescence, and that this effect may be mediated through subtle changes in subcortical brain structures involved in executive motor control.

Of the two facets of effortful control studied here, only inhibitory control and not attention was associated with birth weight. Whether this is due to methodological factors (e.g. limited statistical power; parent report rating scales as opposed to self-report ratings or cognitive tests; differences in measurement reliability), or reflects specificity in long-term consequences of fetal adversity in adolescence is not clear. For inhibitory control we were able to detect a significant indirect effect of birth weight via caudate volume, suggesting that fetal adversity might be linked to behavior in adolescence via alterations in brain development.

We found that birth weight was positively associated with total brain, gray and white matter volume, as well as cortical surface area in both LOFC and MOFC, and in rIFG. With regards to subcortical structures, birth weight was positively associated with caudate volume, but not with other striatal areas or the amygdala.

Table 1. Characteristics of the sample as represented by three groups of fetal growth.

	Low FG group (n = 8)	Medium FG group (n = 12)	High FG group (n = 7)
Age (years)[a]	16.0 (0.36)	15.9 (0.41)	16.0 (0.34)
Age range (years)	15.4–16-6	15.1–16.4	15.5–16.4
Female[b]	3 (37%)	6 (50%)	4 (50%)
Birth weight (kg)[a]	3.2 (0.49)	3.5 (0.28)	4.1 (0.26)
Birth weight range (kg)	2.4–3.6	3.1–4.2	3.7–4.5
Gestational age (weeks)[a]	40.3 (1.56)	39.8 (1.36)	40.1 (1.56)
Gestational age range (weeks)	37.9–42.3	38.1–43.3	38.1–41.7

Note that the only statistically significant differences between groups was in birth weight (see text for details).
[a]M (SD);
[b]n (%); FG: Fetal growth.

Table 2. Associations of birth weight with bilateral structural measures of cortical regions of interest.

	Surface area			Cortical thickness		
	β	p	ΔR²	β	p	ΔR²
LOFC	**0.45**	**.010**	**.17**	−0.24	.24	.05
MOFC	**0.35**	**.029**	**.11**	**−0.51**	**.016**	**.22**
rIFG	**0.35**	**.035**	**.10**	−0.02	.93	.00
ACC	0.24	.20	.05	−0.06	.79	.00

Note. Adjusted for sex and intracranial volume. LOFC: lateral orbitofrontal cortex; MOFC: medial orbitofrontal cortex; rIFG: Right inferior frontal gyrus; ACC: Anterior cingulate cortex.

These findings are largely consistent with recent studies in larger samples that found birth weight effects for surface areas similar to our frontal cortical ROIs [22,23,24] as well as caudate volume [22,48]. Associations in our study reflect relatively large effects with 10–22% of variance in brain structure explained by birth weight. In comparison, Walhovd and colleagues [22] reported effects that explained 3% of variance in total brain volume and 4% in caudate volume. A number of study design factors are possible reasons for the larger effects found in our study. First, we residualized birth weight for gestational age and our results therefore more accurately reflect effects of fetal growth. Second, we selected participants from three groups representing the full spectrum of fetal growth; including the extreme groups might have increased statistical power in our study. Finally, we used data from a longitudinal birth cohort with birth weight recordings done at birth by nurses using digital scales, as opposed to birth weights being recalled by parents or participants at the time of the neuroimaging session, thus reducing unsystematic variance due to recall bias. Nevertheless, our study still had limited statistical power due to the relatively small sample, which might explain some of our negative findings.

In contrast to cortical surface area, a significant association with cortical thickness was found only for the MOFC. Adolescents with lower fetal growth had a thicker MOFC averaged across hemispheres. This finding is consistent with earlier studies of samples covering childhood to young adult age groups showing that cortical thickness was not or only very weakly associated with indicators of fetal growth in both monozygotic and dizygotic twins [23], in a larger sample of adolescents [22], and in both schizophrenia patients and healthy controls [24]. In children and adolescents born small-for-gestational age, thickening of frontal cortical areas was found, although the effects where rather small [58,59]. As brain development is characterized by progressive cortical thinning during adolescence [60] these results might indicate a maturational delay of orbitofrontal cortex in adolescents with low fetal growth. Alternatively, the weak associations found here might be due to opposing effects of fetal growth and overall brain size on cortical thickness. However, we also found birth

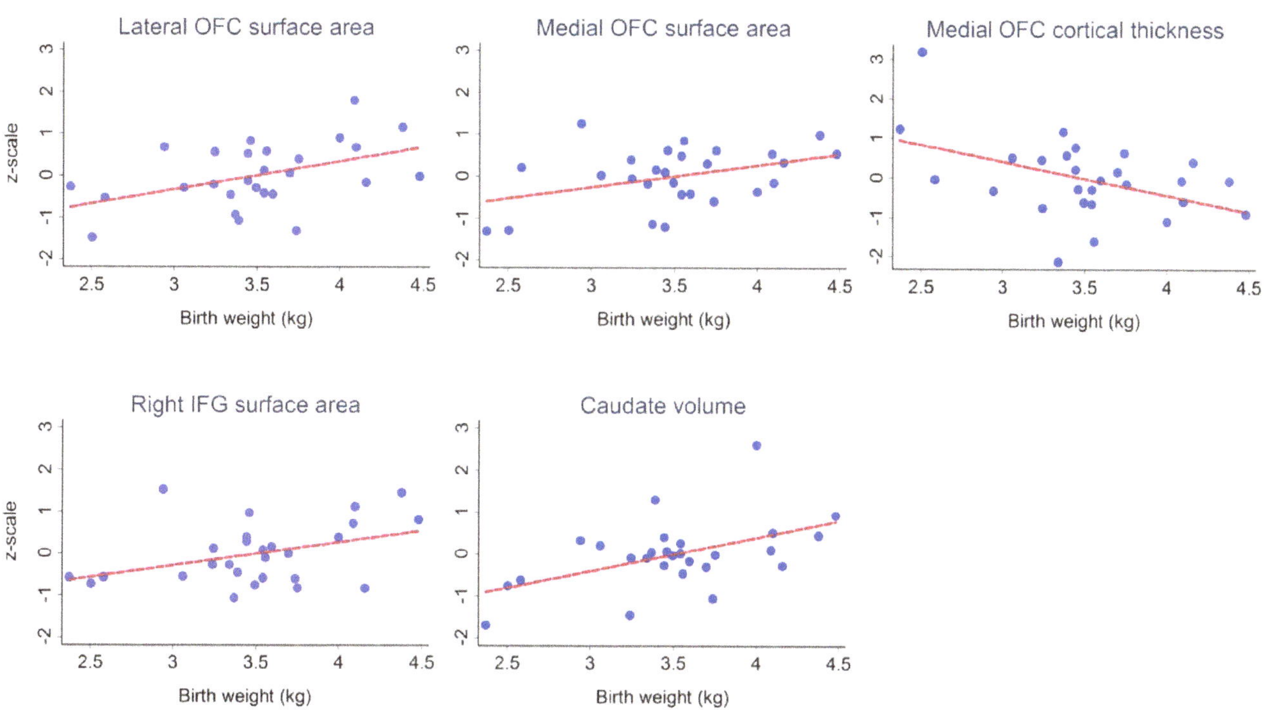

Figure 2. Scatter plots showing statistically significant associations between birth weight and neuroanatomical variables residualized for sex and intracranial volume.

Table 3. Associations of birth weight with volume of subcortical gray matter regions of interest.

	β	p	ΔR^2
Amygdala	0.03	.90	.00
Caudate	**0.50**	**.005**	**.21**
Putamen	−0.01	.95	.00
Pallidum	0.11	.55	.01

Note. Adjusted for sex and intracranial volume.

weight to be more strongly, and positively, associated with white matter volume than gray matter volume. Although speculative, together with our cortical thickness finding this could indicate a less extensive architecture of white matter tracts in adolescents with low fetal growth, suggesting that future studies examining connectivity of gray and white matter areas using Diffusion Tensor Imaging might reveal important additional information on potential effects of fetal adversity on brain structure in adolescence.

It has been suggested that the striatum is particularly vulnerable to perinatal hypoxic-ischemic events [61] and intraventricular hemorrhage [33], leading to reduced cognitive and behavioral control in affected individuals. In addition, experimental animal studies have shown that an adverse intrauterine environment due to hypoxic-ischemic injury and inflammatory insults can lead to neuronal death, white matter damage, and reduced brain growth [62,63]. In guinea pigs, reduced uteroplacental blood flow has been shown to lead to reduced brain weight and reduced basal ganglia volume lasting into adolescence [64]. Therefore, long-term consequences of fetal adversity are possible and the behavioral consequences suggested by our results are plausible. However, what remains unclear is to what extent our findings represent maturational delay or impairment of normal brain development. Also, our study does not allow any causal conclusions, as alternative explanations cannot be ruled out. It is well known that genetic and postnatal environmental factors contribute to brain development [65,66]. As effects of birth weight on brain structure where demonstrated within monozygotic twin pairs [23], genetic effects seem to be an unlikely alternative explanation. Including maternal smoking and drinking alcohol, parity and social class in our models did not change any of the associations observed. However, continuation of adversity in postnatal life and residual confounding variables could not be controlled in more detail in our study.

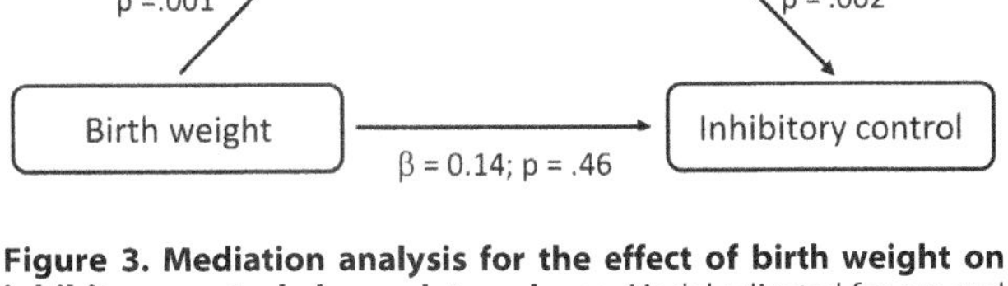

Figure 3. Mediation analysis for the effect of birth weight on inhibitory control via caudate volume. Model adjusted for sex and intracranial volume. Coefficients shown are standardized regression coefficients. The total indirect effect of birth weight on inhibitory control was statistically significant at p = .025. Omitting caudate volume from the analysis, birth weight was associated with inhibitory control, β = 0.41, p = .043.

The finding of a positive association between caudate volume and inhibitory control in daily life is consistent with neuroscience models that postulate a major involvement of striatal areas in inhibitory motor control [33,34,41,67,68] and findings of reduced caudate volume in ADHD [69]. However, contrary to our expectations, none of the other brain structures investigated were associated with inhibitory control. This could be due to limited reliability of the behavioral scale, limited statistical power, or it might indicate structural differences that do not translate into function. Using fMRI with an inhibitory control task could provide some clarification of this question, which might be highly relevant as the neural mechanisms of stopping have an effect on the broader construct of self-control [67], which itself is associated with behavioral problems, adjustment, and health and wealth later in life [2,9].

The main limitations of our study were the relatively low internal consistency of the Inhibitory Control scale and limited statistical power due to a relatively small sample. The internal consistency of a scale is dependent on the number of items and the observed scale score variance. For a short scale of five items and a relatively homogenous and small sample the internal consistency observed in this study can be considered acceptable for a group study. Nevertheless, both limitations mean that some relevant associations might have been missed.

In summary, this study demonstrated that an adverse fetal developmental environment might lead to reduced inhibitory control in adolescence, and that reduced caudate volume might mediate this association. As inhibitory control is an integral part of self-control, identifying such pathways originating in prenatal life might in the future help to improve well-being through targeted early preventative action such as educational or nutritional intervention [70,71,72]. However, the exact mechanisms by which prenatal factors might affect behavior and well-being later in life first need to be defined more clearly. Concerning brain development, future studies need to investigate additional effects of fetal adversity such as alterations of neural connectivity and differential functional activation of potentially relevant areas.

Supporting Information

File S1 Combined supporting information, containing results of vertex-wise analyses (Figures S1, S2, and S3) and results of adjustment for potentially confounding covariates (Table S1).

Acknowledgments

We acknowledge generous assistance from Professor Irene Tracey and the Oxford Centre for Clinical Magnetic Resonance Research, John Radcliffe Hospital, Oxford, UK.

Author Contributions

Conceived and designed the experiments: WS KMG DIP. Performed the experiments: WS. Analyzed the data: WS. Wrote the paper: WS KMG DIP.

References

1. Rothbart MK, Bates JE (2006) Temperament. In: Damon W, Lerner R, Eisenberg N, editors.Handbook of child psychology. 6th ed.New York: Wiley. pp. 99–166.
2. Eisenberg N, Spinrad TL, Fabes RA, Reiser M, Cumberland A, et al. (2004) The relations of effortful control and impulsivity to children's resiliency and adjustment. Child Dev 75: 25–46.
3. Nigg JT (2006) Temperament and developmental psychopathology. J Child Psychol Psychiatry 47: 395–422.
4. Olson SL, Sameroff AJ, Kerr DC, Lopez NL, Wellman HM (2005) Developmental foundations of externalizing problems in young children: the role of effortful control. Dev Psychopathol 17: 25–45.
5. Lengua LJ, Bush NR, Long AC, Kovacs EA, Trancik AM (2008) Effortful control as a moderator of the relation between contextual risk factors and growth in adjustment problems. Dev Psychopathol 20: 509–528.
6. Ormel J, Oldehinkel AJ, Ferdinand RF, Hartman CA, De Winter AF, et al. (2005) Internalizing and externalizing problems in adolescence: general and dimension-specific effects of familial loadings and preadolescent temperament traits. Psychol Med 35: 1825–1835.
7. Eisenberg N, Vidmar M, Spinrad TL, Eggum ND, Edwards A, et al. (2010) Mothers' teaching strategies and children's effortful control: A longitudinal study. Dev Psychol 46: 1294–1308.
8. Blair C, Razza RP (2007) Relating effortful control, executive function, and false belief understanding to emerging math and literacy ability in kindergarten. Child Dev 78: 647–663.
9. Moffitt TE, Arseneault L, Belsky D, Dickson N, Hancox RJ, et al. (2011) A gradient of childhood self-control predicts health, wealth, and public safety. Proc Natl Acad Sci U S A 108: 2693–2698.
10. Schlotz W, Phillips DI (2009) Fetal origins of mental health: Evidence and mechanisms. Brain Behav Immun 23: 905–916.
11. Räikkönen K, Pesonen A-K, Roseboom TJ, Eriksson JG (2012) Early determinants of mental health. Best Practice & Research Clinical Endocrinology & Metabolism 26: 599–611.
12. Schlotz W, Jones A, Godfrey KM, Phillips DI (2008) Effortful control mediates associations of fetal growth with hyperactivity and behavioural problems in 7- to 9-year-old children. J Child Psychol Psychiatry 49: 1228–1236.
13. Phua DY, Rifkin-Graboi A, Saw SM, Meaney MJ, Qiu A (2012) Executive functions of six-year-old boys with normal birth weight and gestational age. PLoS ONE 7: e36502.
14. Li-Grining CP (2007) Effortful control among low-income preschoolers in three cities: Stability, change, and individual differences. Dev Psychol 43: 208–221.
15. Lahti J, Raikkonen K, Kajantie E, Heinonen K, Pesonen AK, et al. (2006) Small body size at birth and behavioural symptoms of ADHD in children aged five to six years. J Child Psychol Psychiatry 47: 1167–1174.
16. Heinonen K, Raikkonen K, Pesonen AK, Andersson S, Kajantie E, et al. (2010) Behavioural symptoms of attention deficit/hyperactivity disorder in preterm and term children born small and appropriate for gestational age: a longitudinal study. BMC Pediatr 10: 91.
17. Hultman CM, Torrang A, Tuvblad C, Cnattingius S, Larsson JO, et al. (2007) Birth Weight and Attention-Deficit/Hyperactivity Symptoms in Childhood and Early Adolescence: A Prospective Swedish Twin Study. J Am Acad Child Adolesc Psychiatry 46: 370–377.
18. Linnet KM, Wisborg K, Agerbo E, Secher NJ, Thomsen PH, et al. (2006) Gestational age, birth weight, and the risk of hyperkinetic disorder. Arch Dis Child 91: 655–660.
19. Wiles NJ, Peters TJ, Heron J, Gunnell D, Emond A, et al. (2006) Fetal growth and childhood behavioral problems: results from the ALSPAC cohort. Am J Epidemiol 163: 829–837.
20. Halmoy A, Klungsoyr K, Skjaerven R, Haavik J (2012) Pre- and perinatal risk factors in adults with attention-deficit/hyperactivity disorder. Biol Psychiatry 71: 474–481.
21. Martel MM, Gremillion ML, Roberts B (2012) Temperament and Common Disruptive Behavior Problems in Preschool. Pers Ind Diff 53: 874–879.
22. Walhovd KB, Fjell AM, Brown TT, Kuperman JM, Chung Y, et al. (2012) Long-term influence of normal variation in neonatal characteristics on human brain development. Proc Natl Acad Sci U S A 109: 20089–20094.
23. Raznahan A, Greenstein D, Lee NR, Clasen LS, Giedd JN (2012) Prenatal growth in humans and postnatal brain maturation into late adolescence. Proc Natl Acad Sci U S A 109: 11366–11371.
24. Haukvik UK, Rimol LM, Roddey JC, Hartberg CB, Lange EH, et al. (2014) Normal Birth Weight Variation Is Related to Cortical Morphology Across the Psychosis Spectrum. Schizophr Bull 40: 410–419.
25. Whittle S, Yucel M, Fornito A, Barrett A, Wood SJ, et al. (2008) Neuroanatomical correlates of temperament in early adolescents. J Am Acad Child Adolesc Psychiatry 47: 682–693.
26. Rothbart MK, Sheese BE, Posner MI (2007) Executive Attention and Effortful Control: Linking Temperament, Brain Networks, and Genes. Child Dev Perspect 1: 2–7.
27. Horn NR, Dolan M, Elliott R, Deakin JF, Woodruff PW (2003) Response inhibition and impulsivity: an fMRI study. Neuropsychologia 41: 1959–1966.
28. Cubillo A, Halari R, Smith A, Taylor E, Rubia K (2012) A review of fronto-striatal and fronto-cortical brain abnormalities in children and adults with Attention Deficit Hyperactivity Disorder (ADHD) and new evidence for dysfunction in adults with ADHD during motivation and attention. Cortex 48: 194–215.
29. Nigg JT (2000) On inhibition/disinhibition in developmental psychopathology: views from cognitive and personality psychology and a working inhibition taxonomy. Psychol Bull 126: 220–246.
30. Aron AR (2007) The neural basis of inhibition in cognitive control. Neuroscientist 13: 214–228.
31. Jahfari S, Waldorp L, van den Wildenberg WP, Scholte HS, Ridderinkhof KR, et al. (2011) Effective connectivity reveals important roles for both the hyperdirect (fronto-subthalamic) and the indirect (fronto-striatal-pallidal) fronto-basal ganglia pathways during response inhibition. J Neurosci 31: 6891–6899.
32. Chambers CD, Garavan H, Bellgrove MA (2009) Insights into the neural basis of response inhibition from cognitive and clinical neuroscience. Neurosci Biobehav Rev 33: 631–646.
33. Casey BJ, Tottenham N, Fossella J (2002) Clinical, imaging, lesion, and genetic approaches toward a model of cognitive control. Dev Psychobiol 40: 237–254.
34. Wiecki TV, Frank MJ (2013) A computational model of inhibitory control in frontal cortex and basal ganglia. Psychol Rev 120: 329–355.
35. Aron AR, Behrens TE, Smith S, Frank MJ, Poldrack RA (2007) Triangulating a cognitive control network using diffusion-weighted magnetic resonance imaging (MRI) and functional MRI. J Neurosci 27: 3743–3752.
36. Casey BJ, Castellanos FX, Giedd JN, Marsh WL, Hamburger SD, et al. (1997) Implication of right frontostriatal circuitry in response inhibition and attention-deficit/hyperactivity disorder. J Am Acad Child Adolesc Psychiatry 36: 374–383.
37. Chikazoe J, Jimura K, Asari T, Yamashita K, Morimoto H, et al. (2009) Functional dissociation in right inferior frontal cortex during performance of go/no-go task. Cereb Cortex 19: 146–152.
38. Durston S, Thomas KM, Yang Y, Uluğ AM, Zimmerman RD, et al. (2002) A neural basis for the development of inhibitory control. Developmental Science 5: F9–F16.
39. Brown SM, Manuck SB, Flory JD, Hariri AR (2006) Neural basis of individual differences in impulsivity: contributions of corticolimbic circuits for behavioral arousal and control. Emotion 6: 239–245.
40. Rubia K, Smith AB, Brammer MJ, Taylor E (2003) Right inferior prefrontal cortex mediates response inhibition while mesial prefrontal cortex is responsible for error detection. Neuroimage 20: 351–358.
41. Li CS, Yan P, Sinha R, Lee TW (2008) Subcortical processes of motor response inhibition during a stop signal task. Neuroimage 41: 1352–1363.
42. Durston S, Hulshoff Pol HE, Schnack HG, Buitelaar JK, Steenhuis MP, et al. (2004) Magnetic resonance imaging of boys with attention-deficit/hyperactivity disorder and their unaffected siblings. J Am Acad Child Adolesc Psychiatry 43: 332–340.
43. Sowell ER, Thompson PM, Welcome SE, Henkenius AL, Toga AW, et al. (2003) Cortical abnormalities in children and adolescents with attention-deficit hyperactivity disorder. Lancet 362: 1699–1707.
44. Castellanos FX, Lee PP, Sharp W, Jeffries NO, Greenstein DK, et al. (2002) Developmental trajectories of brain volume abnormalities in children and adolescents with attention-deficit/hyperactivity disorder. JAMA 288: 1740–1748.
45. Matsuo K, Nicoletti M, Nemoto K, Hatch JP, Peluso MA, et al. (2009) A voxel-based morphometry study of frontal gray matter correlates of impulsivity. Hum Brain Mapp 30: 1188–1195.
46. Schilling C, Kuhn S, Romanowski A, Banaschewski T, Barbot A, et al. (2013) Common structural correlates of trait impulsiveness and perceptual reasoning in adolescence. Hum Brain Mapp 34: 374–383.
47. Boes AD, Bechara A, Tranel D, Anderson SW, Richman L, et al. (2009) Right ventromedial prefrontal cortex: a neuroanatomical correlate of impulse control in boys. Social Cognitive and Affective Neuroscience 4: 1–9.
48. Qiu A, Rifkin-Graboi A, Zhong J, Phua DY, Lai YK, et al. (2012) Birth weight and gestation influence striatal morphology and motor response in normal six-year-old boys. Neuroimage 59: 1065–1070.
49. Bechara A (2005) Decision making, impulse control and loss of willpower to resist drugs: a neurocognitive perspective. Nat Neurosci 8: 1458–1463.

50. Rifkin-Graboi A, Bai J, Chen H, Hameed WB, Sim LW, et al. (2013) Prenatal maternal depression associates with microstructure of right amygdala in neonates at birth. Biol Psychiatry 74: 837–844.
51. Buss C, Davis EP, Shahbaba B, Pruessner JC, Head K, et al. (2012) Maternal cortisol over the course of pregnancy and subsequent child amygdala and hippocampus volumes and affective problems. Proc Natl Acad Sci U S A 109: E1312–1319.
52. Godfrey K, Walker-Bone K, Robinson S, Taylor P, Shore S, et al. (2001) Neonatal bone mass: influence of parental birthweight, maternal smoking, body composition, and activity during pregnancy. J Bone Miner Res 16: 1694–1703.
53. Jones A, Godfrey KM, Wood P, Osmond C, Goulden P, et al. (2006) Fetal growth and the adrenocortical response to psychological stress. J Clin Endocrinol Metab 91: 1868–1871.
54. Schlotz W, Jones A, Phillips NM, Godfrey KM, Phillips DI (2007) Size at birth and motor activity during stress in children aged 7 to 9 years. Pediatrics 120: e1237–e1244.
55. Ellis LK, Rothbart MK (2001) Revision of the Early Adolescent Temperament Questionnaire. Biennial Meeting of the Society for Research in Child Development. Minneapolis, Minnesota.
56. Fischl B, Salat DH, Busa E, Albert M, Dieterich M, et al. (2002) Whole brain segmentation: automated labeling of neuroanatomical structures in the human brain. Neuron 33: 341–355.
57. Desikan RS, Segonne F, Fischl B, Quinn BT, Dickerson BC, et al. (2006) An automated labeling system for subdividing the human cerebral cortex on MRI scans into gyral based regions of interest. Neuroimage 31: 968–980.
58. De Bie HM, Oostrom KJ, Boersma M, Veltman DJ, Barkhof F, et al. (2011) Global and regional differences in brain anatomy of young children born small for gestational age. PLoS ONE 6: e24116.
59. Martinussen M, Fischl B, Larsson HB, Skranes J, Kulseng S, et al. (2005) Cerebral cortex thickness in 15-year-old adolescents with low birth weight measured by an automated MRI-based method. Brain 128: 2588–2596.
60. O'Donnell S, Noseworthy MD, Levine B, Dennis M (2005) Cortical thickness of the frontopolar area in typically developing children and adolescents. Neuroimage 24: 948–954.
61. Lou HC (1996) Etiology and pathogenesis of attention-deficit hyperactivity disorder (ADHD): significance of prematurity and perinatal hypoxic-haemodynamic encephalopathy. Acta Paediatr 85: 1266–1271.
62. Mallard EC, Rees S, Stringer M, Cock ML, Harding R (1998) Effects of chronic placental insufficiency on brain development in fetal sheep. Pediatr Res 43: 262–270.
63. Rees S, Harding R, Walker D (2008) An adverse intrauterine environment: implications for injury and altered development of the brain. Int J Dev Neurosci 26: 3–11.
64. Rehn AE, Van Den Buuse M, Copolov D, Briscoe T, Lambert G, et al. (2004) An animal model of chronic placental insufficiency: relevance to neurodevelopmental disorders including schizophrenia. Neuroscience 129: 381–391.
65. Fox SE, Levitt P, Nelson CA 3rd (2010) How the timing and quality of early experiences influence the development of brain architecture. Child Dev 81: 28–40.
66. Paus T (2013) How environment and genes shape the adolescent brain. Horm Behav 64: 195–202.
67. Aron AR, Durston S, Eagle DM, Logan GD, Stinear CM, et al. (2007) Converging evidence for a fronto-basal-ganglia network for inhibitory control of action and cognition. J Neurosci 27: 11860–11864.
68. Jahfari S, Stinear CM, Claffey M, Verbruggen F, Aron AR (2010) Responding with restraint: what are the neurocognitive mechanisms? J Cogn Neurosci 22: 1479–1492.
69. Valera EM, Faraone SV, Murray KE, Seidman LJ (2007) Meta-analysis of structural imaging findings in attention-deficit/hyperactivity disorder. Biol Psychiatry 61: 1361–1369.
70. Muennig P, Schweinhart L, Montie J, Neidell M (2009) Effects of a prekindergarten educational intervention on adult health: 37-year follow-up results of a randomized controlled trial. Am J Public Health 99: 1431–1437.
71. Berglund SK, Westrup B, Hagglof B, Hernell O, Domellof M (2013) Effects of iron supplementation of LBW infants on cognition and behavior at 3 years. Pediatrics 131: 47–55.
72. Makrides M, Anderson A, Gibson RA, Collins CT (2013) Improving the neurodevelopmental outcomes of low-birthweight infants. Nestle Nutrition Institute workshop series 74: 211–221.

16

Abnormal Striatal BOLD Responses to Reward Anticipation and Reward Delivery in ADHD

Emi Furukawa[1]*, Patricia Bado[2,3], Gail Tripp[1], Paulo Mattos[2,3], Jeff R. Wickens[1], Ivanei E. Bramati[2,3], Brent Alsop[4], Fernanda Meireles Ferreira[2], Debora Lima[2], Fernanda Tovar-Moll[2,3], Joseph A. Sergeant[5], Jorge Moll[2]

1 Okinawa Institute of Science and Technology Graduate University (OIST), Okinawa, Japan, **2** D'Or Institute for Research and Education (IDOR), Rio de Janeiro, Brazil, **3** Federal University of Rio de Janeiro, Rio de Janeiro, Brazil, **4** University of Otago, Dunedin, New Zealand, **5** VU University Amsterdam, Amsterdam, The Netherlands

Abstract

Altered reward processing has been proposed to contribute to the symptoms of attention deficit hyperactivity disorder (ADHD). The neurobiological mechanism underlying this alteration remains unclear. We hypothesize that the transfer of dopamine release from reward to reward-predicting cues, as normally observed in animal studies, may be deficient in ADHD. Functional magnetic resonance imaging (fMRI) was used to investigate striatal responses to reward-predicting cues and reward delivery in a classical conditioning paradigm. Data from 14 high-functioning and stimulant-naïve young adults with elevated lifetime symptoms of ADHD (8 males, 6 females) and 15 well-matched controls (8 males, 7 females) were included in the analyses. During reward anticipation, increased blood-oxygen-level-dependent (BOLD) responses in the right ventral and left dorsal striatum were observed in controls, but not in the ADHD group. The opposite pattern was observed in response to reward delivery; the ADHD group demonstrated significantly greater BOLD responses in the ventral striatum bilaterally and the left dorsal striatum relative to controls. In the ADHD group, the number of current hyperactivity/impulsivity symptoms was inversely related to ventral striatal responses during reward anticipation and positively associated with responses to reward. The BOLD response patterns observed in the striatum are consistent with impaired predictive dopamine signaling in ADHD, which may explain altered reward-contingent behaviors and symptoms of ADHD.

Editor: Kenji Hashimoto, Chiba University Center for Forensic Mental Health, Japan

Funding: This study was supported by a joint research agreement between OIST (Okinawa Institute of Science and Technology Graduate University) and IDOR (D'Or Institute for Research and Education). The funders had no role in study design, data collection and analysis, decision to publish, or preparation of the manuscript.

Competing Interests. Dr. Paulo Mattos was on the speakers' bureau and/or acted as consultant for Eli-Lilly, Janssen-Cilag, Novartis, and Shire in the last three years. He received travel awards to participate in scientific meetings from Janssen-Cilag, Novartis, Eli-Lilly, and Shire in 2010 through 2012. The ADHD outpatient program (Grupo de Estudos do éficit de Atenção/Institute of Psychiatry) chaired by Dr. Mattos has also received research support from Novartis and Shire. Prof. dr. J.A. Sergeant has served on the advisory boards of Lilly and Shire, and received grants from Lilly. He has also received speaker's fees from Shire, Lilly, Janssen-Cillag, and Novartis.

* E-mail: furukawa@oist.jp

Introduction

Attention deficit hyperactivity disorder (ADHD) is characterized by elevated levels of inattention, overactivity and/or impulsivity that impair daily functioning. The disorder is common and demonstrates continuity across the life span affecting 5.9–7.1% of children and 5% of adults [1]. The etiology of ADHD is not completely understood. Genetic factors play a role but probably involve multiple genes of moderate effect rather than a single gene. Associations have been established with genetic variations in the dopamine D4 receptor [2], [3] and the dopamine transporter (DAT1) [4], the dopamine D5 receptors, serotonin transporters [5] and dopamine beta-hydroxylase (DBH), 5-hydroxytryptamine (serotonin) receptor 1B (HTR1B) and synaptosomal-associated protein, 25 kDa (SNAP-25) genes [6], [7]. A reduction in dopamine synaptic markers including DAT1 has also been shown in the dopamine reward pathway [8]. Altered dopamine function may lead to changes in reward mechanisms in people with ADHD [9–12].

Consistent with genetic mechanisms affecting reward pathways, a number of experimental studies suggest children with ADHD differ from typically developing children in their responses to reward [13]. This has been measured by effects on cognitive task performance [14–18], psychophysiological variables [16], [19–22] and choice behavior [23–32]. Although there is considerable variability across these studies, a consistent finding in choice behavior is a stronger preference for small immediate rewards over larger delayed rewards [33]. This has been shown in temporal discounting [24], [25], choice delay tasks [23], [26–30] and signal detection procedures [32]. Recent studies with adults with ADHD indicate a similar preference for, or sensitivity to, immediate versus delayed reward compared to controls [34], [35].

The pathophysiological mechanism underlying this behavioral sensitivity to delay of reinforcement in individuals with ADHD is, however, unclear. Normally, when reward is delayed, cues that predict reward can bridge the delay by acting as conditioned reinforcers [36–38]. The neural mechanism underlying this bridging effect may involve the transfer of dopamine cell responses from established reinforcers to cues after repeated pairings, as shown in animal studies [39–42]. This transfer of the dopamine cell firing to earlier cues predicting reinforcement may explain how behavior can be maintained in situations where external reinforcement is delayed.

While a number of brain regions contribute to producing the dopamine responses to reward cues and receipt of reward, the output of the dopamine cells is highly concentrated in the striatum, which receives 100-fold higher density of dopamine innervation than other brain regions [43], [44]. Consistent with this, functional magnetic resonance imaging (fMRI) studies in humans have shown blood-oxygen-level-dependent (BOLD) responses in the ventral striatum during the anticipation of primary and secondary rewards [45], [46] after conditioning. These BOLD responses have been shown to correlate positively with positron emission tomography measures of dopamine release in the striatum [47]. Pharmacological evidence also suggests that dopamine release, by activating postsynaptic D1 receptors in the striatum, leads to increased BOLD signals [48].

We hypothesize that in ADHD, the transfer of the phasic dopamine release from reward to reward-predicting cues is deficient [12]. Previous studies have shown reduced BOLD activity during reward anticipation, consistent with hypodopaminergic function [49–53], and negative associations between such activation and ADHD symptoms (also [54], but not [51]). On the other hand, Paloyelis et al. [55] reported increased responses to reward receipt in the dorsal striatum (caudate nucleus) of adolescents with ADHD. These results are consistent with our hypothesis but do not exclude other possible explanations such as overall hypodopaminergic or hyperdopaminergic function. To specifically test our hypothesis, we studied both anticipatory responses and responses to reward delivery in a simple classical conditioning paradigm similar to those used in the animal studies that first showed the transfer of dopamine cell responses from reward to reward-predicting stimuli [56].

We examined fMRI signals in young adults with lifetime symptoms of ADHD and well-matched controls, as *indirect* measures of dopamine release. We predicted that control participants would demonstrate increased striatal BOLD responses to reward cues together with decreased responses to reward delivery as previously demonstrated (e.g., [57]). Conversely, we predicted reduced BOLD responses to reward cues, but stronger responses to reward delivery in the ADHD group, possibly due to a failure to establish phasic dopamine responses to reward-predicting cues. Alternatively, the hypodopaminergic hypothesis would predict an overall reduction in dopamine signaling [11], and thus reduced responses to both reward cue and reward delivery in those with ADHD symptoms compared to controls.

Materials and Methods

Ethics Statement

The study was approved by the ethics committees of the Institute of Psychiatry of the Federal University of Rio de Janeiro (Brazil) and the D'Or Institute for Research and Education (Brazil). All participants provided written informed consent and received a gift voucher in the amount earned in the fMRI task (amounts varied between R$129 and R$141).

Participants

Participants were recruited from amongst medical students attending the 9th semester of their course at the Federal University of Rio de Janeiro, Brazil, between 2008 and 2011. All participants belonged to upper-middle and upper socioeconomic classes (Class A and B according to IBGE, Brazilian socioeconomic classification, www.ibge.gov.br). Three hundred and ninety seven students completed a screening measure of ADHD symptoms (Portuguese version of the Adult Self Report Scale, [58]). Students who endorsed more than 4 current symptoms of inattention *and/or* hyperactivity/impulsivity were classified as potentially eligible for the ADHD group, and those who endorsed less than 3 current symptoms were classified as potential controls. They were invited to participate in a comprehensive assessment of past and current symptoms of ADHD and comorbidity, by qualified psychiatrists, trained and supervised by a senior psychiatrist/researcher (PM), who also reviewed all diagnostic decisions. Semi-structured interviews were administered to confirm the presence and severity of the ADHD symptoms, or their absence (for controls), and to evaluate disorders with high rates of comorbidity with ADHD in adults. The psychiatrists also reviewed other psychological and medical conditions with the students during the interview.

The Attention Deficit Hyperactivity Disorder module of the Portuguese version of the Kiddie-Schedule for Affective Disorders and Schizophrenia-PL (KSADS-PL) [59] was used to assess 18 symptoms of ADHD listed in the DSM-IV and 5, and only symptoms causing impairments were considered to be present. Comorbidity (Mood Disorders, Anxiety Disorders, Substance-Related Disorders, Psychotic Disorders and Eating Disorders) was assessed using the Mini-International Neuropsychiatric Interview in Portuguese (M.I.N.I.) [60]. The inter-rater reliabilities of the original (.64–.67) [61] and Portuguese (.91–1.00, with adults) versions of the KSADS-PL ADHD section [59] as well as of the M.I.N.I. (.88–1.00), and its agreement with the Composite International Diagnostic Interview (CIDI) (.36–.82) and Structured Clinical Interview (SCID) (.51–.84) [62] have been reported to be adequate.

The eligibility criteria for the fMRI study were: no current drug use, psychotic symptoms, major depression or anxiety disorder; no history of neurological disorder; right-hand dominant [63]; and no MRI contraindications. Eighteen students (10 males, 8 females), meeting DSM-IV diagnostic criteria for ADHD in childhood and demonstrating at least 5 current symptoms of inattention and/or hyperactivity/impulsivity formed the ADHD group. The DSM-5 criteria for the predominantly inattentive presentation based on current symptoms were met by 4 participants, hyperactive/impulsive presentation by 3 participants, and combined presentation by 11 participants. Sixteen students (8 males, 8 females) demonstrating fewer than 3 current or previous symptoms of ADHD, meeting the study eligibility criteria and matched for gender and age, took part as control participants. All participants were medication-naïve for stimulant medications.

One student from the control group and 4 students from the ADHD group were excluded from the final fMRI analyses due to movement-related or other artifacts. The final sample included 14 participants in the ADHD group (8 males, 6 females) and 15 participants in the control group (8 males, 7 females). The mean age (ADHD = 23 years, sd = 1.41; control = 23 years, sd = 1.41) and estimated IQ (ADHD = 113, sd = 8.57; control = 111.53, sd = 7.49; Wechsler Abbreviated Scale of Intelligence, [64]) of the two groups were similar. There were no significant differences in the head motion (3 translation, 3 rotation) parameters between the ADHD (mean = 0.18, max = 2.25) and control (mean = 0.22, max = 2.96) groups [65]. Additionally, no significant stimulus-correlated motions were observed ($r < 0.2$) in either group (http://www.nitrc.org/projects/artifact_detect/) [66].

fMRI Paradigm

A classical conditioning paradigm was developed to examine BOLD responses to reward anticipation and delivery, unconfounded by operant behavioral responses, decision-making or complex reward probability and magnitude estimation (Figure 1). One of two initially neutral stimuli (Cue A or Cue B) was followed by a 6 second delay (anticipation period) after which an outcome stimulus (reward or non-reward) was presented. The delay was kept constant to maintain the temporal predictability of the outcome delivery. A picture of coins was presented as a reward outcome and the participants were told they would receive the equivalent of R$3 for each reward outcome and nothing for the non-reward outcomes. Cue A was followed by reward 66% of the time (44 trials) and non-reward 33% of the time (22 trials) to allow a level of uncertainty. Cue B was always followed by non-reward (22 trials). Participants were asked to press a button when a target appeared after the outcome (Lumina, Cedrus Corporation, CA). The length of the inter-trial delay was varied to reduce the temporal predictability of the next trial (Poisson distribution: min = 4.5 s, max = 14.5 s, average = 6.5 s, sd = 2.05 s).

fMRI Image Acquisition

Participants were scanned in the afternoon, except for 1 ADHD and 2 control participants scanned in the morning. Prior to scanning, participants were given brief instructions followed by a practice using a PowerPoint presentation and a computer key, during which all possible conditions/outcomes of the fMRI paradigm were presented once. Extended training and testing of an explicit awareness of the reward contingency were avoided to discourage cognitive coding of the cues and solicited attention to the cues over reward, as instructed knowledge [67] and extended training [68] have been documented to alter striatal responses. Participants were told to pay attention to two symbols (square or diamond) and subsequent outcomes (reward or non-reward), and to press a button at the end of the trial to indicate their attention to the images. It was emphasized that money awarded in the scanner would be converted to bookstore gift vouchers.

Functional images were acquired in two runs with a 3T Achieva scanner (Philips Medical Systems, The Netherlands). Each run consisted of 44 trials (22 Cue A reward, 11 Cue A non-reward, 11 Cue B non-reward trials), presented in a pseudo-randomized order, using an event-related design. The functional scanning time was 852.5 seconds for the first run and 840.5 seconds for the second run (the difference is due to the varied inter-trial delay periods), for a total of 29 minutes. This yielded 426 functional images for the first run and 420 images for the second run. The trial number, sequence and time were uniform across all the participants. Task stimuli were shown using an LCD display and a mirror adapted to the head coil. Foam padding and straps over the forehead and under the chin were used to restrict head motions.

An 8-channel SENSE head coil, single-shot T2*-weighted fast-field echo, echo-planar imaging sequence (TR = 2000 ms, TE = 22 ms, Matrix = 80×80, FOV = 240 mm, flip angle = 90°, 3 mm isotropic voxel size, 36 slices in ascending order with no gap), a SENSE factor of 2, and "dynamic stabilization" were used to optimize the acquisition of the signals especially in the subcortical areas [69], [70]. Reference anatomical images were acquired using a T1-weighted 3D magnetization-prepared, rapidly acquired gradient echo sequence (TR/TE = 7.2/3.4 s, Matrix/FOV = 240/240 mm, flip angle = 8°, 1 mm isotropic voxel size, 170 sagittal slices).

fMRI Analysis

fMRI data were analyzed with SPM8 (www.fil.ion.ucl.ac.uk/spm/software/spm8, in MATLAB R2009b, www.mathworks.com) employing the general linear model [71], [72]. All trials were included in the analysis as we expected learning at the neural level to be accomplished quickly given the simplicity of the task.

Preprocessing was completed using realignment, slice-time correction (referencing middle slice), co-registration, and normalization to the standard MNI EPI template (Montreal Neurological Institute brain template), resulting in the reconstructed functional images with voxel dimensions of 3 mm^3. Images were spatially smoothed using a 6 mm full-width half-maximum Gaussian spatial kernel to optimize the detection of subcortical BOLD signals [73]. Unwanted low frequencies were removed using high-pass filtering (128 s) [74]. Nine condition-specific regressors (Cue A, Cue B, Cue A delay, Cue B delay, Cue A reward, Cue A non-reward, Cue B non-reward, Button press and Fixation) were convolved with the canonical hemodynamic response function for each participant [75]. Contrasts were performed to examine BOLD responses specific to reward anticipation (Cue A delay vs. Cue B delay) and to reward delivery (Cue A reward vs. Cue B non-reward) while controlling for all other conditions in the first-level analysis. The resulting contrast images were entered into the second-level, one-

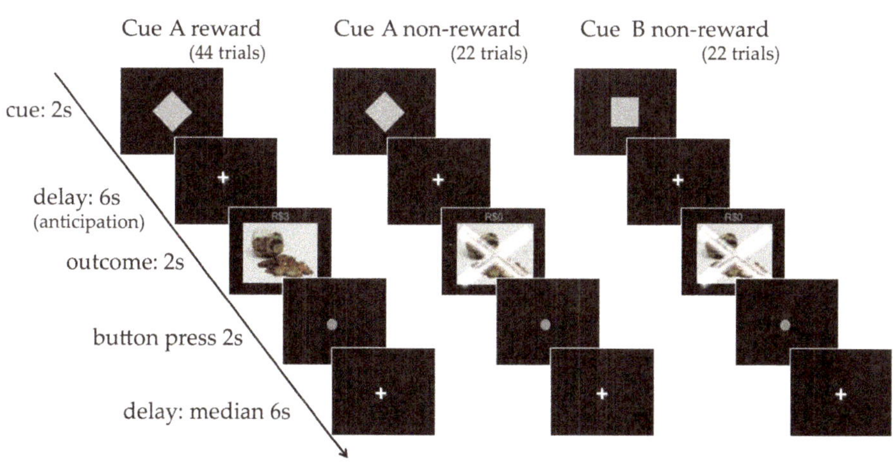

Figure 1. Classical conditioning fMRI paradigm. One of two neutral stimuli (Cue A or Cue B) was followed by an outcome stimulus (reward or non-reward) after a 6-second delay. Cue A was followed by the delivery of the reward 66% of the time and non-reward 33% of the time. Cue B was always followed by non-reward. Participants were told they would receive the equivalent of R$3 for each reward outcome. The length of the inter-trial delay was varied.

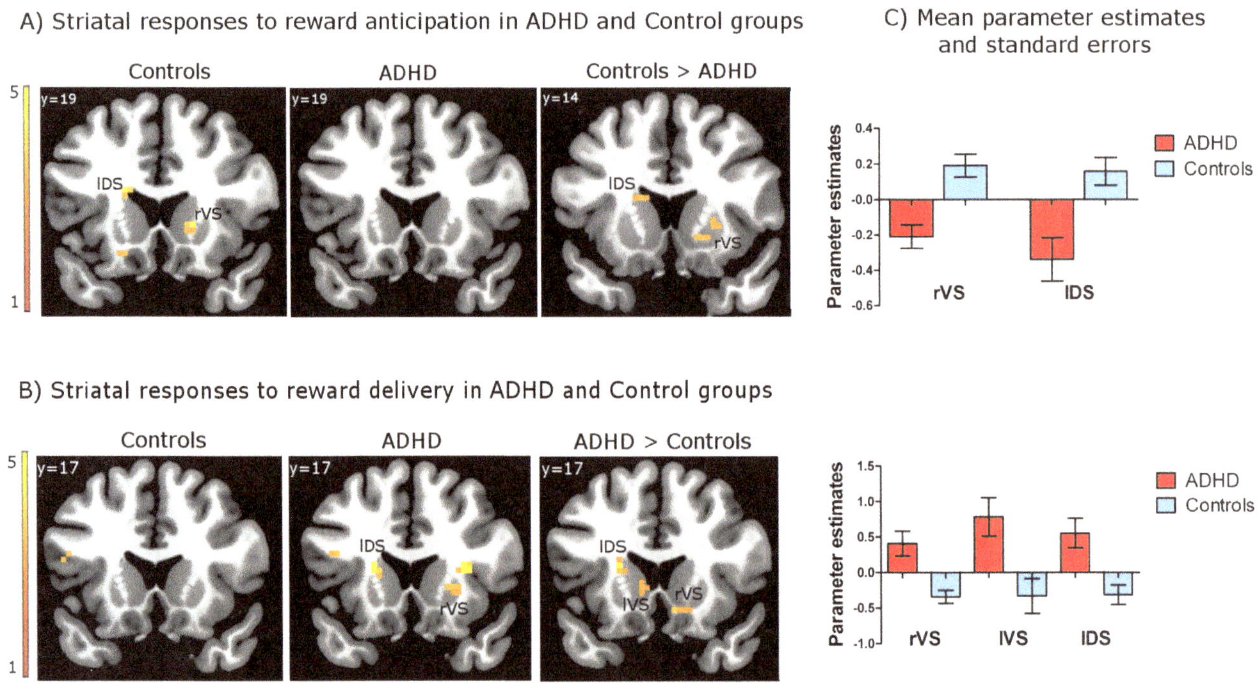

Figure 2. Striatal responses to reward anticipation and reward delivery in the ADHD and control groups. Brain activation displays were generated by overlaying SPM t-maps resulting from the group-level analyses on an MNI standard brain ($p<.005$ uncorrected, cluster size ≥ 5 voxel, for visualization purposes) and applying a gray matter mask. (A) Increased activation in the left dorsal striatum (head of caudate) and right ventral striatum (nucleus accumbens and ventral putamen) during reward anticipation in the control group. (B) Increased activation in the left dorsal striatum (head of caudate), left ventral striatum (ventral regions of the head of caudate), and right ventral striatum (nucleus accumbens and ventral putamen) in response to reward delivery in ADHD. (C) Bar graphs represent mean parameter estimates and standard errors from the GLM analyses examining the effects of reward anticipation (Cue A delay – Cue B delay contrast) and reward delivery (Cue A reward – Cue B non-reward contrast), which were extracted from the local maxima observed within the *a priori*-defined ROIs based on a meta-analysis (Liu et al., 2011); MNI x, y, z = 18, 17, −5 for rVS, −15, 8, 16 for lDS in response to reward anticipation; MNI x, y, z = 9, 17, −11 for rVS, −9, 17, 1 for lVS, −18, 8, 16 for lDS in response to reward delivery. These graphs are provided for illustrative purposes only, and were not used for statistical inferences.

sample t-tests for within-group analysis and two-sample t-tests for between-group analysis with a random-effects model.

The alpha level to identify significant fMRI responses was set to $p<.05$, using family-wise error (FWE) corrections for multiple comparisons with a minimum cluster size of 5 voxels. A whole-brain analysis was conducted first, and *a priori* defined regions of interest (ROIs) were examined, using small volume correction (SVC). Striatal regions consistent with the previous studies of reward sensitivity in ADHD [49–53], [55], [76–78] were examined for the contrasts of interest. MNI coordinates (x, y, z) for each *a priori* ROI were derived from a meta-analysis [79] (ventral striatum [nucleus accumbens]: 12/−12, 10, −6, dorsal striatum [caudate]: 8/−8, 14, 2). For SVC, anatomical ROIs were created in MRIcroN (http://www.mccauslandcenter.sc.edu/mricro/mricron/) by specifying spheres (radius = 10 mm) centered around these *a priori* coordinates, including only gray matter (GM) structures (based on T1-based GM templates) as to discard structures containing mostly cerebrospinal fluid or white matter voxels.

Mean beta values within each anatomical ROI, extracted for each contrast of interest for each participant, were used to examine the group (control vs. ADHD) and condition (reward anticipation vs. delivery) interaction effects in the ventral and dorsal striatum (IBM SPSS Statistics version 20). To examine the relationships between BOLD responses and ADHD symptoms, the number of current inattention and hyperactivity/impulsivity symptoms was modeled separately as a covariate at the second-level SPM analysis (one-sample t-test) for the reward anticipation and outcome in the ADHD group.

Data is available at the BrainMap (www.brainmap.org, searchable by the publication information such as the author, journal name, year of publication, key words).

Results

Analyses focused on striatal responses to reward anticipation and reward delivery in the ADHD and control groups. We predicted that the ADHD group would demonstrate reduced BOLD signals during reward anticipation but greater activation in response to reward delivery, compared to the controls.

Responses to Reward Anticipation

Within-group analyses revealed increased BOLD responses in right ventral striatum (rVS) and left dorsal striatum (lDS) in the control group during reward anticipation (Cue A delay – Cue B delay) (Figure 2, Table 1). In contrast, consistent with our predictions, there were no statistically significant hemodynamic effects during reward anticipation in the ADHD group. Between-group comparisons (Control – ADHD) indicated significantly greater responses in rVS and lDS in the controls, compared to the ADHD group.

Table 1. BOLD responses to reward anticipation and reward delivery in the ADHD and control groups.

Anatomical region	Side	Cluster size	MNI coordinates (x, y, z)			Z-score
Reward anticipation (Cue A delay vs. Cue B delay)						
Control						
Ventral striatum	R	11	18	20	1	3.76*
Dorsal striatum	L	6	−18	20	19	3.50*
ADHD						
No significant activation						
Control>ADHD						
Ventral striatum	R	26	18	17	−5	3.71**
Dorsal striatum	L	24	−15	8	16	3.13**
ADHD>Control						
No significant activation						
Reward delivery (A reward vs. B non-reward)						
Control						
No significant activation						
ADHD						
Putamen	R	8	24	14	1	2.99*
Dorsal striatum	L	27	−21	17	13	4.09*
Control>ADHD						
No significant activation						
ADHD>Control						
Ventral striatum	R	21	9	17	−11	3.31**
Ventral striatum	L	7	−9	17	1	2.79*
Dorsal striatum	L	18	−18	8	16	3.11**

Notes: Coordinates are for the significant local maxima of clusters in the random effects analyses (MNI: Montreal Neurological Institute coordinate system). T statistics were converted to z scores. For the effects surviving SVC, corrected z scores are reported.
*Trend-wise significant, $p = .005$ uncorrected, $k \geq 5$;
**Corrected for small volume, $p = .05$ FWE-corrected.

Responses to Reward Delivery

No significant increase in BOLD activation in the ventral or dorsal striatum was observed in the control group in response to reward delivery (Cue A reward – Cue B non-reward) (Figure 2, Table 1). In contrast, increased responses were observed in the right putamen and left dorsal striatum in the ADHD group. When using a more lenient statistical threshold ($p < .01$, uncorrected), a response in the orbitofrontal cortex was also observed in the ADHD group. However, this was not significant after FWE corrections or SVC. Between-group analysis (ADHD – Control) identified greater hemodynamic effects in bilateral VS and lDS in ADHD participants in response to reward delivery, relative to controls. An additional comparison (Cue A reward – Cue A non-reward) did not show statistically significant effects.

Group×Condition Interaction

Analyses of variance (mixed-design) were conducted to confirm the group (ADHD vs. Control)×condition (reward anticipation vs. delivery) effects. Significant interaction effects for the responses in bilateral VS and lDS and a main effect of the condition for lDS were observed (Table 2).

Relationship between BOLD Responses and ADHD Symptoms

Dimensional analyses were conducted for the ADHD group by modeling the number of symptoms as a predictor variable and BOLD responses to reward anticipation (*Cue A delay*) and reward delivery (*Cue A reward*) as dependent variables, and other conditions as control variables, using within-group one-sample t-tests, SPM second-level analysis. The relationships between the individuals' responses to each condition (rather than contrasts between two conditions) and the number of ADHD symptoms were examined. A higher number of current symptoms of hyperactivity/impulsivity was associated with weaker BOLD signals in left ventral caudate during reward anticipation, together with stronger signals in left ventral putamen in response to reward delivery (Figure 3). A positive association was also found between the number of current inattention symptoms and bilateral VS activation in response to reward delivery; this effect did not survive FWE corrections.

Discussion

The current study revealed altered BOLD responses to a reward-predicting cue and reward delivery among high-functioning young adults with elevated lifetime symptoms of ADHD compared to controls. During reward anticipation, no significant striatal responses were observed in the ADHD group, in contrast to the well-matched controls, who demonstrated increased responses in the ventral and dorsal striatum. Conversely, in response to reward delivery, the ADHD group showed significantly greater hemodynamic effects in the ventral and dorsal striatum than the control group. To our knowledge, this is the first demonstration of a reversal of striatal activation in response to a reward cue and reward delivery in individuals with clinical levels of ADHD symptoms, relative to the control group.

The pattern of BOLD responses observed in control participants is consistent with dopamine release in response to reward and reward-predicting stimuli recorded in the ventral and dorsal striatum in animal studies. These studies, using similar conditioning paradigms, have shown that the phasic responses of dopamine cells transfer from unexpected primary rewards to reward-predicting stimuli [40], [56], [80]. Similarly, in humans, striatal activity has been seen in response to reward-predicting cues [45], [57], [81], [82]. The control participants in the current study showed increased BOLD responses in the striatum during reward anticipation, but very little activity in response to reward delivery, implying that a transfer of phasic responses has occurred.

In contrast to controls, the ADHD group showed the reverse pattern, with no significant increase in striatal responses during reward anticipation but increased responses to reward delivery. This finding is consistent with the hypothesis of an impaired transfer of dopamine cell firing from reward to reward-predicting cues in ADHD [12]. These data are not consistent with overall dopamine hypofunctioning [11], which would predict decreased responses to both reward cues and reward delivery.

The present study is the first to report ADHD versus control group differences in BOLD responses to *both* reward anticipation and delivery within the same study. Previous studies have shown either that cue-evoked BOLD responses are lower among individuals with ADHD [49–53], or that striatal activation is increased in response to reward delivery [55]. We report a reciprocal dissociation that may only have been detected because the current study was designed to test the dopamine transfer deficit hypothesis. We used a simple classical conditioning task modeled on animal studies tailored to measure phasic dopamine release to predictive cues and reward. The paradigms used in other fMRI

Table 2. The interaction effects of the group (control vs. ADHD) and condition (reward anticipation vs. reward delivery).

Factor	Mean (std. error)				F	*p*	Partial eta^2
Right ventral striatum							
Group	Control	−.070 (.073)	ADHD	.029 (.076)	.884	*.355*	.032
Condition	Anticipation	.024 (.039)	Delivery	−.066 (.112)	.475	*.496*	.017
GroupxCondition	Control/Anticipation	.091 (.054)	Control/Delivery	−.232 (.156)	3.165†	*.086*	.105
	ADHD/Anticipation	−.043 (.056)	ADHD/Delivery	.100 (.161)			
Left ventral striatum							
Group	Control	−.104 (.077)	ADHD	.083 (.080)	2.803	*.106*	.094
Condition	Anticipation	−.004 (.045)	Delivery	−.016 (.106)	.010	*.921*	.000
GroupxCondition	Control/Anticipation	.076 (.062)	Control/Delivery	−.284 (.148)	8.526**	*.007*	.240
	ADHD/Anticipation	−.085 (.064)	ADHD/Delivery	.251 (.153)			
Left dorsal striatum							
Group	Control	−.024 (.053)	ADHD	.054 (.054)	1.051	*.314*	.037
Condition	Anticipation	−.099 (.039)	Delivery	.130 (.083)	4.689*	*.039*	.148
GroupxCondition	Control/Anticipation	.001 (.054)	Control/Delivery	−.048 (.116)	6.934*	*.014*	.204
	ADHD/Anticipation	−.200 (.056)	ADHD/Delivery	.308 (.120)			

Note. df = 1, 27;
$^{\dagger}p<.10$,
$^{*}p<.05$,
$^{**}p<.01$.

studies [49–53], [55], [78], [83] differ in important details, such as having a requirement for a behavioral response before reward delivery.

Participants in both the ADHD and control groups in this study were recruited from a population of medication-naïve, high-functioning young adults. This resulted in homogenous groups that differed on the variable of interest only, symptoms of ADHD. While the participants in the ADHD group had not been diagnosed previously, the semi-structured interview revealed clinical levels of lifetime ADHD symptoms, severe enough for a diagnosis. It could be argued that untreated high-functioning adults with elevated ADHD symptoms represent a small portion of affected individuals [84] and that a previously diagnosed population would have more severe symptoms and functional impairments. Therefore, in comparing our results with those from previously diagnosed adults, some allowance should be made for the possibility of more marked changes in the diagnosed and less marked changes in the non-diagnosed adults due to biological adaptation or the effects of medication. Our findings may not generalize to other clinical populations with greater functional impairments. However, the current finding of the reduced VS responses during reward anticipation in the ADHD group is consistent with previous reports in clinical samples [49–53].

The dorsal striatum also showed increased BOLD responses during reward anticipation in controls, and to reward delivery in the ADHD group. Such altered dorsal striatal activation in ADHD samples has not been shown previously, but is consistent with previous research suggesting that individuals with ADHD may value the receipt of reward more highly than its anticipation [83]. At a mechanistic level, animal studies show that the dorsal striatum exhibits neural activity in relation to the learned association of sensory cues with movements [85] and like the ventral striatum [86], receives a strong dopaminergic reward signal [44]. Therefore, we speculate that the dorsal striatum responses in the present study could be related to the dopamine action on striatal neurons becoming active during preparation for the button-press movement required after reward delivery.

The present study focused on BOLD signals in the dorsal and ventral striatum because the highest density of dopamine innervation is found in these areas and our hypotheses were derived from possible underlying mechanisms of dopamine action in ADHD. It should be emphasized that many different brain regions outside of the scope of the present study also contribute to the processing of reward and may be important in the pathophysiology of ADHD. The importance of the dynamic relationships between different brain regions and functions in defining altered reward sensitivity is increasingly recognized [87] and may be a goal to be pursued in further studies. For example, it could be argued that the differences we observed were due to an overall lack of attention in the participants with elevated ADHD symptoms, which might have caused reduced BOLD signals in response to cues but not in relation to reward delivery.

The current paradigm was simple enough to allow the neural learning to occur in the first few trials (e.g., [57]). Thus, we are unable to determine whether the transfer of striatal responses to a reward-predicting cue is slower among individuals with ADHD or if their responses converge to a different asymptote. An important extension to the current study would be to investigate the transfer of dopamine-associated BOLD responses over time and the relationship between changes in neural activity and behavioral learning.

In the present study, we focused on the contrast of reward delivery versus signaled non-reward outcome. Another question of interest is whether brain responses to non-reward (expected or unexpected) are altered in adults with ADHD symptoms. Previous studies in animals and healthy human participants found BOLD "deactivations" in the striatum when expected rewards are omitted [88]. Our additional exploratory analyses contrasting reward delivery with unexpected non-reward indicated no significant change in activation in the ADHD versus control group. In exploring effects of reward omission, the contrast of

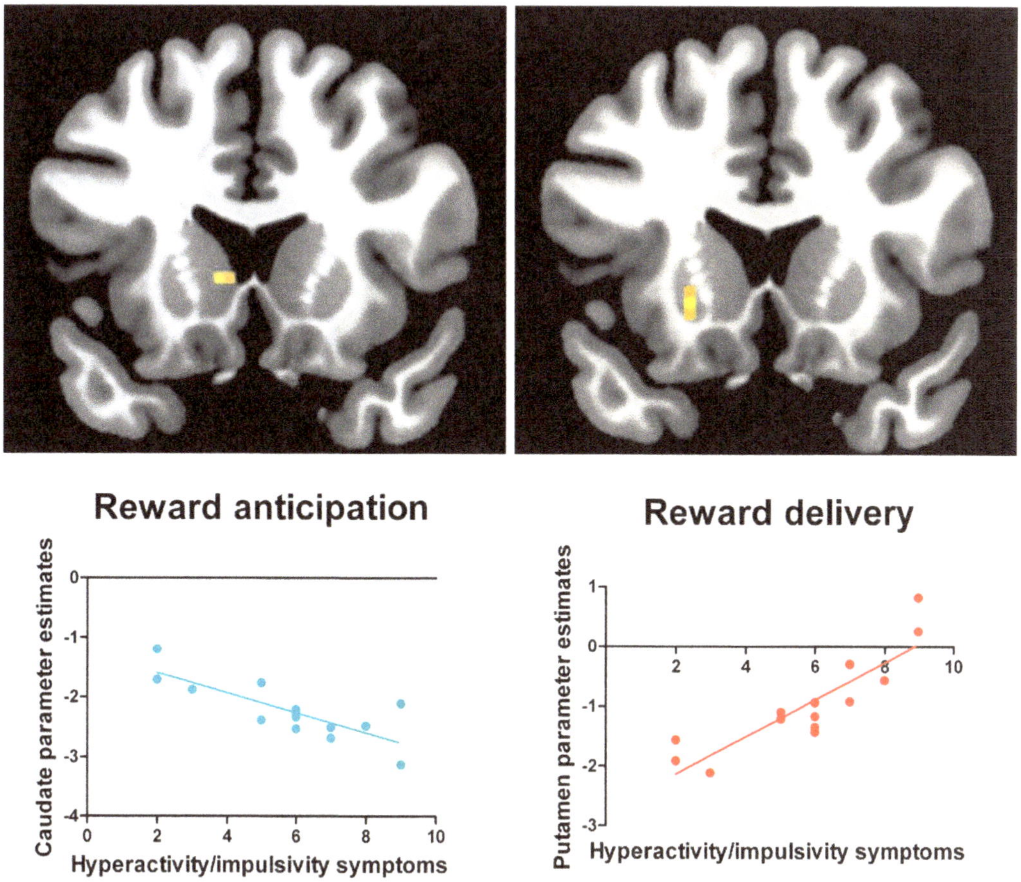

Figure 3. Association between ventral striatal responses and the number of hyperactivity/impulsivity symptoms in the ADHD group. Brain activation displays were generated by overlaying SPM t-maps from the second-level analyses on a MNI standard brain ($p<.005$ uncorrected). Reward anticipation (Cue A delay), t = 4.25 ($p<.005$, uncorrected, MNI local maxima: x, y, z = −6, 14, 4); reward delivery (Cue A reward), t = 5.43 ($p = .04$, FWE corrected, MNI local maxima: x, y, z = −21, 20, −5). The graphs depict the association between the mean parameter estimates of the peak cluster from the one-sample t-tests (y-axis) and the number of symptoms (x-axis) for each participant in the ADHD group. The graphs are provided for illustrative purposes only, and were not used for statistical inferences. MNI: Montreal Neurological Institute.

unexpected versus signaled non-reward suggested greater striatal responses to unexpected non-reward in the ADHD group. The control group showed little activation in response to either expected or unexpected non-reward. Although beyond the scope of the current study, developing predictions and systematically examining the responses to unexpected versus signaled non-reward in ADHD versus healthy controls would provide further insight into how the behaviors of individuals with ADHD are affected by reward and its omission.

Previous studies with ADHD clinical samples have described an inverse relationship between the striatal responses during reward anticipation and hyperactivity/impulsivity symptoms [49], [50], [52]. In contrast, impulsivity traits have been found to positively correlate with anticipatory striatal responses in healthy adolescents and adults [89]. Our results are consistent with the earlier studies using clinical populations, also showing a negative correlation between ventral striatal responses during reward anticipation and the number of current hyperactivity/impulsivity symptoms.

We suggest that among adults with clinical levels of ADHD symptoms, there may be a failure of anticipatory dopamine release in response to reward-predicting cues, which would result in a lack of continuous cellular reinforcement in the striatum when behavioral reward is delayed or discontinuous. Individuals with ADHD may therefore engage in behaviors that provide them with immediate and continuous external reward, which manifest as symptoms of ADHD.

Conversely, in the current study, striatal activation in response to reward delivery was positively associated with current hyperactivity/impulsivity and inattention symptoms. We suggest that in ADHD, there is continued firing of dopamine neurons in response to actual rewards. This would result in reinforcement of "off-task" or alternative behaviors, leading to symptoms of inattention and hyperactivity/impulsivity [12].

Our fMRI results, together with findings from animal studies, suggest a biological basis for abnormal sensitivity to reinforcement in ADHD. The failure of anticipatory dopamine would explain some of the behavioral results reported in the literature including: a stronger preference for immediate over delayed reward [32], [90], poorer performance when reward is not continuous [91], and the need for consistent and immediate reward for shaping behavior [92] amongst those with ADHD. Failure to anticipate reward coupled with continued responses to actual rewards may also offer a biological explanation for the delay aversion observed in children [23], [26–30] and adults [34], [35] with ADHD. For typically developing individuals, reward anticipation serves to maintain appropriate behavior during the periods of waiting. For those with ADHD, the symptoms of inattention, hyperactivity and impulsivity may arise from behaving in ways that lead to immediate reinforcement.

As noted above, the current study is not without limitations. 1) While our high-functioning adult sample displayed elevated levels of lifetime symptoms of ADHD, they had not received a diagnosis of ADHD prior to the clinical interview conducted for the study, thus the generalizability of the current results to the populations with more severe symptoms and functional disabilities may be limited. 2) Our sample size was relatively small, which may have limited statistical power to detect BOLD responses in other areas of brain in the whole-brain analysis. This also prevented us from examining possible interactions with other structures of the reward circuitry. 3) Three of the participants were assessed in the morning, while all others were assessed in the afternoon, possibly affecting their reward-related responses. 4) The present findings do not exclude the possibility that the observed pattern of striatal responses to reward anticipation and delivery may not be specific to ADHD and are present in other pathological conditions associated with altered reward sensitivity. 5) Our study does not exclude the possibility that the behavioral symptoms of ADHD may also relate to, or caused by, different neurobiological processes [93]. Nonetheless, the current study represents a significant step in teasing out the possible underlying mechanism of altered reward sensitivity in ADHD, and the findings argue for behavioral and pharmacological interventions that target the impaired transfer of dopamine release from reward to reward predicting cues.

Author Contributions

Conceived and designed the experiments: EF PB GT PM JRW IEB BA FTM JM. Performed the experiments: PB PM JM DL FTM. Analyzed the data: EF PB PM IEB FMF JAS JM. Wrote the paper: EF PB GT PM JRW IEB BA FMF DL FTM JAS JM.

References

1. Willcutt EG (2012) The prevalence of DSM-IV attention-deficit/hyperactivity disorder: a meta-analytic review. Neurotherapeutics 9: 490–499.
2. Swanson JM, Sunohara GA, Kennedy JL, Regino R, Fineberg E, et al. (1998) Association of the dopamine receptor D4 (DRD4) gene with a refined phenotype of attention deficit hyperactivity disorder (ADHD): a family-based approach. Mol Psych 3: 38–41.
3. Swanson JM, Flodman P, Kennedy J, Spence MA, Moyzis R, et al. (2000) Dopamine genes and ADHD. Neurosci Biobehav Rev 24: 21–25.
4. Gill M, Daly G, Heron S, Hawi Z, Fitzgerald M (1997) Confirmation of association between attention deficit hyperactivity disorder and a dopamine transporter polymorphism. Mol Psych 2: 311–313.
5. Bobb AJ, Castellanos FX, Addington AM, Rapoport JL (2006) Molecular genetic studies of ADHD: 1991 to 2004. Am J Med Genet B Neuropsych Genet 132: 109–125.
6. Faraone SV, Perlis RH, Doyle AE, Smoller JW, Goralnick JJ, et al. (2005) Molecular genetics of attention-deficit/hyperactivity disorder. Biol Psychiatry 57: 1313–1323.
7. Gizer IR, Ficks C, Waldman ID (2009) Candidate gene studies of ADHD: a meta-analytic review. Human genetics 126: 51–90.
8. Volkow ND, Wang GJ, Kollins SH, Wigal TL, Newcorn JH, et al. (2009) Evaluating dopamine reward pathway in ADHD: clinical implications. Jama 302: 1084–1091.
9. Haenlein M, Caul WF (1987) Attention deficit disorder with hyperactivity: a specific hypothesis of reward dysfunction. J Am Acad Child Adolesc Psychiatry 26: 356–362.
10. Sonuga-Barke EJ (2002) Psychological heterogeneity in AD/HD: a dual pathway model of behaviour and cognition. Behav Brain Res 130: 29–36.
11. Sagvolden T, Johansen EB, Aase H, Russell VA (2005) A dynamic developmental theory of attention-deficit/hyperactivity disorder (ADHD) predominantly hyperactive/impulsive and combined subtypes. Behav Brain Sci 28: 397–419.
12. Tripp G, Wickens JR (2008) Research review: dopamine transfer deficit: a neurobiological theory of altered reinforcement mechanisms in ADHD. J Child Psychol Psychiatry 49: 691–704.
13. Luman M, Oosterlaan J, Sergeant JA (2005) The impact of reinforcement contingencies on AD/HD: a review and theoretical appraisal. Clin Psychol Review 25: 183–213.
14. Carlson CL, Tamm L (2000) Responsiveness of children with attention deficit-hyperactivity disorder to reward and response cost: differential impact on performance and motivation. J Consult Clin Psych 68: 73–83.
15. Konrad K, Gauggel S, Manz A, Scholl M (2000) Lack of inhibition: a motivational deficit in children with attention deficit/hyperactivity disorder and children with traumatic brain injury. Child Neuropsychol 6: 286–96.
16. Luman M, Oosterland J, Knol DL, Sergeant JA (2008) Decision making in ADHD: sensitive to frequency but blind to magnitude of penalty? J Child Psychol Psychiatry 49: 712–722.
17. McInerny RJ, Kerns KA (2003) Time reproduction in children with ADHD: motivation matters. Child Neuropsychol 9: 91–108.
18. Slusarek M, Velling S, Bunk D, Eggers C (2001) Motivational effects on inhibitory control in children with AD/HD. J Am Acad Child Adolesc Psychiatry 40: 355–363.
19. Crone EA, Jennings JR, Van der Molen MW (2003) Sensitivity to interference and response contingencies in attention-deficit hyperactivity disorder. J Child Psychol Psychiatry 44: 214–226.
20. Iaboni F, Douglas VI, Ditto B (1997) Psychophysiological response of AD/HD children to reward and extinction. Psychophysiology 34: 116–123.
21. Luman M, Oosterlaan J, Hyde C, Van Meel CS, Sergeant JA (2007) Heart rate and reinforcement in ADHD. J Child Psychol Psychiatry 48: 890–898.
22. Luman M, Oosterlaan J, Sergeant JA (2008) Modulation of response timing in ADHD, effects of reinforcement valence and magnitude. J Abnorm Child Psychol 36: 445–456.
23. Solanto MV, Abikoff H, Sonuga-Barke EJS, Schachar R, Logan GD, et al. (2001) The ecological validity of delay aversion and response inhibition as measures of impulsivity in AD/HD: a supplement to the NIMH Multi-modal treatment study of AD/HD. J Abnorm Child Psychol 29: 215–228.
24. Scheres A, Dijkstra M, Ainslie E, Balkan J, Reynolds B, et al (2006) Temporal and probabilistic discounting of rewards in children and adolescents: effects of age and ADHD symptoms. Neuropsychologia 44: 2092–2103.
25. Scheres A, Tontsch C, Thoeny AL, Kaczkurkin A (2010) Temporal reward discounting in attention-deficit/hyperactivity disorder: the contribution of symptom domains, reward magnitude, and session length. Biol Psychiatry 67: 641–648.
26. Antrop I, Stock P, Verte S, Wiersema JR, Baeyens D, et al. (2006) ADHD and delay aversion: the influence of non-temporal stimulation on choice for delayed rewards. J Child Psychol Psychiatry 47: 1152–1158.
27. Bitsakou P, Psychogiou L, Thompson M, Sonuga-Barke EJS (2009) Delay aversion in attention deficit/hyperactivity disorder: an empirical investigation of the broader phenotype. Neuropsychologica 47: 446–456.
28. Hoerger ML, Mace FC (2006) A computerized test of self-control predicts classroom behavior. J Appl Behav Anal 39: 147–159.
29. Kuntsi J, Oosterlaan J, Stevenson J (2001) Psychological mechanisms in hyperactivity: I. Response inhibition deficit, working memory impairment, delay aversion, or something else? J Child Psychol Psychiatry 42: 199–221.
30. Schweitzer JB, Sulzer-Azaroff B (1995) Self-control in boys with Attention Deficit Hyperactivity Disorder: effects of added stimulation and time. J Child Psychol Psychiatry 36: 671–686.
31. Tripp G, Alsop B (1999) Sensitivity to reward frequency in boys with attention deficit hyperactivity disorder. J Clin Child Psychol 28: 366–375.
32. Tripp G, Alsop B (2001) Sensitivity to reward delay in children with attention deficit hyperactivity disorder (ADHD). J child Psychol Psychiatry 42: 691–698.
33. Sonuga-Barke EJS, Sergeant JA, Nigg J, Willcutt E (2008) Executive dysfunction and delay aversion in attention deficit hyperactivity disorder: nosologic and diagnostic implications. Child Adolesc Psychiatr Clin N Am 17: 367–384.
34. Marx I, Hubner T, Herpertz SC, Berger C, Reuter E, et al. (2010) Cross-sectional evaluation of cognitive functioning in children, adolescents and young adults with ADHD. J Neural Transm 117: 403–429.
35. Marx I, Höpcke C, Berger C, Wandschneider R, Herpertz SC (2013) The impact of financial reward contingencies on cognitive function profiles in adult ADHD. PLoS ONE 8(6): e67002. doi:10.1371/journal.pone.0067002.
36. Ferster CB (1953) The use of the free operant in the analysis behavior. Psychol Bull 50: 263–274.
37. Garrud P, Goodall G, Mackintosh NJ (1981) Overshadowing of a stimulusreinforcer association by an instrumental response. J Exp Psychol 33: 123–135.
38. Winstanley CA, Theobald DEH, Cardinal RN, Robbins TW (2004) Contrasting roles of basolateral amygdala and orbitofrontal cortex in impulsive choice. J Neurosci 19: 4718–4722.
39. Ljungberg T, Apicella P, Schultz W (1992) Responses of monkey dopamine neurons during learning of behavioral reactions. J Neurophysiol 67: 145–163.
40. Pan WX, Schmidt R, Wickens JR, Hyland BI (2005) Dopamine cells respond to predicted events during classical conditioning: evidence for eligibility traces in the reward-learning network. J Neurosci 25: 6235–6242.
41. Schultz W (1998) Predictive reward signal of dopamine neurons. J Neurophysiol 80: 1–27.
42. Schultz W (2002) Getting formal with dopamine and reward. Neuron 36: 241–263.

43. Descarries L, Lemay B, Doucet G, Berger B (1987) Regional and laminar density of the dopamine innervation in adult rat cerebral cortex. Neurosci 21: 807–824.
44. Doucet G, Descarries L, Garcia S (1986) Quantification of the dopamine innervation in adult rat neostriatum. Neurosci 19: 427–445.
45. O'Doherty JP, Dayan P, Schultz J, Deichmann R, Friston K, et al. (2004) Dissociable roles of ventral and dorsal striatum in instrumental conditioning. Science 304: 452–454.
46. Dreher JC, Kohn P, Kolachana B, Weinberger DR, Berman KF (2009) Variation in dopamine genes influences responsivity of the human reward system. Proc Natl Acad Sci 106: 617–622.
47. Schott BH, Minuzzi L, Krebs RM, Elmenhorst D, Lang M, et al. (2008) Mesolimbic functional magnetic resonance imaging activations during reward anticipation correlate with reward-related ventral striatal dopamine release. J Neurosci 28: 14311–14319.
48. Knutson B, Gibbs SEB (2007) Linking nucleus accumbens dopamine and blood oxygenation. Psychopharmacology 191: 813–822.
49. Scheres A, Milham MP, Knutson B, Castellanos FX (2007) Ventral striatal hyporesponsiveness during reward anticipation in attention-deficit/hyperactivity disorder. Biol Psychiatry 61: 720–724.
50. Ströle A, Stoy M, Wrase J, Schwarzer S, Schlagenhauf F, et al. (2008) Reward anticipation and outcomes in adult males with attention-deficit/hyperactivity disorder. NeuroImage 39: 966–972.
51. Plichta MM, Vasic N, Wolf RC, Lesch KP, Brummer D, et al. (2009) Neural hyporesponsiveness and hyperresponsiveness during immediate and delayed reward processing in adult attention-deficit/hyperactivity disorder. Biol Psychiatry 65: 7–14.
52. Carmona S, Hoekzema E, Ramos-Quiroga JA, Richarte V, Canals C, et al. (2012) Response inhibition and reward anticipation in medication-naïve adults with attention-deficit/hyperactivity disorder: a within-subject case-control neuroimaging study. Hum Brain Mapp 33: 2350–2361.
53. Hoogman M, Aarts E, Zwiers M, Slaats-Willemse D, Naber M, et al. (2011) Nitric oxide synthase genotype modulation of impulsivity and ventral striatal activity in adult ADHD patients and healthy comparison subjects. Am J Psychiatry 168: 1099–1106.
54. Stark R, Bauer E, Merz CJ, Zimmermann M, Reuter M, et al. (2011) ADHD related behaviors are associated with brain activation in the reward system. Neuropsychologia 49: 426–434.
55. Paloyelis Y, Mehta MA, Faraone SV, Asherson P, Kuntsi J (2012) Striatal sensitivity during reward processing in attention-deficit/hyperactivity disorder. J Am Acad Child Adolesc Psychiatry 51: 722–732.
56. Schultz W, Dayan P, Montague PR (1997) A neural substrate of prediction and reward. Science 275: 1593–1599.
57. O'Doherty JP, Deichmann R, Critchley HD, Dolan RJ (2002) Neural responses during anticipation of a primary taste reward. Neuron 33: 815–826.
58. Mattos P, Segenreich D, Saboya E, Louzã M, Dias G, et al. (2006) Transcultural adaptation of the Adult Self-Report Scale into Portuguese for evaluation of adult attention-deficit/hyperactivity disorder (ADHD). Revista de Psiquiatria Clínica 33: 188–194.
59. Grevet EH, Bau CHD, Salgado CAI, Ficher A, Victor MM, et al. (2005) Interrater reliability for diagnosis in adults of attention deficit hyperactivity disorder and oppositional defiant disorder using K-SADS-E. Arquivos de Neuro-psiquiatria 63: 307–310.
60. Amorim P (2000) Mini International Neuropsychiatric Interview (MINI): validação de entrevista breve para diagnótico de transtornos mentais. Rev Bras Psiquiatr 22: 106–115.
61. Kaufman J, Birmaher B, Brent D, Rao U, Flynn C, et al. (1997) Schedule for affective disorders and schizophrenia for school-age children-present and lifetime version (K-SADS-PL): initial reliability and validity data. J Am Acad Child Adolesc Psychiatry 36: 980–988.
62. Sheehan DV, Lecrubier Y, Sheehan KH, Amorim P, Janavs J, et al. (1998) The Mini-International Neuropsychiatric Interview (M.I.N.I): the development and validation of a structured diagnostic psychiatric interview for DSM-IV and ICD-10. J Clin Psychiatry 1998: 59 Suppl 20: 22–23.
63. Oldfield RC (1971) The assessment and analysis of handedness: the Edinburgh inventory. Neuropsychologia 9: 97–113.
64. Yates DB, Trentini CM, Tosi SD, Corrêa SK, Poggere LC, et al. (2006) Apresentação da Escala de Inteligência Wechsler abreviada (WASI). Avaliação Psicológica 5: 227–233.
65. Bullmore ET, Brammer MJ, Rabe-Hesketh S, Curtis VA, Morris RG, et al. (1999) Methods for diagnosis and treatment of stimulus-correlated motion in generic brain activation studies using fMRI. Hum Brain Mapp, 7: 38–48.
66. Epstein JN, Casey BJ, Tonev ST, Davidson M, Reiss AL, et al. (2007) Assessment and prevention of head motion during imaging of patients with attention deficit hyperactivity disorder. Psychiatry Res 155: 75–82.
67. Li J, Delgado MR, Phelps EA (2011) How instructed knowledge modulates the neural systems of reward learning. PNAS 108: 55–60.
68. Clark JJ, Collins AL, Sanford CA, Phillips PEM (2013) Dopamine encoding of Pavlovian incentive stimuli diminishes with extended training. J Neurosci 33: 3526–3532.
69. Bellgowan PSF, Bandettini PA, Van Gelderen P, Martin A, Bodurka J (2006) Improved BOLD detection in the medial temporal region using parallel imaging and voxel volume reduction. NeuroImage 29: 1244–1251.
70. Bodurka J, Ye F, Petridou N, Murphy K, Bandettini PA (2007) Mapping the MRI voxel volume in which thermal noise matches physiological noise - implications for fMRI. NeuroImage 34: 542–549.
71. Friston KJ, Frith CD, Turner R, Frackowiak RSJ (1995) Characterizing evoked hemodynamics with fMRI. NeuroImage 2: 157–165.
72. Worsley KJ, Friston KJ (1995) Analysis of fMRI time-series revisited-again. NeuroImage 2: 173–181.
73. Sacchet DM, Knutson B (2013) Spatial smoothing systematically biases the localization of reward-related brain activity. Neuroimage 66: 270–277.
74. Macey PM, Macey KE, Kumar R, Harper RM (2004) A method for removal of global effects from fMRI time series. NeuroImage 22: 360–366.
75. Zarahn E, Aguirre G, D'Esposito M (1997) A trial-based experimental design for fMRI. NeuroImage 6: 122–138.
76. Delgado MR, Stenger VA, Fiez JA (2004) Motivation-dependent responses in the human caudate nucleus. Cereb Cortex 14: 1022–1030.
77. Galvan A, Hare TA, Davidson M, Spicer J, Glover G, et al. (2005) The role of ventral frontostriatal circuitry in reward-based learning in humans. J Neurosci 25: 8650–8656.
78. Stoy M, Schlagenhauf F, Schlochtermeier L, Wrase J, Knutson B, et al. (2011) Reward processing in male adults with childhood ADHD: a comparison between drug-naive and methylphenidate-treated subjects. Psychopharmacology (Berl) 215: 467–481.
79. Liu X, Hairston J, Schrier M, Fan J (2011) Common and distinct networks underlying reward valence and processing stages: a meta-analysis of functional neuroimaging studies. Neurosci Biobehav R 35: 1219–1236.
80. Mirenowicz J, Schultz W (1996) Preferential activation of midbrain dopamine neurons by appetitive rather than aversive stimuli. Nature 379: 449–451.
81. Knutson B, Fong GW, Adams CM, Varner JL, Hommer D (2001) Dissociation of reward anticipation and outcome with event-related fMRI. Neuroreport 12: 3683.
82. Pagnoni G, Zink CF, Montague PR, Berns GS (2002) Activity in human ventral striatum locked to errors of reward prediction. Nat Neurosci 5: 97–98.
83. Wilbertz G, van Elst LT, Delgado MR, Maier S, Feige B, et al. (2011) Orbitofrontal reward sensitivity and impulsivity in adult attention deficit hyperactivity disorder. NeuroImage 60: 353–361.
84. Fayyad J, De Graaf R, Kessler R, Alonso J, Angermeyer M, et al. (2007) Cross-national prevalence and correlates of adult attention-deficit hyperactivity disorder. Br J Psychiatry 190: 402–409.
85. Kimura M (1986) The role of primate putamen neurons in the association of sensory stimuli with movement. Neurosci Res 3: 436–443.
86. Schultz W (1999) The reward signal of midbrain dopamine neurons. News Physiol Sci 14: 249–255.
87. Plichta MM, Wolf I, Hohmann S, Baumeister S, Boecker R, et al. (2013) Simultaneous EEG and fMRI reveals a causally connected subcortical-cortical network during reward anticipation. J Neruosci 33: 14526–14533.
88. O'Doherty JP, Dayan P, Friston KJ, Critchley HD, Dolan RJ (2003) Temporal difference models and reward-related learning in the human brain. Neuron 38: 329–337.
89. Plichta MM, Scheres A (2013) Ventral–striatal responsiveness during reward anticipation in ADHD and its relation to trait impulsivity in the healthy population: A meta-analytic review of the fMRI literature. Neurosci Biobehav http://dx.doi.org doi:10.1016/j.neubiorev.2013.07.012.
90. Sonuga-Barke EJS (2005) Causal models of attention-deficit/hyperactivity disorder: from common simple deficits to multiple developmental pathways. Biol Psychiatry 57: 1231–1238.
91. Douglas VI, Parry PA (1994) Effects of reward and non-reward on frustration and attention in attention deficit disorder. J Abnorm Child Psych 22: 281–302.
92. Barkley RA (2002) Psychosocial treatments for attention-deficit/hyperactivity disorder in children. J Clin Psychiatry 63: 36–43.
93. del Campo N, Fryer TD, Hong YT, Smith R, Brichard L, et al. (2013) A positron emission tomography study of nigro-striatal dopaminergic mechanisms underlying attention: implications for ADHD and its treatment. Brain 136: 3252–3270.

An Inherited Small Microdeletion at 15q13.3 in a Patient with Early-Onset Obsessive-Compulsive Disorder

Carolina Cappi[1]*, Ana Gabriela Hounie[1,5], Daniel B. Mariani[2], Juliana Belo Diniz[1], Aderbal R. T. Silva[1], Viviane N. S. Reis[1], Ariane F. Busso[3], Amanda Gonçalves Silva[3], Felipe Fidalgo[3], Silvia Regina Rogatto[4], Euripedes C. Miguel[1], Ana C. Krepischi[3], Helena Brentani[1]

1 Institute and Department of Psychiatry, São Paulo University Medical School, São Paulo, Brazil, **2** Inter-institutional Grad Program on Bioinformatics, Institute of Mathematics and Statistics, São Paulo University, São Paulo, Brazil, **3** International Research Center, AC Camargo Cancer Center, São Paulo, Brazil, **4** School of Medicine, São Paulo State University, Botucatu, São Paulo, Brazil, **5** Federal University of São Paulo-UPIA-UNIFESP, São Paulo, Brazil

Abstract

Copy number variations (CNVs) have been previously associated with several different neurodevelopmental psychiatric disorders, such as autism, schizophrenia, and attention deficit hyperactivity disorder (ADHD). The present study consisted of a pilot genome-wide screen for CNVs in a cohort of 16 patients with early-onset obsessive-compulsive disorder (OCD) and 12 mentally healthy individuals, using array-based comparative genomic hybridization (aCGH) on 44K arrays. A small rare paternal inherited microdeletion (~64 kb) was identified in chromosome 15q13.3 of one male patient with very early onset OCD. The father did not have OCD. The deletion encompassed part of the *FMN1* gene, which is involved with the glutamatergic system. This finding supports the hypothesis of a complex network of several genes expressed in the brain contributing for the genetic risk of OCD, and also supports the glutamatergic involvement in OCD, which has been previously reported in the literature.

Editor: Chunyu Liu, University of Illinois at Chicago, United States of America

Funding: This study was supported by grants to Dras Cappi and Brentani from the Foundation for Research Support of the State of São Paulo (FAPESP); grant number: 2008/11537-7, and from the Brazilian National Council for Scientific and Technological Development (CNPq; protocol number MCT/CNPq 14/2008). The funders had no role in study design, data collection and analysis, decision to publish, or preparation of the manuscript.

Competing Interests: The authors have declared that no competing interests exist.

* Email: carolinacappi@gmail.com

Introduction

Twin and family studies provide strong evidence of the importance of genetic factors for the expression of obsessive-compulsive disorder (OCD) and other disorders in the obsessive-compulsive spectrum [1]. To date, more than 100 positional and functional candidate genes related to serotonin, dopamine, and glutamate transmission have been implicated in these disorders [2]. However, most of the findings have not been replicated. A recent meta-analysis of all genetic association studies of OCD, which provided sufficient information for data extraction, found that the disorder was associated with serotonin-related polymorphisms (*5-HTTLPR* and *HTR2A*) and that there may be significant sex differences in the genetic bases of the disease, with only male OCD patients carrying polymorphisms involved in catecholamine modulation (*COMT* and *MAOA*) [3]. Secondary analyses of polymorphisms examined in fewer than five data sets identified other candidate polymorphisms associated with trophic factors, neurotransmitters, and with an immunologic factor [3].

The first Genome-Wide Association Study (GWAS) of OCD, which was recently published, analyzed 400 trios, 1,465 cases and 5,557 controls having found no associations between any SNPs (single nucleotide polymorphisms) and OCD at a genome-wide significant level in the combined trio-case-control sample. It is worth mentioning, however, that the top-ranked SNPs were related to transcriptional regulation and to glutamatergic neurotransmission and signaling [4].

Recently, the original genetic model for psychiatric disorders, which explained these conditions as resulting from the effect of common genetic variants (>1% frequency), has been challenged by a model involving high impact variants which are individually rare, but collectively common [5]. Research has shown that, although SNPs outnumber CNVs (copy number variations) in the genome by three orders of magnitude, their relative contribution to genome variation is similar [6]. Therefore, as could be expected from these observations, the study of CNV has allowed a more comprehensive understanding of disease etiology, bringing rare variants to the forefront [7].

Early studies analyzed CNVs ranging from one kilobase (kb) to several megabases (Mb) in size, including large insertions or deletions in the genome. However, the increased accuracy of detection techniques has allowed the identification of smaller CNVs, so that many recent studies involve the analysis of fragments smaller than 1 kb [8].

CNVs are especially relevant to the study of mental disorders, as they have been causally associated with neurodevelopmental disorders and learning disabilities [9]. Specific rare CNVs have also been found to be associated with autism, schizophrenia, and attention-attention deficit hyperactivity disorder (ADHD) [10–14].

The current hypothesis for the etiology of mental disorders suggests that these conditions are polygenic, and that both common and rare variations contribute to their development. Therefore, rather than consisting of risk factors for specific conditions, CNVs are thought to confer broad susceptibility to a variety of neurodevelopmental disorders. Large, rare CNVs are more pathogenic, and are more likely to be under negative evolutionary selection [15]. Although CNVs with smaller effect sizes may also have an important role in the etiology of mental disorders, their individual influences and the impact of their interaction with other CNVs on the development of mental illnesses have been poorly studied [16].

To date, few studies have investigated CNVs in OCD patients. One study was conducted to search for CNVs in these individuals screened for 15q11-13 and 22q11.2 microrearrangements associated with Prader-Willi and DiGeorge Syndromes (DGS). The study was performed in 236 OCD probands using Multiplex Ligation-dependent Probe Amplification (MLPA), which allows the relative quantification of the copy number in at least 50 sequences in a single experiment. The study did not detect any CNVs in these regions, possibly due to the rare prevalence of these chromosomal anomalies in OCD and due to the exclusion of significant mental retardation in the samples studied [17]. Studies have shown that pathogenic CNVs are more prevalent among the individuals with moderate and severe intellectual disability, which are usually exclusionary criteria of research protocols [18].

Another study by Hooper et al., (2012) used cytogenetic analysis and fluorescence in situ hybridization (FISH) to identify an apparently balanced cytogenetic chromosome translocation t(6;22)(q16.2;p13) that segregated from the mother with OCD to her male son with Tourette Syndrome (TS) and OCD. Whole genome mate-pair sequencing and high resolution SNP array analysis was performed in the male proband to identify any related or additional sub-microscopic rearrangements. The largest heterozygous deletion identified in this secondary analysis was a 400 kb deletion located 1.3 Mb telomeric to the chromosome 6q breakpoint. This deletion caused heterozygous loss of all coding sequences of the *GPR63*, *NDUFA4* and *KLHL32* genes which are expressed in the brain [19]. In addition, this deletion coincides with a rearrangement previously reported in a girl diagnosed with Autism Spectrum Disorder (ASD) and developmental delay [20].

In a study of 136 cases of children and adolescents with OCD compared with 106 healthy age-matched controls, Walitza et al., (2011) reported that the deletion (one copy) of a small (100 bp) CNV localized near (68-bp upstream the rs 6311 in the promoter region of the *HTR2A* gene was associated to a very early-onset and to symptom severity of OCD. The frequency of this deletion was increased in the OCD group (n = 8) when compared to healthy controls (n = 1), and carriers of one copy (deletion) of the CNV were associated with a very-early-onset OCD and increased CY-BOCS scores [21].

The first genome-wide CNV analysis in OCD (1,613 patients) and the largest to date in Tourette Syndrome (TS) (1,086 patients) and 720 ancestry-matched controls was conducted to observe the effects of specific neurodevelopmental CNVs. The analyses were restricted to large (>500 kb an rare (<1% frequency in the Database of Genomic Variants-DGV) CNVs, using Illumina genotyping array. The results showed evidence for an increased burden of pathogenic neurodevelopmental deletions in OCD/TS patients compared with controls. Deletion at 16p13.11 was primarily associated with OCD, however 3 de novo CNVs in this region among 6 cases with OCD/TS point to the possibility of pleiotropic effect of this locus. These deletions at 16p13.11 have been extended to other neurodevelopmental disorders, including developmental delay, seizures, and autism [22].

In light of these findings and given our long-standing interest in the contribution of genetic variation to OCD, we conducted a preliminary study to identify rare CNVs in 16 patients with early-onset OCD and 12 controls, using array-based comparative genomic hybridization (aCGH).

Materials and Methods

The present study was approved by the Research Ethics Committees of the University of São Paulo School of Medicine, as well as by the Brazilian National Commission of Research Ethics (CONEP, process number: 16756). All participating subjects gave written informed consent.

The study was conducted in the Outpatient Clinic of the Obsessive-Compulsive Spectrum Disorders Program of the Institute of Psychiatry at the General Hospital of the University of São Paulo, School of Medicine.

Patients were referred from primary psychiatric services, or recruited through television, radio, and newspaper announcements. Healthy controls were recruited from university staff and students, hospital staff or by word of mouth.

Patients and healthy controls were assessed at baseline with the Structured Clinical Interview for DSM-IV Axis I Disorders and additional modules for tic and impulse control disorders, the ADHD and separation anxiety sections of the Kiddie Schedule for Affective Disorders and Schizophrenia (K-SADS), the Yale-Brown Obsessive- Compulsive Scale (Y-BOCS), the Dimensional Yale-Brown Obsessive- Compulsive Scale (DY-BOCS), the Yale Global Tic Severity Scale (YGTSS), and the Beck Depression (BDI) and Anxiety (BAI) Inventories [23,24]. Patients were included if they were aged between 18 and 65 years and had OCD as the primary diagnosis according to DSM-IV criteria. Healthy controls were included if they were aged between 18 and 65 years and did not have OCD, tic or impulse control disorders, ADHD, anxiety disorders or major depression according to the DSM-IV.

Subjects with a primary diagnosis of a psychotic disorder or with any other condition that could impair their understanding of the protocol questions were excluded. Patients with a clinical condition that could hamper the interpretation of the results, such as those whose OCD symptoms began after significant head trauma or were secondary to other neurological disorders and intellectual disability were also excluded.

Genomic DNA extraction

In those patients from whom it was possible to obtain blood samples, peripheral blood leukocytes were used as a source of DNA, which was extracted using the salting out method [25]. For the eight subjects from whom blood samples could not be drawn, DNA was extracted from saliva samples collected using the Oragene kit manufactured by Genotek according to the protocols available at http://www.dnagenotek.com/.

Comparative genomic hybridization based on microarray (aCGH)

Array-CGH analysis was performed using an oligonucleotide 44 K whole-genome microarray platform (design 14950, Agilent Technologies, Santa Clara, USA). The platform was composed of 44,290 60-mer oligonucleotide probes for mapped genes or unique DNA sequences with an average spatial resolution of ~30–35 kb. However, the platform does not cover the pseudoautosomal regions of the X and the Y chromosomes. The genomic DNA of patients and healthy controls was labeled with Cy3-fluorophores, while the reference DNA was labeled with Cy5-fluorophore. These were hybridized to the array in the presence of Cot-1 DNA, a blocking reagent which suppresses the nonspecific hybridization of repetitive sequences.

Test DNA samples were hybridized with gender matched reference DNA, which consisted of a pooled sample of human placenta DNA obtained from ten normal individuals. Purification, hybridization, and washing were carried out according to the manufacturer's instructions. Slides were read by a GenePix 4000B scanner, and the scanned images of the arrays were processed using the Feature Extraction software package (Agilent Technologies, Santa Clara, CA, USA). Fluorescence intensity was measured by the Feature Extraction software, version 9.5, using an Agilent whole human genome 4×44k microarray. Further details on the protocols used are available online (http://www.home.agilent.com/).

These analyses were performed in all patients, healthy controls and additionally, in the parents of one patient who had one rare CNV.

Selection of high-confidence copy number alterations

Constitutive or germline CNVs were identified using the Genomic Workbench software (Agilent Technologies, Santa Clara, CA, USA) with the statistical algorithm ADM-2, and a 6.7 sensitivity threshold. Poor quality hybridizations (QC>0.3) were discarded. For samples that passed quality control, CNV calling (deletions and duplications) was performed using the Nexus Copy Number 5.0 software, with a quality control threshold of < 0.18. CNVs were called in Nexus using the FASST2 segmentation algorithm; with at least three affected probes and default settings (threshold $\log_2$ ratio of 0.3 or 1.14 for gain or high copy gain, and −0.3 and −1.14 for loss and homozygous loss, respectively), and significance threshold set to 1.0E-6.

Samples that did not meet quality thresholds were excluded from further analysis, as were microarrays with low quality according to visual inspection. Although the initial sample was composed of 20 patients and 20 controls, 12 samples were subsequently excluded for quality reasons (4 patients and 8 controls).

CNVs were considered rare if they showed less than 50% overlap with CNVs predicted with frequency of at least 1% according to the March 2010 update of the Database of Genomic Variants (DGV). The confirmation of rare CNVs and determination of the parent of origin were conducted using 60 K SNP array analysis. Furthermore, rare CNVs were confirmed by quantitative PCR (qPCR).

Quantitative PCR (qPCR) validation

Rare CNVs were validated using the SYBR Green system from Applied Biosystems 7500 Real-Time PCR System. Two qPCR primers were designed and mapped against the NCBI reference sequence hg18 to obtain converging evidence for the detected CNVs. Primer sequences were as follows: *FMN1* forward primer: 5′ CAGGTTTGTCTGAAAGTCACC 3′, reverse primer: 5′ CTACTCTTTGTACCTGGGAGGAC -3′. The absolute number of gene copies was normalized using the *GAPDH* and *P2RX7* genes (control genes). Triplicates were analyzed using the comparative $2^{-}\Delta\Delta C^{t}$-cycle threshold method [26]. Values in the 0.8–1.2 range indicated duplication, <0.6 were indicative of deletions, and values>1.4 were considered duplications (Figure 1).

Statistical Analysis

We assessed the impact of CNVs in cases compared to controls using five measures: the number of CNVs per individual, the estimated CNV size, the percentage of CNVs that overlapped with CNVs in the DGV (overlap with>50% of length), and the percentage of CNVs in two different groups of CNV sizes (CNVs>1 Mb and CNVs>100 kb – 999 kb). *P*-values were calculated using two-tailed Fisher exact test and were shown for each comparison between cases and controls. The level of significance considered was alpha = 0.05 (Table 1).

We compared the proportion of subjects in each group harboring CNVs with sizes between 30 kb–500 kb and>500 kb. This last comparison was conducted to observe whether CNVs involved with neurodevelopment disorder were associated with the OCD group [6]. Pearson's Chi-square (two-tailed) p-values were calculated, using a pre-determined p-value threshold that corrected for 2 primary comparisons using a standard Bonferroni approach (p<0.025) [Table 2].

Results

After completing quality control and case-control matching, 12 samples were excluded (4 cases and 8 controls). Therefore, a total of 16 cases and 12 controls were included in the final analyses. The mean age at symptom onset in the patient group was 9.8 years (SD = 4.03) and the mean Y-BOCS score was 30.4 (SD = 4.93).

Characteristics of CNVs in patients and controls

The median CNV size in OCD patients was 435.4 kb and the median number of CNVs per individual was 3, with 11.3% of these events consisting of deletions (the remaining were all duplications). A total of 24.5% of CNVs in OCD patients were>1 Mb, while 67.9% of variants were in the 100-999 kb range. Patients and controls did not significantly differ with respect to these characteristics (Table 1).

Overall, no statistically significant differences in CNV size were found between cases and controls, even when a nominal uncorrected p-value of 0.05 was used. Similar results were obtained with regard to between-group differences in the frequency of CNV occurrence (Table 1 and Table 2).

Rare CNVs analyses

One OCD patient was found to carry a rare CNV consisting of an intragenic ~64 kb microdeletion at 15q13.3 encompassing part of the *FMN1* gene. Array CGH analyses of the patient's parents were performed to verify whether the CNV was *de novo* or inherited. The microdeletion was found to be inherited from a non-affected father (Figure 1).

Discussion

In this study an early-onset OCD patient (age of first obsessive-compulsive symptoms when he was 8 years old) was found to carry a rare intragenic ~64 kb microdeletion at 15q13.3. This microdeletion was present in the father who did not have OCD. The mother also did not have OCD, although his sister also had OCD. Unfortunately the sister did not agree to participate in the study.

This CNV encompasses two exons of the *FMN1* gene, which encodes the protein Formin1. The overexpression of Formin1b produces an increase in the number of primary dendrites in cultured hippocampal neurons and an increase in the number of glutamatergic synaptic inputs [27]. Additionally, it is thought that Formin1 may mediate the effect of the proneural transcription factor Ngn3, which regulates dendritogenesis and synaptogenesis [28].

The genetic findings in OCD has shown dysregulation in genes that are expressed in the brain and are involved in the

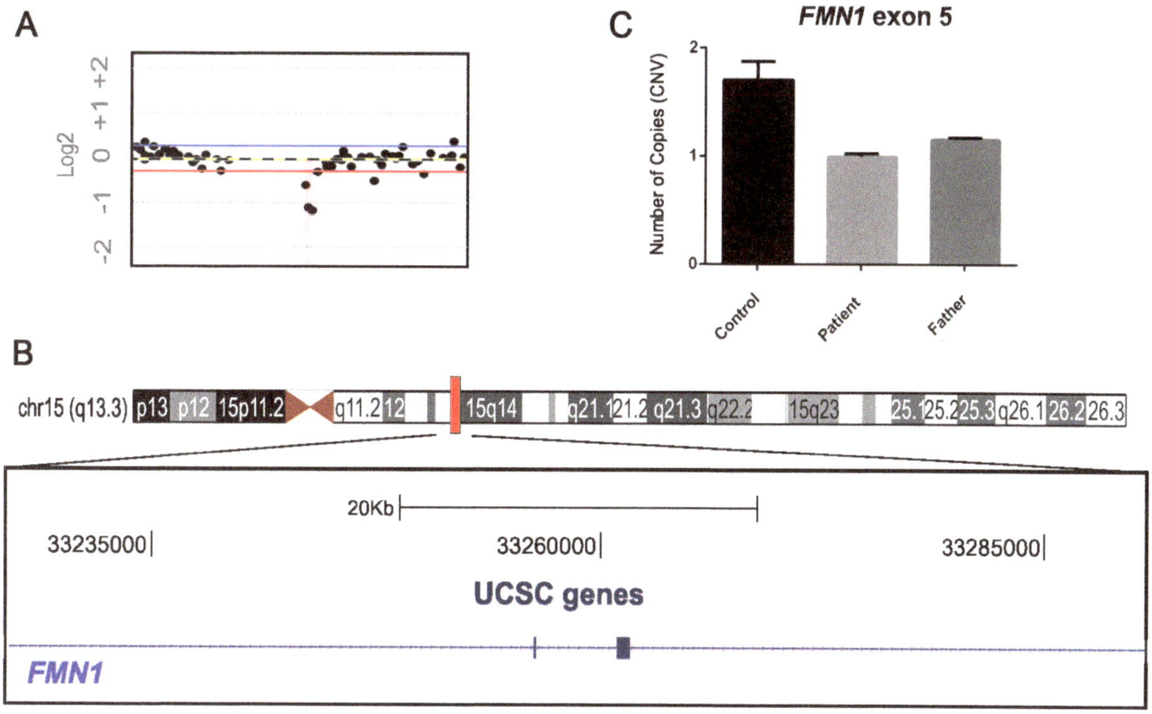

Figure 1. Chromosome 15q 13.3 after CNV and qPCR procedures. A. The microdeletion identified in the *FMN1* region of chromosome 15q13.3 using Genomic Workbench software (Agilent Technologies, Santa Clara, CA, USA). **B.** Genome browser image of the region containing the *FMN1* gene. One rare deletion was identified in the male proband (64 kb loss in OCD case 222_3). **C.** Rare CNVs were validated by SYBR Green-based real time PCR, and it was found that the father and son had only one copy of the exon while the gender-matched control had two copies.

glutamatergic, serotonergic and dopaminergic pathways playing an important part in the expression of OCD [2].

Recent evidence from a number of studies has highlighted the role of glutamatergic synaptic dysfunctions in the cortico-striatal-thalamo-cortical (CSTC) circuit in the etiology of OCD and related disorders [29]. According to a number of independent reports, one of the strongest candidate genes for OCD is the neuronal glutamate transporter gene *SLC1A1* (Solute Carrier, Family 1, Member 1) [30–32]. In fact, this is the only gene whose association with OCD has been replicated in independent samples [4]. However, it is interesting to note that the previously mentioned GWAS of OCD did not find any polymorphisms in the *SLC1A1* gene, although it did associate the disorder with a number of genes involved in glutamatergic processes. These findings corroborate the hypothesis that genes involved in the glutamatergic system may contribute to the pathophysiology of OCD [33,34].

The OCD Collaborative Genetics Study (OCGS) conducted a linkage analysis on 376 affected families using genetic association methods, and found that the SNPs most strongly associated with OCD were in chromosome 15q. Several of those SNPs are located in or near the *FMN1* gene. One SNP (rs2306277) in particular, located in exon 1 of the *FMN1* gene, was predicted by PolyPhen 2 (a tool which predicts the possible impact of an amino acid

Table 1. Characteristics of all copy number variations (CNVs) in obsessive-compulsive disorder (OCD) patients and controls.

	OCD patients (n = 16)	Controls (n = 12)	*P*-value
	All CNVs	All CNVs	
Samples with CNVs	16	12	0.4497
Number of CNVs	53	48	0.6188
Median number of CNVs per genome	3	2	0.6547
Median CNV size (kb)	435.4	389.8	0.1124
% Gain/Loss	88.6/11.3	85.4/14.5	0.8083/0.5287
Overlapping CNVs (%)[1]	58.4	68.7	0.3609
CNVs>1 Mb (%)	24.5	20.8	0.5825
CNVs>100 kb - 999 kb (%)	67.9	79.1	0.3556

P-values were calculated using two-tailed Fisher exact test.
[1]Overlapping CNVs = percentage of CNVs that overlap with CNVs in the DGV (overlap with>50% of length).

Table 2. Frequency of copy number variants of different sizes in patients with obsessive-compulsive disorder (OCD) and controls.

CNV Size Category	Analysis	# OCD (N = 16)	# Controls (N = 12)	*P*-value
All 30–500 kb CNVs	CNVs	53	48	
	Samples	13	11	0.8151
	Proportion	81.2%	91.6%	
All>500 kb CNVs	CNVs	26	26	
	Samples	11	7	0.8644
	Proportion	68.7%	58.3%	

P-values were calculated using Pearson's Chi-square test; Bonferroni-adjusted significance of 0.025.

substitution on the structure and function of a human protein) to be a missense mutation with probable protein damage. The same study also found SNPs associated with OCD in the same chromosomal region (15q), but in the homeobox genes *MEIS2* and *NANOGP8*, which code for transcription factors or closely related proteins, all of which play an important role in neurodevelopment [35]. Other studies have also reported associations between OCD and the 15q region, although none has identified relevant SNPs in the region of the *FMN1* gene itself [36,37].

The main CNVs associated with psychiatric disorders have generally been rare variants in genes involved in synaptogenesis, neuronal and axonal mobility, protein degradation via the ubiquitin-proteasome system (ubiquitin signaling), protein complexes and postsynaptic signaling [11,12,38–48]. Studies have also suggested that the CNVs found in psychiatric probands are often in chromosomal regions associated with microdeletion syndromes, such as loci 16p11.2 and 7q11.23, both associated with Williams Syndrome, locus 15q11-13, associated with Prader-Willi and Angelman Syndromes, and, lastly, locus 22q11.2, which has been associated with DiGeorge syndrome [6].One of the most interesting observations in psychiatric genetic association studies has been the wide variability in the neuropsychiatric phenotype associated with one individual CNV or CNV region [49,50]. These findings are consistent with the hypothesis linking the known pleiotropic effects of these CNVs with shared abnormalities in early neural development [51].

Interestingly, a microduplication at 15q13.3 (including the first four exons of the CHRNA7 gene) was found in a proband with TS, ADHD and OCD and his mother who had subclinical ADHD. The other brother with TS and OCD (without ADHD) did not have this duplication. The authors suggest that this duplication may have an intermediate penetrance effect and may be involved with ADHD development [52].

Studies have described a broad variety of phenotypes associated with 15q13.3 deletion, including schizophrenia, epilepsy, autism, antisocial behaviors and mental retardation [36,37,53–56]. The frequency of these deletions in control individuals has been found to be much lower than in cases. Additionally, the types of deletions and duplications may vary between these individuals. The authors suggest that submicroscopic deletions and duplications in this region are associated with milder phenotypes, have less than 100% penetrance, and tend to be inherited in a larger fraction of cases. Environmental factors may also be important in explaining the lack of penetrance [57]. However, none of the studies cited herein have reported the microdeletion found in the present study. This may suggest a pleiotropic effect whereby multiple variants in the same region are associated with different phenotypes [58]. Perhaps the microdeletion found in the present study in conjunction with environmental factors or other genetic variants may contribute for the manifestation of OCD. The overall rate of *de novo* large CNVs (>500 kb) in OCD trio samples was 1.44%, which is intermediate between healthy controls and autism (1.8% multiplex and 3.9% simplex) and schizophrenia (2%–3%). This finding gives some support to the involvement of CNVs in OCD, despite this study was unable to call CNVs smaller than 500 kb due to technical limitations. There is still the possibility that smaller CNVs may be related to OCD [22].

Several limitations of the present study are worth mentioning. Firstly, the sample size was small, particularly for the purposes of the detection and analysis of rare CNVs. Although this association may have happened by chance alone, other possibilities such as incomplete penetration can be taken into account. Examining the affected sister could help understand this issue.

Furthermore, even though the 44 K platform allows for the observation of large and rare CNVs; the probe spacing may affect the accuracy of CNV length measurements. Future analyses should be conducted using larger sample sizes and a better platform resolution. However, regardless of these limitations, the present findings give further support to the hypothesis that many variations in genes that function in a brain network can be related with OCD, instead of single genes that simply cumulatively add risk.

Acknowledgments

We wish to thank the patients and heathy controls who volunteered to participate in this study.

Author Contributions

Conceived and designed the experiments: HB ACK SRR. Performed the experiments: CC AFB ARTS FF AGS VNSR. Analyzed the data: CC DBM. Contributed reagents/materials/analysis tools: SRR AFB ECM. Wrote the paper: CC AGH JBD ACK HB.

References

1. Pauls DL (2008) The genetics of obsessive compulsive disorder: a review of the evidence. Am J Med Genet C Semin Med Genet 148C: 133–139.
2. Pauls DL, Abramovitch A, Rauch SL, Geller DA (2014) Obsessive-compulsive disorder: an integrative genetic and neurobiological perspective. Nat Rev Neurosci 15: 410–424.

3. Taylor S (2012) Molecular genetics of obsessive-compulsive disorder: a comprehensive meta-analysis of genetic association studies. Mol Psychiatry.
4. Stewart SE, Yu D, Scharf JM, Neale BM, Fagerness JA, et al. (2012) Genome-wide association study of obsessive-compulsive disorder. Mol Psychiatry.
5. Coe BP, Girirajan S, Eichler EE (2012) A genetic model for neurodevelopmental disease. Curr Opin Neurobiol.
6. Malhotra D, Sebat J (2012) CNVs: harbingers of a rare variant revolution in psychiatric genetics. Cell 148: 1223–1241.
7. Conrad DF, Pinto D, Redon R, Feuk L, Gokcumen O, et al. (2010) Origins and functional impact of copy number variation in the human genome. Nature 464: 704–712.
8. Sebat J, Lakshmi B, Troge J, Alexander J, Young J, et al. (2004) Large-scale copy number polymorphism in the human genome. Science 305: 525–528.
9. Merikangas AK, Corvin AP, Gallagher L (2009) Copy-number variants in neurodevelopmental disorders: promises and challenges. Trends Genet 25: 536–544.
10. Sebat J (2007) Major changes in our DNA lead to major changes in our thinking. Nat Genet 39: S3–5.
11. Walsh T, McClellan JM, McCarthy SE, Addington AM, Pierce SB, et al. (2008) Rare structural variants disrupt multiple genes in neurodevelopmental pathways in schizophrenia. Science 320: 539–543.
12. Stefansson H, Rujescu D, Cichon S, Pietiläinen OP, Ingason A, et al. (2008) Large recurrent microdeletions associated with schizophrenia. Nature 455: 232–236.
13. Consortium GP (2010) A map of human genome variation from population-scale sequencing. Nature 467: 1061–1073.
14. Lesch KP, Selch S, Renner TJ, Jacob C, Nguyen TT, et al. (2011) Genome-wide copy number variation analysis in attention-deficit/hyperactivity disorder: association with neuropeptide Y gene dosage in an extended pedigree. Mol Psychiatry 16: 491–503.
15. Rucker JJ, McGuffin P (2012) Genomic structural variation in psychiatric disorders. Dev Psychopathol 24: 1335–1344.
16. Cook EH, Scherer SW (2008) Copy-number variations associated with neuropsychiatric conditions. Nature 455: 919–923.
17. Delorme R, Moreno-De-Luca D, Gennetier A, Maier W, Chaste P, et al. (2010) Search for copy number variants in chromosomes 15q11-q13 and 22q11.2 in obsessive compulsive disorder. BMC Med Genet 11: 100.
18. Engels H, Brockschmidt A, Hoischen A, Landwehr C, Bosse K, et al. (2007) DNA microarray analysis identifies candidate regions and genes in unexplained mental retardation. Neurology 68: 743–750.
19. Hooper SD, Johansson AC, Tellgren-Roth C, Stattin EL, Dahl N, et al. (2012) Genome-wide sequencing for the identification of rearrangements associated with Tourette syndrome and obsessive-compulsive disorder. BMC Med Genet 13: 123.
20. Derwińska K, Bernaciak J, Wiśniowiecka-Kowalnik B, Obersztyn E, Bocian E, et al. (2009) Autistic features with speech delay in a girl with an approximately 1.5-Mb deletion in 6q16.1, including GPR63 and FUT9. Clin Genet 75: 199–202.
21. Walitza S, Bové DS, Romanos M, Renner T, Held L, et al. (2012) Pilot study on HTR2A promoter polymorphism, -1438G/A (rs6311) and a nearby copy number variation showed association with onset and severity in early onset obsessive-compulsive disorder. J Neural Transm 119: 507–515.
22. McGrath LM, Yu D, Marshall C, Davis LK, Thiruvahindrapuram B, et al. (2014) Copy number variation in obsessive-compulsive disorder and tourette syndrome: a cross-disorder study. J Am Acad Child Adolesc Psychiatry 53: 910–919.
23. Miguel EC, Ferrão YA, Rosário MC, Mathis MA, Torres AR, et al. (2008) The Brazilian Research Consortium on Obsessive-Compulsive Spectrum Disorders: recruitment, assessment instruments, methods for the development of multicenter collaborative studies and preliminary results. Rev Bras Psiquiatr 30: 185–196.
24. Hoexter MQ, Shavitt RG, D'Alcante CC, Cecconi JP, Diniz JB, et al. (2009) The drug-naïve OCD patients imaging genetics, cognitive and treatment response study: methods and sample description. Rev Bras Psiquiatr 31: 349–353.
25. Miller SA, Dykes DD, Polesky HF (1988) A simple salting out procedure for extracting DNA from human nucleated cells. Nucleic Acids Res 16: 1215.
26. Livak KJ, Schmittgen TD (2001) Analysis of relative gene expression data using real-time quantitative PCR and the 2(-Delta Delta C(T)) Method. Methods 25: 402–408.
27. Simon-Areces J, Dopazo A, Dettenhofer M, Rodriguez-Tebar A, Garcia-Segura LM, et al. (2011) Formin1 mediates the induction of dendritogenesis and synaptogenesis by neurogenin3 in mouse hippocampal neurons. PLoS One 6: e21825.
28. Salama-Cohen P, Arévalo MA, Grantyn R, Rodríguez-Tébar A (2006) Notch and NGF/p75NTR control dendrite morphology and the balance of excitatory/inhibitory synaptic input to hippocampal neurones through Neurogenin 3. J Neurochem 97: 1269–1278.
29. Arnold PD, Macmaster FP, Hanna GL, Richter MA, Sicard T, et al. (2009) Glutamate system genes associated with ventral prefrontal and thalamic volume in pediatric obsessive-compulsive disorder. Brain Imaging Behav 3: 64–76.
30. Stewart SE, Mayerfeld C, Arnold PD, Crane JR, O'Dushlaine C, et al. (2013) Meta-analysis of association between obsessive-compulsive disorder and the 3′ region of neuronal glutamate transporter gene SLC1A1. Am J Med Genet B Neuropsychiatr Genet.
31. Veenstra-VanderWeele J, Xu T, Ruggiero AM, Anderson LR, Jones ST, et al. (2012) Functional studies and rare variant screening of SLC1A1/EAAC1 in males with obsessive-compulsive disorder. Psychiatr Genet 22: 256–260.
32. Ting JT, Feng G (2008) Glutamatergic Synaptic Dysfunction and Obsessive-Compulsive Disorder. Curr Chem Genomics 2: 62–75.
33. Shugart YY, Samuels J, Willour VL, Grados MA, Greenberg BD, et al. (2006) Genomewide linkage scan for obsessive-compulsive disorder: evidence for susceptibility loci on chromosomes 3q, 7p, 1q, 15q, and 6q. Mol Psychiatry 11: 763–770.
34. Ross J, Badner J, Garrido H, Sheppard B, Chavira DA, et al. (2011) Genomewide linkage analysis in Costa Rican families implicates chromosome 15q14 as a candidate region for OCD. Hum Genet 130: 795–805.
35. Nestadt G, Wang Y, Grados MA, Riddle MA, Greenberg BD, et al. (2012) Homeobox genes in obsessive-compulsive disorder. Am J Med Genet B Neuropsychiatr Genet 159B: 53–60.
36. Crespi B, Stead P, Elliot M (2010) Evolution in health and medicine Sackler colloquium: Comparative genomics of autism and schizophrenia. Proc Natl Acad Sci U S A 107 Suppl 1: 1736–1741.
37. Crespi BJ, Crofts HJ (2012) Association testing of copy number variants in schizophrenia and autism spectrum disorders. J Neurodev Disord 4: 15.
38. Sebat J, Lakshmi B, Malhotra D, Troge J, Lese-Martin C, et al. (2007) Strong association of de novo copy number mutations with autism. Science 316: 445–449.
39. Pinto D, Pagnamenta AT, Klei L, Anney R, Merico D, et al. (2010) Functional impact of global rare copy number variation in autism spectrum disorders. Nature 466: 368–372.
40. Sanders SJ, Ercan-Sencicek AG, Hus V, Luo R, Murtha MT, et al. (2011) Multiple recurrent de novo CNVs, including duplications of the 7q11.23 Williams syndrome region, are strongly associated with autism. Neuron 70: 863–885.
41. Glessner JT, Wang K, Cai G, Korvatska O, Kim CE, et al. (2009) Autism genome-wide copy number variation reveals ubiquitin and neuronal genes. Nature 459: 569–573.
42. Marshall CR, Noor A, Vincent JB, Lionel AC, Feuk L, et al. (2008) Structural variation of chromosomes in autism spectrum disorder. Am J Hum Genet 82: 477–488.
43. Gilman SR, Iossifov I, Levy D, Ronemus M, Wigler M, et al. (2011) Rare de novo variants associated with autism implicate a large functional network of genes involved in formation and function of synapses. Neuron 70: 898–907.
44. Consortium IS (2008) Rare chromosomal deletions and duplications increase risk of schizophrenia. Nature 455: 237–241.
45. Sebat J, Levy DL, McCarthy SE (2009) Rare structural variants in schizophrenia: one disorder, multiple mutations; one mutation, multiple disorders. Trends Genet 25: 528–535.
46. Kirov G, Grozeva D, Norton N, Ivanov D, Mantripragada KK, et al. (2009) Support for the involvement of large copy number variants in the pathogenesis of schizophrenia. Hum Mol Genet 18: 1497–1503.
47. Xu B, Woodroffe A, Rodriguez-Murillo L, Roos JL, van Rensburg EJ, et al. (2009) Elucidating the genetic architecture of familial schizophrenia using rare copy number variant and linkage scans. Proc Natl Acad Sci U S A 106: 16746–16751.
48. Malhotra D, McCarthy S, Michaelson JJ, Vacic V, Burdick KE, et al. (2011) High frequencies of de novo CNVs in bipolar disorder and schizophrenia. Neuron 72: 951–963.
49. Williams NM, Zaharieva I, Martin A, Langley K, Mantripragada K, et al. (2010) Rare chromosomal deletions and duplications in attention-deficit hyperactivity disorder: a genome-wide analysis. Lancet 376: 1401–1408.
50. Fernandez TV, Sanders SJ, Yurkiewicz IR, Ercan-Sencicek AG, Kim YS, et al. (2012) Rare copy number variants in tourette syndrome disrupt genes in histaminergic pathways and overlap with autism. Biol Psychiatry 71: 392–402.
51. Ahn K, Gotay N, Andersen TM, Anvari AA, Gochman P, et al. (2013) High rate of disease-related copy number variations in childhood onset schizophrenia. Mol Psychiatry.
52. Melchior L, Bertelsen B, Debes NM, Groth C, Skov L, et al. (2013) Microduplication of 15q13.3 and Xq21.31 in a family with Tourette syndrome and comorbidities. Am J Med Genet B Neuropsychiatr Genet 162B: 825–831.
53. Coppola A, Bagnasco I, Traverso M, Brusco A, Di Gregorio E, et al. (2013) Different electroclinical picture of generalized epilepsy in two families with 15q13.3 microdeletion. Epilepsia 54: e69–73.
54. Pagnamenta AT, Wing K, Sadighi Akha E, Knight SJ, Bölte S, et al. (2009) A 15q13.3 microdeletion segregating with autism. Eur J Hum Genet 17: 687–692.
55. Le Pichon JB, Yu S, Kibiryeva N, Graf WD, Bittel DC (2013) Genome-wide gene expression in a patient with 15q13.3 homozygous microdeletion syndrome. Eur J Hum Genet.
56. Barrett MT, Scheffer A, Ben-Dor A, Sampas N, Lipson D, et al. (2004) Comparative genomic hybridization using oligonucleotide microarrays and total genomic DNA. Proc Natl Acad Sci U S A 101: 17765–17770.
57. Ben-Shachar S, Lanpher B, German JR, Qasaymeh M, Potocki L, et al. (2009) Microdeletion 15q13.3: a locus with incomplete penetrance for autism, mental retardation, and psychiatric disorders. J Med Genet 46: 382–388.
58. Solovieff N, Cotsapas C, Lee PH, Purcell SM, Smoller JW (2013) Pleiotropy in complex traits: challenges and strategies. Nat Rev Genet 14: 483–495.

18

Multidimensional Measures of Impulsivity in Obsessive-Compulsive Disorder: Cannot Wait and Stop

Sung Yun Sohn, Jee In Kang, Kee Namkoong, Se Joo Kim*

Department of Psychiatry and Institute of Behavioral Science in Medicine, Yonsei University College of Medicine, Seoul, Korea

Abstract

Objective: Although the relationship between obsessive compulsive disorder (OCD) and impulsivity has long been debated, impulsivity has not been systematically examined in clinical samples of OCD. Meanwhile, recent findings suggest that impulsivity is multi-dimensional construct that can be examined through several constructs. Therefore, this study is aimed to evaluate multiple facets of impulsivity in OCD.

Method: The recruitment includes 80 OCD and 76 healthy control participants. Participants completed a test battery comprising three behavioral tasks of stop signal task (SST), delay discounting task (DDT) and balloon analog risk test (BART), and one self-report measure of the Barratt Impulsiveness scale (BIS-11).

Results: OCD subjects showed significantly lower stop signal reaction time of SST reflecting higher action impulsivity and higher delay discounting parameter of DDT suggesting increased choice impulsivity but significantly lower adjusted mean pump of BART implying lower risk taking propensity of BART than healthy control.

Conclusion: Increased Action and choice impulsivity, and decreased risk taking propensities were found in OCD. These findings seem to be consistent with clinical characteristics of OCD such as greater preference for or avoid risky situations (avoidance), inability to wait tension relief may provoke safety behaviors (compulsion) and inability to stop already started behaviors (repetition).

Editor: Carles Soriano-Mas, Bellvitge Biomedical Research Institute-IDIBELL, Spain

Funding: This research was supported by grants (to S. J. Kim) from the National Research Foundation of Korea (NRF) funded by the Ministry of Education, Science and Technology (2010-0022363). The funders had no role in study design, data collection and analysis, decision to publish, or preparation of the manuscript.

Competing Interests: The authors have declared that no competing interests exist.

* Email: kimsejoo@yuhs.ac

Introduction

Obsessive-compulsive disorder (OCD) is a common psychiatric condition characterized by obsessions and compulsions. *Obsessions* are repetitive, unwanted, intrusive thoughts, images, or impulses causing uneasiness, apprehension, or distress in one's mind. *Compulsion* is repetitive ritualistic behavior and is defined as actions inappropriate to the situation that nevertheless persist and which often result in undesirable consequences [1].

Like compulsivity, impulsivity is a common feature in various psychiatric disorders. Impulsivity involves actions that are insufficiently conceived, prematurely expressed, excessively risky or inappropriate to the situation, and that often lead to undesirable outcomes [1]. According to the traditional conception, compulsive disorders and impulsive disorders represent opposite ends of a single dimension, with the former on harm avoidant and the latter on risk seeking [2,3]. However, recent research suggest that, rather than being polar opposites, compulsivity and impulsivity may represent orthogonal factors that each contribute in varying degrees to various psychiatric conditions, including obsessive-compulsive spectrum disorders (OCSDs) [4]. Phenomenologically, OCSDs are characterized by difficulties suppressing repetitive behaviors that are inappropriate to the situation, suggesting underlying impairment in inhibitory control [5]. In the fifth edition of the Diagnostic and Statistical Manual of Mental Disorders (DSM-5), OCD has been reclassified within a new chapter of obsessive-compulsive and related disorders (OCRDs) that includes trichotillomania and skin picking, in which impulsive features are core characteristics [6]. In some aspects, both impulsive and compulsive disorders show similar clinical features, such as difficulties in delaying or inhibiting repetitive behaviors [7]. Compulsive and impulsive disorders are often comorbid and influence each other's development. A number of studies reported high prevalence of impulse control disorders (ICDs) in OCD [8] and high prevalence of OCD in ICDs [9]. In addition, the impulsiveness in OCD seems to have various significant clinical implications. Comorbid ICDs in patients with OCD are associated with poor clinical characteristics, such as early age at onset, great number and severity of symptoms, poor insight, insidious onset, impaired functioning, and poor treatment response seen at long-term follow-up [10]. OCD subjects with higher impulsivity show higher learning problems, low frustration tolerance, poor inter-personal relationships, attention-seeking behavior in childhood, higher neuroticism, and a higher incidence of somatic symptoms

[11]. Additionally, based on neuroimaging and lesion studies, one of the major areas involving impulsivity is the ventral striatal loop [12], which is a target area of deep brain stimulation to improve obsessive-compulsive (OC) symptoms in refractory [13]. Despite this substantial evidence suggesting the importance of impulsivity in OCD, there have been few studies on this relationship and these have mainly used self-rating measures [3,14].

Impulsivity is not a unidimensional construct and it has been suggested that there are several distinct facets of impulsivity, including behavioral disinhibition (impulsive action), impulsive decision making (impulsive choice), and unduly risk taking [15,16,17]. Behavioral disinhibition is defined as an active process that involves suppression of a prepotent response that has been actively investigated by using the stop signal task (SST) [15]. Impulsive decision making is characterized by making choices for smaller immediate rewards rather than waiting for larger delayed rewards. The delay discounting task (DDT) is a well-known behavioral task that measures delay discounting, which refers to the devaluing of a reward due to its location in the future; in other words, DDT assesses the tendency to discount future rewards [18]. Risky decision making is the tendency to engage in behaviors with some potential for danger or harm while also providing an opportunity to obtain some form of reward [19]. The balloon analogue risk task (BART) is a computerized measure that assesses the tendency to engage in simulated risk taking behavior in a context in which unduly risky behavior results in poor outcomes [17]. Considering the multidimensionality of impulsivity, it would be fruitful to simultaneously evaluate the various dimensions of impulsivity (impulsive choice, impulsive action, and risk taking) as well as by using a self-rating measure. These approaches may help in providing a more integrative understanding about the various subtypes of impulsivity and their interrelations in OCD.

Therefore, the central aim of this study is to explore how subconstructs of impulsivity pertain to OCD. We systematically assessed impulsivity using both a subjective self-report and an objective behavioral approach with multiple measures. Based on fact that avoidance behavior and difficulties of inhibiting or delaying compulsive urges are characteristic features of OCD, we hypothesized that OCD subjects show higher impulsive actions and choices and make lower risky decisions than normal controls.

Materials and Methods

Participants

The study group comprised 80 patients with OCD and 76 healthy control participants who were matched for age and sex. The primary diagnosis of OCD and other comorbid psychiatric conditions in patients were determined by the patient version of the Structured Clinical Interview for the DSM-IV (SCID-IV) [20], assessed by a trained psychiatrist (S. J. Kim). Healthy control subjects also underwent SCID-IV and were required to be free of a lifetime history of psychiatric illness.

Exclusion criteria for OCD patients demanded the absence of significant medical or neurologic illness and any other Axis I disorders except for comorbid major depressive disorder. All participants gave written informed consent according to the procedures approved by the Severance Hospital Institutional Review Board.

Procedure and clinical assessments

To assess OCD symptoms, we administered the Yale-Brown Obsessive-Compulsive Scale (Y-BOCS) [21] and the Obsessive-Compulsive Inventory Revised-Korean, (OCI-R-K) [22]. Depressive symptoms were assessed using the Montgomery-Åsberg Depression Rating Scale (MADRS) [23]. In addition, the vocabulary and block design of the Korean version of the Wechsler Adult Intelligence Scale was applied to all participants to estimate IQ. The participants were excluded if their IQ was below average (IQ <90) [24], as some studies had suggested associations between intelligence and the performances of SST [25], DDT [26], and BART [27].

Action impulsivity: Stop Signal Task (SST) [28]

Response inhibition (action impulsivity) was assessed using the SST, which consists of 120 total trials. In each trial, participants were presented with the *go* stimulus (the letter "X" or "O") for 1,000 ms with participants instructed to press the Z key for an X and the/key for an O as quickly and as accurately as possible (go trials). For stop trials (25% of trials), a go stimulus was followed by a stop signal (a beep) after a variable delay, which signaled participants to withhold a response. The onset of the stop signal was varied by a tracking algorithm, in which the stop signal delay was initially 250 ms and was decreased by 50 ms after a previous stop task failure and increased by 50 ms after a previous success. To yield reliable stop signal reaction time (SSRT), we used outlier criteria as follows: (1) percent inhibition on stop trials less than 25% or greater than 75%, (2) percent go-response less than 60%, (3) percent go-errors greater than 10%, and (4) SSRT estimate that is negative or less than 50 ms [29]. A stop signal delay (SSD) indexed the time delay the participant needed in order to inhibit their response. Go reaction time (GORT) is the time taken to press the button when there is no auditory signal. The main dependent variable, SSRT, is a sensitive measure of response inhibition and was extracted by the quantile method which does not require an assumption of 50% inhibition [28]. Longer SSRT reflects worse inhibitory control (slower inhibitory process). In this study, we used the Korean version of the SST [30].

Choice impulsivity: Delay Discounting Task (DDT) [31]

Delay discounting (choice impulsivity) was assessed using a binary choice procedure. In each trial, the computer screen showed a series of choices between two virtual money rewards: immediate smaller reward and delayed larger reward. The delayed reward was fixed at 1,000,000 Korean Won (???), which is approximately 100 US dollars. At the first session, the amount of delay was held constant as within 1 week, and the 26 immediate rewards were presented on the screen in descending order, one per each trial. In the next session, the sequence of immediate monetary rewards ascended in amount until the largest reward was presented, with a particular temporal delay. The next sessions were repeated with incrementally larger temporal delays of 1 week, 2 weeks, 1 month, 6 months, 1 year, 3 years, and 10 years. Within each session, the amount of the immediate monetary value that was preferred equivalently to the large delayed monetary value was defined as the point of subjective equivalence (i.e., an indifference point). Indifference points across the delays were calculated using the hyperbolic decay function, yielding k values reflecting the delay discounting rate [32]. Higher k values indicate higher sensitivity to delayed rewards or choice impulsivity. In this study, we used the Korean version of the DDT [33].

Risk Taking: Balloon Analogue Risk Task (BART) [34]

During the BART, participants were required to press a button to inflate a series of 30 balloons. With each button click the balloon inflated and participants earned money (50 ???) for each pump. This money was added in a temporary bank for that balloon. Participants were told that at some point the balloon would pop and they would lose all the money in the temporary bank. When a balloon exploded, an explosion sound and a picture of the exploding balloon were generated by the computer. Participants were instructed that they could collect from the temporary account to their permanent account at any point before the balloon exploded by pressing a button marked "Collect." After each time a participant collected or popped a balloon, a new balloon appeared. Participants did not actually receive the money, but were instructed to imagine that they would have earned money in a permanent bank in real life. Risk taking propensity was measured by calculating the adjusted mean pumps (AMP), the average number of inflations over the trials in which the balloons did not explode. A larger adjusted value represents a higher risk taking propensity. As the Korean version of the BART was not available, we used the original version of BART [34], which was translated into Korean.

Self-report impulsivity questionnaire: Barratt Impulsiveness Scale (BIS) [35]

The BIS-11 is a self-rating questionnaire. The scale consists of three factors of impulsivity: (1) motor impulsiveness, (2) attentional (cognitive) impulsiveness, and (3) non-planning impulsiveness. In this study, the Korean version of the BIS-11 [36] was used.

Statistical analyses

Statistical tests were two-tailed with level of significance set at $p = 0.05$. Demographic characteristics (age, estimated IQ) were compared across groups using the Mann-Whitney U test or *t*-test for continuous variables. Gender was compared using χ^2 analysis. The primary analyses were *t*-tests with k parameters, adjusted value, SSRT, BIS total score, and BIS subscale as the dependent variables. Because the k parameters were not normally distributed, the distributions of the k parameters were normalized by using the natural log transformation. In addition, we explored associations between the task parameters, BIS scores, and OCD symptom dimensions in patients using Pearson's correlation analyses. All analyses were performed using SPSS version 20.0 (SPSS Inc., USA).

Results

Sample characteristics

Demographic and clinical characteristics for participants are presented in Table 1. A total of 80 OCD patients underwent testing. There were no significant differences in age, sex, or estimated IQ between OCD patients and healthy controls. Patients with OCD presented in the moderately ill range. The mean age at onset of OCD was 18.9±9.3 years. In the OCD groups (n = 80), 78 were currently taking psychiatric medications, all were taking serotonin reuptake inhibitors (SRIs), 31 were taking an SRI with a non-SRI (i.e., benzodiazepine, n = 24; benzodiazepine and antipsychotic, n = 7).

Group comparisons

Behavioral performance and self-report impulsivity are presented in Table 2. Results on the SST were analyzed after first excluding data from 20 OCD patients and 24 normal controls by the outlier criteria method described in [29].

OCD participants had significantly longer SSRTs than did those in the control group ($p = 0.04$). No significant differences between the groups were found on GORT, and there were no impairments in responding ($p = 0.88$). OCD participants exhibited significantly higher AMP than did controls ($p = 0.01$). The mean log k was significantly higher in the OCD group than in the healthy control group ($p = 0.005$). On the BIS, the OCD group evidenced greater levels of total impulsivity than the healthy controls ($p<0.001$). OCD patients reported significantly higher levels of attentional impulsivity and motor impulsivity than did those in the control group (all $p<0.001$). There were no significant group differences in non-planning impulsivity.

Correlations between measures of impulsivity

Correlational analyses among clinical variables and impulsivity measures were performed for OCD patients. The results are presented in Table 3. The severities of obsessive-compulsive symptoms (Y-BOCS) and depressive symptoms (MADRS) were not significantly correlated with any task measures (all $p>0.05$). In addition, the three behavioral measures (SSRT, DDT, and BART) were not significantly correlated with each other (all $p>0.05$). The correlations between the behavioral measures and the BIS also were not significant (all $p>0.05$). We obtained the same results when we performed correlational analyses for the controls and for the combination of both OCD and control participants (data not presented).

Discussion

The main aim of this study was to investigate the relationship between impulsivity and OCD. To the best of our knowledge, this is the first study using behavioral measures of multiple facets of impulsivity (action impulsivity, choice impulsivity, and risk taking) in OCD. Compared to controls, OCD patients showed higher action and choice impulsivity but lower risk taking propensity. On the self-report questionnaire, BIS-11, OCD participants showed higher scores on attentional and motor but not non-planning impulsivity subscales than did controls.

On the SST, OCD participants showed slower SSRTs than controls did, which indicates that more time was required for OCD patients to inhibit a response and which reflects difficulties with motor inhibitory control. Consistent with this finding, several previous studies also reported impaired response inhibition in OCD [5,37,38,39,40]. Moreover, greater SSRT has also been found in first-degree relatives of those with OCD that did not differ from that of OCD patients [5,41]. These findings suggest the possibility of impaired motor inhibition for the endophenotype of OCD. In an imaging study, behavioral impairment indicated by the SST was significantly associated with decreased grey matter in orbitofrontal regions and increased grey matter in cingulate, parietal, and striatal regions [42,43], which have been considered to be implicated in the pathophysiology of OCD [42]. A recent study using non-clinical samples of participants with high SSRT showed increased uncertainty and memory distrust as a consequence of repeated checking compared to participants with lower SSRT [44]. The authors suggested that longer SSRT reflecting poor inhibitory control might increase the liability for harmful effects of neutral compulsive-like behaviors, and the inhibitory deficit might contribute to the development and maintenance of OCD, especially compulsive behaviors [44]. Because the go cues always precede the stop signal in the SST, the increased SSRT of OCD patients indicates that OCD patients fail to inhibit already started actions [45]. These findings are consistent with clinical manifestations because OCD subjects generally are not able to inhibit their compulsive behaviors even though they know them to be senseless, and moreover, once compulsive behaviors begin, usually they become more and more severe.

In the current study, the delay discounting parameter measured by the DDT was higher in the participants with OCD than in the controls. This result suggests that people with OCD tend to choose immediate smaller rewards over larger but postponed ones. This

Table 1. Demographic and Clinical Characteristics of OCD and Healthy Control Subjects.

	OCD (n = 80)		HC (n = 76)		U/χ2/t	*p*
	Mean	SD	Mean	SD		
Age (Years)[a]	27.8	8.1	25.5	4.1	2797	0.39
Male (%)[b]	73.8		65.8		1.17	0.28
IQ Estimate[c]	111.7	10.8	112.0	10.5	−0.176	0.86
Y-BOCS	21.7	6.9				
MADRS	16.4	9.7				
OCI-R-Total Score	34.6	14.2				
Washing	5.3	3.8				
Obsessing	7.8	2.8				
Checking	6.0	3.4				
Ordering	5.1	3.6				
Hoarding	4.4	3.6				
Neutralizing	6.1	3.7				

HC, healthy control subjects; OCD, Obsessive-Compulsive disorder; Y-BOCS, Yale-Brown Obsessive Compulsive Scale; MADRS: Montgomery-Asberg Depression Rating Scale; OCI-R, Obsessive Compulsive Inventory-Revised.
a. Mann-Whitney U test because the data were not normally distributed.
b. χ2-test.
c. Independent samples two tailed t-test.

result is in consistent with the clinical characteristics of OCD because most OCD subjects cannot stop or delay their urge to do compulsive behaviors that immediately reduce their tension, even though they result in more negative consequences in the future. To date, there has been only one study of the association between delay discounting and OCD. Pinto et al. [46] examined the asymmetric discounting (intertemporal choice) task in 25 participants with OCD, 25 with OC personality disorders (OCPD), 25 with comorbid OCD + OCPD, and 25 healthy controls. Contrary to our study, they did not find any differences of performance between OCD and controls, although individuals with OCPD show less temporal discounting than did the controls or those with OCD [46]. Although the reasons for the discrepant results are not clear, there were several differences between the two studies. Pinto et al. [46] used a single delay (i.e., 3 months) and discount factor (δ) as a discount parameter, but we used multiple time delays and k parameter, which have been most widely used for delay discounting. In addition, they focused on OCPD rather than OCD and analyzed OCD and OCPD separately, whereas we did not consider the comorbidity of OCPD. Finally, there might be cultural differences between the OCD subjects participating in the two studies. In our study, the participants were all Korean, but in their study, the participants were recruited from one anxiety clinic in North America, and the ethnicities were not presented. However, there has been some evidence suggesting cultural influences on the performance of delay discounting [34]. One recent study reported cultural differences of neural substrates of delay discounting [47]. In addition, the cultural backgrounds may lead to some differences of attitudes toward delay, the perception of time, or the perceived magnitude of the monetary outcome, all of which can influence the delay discounting performance [34]. These several differences between the two studies caused discrepancies, but further studies are needed to better explain these inconsistent results.

OCD participants showed significantly decreased risk taking on the BART, which suggest that people with OCD avoid taking risks. Risk taking involves the potential for danger or harm as well as the opportunity to obtain some form of reward [19]. The BART scores successfully predicted naturalistic risk taking [48]. namely, the likelihood of engaging in real-world activities that involve potential negative outcomes [49]. Although no previous study has used the BART to investigate OCD, our results are generally consistent with previous research showing lower risk taking or more risk averting properties in people with OCD [50,51,52]. OCD participants had lower risk taking than controls in everyday activities, as measured by the self-reported Everyday Risk Inventory, in both American [52] and Australian samples [51]. Recently, Admon et al. [50] found that people with OCD were reluctant to make risky choices during an interactive risky choice game. Risk taking propensity is determined by both increased reward seeking and decreased sensitivity to loss [53]. Several studies reported decreased sensitivity to reward, and increased sensitivity to loss in OCD [54]. Therefore, the lower risk taking among OCD participants in our study might result from increased sensitivity to loss. This finding is also in line with the maladaptive behavior of OCD patients involving excessive aversion to slight risk, which is commonly thought to result from their perception of situations as highly threatening.

We found that the OCD participants showed significantly higher total scores than controls did on the attentional and motor subscale scores but not on the non-planning subscale of the BIS-11. Most previous studies have also consistently reported higher total and attentional subscale scores of the BIS-11 in OCD [37,55,56]. In terms of motor subscale of BIS-11, there are some controversies. Contrary to ours, some previous studies could not find any difference of motor impulsiveness of BIS-11 between OCD patients and controls [37,55,57]. However, in one recent Korean study, the motor impulsiveness of the BIS-11 in OCD patients was significantly higher than in controls and was correlated with hoarding or aggressive/checking dimensions of obsessive-compulsive symptoms [56]. In another Korean study, although the difference in motor impulsiveness between OCD patients and controls did not reach statistical significance, the effect size ($d = 0.81$) was bigger than in ours ($d = 0.73$), which

Table 2. Comparison of impulsiveness in patients with OCD and healthy controls.

	OCD (n = 80)		HC (n = 76)		t	*p*	*Cohen's d*
	Mean	**SD**	**Mean**	**SD**			
BART							
AMP	27.75	18.25	34.64	16.51	2.469	0.015*	0.40
DDT							
log k	−4.04	2.50	−5.09	1.81	−3.010	0.003**	0.48
BIS							
BIS_A	16.65	2.73	14.36	2.27	−5.725	<0.001**	0.91
BIS_M	17.14	3.96	14.36	3.50	−4.639	<0.001**	0.74
BIS_NP	22.41	4.30	21.43	3.29	−1.589	0.114	0.26
BIS_T	56.20	9.21	50.14	7.34	−4.553	<0.001**	0.73
SST (OCD, n = 60; HC, n = 52)							
GORT	518.83	128.28	522.31	112.77	0.151	0.880	0.03
SSD	353.17	106.34	373.85	104.80	1.034	0.304	0.20
SSRT	165.67	48.94	148.46	35.83	−2.141	0.035*	0.40
STOPACC	0.62	0.10	0.61	0.13	0.711	0.479	0.09

BART, Balloon Analogue Risk Task; AMP, Adjusted Mean Pumps; DDT, Delay Discounting Task; BIS, Barratt Impulsiveness Scale; BIS_A, Barratt Impulsiveness Scale – Attentional; BIS_NP, Barratt Impulsiveness Scale – Non-planning; BIS_M, Barratt Impulsiveness Scale – Motor; BIS_T, Barratt Impulsiveness Scale – Total; SST, Stop Signal Task; GORT, Go Reaction Time; SSD, Stop Signal Delay; SSRT, Stop Signal Reaction Time; STOPACC, stop accuracy.

* $p < .05$, significant difference. ** $p < .01$, significant difference.

Table 3. Pearson Correlation matrix (n = 80) comparing all measures of impulsivity in patients with OCD.

	1	2	3[a]	4	5	6	7
1 AMP	-	−0.127	0.054	0.161	0.133	0.156	0.178
2 log k		-	0.191	0.083	−0.214	0.005	−0.070
3 SSRT[a]			-	−0.048	−0.041	−0.018	−0.041
4 BIS_A				-	0.404**	0.462**	0.686**
5 BIS_M					-	0.692**	0.873**
6 BIS_NP						-	0.902**
7 BIS_T							-

AMP, Adjusted Mean Pumps; SSRT, Stop Signal Reaction Time; BIS_A, Barratt Impulsiveness Scale – Attentional; BIS_NP, Barratt Impulsiveness Scale – Non-planning; BIS_M, Barratt Impulsiveness Scale – Motor; BIS_T, Barratt Impulsiveness Scale – Total.
a. analysis was performed with 60 OCD patients remained after excluded by outlier criteria of SST.
*p<.05, significant difference ** p<.01, significant difference.

means that the main reason for their being no difference in motor impulsiveness was the small sample size (OCD patients, n = 18; controls, n = 33). Consistent with previous findings, our study showed no difference in non-planning impulsiveness between OCD and control participants [55,57].

To our knowledge, this is the first study of OCD that used the SST, DDT, and BART altogether. All of the three behavioral measures of impulsivity demonstrated differences between groups. In OCD subjects, the performances of the SST, DDT, and BART were not correlated with each other. This finding suggested that there were no associations between behavioral disinhibition, impulsive decision making, and unduly risk taking. Several investigations that used multiple measures of impulsivity simultaneously in the study of other psychiatric disorders, such as substance use disorders or impulse control disorders, also showed inconsistent profiles between measures (i.e., increased in one dimension but null findings in other dimensions of impulsivity) [17]. In our study, increased behavioral disinhibition and impulsive decision making but decreased risk taking were observed in OCD subjects. Such a result might be possible when each task reflects a distinct underlying process. The null correlations between task parameters are consistent with some prior investigations [58,59], which also suggest that various assessments of impulsivity are distinct from each other and that there might be different neurobiological mechanisms underlying each process [60]. Although speculative, it is conceivable that each process could contribute to the OCD phenotype in different ways. In the simple case of a patient with pathologic doubt and checking, risk aversion could lead to a greater preference for avoiding risky situations, whereas a concomitant inability to wait for tension relief may provoke safety behaviors (e.g., checking the gas valve), and the inability to stop already started behaviors leads to repeating those behaviors. As aforementioned, our study supports the utility of implementing multiple behavioral tasks for measuring impulsivity because of its conceptual complexity.

One limitation of the present study was that all of the patients were taking SRIs and some of the patient were also taking benzodiazepines and/or atypical antipsychotics when they were tested, which may have had confounding effects on our results. To rule out these potential confounding effects, further research using drug naïve or drug free OCD subjects is warranted. Another limitation is that we may not have completely excluded OCD subjects with comorbid childhood onset psychiatric conditions, especially ADHD. Given that such comorbid conditions were ruled out by a lifetime history-taking method relying solely on patients' self-reports, it may have been possible that some hidden adult ADHD patients were included in both the OCD and healthy control groups. Considering that ADHD tends to be highly comorbid with OCD and impaired response inhibition [61,62], our results may have at least been partially influenced by unscreened participants with ADHD or other childhood onset psychiatric conditions. The other study limitation is that a portion of participants (n = 20 in OCDs and n = 24 in healthy controls) was excluded because of invalid SST performance. A similar rate of exclusion due to invalid results on the SST has been observed in several other studies [61,63,64]. In our study, majority (n = 32) of the outliers were excluded due to high stop response inhibition rate (>70%), which reflects participants' trading speed in the go task for success in the stop task [65,66]. Other researchers also pointed out that participants are likely to trade-off speed for accuracy, instead of equally considering both aspects of the instructions, that is, fast responses in go trials and inhibition in stop trials [65,67]. Considering these findings including our outliers, our instruction might not be sufficient for the participants to balance go-process and stop-process. Some researchers suggested several strategies for preventing this trade- off such as keeping the proportion of stop signal as low as possible [68] or providing clear instruction (e.g., by stressing speed in the go task and explaining the staircase-tracking procedure) and implementing feedback procedures (feedback after every trial or every block) [69]. Therefore, future studies with these strategies can minimize the outliers for reliable SST.

In summary, this study showed increased action and choice impulsivity but lower risk taking characteristics in OCD patients who have difficulty in waiting for advantageous outcomes and stopping already started behavior. Our multimodal tasks results support each task as a measure of a distinct underlying process of impulsivity.

Author Contributions

Conceived and designed the experiments: SJK KN JIK. Performed the experiments: SYS. Analyzed the data: SYS SJK JIK. Wrote the paper: SYS SJK KN JIK.

References

1. Dalley JW, Everitt BJ, Robbins TW (2011) Impulsivity, compulsivity, and top-down cognitive control. Neuron 69: 680–694.
2. Fineberg NA, Potenza MN, Chamberlain SR, Berlin HA, Menzies L, et al. (2010) Probing compulsive and impulsive behaviors, from animal models to endophenotypes: a narrative review. Neuropsychopharmacology 35: 591–604.
3. Stein DJ, Hollander E, Simeon D, Cohen L (1994) Impulsivity scores in patients with obsessive-compulsive disorder. J Nerv Ment Dis 182: 240–241.
4. Fineberg NA, Chamberlain SR, Goudriaan AE, Stein DJ, Vanderschuren LJ, et al. (2014) New developments in human neurocognition: clinical, genetic, and brain imaging correlates of impulsivity and compulsivity. CNS Spectr 19: 69–89.
5. Chamberlain SR, Fineberg NA, Menzies LA, Blackwell AD, Bullmore ET, et al. (2007) Impaired cognitive flexibility and motor inhibition in unaffected first-degree relatives of patients with obsessive-compulsive disorder. Am J Psychiatry 164: 335–338.
6. American Psychiatric Association (2013) Diagnostic and statistical manual of mental disorders: DSM-5. Washington, D.C.: Amer Psychiatric Pub Inc.
7. Stein DJ, Mullen L, Islam MN, Cohen L, DeCaria CM, et al. (1995) Compulsive and impulsive symptomatology in trichotillomania. Psychopathology 28: 208–213.
8. Fontenelle LF, Mendlowicz MV, Versiani M (2005) Impulse control disorders in patients with obsessive-compulsive disorder. Psychiatry Clin Neurosci 59: 30–37.
9. Grant JE, Potenza MN (2006) Compulsive aspects of impulse-control disorders. Psychiatr Clin North Am 29: 539–551, x.
10. Matsunaga H, Kiriike N, Matsui T, Oya K, Okino K, et al. (2005) Impulsive disorders in Japanese adult patients with obsessive-compulsive disorder. Compr Psychiatry 46: 43–49.
11. Hoehn-Saric R, Barksdale VC (1983) Impulsiveness in obsessive-compulsive patients. Br J Psychiatry 143: 177–182.
12. Robbins TW, Gillan CM, Smith DG, de Wit S, Ersche KD (2012) Neurocognitive endophenotypes of impulsivity and compulsivity: towards dimensional psychiatry. Trends Cogn Sci 16: 81–91.
13. Denys D, Mantione M, Figee M, van den Munckhof P, Koerselman F, et al. (2010) Deep brain stimulation of the nucleus accumbens for treatment-refractory obsessive-compulsive disorder. Arch Gen Psychiatry 67: 1061–1068.
14. Hwang J, Shin Y-C, Lim S-W, Park H, Shin N, et al. (2012) Multidimensional Comparison of Personality Characteristics of the Big Five Model, Impulsiveness, and Affect in Pathological Gambling and Obsessive–Compulsive Disorder. J Gambl Stud 28: 351–362.
15. Courtney KE, Arellano R, Barkley-Levenson E, Galvan A, Poldrack RA, et al. (2012) The relationship between measures of impulsivity and alcohol misuse: an integrative structural equation modeling approach. Alcohol Clin Exp Res 36: 923–931.
16. de Wit H (2009) Impulsivity as a determinant and consequence of drug use: a review of underlying processes. Addict Biol 14: 22–31.
17. Fernie G, Cole JC, Goudie AJ, Field M (2010) Risk-taking but not response inhibition or delay discounting predict alcohol consumption in social drinkers. Drug Alcohol Depend 112: 54–61.
18. Kirby KN, Maraković NN (1995) Modeling Myopic Decisions: Evidence for Hyperbolic Delay-Discounting within Subjects and Amounts. Organ Behav Hum Decis Process 64: 22–30.
19. Leigh BC (1999) Peril, chance, adventure: concepts of risk, alcohol use and risky behavior in young adults. Addiction 94: 371–383.
20. First MB (2002) User's guide for the structured clinical interview for DSM-IV-TR axis I disorders: SCID-I. New York: New York State Psychiatric Institute.
21. Goodman WK, Price LH, Rasmussen SA, Mazure C, Fleischmann RL, et al. (1989) The Yale-Brown Obsessive Compulsive Scale. I. Development, use, and reliability. Arch Gen Psychiatry 46: 1006–1011.
22. Foa EB, Huppert JD, Leiberg S, Langner R, Kichic R, et al. (2002) The Obsessive-Compulsive Inventory: development and validation of a short version. Psychol Assess 14: 485-496.
23. Montgomery SA, Asberg M (1979) A new depression scale designed to be sensitive to change. Br J Psychiatry 134: 382–389.
24. Weiss LG, Saklofske DH, Prifitera A, Hodldnack JA editors. (2006) WISC-IV Advanced Clinical Interpretation. Practical Resources for the Mental Health Professional. Burlington: Burlington Academic Press.
25. Albrecht B, Banaschewski T, Brandeis D, Heinrich H, Rothenberger A (2005) Response inhibition deficits in externalizing child psychiatric disorders: an ERP-study with the Stop-task. Behav Brain Funct 1: 22.
26. de Wit H, Flory JD, Acheson A, McCloskey M, Manuck SB (2007) IQ and nonplanning impulsivity are independently associated with delay discounting in middle-aged adults. Pers Individ Dif 42: 111–121.
27. Ashenhurst JR, Jentsch JD, Ray LA (2011) Risk-taking and alcohol use disorders symptomatology in a sample of problem drinkers. Exp Clin Psychopharmacol 19: 361–370.
28. Band GP, van der Molen MW, Logan GD (2003) Horse-race model simulations of the stop-signal procedure. Acta Psychol (Amst) 112: 105–142.
29. Congdon E, Mumford JA, Cohen JR, Galvan A, Canli T, et al. (2012) Measurement and reliability of response inhibition. Front Psychol 3: 37.
30. Won JY, Kim EJ (2008) Validation of stop-signal task. Korean J Psychol17: 217–234.
31. Hurst RM, Kepley HO, McCalla MK, Livermore MK (2011) Internal consistency and discriminant validity of a delay-discounting task with an adult self-reported ADHD sample. J Atten Disord 15: 412–422.
32. Mazur JE (1987) An adjusting procedure for studying delayed reinforcement. In: Commons ML, Mazur JE, Nevin JA, Rachlin H, editors. Quantitative analyses of behavior: Vol. 5: The effect of delay and of intervening events on reinforcement value. Hillsdale, NJ: Erlbaum; 1987. p. 55–73.
33. Choi BY, Chung KM (2011) Utility of delay discounting task as a measure of impulsivity. Korean J Psychol 30: 845–869.
34. Lejuez CW, Read JP, Kahler CW, Richards JB, Ramsey SE, et al. (2002) Evaluation of a behavioral measure of risk taking: the Balloon Analogue Risk Task (BART). J Exp Psychol Appl 8: 75–84.
35. Patton JH, Stanford MS, Barratt ES (1995) Factor structure of the Barratt impulsiveness scale. J Clin Psychol 51: 768–774.
36. Lee HS (1992) Impulsiveness test guide. Seoul: Korean guidance.
37. Boisseau CL, Thompson-Brenner H, Caldwell-Harris C, Pratt E, Farchione T, et al. (2012) Behavioral and cognitive impulsivity in obsessive-compulsive disorder and eating disorders. Psychiatry Res 200: 1062–1066.
38. Chamberlain SR, Fineberg NA, Blackwell AD, Clark L, Robbins TW, et al. (2007) A neuropsychological comparison of obsessive-compulsive disorder and trichotillomania. Neuropsychologia 45: 654–662.
39. Chamberlain SR, Fineberg NA, Blackwell AD, Robbins TW, Sahakian BJ (2006) Motor inhibition and cognitive flexibility in obsessive-compulsive disorder and trichotillomania. Am J Psychiatry 163: 1282–1284.
40. Morein-Zamir S, Fineberg NA, Robbins TW, Sahakian BJ (2010) Inhibition of thoughts and actions in obsessive-compulsive disorder: extending the endophenotype? Psychol Med 40: 263–272.
41. Menzies L, Achard S, Chamberlain SR, Fineberg N, Chen CH, et al. (2007) Neurocognitive endophenotypes of obsessive-compulsive disorder. Brain 130: 3223–3236.
42. Del Casale A, Kotzalidis GD, Rapinesi C, Serata D, Ambrosi E, et al. (2011) Functional neuroimaging in obsessive-compulsive disorder. Neuropsychobiology 64: 61–85.
43. Menzies L, Chamberlain SR, Laird AR, Thelen SM, Sahakian BJ, et al. (2008) Integrating evidence from neuroimaging and neuropsychological studies of obsessive-compulsive disorder: the orbitofronto-striatal model revisited. Neurosci Biobehav Rev 32: 525–549.
44. Linkovski O, Kalanthroff E, Henik A, Anholt G (2013) Did I turn off the stove? Good inhibitory control can protect from influences of repeated checking. J Behav Ther Exp Psychiatry 44: 30–36.
45. Eagle DM, Bari A, Robbins TW (2008) The neuropsychopharmacology of action inhibition: cross-species translation of the stop-signal and go/no-go tasks. Psychopharmacology (Berl) 199: 439–456.
46. Pinto A, Steinglass JE, Greene AL, Weber EU, Simpson HB (2013) Capacity to Delay Reward Differentiates Obsessive-Compulsive Disorder and Obsessive Compulsive Personality Disorder. Biol Psychiatry.
47. Kim B, Sung YS, McClure SM (2012) The neural basis of cultural differences in delay discounting. Philos Trans R Soc Lond B Biol Sci 367: 650–656.
48. Schonberg T, Fox CR, Poldrack RA (2011) Mind the gap: bridging economic and naturalistic risk-taking with cognitive neuroscience. Trends Cogn Sci 15: 11–19.

49. Congdon E, Bato AA, Schonberg T, Mumford JA, Karlsgodt KH, et al. (2013) Differences in neural activation as a function of risk-taking task parameters. Front Neurosci 7: 173.
50. Admon R, Bleich-Cohen M, Weizmant R, Poyurovsky M, Faragian S, et al. (2012) Functional and structural neural indices of risk aversion in obsessive-compulsive disorder (OCD). Psychiatry Res 203: 207–213.
51. Cicolini T, Rees CS (2003) Measuring Risk-Taking In Obseessive-Compulsive Disorder: An Extension Of The Everyday Risk Inventory With An Australian Sample. Behavioural and Cognitive Psychotherapy 31: 247–259.
52. Steketee G, Frost RO (1994) Measurement of Risk-Taking in Obsessive-Compulsive Disorder. Behav Cogn Psychother: 287–298.
53. Barkley-Levenson EE, Van Leijenhorst L, Galvan A (2013) Behavioral and neural correlates of loss aversion and risk avoidance in adolescents and adults. Dev Cogn Neurosci 3: 72–83.
54. Fitzgerald KD, Welsh RC, Gehring WJ, Abelson JL, Himle JA, et al. (2005) Error-related hyperactivity of the anterior cingulate cortex in obsessive-compulsive disorder. Biol Psychiatry 57: 287–294.
55. Ettelt S, Ruhrmann S, Barnow S, Buthz F, Hochrein A, et al. (2007) Impulsiveness in obsessive-compulsive disorder: results from a family study. Acta Psychiatr Scand 115: 41–47.
56. Roh D, Kim SJ, KIM C-H (2009) The relationship between clinical characteristics and impulsiveness in obsessive-compulsive disorder. J Korean Neuropsychiatr Assoc 2009: 336–343
57. Benatti B, Dell'osso B, Arici C, Hollander E, Altamura AC (2014) Characterizing impulsivity profile in patients with obsessive-compulsive disorder. Int J Psychiatry Clin Pract 2014: 156–160.
58. Reynolds B, Ortengren A, Richards JB, de Wit H (2006) Dimensions of impulsive behavior: Personality and behavioral measures. Pers Individ Dif 40: 305–315.
59. Xu S, Korczykowski M, Zhu S, Rao H (2013) Assessment of risk-taking and impulsive behaviors: A comparison between three tasks. Soc Behav Pers 41: 477–486.
60. Dalley JW, Roiser JP (2012) Dopamine, serotonin and impulsivity. Neuroscience 215: 42–58.
61. Crosbie J, Arnold P, Paterson A, Swanson J, Dupuis A, et al. (2013) Response inhibition and ADHD traits: correlates and heritability in a community sample. J Abnorm Child Psychol 41: 497–507.
62. Abramovitch A, Dar R, Hermesh H, Schweiger A (2012) Comparative neuropsychology of adult obsessive-compulsive disorder and attention deficit/hyperactivity disorder: implications for a novel executive overload model of OCD. J Neuropsychol 6: 161–191.
63. Sjoerds Z, van den Brink W, Beekman AT, Penninx BW, Veltman DJ (2013) Response inhibition in alcohol-dependent patients and patients with depression/anxiety: a functional magnetic resonance imaging study. Psychol Med: 1–13.
64. Solanto MV, Abikoff H, Sonuga-Barke E, Schachar R, Logan GD, et al. (2001) The ecological validity of delay aversion and response inhibition as measures of impulsivity in AD/HD: a supplement to the NIMH multimodal treatment study of AD/HD. J Abnorm Child Psychol 29: 215–228.
65. Verbruggen F, Logan GD (2009) Models of response inhibition in the stop-signal and stop-change paradigms. Neurosci Biobehav Rev 33: 647–661.
66. Leotti LA, Wager TD (2010) Motivational influences on response inhibition measures. J Exp Psychol Hum Percept Perform 36: 430–447.
67. Sella F, Bonato M, Cutini S, Umilta C (2013) Living on the edge: strategic and instructed slowing in the stop signal task. Psychol Res 77: 204–210.
68. Verbruggen F, Logan GD (2009) Proactive adjustments of response strategies in the stop-signal paradigm. J Exp Psychol Hum Percept Perform 35: 835–854.
69. Verbruggen F, Chambers CD, Logan GD (2013) Fictitious inhibitory differences: how skewness and slowing distort the estimation of stopping latencies. Psychol Sci 24: 352–362.

19

Mental and Substance Use Disorders in Sub-Saharan Africa: Predictions of Epidemiological Changes and Mental Health Workforce Requirements for the Next 40 Years

Fiona J. Charlson[1,2,3]*, Sandra Diminic[1,2], Crick Lund[4], Louisa Degenhardt[5,6], Harvey A. Whiteford[1,2,3]

1 School of Population Health, University of Queensland, Brisbane, Queensland, Australia, **2** Queensland Centre for Mental Health Research, Brisbane, Queensland, Australia, **3** Institute of Health Metrics and Evaluation, University of Washington, Seattle, Washington, United States of America, **4** Alan J Flisher Centre for Public Mental Health, Department of Psychiatry and Mental Health, University of Cape Town, Cape Town, South Africa, **5** National Drug and Alcohol Research Centre, University of New South Wales, Sydney, New South Wales, Australia, **6** Melbourne School of Population and Global Health, University of Melbourne, Melbourne, Victoria, Australia

Abstract

The world is undergoing a rapid health transition, with an ageing population and disease burden increasingly defined by disability. In Sub-Saharan Africa the next 40 years are predicted to see reduced mortality, signalling a surge in the impact of chronic diseases. We modelled these epidemiological changes and associated mental health workforce requirements. Years lived with a disability (YLD) predictions for mental and substance use disorders for each decade from 2010 to 2050 for four Sub-Saharan African regions were calculated using Global Burden of Disease 2010 study (GBD 2010) data and UN population forecasts. Predicted mental health workforce requirements for 2010 and 2050, by region and for selected countries, were modelled using GBD 2010 prevalence estimates and recommended packages of care and staffing ratios for low- and middle-income countries, and compared to current staffing from the WHO Mental Health Atlas. Significant population growth and ageing will result in an estimated 130% increase in the burden of mental and substance use disorders in Sub-Saharan Africa by 2050, to 45 million YLDs. As a result, the required mental health workforce will increase by 216,600 full time equivalent staff from 2010 to 2050, and far more compared to the existing workforce. The growth in mental and substance use disorders by 2050 is likely to significantly affect health and productivity in Sub-Saharan Africa. To reduce this burden, packages of care for key mental disorders should be provided through increasing the mental health workforce towards targets outlined in this paper. This requires a shift from current practice in most African countries, involving substantial investment in the training of primary care practitioners, supported by district based mental health specialist teams using a task sharing model that mobilises local community resources, with the expansion of inpatient psychiatric units based in district and regional general hospitals.

Editor: Suxia Li, Peking University, China

Funding: The Global Burden of Diseases, Injuries, and Risk Factors Study 2010 (GBD 2010) receives funding from the Bill & Melinda Gates Foundation. The funders had no role in study design, data collection and analysis, decision to publish, or preparation of the manuscript.

Competing Interests: The authors have declared that no competing interests exist.

* Email: fiona_charlson@qcmhr.uq.edu.au

Introduction

The recent Global Burden of Disease Study (GBD 2010) is the largest systematic assessment of disease and injury-specific epidemiology undertaken since its 1990 predecessor [1]. The GBD methodology incorporates the years of life lost through premature mortality (YLL) and years lived with disability (YLD) into a single metric (the Disability Adjusted Life Year (DALY)). Calculating disease burden worldwide and for 21 regions for 1990, 2005, and 2010 with methods to enable meaningful comparisons over time, it has delivered much needed information and key global health messages. The most notable of these is that the world has undergone a rapid health transition over the 1990 to 2010 period – populations have aged, infectious and childhood diseases are making way for non-communicable and chronic disorders, and disease burden is increasingly defined by disability rather than premature death [2].

The health transitions observed globally in GBD 2010 were not as apparent across Sub-Saharan Africa (SSA). Improvements in life-expectancies have trailed other regions, largely due to the HIV/AIDS epidemic, maternal deaths, and child mortality caused by infectious diseases and malnutrition. However these trends are at a turning point and the next 40 years are predicted to see significant reductions in child mortality and lowering mortality from HIV/AIDS and malaria, signalling the inevitable health transitions we have seen across the rest of the globe and a surge in the impact of chronic and non-communicable diseases, defined by long-term disability [3–6].

Mental and substance use disorders are the leading cause of disability, accounting for 23% of all disability-associated burden (years lived with a disability, YLD) globally and 19% in Sub-Saharan Africa in 2010 [7,8]. Major depressive disorder (MDD) makes the largest contribution, accounting for approximately 40% of YLDs in this group, yet the very limited mental health services in Sub-Saharan Africa are frequently restricted to tertiary psychiatric facilities treating those with acute psychoses, and to humanitarian responses to traumatic events such as gender-based violence and societal conflict [9].

For most, the idea of a non-communicable disease epidemic in Sub-Saharan Africa may seem intangible, or at the very least, too far off to contemplate – particularly given the fact that communicable, maternal, neonatal and nutritional diseases still account for approximately 68% of DALYs in the region [7]. So, how imminent is this health transition, and what might it look like for Sub-Saharan Africa? Using UN population data [10] and the findings of GBD 2010, we estimate the change in burden of mental and substance use disorders in context of the broader epidemiological transition which will take place in Sub-Saharan Africa from 2010 to 2050, and model the predicted increase in the mental health workforce required to meet future needs.

Methods

GBD 2010

As part of the GBD 2010 study [4], burden of disease estimates were produced for 20 mental and substance use disorders [8]. In brief, this process consisted of systematic reviews for empirical epidemiological data for each disorder as described by the Diagnostic and Statistical Manual of Mental Disorders (DSM) and/or the International Classification of Diseases (ICD) [11,12]. Internally consistent epidemiological models were created for each disorder using DisMod-MR, a Bayesian meta-regression tool. Adjustments to the data were made via various methods including the application of covariates and severity distributions, and comorbidity adjustments were applied to sequela-specific disability weights in the calculation of YLDs (more detailed information can be found in Murray et al 2012 [4] and Whiteford et al 2013 [8]).

For the GBD 2010, YLDs per person from a sequela (e.g. severe major depression) are equal to the prevalence of the sequela multiplied by the disability weight for the health state associated with that sequela. YLDs for a disease or injury are the sum of the YLDs for each sequela (e.g., mild, moderate and severe depression) associated with the disease or injury [13].

Disability (YLD) estimates 2010 to 2050

YLD predictions for each 10-year period from 2010 to 2050 were calculated for the East, West, Central and Southern Sub-Saharan African regions (as defined by the Global Burden of Disease Study; refer to appendix S1 for a list of countries and regions). We applied UN population data forecasts (see appendix S1 for UN population data) to 2010 age-specific YLD rates ascertained from the GBD 2010 to calculate changes in YLDs for mental and substance use disorders in the context of communicable (includes communicable, maternal, neonatal and nutritional diseases) and non-communicable diseases for each Sub-Saharan region and 10-year time period (see appendix S1 for full list of mental and substance use disorders). By using 2010 YLD rates we assume that age-specific prevalence and disability weights will remain constant throughout the time period. It has been shown that prevalence and disability weights are unlikely to change

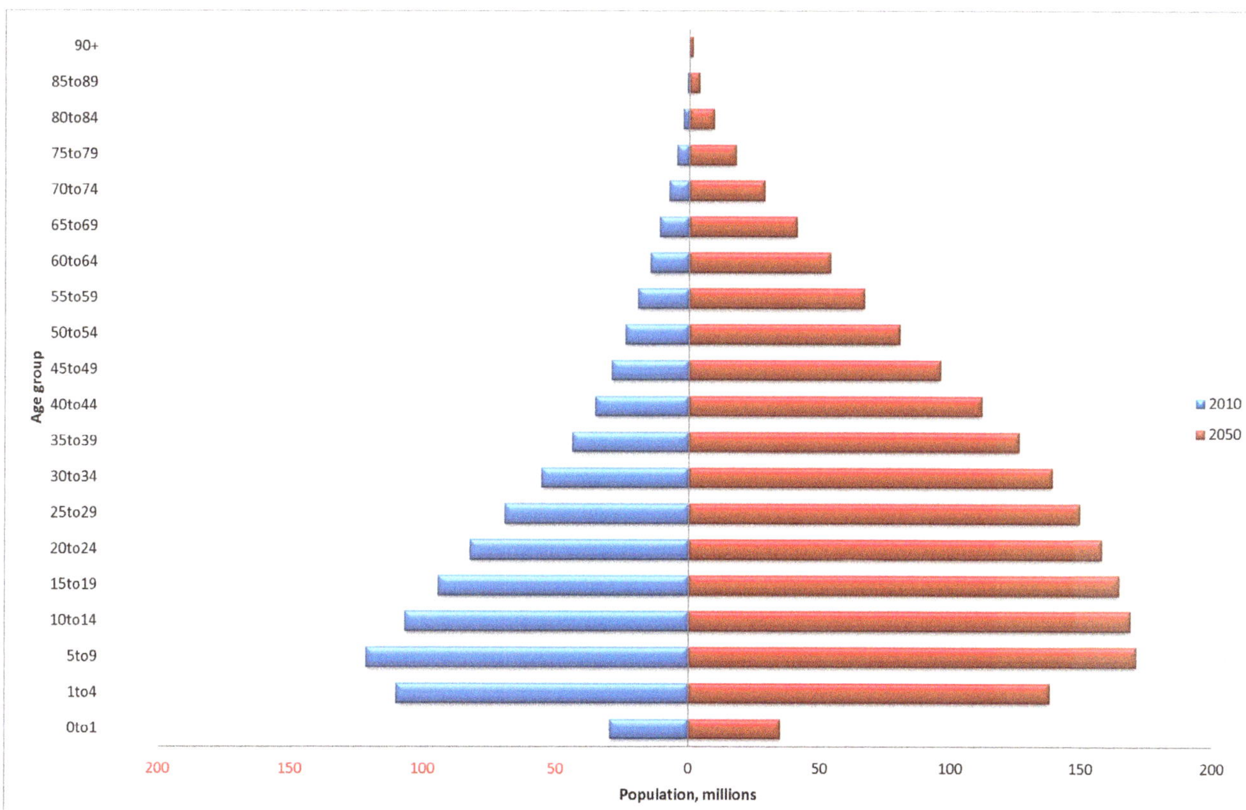

Figure 1. Population age distribution in Sub-Saharan Africa, 2010 and 2050. Source: United Nations Population Data [36].

significantly over time for the majority of mental disorders; however, there will likely be changes for substance use disorders and the implications of this assumption are addressed in the discussion [8].

Service requirements for 2010 and 2050

Recommended packages of care and service requirements in low- and middle-income countries[14–16] formed the basis of estimation methods of full time equivalent (FTE) staffing requirements. Guided by the priority disorders identified in Bruckner et al [14], 7 mental and substance use disorders which were included in GBD 2010 were selected for modelling. Selected disorders were schizophrenia, bipolar disorder, depression, alcohol dependence disorder, opioid dependence disorder, conduct disorder and attention deficit hyperactivity disorder (ADHD) (the latter two for 5–19 year olds only). The seven disorders selected are not intended to represent the only important conditions (dementia and epilepsy are examples of other important conditions that could be added to future modelling).

Prevalence estimates for 2010 and 2050

Disorder prevalence estimates are central to the estimation of FTE staff requirements. The more recent prevalence estimates from GBD 2010 were used over the prevalence estimates reported in Bruckner et al. Pooled prevalence estimates for each disorder and each of four Sub-Saharan Africa regions (East, West, Southern and Central) were calculated using 2010 age and sex-standardised prevalence estimates derived from DisMod-MR modelling. Predicted pooled prevalence for 2050 was also calculated using 2010 age and sex-standardised prevalence estimates and UN population data for 2050 (see appendix S1 for UN population figures). Pooled prevalence for the paediatric disorders (ADHD and conduct disorder) were based on only prevalence estimates from the 5–19 year age groups. Using similar methods, pooled prevalence estimates for the entire Sub-Saharan Africa (4 regions) were also calculated. Prevalence estimates at the regional level were applied to each country within that region.

Adjustments to prevalence estimates were necessary to account for comorbidity between disorders. To allow for comorbidity between depression, alcohol and opioid use disorders, the separate and combined prevalence of MDD, alcohol use, alcohol dependence, drug use and drug dependence were sourced from South African survey data published by Williams et al [17]. The GBD prevalence estimates for depression, alcohol and opioid use disorders were reduced in proportion to their weighting relative to the prevalence of any depressive or substance use disorder. This was translated into the formula: (disorder prevalence divided by sum of prevalences of individual depressive and substance use disorders) multiplied by (prevalence of any depressive or substance use disorder). Across the board, rates were adjusted down to 87.6% of the original total. This method was based on Lund et al [18].

It was assumed that conduct disorder and ADHD held no comorbidity with other disorders. However it was considered implausible to assume no comorbidity in the model between conduct disorder and ADHD. Data from the US National Comorbidity Survey Replication – Adolescent [19] were therefore used to estimate comorbidity between these childhood disorders, as no African data were available. As per the method for depressive and substance use disorders above, the raw prevalence of ADHD, conduct and oppositional defiant disorders, as well as the prevalence of any of these behavioural disorders, was used to calculate a comorbidity weighting (prevalence/sum of individual behavioural disorders) x (prevalence of any behavioural disorder). The GBD prevalence rates for ADHD and conduct disorder were adjusted down to 69.8% of the originals. A table summarising the pooled prevalence of selected mental and substance use disorders in Sub-Saharan Africa from GBD 2010, by region and adjusted for comorbidity can be found in the appendix S1.

For the purpose of the modelling (and due to a lack of data to estimate otherwise) it was assumed that bipolar disorder and schizophrenia held no significant comorbidity with any other mental disorders. Although these two disorders experience high comorbidity with substance use disorders, it was considered that the treatment patients would require for their substance use disorder would be in addition to that for their bipolar disorder or schizophrenia and therefore comorbidity adjustments were not made. The implications of this are explored in the discussion.

Treatment packages

Treatment coverage targets and care packages (service coverage and utilization rate for each type of service) for the priority disorders were taken from Bruckner et al [14] (see appendix S1 for more details). A slight modification to the Bruckner et al model was made where an equivalent psychosocial treatment package as that for alcohol use disorders was added for opioid use disorders in line with WHO opioid treatment guidelines [20].

For each disorder, region or country and service type, the number of bed-days for inpatient or residential or number of sessions for outpatient care was equal to the *population X adjusted prevalence X treatment coverage target X service coverage X utilisation rate,* where: *treatment coverage target* is the percentage of prevalent cases requiring or presenting for any treatment; *service coverage* is the percentage of treated cases needing care in this specific service setting in a year; and *utilisation rate* is the average number of bed days used per case per year for cases treated in inpatient services, or the average number of consultations or sessions per case per year for cases treated in outpatient services.

Staffing ratios

Staffing ratios recommended by the mhGAP costing tool [16] allowed estimation of staffing by health professional type – psychiatrist, other physician/doctor, nurse, psychologist, other psychosocial worker, and other provider/worker. The overall 'nurse' category was further split into psychiatric nurses and general nurses using a ratio of 1:4, based on consultation with African mental health experts in four countries (further field testing is needed to validate this in future, as the figure will vary by country and setting).

FTE staffing estimates by service type

FTE modelling was conducted for both 2010 and 2050, for each of the four Sub-Saharan African regions and a small selection of countries within each region. The selection of countries was done without prejudice and merely as examples to highlight the stark differences that can be observed across countries within the same region. The countries selected for modelling FTE were: Sub-Saharan Africa East – Zambia, Ethiopia, Burundi; Sub-Saharan Africa West – Ghana, Nigeria, Chad; Sub-Saharan Africa Central – Democratic Republic of Congo (DRC), Angola; Sub-Saharan Africa Southern – South Africa, Zimbabwe.

For each region/country, the number of bed-days for inpatient/residential services and sessions for outpatient services were converted into FTE mental health staff requirements using the following formulae. The number of FTE staff required to deliver inpatient/residential mental health care was calculated as: number of bed-days/0.85 (85% bed occupancy rate as per Bruckner et al)/365

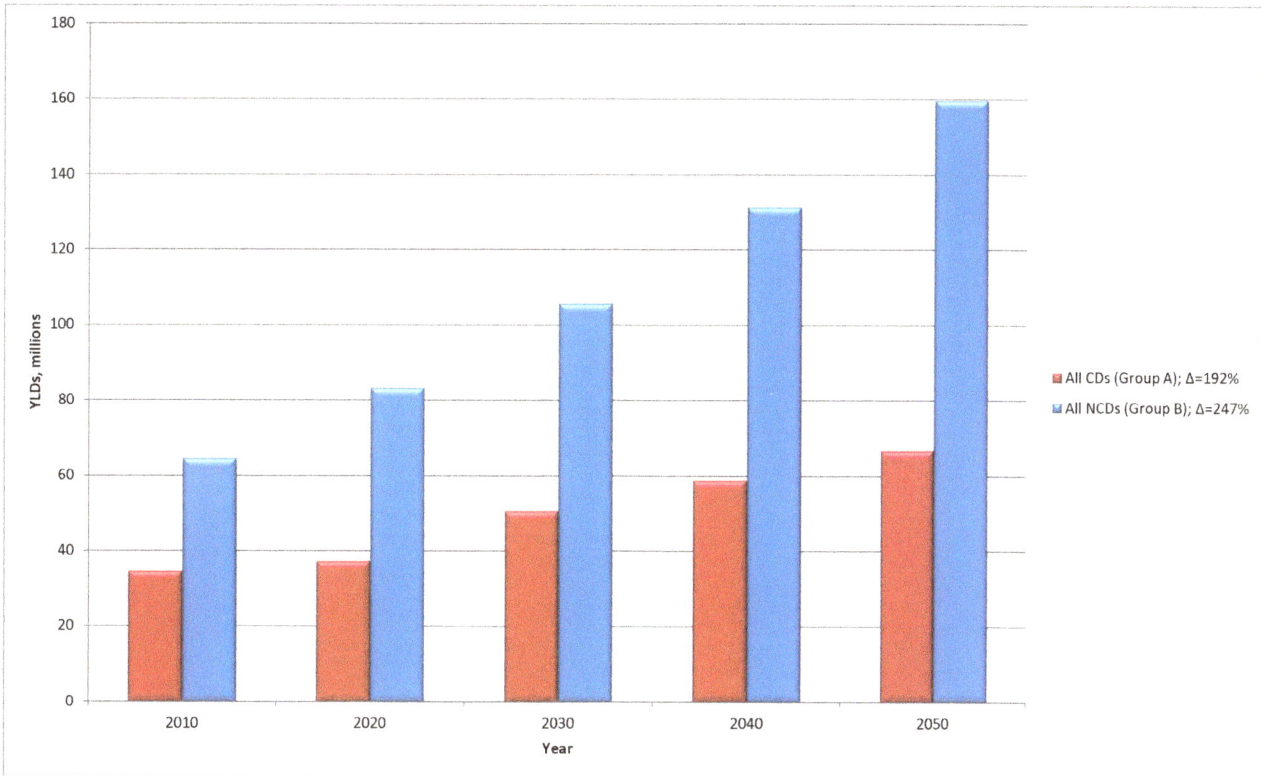

Figure 2. Change in disability burden distribution of communicable and non-communicable diseases in Sub-Saharan Africa. Note: CDs include all communicable, maternal, neonatal and nutritional diseases; NCDs include all non-communicable diseases (including mental and substance use disorders).

service days per annum/25 beds in unit x number of staff per unit (7.5 per 25 beds as per mhGAP) x staffing ratio (proportion of nurses, doctors, and other professionals in that setting from mhGAP).

The number of FTE staff required to deliver outpatient mental health care was calculated as: number of sessions/number of consultations per day/240 working days per year (from mhGAP) X staffing ratio (from mhGAP) [14,21]. Consultations per day were derived from mhGAP as a weighted average across providers in each category of outpatient care: outpatient care −8 consultations per day; primary care −9 consultations per day; psychosocial (ancillary) care −7 consultations per day. Group day programs were assumed to be delivered to an average of 10 users per day.

Finally, gaps between the estimated target FTE staff for 2010 and the current mental health service FTE staffing levels in the selected countries, as reported by the WHO Mental Health Atlas [9], were estimated.

Results

Burden of disease

The population distribution in Sub-Saharan Africa is expected to change dramatically over the next 40 years (Figure 1). An expected doubling of population size from approximately 0.9 billion to 1.8 billion will be accompanied by a significant ageing. As a result, a population dominated by under 25 s in 2010 (63%) will be represented by over 25 s in 2050 (53%).

This change in demographics will result in a rapidly growing disparity between the disability burden associated with communicable compared to non-communicable diseases, with a one and a half fold increase in non-communicable compared to communicable diseases (Figure 2). Interestingly, although considering only population ageing and growth would see communicable diseases experience a doubling in burden, the burden in under 5 s – traditionally the most important group for communicable diseases – could see only a relatively modest increase over time of around 24% (appendix S1).

In terms of individual disorders, the largest contributor to burden of disease is MDD (Figure 3). This is followed by schizophrenia which is considered to be one of the most disabling conditions across all diseases in GBD. The childhood disorders of conduct disorder and ADHD will see relatively little increase in burden as the populations of SSA ages significantly over the next 40 years.

In terms of mental and substance use disorders, all Sub-Saharan African regions would experience an increase in burden of around 130% in the absence of a change in disorder prevalence rates (Figure 4). This increase would vary across regions, with the largest (196%) seen in Sub-Saharan Africa Central and the lowest (28%) in Sub-Saharan Africa Southern (East = 139% and West = 129%).

Mental and substance use disorders were the leading cause of YLDs in Sub-Saharan Africa in 2010 (18.94% of total) and an estimated rise from approximately 20 million YLDs to 45 million YLDs could be experienced by 2050. Based on the individual effects of demographic changes alone, by 2050 mental and substance use disorders may be equivalent to approximately two thirds the YLDs of the entire communicable diseases group (67 million YLDs, appendix S1).

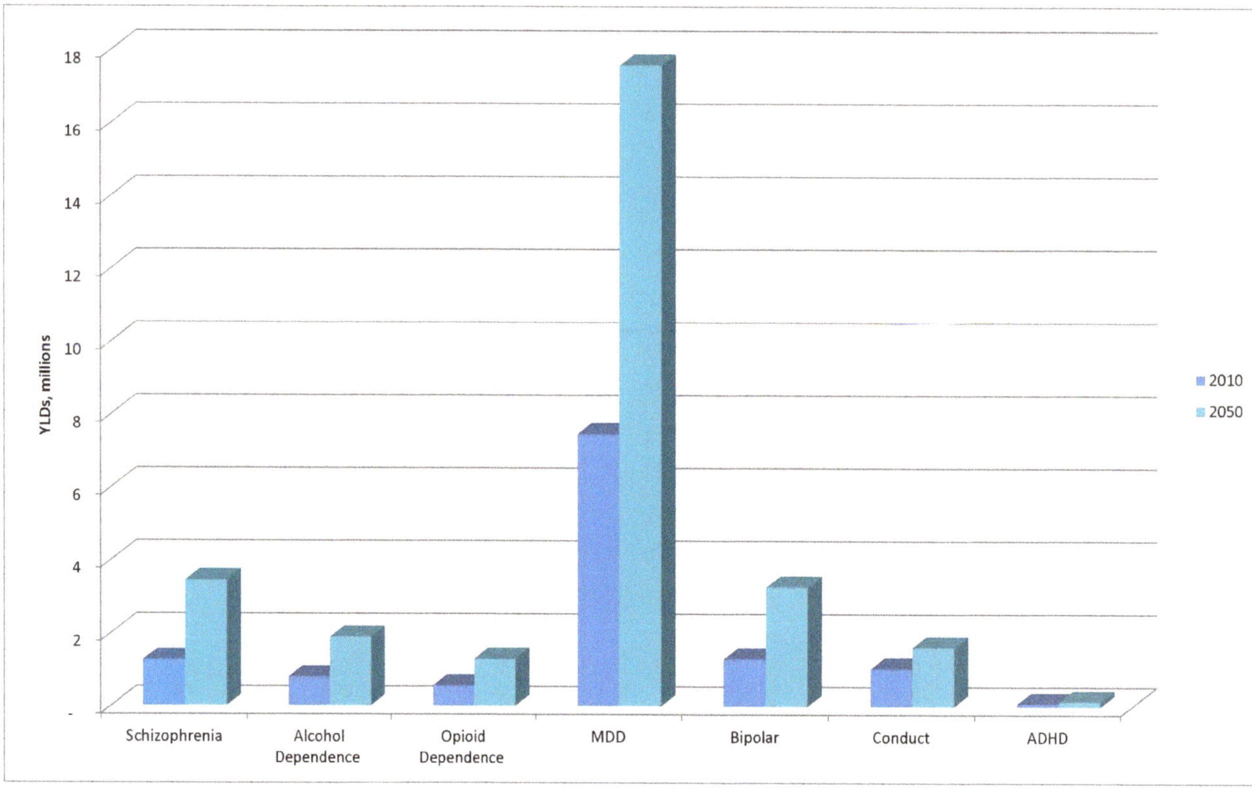

Figure 3. Disability burden for individual mental and substance use disorders, 2010 to 2050.

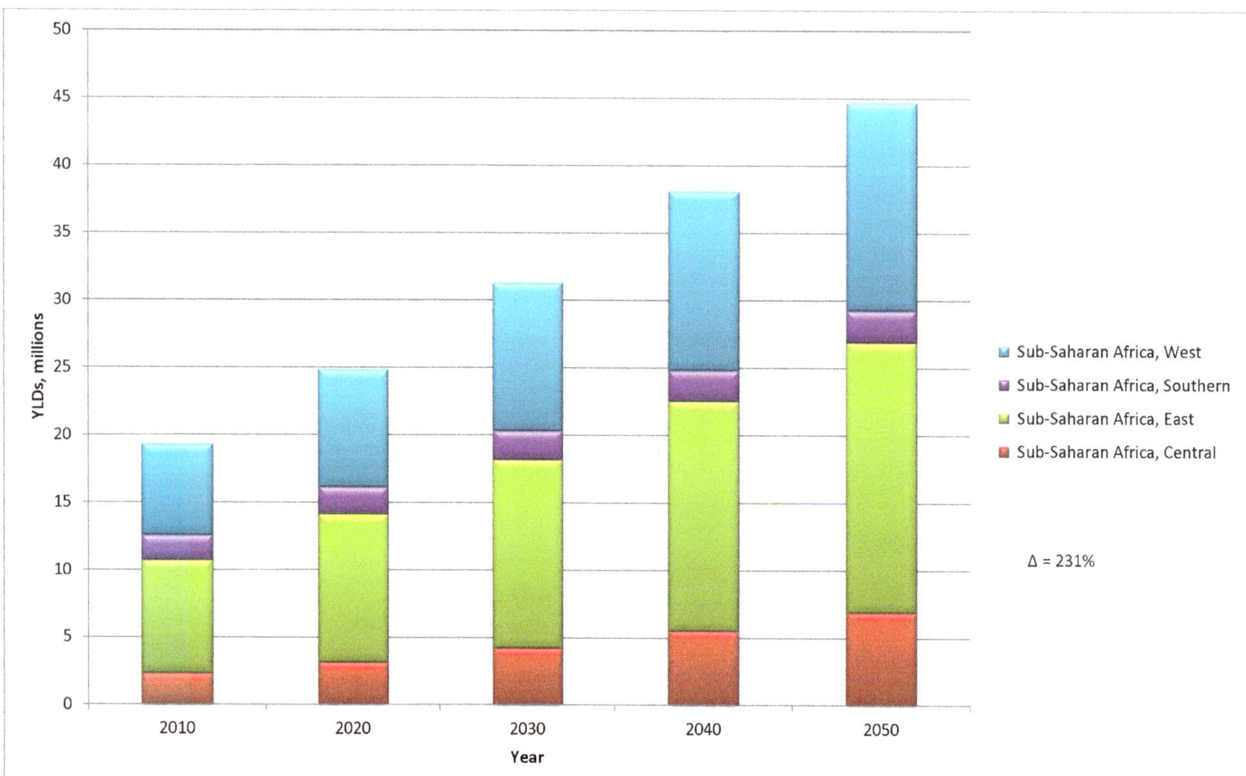

Figure 4. Disability burden of mental and substance use disorders in Sub-Saharan Africa over time, all ages.

Importantly, the shifting population distribution of Sub-Saharan Africa seen in Figure 1 translates directly to the mental and substance use burden changes seen in Figure 5, which shows the increase in burden by age group. This is important for this group of disorders, where the 20–54 age group is typically most affected.

Health service requirements

The overall predicted increase in target FTE per 100,000 population in each region from 2010 to 2050 is 24.0 to 24.3, due to demographic changes influencing overall prevalence (Table 1). This seemingly modest increase can be misleading though and only when converted to absolute FTE do the estimates become more meaningful in terms of health system planning. Target FTE for Sub-Saharan Africa Southern in 2050 will increase by around 3,700 from the 2010 target, whilst the target FTE for Sub-Saharan Africa East, a far more populous region, will need to increase by 95,400 over the 2010 to 2050 time period to meet the growth in burden of disease.

Not only are there significant differences in target FTE increases across the 4 regions, but also within the countries of each region (Figure 6). The highly populous countries of Ethiopia, Nigeria and DRC highlight well the impact of population growth and ageing on health system requirements when compared against their neighbouring countries. Nigeria is predicted to require an additional 65,000 FTE staff to provide mental health care by 2050. In contrast, increases required in South Africa and Zimbabwe are expected to be much smaller.

Perhaps more important than predicted increases in target FTE is the gap between the estimated minimum FTE staffing requirements for 2010 and the actual FTE staffing numbers that currently exist within countries as reported by the WHO Mental Health Atlas. The health challenges in Sub-Saharan Africa are clearly demonstrated here with some countries reportedly having only a fraction of current target staffing levels. Although current FTE estimates from the WHO Mental Health Atlas and FTE targets proposed in this paper are not strictly comparable across the board, two groups of mental health workers, psychiatrists and psychologists, can provide a reasonable indication of any shortfall in mental health workers within a country (Table 2). Our estimates highlight a very significant shortfall of mental health workers across all SSA countries, with large variations within the same geographical regions. Even South Africa, with clearly the best mental health staffing capacity, appears to be lacking in crucial areas such as numbers of psychiatrists. Particularly notable is Nigeria, a country with low current capacity and one of the highest predicted increases in requirements.

Discussion

We used UN population data to forecast the change in disability-associated burden of seven of the major mental and substance use disorders in Sub-Saharan Africa from 2010 to 2050. It is estimated that during this 40 year period the population will double in size and age significantly, making way for the dramatic health transition seen in other regions of the world. Predictions clearly highlight the anticipated shift from communicable diseases characterised by high mortality to non-communicable diseases with a chronic and disabling course.

Naturally, modelling burden estimates holding YLD rates constant makes several assumptions, including that disorder prevalence and disability weights remain constant. Whilst this is entirely plausible for many non-communicable diseases, indeed the prevalence of many mental disorders has been shown to not change significantly over time [8], this may not be true for others. Drug use disorder prevalence, for example, is expected to increase in the Sub-Saharan Africa regions in the coming years, largely driven by changing routes of drug trafficking [22,23].

Modelling changes in communicable diseases is also not straight forward. Different factors are at play and will influence the estimates. Firstly, the successes of public health campaigns such as expanded programs on immunisation and insecticide treated nets to combat malaria should continue to reduce the prevalence of infectious diseases. Secondly, improvements in health systems and treatments may not reduce the prevalence of some communicable diseases but shift the burden from premature mortality to a more chronic health loss; the push towards universal access to anti-retroviral therapies makes HIV the definitive example of this and will shape the future burden of disease in Sub-Saharan Africa substantially. In terms of disability, it is possible that the gains made by declines in prevalence of communicable, maternal, neonatal and nutritional diseases over the next 40 years will be partially offset by the increase in burden of chronic HIV. Whatever the scenario for communicable disease may be, it is clear that the balance in the contribution of communicable and non-communicable diseases to disease burden is set to change dramatically.

The consequences of a rising burden on non-communicable disease (NCD) are far-reaching. For the mental and substance use disorders, largest group of NCD's the impacts are long-lasting at the level of the individual, family and community [24]. Quality of life is impacted and economic costs are significant. A recent study estimates that the cumulative global impact of mental disorders may amount to US$16 trillion of lost economic output over the next 20 years, equivalent to 25% of global GDP in 2010 [25].

The secondary health outcomes of mental disorders also need to be considered. For example, major depression has been shown to be an independent risk factor for other important non-communicable disorders such as ischaemic heart disease [26] and a consistent association between HIV and poor mental health has been reported [27]. The strong and often bidirectional relationships that exist between mental and substance use disorders with communicable disease, non-communicable disease and injuries emphasises the critical role of mental health [27].

Due to the pressures of communicable disease and malnutrition, mental health in Africa has been low on the priority list to-date. In terms of policy, a recent WHO report has revealed only 42.2% of countries within the WHO Africa region report having a dedicated mental health policy, 67% possess a mental health plan and 44% report having dedicated mental health legislation [9]. African countries reportedly spend less than 1% of their health budgets on mental health [28].

As a result mental health services are poorly resourced and generally accessible to only the most severely ill and then as inpatients in urban facilities. Mental health care provided outside the hospital by health and social workers based in the community is only available in half of African countries [28]. Globally, treatment rates for people with mental and substance use disorders remain low [29,30], with treatment gaps over 90% in low and middle income countries [29]. Perhaps an exception to this is in traumatised populations where non-government organisations are present, providing temporary mental health services during emergency or post-conflict response efforts. However, these services are not sustainable and it is important to prepare for chronic disease and disability services beyond acute care.

In keeping with the recommendations of WHO, reaching FTE targets set in this paper requires a shift from current practice in most African countries, where psychiatric hospitals are the main site of service delivery, and consume the vast majority of the

Table 1. Mental health workforce requirements for Sub-Saharan Africa, year 2010 and 2050[1,2].

	Sub-Saharan Africa, East			Sub-Saharan Africa, West			Sub-Saharan Africa, Central			Sub-Saharan Africa, Southern		
	Target FTE 2010	Target FTE 2050	Suggested increase[3]	Target FTE 2010	Target FTE 2050	Suggested increase	Target FTE 2010	Target FTE 2050	Suggested increase[3]	Target FTE 2010	Target FTE 2050	Suggested increase[3]
Provider type												
Psychiatrist	1.8	1.9	7,400	1.7	1.8	6,200	1.9	1.9	2,900	1.8	1.9	300
Medical officer/clinical officer	2.5	2.5	9,900	2.3	2.4	8,200	2.5	2.6	4,000	2.5	2.5	400
Psychiatric nurse	2.1	2.2	8,500	2.0	2.0	7,100	2.2	2.2	3,400	2.1	2.2	300
General nurse	8.5	8.6	33,800	8.1	8.2	28,200	8.6	8.8	13,500	8.6	8.7	1,300
Psychologist	2.0	2.1	8,100	1.9	2.0	6,800	2.1	2.1	3,200	2.0	2.1	300
Psychosocial provider	3.5	3.6	14,100	3.3	3.4	11,700	3.6	3.7	5,600	3.5	3.6	500
Other primary care	3.5	3.5	13,800	3.2	3.3	11,200	3.5	3.6	5,500	3.5	3.5	500
Service type												
Outpatient care	10.9	11.0	42,800	10.2	10.2	34,900	11.1	11.3	17,200	11.0	11.1	1,600
Psychosocial care	2.5	2.6	10,400	2.2	2.3	8,100	2.6	2.7	4,200	2.6	2.6	400
Inpatient care	10.5	10.7	42,300	10.2	10.4	36,400	10.6	10.9	16,700	10.6	10.9	1,700
Total	24.0	24.3	95,400	22.6	22.9	79,400	24.4	24.8	38,100	24.2	24.6	3,700

[1]FTE are expressed as a rate per 100,000 population.
[2]The suggested increase to 2050 was calculated by subtracting the target full time equivalent for 2050 in absolute numbers from that of 2010. [3]Rounded to nearest hundred.

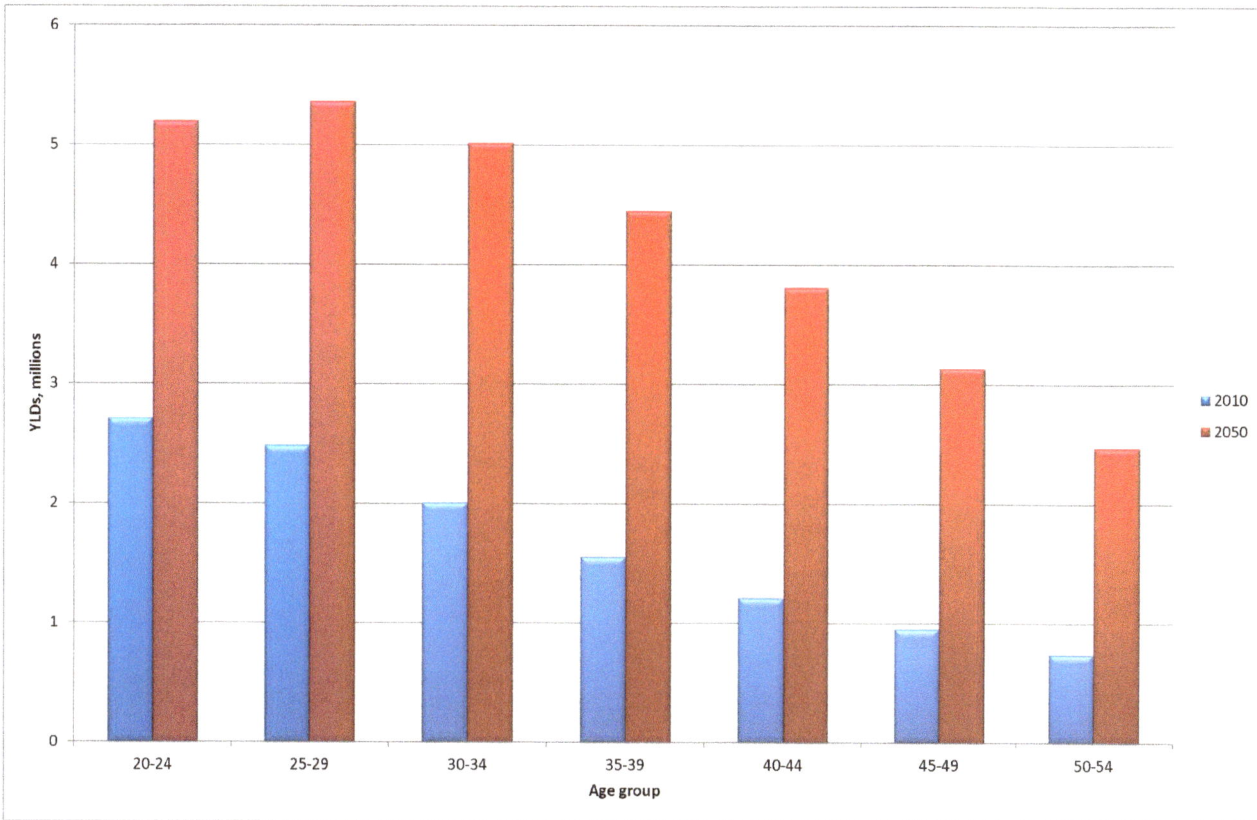

Figure 5. Change in disability burden of mental and substance use disorders over time, 20–54 years by age group, all Sub-Saharan Africa.

country's mental health budget [9]. Instead a new model is required which involves substantial investment in the training of primary care practitioners, supported by district based mental health specialist teams, using a task sharing model that mobilises local community resources [31,32]. The new model also requires substantial investment in smaller inpatient psychiatric units, based in district and regional general hospitals as reflected in the inpatient services targets which demand the biggest increase in resources in this model.

Health transitions in other regions of the world have been rapid [4]. The health system reforms required to deal with dramatic changes in burden of disease are intimidating and will take long term careful planning. However the human and economic costs of not preparing for this will be substantial. Sub-Saharan Africa is in a particularly challenging position as it will soon be caught in the rising tide of non-communicable disease, yet it still has a considerable way to go in the fight against communicable, maternal, neonatal and nutritional diseases. A logical starting point in the preparation might be to implement packages of care for key mental disorders which have been designed for low- and middle-income countries and provide realistic goals given challenging environments such as those in Sub-Saharan Africa [21,33]. Fundamental in scaling up services is increasing the mental health workforce [14] and integrating mental health into primary health care [34,35]. A continuing commitment to addressing key research priorities is also vital [34].

Limitations

As highlighted previously, this modelling is limited to disability-associated burden only and makes the assumption of unchanged disease prevalence and disability weights over time. Whilst this may be a reasonable representation for the future of many non-communicable diseases, changes in disease profiles of communicable diseases will be likely. As mental and substance use disorders are highly disabling conditions which carry a relatively small amount of directly-associated mortality and there will be a future shift to chronic, disabling diseases it was seen appropriate to selectively present disability-associated burden forecasts.

One obvious omission from this paper which is particularly relevant to the Sub-Saharan African context is that of neurological disorders. Neurological disorders were modelled separately from mental and substance use disorders in GBD 2010 and were not included in our modelling. Given epidemiological transition and ageing population, the inclusion of neurological disorders (dementia in particular) would add substantially to the predicted changes in burden and FTE requirements and have significant implications for concomitant service requirements.

Other assumptions of our estimates are that predicted demographic changes are correct. The estimation process of mental disorder YLD rates ascertained in GBD 2010 additionally carried some limitations which have been discussed elsewhere [8]. In particular, the lack of data from the Sub-Saharan region was problematic and more epidemiological data is required from these regions.

Comorbidity adjustments were not made between bipolar disorder and schizophrenia and substance use disorders when

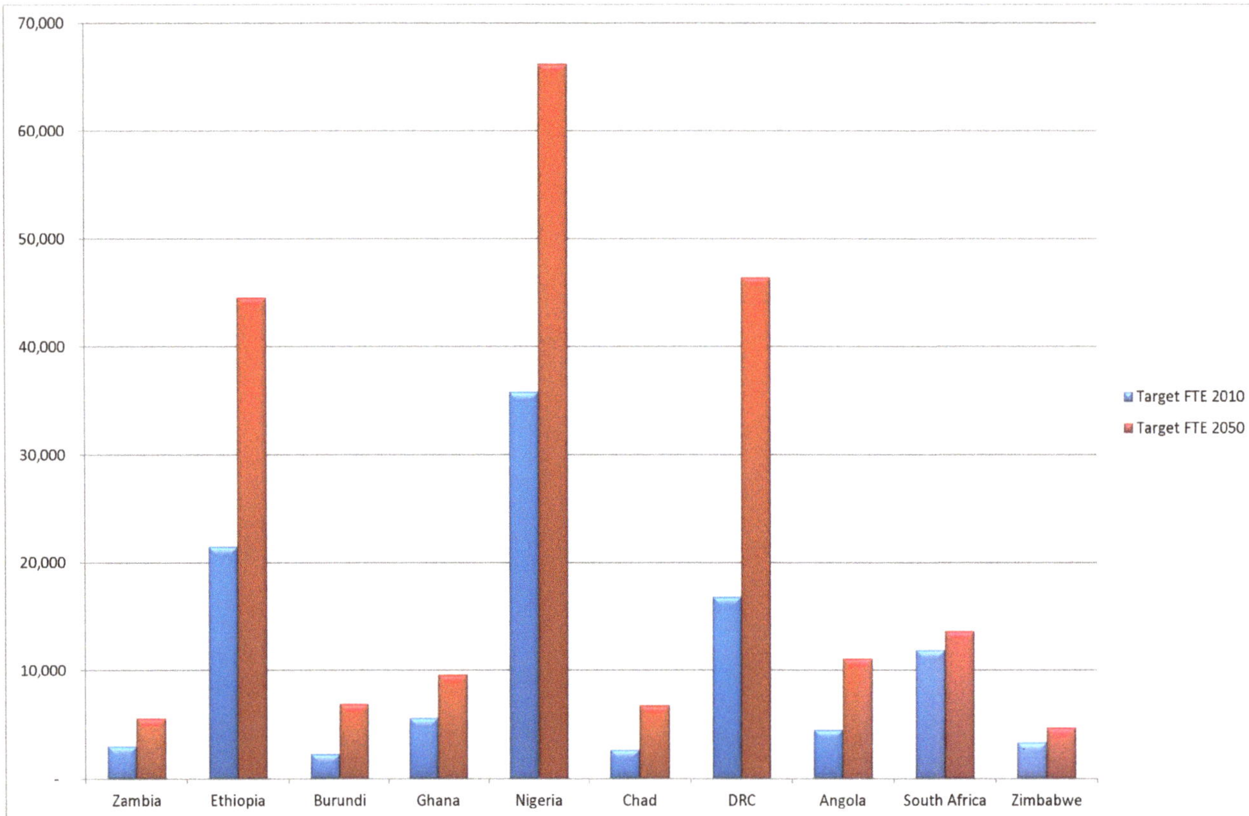

Figure 6. Predicted increase in FTE staff requirements for mental health care for selected Sub-Saharan African countries, 2010 to 2050. Note: SSA East – Zambia, Ethiopia, Burundi; SSA West – Ghana, Nigeria, Chad; SSA Central – DRC, Angola; SSA Southern – South Africa, Zimbabwe.

the known comorbidity is high. There was no clear way to adjust prevalence between these disorders in a way that would reflect the reality of how service requirements would likely reduce (that is, a reduction in substance use services) given the clinical reality that any reduction in service requirements for a patient experiencing bipolar disorder or schizophrenia and a substance use disorder

Table 2. Current and target 2010 FTE psychiatrists and psychologists per 100,000 population for selected countries in Sub-Saharan Africa.

Country	Psychiatrists			Psychologists		
	Current	2010 target	% target FTE	Current	2010 target	% target FTE
Sub-Saharan Africa East						
Zambia	0.03	0.8	4%	0.02	0.3	7%
Ethiopia	0.04	0.8	5%	0.02	0.3	7%
Burundi	0.01	0.8	1%	0.01	0.3	3%
Sub-Saharan Africa West						
Ghana	0.07	0.8	9%	0.04	0.3	13%
Nigeria	0.06	0.8	8%	0.02	0.3	7%
Chad	0.01	0.8	1%	0.01	0.3	3%
Sub-Saharan Africa Central						
DRC	0.07	0.8	8%	0.015	0.3	5%
Angola	0.002	0.8	0.3%	0.003	0.3	1%
Sub-Saharan Africa Southern						
South Africa	0.27	0.8	34%	0.31	0.3	103%
Zimbabwe	0.06	0.8	8%	0.04	0.3	13%

would be minimal given the very different packages of care, intensity of treatment required and the low prevalence of these two mental disorders. Although there is potential that treatment services for substance use disorders have been overestimated to a small degree, it should be noted that estimated staffing requirements for the treatment of opioid and alcohol use disorders will likely be conservative due to using dependence (lower) prevalence estimates, as provided by GBD 2010, with treatment targets and care packages from Bruckner et al designed for the broader category of abuse and dependence.

It is important to recognise that the model used for estimating service requirements in this paper is one developed for both low- and middle-income countries and may need substantial modification to suit the Sub-Saharan African context. Furthermore, it is recognised that each country will have its own health service and workforce configuration and unique challenges, and therefore targets should ideally be tailored to the country context.

Finally, the Mental Health Atlas only records mental health labelled staff working in dedicated facilities/clinics whereas the care packages presented by Bruckner and colleagues represent the total package of care that person needs, including care that might be provided by non-mental health specialists working in general primary care clinics. These key differences make general comparisons against the staffing targets modelled above difficult yet the data is nonetheless informative.

Conclusion

With a rapid epidemiological transition predicted for Sub-Saharan African over the coming decades it is now time to begin planning for health services able to address a dramatic increase in burden of non-communicable disease. Mental and substance use disorders are already the leading cause of disability in Sub-Saharan Africa yet services are drastically under-resourced. Packages of care and service models advocating for a task shifting approach and the embedding of mental health services within the primary health care system are available for LMICs. Investment and health system reform should be a priority for policy makers in Sub-Saharan Africa.

Acknowledgments

We would like to thank Dan Chisholm (World Health Organisation) for his provision of mhGAP costing tool and his guidance in modelling treatment packages. We would also like to thank Oye Gureje (University of Ibadan, Nigeria), Abebaw Fekadu (Addis Ababa University, Ethiopia) and Fred Kigozi (Makerere University, Uganda) for their advice in preparing this paper.

Author Contributions

Conceived and designed the experiments: FJC HAW SD CL LD. Analyzed the data: FJC SD. Contributed to the writing of the manuscript: FJC SD CL LD HAW.

References

1. (2013) The Global Burden of Disease Study 2010. The Lancet 380: 2053–2260.
2. Institute of Health Metrics and Evaluation (2013) The Global Burden of Disease: Generating Evidence, Guiding Policy. Washington.
3. Lozano R, Wang H, Foreman KJ, Rajaratnam JK, Naghavi M, et al. (2011) Progress towards Millennium Development Goals 4 and 5 on maternal and child mortality: an updated systematic analysis. The Lancet 378: 1139–1165.
4. Murray CJ, Vos T, Lozano R, Naghavi M, Flaxman AD, et al. (2012) Disability-adjusted life years (DALYs) for 291 diseases and injuries in 21 regions, 1990–2010: a systematic analysis for the Global Burden of Disease Study 2010. The Lancet 380: 2197–2223.
5. Murray CJL, Rosenfeld LC, Lim SS, Andrews KG, Foreman KJ, et al. (2012) Global malaria mortality between 1980 and 2010: a systematic analysis. The Lancet 379: 413–431.
6. Ortblad KF, Lozano R, Murray CJL (2013) The burden of HIV: insights from the Global Burden of Disease Study 2010. AIDS 27: 2003–2017 2010.1097/QAD.2000b2013e328362ba328367.
7. Institute of Health Metrics and Evaluation (2013) GBD Compare.
8. Whiteford HA, Degenhardt L, Rehm J, Baxter AJ, Ferrari AJ, et al. (2013) Global burden of disease attributable to mental and substance use disorders: findings from the Global Burden of Disease Study 2010. The Lancet 382: 1575–1586.
9. World Health Organization (2011) Mental Health Atlas. Geneva, Switzerland.
10. United Nations (2011) World Population Prospects - The 2010 Revision. New York: United Nations.
11. American Psychiatric Association (APA) (1994) Diagnostic and Statistical Manual of Mental Disorders. Washington, D.C.: American Psychiatric Association Press.
12. World Health Organization (1993) The ICD-10 Classification of Mental and Behavioural Disorders - Diagnostic Criteria for Research. Geneva: World Health Organization.
13. Vos T, Flaxman AD, Naghavi M, Lozano R, Michaud C, et al. (2012) Years lived with disability (YLDs) for 1160 sequelae of 289 diseases and injuries 1990?2010: a systematic analysis for the Global Burden of Disease Study 2010. The Lancet 380: 2163–2196.
14. Bruckner TA, Scheffler RM, Shen G, Yoon J, Chisholm D, et al. (2011) The mental health workforce gap in low-and middle-income countries: a needs-based approach. Bulletin of the World Health Organization 89: 184–194.
15. World Health Organization (2008) mhGAP Mental Health Gap Action Programme: Scaling up care for mental, neurological, and substance use disorders. Available: http://www.who.int/mental_health/mhgap_final_english.pdf.
16. Chisholm D (2014) The default distribution in the mhGAP costing tool.
17. Williams D, Herman A, Stein D, Heeringa S, Jackson P, et al. (2008) Twelve-month mental disorders in South Africa: prevalence, service use and demographic correlates in the population-based South African Stress and Health Study. Psychological Medicine 38: 211.
18. Lund C, Flisher AJ (2009) A model for community mental health services in South Africa. Tropical Medicine & International Health 14: 1040–1047.
19. Merikangas KR, He J-p, Burstein M, Swanson SA, Avenevoli S, et al. (2010) Lifetime prevalence of mental disorders in US adolescents: results from the National Comorbidity Survey Replication-Adolescent Supplement (NCS-A). Journal of the American Academy of Child & Adolescent Psychiatry 49: 980–989.
20. World Health Organization (2009) Guidelines for the psychosocially assisted pharmacological treatment of opioid dependence. Geneva.
21. Chisholm D, Lund C, Saxena S (2007) Cost of scaling up mental healthcare in low- and middle-income countries. British Journal of Psychiatry 191: 528–535.
22. Dewing S, Plüddemann A, Myers BJ, Parry CD (2006) Review of injection drug use in six African countries: Egypt, Kenya, Mauritius, Nigeria, South Africa and Tanzania. Drugs: Education, Prevention, and Policy 13: 121–137.
23. Cockayne J, Williams P (2009) The invisible tide: towards and international strategy to deal with drug trafficking through West Africa: International Peace Institute (IPI).
24. World Health Organization (2001) The World Health Report: 2001: Mental Health: New Understanding, New Hope. Available: http://www.who.int/whr/2001/en/.
25. Bloom DE, Cafiero E, Jané-Llopis E, Abrahams-Gessel S, Bloom LR, et al. (2012) The global economic burden of noncommunicable diseases. Program on the Global Demography of Aging.
26. Charlson FJ, Moran AE, Freedman G, Norman RE, Stapelberg NJ, et al. (2013) The contribution of major depression to the global burden of ischemic heart disease: a comparative risk assessment. BMC Medicine 11: 250.
27. Prince M, Patel V, Saxena S, Maj M, Maselko J, et al. (2007) No health without mental health. The Lancet 370: 859–877.
28. Saxena S, Thornicroft G, Knapp M, Whiteford H (2007) Resources for mental health: scarcity, inequity, and inefficiency. The Lancet 370: 878–889.
29. Wang PS, Aguilar-Gaxiola S, Alonso J, Angermeyer MC, Borges G, et al. (2007) Use of mental health services for anxiety, mood, and substance disorders in 17 countries in the WHO world mental health surveys. The Lancet 370: 841–850.
30. Mathers BM, Degenhardt L, Ali H, Wiessing L, Hickman M, et al. (2010) HIV prevention, treatment, and care services for people who inject drugs: a systematic review of global, regional, and national coverage. The Lancet 375: 1014–1028.

31. Kakuma R, Minas H, van Ginneken N, Dal Poz MR, Desiraju K, et al. (2011) Human resources for mental health care: current situation and strategies for action. Lancet 378: 1654–1663.
32. Patel V, Thornicroft G (2009) Packages of care for mental, neurological, and substance use disorders in low-and middle-income countries: PLoS Medicine Series. PLoS medicine 6: e1000160.
33. Patel V, Simon G, Chowdhary N, Kaaya S, Araya R (2009) Packages of care for depression in low-and middle-income countries. PLoS medicine 6: e1000159.
34. Collins PY, Patel V, Joestl SS, March D, Insel TR, et al. (2011) Grand challenges in global mental health. Nature 475: 27–30.
35. Eaton J, McCay L, Semrau M, Chatterjee S, Baingana F, et al. (2011) Scale up of services for mental health in low-income and middle-income countries. The Lancet 378: 1592–1603.
36. United Nations (2011) World Population Prospects - The 2010 Revision. New York.

20

Executive Function and Mental Health in Adopted Children with a History of Recreational Drug Exposures

Brian J. Piper[1,2*], Hilary M. Gray[2,3], Selena M. Corbett[2,4], Melissa A. Birkett[5], Jacob Raber[2,6]

1 Department of Basic Pharmaceutical Sciences, Husson University, Bangor, Maine, United States of America, **2** Department of Behavioral Neuroscience, Oregon Health and Science University, Portland, Oregon, United States of America, **3** School of Community Health and Department of Counselor Education, Portland State University, Portland, Oregon, United States of America, **4** College of Osteopathic Medicine of the Pacific Northwest, Western University of Health Sciences, Pomona, California, United States of America, **5** Department of Psychological Sciences, Northern Arizona University, Flagstaff, Arizona, United States of America, **6** Department of Neurology and Radiation Medicine, and Division of Neuroscience, ONPRC, Oregon Health and Science University, Portland, Oregon, United States of America

Abstract

Adoptive children are at increased risk for problematic behaviors but the origin of these individual differences in neurobehavioral function is unclear. This investigation examined whether adopted children with prenatal exposure to a wide variety of recreational drugs exhibited higher scores (i.e. more problems) with executive function and psychiatric symptomology. Caregivers of children ages 5 to 18 completed an online survey with items about use of alcohol, nicotine, or methamphetamine during pregnancy followed by the Behavior Rating Inventory of Executive Function (BRIEF, N = 437 including 59 adoptive parents) or the Child Behavior Checklist (CBCL, N = 549 including 54 adoptive parents). Relative to a comparison group of children raised by their biological parents, adoptive children that were polysubstance exposed during prenatal development exhibited higher rates of academic difficulties and were behind their classmates in math and reading. Adoptive children had statistically and clinically significant higher BRIEF ratings and this pattern was similar for boys and girls. CBCL ratings were significantly increased in adoptive children, particularly for Externalizing and Attention problems. Adoptive children with a history of polysubstance exposures including alcohol, nicotine, and methamphetamine are at heightened risk for difficulties with executive function as well as various psychopathologies. These findings suggest that increased monitoring to identify and implement remediation strategies may be warranted for adopted children with a history of *in utero* drug exposures.

Editor: Kenji Hashimoto, Chiba University Center for Forensic Mental Health, Japan

Funding: This work was supported by the National Institute of Drug Abuse (L30 DA027582, T32 DA07262), the National Institute of Environmental Health Sciences (T32 ES007060-31A1), the Oregon Clinical Translational Research Institute (UL1 RR024140, and the Husson University School of Pharmacy. The funders had no role in study design, data collection and analysis, decision to publish, or preparation of the manuscript.

Competing Interests: The authors have declared that no competing interests exist.

* Email: piperbj@husson.edu

Introduction

An extensive and long-standing literature has thoroughly documented that adoptive children are over-represented in clinical settings and have academic difficulties [1]. Meta-analyses of parental reports using instruments like the Child Behavior Checklist (CBCL) have documented that domestic adoptees had more total problems, Externalizing problems, and Internalizing problems than international adoptees [2]. The origins and processes responsible for these individual differences has become an area of increasing interest with an emphasis on psychological, endocrine, and genetic factors [1]. The teratogenic potential of prenatal exposure to recreational drugs to contribute to adverse outcomes [3] has received less systematic attention among offspring that are subsequently put-up for adoption. This oversight may be due to a variety of factors including that exact information regarding the timing and extent of drug use may be impractical to obtain from the birth mother [4]. Alternatively, among polysubstance abusing women who may have multiple legal problems who subsequently become involved with child welfare agencies, it may be challenging to isolate the unique contribution of an individual agent from other comorbid conditions including under-utilization of medical services, poor nutrition/decreased rates of breast feeding, maternal stress, domestic violence, trauma, age of the child at adoption, or a sub-optimal socio-economic environment. However, there are at least three reasons why adopted children are an important population to study. First, a mother whose drug use patterns are extensive enough to contribute to the loss of her legal rights to child custody may provide important insights into the risks associated with a particular drug that may not be as readily apparent among the offspring of women with less intense use patterns. Second, adoptive children provide an important natural experiment, analogous to standard practices by preclinical investigations, to begin to untangle the importance of the prenatal and postnatal environment. Third, we have found that adoptive parents, as a group, are strong advocates for their children and valuable participants in research studies which could form the empirical foundation for remediation efforts. Together, these factors form the impetus for this report.

Executive function refers to neurocognitive processes responsible for generating and regulating behavior which includes selective attention, forming plans, working memory, solving problems, and mental flexibility. Executive function elements show a dose-dependent sensitivity to *in utero* exposure to a wide variety of recreational drugs, most prominently alcohol [5,6] but also nicotine [7,8], and methamphetamine [9,10]. Interestingly, girls, but not boys, prenatally exposed to cocaine showed more problems with executive function as determined by a parent completed questionnaire, the Behavior Rating Inventory of Executive Function (BRIEF) [11]. As executive function is an important capacity that also contributes to a wide variety of psychiatric conditions (e.g. Bipolar Disorder), this paper reports on two complementary investigations describing parentally rated behavior in adopted and non-adopted offspring with the BRIEF (Study I) and CBCL (Study II). We hypothesized that there are pronounced abnormalities in executive function and psychopathology, largely independent of child age and sex, among adoptive children with a history of prenatal drug exposures.

Materials and Methods

Caregivers of children ages 5 to 18 (Study I, N = 437) or 6 to 18 (Study II, N = 539) were recruited for a child behavior investigation which was displayed on the volunteer and community sections of Craigslist (craigslist.org) as well as the Oregon Post-Adoption Resource Center website (orparc.org) and newsletter. Paper flyers were prominently and frequently posted on community boards throughout Oregon Health Science University (OHSU), the Portland metro area, and western Oregon/western Washington (e.g. laundromats, libraries). Participants were not offered an incentive for their participation. This anonymous online survey was administered by Research Electronic Data Capture (REDCap), version 1.3.9, an application for procuring online databases with maximal security for sensitive information [12]. Exclusion criteria were incomplete/unfinished questionnaires and a child age that was outside the range of the instruments (5 to 18 for the BRIEF, 6 to 18 for the CBCL). The Institutional Review Board of OHSU (Study I & II, protocol #5720) as well as Northern Arizona University (Study II, protocol #11.0169) approved all of the procedures including the consent form.

Measures

After completing an online consent, the caregivers began the survey which typically took about twenty minutes. The first half of the items were organized from less to more sensitive and included questions about maternal and child demographics (e.g. age, sex, ethnicity), academic performance (e.g. "Please rate your child's performance in reading with relation to their scores on the state's standardized test." with options of below, at, or above grade level), and child psychiatric and neurological conditions (e.g. diagnosis of Attention Deficit Hyperactivity Disorder). An additional item was added for study II (What percent of your child's life have they lived with you?). Questions on maternal drug use were organized into two periods: during pregnancy and specifically during the third trimester. Because pre-adoption histories may not be known with certainty in all cases, the response options for the drugs most likely to be used during pregnancy (alcohol and nicotine) were, yes, no, suspect, or don't know. The Behavior Rating Inventory of Executive Function (BRIEF) accounted for the remaining 86 items in Study I and the Child Behavior Checklist (CBCL) accounted for the final 118 items in Study II. As data collection was anonymous, there is no simple method to determine if any parents from Study I also participated in Study II.

The BRIEF is a rating instrument completed by parents for the neuropsychological assessment of children and adolescents which focuses on the child's everyday activities at home and at school. Each behavior is rated as never, sometimes, or often a problem (1 to 3 points, respectively) in the last six months. The eight BRIEF scales form two measures of executive functioning (Metacognition and Behavioral Regulation) and these are totaled for an overall measure (the Global Executive Composite or GEC). The Metacognition Index consists of the following five scales: 1) Working Memory, the capacity to hold information to complete a task; 2) Monitor, self-monitoring habits; 3) Organization of Materials, the extent of orderliness of play and work areas; 4) Plan/Organize, the capability to foresee future events, construct goals, and implement the appropriate steps to complete a task; and: 5) Initiate, the ability to act independently to produce ideas, responses, or problem solving strategies. The Behavioral Regulation Index is composed of three scales: 1) Emotional Control, the ability to regulate emotions appropriately; 2) Shift, the capability to change from one activity to another; and 3) Inhibit, the capacity to regulate one's behavior at the appropriate time and not act on impulse. Negativity scale scores were obtained by summing the number of select items (maximum = 9) with an "often" response. An inconsistency scale score was determined by calculating the difference between ten item pairs (range = 0 to 20) with a score ≥9 interpreted as inconsistent. Standardized (T_{50} scores) were calculated based on age/sex norms with higher scores indicating greater severity. A small (4.7%) portion of the BRIEF standardization sample (N = 1,417) consisted of grandparents and adoptive/foster parents. The BRIEF has excellent internal consistency (Cronbach's alpha = 0.80 to 0.98) and very good test-retest reliability (r>0.70) [13,14]. Additional information about the psychometric properties of the BRIEF including about the moderately large (N = 1,419) normative sample and the traumatic brain injury validation sample is available elsewhere [13,14].

The CBCL 6–18 parent form measures a child's problems and can be completed in approximately 20 minutes [16,17]. Items about the child's behavior are rated by caregiver as being 0 = not true (as far as you know); 1 = somewhat or sometimes true; or 2 = very true or often true. There are separate scoring profiles based on age (6 to 11 or 12 to 18) and sex. The Syndrome scales are Anxious/Depressed, Withdrawn/Depressed, Somatic Complaints, Social Problems, Thought Problems, Attention Problems (including both Inattention and Hyperactivity-Impulsivity items), Rule-Breaking Behavior, Aggressive Behavior, and Other Problems. The Internalizing broadband scale is the sum of Anxious/Depressed, Withdrawn/Depressed and Somatic Complaints scores. Similarly, the Externalizing broadband scale is the sum of the Rule-Breaking Behavior, and Aggressive Behavior scores. Additional information about the Syndrome scales may be found elsewhere [16]. The CBCL has very good internal consistency (Cronbach's alpha for total problems = .97) and one-week test-retest reliability (r = .94) whereas cross-informant correlations are appreciably lower [16]. The full survey, excluding copyrighted materials, is available in the Materials S1.

Data analyses

Statistical analyses were completed with the Systat (Chicago, IL), version 13.0, with data expressed as mean ±SD for tables with ±SEM for figures, and $p<.05$ considered statistically significant. Foster parents were relatively infrequently encountered (N = 3 in Study I and N = 8 in Study II) so were not included in this report. Respondents were divided into two groups, Adoptive (N = 59) and a Comparison group (N = 378) composed of biological mothers (N = 366) or biological fathers (N = 12) for Study I. Similarly,

Study II consisted of an Adoptive (N = 54) group and a Comparison group (N = 485) with biological mothers (N = 469) and biological fathers (N = 26). Please note that demographic information and child ratings from the biological mothers is reported elsewhere [8,15]. Unfortunately, given the use pattern of substances reported, as well as the occurrence of some children where the maternal history was unknown, made it impossible to create a subgroup of adopted children that were unexposed to alcohol, nicotine, or methamphetamine during pregnancy. Analyses were completed on the BRIEF standardized scores and on the percentage of children with clinically significant (T_{50}≥65) problems in that domain. CBCL analyses were conducted using the total (raw) scores and using the percentage meeting clinically significant thresholds (i.e. age and sex corrected). Additional analyses were completed for children (age<13) and adolescents (age≥13) separately. Categorical level analyses were completed with a chi-square, or Likelihood ratios if the N/cell was <5. The Odds Ratio (OR) was listed only for significant associations among dichotomous variables. The data for Study I and Study II are available as Materials S1. Key findings were expressed in terms of effect size (Cohen's *d*) with values of ≈0.20, ≈0.50, or ≥0.80 interpreted as small, medium, or large, respectively.

Results

Sample characteristics in Study I

The majority of respondents were from Oregon (48.9%) or Washington (15.2%). Approximately two-thirds (65.8%) of the Comparison group were recruited from Craigslist relative to only one-third (32.2%) of Adoptive parents ($\chi^2(1) = 24.4$, $p < .001$). Table 1 shows that the Adopted (N = 59) and Comparison (N = 378) groups did not differ significantly in terms of child sex or likelihood of the child being born premature. Adopted children were more likely (OR = 2.8) to be non-white (15.3% Black, 13.6% Alaska Native). Children that were Adopted were significantly more commonly diagnosed with many conditions including Fetal Alcohol Syndrome, a Cognitive Delay (OR = 13.7), Post-Traumatic Stress Disorder (OR = 13.4), Attachment Disorder (OR = 8.6), Motor Development Disorder (OR = 7.1), a Hearing Impairment (OR = 6.8), a birth defect (OR = 6.6), Sensory Integration Disorder (OR = 5.2), a Developmental Disorder (OR = 3.9), Speech Delay (OR = 2.8), or ADHD (OR = 2.2).

The majority (76.3%) of adoptive parents were able to confidently provide information about illicit drug exposures including methamphetamine, marijuana, or cocaine. Two-thirds of the birth mothers of Adoptive children relative to only one out of every twenty-five Comparison moms used methamphetamine during pregnancy (OR = 41.0). The biological mothers of Adoptive children more commonly smoked cigarettes (OR = 25.9) and marijuana (OR = 6.2) as well as consumed alcohol (OR = 30.4) during pregnancy. Examination of maternal drug use patterns specific to the third-trimester revealed continued polysubstance use, particularly of nicotine and alcohol (Table 2). Academically, Adoptive children were more likely to be behind Comparison children in school (OR = 5.2) and also behind their peers on math (OR = 3.0) and reading (OR = 3.3).

Behavior Rating Inventory of Executive Function (BRIEF)

Mean inconsistency ratings did not differ between groups (Adoptive = 3.6±2.1, Comparison = 3.3±1.9) but Adoptive (2.5±2.2) children scored higher than Comparison (1.1±1.8) children on Negativity ($t(435) = 5.59$, $P < .0005$). Similarly, Negativity scores were more likely to be Highly Elevated (≥7) among Adopted (8.5%) than Comparison (1.6%) children ($\chi^2(1) = 9.87$, $P < .005$). Adopted boys exhibited statistically significant elevations on the total (Global Executive Composite, *d* = .69), both broadband scores (*d* = .64 to .66), and all scales (*d* = .42 to .79). The mean BRIEF scores were in the clinically significant (T_{50}≥65) range for Adopted boys on all scales except Organization of Materials (*d* = .42) and Emotional Control (*d* = .49, Figure 1A).

Similarly, Adopted girls demonstrated statistically significantly higher scores than girls living with their biological parents (mother and/or father) on the Global Executive Composite (*d* = 1.25), the broadband scores (Metacognition *d* = .99, Behavioral Regulation Index *d* = 1.45), and the narrowband scales (*d* = .53 to 1.42). Notably, only Organization of Materials (*d* = .53) was below the clinical cut-off (Figure 1B). Although the means were generally higher among Adopted girls relative to Adopted boys, Emotional Control was the only significant sex difference ($t(55) = 2.45$, $P < .05$). Among the Comparison group, boys were rated as having more problems on Organization of Materials ($t(374) = 2.00$, $P < .05$) and Shift ($t(373) = 2.19$, $P < .05$). The same general pattern of group differences between Adoptive and Comparison children was retained when the children with ADHD were excluded (Figure S1A, *d* = .61 to 1.19). There was no evidence that these group differences dissipated with increasing age. In fact, the effect size was larger in adolescents relative to children on ten out of eleven BRIEF scales (Table S1). The percentage of each group that was above the clinical cut-off is shown in Table 3.

Sample characteristics in Study II

Geographically, three-fifths of participants were from the West-Coast of the United States (36.5% Oregon, 12.9% Washington, 11.6% California). Table 1 shows that the Adoptive (N = 54) and Comparison (N = 495) groups did not differ significantly based on child age, sex, ethnicity, or prematurity but that Adoptive children again exhibited more academic difficulties (OR = 3.0), specifically in being behind peers in math (OR = 2.7) and reading (OR = 2.5). The Adopted children typically began living with their current family before the age of three (Mean = 2.7±0.4, Median = 1.9, Min = 0, Max = 11.7 years). Adopted children were more likely to have a wide variety of psychiatric, neurological, and other medical conditions including Fetal Alcohol Syndrome (OR = 30.0), an Attachment Disorder (OR = 23.4), an Anxiety Disorder (OR = 2.4) specifically Post-Traumatic Stress Disorder (OR = 10.0), a Cognitive Delay (OR = 8.0), Sensory Integration Disorder (OR = 7.8), Tourette Disorder (OR = 6.3), Bipolar Disorder (OR = 5.5), a visual impairment (OR = 3.3), or ADHD (OR = 2.6). The birth mother of Adoptive children had lower incomes and education but family income did not currently differ between Adoptive and Comparison children. Only half of Adoptive respondents were able to provide information about prenatal exposures to illicit drugs (methamphetamine, marijuana, cocaine, Oxycontin) and even fewer could definitively answer items regarding alcohol or nicotine. The majority of Adoptive, relative one fifth or less of Comparison children, had been exposed to alcohol, nicotine or methamphetamine during pregnancy. Prenatal marijuana, cocaine, barbiturates, and Oxycontin exposures were also more common among Adoptive children. Methamphetamine and nicotine exposures were also prevalent in Adopted, but not Comparison, children in the third trimester (Table 2).

Child Behavior Checklist (CBCL)

Adopted boys were rated at having more Attention (*d* = .86), Externalizing (*d* = .91), and Internalizing (*d* = .63) problems than Comparison boys. Other group differences included Aggressive Behavior (*d* = .98), Impulsivity (*d* = .97), Social Problems (*d* = .97), and Anxiety/Depression (*d* = .77, Figure 2A). Adopted girls

Table 1. Child and maternal characteristics among respondents completing study I (BRIEF: Behavioral Rating Inventory of Executive Function) or II (CBCL: Child Behavior Checklist).

	Study I: BRIEF				Study II: CBCL			
Child	**Adoptive**		**Comparison**		**Adoptive**		**Comparison**	
Sex (% female, N)	44.1	59	50.2	378	57.4	54	49.0	492
Age (Mean, SD, N)	9.2, 3.9*	59	10.5, 4.0	378	11.0, 3.7	54	11.5, 3.8	495
Ethnicity (% non-white, N)	35.6**	59	16.6	378	31.5	54	23.9	493
Born premature (%, N)	11.3	52	15.4	377	26.5	43	15.6	483
ADHD (%, N)	35.6*	59	20.4	378	31.5**	54	14.9	495
Fetal Alcohol Syndrome (%, N)	10.2***	59	0.0	378	11.1***	54	0.4	495
School performance (% below, N)	31.0***	58	8.0	376	32.0**	53	13.6	494
Math (% below, N)	44.7**	47	26.6	352	38.8**	49	18.8	462
Reading (% below, N)	42.9***	49	18.3	349	36.0**	50	18.3	465
Family								
Age when BM pregnant (Mean, SD, N)	23.4, 6.1*	53	25.6, 6.5	366	24.8, 7.4	52	25.8, 7.0	492
Education of BM (% < High-school, N)	97.9***	47	29.2	359	95.2***	42	26.4	493
Income of BM (% <$10 K, N)	80.0***	25[D]	17.6	369	88.9***	27[D]	21.1	468
Family income (%, >$50 K, N)	53.8	52	47.7	369	64.8	54	43.5	464
Prenatal Drug Exposure								
Nicotine (% exposed, N)	88.9***	36[SD]	23.6	369[SD]	61.9***	21[SD]	20.	489[SD]
Alcohol (% exposed, N)	87.5***	24[SD]	18.7	374	80.0***	15[SD]	13.9	489[SD]
Methamphetamine (% exposed, N)	71.1***	45[D]	4.2	378	74.1***	27[D]	4.3	492
Marijuana (% exposed, N)	46.7***	45[D]	11.4	378	25.9*	27[D]	10.6	492
Cocaine (% exposed, N)	15.6**	45[D]	3.2	378	22.2***	27[D]	1.8	492
Barbiturates (% exposed, N)	4.4*	45[D]	0.	378	11.1***	27[D]	0.2	492
Oxycontin (% exposed, N)	2.2	45[D]	0.0	378	7.4**	27[D]	0.2	492

BM: Birth-mother. Caregivers choosing the [S]suspect or [D]don't know options were excluded (chi-square or t-test *$P<.05$, **$P<.005$, ***$P\leq.0001$).

Table 2. Third-trimester drug exposure among adoptive and comparison children in Study I (BRIEF: Behavioral Rating Inventory of Executive Function) or II (CBCL: Child Behavior Checklist).

	Study I: BRIEF				Study II: CBCL			
	Adoptive	N	Comparison	N	Adoptive	N	Comparison	N
Nicotine	86.1%***	36[SD]	19.1%	378	61.9%	21[SD]	16.8%	489
Alcohol	68.4%***	19[SD]	9.9%	375	33.3%	15[SD]	0.8%	489
Methamphetamine	45.0%***	40[D]	1.6%	378	63.3%***	30[D]	1.2%	492
Marijuana	40.0%***	40[D]	6.3%	378	20.0%**	30[D]	5.5%	492
Cocaine	20.0%***	40[D]	0.8%	378	16.7%***	30[D]	0.4%	492
Methadone	7.5%**	40[D]	0.3%	378	3.3%	30[D]	0.0%	492
Barbiturates	5.0%*	40[D]	0.3%	378	6.7%**	30[D]	0.0%	492
Heroin	5.0%*	40[D]	0.3%	378	3.3%	30[D]	0.0%	492
Oxycontin	2.5%	40[D]	0.0%	378	3.3%	30[D]	0.0%	492

Caregivers choosing the [S]suspect or [D]don't know options were excluded (chi-square *$P<.05$, **$P<.005$, ***$P<.0005$).

exhibited a generally similar pattern with more Attention ($d = .73$), Externalizing ($d = .71$), and Internalizing ($d = .38$) problems than Comparison girls (Figure 2B). The same pattern of group differences between Adopted and Comparison children was observed with children with ADHD excluded (Figure S1B, $d = 0.89$ to 1.27). Among Comparison children, boys showed the anticipated increase in Attention Problems ($t(482) = 2.91$, $P<.005$), specifically Inattention Problems ($t(486) = 2.45$, $P<.05$) as well as Thought Problems ($t(481) = 2.13$, $P<.05$) relative to Comparison girls. Conversely, Comparison girls exhibited the expected increase relative to boys for Anxiety and Depression ($t(486) = -2.77$, $P<.01$). However, no sex differences were present among Adopted children. Adopted boys and girls more frequently had clinically significant Attention and Aggression problems but only boys had more Social and Anxiety/Depression problems and only girls had more Thought Problems (Table 4). The presence of clinically significant problems was equally common among children and adolescents (Table S2). Among the Adoptive children, there were no appreciable CBCL differences between children adopted at younger (<1.5) versus older ages ($P>.11$).

Discussion

The principal findings of this report are that adoptive children, the majority of whom had a history of prenatal exposure to methamphetamine, nicotine, and alcohol, exhibited a pronounced and diffuse elevation in problems with executive function as well as psychiatric symptomology. Importantly, adoptive children have been included in the samples of several behavioral teratology reports [4], specifically of children exposed to alcohol [18], cocaine [19], and methamphetamine [10,20]. These reports can be compared with studies of adoptive children without a known history of substance exposure. A meta-analysis of over 100,000 children determined that there were small, but significant, increases in Externalizing ($d = .24$) and Internalizing ($d = 0.16$) in adopted, relative to nonadopted children [2]. Interestingly, preschoolers with a history of methamphetamine/nicotine exposure showed a relatively focused behavioral profile with higher (i.e. more problematic) ratings, primarily made by their biological parents, for emotional reactivity ($d = .16$) and anxiety/depression ($d = .16$) but no significant elevations at this age (3 and 5) in Attention or Externalizing problems [20]. There is also a large, albeit contentious, literature reviewed in [15] documenting CBCL elevations in the offspring of women that smoked but used other recreational drugs at low levels. For example, New Zealand toddlers whose mothers smoked cigarettes were more likely to be rated as having clinically significant Somatic (OR = 2.4) and Externalizing (OR = 1.8) problems [21]. Prenatal alcohol, unlike cocaine, has generally been reported to be associated with CBCL abnormalities which are not mediated by the postnatal environment [22]. Importantly, the issue of the threshold alcohol dose necessary to induce CBCL increases has not been conclusively determined but the pattern of alcohol intake is likely a key variable [22–24]. The present CBCL ratings, either expressed as the mean or as the percentage above the clinically significant cut-off, were increased in polysubstance exposed adoptive children and is generally consistent with a large body of evidence [22]. Importantly, the magnitude of group differences with effect sizes in the moderate to large size in this sample is indicative a particularly severe pattern of psychopathology.

Polysubstance exposed adoptive children also exhibited statistically and clinically significantly higher (i.e. more problematic) executive function ratings. In contrast to the substantial wealth of prior research with the CBCL, the available information using the

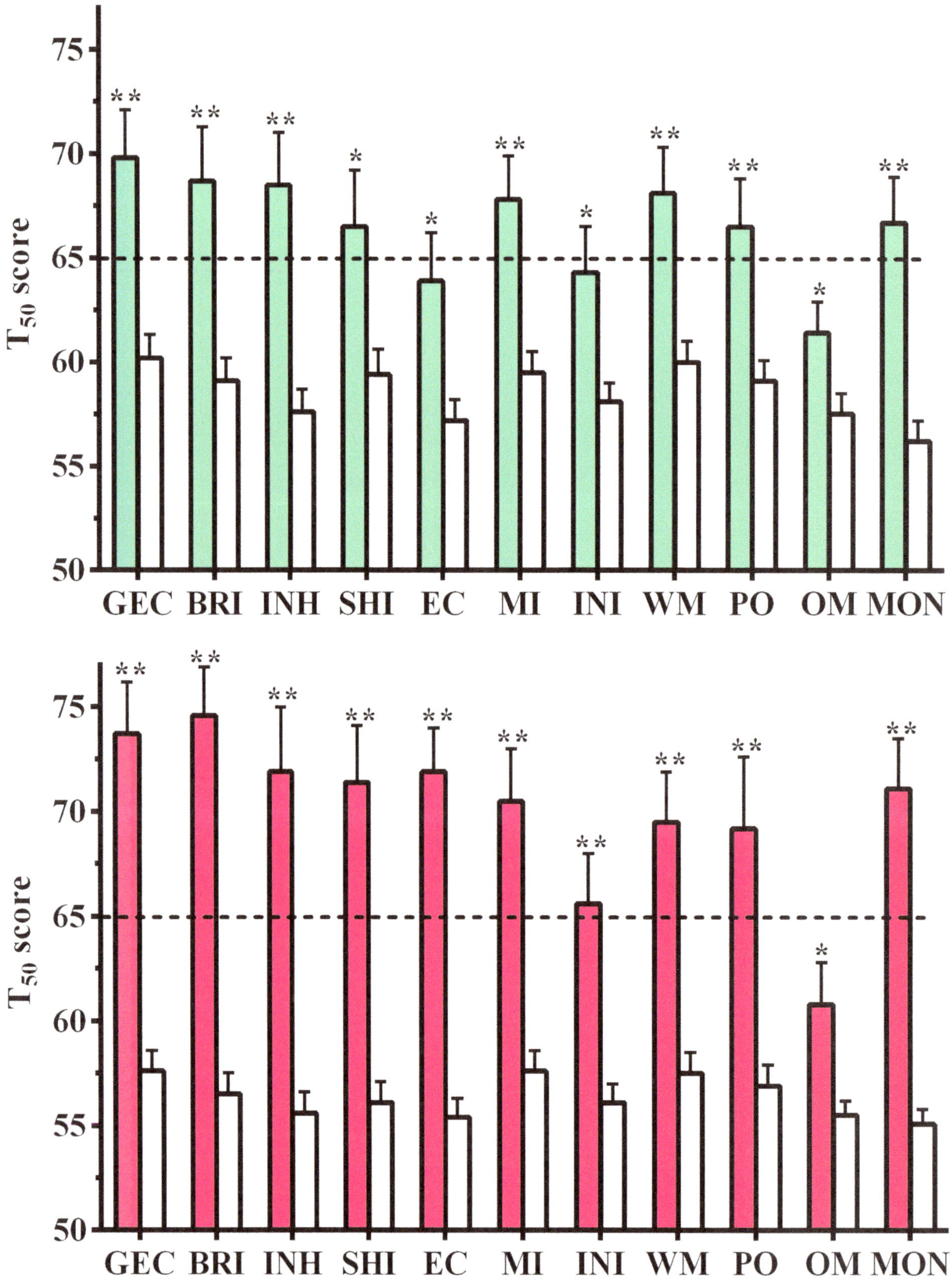

Figure 1. Behavioral Rating Inventory of Executive Function parental ratings of Adoptive (filled bars) and Comparison (open bars) boys (top) and girls (bottom). Global Executive Composite (GEC), Behavioral Regulation Index (BRI), Inhibit (INH), Shift (SHI), Emotional Control (EC), Metacognition Index (MI), Initiate (INI), Working Memory (WM), Plan Organize (PO), Organization of Materials (OM), and Monitor (MON), (**P*<.05, ***P*<.005).

Table 3. Percentage of Adopted and Comparison boys and girls with clinically significant ($T_{50} \geq 65$) problems on the Behavioral Rating Inventory of Executive Function.

	Boys			Girls		
	Adoptive (%)	Comparison (%)	Odds Ratio	Adoptive (%)	Comparison (%)	Odds Ratio
Global Executive Composite	72.7*	42.5	3.61	76.0**	27.5	8.34
Behavioral Regulation Index	69.7**	35.5	4.18	80.0**	27.0	10.82
Inhibit	69.7**	32.3	4.83	68.0**	24.3	6.61
Shift	54.5	36.6	2.08	68.0**	26.5	5.91
Emotional Control	51.5*	30.5	2.42	79.2**	22.8	12.90
Metacognition Index	66.7*	38.7	3.17	72.0**	25.9	7.35
Initiate	54.5*	34.9	2.23	56.0*	25.4	3.74
Working Memory	57.6	39.6	2.07	72.0**	28.0	6.60
Plan Organize	60.6*	35.5	2.80	58.3*	28.7	3.47
Organization of Materials	48.5*	29.4	2.26	40.0	22.8	2.26
Monitor	69.7%**	30.6%	5.20	72.0%**	22.8%	8.73

Adopted Boys N=25; Comparison Boys N=189; Adopted Girls N=33; Comparison Girls N=186. (chi-square *$P<.05$, or **$P<.0005$).

BRIEF is much more limited. Importantly, the preschool version of this instrument has been employed to examine internationally adopted children, albeit with an unknown prenatal history, and identified relatively subtle group differences. Only 11% of adoptees from a variety of countries fell into the problem range on the Global Executive Composite [25]. Perhaps unexpectedly, three scales were significantly lower (i.e. less problems) relative to the BRIEF standardization sample among Russian born preschoolers adopted into families in the United States. Further, the BRIEF means were within a half standard deviation ($T_{50}<55$) among school aged children unless they were adopted after age 1.5 in which case the averages were still below the clinical cut-off [26]. The BRIEF profile observed among Adopted and polysubstance exposed children is much more pronounced than that observed among adopted children that did not have an in utero exposure history. Overall, these findings indicate that adoption per se is only responsible for a portion of the variance in BRIEF ratings and that other factors associated with the birth-mother may be responsible. Use of licit and illicit drugs is likely a key factor although we cannot discount the involvement of stress or other sub-optimal aspects of the prenatal environment either acting alone or synergistically with the teratogens.

The large group difference identified between Adopted/polysubstance exposed and comparison children is also of interest when considering findings observed following exposure to other recreational drugs and at different ages. There were significant BRIEF elevations among methamphetamine/alcohol/nicotine exposed children (ages 7 to 9) living with their birth parents which tended to be more severe among adoptive/exposed children [10]. The present results with both the BRIEF and CBCL substantially elaborates upon earlier outcomes [10] and indicates that the atypical profile is not limited to the period shortly after starting school and persists into adolescence. The BRIEF profile, specifically with mean elevations two standard deviations above that of the standardization sample and with the majority of Adopted children meeting the criteria for a clinically significant impairment on all scales with the exception of Organization of Materials, shows striking similarities to that described previously for children diagnosed with Fetal Alcohol Spectrum Disorders [6]. Although only a small subset (10–11%) of our sample included children with Fetal Alcohol Syndrome (FAS), this condition is not trivial to diagnose [27]. Some caregivers are also hesitant to have a formal evaluation given due to concerns of child stigmatization so it is very possible that some children were undiagnosed.

Sex differences are clearly evident in the prevalence of a wide variety of psychiatric conditions including disorders like ADHD which rely on executive function [28]. The question of whether one sex is more vulnerable to prenatal substance exposure has been the focus of substantial empirical attention with some, albeit sporadic, findings [11,29]. For example, preschool girls, but not boys, exposed throughout pregnancy to methamphetamine and nicotine demonstrated elevated N-acetyl compounds and decreased myoinositol in the frontal white matter [30]. In Study I adopted females showed higher mean ratings than adopted males on Emotional Control but no appreciable sex differences were evident when using clinical cut-offs with the BRIEF. In Study II, both sexes showed an equivalent pattern when the mean raw scores (i.e. not corrected for age and sex) were evaluated but there was some indications of a sex difference when the percentage of children that met clinically significant criteria (i.e. corrected for age and sex) were examined with boys, but not girls, more commonly meeting this criteria for Anxious/Depressed and Social Problems with the CBCL.

There are many ambiguities and uncertainties associated with studies of adopted children and some limitations as well as future directions are noteworthy. One ongoing challenge in determination of the risks associated with recreational drug use during pregnancy, and particularly among children who were subsequently adopted, is the veracity of information about the timing and intensity of substance abuse. Although hair analysis provides a long window of detection (months) and this technology is rapidly advancing for detection of methamphetamine [31], nicotine [32], as well as other drugs [33], collection of this biological matrix was not a common practice when the children in this study were born. Similarly, meconium testing for alcohol metabolites may prove to be the most sensitive index to complement self-reports [34]. Although it may be tempting to speculate that specific agents, especially alcohol, contribute to the neurobehavioral profile observed, inferences of this type should be made with substantial caution given the indirect, and frequently incomplete, nature of

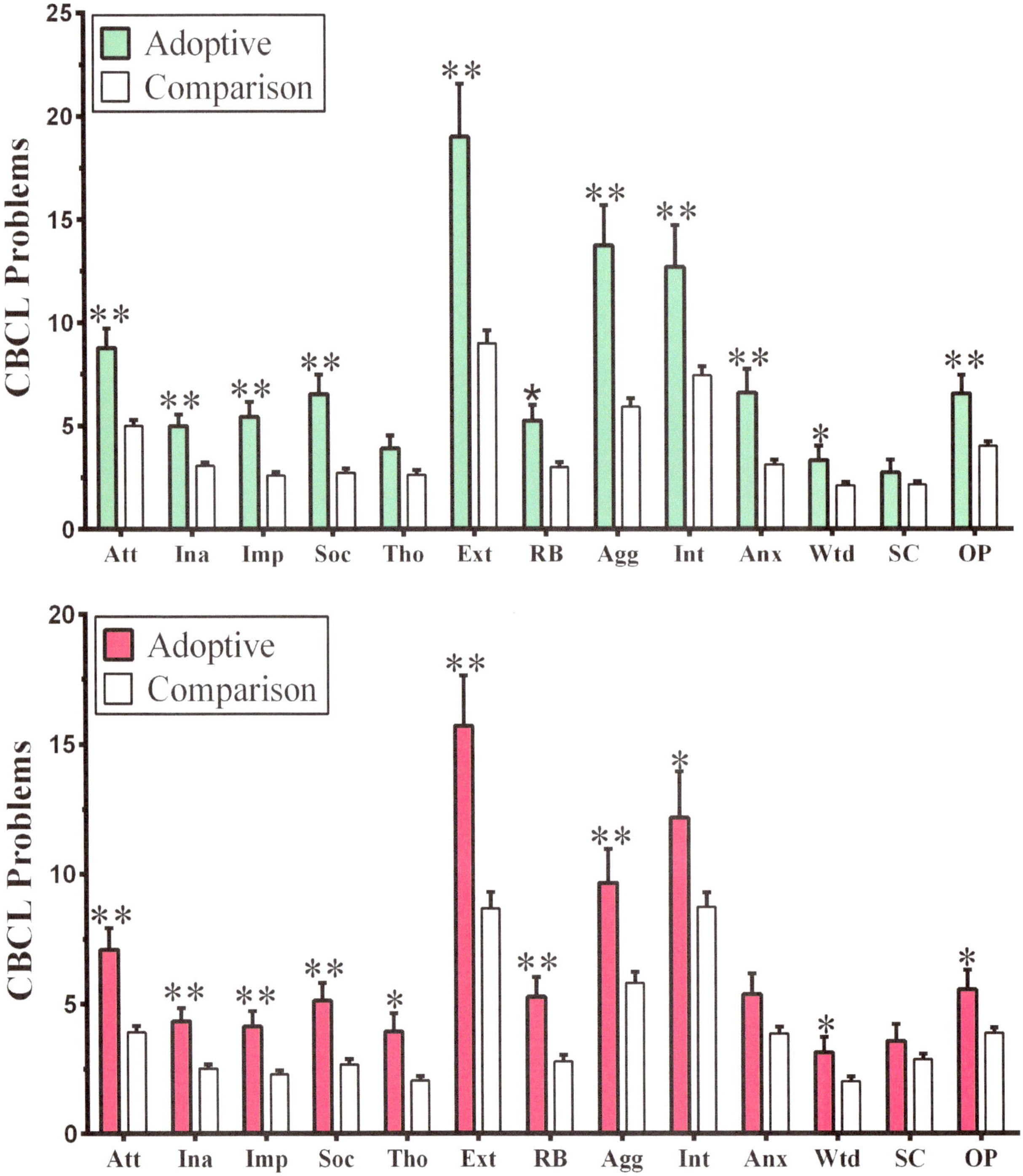

Figure 2. Child Behavior Checklist (CBCL) ratings of Adoptive and Comparison boys (top) and girls (bottom). Attention (Att), Inattention (Ina), Impulsivity (Imp), Social (Soc) Problems, Thought (Tho) Problems, Externalizing (Ext), Rule Breaking (RB), Aggression (Agg), Internalizing (Int), Anxious-Depressed (Anx), Withdrawn-Depressed (Wtd), Somatic Complaints (SC), or Other Problems (OP), (*$P<.05$, *$P<.005$).

the information provided by adoptive mothers. Obtaining medical records of the birth mother without her consent in order to verify the adoptive mother's reports of prenatal drug exposures is not feasible due to Health Insurance Accountability and Portability Act regulations and was not attempted for this anonymous online investigation. In theory, while longitudinal research which involves a representative sample of biological mothers abusing drugs and the adoptive mothers would extend upon the current findings, a variety of logistical and ethical challenges considerably limits the likelihood of such a hypothetical study being conducted in the immediate future. Atypical CBCL and BRIEF scores among polysubstance exposed adoptive children may also be compared to ratings made by birth parents of children that did, and did not, have a history of recreational drug exposures, particularly to nicotine [8,15]. While the present dataset is novel and well powered, future research that corroborates and extends upon the

Table 4. Percentage of Adopted and Comparison boys and girls with clinically significant (T_{50}>63) problems on the Child Behavior Checklist.

	Boys			Girls		
	Adoptive (%)	Comparison (%)	Odds Ratio	Adoptive (%)	Comparison (%)	Odds Ratio
Internalizing						
Anxious/Depressed	21.7*	4.4	6.03	13.3	8.8	1.60
Withdrawn/Depressed	17.4	7.6	2.57	12.9	7.9	1.73
Somatic Complaints	8.7	6.4	1.39	13.3	10.8	1.27
Social	30.4*	6.5	6.29	10.0	6.8	1.54
Thought	17.4	9.4	2.04	23.3*	8.4	3.30
Attention	22.7*	7.3	3.74	32.3**	10.1	4.23
Externalizing						
Rule-Breaking	17.4	8.5	2.27	13.8	8.0	1.84
Aggression	39.1*	10.9	5.26	20.0*	7.2	3.24

Adopted Boys N = 22; Comparison Boys N = 247; Adopted Girls N = 33; Comparison Girls N = 186. (chi-square *$P<.05$, or **$P<.0005$).

maternal reports of psychopathology is needed including teacher reports as well as direct neurobehavioral and neurophysiological assessments of the children. Additional studies are also needed to identify the most optimal postnatal environment and psychoeducational interventions for polysubstance exposed adopted children with the goal of ameliorating deficits in executive function and enhancing mental health.

In conclusion, adoptive children with histories of prenatal exposure to recreational drugs had statistically and substantially greater difficulties with executive (or self-regulatory) and behavioral functioning as assessed by parent ratings relative to a nonadopted comparison group, and the proportion of adopted children with clinically significant psychopathology (i.e., scores> 63) was also much greater. The CBCL and BRIEF have been employed previously with adopted children and do not show group differences of the magnitude reported here indicating that other factors are responsible. Adoptive children are not a homogenous group [35] and generalizations based on this descriptive cross-sectional dataset should be limited exclusively to the adoptive offspring of birth mothers that used alcohol and other recreational substances during pregnancy. This report does contribute to a wide body of evidence [3,4,6,22,36] which supports continued vigilance to minimize the prevalence of children exposed prenatally to alcohol and other recreational drugs during pregnancy.

Supporting Information

Figure S1 Behavioral Rating Inventory of Executive Function (N = 335, top) and Child Behavior Checklist (N = 450, bottom) ratings with of Adoptive (filled bars) and Comparison (open bars) with ADHD children excluded (*$P<.05$, **$P<.005$). BRIEF Indexes and Scales: Global Executive Composite (GEC), Behavioral Regulation Index (BRI), Inhibit (INH), Shift (SHI), Emotional Control (EC), Metacognition Index (MI), Initiate (INI), Working Memory (WM), Plan Organize (PO), Organization of Materials (OM), and Monitor (MON). CBCL Indexes and Scales: Attention (Att), Inattention (Ina), Impulsivity (Imp), Social (Soc), Thought (Tho), Externalizing (Ext), Rule Breaking (RB), Aggression (Agg), Internalizing (Int), Anxious-Depressed (Anx), Withdrawn-Depressed (Wtd), Somatic Complaints (SC), or Other Problems (OP).

Table S1 Behavioral Rating Inventory of Executive Function standardized (T_{50}) scores by offspring age and parental relationship.

Table S2 Percentage of Adopted and Comparison children with clinically significant (T_{50}>63) problems on the Child Behavior Checklist by offspring age and parental relationship.

Data S1 Raw data from Study I.

Data S2 Raw data from Study II.

Materials S1

Acknowledgments

We would like to express a special thanks to the caregivers that participated in this project and to Kendra Jacobson Morris, MA of the Oregon Post Adoption Resource Center for feedback on an earlier version of this manuscript.

Author Contributions

Conceived and designed the experiments: BJP SMC HMG JR MAB. Performed the experiments: BJP HMG SMC. Analyzed the data: BJP. Contributed reagents/materials/analysis tools: MAB JR. Contributed to the writing of the manuscript: BJP JR MAB HMG SMC.

References

1. Palacios J, Brodzinsky D (2010) Adoption research: Trends, topics, outcomes. Int J Behav Devel. 34: 270–284.
2. Juffer F, van IJzendoorn MH (2005) Behavior problems and mental health referrals of international adoptees: A meta-analysis. JAMA 293: 2501–2515.

3. Meyer JS, Piper BJ (2011) Developmental neurotoxicology of abused drugs. In Gupta RC, ed. Reproductive & Developmental Toxicology. Amsterdam: Elsevier: 2011: 341–353.
4. Davies JK, Bledsoe JM (2005) Prenatal alcohol and drug exposure in adoption. Pediatr Clin North Am 52: 1369–1393.
5. Kesmodel US, Bertrand J, Støvring H, Skarpness B, Denny CH, et al. (2012) The effect of different alcohol drinking patterns in early to mid pregnancy on the child's intelligence, attention, and executive function. BJOG 19: 1180–1190.
6. Rasmussen C, McAuley R, Andrew G (2007) Parental ratings of children with Fetal Alcohol Spectrum Disorder on the Behavior Rating Inventory of Executive Function (BRIEF). J FAS Int 5: e2.
7. Julvez J, Ribas-Fito N, Torrent M, Forns M, Garcia-Esteban R, et al. (2007) Maternal smoking habits and cognitive development of children at age 4 years in a population-based birth cohort. Int J Epidem 36: 825–832.
8. Piper BJ, Corbett SM (2012) Executive function in the offspring of women that smoked during pregnancy. Nicotine Tob Res 14: 191–199.
9. Kiblawi ZN, Smith LM, Lagasse LL, Derauf C, Newman E, et al. (2013) The effect of prenatal methamphetamine exposure on attention as assessed by Continuous Performance tests: Results from the infant development, environment, and lifestyle study. J Dev Behav Pediatr 34: 31–37.
10. Piper BJ, Acevedo SF, Kolchugina GK, Butler RW, Corbett SM, et al. (2011) Abnormalities in parentally rated executive function in methamphetamine/polysubstance exposed children. Pharm Biochem Behav 98: 432–439.
11. Minnes S, Singer LT, Min MO, Lang AM, Ben-Harush A, et al. (2014) Comparison of 12-year old children with prenatal exposure to cocaine and non-exposed controls on caregiver ratings of executive function. J Youth Adoles 43: 52–69.
12. Harris PA, Taylor R, Thielke R, Payne J, Gonzalez N, et al. (2009) Research Electronic Data Capture (REDCap)–a metadata-driven methodology and workflow process for providing translational research informatics support. J Biomed Inform 42: 377–381.
13. Baron IS (2000) Test review: Behavior Rating Inventory of Executive Function. Child Neuropsychol 6: 235–238.
14. Gioia GA, Isquith PK, Guy SC, Kenworthy L (2000) Behavior Rating Inventory of Executive Function Professional Manual. Psychological Assessment Resources, Lutz: Florida.
15. Piper BJ, Gray HM, Birkett MA (2012) Maternal smoking cessation and reduced academic and behavioral problems in offspring. Drug Alcohol Depend 121: 62–67.
16. Achenbach TM, Rescorla LA (2001) Manual for the ASEBA school age forms and profiles. Burlington, VT, ASEBA.
17. Achenbach TM, Ruffle TM (2000) The child behavior checklist and related forms for assessing behavioral/emotional problems and competencies. Pediatr Rev; 21: 265–271.
18. Landgren M, Svensson L, Strömland K, Andersson Grönlund M (2010) Prenatal alcohol exposure and neurodevelopmental disorders in children adopted from Eastern Europe. Pediatrics 125: e1178.
19. Nulman I, Rovet J, Greenbaum R, Loebstein M, Wolpin J, et al. (2001) Neurodevelopment of adopted children exposed in utero to cocaine: The Toronto Adoption study. Clin Invest Med 24: 129–137.
20. LaGasse L, Derauf C, Smith LM, Newman E, Shah R, et al. (2012) Methamphetamine exposure and childhood behavior problems at 3 and 5 years of age. Pediatrics 129: 681–688.
21. Carter S, Paterson J, Gao W, Iusitini L (2008) Maternal smoking during pregnancy and behaviour problems in a birth cohort of 2-year-old Pacific children in New Zealand. Early Hum Dev 84: 59–66.
22. Dixon DR, Kurtz PF, Chin MD (2008) A systematic review of challenging behaviors in children exposed prenatally to substances of abuse. Res Devel Disabil 28: 483–502.
23. O'Leary CM, Nassar N, Zubrick SR, Kurinczuk JJ, Stanley F, et al. (2009) Evidence of a complex association between dose, pattern and timing of prenatal alcohol exposure and child behavior problems. Addiction 105: 74–86.
24. Robinson M, Oddy WH, McLean NJ, Jacoby P, Pennell CE, et al. (2010) Low-moderate prenatal alcohol exposure and risk to child behavioural development: A prospective cohort study. BJOG 117: 1139–1152.
25. Jacobs E, Miller LC, Tirella LG (2010) Developmental and behavioral performance of internationally adopted preschoolers: A pilot study. Child Psychiatry Hum Dev 41: 15–29.
26. Merz EC, McCall RB (2011) Parent ratings of executive functioning in children adopted from psychologically depriving institutions. J Child Psychol Psychiatry 52: 537–546.
27. Hoyme HE, May PA, Kalberg WO, Kodituwakku P, Gossage JP, et al. (2005) A practical approach to diagnosis of Fetal Alcohol Spectrum Disorders: Clarification of the 1996 Institute of Medicine criteria. Pediatrics 115: 39–47.
28. Langberg JM, Dvorsky MR, Evans SW (2013) What specific facets of executive function are associated with academic functioning in youth with Attention-Deficit/Hyperactivity Disorder? J Abnorm Child Psychol 41: 1145–1159.
29. Sayal K, Heron J, Golding J, Emond A (2007) Prenatal alcohol exposure and gender differences in childhood mental health problems: A longitudinal population based study. Pediatrics 119: e426–434.
30. Chang L, Cloak C, Jiang CS, Farnham S, Tokeshi B, et al. (2009) Altered neurometabolites and motor integration in children exposed to methamphetamine in utero. Neuroimage 48: 391–397.
31. Han E, Yang H, Seol I, Park Y, Lee B, et al. (2013) Segmental hair analysis and estimation of methamphetamine use pattern. Int J Legal Med 127: 405–411.
32. Almeida ND, Koren G, Platt RW, Kramer MS (2011) Hair biomarkers as measures of maternal tobacco smoke exposure and predictors of fetal growth. Nicotine Tob Res 13: 328–335.
33. Lendoiro E, González-Colmenero E, Concheiro-Guisán A, de Castro A, Cruz A, et al. (2013) Maternal hair analysis for the detection of illicit drugs, medicines, and alcohol exposure during pregnancy. Ther Drug Monit 35: 296–304.
34. Morini L, Marchei E, Tarani L, Trivelli M, Rapisardi G, et al. (2013) Testing ethylglucuronide in maternal hair and nails for the assessment of fetal exposure to alcohol: comparison with meconium testing. Ther Drug Monit 35: 402–407.
35. Grotevant HD, McDermott JM (2014) Adoption: Biological and social processes linked to adaptation. Annu Rev Psychol 65: 235–265.
36. Lange S, Shield K, Rehm J, Popova S (2013) Prevalence of Fetal Alcohol Spectrum Disorders in child care settings: A meta-analysis. Pediatrics 132: e980–e995.

Early-Life Exposure to Polycyclic Aromatic Hydrocarbons and ADHD Behavior Problems

Frederica P. Perera[1,2]*, Hsin-wen Chang[2,3], Deliang Tang[1,2], Emily L. Roen[1,2], Julie Herbstman[1,2], Amy Margolis[2,4], Tzu-Jung Huang[2,3], Rachel L. Miller[1,2,5,6], Shuang Wang[2,3], Virginia Rauh[2,7]

1 Department of Environmental Health Sciences, Mailman School of Public Health, Columbia University, New York, New York, United States of America, **2** Columbia Center for Children's Environmental Health, Columbia University, New York, New York, United States of America, **3** Department of Biostatistics, Mailman School of Public Health, Columbia University, New York, New York, United States of America, **4** Division of Child & Adolescent Psychiatry and the Center for Developmental Neuropsychiatry, Department of Psychiatry, the New York State Psychiatric Institute and the College of Physicians and Surgeons, Columbia University, New York, New York, United States of America, **5** Division of Pulmonary, Allergy and Critical Care of Medicine, Department of Medicine, College of Physicians and Surgeons, Columbia University, New York, New York, United States of America, **6** Division of Pediatric Allergy and Immunology, Department of Pediatrics, College of Physicians and Surgeons, Columbia University, New York, New York, United States of America, **7** The Heilbrunn Department of Population and Family Health, Columbia University, New York, New York, United States of America

Abstract

Importance: Polycyclic aromatic hydrocarbons are widespread urban air pollutants from combustion of fossil fuel and other organic material shown previously to be neurotoxic.

Objective: In a prospective cohort study, we evaluated the relationship between Attention Deficit Hyperactivity Disorder behavior problems and prenatal polycyclic aromatic hydrocarbon exposure, adjusting for postnatal exposure.

Materials and Methods: Children of nonsmoking African-American and Dominican women in New York City were followed from *in utero* to 9 years. Prenatal polycyclic aromatic hydrocarbon exposure was estimated by levels of polycyclic aromatic hydrocarbon- DNA adducts in maternal and cord blood collected at delivery. Postnatal exposure was estimated by the concentration of urinary polycyclic aromatic hydrocarbon metabolites at ages 3 or 5. Attention Deficit Hyperactivity Disorder behavior problems were assessed using the Child Behavior Checklist and the Conners Parent Rating Scale- Revised.

Results: High prenatal adduct exposure, measured by elevated maternal adducts was significantly associated with all Conners Parent Rating Scale-Revised subscales when the raw scores were analyzed continuously (N = 233). After dichotomizing at the threshold for moderately to markedly atypical symptoms, high maternal adducts were significantly associated with the Conners Parent Rating Scale-Revised DSM-IV Inattentive (OR = 5.06, 95% CI [1.43, 17.93]) and DSM-IV Total (OR = 3.37, 95% CI [1.10, 10.34]) subscales. High maternal adducts were positivity associated with the DSM-oriented Attention Deficit/Hyperactivity Problems scale on the Child Behavior Checklist, albeit not significant. In the smaller sample with cord adducts, the associations between outcomes and high cord adduct exposure were not statistically significant (N = 162).

Conclusion: The results suggest that exposure to polycyclic aromatic hydrocarbons encountered in New York City air may play a role in childhood Attention Deficit Hyperactivity Disorder behavior problems.

Editor: Robert L. Tanguay, Oregon State University, United States of America

Funding: Funding was provided by the National Institute for Environmental Health Sciences (NIEHS) and the U.S. Environmental Protection Agency (US EPA): NIEHS/EPA P01ES09600/R82702701, NIEHS/EPA P01ES09600/RD832141, NIEHS/EPA P01ES09600/RD834509, NIEHS R01ES08977. This publication was also made possible in part by US EPA grants RD832096, the John & Wendy Neu Family Foundation, the New York Community Trust, Trustees of the Blanchette Hooker Rockefeller Fund, and an anonymous foundation. Funding from all the institutions listed was used towards the design and conduct of the study; collection, management, analysis, and interpretation of the data; and the preparation, review, and approval of the manuscript. Its contents are solely the responsibility of the grantee and do not necessarily represent the official views of the US EPA. Further, US EPA does not endorse the purchase of any commercial products or services mentioned in the publication. Findings expressed in this paper are the opinions of the authors and do not necessarily reflect the official opinion of the Centers for Disease Control and Prevention.

Competing Interests: The authors have declared that no competing interests exist.

* Email: fpp1@columbia.edu

Introduction

Polycyclic aromatic hydrocarbons (PAH), such as benzo[a]pyrene (B[a]P), are toxic air pollutants released during incomplete combustion of fossil fuel, tobacco, and other organic material [1]. They are also found in the diet. In New York City (NYC) and other urban areas, traffic and residential heating are major local sources. There is also some contribution from coal-burning sources in states upwind. Urban, minority populations in the U.S. often have disproportionate exposure to air pollution and are at greater risk for adverse health and developmental outcomes from this exposure [2–5]. All of the mothers in the Columbia Center for Children's Environmental Health (CCCEH) NYC cohort had detectable levels of PAH in prenatal personal air samples; 42% had detectable levels of B[a]P-DNA adducts in maternal blood; and 46% had detectable levels of B[a]P-DNA adducts in cord blood. B[a]P is considered a representative PAH and is highly correlated with other PAH class members [6]. PAH-DNA adducts reflect individual exposure to PAH, integrating exposure over a 2–3 month period [7]and via different routes (primarily inhalation and ingestion). Adducts provide a biologic dosimeter as they not only reflect inter-individual differences in exposure and uptake of PAH but also in detoxification and DNA repair [8,9].

Because of the heightened susceptibility of the fetus and young child, exposures to PAH and other environmental pollutants during the prenatal and early postnatal stages are of particular concern [10–13]. During the fetal period and early childhood years, the brain is rapidly developing and vulnerable to neurotoxic insults that may manifest as adverse outcomes in childhood and adulthood [14,15]. Laboratory studies of PAH exposure during the prenatal, neonatal, or adult periods have reported a range of neurodevelopmental and behavioral effects, [16,17] including hyperactivity [18,19]. In the present CCCEH cohort, prenatal exposure to PAH measured by prenatal air monitoring or B[a]P-DNA adducts in maternal or umbilical cord blood at delivery was associated with developmental delay at age 3 [20], reduced IQ at age 5 [21], and symptoms of anxiety/depression and attention problems at ages 6–7 [6].

Attention-deficit/hyperactivity disorder (ADHD) is the most common behavioral disorder diagnosed in children [22] and is often accompanied by anxiety and depression [23–26]. In our cohort, ADHD behavior problems and anxiety/depression at age 9 were significantly correlated ($r = 0.43$, $p<0.0001$). Children with ADHD are at increased risk of substance abuse, conduct, and mood disorders [27–30]. Family history, certain environmental contaminants, alcohol use, maternal smoking during pregnancy, pregnancy and delivery complications, and psychosocial adversity have been implicated or identified as risk factors for ADHD [31,32].

Prior data on air pollution and ADHD are suggestive. For example, a cross-sectional study found an association between ambient particulate matter (PM_{10}) and childhood ADHD [33]. In a longitudinal study, estimated exposure during infancy to elemental black carbon, based on air sampling data and land use regression modeling, was significantly associated with ADHD-related symptoms [34]. Another cohort study reported an association between attention and children's lifetime exposure to black carbon based on children's residence and a spatiotemporal model [35]. Ours is the first report of associations between individual measures of early-life exposure to PAH pollutants and ADHD behavior problems in children.

Methods

Sample selection

A complete description of the NYC cohort appears elsewhere [20,36]. Briefly, African-American and Dominican women who resided in Washington Heights, Harlem, or the South Bronx in NYC, U.S., were recruited between 1998 and 2006 through local prenatal care clinics. Enrollment was restricted to women who were non-active cigarette smokers; ages 18–35; non-users of other tobacco products or illicit drugs; free of diabetes, hypertension, or known HIV; and who had initiated prenatal care by the 20th week of pregnancy. The Institutional Review Board of the Columbia University Medical Center approved the study. Mothers signed a consent form, approved by the IRB, for themselves and their children at the time of enrollment and at every subsequent visit. The children sign an IRB-approved assent form beginning at age 7. The consent and assent forms are available in English and Spanish and clearly explain the study goals and procedures.

The sample included in the present analysis is composed of the children who had available data on at least one adduct measure (maternal or newborn), the CPRS and the CBCL assessments, and all covariates of interest ($N = 250$).

Maternal/child characteristics and home caretaking environment

Demographic, health and environmental conditions. A 45-minute structured questionnaire was administered by a trained bilingual interviewer during the last trimester of pregnancy to obtain demographic information, residential history, and health and environmental data such as active smoking (to confirm non-active smoking status) and passive smoking [36]. The questionnaire also elicited information on dietary PAH (consumption of broiled, fried, grilled or smoked meat), and socioeconomic information related to income and education. Postnatal interviews were administered in person at 6 months and annually thereafter to determine changes in residence, exposure to environmental tobacco smoke (ETS), and health and environmental conditions.

Maternal demoralization. Maternal demoralization, a measure of maternal nonspecific psychological distress that has been linked to neurodevelopment [37–39], was measured at each visit by the Psychiatric Epidemiologic Research Instrument Demoralization Scale (PERI-D) [40].

Non-verbal intelligence. The Test of Non-Verbal Intelligence-Second Edition (C-TONI-2) [41] was administered to the mothers when the child was about 3 years old.

Home assessment. Caldwell and Bradley's Home Observation for Measurement of the Environment (HOME) [42] was administered in the home by research workers, also when the child was about 3 years old, to assess physical and interactive characteristics of the child rearing environment.

Maternal ADHD. At the child's 7 year visit, mothers completed the Conners Adult ADHD Rating Scales (CAARS) [43]. Given the high heritability rate of ADHD [44], maternal ADHD symptoms on the CAARS were included as a covariate in our analyses.

Child anxiety/depression. Childhood ADHD and anxiety/depression are frequently comorbid conditions [24]. The continuous score for symptoms of anxiety/depression on the CBCL at age 9 [45] was included as a covariate.

Independent variables

Prenatal exposure: PAH-DNA adducts. Following delivery, maternal blood and umbilical cord blood samples were collected. Within several hours following collection, samples were transported to the CCCEH Molecular Epidemiology Laboratory, processed, and stored at −70°C. B[a]P–DNA adducts in extracted white blood cell DNA were analyzed using the high performance liquid chromatography (HPLC)/fluorescence method which detects B[a]P tetraols [12,46]. Not all participants had adequate DNA quantity for adduct analysis.

Postnatal exposure: urinary PAH metabolites. At the CDC, a suite of PAH metabolites was measured in spot urine (collected from the child at ages 3 and 5) using automated liquid-liquid extraction and gas chromatography/isotope dilution high-resolution mass spectrometry [47–49]. Although PAH urinary metabolite have a short lifetime (half-life of 6–35 hours) [50], in conditions of chronic exposure they provide a useful measure of exposure to PAH [47,48]. Specific gravity (SG) measurements were used to control for urinary dilution of the samples using the following formula: freshweight metabolites for the subject*(mean SG-1)/(SG for that subject-1) [51,52].

Behavioral outcomes

ADHD behavior problems were assessed using two complementary parent-report instruments: the CBCL for ages 6–18 (CBCL) [53] and the CPRS- Revised: Long Version [54]. The CBCL is a screening instrument assessing childhood competencies, adaptive functioning, and problems [45]. The CPRS is a focused assessment of childhood ADHD and its common comorbid disorders [54,55]. Both are widely used instruments that measure ADHD problems and attention function and have been used to study their associations with diverse environmental contaminants [56–59]. Both instruments yield scales derived from the DSM-IV [60] that are intended to screen for ADHD-behavior problems and indicate those children requiring follow-up. Mothers self-administered the 80-item CPRS [54] and the 118-item CBCL [53] when their children were 9 years old, under the guidance of trained research workers. Outcomes analyzed included the CBCL DSM-oriented Attention Deficit/Hyperactivity Problems scale, and the CPRS ADHD Index and DSM-IV subscales (denoted as "Total", "Inattentive", and "Hyperactive-Impulsive"). The "Total" DSM-IV measure comprises the "Inattentive" and "Hyperactive-Impulsive" subscales. For both instruments, the child's responses were scored and summed to a raw score. T-scores were derived from raw scores based on the normative comparison sample as described in the administration manual and used to determine the child's classification [53,54]. On the CBCL DSM-oriented Attention Deficit/Hyperactivity Problems score, children above the 93rd percentile were classified as "borderline clinical", and those below the 93rd percentile were classified in the normal range [53]. The CPRS DSM-IV subscales and ADHD Index scores were dichotomized based on the classification of a T score >65 as "moderately to markedly atypical" and a T score ≤65 as "in the normal range" [54].

Statistical Analysis

As in prior analyses [6], adduct levels were dichotomized as detectable/non-detectable ("high/low"), with detectable levels observed in 42% of maternal and 46% of cord blood samples in the whole cohort. Dichotomization of exposure variables is less vulnerable to measurement error and permits comparison of the most highly exposed children to children with lower exposure. In our analyses, (1-hydroxynaphthalene, 2-hydroxynaphthalene, 2-hydroxyfluorene, 3-hydroxyfluorene, 9-hydroxyfluorene, 1-hydroxyphenanthrene, 2-hydroxyphenanthrene, 3-hydroxyphenanthrene, 4-hydroxyphenanthrene) were summed to provide a composite measure denoted "PAH metabolites". PAH metabolites in child urine at ages 3 or 5 were dichotomized at the respective medians for the entire cohort and treated as "high/low". In terms of data analysis, the age 5 metabolite level was preferentially selected, but if that measure was missing, the age 3 metabolite level was used. In secondary analyses, adducts and PAH metabolites were also treated as a continuous variable after log transformation.

Covariates were selected based on whether they were significant contributors to the model (at p≤0.1) for at least one of the outcomes and included: prenatal ETS exposure, child's sex, child's ethnicity, child's gestational age, mother's intelligence, mother's completed years of education prior to birth of the child, maternal prenatal demoralization, maternal ADHD symptoms, child's exact age at assessment (in months), the quality of the early home caretaking environment, and season at time of monitoring (heating vs. non-heating) (Table 1). We further adjusted for child anxiety/depression at age 9 since it is a well-documented comorbid condition with ADHD and symptoms overlap [24]. Moreover, we have previously found associations of PAH with child anxiety/depressive symptoms [6]. Dietary PAH, measured prenatally during the third trimester, was not a predictor of outcomes at p≤0.1. The associations between the dichotomized PAH exposure variables and continuous raw scores and dichotomized T scores for ADHD-related behavior were analyzed by Poisson and logistic regression, respectively.

Results

Maternal and cord adducts were not significantly correlated with prenatally air monitored PAH, ETS, or dietary PAH.

Table 1 presents the socio-demographic, outcome, and exposure characteristics of the children who had available data on maternal or cord adducts, stratifying on whether or not they had data on neurobehavioral outcomes and covariates of interest and were thus included (N = 250) or not included (N = 364) in the analysis. The two groups were similar except that the group included had a higher proportion of females and were younger at the CPRS assessment, though all assessments were given at approximately age 9. The level of adducts and percentage characterized as high vs. low did not differ between those included and not included. Comparing the group included (N = 250) with those children who did not have maternal or cord adduct data (N = 111), there were differences in terms of exact age at assessment for the CBCL and CPRS, home inventory scores, and percentage of mothers that had completed high school (data not shown).

Table 2 summarizes the distribution of CBCL and CPRS scores in the entire sample. Table 3 shows the number of children in the borderline or clinical range on the CBCL, and the number in the moderately to markedly atypical range on the CPRS. Consistent with other studies, there was substantial overlap between the number of children categorized in the moderately to markedly atypical range on the Hyperactive-Impulsive and Inattentive problems, as shown in Figure 1.

Table 4 summarizes the associations between maternal (N = 233) and cord adduct (N = 162) exposure and CBCL DSM-oriented Attention Deficit/Hyperactivity problems and all CPRS outcomes, adjusting for postnatal PAH exposure and selected covariates. When considering outcomes analyzed as continuous raw scores, all CPRS subscales were positively and significantly associated with high maternal adduct exposure. After dichotomizing the outcome measures, those with high maternal adducts had odds of being categorized as moderately to markedly atypical on the DSM-IV Inattentive and DSM-IV Total scales 5.06 (95% CI [1.43, 17.93]) and 3.37 (95% CI [1.10, 10.34]) times greater than those with low maternal adducts. High maternal adduct exposure

Table 1. Characteristics of the children included in the analysis and those not included due to missing data.

	Subjects included in the analysis (N = 250)[a]	Subjects not included in the analysis (N = 364)[b]	
Variables	Mean ±SD or %	Mean ±SD or %	p-value
High maternal adducts[c]	37.34%	44.25%	0.10
High cord adducts[c]	39.51%	49. 37%	0.07
High urinary PAH metabolites at ages 3 or 5[d]	49.20%	55.07%	0.22
Log-transformed urinary PAH metabolites at ages 3 or 5[e]	9.02±0.89	9.03±0.80	0.86
Log-transformed maternal adduct (per 10^8 nucleotides)	−1.73±0.47	−1.68±0.48	0.20
Log-transformed cord adduct (per 10^8 nucleotides)	−1.67±0.53	−1.59±0.53	0.13
CBCL DSM-oriented Attention Deficit/Hyperactivity Problems (% with borderline or clinical diagnosis)[f]	7.20%	10.66%	0.32
CPRS subscales (% categorized as moderately to markedly atypical)[g]			
ADHD Index	8.40%	7.87%	1.00
DSM-IV Inattentive	8.40%	5.51%	0.41
DSM- IV Hyperactive- Impulsive	10.80%	14.17%	0.40
DSM-IV Total	10.40%	7.87%	0.47
Prenatal ETS exposure (% yes)	33.20%	37.36%	0.30
Child sex (% female)	**57.60%**	**48.35%**	**0.03***
Child ethnicity (AA%)[h]	40.00%	33.24%	0.09
Gestational age (in weeks)[i]	39.35±1.37	39.34±1.44	0.94
Maternal intelligence[j]	20.82±8.78	20.25±8.62	0.47
Maternal education (%≥ high school education)	64.80%	59.83%	0.24
Maternal demoralization score	1.15±0.61	1.18±0.67	0.67
Maternal ADHD (CAARS ADHD index raw score)[k]	38.79±8.87	37.67±7.16	0.15
CBCL age (in months)[l]	108.01±1.83	108.78±4.60	0.14
CPRS age (in months)[l]	**107.96±2.02**	**109.15±4.97**	**0.03***
Home environment[m]	40.09±5.94	39.33±6.09	0.18
Heating season (% yes)[n]	54.0%	56.52%	0.64
Child anxiety/depression (CBCL anxiety/depression raw score)[o]	2.74±3.02	2.53±2.80	0.53

[a]Subjects were included if they had data for maternal adducts and/or cord adducts, as well as data on CBCL, CPRS outcome and all covariates of interest.
[b]Subjects not included are those that had available data on cord and/or maternal adducts but were missing data on the CBCL, CPRS outcomes and/or any covariates included in the final model.
[c]Adduct levels were dichotomized as detectable/non-detectable ("high/low").
[d]PAH metabolites in child urine at ages 3 or 5 were dichotomized at the respective medians ("high/low").
[e]Children with urinary PAH metabolite measurement at ages 3 or 5.
[f]Based on T score. Borderline or clinical defined as percentile ≥93rd.
[g]Based on T score. Moderately to markedly atypical defined as T-score >65.
[h]Percent African American; the remainder are Dominican.
[i]Based on medical record data.
[j]Nonverbal intelligence measured by the TONI-2.
[k]Measure of maternal ADHD.
[l]Age at administration.
[m]HOME Inventory as a measure of the home caretaking environment.
[n]Third trimester in heating season.
[o]Based on CBCL Anxious/Depressed Syndrome Scale measured at age 9.
*p-value <0.05.

was also significantly and positively associated with the CDCL DSM-oriented Attention Deficit/Hyperactivity Problems scale, though results did not reach statistical significance.

In separate models with log transformed adduct and metabolite values as the exposure variables, the direction and significance of the associations between adducts and outcomes were the same as the models with the dichotomized exposure with the exception of the CBCL DSM-oriented attention deficit hyperactivity scale raw score and CPRS DSM-IV Total scale raw score, which became borderline significant (p = 0.06, and p = 0.08, respectively) (data not shown).

Parallel analyses in the smaller number of subjects with available cord adduct data (N = 162) exposure found non-significant or borderline significant associations with all outcomes (Table 4).

Discussion

The present results suggest that high prenatal exposure, taking into account the potential effects of postnatal PAH exposure, may

Table 2. Distribution of CBCL and CPRS Scores in children at age 9 (N = 250[a]).

Outcomes	Score Range		Mean of Scores		Percent in Borderline or clinical or Moderately to markedly atypical range[b]
	T Score	Raw Score	T score	Raw score	
CBCL DSM-oriented Attention Deficit/ Hyperactivity Problems	50–80	0–14	53.9	3.1	7.2
CPRS subscales					
ADHD Index	40–89	0–34	49.8	6.4	8.4
DSM-IV Total	40–90	0–48	50.8	9.2	10.4
DSM-IV Hyperactive- Impulsive	41–90	0–25	52.8	4.7	10.8
DSM-IV Inattentive	40–88	0–25	48.9	4.5	8.4

[a]Children included in analysis with all covariates.
[b]CBCL "borderline or clinical" defined as percentile ≥93rd; CPRS "moderately to markedly atypical" defined as T-score >65.

increase the risk of ADHD behavior problems. ADHD is a disorder that is known to impact school performance, social relationships, and occupational performance [61–66]. In the U.S. the annual societal cost of illness for ADHD is estimated to be between $36 and $52 billion, and the annual cost per individual is estimated to be $12,005 to $17,458 (2005) [67,68].

To our knowledge, there have been no prior epidemiological studies on the role of pre- and post-natal PAH exposure, here measured by chemical-specific biomarkers, on ADHD in school-age children. Prior experimental research and limited epidemiological studies have suggested links between PM and air pollution (elemental carbon and black carbon) and ADHD symptoms [33–35]. In the present longitudinal study high maternal adduct levels were not significantly associated with Attention Deficit/Hyperactivity problems on the CBCL screening test, but on the more detailed CPRS, consistently significant associations with a number of ADHD-related outcomes were seen. In particular, significant associations between high maternal adducts and the DSM-IV Total and DSM-IV Inattentive scales were observed in models treating CPRS scores as continuous and dichotomous outcomes. Consistency in the results across both of these outcome measures strengthens the conclusion that inattention is associated with prenatal PAH exposure.

The maternal and cord adducts were significantly but only modestly correlated ($r = 0.28$, $p<0.0001$), probably because of the immaturity of the metabolic/detoxification and DNA repair systems in the fetus compared to the adult [69] and the differing genetic profiles of the mother and the child. The stronger relationship between the maternal adducts and ADHD-related outcomes than between the cord adducts and the same outcomes could be attributable to the effects of exposure on placental function and/or the fact that high levels of maternal adducts indicate that the mother has been highly exposed and is an efficient activator of PAH, resulting in higher transplacental exposure to reactive PAH intermediates. We used urinary PAH metabolites to assess postnatal exposure. This biomarker has been employed in many studies as an indicator of PAH exposure in the general population [70]. Although they represent recent exposure [71], the metabolites can provide a chronic measure of ambient PAH in populations with constant exposure [72].

The mechanisms by which PAH exposure might affect the developing brain are not fully understood. Several pathways have been suggested including endocrine disruption [73–75], binding to receptors for placental growth factors resulting in decreased exchange of oxygen and nutrients [76], binding to the human Ah receptor to induce P450 enzymes [77], DNA damage resulting in activation of apoptotic pathways [78–80], oxidative stress due to inhibition of the brain antioxidant scavenging system [81], and epigenetic alterations [82]. The prenatal period is critical because of the extensive structural and cellular-level changes that occur during this stage of development. However, because brain development and growth occurs throughout childhood, postnatal exposures to environmental pollutants may also affect children's neurodevelopment and behavior [83].

The strengths of the study include our ability to account for a number of potential confounding variables and to draw upon

Table 3. Number of children scoring in the borderline or clinical range on the CBCL and in the moderately to markedly atypical range on the CPRS in the analyses with maternal adducts or cord adducts[a].

	Maternal Adducts (N = 233)	Cord Adducts (N = 162)
CBCL DSM-oriented Attention Deficit/Hyperactivity Problems (Borderline or clinical[b])	18	15
CPRS subscales (Moderately to markedly atypical[b])		
ADHD Index	20	14
DSM-IV Total	25	19
DSM-IV Hyperactive Impulsive	26	19
DSM-IV Inattentive	20	15

[a]Children included in analysis with all covariates.
[b]CBCL- Borderline or clinical defined as percentile ≥93rd; CPRS- Moderately to markedly atypical defined as T-score >65.

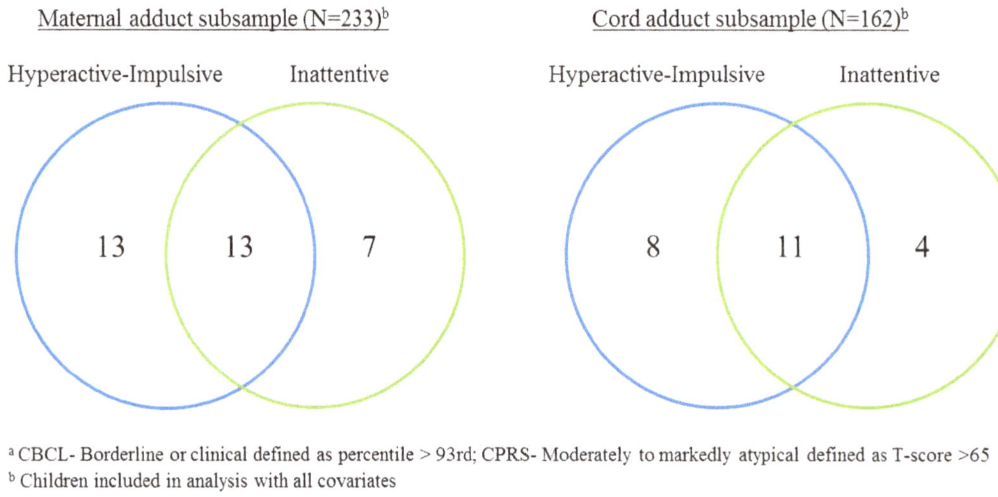

Figure 1. Number of children categorized as moderately to markedly atypical on the CPRS DSM-IV Hyperactive Impulsive and CPRS DSM-IV Inattentive Subscales[a].

individual pre- and post-natal exposure data from biomarker and questionnaire data. We were able to use two complementary age-appropriate instruments to measure ADHD-related behaviors. The CBCL screens for various childhood behavior problems, including ADHD [53]. The CPRS tests specifically for ADHD and related problem behaviors and is intended to be more diagnostic than the CBCL [54]. Due to the prospective nature of our cohort study we were able to assess the association between environmental exposures sustained prenatally and future development of ADHD-related behaviors in childhood.

A limitation of the study is that unmeasured factors such as other pollutants, stress, and noise may have contributed to residual confounding. In addition, the number of children with moderately to markedly atypical outcomes on the CPRS (cases) was small, resulting in fairly wide confidence intervals around the odds ratios. However, the confidence intervals around the effect estimates for the continuous outcomes are much tighter. Although of interest, we

Table 4. Associations between PAH Exposure and CBCL DSM-oriented Attention Deficit/Hyperactivity problems and ADHD Behavior Problems on the CPRS Subscales adjusting for postnatal exposure[a].

	Maternal Adduct (N = 233)	Cord Adduct (N = 162)
Outcomes analyzed continuously		
	$\beta_{adducts}$(95% CI[b])	$\beta_{adducts}$ (95% CI[b])
CBCL DSM-oriented Attention Deficit/Hyperactivity Problems	0.13 (−0.03, 0.29)	−0.04 (−0.23, 0.15)
CPRS subscales		
ADHD Index	**0.14 (0.03, 0.25)***	−0.06 (−0.19, 0.07)
DSM-IV Total	**0.16 (0.07, 0.26)***	0.009 (−0.10, 0.12)
DSM-IV Hyperactive-Impulsive	**0.16 (0.03, 0.29)***	0.10 (−0.05, 0.26)
DSM-IV Inattentive	**0.17 (0.04, 0.31)***	−0.09 (−0.25, 0.06)
Outcomes analyzed dichotomously[c]		
	OR[b] (95% CI[b])	OR[b] (95% CI[b])
CBCL DSM-oriented Attention Deficit/Hyperactivity Problems	1.48 (0.38, 5.79)	1.17 (0.24, 5.66)
CPRS subscales		
ADHD Index	1.83 (0.61, 5.54)	0.93 (0.22, 4.01)
DSM-IV Total	**3.37 (1.10, 10.34)***	1.70 (0.47, 6.17)
DSM-IV Hyperactive-Impulsive	1.58 (0.55, 4.52)	1.04 (0.30, 3.61)
DSM-IV Inattentive	**5.06 (1.43, 17.93)***	1.32 (0.31, 5.56)

[a]Adjusting for postnatal PAH exposure (measured by metabolites at ages 3 or 5, adjusted for specific gravity), prenatal ETS, child sex, maternal education, child ethnicity, gestational age, maternal demoralization, heating season, HOME caretaking environment, maternal intelligence, child age at assessment, maternal ADHD, child anxiety/depression at age 9.
[b]OR stands for odds Ratio; CI stands for Confidence Interval.
[c]CBCL- Borderline or clinical defined as percentile ≥93rd; CPRS- Moderately to markedly atypical defined as T-score >65.
*p-value <0.05.

did not have complete data on exposure to lead or mercury and were unable to account for this in our models. We were also unable to evaluate the effects of individual postnatal PAH metabolites that may have differing toxicities; however benzo[a]pyrene is an important, toxic member of the class of PAH. Finally, generalizability was reduced by the ethnicity restriction of our cohort (African-American and Dominican) and our exclusion of active smokers, illicit drug users, and women with pre-existing disease.

Conclusions

In conclusion, this study provides evidence that early exposure to environmental PAH may contribute to ADHD behavior problems in children. The results require confirmation but are of concern since children with ADHD are at greater risk of risk-taking behaviors [84], poor academic performance [85], and lower earnings in adulthood [86,87]. ADHD imposes large costs on society, estimated to range between $36 billion and $52 billion annually [67,68].

PAH are widespread in urban environments worldwide largely as a result of fossil fuel combustion. Fortunately, it is possible to reduce airborne PAH concentrations using currently available pollution controls, greater energy efficiency, the use of alternative energy sources, and regulatory intervention to control polluting sources.

Acknowledgments

Funding was provided by the National Institute for Environmental Health Sciences (NIEHS) and the U.S. Environmental Protection Agency (US EPA): NIEHS/EPA P01ES09600/R82702701, NIEHS/EPA P01ES09600/RD832141, NIEHS/EPA P01ES09600/RD834509, NIEHS R01ES08977. This publication was also made possible in part by US EPA grants RD832096, the John & Wendy Neu Family Foundation, the New York Community Trust, Trustees of the Blanchette Hooker Rockefeller Fund, and an anonymous foundation. Funding from all the institutions listed was used towards the design and conduct of the study; collection, management, analysis, and interpretation of the data; and the preparation, review, and approval of the manuscript. Its contents are solely the responsibility of the grantee and do not necessarily represent the official views of the US EPA. Further, US EPA does not endorse the purchase of any commercial products or services mentioned in the publication. Findings expressed in this paper are the opinions of the authors and do not necessarily reflect the official opinion of the Centers for Disease Control and Prevention.

Analysis of PAH metabolites was conducted at the Centers for Disease Control and Prevention, National Center for Environmental Health, Division of Laboratory Sciences, 4770 Buford Highway, Atlanta, Georgia 30341, United States, in the laboratory of Andreas Sjodin, PhD. We also thank Joanne Chin, MFA, at the Columbia Center for Children's Environmental Health, 722 W. 168th Street, New York, NY 10032, United States, for assistance in manuscript preparation.

Author Contributions

Acquired the data: FPP HC AM TH SW VR. Interpreted the data: FPP HC AM TH SW VR. Drafted the article or revised it critically for important intellectual content: FPP ELR AM SW VR. Final approval of the version to be published: FPP HC DT ELR JH RLM AM TH SW VR.

References

1. Bostrom CE, Gerde P, Hanberg A, Jernstrom B, Johansson C, et al. (2002) Cancer risk assessment, indicators, and guidelines for polycyclic aromatic hydrocarbons in the ambient air. Environ Health Perspect 110: 451–488.
2. Perera FP, Illman SM, Kinney PL, Whyatt RM, Kelvin EA, et al. (2002) The challenge of preventing environmentally related disease in young children: community-based research in New York City. Environ Health Perspect 110: 197–204.
3. Woodruff TJ, Parker JD, Kyle AD, Schoendorf KC (2003) Disparities in exposure to air pollution during pregnancy. Environmental Health Perspectives 111: 942–946.
4. Jerrett M (2009) Global Geographies of Injustice in Traffic-Related Air Pollution Exposure. Epidemiology 20: 231–233 210.1097/EDE.1090b1013e31819776a31819771.
5. Morello-Frosch R, Zuk M, Jerrett M, Shamasunder B, Kyle AD (2011) Understanding The Cumulative Impacts Of Inequalities In Environmental Health: Implications For Policy. Health Affairs 30: 879–887.
6. Perera FP, Tang D, Wang S, Vishnevetsky J, Zhang B, et al. (2012) Prenatal Polycyclic Aromatic Hydrocarbon (PAH) Exposure and Child Behavior at age 6–7. Environ Health Perspect.
7. Mooney LA, Santella RM, Covey L, Jeffrey AM, Bigbee W, et al. (1995) Decline of DNA damage and other biomarkers in peripheral blood following smoking cessation. Cancer Epidemiol Biomarkers Prev 4: 627–634.
8. Godschalk RWL, Van Schooten FJ, Bartsch H (2003) A critical evaluation of DNA adducts as biological markers for human exposure to polycyclic aromatic compounds. Journal of Biochemistry and Molecular Biology 36: 1–11.
9. Veglia F, Loft S, Matullo G, Peluso M, Munnia A, et al. (2008) DNA adducts and cancer risk in prospective studies: a pooled analysis and a meta-analysis. Carcinogenesis 29: 932–936.
10. Anderson LM, Diwan BA, Fear NT, Roman E (2000) Critical windows of exposure for children's health: cancer in human epidemiological studies and neoplasms in experimental animal models. Environ Health Perspect 108: 573–594.
11. National Research Council (1993) Toxicity Testing and Strategies to Determine Needs and Priorities. Washington, D.C.: National Academy Press.
12. Perera FP, Tang D, Jedrychowski W, Hemminki K, Santella RM, et al. (2004) Biomarkers in maternal and newborn blood indicate heightened fetal susceptibility to procarcinogenic DNA damage. Environ Health Perspect 112: 1133–1136.
13. Grandjean P, Landrigan PJ (2006) Developmental neurotoxicity of industrial chemicals. Lancet 368: 2167–2178.
14. Stein J, Schettler T, Wallinga D, Valenti M (2002) In harm's way: toxic threats to child development. J Dev Behav Pediatr 23: S13–22.
15. Shonkoff JP, Garner AS, Committee on Psychosocial Aspects of Child And Family Health, Committee on Early Childhood, Adoption, and Dependent Care, Section on Developmental and Behavioral Pediatrics (2012) The Lifelong Effects of Early Childhood Adversity and Toxic Stress. Pediatrics 129: E232–E246.
16. Brown LA, Khousbouei H, Goodwin JS, Irvin-Wilson CV, Ramesh A, et al. (2007) Down-regulation of early ionotrophic glutamate receptor subunit developmental expression as a mechanism for observed plasticity deficits following gestational exposure to benzo(a)pyrene. Neurotoxicology 28: 965–978.
17. Wormley DD, Ramesh A, Hood DB (2004) Environmental contaminant-mixture effects on CNS development, plasticity, and behavior. Toxicol Appl Pharmacol 197: 49–65.
18. Grova N, Valley A, Turner JD, Morel A, Muller CP, et al. (2007) Modulation of behavior and NMDA-R1 gene mRNA expression in adult female mice after sub-acute administration of benzo(a)pyrene. Neurotoxicology 28: 630–636.
19. Schellenberger MT, Grova N, Farinelle S, Willième S, Schroeder H, et al. (2013) Modulation of benzo[a]pyrene induced neurotoxicity in female mice actively immunized with a B[a]P–diphtheria toxoid conjugate. Toxicology and Applied Pharmacology 271: 175–183.
20. Perera FP, Rauh V, Whyatt RM, Tsai WY, Tang D, et al. (2006) Effect of prenatal exposure to airborne polycyclic aromatic hydrocarbons on neurodevelopment in the first 3 years of life among inner-city children. Environ Health Perspect 114: 1287–1292.
21. Perera FP, Li Z, Whyatt R, Hoepner L, Wang S, et al. (2009) Prenatal polycyclic aromatic hydrocarbon exposure and child intelligence at age 5. Pediatrics 124: e195–e202.
22. Bostic JQ, Prince JB (2008) Child and adolescent psychiatric disorders. In: Stern TA, Rosenbaum JF, Fava M, Biederman J, Rauch SL, editors.Massachusetts General Hospital Comprehensive Clinical Psychiatry. 1st ed. Philadelphia, PA: Elsevier Mosby.
23. Wilens TE, Biederman J, Brown S, Tanguay S, Monuteaux MC, et al. (2002) Psychiatric Comorbidity and Functioning in Clinically Referred Preschool Children and School-Age Youths With ADHD. Journal of the American Academy of Child & Adolescent Psychiatry 41: 262–268.
24. Spencer TJ, Biederman J, Mick E (2007) Attention-deficit/hyperactivity disorder: diagnosis, lifespan, comorbidities, and neurobiology. J Pediatr Psychol 32: 631–642.
25. Biederman J, Faraone SV, Keenan K, Benjamin J, Krifcher B, et al. (1992) Further Evidence for Family-Genetic Risk-Factors in Attention-Deficit Hyperactivity Disorder - Patterns of Comorbidity in Probands and Relatives in Psychiatrically and Pediatrically Referred Samples. Archives of General Psychiatry 49: 728–738.
26. Spencer T, Biederman J, Wilens T (1999) Attention-deficit/hyperactivity disorder and comorbidity.Pediatr Clin North Am 46: 915–927, vii.
27. Charach A, Yeung E, Climans T, Lillie E (2011) Childhood Attention-Deficit/Hyperactivity Disorder and Future Substance Use Disorders: Comparative

Meta-Analyses. Journal of the American Academy of Child and Adolescent Psychiatry 50: 9–21.

28. Lee SS, Humphreys KL, Flory K, Liu R, Glass K (2011) Prospective association of childhood attention-deficit/hyperactivity disorder (ADHD) and substance use and abuse/dependence: a meta-analytic review. Clin Psychol Rev 31: 328–341.
29. Groenman AP, Oosterlaan J, Rommelse N, Franke B, Roeyers H, et al. (2013) Substance use disorders in adolescents with attention deficit hyperactivity disorder: a 4-year follow-up study. Addiction 108: 1503–1511.
30. Shaw M, Hodgkins P, Caci H, Young S, Kahle J, et al. (2012) A systematic review and analysis of long-term outcomes in attention deficit hyperactivity disorder: effects of treatment and non-treatment. BMC Med 10: 99.
31. Banerjee TD, Middleton F, Faraone SV (2007) Environmental risk factors for attention-deficit hyperactivity disorder. Acta Paediatr 96: 1269–1274.
32. Froehlich TE, Anixt JS, Loe IM, Chirdkiatgumchai V, Kuan L, et al. (2011) Update on environmental risk factors for attention-deficit/hyperactivity disorder. Curr Psychiatry Rep 13: 333–344.
33. Siddique S, Banerjee M, Ray MR, Lahiri T (2011) Attention-deficit hyperactivity disorder in children chronically exposed to high level of vehicular pollution. Eur J Pediatr 170: 923–929.
34. Newman NC, Ryan P, Lemasters G, Levin L, Bernstein D, et al. (2013) Traffic-related air pollution exposure in the first year of life and behavioral scores at 7 years of age. Environ Health Perspect 121: 731–736.
35. Chiu YHM, Bellinger DC, Coull BA, Anderson S, Barber R, et al. (2013) Associations between Traffic-Related Black Carbon Exposure and Attention in a Prospective Birth Cohort of Urban Children. Environ Health Perspect 121: 859–864.
36. Perera FP, Rauh V, Tsai WY, Kinney P, Camann D, et al. (2003) Effects of transplacental exposure to environmental pollutants on birth outcomes in a multi-ethnic population. Environ Health Perspect 111: 201–205.
37. Schuurmans C, Kurrasch DM (2013) Neurodevelopmental consequences of maternal distress: what do we really know? Clinical Genetics 83: 108–117.
38. Bergman K, Sarkar P, O'Connor TG, Modi N, Glover V (2007) Maternal Stress During Pregnancy Predicts Cognitive Ability and Fearfulness in Infancy. Journal of the American Academy of Child & Adolescent Psychiatry 46: 1454–1463.
39. Barry TD, Dunlap ST, Cotten SJ, Lochman JE, Wells KC (2005) The Influence of Maternal Stress and Distress on Disruptive Behavior Problems in Boys. Journal of the American Academy of Child & Adolescent Psychiatry 44: 265–273.
40. Dohrenwend BS, Krasnoff L, Askenacy A, Dohrenwend B (1978) Exemplification of a method for scaling life events: the PERI life events scale. J Health Soc Behavior 19: 205–229.
41. Brown L, Sherbenou RJ, Johnson SK (1990) Test of non-verbal intelligence: a language-free measure of cognitive ability. 2nd edition. Austin, Tx: PRO-ED, Inc.
42. Caldwell BM, Bradley RH (1979) Home observation for measurement of the environment. Little Rock, AK: University of Arkansas Press.
43. Conners C, Erhardt D, Sparrow E (1999) Conners' Adult ADHD rating scales: Technical manual. New York: Multi-Health Systems.
44. Todd RD, Rasmussen ER, Neuman RJ, Reich W, Hudziak JJ, et al. (2001) Familiality and heritability of subtypes of attention deficit hyperactivity disorder in a population sample of adolescent female twins. Am J Psychiatry 158: 1891–1898.
45. Achenbach T, Rescorla L (2001) Child Behavior Checklist for age 6–18. Burlington VT: ASEBA, 6-1-01 Edition.
46. Alexandrov K, Rojas M, Geneste O, Castegnaro M, Camus AM, et al. (1992) An improved fluorometric assay for dosimetry of benzo(a)pyrene diol-epoxide-DNA adducts in smokers' lung: comparisons with total bulky adducts and aryl hydrocarbon hydroxylase activity. Cancer Res 52: 6248–6253.
47. Li Z, Romanoff LC, Trinidad DA, Hussain N, Jones RS, et al. (2006) Measurement of urinary monohydroxy polycyclic aromatic hydrocarbons using automated liquid-liquid extraction and gas chromatography/isotope dilution high-resolution mass spectrometry. Anal Chem 78: 5744–5751.
48. Li Z, Sandau CD, Romanoff LC, Caudill SP, Sjodin A, et al. (2008) Concentration and profile of 22 urinary polycyclic aromatic hydrocarbon metabolites in the US population. Environ Res 107: 320–331.
49. Miller RL, Garfinkel R, Lendor C, Hoepner L, Li Z, et al. (2010) Polycyclic aromatic hydrocarbon metabolite levels and pediatric allergy and asthma in an inner-city cohort. Pediatr Allergy Immunol 21: 260–267.
50. Jongeneelen FJ, van Leeuwen FE, Oosterink S, Anzion RB, van der Loop F, et al. (1990) Ambient and biological monitoring of cokeoven workers: determinants of the internal dose of polycyclic aromatic hydrocarbons. Br J Ind Med 47: 454–461.
51. Hauser R, Meeker JD, Park S, Silva MJ, Calafat AM (2004) Temporal variability of urinary phthalate metabolite levels in men of reproductive age. Environ Health Perspect 112: 1734–1740.
52. Perera F, Vishnevetsky J, Herbstman JB, Calafat AM, Xiong W, et al. (2012) Prenatal bisphenol a exposure and child behavior in an inner-city cohort. Environ Health Perspect 120: 1190–1194.
53. Achenbach T, Rescorla L (2001) Manual for the ASEBA School-Age Forms & Profiles. Burlington, VT: University of Vermont, Research Center for Children, Youth & Families.
54. Conners CK (1997) Conners' Rating Scales- Revised (CRS-R): User's Manual Toronto, ON: Multi-Health Systems Inc.
55. Conners CK, Parker JDA, Sitarenios G, Epstein JN (1998) The Revised Conners' Parent rating Scale (CPRS-R): Factor structure, reliability, and criterion validity. Journal of Abnormal Child Psychology 26: 2567–2268.
56. Rodriguez-Barranco M, Lacasana M, Aguilar-Garduno C, Alguacil J, Gil F, et al. (2013) Association of arsenic, cadmium and manganese exposure with neurodevelopment and behavioural disorders in children: a systematic review and meta-analysis. Sci Total Environ 454–455: 562–577.
57. Cornelius MD, De Genna NM, Leech SL, Willford JA, Goldschmidt L, et al. (2011) Effects of prenatal cigarette smoke exposure on neurobehavioral outcomes in 10-year-old children of adolescent mothers. Neurotoxicol Teratol 33: 137–144.
58. Bouchard M, Laforest F, Vandelac L, Bellinger D, Mergler D (2007) Hair manganese and hyperactive behaviors: pilot study of school-age children exposed through tap water. Environ Health Perspect 115: 122–127.
59. Wasserman GA, Staghezza-Jaramillo B, Shrout P, Popovac D, Graziano J (1998) The effect of lead exposure on behavior problems in preschool children. Am J Public Health 88: 481–486.
60. American Psychiatric Association, American Psychiatric Association, Task Force on DSM-IV (2000) Diagnostic and statistical manual of mental disorders: DSM-IV-TR. Washington, DC: American Psychiatric Association. xxxvii, 943 p. p.
61. de Graaf R, Kessler RC, Fayyad J, ten Have M, Alonso J, et al. (2008) The prevalence and effects of adult attention-deficit/hyperactivity disorder (ADHD) on the performance of workers: results from the WHO World Mental Health Survey Initiative. Occup Environ Med 65: 835–842.
62. Kupper T, Haavik J, Drexler H, Ramos-Quiroga JA, Wermelskirchen D, et al. (2012) The negative impact of attention-deficit/hyperactivity disorder on occupational health in adults and adolescents. Int Arch Occup Environ Health 85: 837–847.
63. Wu SY, Gau SS (2013) Correlates for academic performance and school functioning among youths with and without persistent attention-deficit/hyperactivity disorder. Res Dev Disabil 34: 505–515.
64. Jacobson LA, Ryan M, Denckla MB, Mostofsky SH, Mahone EM (2013) Performance Lapses in Children with Attention-Deficit/Hyperactivity Disorder Contribute to Poor Reading Fluency. Arch Clin Neuropsychol.
65. Ek U, Westerlund J, Holmberg K, Fernell E (2011) Academic performance of adolescents with ADHD and other behavioural and learning problems -a population-based longitudinal study. Acta Paediatr 100: 402–406.
66. Strine TW, Lesesne CA, Okoro CA, McGuire LC, Chapman DP, et al. (2006) Emotional and behavioral difficulties and impairments in everyday functioning among children with a history of attention-deficit/hyperactivity disorder. Prev Chronic Dis 3: A52.
67. CDC (2013) ADHD, Data and Statistics, National Center on Birth Defects and Developmental Disabilities.
68. Pelham WE, Foster EM, Robb JA (2007) The economic impact of attention-deficit/hyperactivity disorder in children and adolescents. J Pediatr Psychol 32: 711–727.
69. Perera FP, Tang D, Whyatt R, Lederman SA, Jedrychowski W (2005) DNA damage from polycyclic aromatic hydrocarbons measured by benzo[a]pyrene-DNA adducts in mothers and newborns from Northern Manhattan, the World Trade Center Area, Poland, and China. Cancer Epidemiol Biomarkers Prev 14: 709–714.
70. Castano-Vinyals G, D'Errico A, Malats N, Kogevinas M (2004) Biomarkers of exposure to polycyclic aromatic hydrocarbons from environmental air pollution. Occup Environ Med 61: e12.
71. Strickland P, Kang D, Sithisarankul P (1996) Polycyclic aromatic hydrocarbon metabolites in urine as biomarkers of exposure and effect. Environ Health Perspect 104 Suppl 5: 927–932.
72. Zhao ZH, Quan WY, Tian DH (1990) Urinary 1-Hydroxypyrene as an Indicator of Human Exposure to Ambient Polycyclic Aromatic-Hydrocarbons in a Coal-Burning Environment. Science of the Total Environment 92: 145–154.
73. Archibong AE, Inyang F, Ramesh A, Greenwood M, Nayyar T, et al. (2002) Alteration of pregnancy related hormones and fetal survival in F-344 rats exposed by inhalation to benzo(a)pyrene. Reprod Toxicol 16: 801–808.
74. Bui QQ, Tran MB, West WL (1986) A comparative study of the reproductive effects of methadone and benzo(a)pyrene in the pregnant and pseudopregnant rat. Toxicology 42: 195–204.
75. Takeda K, Tsukue N, Yoshida S (2004) Endocrine-disrupting activity of chemicals in diesel exhaust and diesel exhaust particles. Environ Sci 11: 33–45.
76. Dejmek J, Solansky I, Benes I, Lenicek J, Sram RJ (2000) The impact of polycyclic aromatic hydrocarbons and fine particles on pregnancy outcome. Environ Health Perspect 108: 1159–1164.
77. Manchester DK, Gordon SK, Golas CL, Roberts EA, Okey AB (1987) Ah receptor in human placenta: stabilization by molybdate and characterization of binding of 2,3,7,8-tetrachlorodibenzo-p-dioxin, 3-methylcholanthrene, and benzo(a)pyrene. Cancer Res 47: 4861–4868.
78. Meyn MS (1995) Ataxia-telangiectasia and cellular responses to DNA damage. Cancer Res 55: 5991–6001.
79. Nicol CJ, Harrison ML, Laposa RR, Gimelshtein IL, Wells PG (1995) A teratologic suppressor role for p53 in benzo[a]pyrene-treated transgenic p53-deficient mice. Nat Genet 10: 181–187.
80. Wood KA, Youle RJ (1995) The role of free radicals and p53 in neuron apoptosis in vivo. J Neuroscience 15: 5851–5857.

81. Saunders CR, Das SK, Ramesh A, Shockley DC, Mukherjee S (2006) Benzo(a)pyrene-induced acute neurotoxicity in the F-344 rat: role of oxidative stress. J Appl Toxicol 26: 427–438.
82. Wilson VL, Jones PA (1983) Inhibition of DNA methylation by chemical carcinogens in vitro. Cell 32: 239–246.
83. Stiles J, Jernigan TL (2010) The basics of brain development. Neuropsychol Rev 20: 327–348.
84. Garzon DL, Huang H, Todd RD (2008) Do Attention Deficit/Hyperactivity Disorder and Oppositional Defiant Disorder Influence Preschool Unintentional Injury Risk? Archives of Psychiatric Nursing 22: 288–296.
85. Wood JJ (2006) Effect of anxiety reduction on children's school performance and social adjustment. Dev Psychol 42: 345–349.
86. Knapp M, King D, Healey A, Thomass C (2011) Economic Outcomes in Adulthood and their Associations with Antisocial Conduct, Attention Deficit and Anxiety Problems in Childhood. Journal of Mental Health Policy and Economics 14: 137–147.
87. Kotsopoulos N, Connolly MP, Sobanski E, Postma MJ (2013) The fiscal consequences of ADHD in Germany: a quantitative analysis based on differences in educational attainment and lifetime earnings. J Ment Health Policy Econ 16: 27–33.

22

Multimodal Magnetic Resonance Imaging Study of Treatment-Naïve Adults with Attention-Deficit/ Hyperactivity Disorder

Tiffany M. Chaim[1,2,3]*, Tianhao Zhang[4], Marcus V. Zanetti[1,2], Maria Aparecida da Silva[3], Mário R. Louzã[3], Jimit Doshi[4], Mauricio H. Serpa[1,2], Fabio L. S. Duran[1,2], Sheila C. Caetano[1,2], Christos Davatzikos[4], Geraldo F. Busatto[1,2]

1 Laboratory of Psychiatric Neuroimaging, Department and Institute of Psychiatry, Faculty of Medicine, University of São Paulo, Sao Paulo, Sao Paulo, Brazil, **2** Center for Interdisciplinary Research on Applied Neurosciences, University of São Paulo, Sao Paulo, São Paulo, Brazil, **3** Program for Attention Deficit Hyperactivity Disorder, Department and Institute of Psychiatry, Faculty of Medicine, University of São Paulo, Sao Paulo, Sao Paulo, Brazil, **4** Section of Biomedical Image Analysis, Department of Radiology, University of Pennsylvania, Philadelphia, Pennsylvania, Unites States of America

Abstract

Background: Attention-Deficit/Hiperactivity Disorder (ADHD) is a prevalent disorder, but its neuroanatomical circuitry is still relatively understudied, especially in the adult population. The few morphometric magnetic resonance imaging (MRI) and diffusion tensor imaging (DTI) studies available to date have found heterogeneous results. This may be at least partly attributable to some well-known technical limitations of the conventional voxel-based methods usually employed to analyze such neuroimaging data. Moreover, there is a great paucity of imaging studies of adult ADHD to date that have excluded patients with history of use of stimulant medication.

Methods: A newly validated method named optimally-discriminative voxel-based analysis (ODVBA) was applied to multimodal (structural and DTI) MRI data acquired from 22 treatment-naïve ADHD adults and 19 age- and gender-matched healthy controls (HC).

Results: Regarding DTI data, we found higher fractional anisotropy in ADHD relative to HC encompassing the white matter (WM) of the bilateral superior frontal gyrus, right middle frontal left gyrus, left postcentral gyrus, bilateral cingulate gyrus, bilateral middle temporal gyrus and right superior temporal gyrus; reductions in trace (a measure of diffusivity) in ADHD relative to HC were also found in fronto-striatal-parieto-occipital circuits, including the right superior frontal gyrus and bilateral middle frontal gyrus, right precentral gyrus, left middle occipital gyrus and bilateral cingulate gyrus, as well as the left body and right splenium of the corpus callosum, right superior corona radiata, and right superior longitudinal and fronto-occipital fasciculi. Volumetric abnormalities in ADHD subjects were found only at a trend level of significance, including reduced gray matter (GM) in the right angular gyrus, and increased GM in the right supplementary motor area and superior frontal gyrus.

Conclusions: Our results suggest that adult ADHD is associated with neuroanatomical abnormalities mainly affecting the WM microstructure in fronto-parieto-temporal circuits that have been implicated in cognitive, emotional and visuomotor processes.

Editor: Juan Zhou, Duke-NUS Graduate Medical School, Singapore

Funding: The present investigation was supported by a 2010 NARSAD Independent Investigator Award (NARSAD: The Brain and Behavior Research Fund) awarded to Geraldo F. Busatto. Geraldo F. Busatto is also partially funded by CNPq-Brazil. The funders had no role in study design, data collection and analysis, decision to publish, or preparation of the manuscript.

Competing Interests: The authors have declared that no competing interests exist.

* Email: chaim.tiffany@gmail.com

Introduction

Attention-deficit and hyperactivity disorder (ADHD) is a frequent and underdiagnosed mental disorder in the general adult population, with a reported prevalence of up to 5.8% in this age range [1–4].

The neuroanatomical circuitry underlying adult ADHD is still relatively understudied. Only a few brain morphometric investigations using magnetic resonance imaging (MRI) have evaluated adult ADHD subjects to date, most of which enrolling patients under pharmacological treatment with stimulant agents. These MRI studies have suggested the presence of gray matter (GM) volume abnormalities in prefrontal-striatal-parietal networks [6–8], known to have a central role in attentional processing and executive functioning in general [8]. Other brain regions have also been variably found to present volume abnormalities in adult ADHD patients, including the anterior cingulate cortex, occipital cortex and thalamus [8,11,12]. Using diffusion tensor imaging (DTI), MRI studies may also help to unravel the nature of WM microstructural pathological features underlying ADHD in adults, allowing the combined measurement of different indices of white matter microstructural integrity, namely: fractional anisotropy (FA), which provides information on axonal integrity and homogeneity of fiber orientations [13,14]; and measures of diffusivity, which reflect deficits in cellular density, myelin breakdown or changes in extracellular volumes [13,15,16]. The few available DTI studies of adult ADHD subjects to date have reported alterations in tracts that interconnect the above GM regions and which are known to be important for attention and decision making processes, such as the superior longitudinal fasciculus [5,9,10].

Thus although not yet numerous, the above MRI studies have provided preliminary evidence that the neuropathology underlying ADHD in adults may involve abnormalities both of GM and WM tracts. However, there has been a great paucity of studies evaluating treatment-naïve adult ADHD subjects to date [17,18], and no MRI study of such population has acquired both morphometric and DTI data from the same individuals at the same point in time.

Because widely distributed brain networks may be implicated in ADHD, voxel-based methods that systematically search for abnormalities across the entire brain may be more suitable for analyzing data in MRI studies of ADHD, rather than region of interest (ROI)-based methods that are unavoidably restricted to a few selected portions of the brain. However, significant findings have varied considerably across the few MRI studies of ADHD to date that used voxelwise methods, particularly in regard to their specific brain location [7,19,20]. Such discrepancies might be, at least in part, attributed to some well-known technical limitations of conventional voxel-based image analysis approaches. For instance, voxel-based morphometry (VBM) methods include a step of image blurring by Gaussian smoothing, in order to account for registration errors and to conform the imaging data to a normal distribution, which is important to validate the assumptions of the statistical parametric mapping approach usually employed in VBM studies [21]. This is conventionally performed in a homogeneous fashion across the whole brain, without accounting for either the wide differences in shape and size of separate brain portions or inter-subject variations; such uniform smoothing methods may increase the risk of both false positive and false negative results [22]. Moreover, the size of the Gaussian kernel is chosen in each study in a somewhat *ad hoc* way, even though it significantly affects the detected group differences. Finally, and most importantly, conventional VBM methods employ a "mass univariate" statistical approach, considering each voxel individually in its separate brain compartment without weighting possible inter-relationships with neighboring voxels and voxels from other brain tissues [23]. For example, in a situation where a specific disorder under study is associated with an enlargement of a given brain area (such as the temporal horn of the lateral ventricle), the VBM analysis may misinterpret such abnormality as a volumetric reduction of a neighboring region (such as the hippocampus). This statistical approach substantially reduces sensitivity to detect group differences and can also produce mislocalization of regions of significant brain tissue density or volumetric changes.

A recently developed voxelwise image analysis methodology, known as optimally-discriminative voxel-based analysis (ODVBA), attempts to minimize the above technical limitations. The ODVBA approach employs a spatially adaptive smoothing filtering and a high-dimensional multivariate local discriminative analysis technique in order to achieve improved sensitivity and accuracy to detect regional brain abnormalities [22]. This methodology has been validated in a recently published study by two of the authors (T.Z and C.D) [24]. In this study, the ODVBA was evaluated using datasets of previously published investigations in schizophrenia and minor cognitive impairment (MCI) in comparison to other established methods, including: the conventional VBM method (Gaussian smoothing plus general linear model – GLM); extant spatially adaptive smoothing methods; and cluster enhancing methods. The experimental results indicated that ODVBA was considerably more sensitive in detecting group differences, demonstrating the highest significance in group differences within the identified voxels. In terms of the spatial extent of detected areas of group differences, agreement of anatomical boundaries and classification, the ODVBA performed better than the other tested voxel-based methods and competitively with the cluster enhancing methods [24]. The findings obtained with the ODBVA approach in those clinical samples were consistent with the previous literature, including widespread GM losses both in schizophrenia and MCI involving several cortical and limbic regions, as well as a greater degree of GM losses in MCI patients who later converted to Alzheimers disease compared to non-converters [24].

In the present MRI study, we employed the ODBVA approach to compare treatment-naïve adults with ADHD and age and gender-matched healthy controls (HC). Given the relevance of assessing both localized morphological abnormalities and microstructural changes in large-scale brain networks associated with ADHD [5,25,26], we adopted a multi-modal MRI approach, applying the same voxelwise routines to compare both GM and WM volumes and DTI indices (FA and Trace – TR, an index of diffusivity) between groups. Such combined approach aimed to ascertain whether there are similarities or differences in the topography and severity of GM/WM volumetric versus microstructural WM abnormalities in never-medicated adult ADHD patients. This integrative mapping of morphological and microstructural abnormalities in such population may provide further insights into the neural underpinnings of the clinical manifestations of ADHD in adulthood, including its cognitive and behavioral problems. Also, by combining two DTI indices (FA and TR), we wished to improve understanding about the mechanisms underlying the microstructural WM abnormalities in never-medicated adult ADHD patients. Based on findings from the previous MRI literature cited above [5–9], we hypothesized the presence of widespread volumetric abnormalities in the adult ADHD group relative to healthy controls, mainly affecting prefrontal, striatal and parietal regions, as well as microstructural WM abnormalities as assessed with DTI in the tracts which interconnect such brain network, including the caudate nucleus, superior corona radiata, superior longitudinal fasciculus and the cingulum bundle.

Methods and Materials

Participants

Twenty-two treatment-naive patients with ADHD aged 18–50 years were consecutively evaluated at the outpatient ADHD clinic of the Institute of Psychiatry, University of São Paulo, Brazil. Subjects were interviewed with the Structured Clinical Interview (SCID) for the DSM-IV [27], and the Schedule for Affective Disorders and Schizophrenia for school-age children-present and lifetime version (K-SADS-PL) [28] Adapted Module (version 6.0) in order to confirm the diagnosis of ADHD and also to access potential axis I comorbidities. For the assessment of symptom severity, we used the Adult ADHD Self-Report Scale (ASRS-18) [29].

Healthy volunteers matched for age and gender with ADHD patients were recruited through advertisement in the local community and constituted our HC group. All subjects in the HC group also underwent clinical interviewing, including the SCID and the K-SADS-PL screening, in order to exclude psychiatric disorders and previous use of psychopharmacological agents.

In addition to the clinical instruments mentioned above, both patients and HC were screened for substance use with the Alcohol Use Disorders Identification Test (AUDIT) [30] and the South Westminster Questionnaire [31]. Diagnostic criteria for substance abuse or dependence were assessed using the SCID [32]. Handedness was assessed using the Edinburgh inventory [33]. Moreover, a general medical history, including information about cerebrovascular risk factors, and data on the use of psychotropic and general medications, was obtained through interviews with patients and/or their family.

Exclusion criteria for both groups were: substance abuse or dependence (current and lifetime); the presence of medical conditions or neurological disorders which could affect the central nervous system; history of mental retardation as assessed by clinical interviews with the patients and a close relative if necessary; past history of head trauma with loss of consciousness; and contraindications for MRI scanning.

This study was approved by our local ethics committee: "*Comissão de Ética para Análise de Projetos de Pesquisa*" – CAPPesq from the board of the University o Sao Paulo Medical School, and "*Comissão Nacional de Ética em Pesquisa – Conep*". After complete description of the study to the subjects, written informed consent was obtained.

Image acquisition

All subjects (ADHD patients and HC) underwent MRI scanning using a 1.5T Siemens Espree system (Siemens, Erlagen, Germany).

Morphological data was acquired using a T1-weighted magnetization-prepared rapid gradient echo sequence (MPRAGE) using the following parameters: TR = 2,400 ms, TE = 3.65 ms, NEX = 1, field of view (FOV) = 240 mm, flip angle = 8o, matrix = 192×192 pixels, slice thickness = 1.2 mm (no gap between slices), voxel size = 1.3×1.3×12 mm, resulting in 160 slices covering the whole brain.

The DTI sequence was acquired using cardiac gating, a 12-channel head coil and parallel imaging. DTI was based on an echo-planar image (EPI) acquisition and consisted of one image without diffusion gradient (b = 0 s/mm^2) plus diffusion-weighted images (DWI) acquired along 64 non-colinear directions (b = 1,000 s/mm^2) using the following parameters: TR = 8,000 ms, TE = 110 ms, NEX = 2, FOV = 240 mm, matrix = 120×120 pixels, slice thickness = 2.7 mm (no gap between slices), voxel size = 2.0×2.0×2.7 mm, resulting in 50 slices covering the whole brain.

The two sequences were acquired in up to 25 minutes. The imaging protocol also included a T2-weighted turbo spin-echo transaxial sequence (24 slices, slice thickness = 5 mm, 1 mm gap) and a fluid attenuated inversion recovery (FLAIR) transaxial sequence (24 slices, slice thickness = 5 mm, 1 mm gap). Individual image inspection of the datasets of each subject was performed visually by an expert neuroradiologist aiming to identify silent gross brain lesions and artifacts that could interfere with image processing and analysis.

Processing and analysis of neuroimaging data

The T1-weighted images were pre-processed by correcting for signal inhomogeneities followed by skull-stripping and cerebellum removal. The MNI_N3 Software Package [34], available in: http://www.bic.mni.mcgill.ca/software/N3/, was used for correcting for signal inhomogeneities. Then, the skull-stripping and cerebellum removal were performed using a novel automated method known as Multi-Atlas Skull-Stripping (MASS version 1.0) [35], This method has been validated on three different public data sets and has been shown to achieve a higher accuracy than other state-of-the-art brain extraction methods [35]. It uses a set of selected atlases that are built from the actual dataset under study, based on a classification process that identifies a subgroup of images that best represent the neuroanatomical variations within the sample. Finally, each resulting image was subsequently inspected for imperfections in the skull-stripping and cerebellum removal process (cortical erosions or extra-cerebral tissue remains, for example) and corrections were eventually made manually using the Rordens MRIcro 6/2013 program, available in: http://www.mccauslandcenter.sc.edu/mricro/mricron/index.html. As the segmentation algorithms used to extract the GM and WM have been shown to be inaccurate in the cerebellum, due to reduced contrast, our group routinely performs the cerebellum removal. Moreover, the removal of the cerebellum improves our ability to accurately segment GM/WM throughout the brain.

The images were subsequently segmented into their 3 principal brain tissues (GM, WM, and cerebrospinal fluid space) through an automated, iterative algorithm for energy minimization called Multiplicative Intrinsic Component Optimization (MICO) [36], available in http://www.rad.upenn.edu/sbia/software/request.php?software=mico. The skull-stripped and cerebellum-removed images were then spatially registered to the single-subject brain template of Montreal Neurological Institute (MNI) through a robust method for elastic registration called Deformable Registration via Attribute Matching and Mutual-Saliency weighting (DRAMMS version 1.1.0) [37], available in http://www.rad.upenn.edu/sbia/software/dramms/download.html. The deformation field resulting from this spatial registration was then applied to the segmented images in order to generate mass-preserved volumetric maps, named Regional Analysis of Volumes Examined in Normalized Space (RAVENS) maps of the GM, WM, and cerebrospinal fluid compartments [38]. In RAVENS maps, the tissue density reflects the amount of tissue present in each subject's image at a given location, after mapping to the standardized template space. For example, a region of decreased density indicates a reduced volume in this structure. Lastly, the RAVENS maps were corrected for the total brain volume (given by the sum of all voxels of brain tissue and cerebrospinal fluid space).

The diffusion tensor images were reconstructed from the DWI data using multivariate linear fitting [39]. Spatial normalization of all the tensor images was then carried out via an elastic registration method known as FNIRT [40], against a standard DTI template known as the EVE [41]. For the brain DTI registration we used the FMRIB's nonlinear image registration tool, which is part of the FMRIB Software Library (FSL 4.1.5) [40], available in http://fsl.fmrib.ox.ac.uk/fsl/fslwiki/FslInstallation. Following the spatial normalization, Fractional Anisotropy (FA) and Trace (TR) images were derived for each subject. While FA provides a measure of diffusion directional anisotropy, TR affords indices of diffusivity, similarly to other commonly employed DTI measures such as mean diffusivity (MD) [42]. TR measures mean diffusivity by adding the Eigen values of the tensor. Thus, it provides a rotationally invariant index of the overall amount of diffusivity within each image voxel [42]. Whereas the TR index provides an estimate of the displacement of water molecules in a medium, measure of FA reflect the degree of water diffusion directionality and, thus, are sensitive to the degree of myelination, density and organization of WM tracts, all of which may reflect maturational processes [22,42,43]. One final point to consider is that although the FA and TR indices are thought to reflect *micro*-structural brain abnormalities, the relatively large voxel size of the DTI acquisition (2.0*2.0*2.7 mm) implies that FA differences between groups may not always indicate a *micro*-structural change.

Statistical analyses were performed voxel-by-voxel using the Optimally-Discriminative Voxel-Based Analysis (ODVBA 2.0) Software Package [22], in-house program in SBIA, UPenn, on four different measures: 1) RAVENS maps of GM; 2) RAVENS maps of WM; 3) FA; and 4) TR. ODVBA is a new optimally-discriminative framework for determining the adaptive smoothing kernel and examining group differences. The main premise of ODVBA is that it using a machine learning paradigm to effectively apply a form of matched filtering, to optimally detect a group difference. The framework of ODVBA mainly contains three phases: regional nonnegative discriminative projection, determining each voxel's statistic, and permutation tests. At first, regional discriminative analysis, restricted by appropriate nonnegativity constraints, is applied to a spatial neighborhood around each voxel, aiming to find the coefficients that best highlight the difference between two groups in that neighborhood. Secondly, since each voxel belongs to a large number of such neighborhoods, each centered on one of its neighboring voxels, the group difference at each voxel is determined by a composition of contributions from all neighborhoods to which it participates. Finally, the statistical significances (p values) are obtained by using permutation tests [44]. In this paper, the number of permutations is 2,000.

For the detection of differences in morphometry, anisotropy and diffusivity measures between adult ADHD and HC, we used a strict statistical threshold of $p<0.05$ with false-discovering rate (FDR) correction for multiple comparisons. Findings that were significant only at an uncorrected threshold of $p<0.001$ are reported as trends. The significance maps are partitioned and analyzed according to 1) the automated anatomical labeling (AAL) atlas [45] for GM analysis, and 2) the JHU-MNI-ss atlas (or EVE atlas) [46], for WM, FA, and TR analysis. On each anatomical region, we calculated the cluster size and the t statistic (based on the means of the detected area per region).

In addition to the above described between-group comparisons, we conducted a voxel-based search for significant linear correlations between the severity of symptoms as assessed by the ASRS-18 within the ADHD group and each of the four maps (GM, WM, FA and TR), in a regression analysis using the general linear model (GLM) [47].

Results

Demographic and Clinical Data

Table 1 summarizes the clinical and demographic characteristics of ADHD patients and HC. All ADHD patients had a history of clinically relevant symptoms starting before the age of 7 years, as assessed with the K-SADS-PL.

As mentioned above, both groups were matched for age and gender, and all participants had no current of past history of substance use disorders. ADHD patients and HC did not differ with regard to years of education and handedness.

From the 22 patients with ADHD, 10 had the combined subtype whereas 12 presented the inattentive subtype of the disorder. Also, 7 out of the 22 ADHD patients fulfilled criteria for comorbid axis I disorders: 4 for bipolar disorder, 2 for major depressive disorder and 1 for anxiety disorder NOS.

Multimodal Image Analysis

Significant group differences (at the corrected $p<0.05$ level) and/or trends ($p<0.001$ uncorrected) were detected in four comparisons between ADHD patients and HC: 1) GM of ADHD < GM of HC; 2) GM of ADHD > GM of HC; 3) FA of ADHD > FA of HC; 4) TR of ADHD < TR of HC. These differences are detailed in the sub-items below.

GM of ADHD < GM of HC

There were foci of lower GM values in ADHD patients compared to HC, but these were significant only at the trend level of $p<0.001$, uncorrected for multiple comparisons. These foci were located mainly in the parietal cortex (right angular gyrus), as presented in Table 2. Figure 1 shows the representative slices in the sagittal view.

GM of ADHD > GM of HC

There were also foci of higher GM values in ADHD patients compared to HC that achieved trend levels of statistical significance ($p<0.001$, uncorrected). These foci of increased GM values in the ADHD group were detected mainly in the right supplementary motor area right superior frontal gyrus. (Table 2, Figure 1).

FA of ADHD > FA of HC

Several areas of significantly increased FA values in the ADHD sample compared with HC were detected at the strict threshold of $p<0.05$ (corrected for multiple comparisons), in WM underlying the bilateral superior frontal gyrus, right middle frontal gyrus, bilateral cingulate gyrus, bilateral middle temporal gyrus and left postcentral gyrus (Table 3, Figure 2). There were additional foci of increased FA values in ADHD patients that were significant at the trend level of $p<0.001$ (uncorrected), located in WM regions underlying the right superior temporal gyrus and right precentral gyrus, as well as the left posterior thalamic radiation, left inferior longitudinal/left inferior fronto-occipital fasciculi (sagital stratum), left body of the corpus callosum, and left superior corona radiata (Table 3).

TR of ADHD < TR of HC

Several areas of significantly lower TR values in ADHD subjects compared with HC were seen at the corrected $p<0.05$ level. These were detected in WM regions underlying the right superior frontal gyrus, bilateral middle frontal gyrus, right precentral gyrus, left middle occipital gyrus and bilateral cingulate gyrus, as well as the bilateral body and right splenium of the corpus callosum, right superior corona radiata, right superior longitudinal fasciculus, right superior fronto-occipital fasciculus, and right caudate nucleus (Table 4, Figure 3). There were additional foci of lower TR values in ADHD patients that were significant at the trend level of $p< 0.001$ (uncorrected), located in WM regions underlying the right angular gyrus as well as the bilateral thalamus and left genu of the corpus callosum (Table 4).

Other group comparisons

There were no statistically significant differences (or trends) between groups when we compared: 1) WM of ADHD < WM of HC; 2) WM of ADHD > WM of HC; 3) FA of ADHD < FA of HC; and 4) TR of ADHD > TR of HC.

Table 1. Demographic and clinical characteristics of subjects with ADHD and HC.

Variables	ADHD (n = 22)	HC (n = 19)	Statistical test
Mean age, years (SD)	28.8 (4.9)	28.7 (5.4)	-
Gender, no. of males (%)	14 (63.6%)	12 (63.1%)	-
Years of Education (mean; SD)	13.8 (2.5)	12.3 (3.8)	F = 0.98, $P = 0.33$, df = 39
Handedness, number of right-handed (%)	20 (90.9%)	18 (94.7%)	$\chi^2 = 0.220$, df = 1, p = 0.639
Mean ASRS-18 Score (SD)			
Part A: Inattentive Symptoms	30.8 (2.8)	-	-
Part B: Hyperactive/Impulsive Symptoms	25.9 (5.5)	-	-

ADHD: Attention-Deficit/Hyperactivity Disorder; HC: Healthy Controls; SD: Standard Deviation; ASRS-18: Adult ADHD Self-Report Scale.

Comparisons between ADHD patients with no comorbidities (n = 15) versus HC (n = 19)

None of the findings reported in the above comparisons retained statistical significance after correction for multiple comparisons ($p<0.05$). However, the following results remained as trends ($p<0.001$, uncorrected) (see Tables 2, 3 and 4): 1) GM of ADHD > GM of HC: right supplementary motor area; 2) FA of ADHD > FA of HC: WM underlying the right superior frontal gyrus, right cingulate gyrus, and left postcentral gyrus; and 3) TR of ADHD < TR of HC: right splenium of the corpus callosum and WM underlying the right cingulate gyrus.

Correlations between ADHD symptom severity and brain imaging measures

The investigation of correlations between ASRS-18 scores within the ADHD group and brain imaging measures revealed no significant results at $p<0.05$ (corrected for multiple comparisons).

Discussion

This MRI study investigated brain morphometric and DTI differences between adults with ADHD and age- and gender-matched healthy subjects. In contrast with the vast majority of imaging studies of adult ADHD patients conducted to date, we were able to investigate a group of adult ADHD subjects who had never been exposed to treatment. Samples of treatment-naïve adults with ADHD provide information of critical relevance on brain abnormalities which are genuine to the disease and cannot be attributed to medication effects [26,62–64]. In addition, we employed ODVBA, a newly-validated image analysis methodology aimed at increasing: sensitivity to detect group differences; and accuracy in the localization of brain regions of significant volumetric and WM integrity changes [22]. By evaluating concurrently brain morphology and WM connectivity in the same sample of adult, treatment-naïve ADHD patients, we were able to detect macro- and *micro*-structural changes in a whole-brain fashion, thus potentially affording a more thorough understanding of the network of anatomical abnormalities underlying the clinical manifestations of ADHD [5,48].

GM Volume Abnormalities

The present results suggest that adult ADHD is associated with subtle GM volume abnormalities affecting fronto-parietal networks, since there was a statistical trend towards GM reductions in the right angular gyri in our ADHD sample compared to controls, as well as GM volume increases in the right superior frontal gyrus, and right supplementary motor area. These cortical areas are interconnected and participate critically in a number of cognitive processes of relevance to ADHD such as attention, executive functioning and visuomotor coordination [49,50]. Dysfunction in this circuitry has been linked to behavioral symptoms that are prominent in ADHD, such as altered response inhibition and difficulties with waiting situations [51].

Regions of GM reduction affecting the parietal cortex in adults with ADHD were also found by Makris et al. (2007), who observed a decrease in thickness in the inferior parietal lobule of the right hemisphere [52]. Also, a recent study evaluating a cohort of adults with childhood-onset ADHD found reduced cortical thickness in similar parietal areas, known as the dorsal attentional network [8]. The angular gyrus lies in the caudal inferior portion of the parietal lobe and brings to the prefrontal cortex visual and linguistic information [53]. Likewise, the prefrontal cortex via bidirectional connections sends to the posterior parietal region information for the adjustment of the focus of attention in different parts of the space [5]. The angular gyrus, frequently associated with semantic aspects of language processing [53], has also been implicated in impulsive personality traits [54].

ADHD in children is known to be linked to a retarded cortical maturation relative to normal development [55–57]. In children with ADHD, both a delay in attaining peak cortical thickness throughout most of the brain [56] and a slower rate of cortical thinning affecting mainly prefrontal regions, including the premotor area [57], have been observed relative to normal controls. Thus, the trend towards increased GM in frontal regions observed in the adults with ADHD here might be a residue of to abnormal neurodevelopmental processes that occur since childhood [58].

Despite the improved sensitivity of the ODBVA methodology employed herein [24], we found modest GM deficits in adult ADHD subjects relative to controls. The subtlety of our findings of volumetric changes are consistent with the results of previous morphometric MRI studies evaluating GM differences between treatment naïve adult ADHD and HC samples of comparable size to ours, which have reported circumscribed GM deficits in ADHD samples when using strict statistical thresholds with correction for multiple comparisons [59,60,61]. It should also be noted that the vast majority of previous imaging studies in ADHD have been conducted with medicated patients. The use of stimulant medication may be associated with changes in regional brain volumes and/or cortical thickness affecting the anterior cingulate cortex, dorsolateral frontal cortex, parieto-occipital region and striatum [26,62–64].

Table 2. Comparison of GM volumes between ADHD and HC.

Group comparison	Anatomical Regions (Hemisphere)	Talairach Coordinates*			$p<0.05$ (FDR)		$p<0.001$		$p<0.001$ (nonCom)	
		x	*y*	*z*	*N*	*t*	*N*	*t*	*N*	*t*
ADHD < HC	Angular gyrus (right)	41.58	−51.21	24.67	/	/	12	6.68	/	/
ADHD > HC	Supplementary motor area (right)	7.92	14.75	61.9	/	/	21	4.93	24	5.30
	Superior frontal gyrus (right)	15.84	18.44	58.03	/	/	12	6.19	/	/

GM: Gray Matter; ADHD: Attention-Deficit/Hyperactivity Disorder; HC: Healthy Controls; FDR: False Discovery Rate; nonCom: comparison excluding the comorbidities AHD patients; *N*: number of significant voxels in each anatomical region; *t*: value calculated based on the means of Regional Analysis of Volumes Examined in Normalized Space (RAVENS) values of the significant voxels.
*Talairach coordinates represent center-of-mass obtained with the significance level of $p<0.001$.

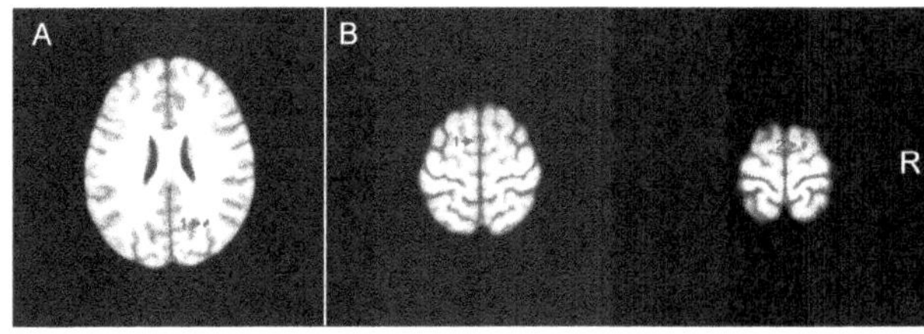

Figure 1. Voxel clusters of relatively reduced gray matter (A) and increased gray matter (B) in attention-deficit/hyperactivity disorder subjects compared to healthy controls are shown in red, overlaid on transaxial sections from a reference brain spatially normalized to the Montreal Neurological Institute stereotactic space, in neurological convention. Statistical maps are displayed with a statistical threshold of $p<0.001$, uncorrected for multiple comparisons. A)1) Angular gyrus (Right); B)1) Supplementary motor area (right); B)2) Superior frontal gyrus (right). R: Right.

WM Morphometric and DTI Analyses

No significant focus of WM volume abnormality was observed in the ADHD group relative to controls, even when a flexible statistical threshold of uncorrected $p<0.001$ was used. Few MRI studies investigated the presence of WM morphological changes in ADHD to date. Studies evaluating children and adolescents with ADHD reported an overall reduction of total cerebral WM as well as mostly bilateral reductions in all four lobes compared to healthy subjects [65–69]. In one study of ADHD adults, a trend towards an increase in total WM volume has been reported [70].

Conversely, our analyses of DTI data revealed a widespread pattern of microstructural WM differences between the ADHD and HC groups, as measured, respectively, by FA and TR indices, with findings retaining statistical significance after correction for multiple comparisons. These changes in DTI indices in our sample of adults with ADHD relative to HC were located in fronto-striatal-parieto-temporo-occipital circuits, involving WM regions underlying the frontal, parietal, temporal and occipital lobes, as well as the superior corona radiata, caudate nucleus, superior longitudinal and superior fronto-occipital fasciculi, besides portions of the corpus callosum responsible for the inter-hemispheric connection of frontal, parietal and occipital regions (Tables 3 and 4). The findings of DTI abnormalities affecting these wide WM tracts in adult ADHD patients relative to HC provide support to the hypothesis of impaired connection in widespread brain areas in the pathophysiology of ADHD [23].

It is interesting to note that some of the WM tracts implicated in the present study (eg. the superior longitudinal fasciculi and the body of the corpus callosum) are among the tracts that mature most tardive in normal life, with the age of peak FA and minimum TR varying from 30 to 40 years in healthy aging. Conversely, other WM tracts also implicated herein (eg. splenium of the corpus callosum) show an early developing pattern of maturation in normal life, with the age of peak FA and minimum TR varying from 20 to 30 years in healthy aging [71]. DTI abnormalities affecting these WM circuits have been previously reported by studies of adolescent and adult ADHD [5,9,23,72–76]. It is intriguing, however, that the direction of FA alterations observed in ADHD patients relative to controls varies considerably across different investigations, with some studies reporting areas of FA increase [74,77,78], others observing foci of FA decrease [9,5,73,75] and one paper showing mixed findings [23]. As the age of peak FA and minimum TR of the WM tracts most frequently implicated in ADHD varies from 20 to 40 years in normal aging [71], differences in the age range of the participants enrolled in the above-mentioned studies might at least partially

Table 3. Statistics obtained from the analysis of FA on ADHD >HC.

Anatomical Regions (Hemisphere)	Talairach Coordinates*			p<0.05 (FDR)		p<0.001		p<0.001 nonCom	
	x	*y*	*z*	*N*	*t*	*N*	*t*	*N*	*t*
Superior frontal gyrus (right)	11.88	59.04	15.46	40	6.93	85	9.3247	31	6.49
Superior frontal gyrus (left)	−7.92	58.49	4.44	28	5.97	65	8.1677		
Cingulate gyrus (right)	11.88	−48.35	42.95	22	6.38	50	7.1731	28	6.04
Cingulate gyrus (left)	−3.96	−19.38	39.65	21	5.61	35	6.3222	\	\
Middle temporal gyrus (right)	59.4	−31	1.55	18	5.25	33	5.0418	\	\
Postcentral gyrus (left)	−33.66	−33.96	58.81	15	3.67	31	4.6798	101	4.49
Middle frontal gyrus (right)	27.72	57.84	30.26	16	3.94	31	5.064	\	\
Middle temporal gyrus (left)	−41.58	−36.44	9.19	19	5.44	27	5.9271	\	\
Superior corona radiata (left)	−21.78	−2.03	36.94	\	\	48	3.9058	\	\
Body of corpus callosum (left)	−13.86	−7.75	39.07	\	\	18	4.8708	\	\
Superior temporal gyrus (right)	47.52	−38.01	16.64	\	\	17	3.0803	\	\
Precentral gyrus (right)	25.74	−7.11	51.94	\	\	15	8.5404	\	\
Posterior thalamic radiation (left)	−31.68	−60.89	25.15	\	\	14	5.8836	\	\
Inferior longitudinal and Inferior fronto-occipital fasciculi (Sagital stratum) (left)	−39.6	−34.69	5.42	\	\	11	4.757	\	\

FA: Fractional Anisotropy; ADHD: Attention-Deficit/Hyperactivity Disorder; HC: Healthy Controls; FDR: False Discovery Rate; nonCom: comparison excluding the comorbidities AHD patients; *N*: number of significant voxels in each anatomical region; *t*: value calculated based on the means of fractional anisotropy (FA) values of the significant voxels; WM: white matter.
*Talairach coordinates represent center-of-mass obtained with the significance level of $p<0.001$

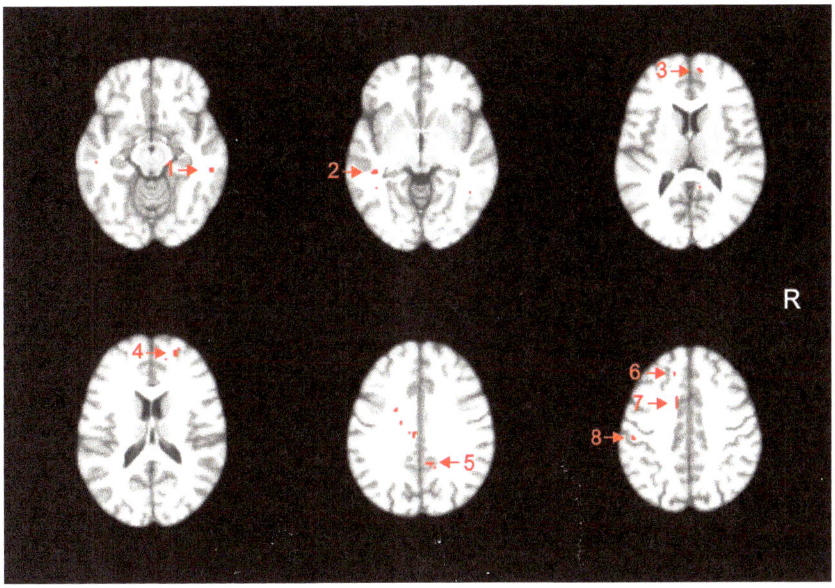

Figure 2. Voxel clusters of relatively increased fractional anisotropy in attention-deficit/hyperactivity disorder subjects compared to healthy controls are shown in red, overlaid on transaxial sections from a reference brain spatially normalized to the Montreal Neurological Institute stereotactic space, in neurological convention. Statistical maps are displayed with a statistical threshold of $p<0.05$, corrected for multiple comparisons (false-discovery rate). 1) Middle temporal gyrus white matter (WM) (right); 2) Middle temporal gyrus WM (left); 3) Superior frontal gyrus WM (right); 4) Middle frontal gyrus (right); 5) Cingulate gyrus (right); 6) Superior frontal gyrus (left); 7) Cingulate gyrus (left); 8) Postcentral gyrus (left). R: right.

account for their discrepant results. One other potential source of heterogeneity in the literature about ADHD is the wide variation observed in the methodology employed for the analysis of DTI data. Also, it is conceivable that WM tracts interconnecting the anterior cingulate cortex, dorsolateral frontal cortex, parieto-occipital region and striatum would suffer influence from chronic medication usage and, thus, be a major source of bias in DTI studies of ADHD. To our knowledge, no study to date has evaluated the impact of stimulant medication use on DTI indices.

Although findings of increased FA [17,79] and reduced diffusivity [79] have been previously reported in ADHD samples including adult patients, our study is the first to report increased FA and reduced TR (with results corrected for multiple comparisons) in adult treatment-naïve patients with ADHD. The FA and TR findings observed in our sample of ADHD adults might suggest that, although a delay in the maturation of WM circuits is observed in the brain development of adolescents with ADHD [80], higher FA and lower TR indices are achieved in adulthood in subjects with persistent ADHD symptoms.

Higher values of FA are typically interpreted as reflecting more highly organized fibers oriented in the same direction [81–83], and this might be taken as indicative of healthier white matter [16]. However, recent DTI studies of brain disorders such as Williams syndrome, Alzheimers disease and bipolar disorder have suggested that higher FA values may be actually indicative of WM pathology [84–88]. Findings of increased FA in such previous MRI studies have been speculated to indicate less neuronal branching and/or abnormally increased density of WM fibers oriented in the same direction [84–88]. In brain areas with significant crossing and branching of neuronal fibers, FA values might be relatively lower due to diffusion in multiple directions. In contrast, areas with less fiber crossing/branching could reduce the magnitude of diffusion in secondary and tertiary directions, leading to relatively greater FA values [89]. According to such reasoning, one possible explanation for our findings is that our pattern of higher FA in adult, treatment-naïve ADHD patients could be due to an aberrant reduction in fiber branching in brain regions where that pattern should be present [74,78], or to an abnormally increased density of fibers in the same orientation.

In regard to the decrement in TR, this measure reflects the rate of water diffusion through the WM, which was reduced in our adult ADHD patients. Besides the hypothesis of abnormally increased fiber density raised above, findings of decreased TR in brain diseases have been previously suggested to reflect processes of atypical myelination [90,91]. While a reduction in fiber branching would result in higher TR, increased density of fibers and an atypical higher degree of myelination would decrease TR indices. Overall, we thus suggest that the combination of increased FA and decreased TR in fronto-striatal-parietal- temporo-occipital circuits of treatment-naïve adults with ADHD, as shown by our DTI analyses, may indicate that an abnormal increased density of WM fibers oriented in the same direction, less neuronal branching, and/or a higher degree of abnormal myelination in these WM tracts, contribute to the continuing clinical manifestations of ADHD into adulthood. Neuropathological studies investigating WM histopathological changes in the brains of adult ADHD patients would be important to confirm such potential explanations. However, postmortem investigations of such kind have not been carried out to date. Finally, it should be noted that the size of the clusters of increased FA and reduced TR in our study were relatively small, and there are previous studies in modestly-sized samples of ADHD patients that reported findings in the opposite direction (reduced FA and increased diffusivity) [5,9,18,25,26,72,73]. Therefore, caution must be exercized in the interpretation of our DTI results and replication of these findings in larger samples is clearly warranted.

Table 4. Statistics obtained from the analysis of TR on ADHD < HC.

Anatomical Regions (Hemisphere)	Talairach Coordinates*			p<0.05 (FDR)		p<0.001		p<0.001 nonCom	
	x*	y*	z*	N	t	N	t	N	t
Superior frontal gyrus WM (right)	25.74	33.11	40.71	25	4.7117	62	5.1361	\	\
Middle frontal gyrus WM (right)	27.72	27.21	39.16	16	5.1947	55	6.177	\	\
Precentral gyrus WM (right)	37.62	3.97	37.04	26	5.2873	55	6.0633	\	\
Splenium of corpus callosum WM (right)	9.9	33.49	29.31	29	4.6834	54	4.9279	23	5.1769
Cingulate gyrus WM (right)	3.96	13.66	37.52	27	4.2316	53	4.4117	11	3.7164
Caudate Nucleus (right)	17.82	7.1	25.43	27	3.0545	44	2.9972	\	\
Body of corpus callosum (right)	3.96	9.87	35.49	21	5.5169	42	4.9758	\	\
Cingulate gyrus WM (left)	7.92	8.11	45.65	23	5.48	39	5.5251	\	\
Middle frontal gyrus WM (left)	27.72	55.26	17.49	20	7.571	39	8.8648	\	\
Superior longitudinal fasciculus (right)	35.64	9.78	37.33	26	6.3192	35	7.0118	\	\
Body of corpus callosum (left)	5.94	5.62	34.72	12	5.3907	32	5.2589	\	\
Superior corona radiata (right)	23.76	9.22	29.01	17	7.1591	28	6.1386	\	\
Middle occipital gyrus WM (left)	17.82	104.53	7.07	15	3.7411	24	3.7598	\	\
Superior fronto-occipital fasciculus (right)	19.8	3.4	29.31	15	3.771	16	3.7668	\	\
Thalamus (right)	3.96	9.13	11.51	\	\	18	4.2025	\	\
Angular gyrus WM (right)	45.54	65.7	45.66	\	\	16	6.2677	\	\
Thalamus (left)	1.98	14.85	13.63	\	\	15	3.0199	\	\
Genu of corpus callosum (left)	5.94	26.1	17.11	\	\	14	5.1061	\	\

TR: Trace; ADHD: Attention-Deficit/Hyperactivity Disorder; HC: Healthy Control; FDR: False Discovery Rate; nonCom: comparison excluding the comorbidities AHD patients; N: number of significant voxels in each anatomical region; t: value calculated based on the means of trace (TR) values of the significant voxels; WM: white matter.

*Talairach coordinates represent center-of-mass obtained with the significance level of p<0.001.

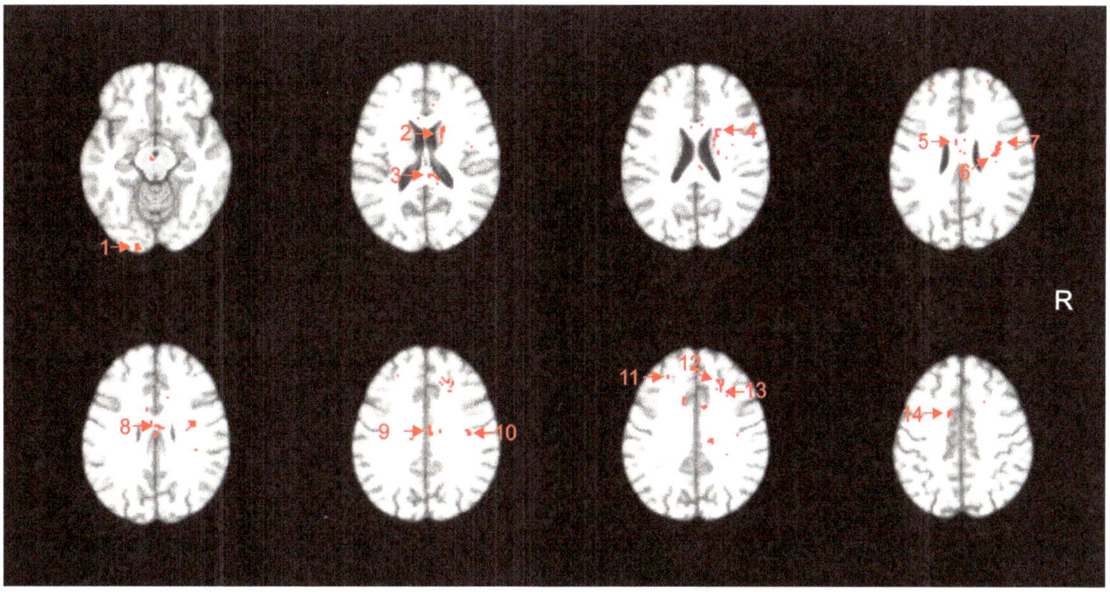

Figure 3. Voxel clusters of relatively decreased Trace in attention-deficit/hyperactivity disorder subjects compared to healthy controls (HC) are shown in red, overlaid on transaxial sections from a reference brain spatially normalized to the Montreal Neurological Institute stereotactic space, in neurological convention. Statistical maps are displayed with a statistical threshold of $p<0.05$, corrected for multiple comparisons (false-discovery rate). 1) Middle occipital gyrus white matter (WM) (left); 2) Caudate nucleus (right); 3) Splenium of corpus callosum (right); 4) Superior fronto-occipital fasciculus (right); 5) Body of the corpus callosum WM (left); 6) Superior corona radiata (right); 7) Superior longitudinal fasciculus (right); 8) Body of the corpus callosum (right); 9) Cingulate gyrus WM (right); 10) Precentral gyrus WM (right); 11) Middle frontal gyrus WM (left); 12) Superior frontal gyrus WM (right); 13) Middle frontal gyrus WM (right); 14) Cingulate gyrus WM (left). R: right.

Integration of findings of gray matter and white matter abnormalities in ADHD patients

Part of the WM tracts in which we found the greater degree of FA and/or TR differences between ADHD patients and HC are known to interconnect the brain regions where we also detected trend GM volume changes in the ADHD group, namely the fronto-striatal-parieto-temporo-occipital networks. Therefore, taking together the different GM and WM measurements evaluated in the present study, the findings obtained suggest that the persistence of ADHD symptoms into adulthood relates to: circumscribed GM volume abnormalities, subtler than those detected in children and adolescent with ADHD and which are thought to reflect delayed maturation processes [56,57]; and widespread microstructural alterations in the WM tracts connecting these and other GM regions.

We used exactly the same image processing pipelines and statistical inference approach to the analysis of both morphometric and DTI data obtained from the same individuals in a single MRI scanning session. This allowed us to demonstrate that microstructural WM differences from HC are more widespread and significant than macroscopic GM or WM volumetric changes in never-medicated adult ADHD patients. To the best of our knowledge, such prominence of WM microstructural changes in treatment-naïve ADHD adults has not been reported previously in studies combining DTI and brain volumetric measurements. This pattern of results is consistent with the notion that ADHD-related impairments in cortico-subcortical circuits may originate from alterations in microstructural connectivity [76]. If replicated in subsequent studies, our findings could indicate that microstructural WM abnormalities represent a key neuroanatomical feature underlying the persistence of ADHD symptoms into adulthood.

We did not find any significant results in our correlation analysis between brain imaging measures and the severity of ADHD symptoms. This may relate to an increased risk of type II statistical errors, due to the relatively small size of the ADHD sample. Also, the inclusion of ADHD patients with comorbidities may have increased the clinical heterogeneity of our ADHD sample. However, comorbid psychiatric disorders are very frequent in ADHD [92]; a pure never-medicated ADHD group is very difficult to recruit and would not have been representative of the overall adult ADHD population that usually demands clinical management [93]. We attempted to investigate GM and WM abnormalities in the subgroup with "pure" ADHD features compared to HC, but the results were considerably less significant in comparison to the findings of the analyses for the overall ADHD sample. This may have occurred due to loss of statistical power, given the significant proportion of individuals presenting with comorbid psychiatric conditions in the present study ($n = 7$). However, one alternative explanation of potential clinical relevance is that the presence of comorbidities is related to an accentuation of the brain abnormalities in never-medicated adult ADHD subjects; this would be consistent with the notion that the presence of comorbid diagnoses is associated with greater ADHD severity [94–96]. MRI studies with larger ADHD samples including both subjects with "pure" ADHD and ADHD with comorbidities are needed in order to extend the preliminary findings reported herein.

Finally, two additional methodological limitations should be acknowledged. First, regarding to the protocol used for the acquisition of DTI data, we acquired only one reference "B0" (non-diffusion) image. Although this is a standard strategy [17,18,72,73,77,86], it has been recently advised that 1/8th to 1/10th of images during DTI acquisitions should be B0 scans, as this provides greater accuracy in the estimation of tensors and FA values [97–99]. Also, we chose to report only TR values rather than adding traditionally used diffusivity indices such as radial diffusivity (RD) and axial diffusivity (AD). Although all diffusion parameters are overall sensitive to tissue properties such as myelination, axonal orientation and axonal density, no DTI measure can be taken as more specific to a given property [13,43]. Recent studies using synthetic models of crossing fibers have shown that pathological changes to the WM microstructure may result in unpredictable changes to AD and RD measurements, unrelated to the underlying original tissue organization, thus suggesting that such diffusivity indices may not always be reliable [100].

In conclusion, the use of the newly-validated ODVBA image analysis methodology in the present multimodal MRI study revealed the presence of widespread microstructural WM changes in tracts connecting distributed cortical regions in treatment-naïve ADHD adults, as well as subtle regional brain volume abnormalities confined to the GM compartment. Further application of such study design in larger samples is warranted to confirm these preliminary findings and to further investigate how they relate to specific ADHD symptom dimensions, associated neuropsychological deficits, treatment response patterns and other aspects of clinical outcome.

Acknowledgments

The present investigation was supported by a 2010 NARSAD Independent Investigator Award (NARSAD: The Brain and Behavior Research Fund) awarded to Geraldo F. Busatto. Geraldo F. Busatto is also partially funded by CNPq-Brazil. Marcus V. Zanetti is funded by FAPESP, Brazil (no. 2013/03905-4).

Author Contributions

Conceived and designed the experiments: TMC TZ MVZ MAS JD CD GFB. Performed the experiments: TMC MVZ MAS MHS. Analyzed the data: TMC TZ MVZ MAS JD MHS FLSD SCC CD GFB. Contributed reagents/materials/analysis tools: TMC TZ MVZ MAS JD MHS FLSD SCC CD GFB. Wrote the paper: TMC TZ MVZ MAS MRL JD MHS FLSD SCC CD GFB.

References

1. Polanczyk G, Rohde LA (2007) Epidemiology of attention-deficit/hyperactivity disorder across the lifespan. Curr Opin Psychiatry 20: 386–92.
2. Simon V, Czobor P, Bálint S, Mészáros A, Bitter I (2009) Prevalence and correlates of adult attention-deficit hyperactivity disorder: meta-analysis. Br J Psychiatry 194: 204–11.
3. Polanczyk G, Laranjeira R, Zaleski M, Pinsky I, Caetano R, et al. (2010) ADHD in a representative sample of the Brazilian population: estimated prevalence and comparative adequacy of criteria between adolescents and adults according to the item response theory. Int J Methods Psychiatr Res 19: 177–84.
4. de Zwaan M, Gruss B, Müller A, Graap H, Martin A, et al. (2012) The estimated prevalence and correlates of adult ADHD in a German community sample. Eur Arch Psychiatry Clin Neurosci 262: 79–86.
5. Makris N, Buka SL, Biederman J, Papadimitriou GM, Hodge SM, et al. (2008) Attention and executive systems abnormalities in adults with childhood ADHD: A DT-MRI study of connections. Cereb Cortex 18: 1210–20.
6. Almeida Montes LG, Ricardo-Garcell J, Barajas De La Torre LB, Prado Alcántara H, Martínez García RB, et al. (2010) Clinical correlations of gray matter reductions in the caudate nucleus of adults with attention deficit hyperactivity disorder. J Psychiatry Neurosci 35: 238–46.
7. Seidman LJ, Biederman J, Liang L, Valera EM, Monuteaux MC, et al. (2011) Gray matter alterations in adults with attention-deficit/hyperactivity disorder identified by voxel based morphometry. Biol Psychiatry 69: 857–66.
8. Proal E, Reiss PT, Klein RG, Mannuzza S, Gotimer K, et al. (2011) Brain gray matter deficits at 33-year follow-up in adults with attention-deficit/hyperactivity disorder established in childhood. Arch Gen Psychiatry 68: 1122–34.
9. Cortese S, Imperati D, Zhou J, Proal E, Klein RG, et al. (2013) White Matter Alterations at 33-Year Follow-Up in Adults with Childhood Attention-Deficit/Hyperactivity Disorder. Biol Psychiatry 74: 591–8.
10. Casey BJ, Epstein JN, Buhle J, Liston C, Davidson MC, et al. (2007) Frontostriatal connectivity and its role in cognitive control in parent-child dyads with ADHD. Am J Psychiatry 164: 1729–36.
11. Amico F, Stauber J, Koutsouleris N, Frodl T (2011) Anterior cingulate cortex gray matter abnormalities in adults with attention deficit hyperactivity disorder: a voxel-based morphometry study. Psychiatry Res 191: 31–5.
12. Ahrendts J, Rüsch N, Wilke M, Philipsen A, Eickhoff SB, et al. (2011) Visual cortex abnormalities in adults with ADHD: a structural MRI study. World J Biol Psychiatry 12: 260–70.
13. Alexander AL, Lee JE, Lazar M, Field AS (2007) Diffusion tensor imaging of the brain. Neurotherapeutics 4: 316–29.
14. Assaf Y1, Pasternak O (2008) Diffusion tensor imaging (DTI)-based white matter mapping in brain research: a review. J Mol Neurosci 34: 51–61.
15. Tievsky AL, Ptak T, Farkas J (1999) Investigation of apparent diffusion coefficient and diffusion tensor anisotropy in acute and chronic multiple sclerosis lesions. AJNR Am J Neuroradiol 20: 1491–1499.
16. Beaulieu (2002) The basis of anisotropic water diffusion in the nervous system - a technical review. NMR Biomed 15: 435–55.
17. Konrad A, Dielentheis TF, El Masri D, Bayerl M, Fehr C, et al. (2010) Disturbed structural connectivity is related to inattention and impulsivity in adult attention deficit hyperactivity disorder. Eur J Neurosci 31: 912–9.
18. Konrad A1, Dielentheis TF, El Masri D, Dellani PR, Stoeter P, et al. (2012) White matter abnormalities and their impact on attentional performance in adult attention-deficit/hyperactivity disorder. Eur Arch Psychiatry Clin Neurosci 262: 351–60.
19. Depue BE, Burgess GC, Bidwell LC, Willcutt EG, Banich MT (2010) Behavioral performance predicts grey matter reductions in the right inferior frontal gyrus in young adults with combined type ADHD. Psychiatry Res 182: 231–7.
20. Frodl T, Skokauskas N (2012) Meta-analysis of structural MRI studies in children and adults with attention deficit hyperactivity disorder indicates treatment effects. Acta Psychiatr Scand 125: 114–26.
21. Ashburner J (2009) Computational anatomy with the SPM software. Magn Reson Imaging 27: 1163–74.
22. Zhang T, Davatzikos C (2011) ODVBA: optimally-discriminative voxel-based analysis. IEEE Trans Med Imaging 30: 1441–54.
23. Davatzikos C (2004) Why voxel-based morphometric analysis should be used with great caution when characterizing group differences. Neuroimage 23: 17–20.
24. Zhang T, Davatzikos C (2013) Optimally-Discriminative Voxel-Based Morphometry significantly increases the ability to detect group differences in schizophrenia, mild cognitive impairment, and Alzheimer's disease. Neuroimage 79: 94–110.
25. Cao Q, Sun L, Gong G, Lv Y, Shuai L, et al. (2010) The macrostructural and microstructural abnormalities of corpus callosum in children with attention deficit/hyperactivity disorder: a combined morphometric and diffusion tensor MRI study. Brain Res 1310: 172–80.
26. Dramsdahl M, Westerhausen R, Haavaik J, Hugdal K, Plessen KJ (2012) Adults with attention-deficit/hyperactivity disorder - a diffusion-tensor imaging study of the corpus callosum. Psychiatry Res 201: 168–73.
27. American Psychiatric Association (1994) *Diagnostic and Statistical Manual of Mental Disorders*, 4th ed. Washington, DC: American Psychiatric Press.
28. Kaufman J, Birmaher B, Brent DA, Rao U, Flynn C, et al. (1997) K-Schedule for Affective Disorders and Schizophrenia for School-Age Children-Present and Lifetime Version (K-SADS-PL): initial reliability and validity data. J Am Acad Child Adolesc Psychiatry 36: 980–8.
29. Adler LA, Spencer T, Faraone SV, Kessler RC, Howes MJ, et al. (2006) Validity of pilot Adult ADHD Self- Report Scale (ASRS) to Rate Adult ADHD symptoms. Ann Clin Psychiatry 18: 145–8.
30. Saunders JB, Aasland OG, Babor TF, de la Fuente JR, Grant M (1993) Development of the Alcohol Use Disorders Identification Test (AUDIT): WHO Collaborative Project on Early Detection of Persons with Harmful Alcohol Consumption – II. Addiction 88: 791–804.
31. Menezes PR, Johnson S, Thornicroft G, Marshall J, Prosser D, et al. (1996) Drug and alcohol problems among individuals with severe mental illness in south London. Br J Psychiatry 168: 612–9.
32. First MB, Spitzer RL, Gibbon M, Williams JBW (1995) Structured Clinical Interview for DSM-IV Axis I Disorders, Patient Edition (SCID-I/P). New York, NY: Biometrics Research, New York State Psychiatry Institute.
33. Oldfield RC (1971) The assessment and analysis of handedness: the Edinburgh inventory. Neuropsychologia 9: 97–113.
34. Sled JG, Zijdenbos AP, Evans AC (1998) A nonparametric method for automatic correction of intensity nonuniformity in MRI data. IEEE Trans Med Imaging 17: 87–97,
35. Doshi J, Erus G, Ou Y, Gaonkar B, Davatzikos C (2013) Multi-Atlas Skull-Stripping, MASS. Acad Radiol, in press.
36. Li C, Gatenby C, Wang L, Gore JC (2009) A robust parametric method for bias field estimation and segmentation of MR images. Proc IEEE Comput Soc Conf Comput Vis Pattern Recognitpp. 218–223.
37. Ou Y, Sotiras A, Paragios N, Davatzikos C (2011) DRAMMS: Deformable registration via attribute matching and mutual-saliency weighting. Med Image Anal 15: 622–639.
38. Davatzikos C, Genc A, Xu D, Resnick SM (2001) Voxel-Based Morphometry Using the RAVENS Maps: Methods and Validation Using Simulated Longitudinal Atrophy. NeuroImage 14: 1361–1369.

39. Pierpaoli C, Basser P (1996) Toward a quantitative assessment of diffusion anisotropy. Magn ResonMed 36: 893–906.
40. Andersson J, Jenkinson M, Smith S (2007) Non-linear registration, aka spatial normalization. FMRIB Analysis Group of the University of Oxford. FMRIB technical report TR07JA1. Available: http://http://www.fmrib.ox.ac.uk/analysis/techrep/. Accessed 05 November 2013.
41. Wakana S, Jiang H, Nagae-Poetcher L, van Zijl PCM, Mori S (2004) Fiber tract-based atlas of human white matter anatomy. Radiology 230: 77–87.
42. Jones DK (2008) Studying connections in the living human brain with diffusion MRI. Cortex 44: 936–52.
43. Jones DK, Knösche TR, Turner R (2013) White matter integrity, fiber count, and other fallacies: the do's and don'ts of diffusion MRI. Neuroimage 73: 239–54.
44. Nichols TE, Holmes AP (2002) Nonparametric permutation tests for functional neuroimaging: a primer with examples. Hum Brain Mapp 15: 1–25.
45. Tzourio-Mazoyer N, Landeau B, Papathanassiou D, Crivello F, Etard O, et al. (2002) Automated anatomical labeling of activations in GLM using a macroscopic anatomical parcellation of the MNI MRI single-subject brain. NeuroImage 15: 273–289.
46. Oishi K, Faria A, Jiang H, Li X, Akhter K, et al. (2009) Atlas-based whole brain white matter analysis using large deformation diffeomorphic metric mapping: application to normal elderly and Alzheimer's disease participants. Neuroimage 46: 486–499.
47. Friston KJ, Holmes AP, Worsley KJ, Poline JP, Frith CD, et al. (1994) Statistical parametric maps in functional imaging: a general linear approach. Human brain mapping 2: 189–210.
48. Konrad K, Eickhoff SB (2010) Is the ADHD brain wired differently? A review on structural and functional connectivity in attention deficit hyperactivity disorder. Hum Brain Mapp 31: 904–16.
49. Rubia K, Smith A (2004) The neural correlates of cognitive time management: a review. ActaNeurobiolExp 64: 329–340.
50. Mahone EM, Croceti D, Ranta ME, Gaddis A, Catalo M, et al. (2011) A Preliminary Neuroimaging Study of Preschool Children with ADHD. Clin Neuropsych 25: 1009–1028.
51. Krain AL, Castellanos FX (2006) Brain development and ADHD. Clin Psychol Rev 26: 433–444.
52. Makris N, Biederman J, Valera EM, Bush G, Kaiser J, et al. (2007) Cortical thinning of the attention and executive function networks in adults with attention-deficit/hyperactivity disorder. Cerb Cortex 17: 1364–75.
53. Caspers S, Schleicher A, Bacha-Trams M, Palomero-Gallagher N, Amunts K, et al. (2013) Organization of the Human Inferior Parietal Lobule Based on Receptor Architectonics. Cereb Cortex 23: 615–28.
54. Siever LJ, Buchsbaum MS, New AS, Spiegel-Cohen J, Wei T, et al. (1999) d,l-fenfluramine response in impulsive personality disorder assessed with [18F]fluorodeoxyglucose positron emission tomography. Neuropsychopharmacology 20: 413–23.
55. Giedd JN, Blumenthal J, Jeffries NO, Castellanos FX, Liu H, et al. (1999) Brain development during childhood and adolescence: a longitudinal MRI study. Nat Neurosci 2: 861–3.
56. Shaw P, Eckstrand K, Sharp W, Blumenthal J, Lerch JP, et al. (2007) Attention-deficit/hyperactivity disorder is characterized by a delay in cortical maturation. Proc Natl Acad Sci USA 104: 19649–54.
57. Shaw P, Gilliam M, Liverpool M, Weddle C, Malek M, et al. (2011) Cortical development in typically developing children with symptoms of hyperactivity and impulsivity: support for a dimensional view of attention deficit hyperactivity disorder. Am J Psychiatry 168: 143–51.
58. Duerden EG, Tannock R, Dockstader C (2012) Altered cortical morphology in sensorimotor processing regions in adolescents and adults with attention-deficit/hyperactivity disorder. Brain Res 1445: 82–91.
59. Makris N, Seidman LJ, Valera EM, Biederman J, Monuteaux MC, et al. (2010) Anterior cingulate volumetric alterations in treatment-naïve adults with ADHD: a pilot study. J Atten Disord 13: 407–13.
60. Frodl T, Skokauskas N (2012) Meta-analysis of structural MRI studies in children and adults with attention deficit hyperactivity disorder indicates treatment effects. Acta Psychiatr Scand 125: 114–26.
61. Makris N, Liang L, Biederman J, Valera EM, Brown AB, et al. (2013) Toward Defining the Neural Substrates of ADHD: A Controlled Structural MRI Study in Medication-Naive Adults. J Atten Disord Available: http://jad.sagepub.com/content/early/2013/10/25/1087054713506041. Accessed 15 June 2014.
62. Semrud-Clikeman M, Pliszka SR, Lancaster J, Liotti M (2006) Volumetric MRI differences in treatment-naïve vs chronically treated children with ADHD. Neurology 67: 1023–7.
63. Shaw P, Sharp WS, Morrison M, Eckstrand K, Greenstein DK, et al. (2009) Psychostimulant treatment and the developing cortex in attention deficit hyperactivity disorder. Am J Psychiatry 166: 58–63.
64. Hoekzema E, Carmona S, Ramos-Quiroga JA, Canals C, Moreno A, et al. (2012) Stimulant drugs trigger transient volumetric changes in the human ventral striatum. Brain Struct Funct 219: 23–34.
65. Filipek PA, Semrud-Clikeman M, Steingard RJ, Renshaw PF, Kennedy DN, et al. (1997) Volumetric MRI analysis comparing subjects having attention-deficit hyperactivity disorder with normal controls. Neurology 48: 589–601.
66. Castellanos FX, Lee PP, Sharp W, Jeffries NO, Greenstein DK, et al. (2002) Developmental trajectories of brain volume abnormalities in children and adolescents with attention-deficit/hyperactivity disorder. JAMA 288: 1740–8.
67. Mostofsky SH, Cooper KL, Kates WR, Denckla MB, Kaufmann WE (2002) Smaller prefrontal and premotor volumes in boys with attention-deficit/hyperactivity disorder. Biol Psychiatry 52: 785–94.
68. Kates WR, Frederikse M, Mostofsky SH, Folley BS, Cooper K, et al. (2002) MRI parcellation of the frontal lobe in boys with attention deficit hyperactivity disorder or Tourette syndrome. Psychiatry Res 116: 63–81.
69. McAlonan GM, Cheung V, Cheung C, Chua SE, Murphy DG, et al. (2007) Mapping brain structure in attention deficit-hyperactivity disorder: a voxel-based MRI study of regional grey and white matter volume. Psychiatry Res 154: 171–80.
70. Seidman LJ, Valera EM, Makris N, Monuteaux MC, Boriel DL, et al. (2006) Dorsolateral prefrontal and anterior cingulate cortex volumetric abnormalities in adults with attention-deficit/hyperactivity disorder identified by magnetic resonance imaging. Biol Psychiatry 60: 1071–80.
71. Lebel C, Gee M, Camicioli R, Wieler M, Martin W, et al. (2012) Diffusion tensor imaging of white matter tract evolution over the lifespan. Neuroimage 60: 340–52.
72. Hamilton LS, Levitt JG, O'Neill J, Alger JR, Luders E, et al. (2008) Reduced white matter integrity in attention-deficit hyperactivity disorder. Neuroreport 19: 1705–8.
73. Pavuluri MN, Yang S, Kamineni K, Passarotti AM, Srinivasan G, et al. (2009) Diffusion tensor imaging study of white matter fiber tracts in pediatric bipolar disorder and attention-deficit/hyperactivity disorder. Biol Psychiatry 65: 586–93.
74. Silk TJ, Vance A, Rinehart N, Bradshaw JL, Cunnington R (2009) White-matter abnormalities in attention deficit hyperactivity disorder: a diffusion tensor imaging study. Hum Brain Mapp 30: 2757–65.
75. Chuang TC, Wu MT, Huang SP, Weng MJ, Yang P (2013) Diffusion tensor imaging study of white matter fiber tracts in adolescent attention-deficit/hyperactivity disorder. Psychiatry Res 211: 186–7.
76. van Ewijk H, Heslenfeld DJ, Zwiers MP, Buitelaar JK, Oosterlaan J. (2012) Diffusion tensor imaging in attention deficit/hyperactivity disorder: a systematic review and meta-analysis. Neurosci Biobehav Rev 36: 1093–106.
77. Davenport ND, Karatekin C, White T, Lim KO (2010) Differential fractional anisotropy abnormalities in adolescents with ADHD or schizophrenia. Psychiatry Res 181: 193–8.
78. Tamm L, Barnea-Goraly N, Reiss AL (2012) Diffusion tensor imaging reveals white matter abnormalities in Attention-Deficit/Hyperactivity Disorder. Psychiatry Res 202: 150–4.
79. van Ewijk H, Heslenfeld DJ, Zwiers MP, Faraone SV, Luman M, et al. (2014) Different mechanisms of white matter abnormalities in attention-deficit/hyperactivity disorder: a diffusion tensor imaging study. J Am Acad Child Adolesc Psychiatry 53: 790–9.
80. Arnsten AF, Rubia K (2012) Neurobiological circuits regulating attention, cognitive control, motivation, and emotion: disruptions in neurodevelopmental psychiatric disorders. J Am Acad Child Adolesc Psychiatry 51: 356–67.
81. Basser PJ, Mattiello J, LeBihan D (1994) MR diffusion tensor spectroscopy and imaging. Biophysical Journal 66: 259–267.
82. Basser PJ, Pierpaoli C (1996) Microstructural and physiological features of tissues elucidated by quantitative-diffusion-tensor MRI. Journal of Magnetic Resonance B 111: 209–219.
83. Werring DJ, Toosy AT, Clark CA, Parker GJ, Barker GJ, et al. (2000) Diffusion tensor imaging can detect and quantify corticospinal tract degeneration after stroke. Journal of Neurology, Neurosurgery, and Psychiatry 69 269–272.
84. Hoeft F, Barnea-Goraly N, Haas BW, Golarai G, Ng D, et al. (2007) More is not always better: increased fractional anisotropy of superior longitudinal fasciculus associated with poor visuospatial abilities in Williams syndrome. Journal of Neuroscience 27: 11960–11965.
85. Yurgelun-Todd DA, Silveri MM, Gruber SA, Rohan ML, Pimentel PJ (2007) White matter abnormalities observed in bipolar disorder: a diffusion tensor imaging study. Bipolar Disord 9: 504–12.
86. Versace A, Almeida JR, Hassel S, Walsh ND, Novelli M, et al. (2008) Elevated Left and Reduced Right Orbitomedial Prefrontal Fractional Anisotropy in Adults With Bipolar Disorder Revealed by Tract-Based Spatial Statistics. Arch Gen Psychiatry 65: 1041–52.
87. Heng S, Song AW, Sim K (2010) White matter abnormalities in bipolar disorder: insights from diffusion tensor imaging studies. J Neural Transm 117: 639–54.
88. Teipel SJ, Grothe MJ, Filippi M, Fellgiebel A, Dyrba M, et al. (2014) Fractional Anisotropy Changes in Alzheimer's Disease Depend on the Underlying Fiber Tract Architecture: A Multiparametric DTI Study using Joint Independent Component Analysis. J Alzheimers Dis 41: 69–83.
89. Suzuki Y, Matsuzawa H, Kwee IL, Nakada T (2003) Absolute eigenvalue diffusion tensor analysis for human brain maturation. NMR in Biomedicine, 16 257–260.
90. Phillips MD, McGraw P, Lowe MJ, Mathews VP, Hainline BE (2001). Diffusion- weighted imaging of white matter abnormalities in patient with phenylketonuria, Am. J. Neuroradiol., 22 1583–1586.
91. White DA, Connor LT, Nardos B, Shimony JS, Archer R, et al. (2010) Age-related decline in the microstructural integrity of white matter in children with early- and continuously-treated PKU: a DTI study of the corpus callosum. Mol Genet Metab. 99 Suppl 1: S41–6.

92. Elia J, Ambrosini P, Berrettini W (2008) ADHD characteristics: I. Concurrent co-morbidity patterns in children & adolescents. Child Adolesc Psychiatry Ment Health 2: 15.
93. Kobel M, Bechtel N, Specht K, Klarhöfer M, Weber P, et al. (2010) Structural and functional imaging approaches in attention deficit/hyperactivity disorder: does the temporal lobe play a key role? Psychiatry Res 183: 230–6.
94. Marin A, Scott D, Groll DL (2013) Bipolar disorder comorbid with attention-deficit/hyperactivity disorder in adult inpatients with acute relapse. Prim Care Companion CNS Disord 15.
95. Onnink AM, Zwiers MP, Hoogman M, Mostert JC, Kan CC, et al. (2014) Brain alterations in adult ADHD: effects of gender, treatment and comorbid depression. Eur Neuropsychopharmacol 24: 397–409.
96. Di Trani M, Di Roma F, Elda A, Daniela L, Pasquale P, et al. (2014) Comorbid Depressive Disorders in ADHD: The Role of ADHD Severity, Subtypes and Familial Psychiatric Disorders. Psychiatry Investig 11: 137–42.
97. Rodern C (2013) Advanced DTI processing. Avaliable: http://www.mccauslandcenter.sc.edu/CRNL/tools/advanced-dti. Accessed 22 September 2014.
98. Nir TM, Jahanshad N, Villalon-Reina JE, Toga AW, Jack CR, et al. (2013) Effectiveness of regional DTI measures in distinguishing Alzheimer's disease, MCI, and normal aging. Neuroimage Clin 3: 180–95.
99. Lim JS, Park YH, Jang JW, Park SY, Kim S (2014) Differential White Matter Connectivity in Early Mild Cognitive Impairment According to CSF Biomarkers. PLoS One 9: e91400.
100. Wheeler-Kingshott ACM, Cercignani M (2009) About "Axial" and "Radial" Diffusivities. Magnetic Resonance in Medicine 61: 1255–1260.

Permissions

All chapters in this book were first published in PLOS ONE, by The Public Library of Science; hereby published with permission under the Creative Commons Attribution License or equivalent. Every chapter published in this book has been scrutinized by our experts. Their significance has been extensively debated. The topics covered herein carry significant findings which will fuel the growth of the discipline. They may even be implemented as practical applications or may be referred to as a beginning point for another development.

The contributors of this book come from diverse backgrounds, making this book a truly international effort. This book will bring forth new frontiers with its revolutionizing research information and detailed analysis of the nascent developments around the world.

We would like to thank all the contributing authors for lending their expertise to make the book truly unique. They have played a crucial role in the development of this book. Without their invaluable contributions this book wouldn't have been possible. They have made vital efforts to compile up to date information on the varied aspects of this subject to make this book a valuable addition to the collection of many professionals and students.

This book was conceptualized with the vision of imparting up-to-date information and advanced data in this field. To ensure the same, a matchless editorial board was set up. Every individual on the board went through rigorous rounds of assessment to prove their worth. After which they invested a large part of their time researching and compiling the most relevant data for our readers.

The editorial board has been involved in producing this book since its inception. They have spent rigorous hours researching and exploring the diverse topics which have resulted in the successful publishing of this book. They have passed on their knowledge of decades through this book. To expedite this challenging task, the publisher supported the team at every step. A small team of assistant editors was also appointed to further simplify the editing procedure and attain best results for the readers.

Apart from the editorial board, the designing team has also invested a significant amount of their time in understanding the subject and creating the most relevant covers. They scrutinized every image to scout for the most suitable representation of the subject and create an appropriate cover for the book.

The publishing team has been an ardent support to the editorial, designing and production team. Their endless efforts to recruit the best for this project, has resulted in the accomplishment of this book. They are a veteran in the field of academics and their pool of knowledge is as vast as their experience in printing. Their expertise and guidance has proved useful at every step. Their uncompromising quality standards have made this book an exceptional effort. Their encouragement from time to time has been an inspiration for everyone.

The publisher and the editorial board hope that this book will prove to be a valuable piece of knowledge for researchers, students, practitioners and scholars across the globe.

List of Contributors

Yongsheng Han
Department of Neurology, The First Affiliated Hospital of Anhui Medical University, Hefei, Anhui Province, PR China
Institute of Neurology, Anhui University of Chinese Medicine, Hefei, Anhui Province, PR China

Fangfang Zhang, Yanghua Tian, Panpan Hu and Kai Wang
Department of Neurology, The First Affiliated Hospital of Anhui Medical University, Hefei, Anhui Province, PR China

Bo Li
Institute of Neurology, Anhui University of Chinese Medicine, Hefei, Anhui Province, PR China

Ruosi Wang
State Key Laboratory of Cognitive Neuroscience and Learning & IDG/McGovern Institute for Brain Research, Beijing Normal University, Beijing, China

Xiang-zhen Kong, Zonglei Zhen, Xueting Li, Huan-hua Lu, Ling Liu and Yong He
State Key Laboratory of Cognitive Neuroscience and Learning & IDG/McGovern Institute for Brain Research, Beijing Normal University, Beijing, China
Center for Collaboration and Innovation in Brain and Learning Sciences, Beijing Normal University, Beijing, China

Jia Liu
School of Psychology, Beijing Normal University, Beijing, China
Center for Collaboration and Innovation in Brain and Learning Sciences, Beijing Normal University, Beijing, China

Yufeng Zang
Center for Cognition and Brain Disorders, Hangzhou Normal University, Hangzhou, China

Javier Sanchez-Lopez and Thalia Fernandez
Departamento de Neurobiología Conductual y Cognitiva del Instituto de Neurobiología, Universidad Nacional Autónoma de México, Juriquilla, Querétaro, México

Juan Silva-Pereyra
Proyecto en Neurociencias de la Facultad de Estudios Superiores Iztacala, Universidad Nacional Autónoma de México, Tlalnepantla, Estado de Mexico, México

Juan A. Martinez Mesa
Departamento de Psicología del Deporte, Instituto de Medicina del Deporte de Cuba, Cerro, Ciudad de La Habana, Cuba

Francesco Di Russo
Dipartimento di Scienze Motorie Umane e della Salute, Universitádegli Studi di Roma "Foro Italico," Roma, Lazio, Italia
Unitádi Neuropsicologia, IRCCS Fondazione Santa Lucia, Roma, Lazio, Italia

Stefan Spulber, Pascal Kilian, Natalia Onishchenko and Sandra Ceccatelli
Dept of Neuroscience, Karolinska Institutet, Stockholm, Sweden

Wan Norhamidah Wan Ibrahim
Dept of Neuroscience, Karolinska Institutet, Stockholm, Sweden
Department of Biology, Faculty of Science, Universiti Putra Malaysia, Serdang, Selangor, Malaysia

Mazhar Ulhaq and Leif Norrgren
Department of Biomedicine and Veterinary Public Health, Swedish University of Agricultural Sciences, Uppsala, Sweden

Sara Negri and Marcello Di Tuccio
Environmental Research Center, Salvatore Maugeri Foundation - IRCCS, Pavia, Italy

Ricardo Saute
Faculty of Medicine, Pontificia Universidade Catolica do Rio Grande do Sul (PUCRS), Porto Alegre, Brazil

Kevin Dabbs, Jana E. Jones, Daren C. Jackson and Bruce P. Hermann
Department of Neurology, University of Wisconsin School of Medicine and Public Health, Madison, Wisconsin, United States of America

Michael Seidenberg
Department of Psychology, Rosalind Franklin University of Science and Medicine, North Chicago, Illinois, United States of America

Lucia A. Ruocco, Concetta Treno, Ugo A. Gironi Carnevale and Adolfo G. Sadile
Department of Experimental Medicine, School of Medicine, II University of Naples, Napoli, Italy

Claudio Arra
Animal facility, National Cancer Institute, Napoli, Italy

Gianpiero Boatto and Maria Nieddu
Department of Chemistry and Pharmacy, University of Sassari, Sassari, Italy

Cristina Pagano, Placido Illiano, Fabiana Barbato and Angela Tino
Istituto di Cibernetica "Eduardo Caianiello" - CNR, Pozzuoli, Napoli, Italy

Ezio Carboni
Department of Biomedical Sciences, University of Cagliari, Cagliari, Italy

Giovanni Laviola and Walter Adriani
Section of Behavioural Neuroscience, Department of Cell Biology and Neurosciences, Istituto Superiore di Sanità, Roma, Italy

Enza Lacivita and Marcello Leopoldo
Department of Medicinal Chemistry, University of Bari, Bari, Italy

Ilina Singh
Department of Social Science, Health & Medicine, Kings College London, London, United Kingdom

Imre Bard and Jonathan Jackson
Department of Methodology, London School of Economics & Political Science, London, United Kingdom

Huang
Department of Psychiatry, Chi Mei Medical Center, Tainan, Taiwan
School of Medicine, Kaohsiung Medical University, Kaohsiung, Taiwan

Chin-Chen Chu
Department of Anesthesiology, Chi Mei Medical Center, Tainan, Taiwan
Department of Recreation and Health-Care Management, Chia-Nan University of Pharmacy and Science, Tainan, Taiwan

Tain-Junn Cheng
Department of Neurology and Occupational Medicine, Chi Mei Medical Center, Tainan, Taiwan
Department of Occupational Safety, College of Environment, Chia Nan University of Pharmacy and Science, Tainan, Taiwan
Department of Occupational and Environmental Medicine, National Cheng Kung University Hospital, Tainan, Taiwan

Shih-Feng Weng
Department of Medical Research, Chi Mei Medical Center, Tainan, Taiwan
Department of Hospital and Health Care Administration, Chia Nan University of Pharmacy and Science, Tainan, Taiwan

Ivo Marx
Department of Psychiatry and Psychotherapy, University Medicine Rostock, Rostock, Germany

John Krause
Department of Psychiatry and Psychotherapy, University Medicine Rostock, Rostock, Germany
Department of Forensic Psychiatry, University Medicine Rostock, Rostock, Germany

Christoph Berger
Department of Psychiatry and Psychotherapy, University Medicine Rostock, Rostock, Germany
Department of Child and Adolescent Psychiatry, Psychotherapy and Neurology, University Medicine Rostock, Rostock, Germany

Frank Häßler
Department of Child and Adolescent Psychiatry, Psychotherapy and Neurology, University Medicine Rostock, Rostock, Germany

Kathleen M. Gates
Department of Psychology, University of North Carolina, Chapel Hill, North Carolina, United States of America

Peter C. M. Molenaar
Department of Human Development and Family Studies, The Pennsylvania State University, State College, Pennsylvania, United States of America

Swathi P. Iyer
Department of Behavioral Neuroscience, Oregon Health & Sciences University, Portland, Oregon, United States of America

Joel T. Nigg
Department of Behavioral Neuroscience, Oregon Health & Sciences University, Portland, Oregon, United States of America
Department of Psychiatry, Oregon Health & Sciences University, Portland, Oregon, United States of America

Damien A. Fair
Department of Behavioral Neuroscience, Oregon Health & Sciences University, Portland, Oregon, United States of America
Department of Psychiatry, Oregon Health & Sciences University, Portland, Oregon, United States of America
Advanced Imaging Research Center, Oregon Health & Sciences University, Portland, Oregon, United States of America

Lourdes Ezpeleta, Roser Granero, Núria de la Osa and Josep M. Domènech
Unitat d'Epidemiologia i de Diagnòstic en Psicopatologia del Desenvolupament, Departament de Psicologia Clínica i de la Salut, Universitat Autònoma de Barcelona, Barcelona, Spain

José Blas Navarro and Eva Penelo
Departament de Psicobiologia i Metodologia de les Ciències de la Salut, Universitat Autònoma de Barcelona, Barcelona, Spain

John M. D. Thompson and Edwin A. Mitchell
Department of Paediatrics, The University of Auckland, Auckland, New Zealand

Karen E. Waldie
School of Psychology, The University of Auckland, Auckland, New Zealand

Clare R. Wall
Discipline of Nutrition, The University of Auckland, Auckland, New Zealand

Rinky Murphy
Department of Medicine, The University of Auckland, Auckland New Zealand

Cristina F. B. Murphy, Luciana O. Pagan-Neves, Haydée F. Wertzner and Eliane Schochat
Department of Physical Therapy, Speech-Language Pathology and Occupational Therapy, School of Medicine, University of São Paulo, São Paulo, Brazil

Peter Deschamps
Department of Psychiatry, Brain Center Rudolf Magnus, University Medical Center Utrecht, Utrecht, The Netherlands

Nicolette Munsters, Leon Kenemans and Dennis Schutter
Department of Experimental Psychology, Helmholtz Research Institute, Utrecht University, Utrecht, The Netherlands

Walter Matthys
Department of Psychiatry, Brain Center Rudolf Magnus, University Medical Center Utrecht, Utrecht, The Netherlands
Department of Child and Adolescent Studies, Utrecht University, Utrecht, The Netherlands

Wolff Schlotz
Institute of Psychology, University of Regensburg, Regensburg, Germany
MRC Lifecourse Epidemiology Unit, Southampton, United Kingdom
Faculty of Social and Human Sciences, University of Southampton, Southampton, United Kingdom

Keith M. Godfrey
MRC Lifecourse Epidemiology Unit, Southampton, United Kingdom
NIHR Southampton Biomedical Research Centre, University of Southampton and University Hospital Southampton NHS Foundation Trust, Southampton, United Kingdom

David I. Phillips
MRC Lifecourse Epidemiology Unit, Southampton, United Kingdom

Emi Furukawa, Gail Tripp and Jeff R. Wickens
Okinawa Institute of Science and Technology Graduate University (OIST), Okinawa, Japan

Patricia Bado, Paulo Mattos, Ivanei E. Bramati and Fernanda Tovar-Moll
D'Or Institute for Research and Education (IDOR), Rio de Janeiro, Brazil
Federal University of Rio de Janeiro, Rio de Janeiro, Brazil

Brent Alsop
University of Otago, Dunedin, New Zealand

Fernanda Meireles Ferreira and Debora Lima and Jorge Moll
D'Or Institute for Research and Education (IDOR), Rio de Janeiro, Brazil

Joseph A. Sergeant
VU University Amsterdam, Amsterdam, The Netherlands

Carolina Cappi, Juliana Belo Diniz, Aderbal R. T. Silva, Viviane N. S. Reis, Euripedes C. Miguel and Helena Brentani
Institute and Department of Psychiatry, São Paulo University Medical School, São Paulo, Brazil

Ana Gabriela Hounie
Institute and Department of Psychiatry, São Paulo University Medical School, São Paulo, Brazil
Federal University of São Paulo-UPIA-UNIFESP, São Paulo, Brazil

Daniel B. Mariani
Inter-institutional Grad Program on Bioinformatics, Institute of Mathematics and Statistics, São Paulo University, São Paulo, Brazil,

Ariane F. Busso, Amanda Gonçalves Silva, Felipe Fidalgo and Ana C. Krepischi
International Research Center, AC Camargo Cancer Center, São Paulo, Brazil

Silvia Regina Rogatto
School of Medicine, São Paulo State University, Botucatu, São Paulo, Brazil

Sung Yun Sohn, Jee In Kang, Kee Namkoong and Se Joo Kim
Department of Psychiatry and Institute of Behavioral Science in Medicine, Yonsei University College of Medicine, Seoul, Korea

Sandra Diminic
School of Population Health, University of Queensland, Brisbane, Queensland, Australia
Queensland Centre for Mental Health Research, Brisbane, Queensland, Australia

Crick Lund
Alan J Flisher Centre for Public Mental Health, Department of Psychiatry and Mental Health, University of Cape Town, Cape Town, South Africa

Louisa Degenhardt
National Drug and Alcohol Research Centre, University of New South Wales, Sydney, New South Wales, Australia
Melbourne School of Population and Global Health, University of Melbourne, Melbourne, Victoria, Australia

Fiona J. Charlson and Harvey A. Whiteford
School of Population Health, University of Queensland, Brisbane, Queensland, Australia
Queensland Centre for Mental Health Research, Brisbane, Queensland, Australia
Institute of Health Metrics and Evaluation, University of Washington, Seattle, Washington, United States of America

Brian J. Piper
Department of Basic Pharmaceutical Sciences, Husson University, Bangor, Maine, United States of America
Department of Behavioral Neuroscience, Oregon Health and Science University, Portland, Oregon, United States of America

Hilary M. Gray
Department of Behavioral Neuroscience, Oregon Health and Science University, Portland, Oregon, United States of America
School of Community Health and Department of Counselor Education, Portland State University, Portland, Oregon, United States of America

Selena M. Corbett
Department of Behavioral Neuroscience, Oregon Health and Science University, Portland, Oregon, United States of America
College of Osteopathic Medicine of the Pacific Northwest, Western University of Health Sciences, Pomona, California, United States of America

Melissa A. Birkett
Department of Psychological Sciences, Northern Arizona University, Flagstaff, Arizona, United States of America

Jacob Raber
Department of Behavioral Neuroscience, Oregon Health and Science University, Portland, Oregon, United States of America
Department of Neurology and Radiation Medicine, and Division of Neuroscience, ONPRC, Oregon Health and Science University, Portland, Oregon, United States of America

Frederica P. Perera, Deliang Tang, Emily L. Roen and Julie Herbstman
Department of Environmental Health Sciences, Mailman School of Public Health, Columbia University, New York, New York, United States of America
Columbia Center for Children's Environmental Health, Columbia University, New York, New York, United States of America

Hsin-wen Chang, Tzu-Jung Huang and Shuang Wang
Columbia Center for Children's Environmental Health, Columbia University, New York, New York, United States of America
Department of Biostatistics, Mailman School of Public Health, Columbia University, New York, New York, United States of America

Amy Margolis
Columbia Center for Children's Environmental Health, Columbia University, New York, New York, United States of America
Division of Child & Adolescent Psychiatry and the Center for Developmental Neuropsychiatry, Department of Psychiatry, the New York State Psychiatric Institute and the College of Physicians and Surgeons, Columbia University, New York, New York, United States of America

Rachel L. Miller
Department of Environmental Health Sciences, Mailman School of Public Health, Columbia University, New York, New York, United States of America
Columbia Center for Children's Environmental Health, Columbia University, New York, New York, United States of America
Division of Pulmonary, Allergy and Critical Care of Medicine, Department of Medicine, College of Physicians and Surgeons, Columbia University, New York, New York, United States of America
Division of Pediatric Allergy and Immunology, Department of Pediatrics, College of Physicians and Surgeons, Columbia University, New York, New York, United States of America

Virginia Rauh
Columbia Center for Children's Environmental Health, Columbia University, New York, New York, United States of America
The Heilbrunn Department of Population and Family Health, Columbia University, New York, New York, United States of America

Tiffany M. Chaim
Laboratory of Psychiatric Neuroimaging, Department and Institute of Psychiatry, Faculty of Medicine, University of São Paulo, Sao Paulo, Sao Paulo, Brazil
Center for Interdisciplinary Research on Applied Neurosciences, University of São Paulo, Sao Paulo, São Paulo, Brazil
Program for Attention Deficit Hyperactivity Disorder, Department and Institute of Psychiatry, Faculty of Medicine, University of São Paulo, Sao Paulo, Sao Paulo, Brazil

Tianhao Zhang, Jimit Doshi and Christos Davatzikos
Section of Biomedical Image Analysis, Department of Radiology, University of Pennsylvania, Philadelphia, Pennsylvania, Unites States of America

Marcus V. Zanetti, Mauricio H. Serpa, Fabio L. S. Duran, Sheila C. Caetano and Geraldo F. Busatto
Laboratory of Psychiatric Neuroimaging, Department and Institute of Psychiatry, Faculty of Medicine, University of São Paulo, Sao Paulo, Sao Paulo, Brazil
Center for Interdisciplinary Research on Applied Neurosciences, University of São Paulo, Sao Paulo, São Paulo, Brazil

Maria Aparecida da Silva and Mário R. Louzã
Program for Attention Deficit Hyperactivity Disorder, Department and Institute of Psychiatry, Faculty of Medicine, University of São Paulo, Sao Paulo, Sao Paulo, Brazil

Index